The Classical Tradition

Art, Literature, Thought

The Classical Tradition
Art, Literature, Thought

Michael Silk, Ingo Gildenhard, and Rosemary Barrow

WILEY Blackwell

This edition first published 2017

Edition history: Michael Silk, Ingo Gildenhard, and Rosemary Barrow (hardback, 2014)

Registered Office
John Wiley & Sons, Inc., 111 River Street, Hoboken, NJ 07030, USA
John Wiley & Sons Ltd, The Atrium, Southern Gate, Chichester, West Sussex, PO19 8SQ, UK

Editorial Offices
1606 Golden Aspen Drive, Suites 103 and 104, Ames, Iowa 50010, USA

For details of our global editorial offices, customer services, and more information about Wiley products visit us at www.wiley.com.

Wiley also publishes its books in a variety of electronic formats and by print-on-demand. Some content that appears in standard print versions of this book may not be available in other formats.

Library of Congress Cataloging-in-Publication Data
Silk, Michael.
The Classical Tradition : Art, Literature, Thought / Michael Silk, Ingo Gildenhard, and Rosemary Barrow.
pages cm
Includes bibliographical references and index.
ISBN 978-1-4051-5549-6 (hardback) ISBN 978-1-4051-5550-2 (paperback)
1. Classical literature–History and criticism. 2. Civilization, Classical–Influence.
I. Gildenhard, Ingo, 1970– II. Barrow, R. J. (Rosemary J.) III. Title.
PA3013.S55 2014
880.09–dc23

2013028383

Cover Image: Calum Colvin, *Brief Encounter*. By permission of the artist.
Cover Design: Nicki Averill

Set in 10.5/13 pt Minion by SPi Global, Pondicherry, India

10 9 8 7 6 5 4 3 2 1

Contents

Figures

Plates

Colour plates appear at the back of the book

Prologue

During the writing of this book, colleagues who have enquired about the work in progress, and then learnt the title, have usually assumed that our collaboration must be intended to produce some sort of ambitious survey of classical receptions. What we are attempting is significantly different, but actually more ambitious: a rereading of a formative aspect of Western culture and, thus, a rereading, however partial, of Western culture itself in the perspective of the classical. Our scope is therefore wider, though our focus is certainly more coherent – but our potential readership is in any event more open-ended. We hope to appeal to a diverse readership among all who are concerned to make sense of almost two millennia of cultural developments and achievements, whether as advanced students, general readers, or fellow scholars; and if we have a particular hope, it must be that the outcomes of our efforts will be of serious interest to those with scholarly expertise across a broad spectrum of contemporary, modern, early modern, and medieval studies, along with the classics and its receptions, as well. We invite them, not least, to ponder the wider contexts into which we have placed their special concerns.

Although in various senses we do go 'back to basics', ours is not an introduction to the field. We do aim to offer an overview of the classical tradition, and a point of reference for a wide variety of different matters, but the book is not a survey, even if many of its sections do survey relevant material in whole or part. Nor is it a catalogue: we make no pretence to complete coverage of our field.

As we explain more fully in the opening section (§1), the book is a continuous work, and not a sequence of separate essays. It is not for us to dissuade readers from selective reading, but such readers should at least bear in mind that texts, works of art, topics, perspectives, may be presented in one section and presupposed in another.

We do not – let us stress at the outset – assume that the more classical is superior to the less, nor, indeed, that the less is superior to the more. If we assume anything, it is that a rereading like ours is as desirable as its subject is important.

If this was a research proposal, we would stress the extent to which we have sought to offer fresh appraisals of a wide range of material and to make new connections among a multitude of artists, writers, thinkers, works, and developments, well-known and lesser-known, that are not normally brought together in one volume, let alone in one (re)reading. Our ultimate concern, however, is with what is sometimes sceptically referred to as the grand sweep or the big picture. In today's academy, professional compartmentalization, allied to various strands of relativism (not least, postmodern suspicion of 'metanarratives'), has encouraged a timidity in the face of such large readings which we see as, ultimately, absurd. Anyone who supposes they can do without grand sweeps or big pictures is deceiving themselves. Everyone relies on them. The question is whether it is enough simply to rely on them in the form of outdated surveys or, perhaps, fashionable critiques – or, instead, seek to improve on them. Assuming we have made some headway in that direction, however, we do not suppose that there can be anything definitive about any such improvement, and if our efforts provoke others to improve on ours, we shall be the first to applaud.

Ours has been a collaboration in the fullest sense of the word. Over a period of years, the co-authors have debated the contents, the arguments, the organization, and the minutest detail of the book, and while our respective spheres of special expertise have naturally helped to determine which of us produced an initial draft for which section, the fact is that every section has been redrafted several times, and that all three of us have contributed to every section as it now stands. The book has been a joint project, and we are, all three of us, committed to it, as a whole, in its final form.

'Art, literature, thought': we have sought to achieve a balance between our treatment of the three, not necessarily in quantifiable terms, but certainly in the sense that all three have been kept in view, as appropriate, throughout the book. 'Thought', perhaps, deserves a special comment. In our usage, the word in effect subsumes thought about antiquity, thought about art, thought about literature, and indeed thought about thought, as well as, for instance, specifiable aspects of cultural, ethical, and political thought; it would, however, be misleading to claim that technical philosophical or scientific issues, in particular, bulk large in our discussions.

Out of the many cultural traditions that have contributed to 'the' classical tradition, our concern (as we explain in §1) is primarily with four: the Italian, French, German, and those of the English-speaking world (in linguistic terms, this subsumes not only the corresponding four languages, but also post-classical, transnational Latin). In general, we have sought, once again, to keep a balance between our treatment of the four – but with one significant exception. Where close literary readings are called for, it will usually be literature in the English language that is to the fore – if only for reasons of simplicity of exposition and appropriateness for a readership whose common language is English.

Practical Information

(*a*) *Arrangement by sections*: our book is divided, not into chapters, but into thirty-five continuously numbered sections (of varying lengths), which are grouped into five 'Parts' (again of varying lengths), followed by an epilogue. This arrangement is designed to follow the contours of our subject and our treatment of it, with no loss to practical convenience. It may be noted that the sections ('§§') are often used as a basis for cross-reference: 'cf. §24' or simply '(§24)'.

(*b*) *Annotation*: though there is a good deal of annotation here, it is in fact highly selective. Across the many areas we confront, we have not sought to annotate every point where there is a diversity of published views, or an occasion for citing secondary literature (cf. (*c*) below). Our policy, however, has been to use the notes not only for essential reference, but to flag up some of the many tangential issues in which our discussions are implicated.

(*c*) *Secondary literature*: publications are cited in the notes in a version of Harvard style – 'Trask (2000) 278' (or, within brackets, 'Trask 2000: 278') – with full citation in the Bibliography (pp. 432–74). Some items (usually primary sources) are not cited in Harvard style, and not included in the Bibliography. With secondary literature, we rarely attempt to be comprehensive: our scope precludes it. We source quotations, always. For the rest: in some cases, we cite exemplary items; in others, a specific discussion; in others again, a cross-section. But we have not cited secondary literature for the sake of it. We have often preferred to cite primary sources instead; and in particular we avoid citing any secondary literature for aspects of, or works or individuals from, classical antiquity. In the case of scholarly works published in foreign languages, we have sometimes opted for English translations, where adequate and readily available, but especially where the translation is also a revised version. We have not attempted to match the formal bibliographies in works of reference like France (2000), Grafton, Most, and Settis (2010), Kallendorf (2007), Reid (1993), the monumental *Pauly, Classical Tradition* (2006–10), or the one-volume *Oxford Classical Dictionary* (2012).

(*d*) *Primary texts* from classical antiquity are cited (usually in the notes) in conventional form ('Horace, *Odes*, 1. 13'). Where possible, this is also our procedure with texts from later periods, in whatever language ('Dante, *Inferno*, 4. 85–90'). Line numbers (etc.) in such references (both for classical and for later material) assume numbering (etc.) within the text in its original language. Where the option of such numbering (etc.) is not available for post-classical texts, we cite, if possible, by chapter or section or other manageable and unmistakable subdivision: 'Nietzsche, *Birth of Tragedy*, 15'; 'Rabelais, *Pantagruel*, 8'; 'Vasari, *Lives*, 2, Ghiberti'. For primary texts (post-classical and classical), we avoid, so far as possible, citing by particular editions (to which many readers will have no access) and especially by page numbering in such editions; and unless exceptionally, we avoid including primary material of any kind in the Bibliography. The exceptions usually involve those few cases where reference is made, for some special reason, to particular editions: 'Dryden's preface to his translation of *Ovid's Epistles*: Watson (1962), 1. 268'. In such cases, the publication is Harvard-styled under the editor's name, not the author's, and in the Bibliography is entered correspondingly under the editor's name (but without the ambiguous 'ed.', which is reserved for collections of essays or the like): the whimsical modern practice whereby Dryden, though dead in 1700, can be presented as authoring a publication in 1962 has little to recommend it.

(*e*) *Translation*: in general, all quotations in languages other than English are accompanied by translation (at least on first citation), either in the text or the notes. All translations are our own, unless otherwise indicated; for literary texts, we have made a point of providing our own, wherever possible. Titles of post-classical works in languages other than English are cited in the original, in English, or in both, as seems appropriate, but titles of classical works are often cited only in their most familiar form, whatever that happens to be ('Virgil, *Aeneid*', but 'Cicero, *De Amicitia*').

(*f*) *Orthography*: spelling and punctuation systems in our four languages (as also in post-classical Latin) have changed considerably over time, and in some periods practices are less than consistent. We have found it difficult, and ultimately undesirable, to follow any consistent practice ourselves. Our rule of thumb is that texts later than *c.* 1580/1600 are cited in modernized spelling (etc.) (as is common practice, for instance, with the English of Shakespeare and the King James Bible), though with German material, in particular, we sometimes modernize from Luther onwards (i.e. the best part of a century earlier). The upshot is that (e.g.) Montaigne and Shakespeare are (broadly) modernized, whereas Dante and Chaucer are (broadly) not; and that (e.g.) seventeenth-century English is usually quoted without a plethora of capital letters; whereas (e.g.) we refer to Du Bellay's *Deffence*, in original spelling, and not to his *Défense*. Conversely, some later titles in French and German are left unmodernized ('Leibniz, *Ermahnung an die Teutsche*', not '. . . *Deutsche*'), as are some English verse-usages like Keats's 'light-wingèd Dryad' and 'deep-brow'd Homer'.

(*g*) *Latin titles*: we have sought to distinguish classical and post-classical by generalizing the convention whereby classical titles are fully capitalized ('Cicero, *De Amicitia*'), post-classical only capitalized initially ('Hobbes, *De cive*').

(*h*) *Dates*: where primary texts (books etc.) are cited with a date – 'Gibbon, *Decline and Fall* (1776–88)' – this usually refers to date of publication, unless specified as date of composition. In the body of the book, we usually eschew birth, death, or *floruit* dates for artists, writers (etc.). For reference, such dates are included in the Index, under the name of the artist (etc.). All centuries can be assumed to be AD unless otherwise specified.

(*i*) *Abbreviations*: with the needs of a mixed readership in mind, we have generally avoided abbreviating titles, both of primary works (ancient or other) and especially of modern journals (etc.). Standard abbreviations themselves ('etc.') are largely confined to the notes. Our chief concession to *ad hoc* abbreviation is the intermittent use (but only in the notes) of Roman numerals for centuries ('XXI' = 'twenty-first century').

Acknowledgements

We are indebted to the following, for help with illustrations: Valentina Bandelloni and Alan Kirby, of the Scala Picture Library; Jacklyn Burns, of the J. Paul Getty Museum; Shelley Hales; and especially Calum Colvin, Chris Gollon, and Thomas Gordon Smith, for generously allowing us to reproduce their work; likewise to our respective universities for helping to defray the costs involved. We owe a debt of gratitude to Ian Wong for help with the index. Various friends and colleagues have read some or all of the book in draft: Matthew Bell, Antonio Cartolano, Terence Cave, David Hopkins, Deborah Howard, Sebastian Matzner, Rosa Mucignat. We offer them warm thanks for their comments and advice. We are grateful, too, for the helpful suggestions made by the publisher's readers and, not least, to Haze Humbert and the staff of Wiley-Blackwell, along with Graeme Leonard on the copy-editing side, for their efficiency and patience.

Michael Silk (King's College London)
Ingo Gildenhard (University of Cambridge)
Rosemary Barrow (University of Roehampton)

With great sorrow, we record the fact that during the preparation of this paperback edition, our co-author, Rosemary Barrow, died from cancer at the early age of forty-eight. The book would have been inconceivable without her participation; it remains one of many memorials to her scholarly achievement.

Michael Silk
Ingo Gildenhard

Part I

Overview

§1

The Classical Tradition and the Scope of Our Book

The classical tradition covers a millennium and a half of cultural achievements, historical developments, facts, fictions, and phenomena on many levels. It subsumes the many ways in which, since the end of classical antiquity, the world of ancient Greece and Rome has inspired and influenced, has been constructed and reconstructed, has left innumerable traces (sometimes unregarded), and has, repeatedly, been appealed to, and contested, as a point of reference, and rehearsed and reconstituted (with or without direct reference) as an archetype.

Interest in aspects of the classical tradition is currently as active as it is widespread. The classical canon may no longer dominate the modern mind, as it once determined the responses of elite circles in the past, but we live in a time when Hollywood blockbusters about 'three hundred' Spartans or the tale of 'Troy' attract enthusiastic audiences around the world, when innovative stagings of Greek drama are a familiar presence in many countries, when idealistic notions of, or anxieties about, 'democracy' continue to engender debate, and when the enduring tussle between Britain and Greece over the ownership of the Elgin (or Parthenon) marbles shows how cultural goods tied up with the classical tradition can still be a matter of high politics and national interest. These and countless other achievements, developments, and debates, past and present, are increasingly the focus of a miniature explosion in publishing and what is almost a new academic discipline in its own right.[1] Various, often controversial, factors may have played a part here, not

[1] 'New', though 'the classical tradition' was identified as long ago as Victorian England (John Addington Symonds invokes, and contrasts, 'Christian and Classical Traditions' in his *Renaissance in Italy: The Fine Arts*, 1877, ch. 1), while it was formally institutionalized as a field of study in the Warburg Institute, first in Hamburg (from 1921), then in London (from 1934).

The Classical Tradition: Art, Literature, Thought, First Edition. Michael Silk, Ingo Gildenhard, and Rosemary Barrow.

Published 2017 by John Wiley & Sons Ltd.

least the switch, within classical education in the English-speaking world, from language skills to 'classics in translation' (§§4, 15), but the level of interest in the classical tradition, both among the classically trained and across the arts and humanities, is beyond dispute.

What is 'the classical tradition'? In contemporary usage, 'classical' and 'the classics' may mean a Beethoven symphony, the novels of Tolstoy, the films of René Clair – or a range of notable entities, from permanently-in-fashion dress designs to pre-quantum mechanics.[2] For our purposes, 'the classical' means the world of ancient Greece and Rome, and 'the classical tradition' means reflexes of,[3] uses of, reconstitutions of, or responses to, the ancient world from the disintegration of the Western Roman Empire to our own day. But – given that 'classical' has always had strongly positive connotations, and 'tradition', arguably, too (§2) – this entire domain is inevitably caught up in implications of value. For a start, it is not just any aspect of the Greco-Roman world that inspires and influences, but, overwhelmingly, the special and the privileged – Homer's *Iliad*, Plato's dialogues, the ruined glories of Phidias' marbles – even if the process of inspiring and influencing can sometimes seem to make the whole of antiquity special and privileged anew.

The classical tradition overlaps with the reception (or receptions) of Greece and Rome. They are not the same thing, and for several reasons.[4] First, because the reception of Greece and Rome includes readings and rereadings from within the ancient world itself.[5] There will be all manner of particular differences, but there is no necessary difference in kind or in hermeneutic status, between a response to Virgil's *Aeneid* from Virgil's own time, one from later antiquity, and one from a later age – say, T. S. Eliot's response, in a pair of provoking essays (§35). Yet though these are all instances of the reception of Virgil, only Eliot's essays can meaningfully be referred to the classical tradition. Conversely, the classical tradition is wider in scope. Many of its embodiments are not classical receptions in any meaningful sense. Post-classical versions of classical archetypes sometimes involve reception, sometimes not (§19). Equally, the Romance and Modern Greek languages are momentous post-classical reflexes of Latin and Ancient Greek, and as such clearly belong to the

2 All, on different levels, authoritative. The association of 'classical' with authority is inscribed in its etymology from Latin 'classis' ('fleet'/'army', as well as social 'class'; cf. §3 n. 14) – as it is in (e.g.) the use of 'classical' architecture for buildings required to connote authority, from banks to museums. 'Authority': cf. §5.

3 We borrow – and extend – this use of 'reflex' from historical linguistics, where the word stresses the fact of descent without any implication of purposeful transmission or adjustment: '*reflex* . . . a word or other linguistic form which is directly descended within a particular language from an ancestral form taken as a reference point. For example . . . Italian *donna* "lady" is a reflex of Latin *domina(m)*': Trask (2000) 278. In our extended usage, the word is reapplied from particular linguistic forms to whole language systems and other large behavioural structures. Thus, the Italian language *per se* is (largely) a reflex of Latin *per se* (§13), and medieval Italian carnival (partly) a reflex of ancient ceremonial or ritual (§12).

4 Compare and contrast e.g. Budelmann and Haubold (2008) and Caruso and Laird (2009) 2–3. See further §2.

5 Cf. e.g. Martindale (2006).

classical tradition, but they are not, in themselves, 'receptions' of anything. Whether the same should be said of Medieval Latin, and of Renaissance Latin too, is another matter; both, in any event, belong straightforwardly to the tradition.

Then again, the classical tradition, as a continuum, subsumes not only direct engagements with antiquity, but engagements with earlier engagements. Like Eliot, the poet Milton responds to Virgil's poetry; unlike Eliot, he responds not as critic, but by and within his own poetry, which – from *Lycidas* to *Paradise Lost* – creates (among much else) an idiosyncratic classicizing idiom that looks back to classical Latinity in general and Virgil's Latin among others. In this sense, Milton's poetic language represents a distinctive embodiment of the classical tradition; it is also the object of an Eliotian critique in a notable essay, which, however, makes virtually no reference to antiquity at all. That essay is eminently discussible as itself a critical contribution to the tradition and as significant evidence for Eliot's sense of his own distinctive place within it[6] – but there is nothing in the essay to invite talk of 'reception' of antiquity, nor indeed is the essay commonly discussed as such.

Above all, though, whereas 'classical' and 'tradition' tend to prompt consideration of value, 'reception' does not. In a nutshell, the 'classical' of 'the classical tradition' tends to imply canonicity, even when the post-antique engagement with the antique is anti-canonical (as is the case, most obviously, with engagements within popular culture: §12). Indeed, notwithstanding the fact that it is precisely the value associated with the classical over hundreds of years that has brought its multiple receptions into being, reception studies tend to operate in a relativistic spirit, generally preferring cultural-historical engagement with such issues to critical engagement. All in all: reception *studies* have helped to make what was once the preoccupation of a minority of classicists, and others, fashionable – while reception *theory* has helped to generate better understandings of various aspects of the field – but in no sense has 'reception' itself been shown to redefine, let alone to replace, 'the classical tradition' itself.[7]

The scope of the classical tradition is vast. Its many continuities (and discontinuities) range from high culture to low, from politics to sport, from law to urban planning, from the Romance languages, and the Modern Greek language, to the international, largely Greek-derived terminology of modern science and the continuing use of botanical Latin names for plants – and not just by professional botanists, but by ordinary gardeners too.[8] And if the scope is vast, the variety of usage that arises from particular points of reference is no less so.

Take Augustus and his age. Often regarded as (and seemingly regarding itself as) a 'classical' age in its own right, on the model of fifth-century Athens, with its

[6] Milton, Eliot, and Virgil: §35.

[7] Value: §§2, 18, Epilogue. Reception theory and the field: Martindale (1993), (2006).

[8] In Britain, for instance, herbs like 'salvia' and 'artemisia' are as familiar under those names as under their English names, 'sage' (*salvia officinalis*) and 'wormwood' (*artemisia absinthium*). As these examples suggest, botanical Latin uses classical lexemes or word-shapes, but not necessarily according to the rules of classical Latin usage.

sublimely assured art and architecture and public poetry, the Augustan age has in turn inspired classicizing revivals, along with other responses, in great profusion. It has bequeathed to the Western world the concepts of urban renewal in the grand manner[9] and of 'the classic of all Europe' (Eliot on Virgil again: §35). And the ideals it has been taken to embody have been acclaimed and denied and reinvented, from Charlemagne and Alcuin (who relived the relationship between Augustus and his poets) to the Holy Roman Emperors (who retained 'Imperator Augustus' in their titles), from Cosimo I of Florence (who promoted himself as a Renaissance version of Augustus the autocrat, saving the state from the instabilities of republicanism) to John Dryden (founding father of the English 'Augustan' poets, who reconfigured the same historical schema in his youthful 'Astraea Redux', composed to celebrate the restoration of Charles II), from Joachim Du Bellay (who invoked 'that most happy age of Augustus' as a model for the emergent French aspiration towards a great language and a high culture) to Benito Mussolini (who commemorated his hero's 2000th birthday with a grandiose Fascist exhibition in 1937–8)[10] to W. H. Auden (whose poem 'Secondary Epic' sniped from below at Virgil's lofty vision of Augustus as a carrier of destiny). In this example, and a host of others, it is hard to overstate the rich complexity of a tradition that has Greco-Roman antiquity as its unifying point of reference, but comprehends such a variety of forms and figures, social settings and relations, themes, media, and conflicting ideologies.

The range of our book, and the diversity of its connections and appraisals, reflects this 'infinite variety', but (we repeat) the book makes no attempt to take account of all possible points of reference, in topical, chronological, or geographical terms. While it contains its proper share of facts and figures, attested origins and unmistakable developments, our overall aim is an informed reading of the tradition that responds to diversity by making critical sense of it, and stimulates our readers to form, or sharpen, their own responses and assessments – perhaps in contrast to ours. Our emphasis is on art, literature, and thought: art, with more than passing attention to architecture; literature, with the same attention to theatre, opera, and film; thought, philosophy, and ideas, including, not least, ideas about, or associated with, art and literature themselves. Given the intricate relationships between literature and language, and thought and language, issues of language will impinge significantly on the discussion. So too will the interrelated histories of classical scholarship (§16) and education (§4), and also – interrelated again – of translation (§15). The ideological implications of the tradition will be a recurrent theme, as will the relation between high culture and low (we confront this directly in §12) and the related question of value.

Within art, literature, and thought, we have again made no attempt to scrutinize all media and all periods across all the cultures of the world. The classical tradition at its widest is a global phenomenon (witness Gandhi on Plato, Roman influences

[9] According to Suetonius (*Augustus*, 28), Augustus' proud boast was that 'he found Rome built of brick and left it in marble'. Cf. §25.

[10] *Mostra Augustea della Romanità.*

on the architecture of the mosque, the Greek-tragic evocations of the plays of Soyinka); and it has certainly been in constant dialogue with other cultural traditions throughout its history; but our discussion is concentrated on Western culture and, within Western culture, on the primary and closely related cultural traditions of Italy, France, Germany, and the English-speaking world.[11] Among much else, this means that we have relatively little to say about Byzantium,[12] which sustained the language, learning, and texts of Greek antiquity for a thousand years after the collapse of the Roman empire in the west, and which has considerable importance as a site of the classical tradition in its own right. Our focus is on the classical tradition in its undoubted heartland.

Within these limits, we seek to give a sense of the diverse contents of the tradition, but we are more concerned to ponder its coherence,[13] delineate its profile, and explore its typology. In effect we are asking a series of questions about the tradition overall.

What *is* 'the tradition overall'? How do we identify its boundaries? We confront this question repeatedly, especially in Part I of the book, from §1 (the present section) to §18.

What is its trajectory over time? Here, within the long march (or meandering) from late antiquity to the modern age, we give more than usual attention to the status of the eighteenth century as a transitional era, and to the Romantic generation as a turning-point (see, most immediately, §3 and §5). But the book is anything but a linear history, though many of its sections contain historical sketches.

What definitive forms does the tradition take? Reception, though itself a broad category, is only one such; and any answer to the question must take account, also, of reflexes (of which language is surely the most important: §13), of archetypes (§§19–22), and, as we have already pointed out, of engagements with earlier engagements (exemplified, representatively but not only, in §35). 'Engagements', in their considerable variety, we also categorize in different terms in §14.

What kinds of difference has the tradition made? This is a question we attempt to confront by placing the classical in and against the context of the non-classical. We do so both in large terms (§18) and by a focus on specific case studies (§§28–31).

[11] Initially, but not of course exclusively, European. Here as elsewhere, recent scholarship seeks to take account of the marginalized and the peripheral (as, in conventional terms, they would be regarded), along with the canonical and the central: see e.g. Goff (2005), Goff and Simpson (2008), Hardwick and Gillespie (2007).

[12] Our most significant omission besides is Spain (esp. significant in the Renaissance) and the Hispanic world.

[13] Regarding this 'coherence', we note a revealing comment by the Nigerian playwright, Femi Osofisan, on his *Women of Owu*, an adaptation of Euripides' *Trojan Women*, first performed in 2004. His play addresses, not Western audiences (familiar, perhaps, with the Euripides), but 'a Nigerian audience . . . the audience I am familiar with': Budelmann (2007) 30. In a post-colonial perspective, there will be both new creativities to add to the old and new ways of reading the old, including the classical old: Euripides 'reclaimed' as 'world literature' is different from Euripides as part of the Western classical tradition.

We also do so, more pervasively, by presenting the more 'classical', at any one time or place, as part of a less 'classical' whole. Our very different discussions of popular culture (§12) and Rome (§25) may be taken as representative here.

What kinds of relationship are there – comparative, contrastive, interactive – between the tradition in our four cultures? Between its embodiments in different periods? And (in some respects the most challenging question) between the art, the literature, and the thought of our title? – challenging, if only (though not only) because these three large areas of human creativity and endeavour are seldom brought together in any concerted way in contemporary understandings of the present or past, classical-related or other. These questions are not the kind that allow neat or simple answers, but we have had them in mind throughout.

And, not least, a question that arises directly from the others: what are the different ways in which the tradition can profitably be approached and understood? This question, along with the questions about relationship just cited, has determined the shape of our book. The body of the book is organized as thirty-five sections, of varying lengths, in five parts. Part I (§§1–18) is designed to represent an overview of the tradition and its diversity (this is outlined in detail in §2); Parts II–V present a series of closer readings from alternative standpoints: 'archetypes' (§§19–22), 'the imaginary' (§§23–27), 'making a difference' (§§28–31), 'contrasts and comparisons' (§§32–35).

In a more practical sense, considerations of diversities and alternatives have helped to determine the shape and size of the thirty-five sections. Some sections present their material at relative length, as with the important topic of language (§13). Others, much shorter, we offer as pointers for debate. Two in particular, §10 ('special relationships') and §18 (the classical tradition and *other* traditions), belong here – though in both cases the desire to avoid long lists of illusory counter-examples is also a factor. The shortest sections, designated as 'prefaces' to the several Parts that follow the overview (§§19, 23, 28, 32), seek to provide a theoretical framework for the different kinds of material, and different kinds of discussion, that follow them. But short or long, prefatory or discursive, every section is intended to contribute to a critical reappraisal of the tradition as a whole.

We use the word 'critical' advisedly. Any satisfying treatment of art, of literature, of thought, calls for critical judgement. Such judgement is exercised not least in the choice of examples, and here we are not just selective: we repeatedly argue from particular examples – a technique (this is no coincidence) most familiar in literary criticism. But in any case the classical tradition in these large areas is so implicated in value judgements from the past that any attempt at 'impartiality' now is likely to end up as a quaint evasion. Conversely, though, it may be acknowledged that in art and literature, in particular, achievement is not 'superannuated',[14] and that there is a clear distinction between such areas and those where judgement now is largely superfluous and the classical tradition is a matter of essentially historical interest.

[14] Compare and contrast Eliot's refusal to 'superannuate' Shakespeare, Homer, *or* 'the rock drawing of the Magdalenian draughtsmen' ('Tradition and the Individual Talent', 1920).

The most obvious of the latter is the realm of scientific ideas, where a once common appeal to ancient authority – to the mathematician Euclid, to the medical expert Galen – has been superseded, since the age of Newton, by the dynamic of progressive discovery and the paradigm shift. Between the two extremes of art (visual or verbal) and science, what we are designating 'thought' tends to occupy an intermediate position.

In practice, our concern with critical judgement means attending, as sensitively as we can, not only to the variety of embodiments concealed within 'the' classical tradition, but also to the underlying presuppositions of our own discussion. This means that relevant issues are liable to impinge (they already have) as theoretical issues. For our explorations, theoretical perspectives are a prerequisite – as is a readiness to discriminate between, or beyond, them. Our discussions (or so we would like to think) are both theoretically informed and also actively engaged in current debate on a range of theoretical fronts, from hermeneutics to cultural studies to gender.

§2

Mapping the Field

The vast scope of the classical tradition, and the fact that at least until the nineteenth century it was so central to almost any cultural endeavour in the Western world that it was often taken for granted, explains in part why it lacks adequate disciplinary acknowledgement. Standard academic practice, applying the principle of divide and rule, chops it into chronological and geographical bits – Renaissance Italy, eighteenth-century France, German classicism, post-revolutionary America, Victorian Britain – for treatment by suitably trained experts. Such division of labour underwrites the modern knowledge industry, which favours specialization; but it cannot do justice to the classical tradition, one of whose hallmarks is precisely the way it spans nations and centuries, even though (to invoke a key tenet of reception theory) it is only ever 'realized' at a specific point in space and time.

At which point we might do well to pause and ask what constitutes a tradition as such – a question all the more urgent, given that common and critical understandings of the phenomenon tend to diverge. In everyday usage, 'tradition' carries connotations of longevity, or even invariance, in the reproduction and transmission of cultural practices or cultural goods. By contrast, scholars in various fields would agree that this fixity is at least in part a fiction – even if belief in its reality is a prerequisite for traditions to perform their ideological function for the social groups that sustain them. On critical inspection, any tradition will be seen to subsume continuity and change, stability and flux, repetition and innovation, though the specifics may vary greatly. There are distinctive oral traditions, which practise composition in performance and look to the legendary or timeless past, or else to the experience of recent generations (usually three generations) within

The Classical Tradition: Art, Literature, Thought, First Edition. Michael Silk, Ingo Gildenhard, and Rosemary Barrow.

Published 2017 by John Wiley & Sons Ltd.

'living' memory.[1] There are innumerable traditions of modest cultural practice, from specialized crafts to household activities to unwritten custom in everyday interaction. There are high-profile traditions rooted in ritual and belief, such as those that modern nation-states have fostered, or invented, to give their populations a historical identity.[2] There are traditions centred on the transmission and exegesis of written, perhaps canonical, texts. There are artistic, literary, and intellectual traditions, perpetuated by artists, writers, thinkers, in dialogue with their predecessors, which might be said to limit – yet also, paradoxically, to facilitate – the originality of individual talents.[3] And then there are fundamental traditions that give us our sense of meaning, of who and what each one of us is, traditions of practice and cognition that serve, if not to determine, then certainly to help shape, the specificity and identity of each human being as a being of culture, language, and history.[4]

Among traditions, the classical seems to be a special case, at least in the way we have defined it as made up of 'reflexes of, uses of, reconstitutions of, or responses to, the ancient world' (§1). To begin with, this is a tradition without an obvious owner. One can of course identify numerous individuals and groups who have engaged with aspects of classical antiquity and have thus invested in and perpetuated the classical tradition – while our own focus on the West, and on four cultures and languages within the West, might be said to suggest a certain kind of ownership itself. Even so, the sheer range of responses to antiquity, and the innumerable ways in which antiquity has outlived its chronological demise within art, literature, and thought, defy any attempt to establish clear proprietorship; even less so, once we bring into the reckoning the diverse realms of language and popular culture, education and scholarship, with which art, literature, and thought have been intimately, and very variously, connected; while in recent times, with the dissolution of a long-standing alliance between 'the classical' and 'the elite', the classical tradition itself has become unpredictably diversified, and has (perhaps) gained new vitality through its diversification.

The classical tradition is special in other ways too. Whereas many traditions serve to provide specific groups with a sense of their past and thus a sense of coherence in the present, the classical is ideologically diffuse: witness the fact that over the centuries recourse to antiquity has served a spectrum of national agendas and political movements, from the revolutionary to the established authoritarian, from the fascist to the democratic.[5] Then too, this tradition has fed on the paradox that those

[1] The combination of legendary past and living memory typically gives the temporal profile of such traditions an 'hour-glass shape'.

[2] Compare the case studies in Hobsbawm and Ranger (1983).

[3] We allude again to Eliot's 'Tradition and the Individual Talent'; cf. our Epilogue.

[4] The underlying principle here we owe to Gadamer's *Truth and Method* (*Wahrheit und Methode*, 1960); we qualify it with reference to the inalienable freedom of human development. Nothing will come of nothing – but no formula for such development can be adequate that speaks the language of determinism and loses sight of individual agency and creativity ('a growing and a becoming', in Matthew Arnold's phrase).

[5] Cf. §§26, 34.

who operate within it can do so by denying its premises. Where some have emphasized 'legacy', 'inheritance', 'debt', accumulated over generations, others, from Petrarch to Palladio to Nietzsche, have been prepared to brush aside the intervening centuries for a fresh encounter – perhaps a more 'authentic' encounter – with the ancient past. Indeed, one of the ideals, or fictions, that sustains the tradition is the holy grail of immediate, *un*traditional access to the ancient world and its creativity,[6] the possibility of a privileged dialogical relationship that has helped to ensure the continual reshaping of antiquity itself in the image of the here and now. Much has changed – attitudes to the past and to tradition, not least – since the great Romantic shift around the end of the eighteenth century, but (say) de Chirico's fascination with the mythic Ariadne in the twentieth is, on a personal level at least, no less reflective of the dynamic than Petrarch's preoccupation with classical Latinity in the fourteenth.[7] Conversely (to restate a point made in §1), the history of 'the' classical tradition abounds in instances where ancient texts and artefacts, ideas and ideals, have acquired new identities within *other* cultural traditions (developments intensified in recent years by the forces of globalization) – the upshot of which is a panorama of receptions, some of them remote from 'our' tradition altogether.

In the light of these variabilities, doubts may arise: is the phrase 'classical tradition' too limiting or else too contradictory to be useful? Some classicists, in any case, have criticised the notion on ideological grounds, playing off responsive, 'liberal', and active *reception* against a classical *tradition* conceived of as inherently monolithic, 'conservative', elitist, and caught up in the passive worship of past masters – though it is self-evident that a 'reception' can be passive too,[8] while we have surely made it clear already that our understanding of the classical tradition is rather different. Others have queried whether the classical tradition can be discussed in a meaningful way *as a whole*, as if methodological propriety required us to limit our enquiries to the study of specific acts of reception. Coincidentally or not, in some languages there is no equivalent to 'the classical tradition'; in German, for instance, the closest equivalents are *Antikerezeption* (a 'reception' word) and the paradoxical *Nachleben* ('afterlife'), which has acquired some currency as a loanword in English, and which certainly captures the continuing vitality of classical antiquity (in the sense of its impact or influence) after its 'death'.[9]

Against all these doubts, we insist on 'classical tradition' as a meaningful label and an essential critical concept. Not only is 'reception' too narrow a term to comprehend the full extent of 'the' tradition; it actually obscures the way that

[6] As already in the Renaissance: 'a first attempt . . . by going to the sources themselves to establish a past over which tradition would have no hold': Hannah Arendt, 'Tradition and the Modern Age' (1968: cf. §34).

[7] See, respectively, §§10, 33, 29.

[8] Cf. Goldhill (2002) 297 and esp. Baehr and O'Brien (1994) 86–7: '"reception" implies a relatively weak or passive mode of acceptance or recognition.'

[9] Not only, then, does the term, 'classical tradition', have a history (cf. §1 n.1); it also raises cross-cultural questions. Why do English, Italian (*tradizione classica*), French (*tradition classique*), have the term, if some other European languages do not?

developments that are *not* receptions may themselves facilitate developments that *are*. Our example of language is once again paradigmatic here.[10] In the study of Ancient Greek or Latin, as in the evolution of Ancient Greek into Modern Greek or the evolution of Latin into the Romance languages, the classical tradition has a powerful and pervasive presence beyond reception, but one which has repeatedly provided a crucial enabling condition for new engagements to emerge. The term, in fact, gives decisive shape to a crucial body of data, while the tensions between common and critical understandings of 'tradition' are surely one facet of the study of the classical tradition itself. We propose to continue to think with (but, if necessary, against) the notion in a theoretically informed way, rereading its historically accrued semantics, ideological functions, and past uses,[11] as appropriate.

Meanwhile, the methodological objection to the analysis of 'wholes' (however construed) seems to us merely another mask for the gratuitous suspicion of big pictures and large meanings.[12] Let us make our point more forcibly: all meaning is part of large meaning; and specific realizations cannot be understood at all without some conception of an overall reality to which they are seen to belong. Without the sense of a whole, it is impossible to discriminate between (*or* propose a restatement of) the peripheral and the central or, more simply, to grasp what has mattered when and why. In any case, the extraordinary phenomenon that classical antiquity has remained a source and a – shifting – point of reference down the centuries cries out for critical reflection in its own right, above and beyond specific engagements. And the consideration that any attempt to map the overall territory must be provisional (including any attempt to decide where 'the' territory stops) is no reason for not making the attempt. Quite the contrary: all critical or historical placing must be provisional; it is only by provisional attempts that more satisfying attempts are made possible in the future; and every interpreter of any instance or aspect of the classical tradition relies on some provisional placing in any case (their own or someone else's), whether they acknowledge it or not.

Our aim, in Part I of this book, is to get the overall shape of the tradition into view. To do so, we make free use of particular moments and examples, often pregnant moments and examples, whatever the possible methodological pitfalls involved in identifying a (or especially 'the') representative instance. In §3 ('Eras') we survey the place and status of classical antiquity within alternative historical frames, with special attention to the ways in which the classics have helped to determine how we conceptualize history and situate ourselves in time. The following section, on classics and education (§4), considers the professional experts, the sites of teaching and learning, the premises, and the techniques that have helped to sustain the tradition over the centuries. In §§5–10, from 'authorities' to 'special relationships', we explore shifts in taste and canonicity: *which* texts, *which* figures, *which* aspects of antiquity, have become influential or normative, and *when*, and *why*? Three sections are

10 But not unique: see esp. §12 on popular culture and §§19–22 on archetypes.

11 See Hall (2008a) for a related argument about 'the classical'.

12 See Prologue, above.

devoted to the distinctive trajectories, and problematics, of the visual arts (§11), popular culture (§12), and the Western languages (§13). We then consider the different modes of engagement with 'the classical' that 'tradition' has embodied, both in conspectus (§14) and with separate attention to three main 'modes': translation (§15), 'scientific' (and alternative) responses to the ancient world (§16), and *looking* at the past (§17). Finally (§18), we stand back and consider the place and scope of the classical tradition within Western culture as a whole: what belongs to it and, in particular, what does *not* belong to it?

Part I, it will be apparent, is not just 'background' for the more specific or circumscribed discussions that follow (though we are reasonably confident that it meets that need, among others). It represents an attempt to provide a coherent and theoretically informed refiguration of the classical tradition in its remarkable complexity: its categories and trajectories, definitions and problematics, contexts and relationships (suspected or unsuspected) – and also, not least, the correlations that emerge in some quarters and the seeming absence of correlations in others. Our quest for 'meaning' and our belief in the classical tradition 'as a whole' have not blinded us to the way that, for instance, individual creativities can sometimes defy general tendencies or, again, the way that one medium can work differently from others. Meanings do not have to be tidy, nor wholes the kind that number theorists work with.

§3

Eras

Periodization is inevitable and necessary, but in practice a tricky business, now that we have lost the robust *naiveté* of earlier ages. Today we think we know that any attempt to organize history and time is contingent on the observer – whether our point of reference is Hesiod and his five 'Ages', or the progression from *mythos* to *logos* in the tradition of Vico and Voltaire, or those late twentieth-century thinkers who have made it their business to deconstruct grand historical narratives. There are always possible reasons for huffing and puffing about chronological caesuras, most obviously because change needs to be calibrated against continuity. Not all the different groups in any one society (let alone all the individuals) march in step; 'eras' in literature, or art, or thought, do not necessarily coincide with each other or with 'eras' in political history; and (of direct relevance to the classical tradition) parallel developments in different countries, cultures, languages, do not always take place at the same time. Then again, hindsight tends to superimpose coherence that may well differ from perceptions at the time: modern understandings of the Renaissance as a definitive historical period centred on a broad-based artistic 'rebirth' of antiquity owe more to the classic study by Jacob Burckhardt than to any consensus during the Renaissance itself,[1] while those living in the centuries before the Renaissance did not know that one day they would become 'medieval'. Distinguishing 'eras'

[1] *Die Kultur der Renaissance in Italien* (1860). This usage of 'renaissance' was established by Jules Michelet's *Histoire de France au seizième siècle. La Renaissance* (1855), though in 1550 Vasari (n. 7 below) had already identified a 'rinascità' in the visual arts, and Voltaire (following Pierre Bayle in 1695) a 'renaissance des lettres' in his *Histoire du parlement de Paris* (1769): Ferguson (1948), Pfeiffer (1976) 18.

The Classical Tradition: Art, Literature, Thought, First Edition. Michael Silk, Ingo Gildenhard, and Rosemary Barrow.

Published 2017 by John Wiley & Sons Ltd.

within the classical tradition is no easier than elsewhere. The ways that Greco-Roman antiquity has figured in post-classical culture have changed radically over time, but where best to draw the lines often remains an open question.[2]

For all that, distinguishing between conventionally acknowledged epochs has a great deal more to be said for it than against, both on a heuristic and a pragmatic level, quite apart from keeping the huffers and puffers in business. Accordingly, within the sequence that leads from Greco-Roman antiquity to our postmodern (or post-postmodern) present, we continue to distinguish late antiquity, the Middle Ages, the Renaissance (or 'early modern' period)[3] – and then a series of periods which, indeed, oscillate awkwardly between the political and the literary-historical, art-historical, or history of ideas: the neoclassical era (subsuming the eighteenth-century Enlightenment); the Romantic period; the period of nationalism, empire, and ideology which in Britain, and sometimes elsewhere, is labelled the Victorian age; and then what one might call 'classical' modernity (subsuming the modernist movements, in art and literature) in, roughly, the first half of the twentieth century.

Revealingly, some of these 'period' labels derive from significant shifts in how one or other age assessed (or is perceived to have assessed) the inherent value, the historical position, and the larger cultural significance, of antiquity and the classical. Thus Petrarch 'invented' the Middle Ages as intervening between antiquity and a new age to come (§29), while Burckhardt defined the (Italian) Renaissance as an alliance between two separate cultural epochs of a single people.[4] The classical, then, has played an essential part in providing Western cultural history with its 'characteristic and unique "rhythmical form"',[5] and the more so because patterns of thought from antiquity itself have left their imprint on later constructions.

A case in point is the tendency to subdivide cultural traditions, whole cultures, and periods within cultures into 'early', 'middle', 'late', with latent but unmistakable implications of 'immature', 'mature', 'in decline'. The schema can be traced at least as far back as Aristotle's view of Attic tragedy and Pliny's history of painting[6] – and (in the same spirit) forward to the pioneering art criticism of Giorgio Vasari in the mid-sixteenth century and his sense of Roman art (on the model of the human life

[2] Cf. e.g. the special issue of *Modern Language Quarterly* 62. 4 (2001) on 'Periodization: Cutting Up the Past', and the summary arguments in Schapiro, Janson and Gombrich (1970).

[3] Current scholarly preference for 'early modern' over 'Renaissance' replaces one bit of partisanship with another. If 'Renaissance' privileges classical connections and high culture, 'early modern' does the same for 'moderns' ('us'). Every period label has its own history and implications. On 'early modern', cf. Cave (2006). For some, 'Renaissance' feeds a false stereotype of a secularizing rejection of Christianity. The stereotype is certainly misleading – but so too is the reluctance to acknowledge the secularizing momentum of the status now given to the classical: cf. esp. §§8, 11, 18, 21, 27.

[4] Herzog and Koselleck (1987); Burckhardt, *Kultur der Renaissance* (1860), 3. 1 ('Bündnis zwischen zwei weit auseinanderliegenden Kulturepochen desselben Volkes').

[5] Settis (2006) 106.

[6] Aristotle, *Poetics*, 4; Pliny, *Natural History*, 34. 54–65; 35. 15–29, 56–74; cf. Quintilian's 'history' of sculpture, *Institutio Oratoria*, 12. 10. 7–9 (and also his literary 'histories': §5). Contrast the less specific (and commonplace) principles that 'everything born is destined to decay' (Thucydides, 2. 64. 3) and that all 'human affairs' go in cycles (Herodotus, 1. 207. 2).

cycle) ascending from a 'small beginning' to a 'great height', before declining into 'great ruin';[7] to the larger vision of ancient art developed by Johann Joachim Winckelmann in the eighteenth century; to the youthful Nietzsche's construction of Greek culture in the nineteenth; to Eliot's understanding of Virgil and 'maturity' in the twentieth.[8] Related notions have been applied more widely – for instance, in Oswald Spengler's claim that 'all civilizations pass through ages analogous to spring, summer, autumn, and winter; which is to say that historical organisms are equated with natural ones'.[9] Less explicitly, notions of this kind underlie countless particular readings of particular periods in particular cultures, including those of concern to us. The particular readings, of course, may be disputed. For Petrarch, the Middle Ages were in effect ancient Rome's 'winter'; to many Romantics, they were modernity's 'spring'.

That medieval 'winter' (or 'spring') is, on any reckoning, a period with a special significance for the classical tradition, and is itself, from the first, marked by attempts to identify its own 'historical' relationship to the classical world. If the classical tradition begins where antiquity ends, we can pinpoint its birthday as 4 September 476 – the day when the 'Arian' warlord Odoacer dethrones Auden's 'catholic boy', the Roman emperor Romulus Augustulus, an act conventionally taken to mark the final demise of the Western Roman empire.[10] Within a couple of generations, authors begin to refer to antiquity ('antiquitas') as a thing of the past; in the sixth century, for instance, Cassiodorus distinguishes it from 'our own times' ('nostra tempora') and 'the modern period' ('saecula moderna').[11] However, such ruptures in high politics and historical consciousness should not be allowed to mask cultural continuities or, indeed, earlier moments that proved decisive in shaping antiquity's afterlife, including the formation of canons and the formative selection of artworks, texts, and ideas.

The first such moment is the conscious attempt to establish a corpus of approved texts through selective canonization which takes place hundreds of years earlier in third-century BC Alexandria: when the scholar-poets of that city (Callimachus and others) first set out to assemble and classify the approved literature of the Greek city-states in the creative centre of the new world-empire founded by Alexander, and seek, by selective and contrastive imitation of those works, to recuperate that earlier tradition as something exemplary for their own creative endeavour and

[7] Vasari, *Vite de' più eccellenti architetti, pittori, et scultori* (*Lives of the Most Excellent Painters, Sculptors and Architects*: 1550/68), at the end of the 'proem' attached to Part I. Vasari's own ancient models: Gombrich (1966) 1–10.

[8] Winckelmann: §§11, 29. Nietzsche, in *The Birth of Tragedy* (*Die Geburt der Tragödie*, 1872): Silk and Stern (1981) 155–9. Eliot: §35. Some of these versions of the schema are dependent on others – e.g. Winckelmann's on the ancients': cf. Donohue (1995).

[9] Spengler, summed up by Niebuhr (1943) 313. Compare the late-antique/early-medieval model of the 'ages of man' for a cultural entity like the Church, as in Gregory the Great's *Moralia in Job*, 1. 12. 19 ('boyhood, youth, maturity'). Cf. generally Burke (2010b).

[10] Auden, 'Secondary Epic' (1959). 'The end of antiquity': cf. Curtius (1953) 21–2.

[11] Freund (1957) 28.

(therefore) dissociated from it. And no less special is the moment, in that same century, when Livius Andronicus first translates a Greek text into Latin, thus initiating the momentous process of creating one national literature on the basis of another – an act of paradigmatic importance for the way later ages will come to deal with the classical canon and one which also guarantees the distinctively multilingual character of the classical tradition as a whole.[12]

During the late Roman republic and the early principate – say, between Cicero and Ovid – the Latin language reaches its 'classical' form, which has remained a point of reference and a standard ever since;[13] and the interests of subsequent imperial elites ensure its perpetuation through the study of canonical authors (§4). Likewise, a parallel, but more diffuse, set of developments in the Greek-speaking 'East', from the Alexandrian recuperations to the linguistic Atticism of the first centuries AD, eventually establishes the Attic Greek of Aristophanes, Plato, and Demosthenes as what will eventually be called 'classical' Greek,[14] in contradistinction both to the multifarious dialects of the city states before Alexander and to the Attic-based 'common language', the Hellenistic *koine*, which had been generalized as the *lingua franca* of the Greek world after Alexander and which continued to maintain its existence as the direct ancestor of the Modern Greek language today.[15] The notion of the 'classical' and 'the classics' predates the advent of the classical tradition. And so too do the momentous tussles with an increasingly dominant Christianity that now define the tradition in the West for a millennium, and more.

Even though Christian writers look to the Bible for their basic temporal schemata, above all for the eschatological and chiliastic time-line from the creation of the world to the second coming of Christ,[16] they increasingly turn history into a 'privileged terrain of intellectual combat' with pagan authorities.[17] The integration of classical material into their organization of history constitutes an impressive piece of cultural imperialism.[18] In the fourth century, Constantine the Great offers a messianic rereading of Virgil's fourth *Eclogue*,[19] while Prudentius' hymn to the martyr Saint Lawrence rewrites the teleology of Virgil's *Aeneid* (where history effectively

12 Feeney (1998) 53. Cf. §15.

13 Cf. Stroh (2007).

14 In II AD, Aulus Gellius distinguishes between a 'classical author' ('scriptor classicus') and an 'ordinary' ('proletarius') writer: *Noctes Atticae*, 19. 8. 15. Subsequent history of the terminology: see variously Curtius (1953) 247–74, Pfeiffer (1976) 84, Settis (2010).

15 See Horrocks (1997) and, summarily, Silk (2009a).

16 Implicit is a rejection of the cyclical view of history (n. 6 above); the advent of Christ becomes a focal point and history a linear sequence. 'The cycles have been exploded': Augustine, *De Civitate Dei*, 12. 21.

17 Inglebert (1996) 53.

18 An early example is the *Chronographiae* of Julius Africanus (*c*. 212–21), which the Greek chronicler Eusebius used extensively: Becker (2005), Wallraff (2006).

19 See the *Oratio ad Coetum Sanctorum*, which Eusebius attributed to Constantine and included in his *Vita Constantinii*: Barnes (1981) 73–6. Before Constantine, Tertullian had already characterized Virgil as 'a soul Christian by nature' ('anima naturaliter Christiana': *Apologia* 17).

ends in the reign of Augustus) to proclaim Rome's overcoming of paganism as the ultimate historical achievement.[20] Then, in the early fifth, Orosius makes much of the coincidence that Christ was born in the golden age of Augustus, thereby dissolving 'the antithesis between Christianity and the Roman empire into the transhistorical continuity of all time since Christ's birth'[21] – and this, despite the recent convulsive shock to the empire, when the Christian Visigoths sacked Rome in 410: an event that would inspire Augustine to compose his *City of God*, separating the historical from the spiritual realm, the real from the ideal.[22]

Throughout late antiquity and the Middle Ages, the interlocking of pagan and Christian chronotopes continues. The most striking examples are, perhaps, the various synchronicities that Christian authors of universal history establish between Greco-Roman myth and the events narrated in the Bible. As Momigliano put it: 'The new history could not suppress the old. Adam and Eve and what follows had in some way to be presented in a world populated by Deucalion, Cadmus, Romulus, and Alexander the Great.'[23] Constantine's confidant Eusebius claimed that Ogygus, supposedly the first man in Attica, was a contemporary of Moses, thus implying that the pagans arrived on the stage of history rather late.[24] More than eleven centuries after Eusebius, the Dominican Giovanni Nanni is eager to rewrite ancient history, in the same polemical spirit, with a series of new equations (Noah with Janus, in particular),[25] while, two centuries after that, Milton is still playing the same game in *Paradise Lost* – though prepared now to backdate the pagan in the interests of Christology. In one memorable example, the divine (but now demonic) architect of Milton's Hell-city ('Pandaemonium') comes under the spotlight, equated with the Greco-Roman Hephaestus/Vulcan, or as Milton calls him, 'Mulciber'. This composite figure, Milton declares, 'fell | From heaven', according to pagan myth 'thrown by angry Jove' – but *not* according to higher authority: 'thus they relate, | Erring; for he with this rebellious rout | Fell long before.'[26] In the visual arts of Milton's day the synchronistic habit gives further scope for a range of unforeseen equations and correlations: 'for a learned seventeenth-century viewer, such as Loménie de Brienne, the infant in Poussin's *Finding of Moses* was not only Moses, but also Pan, Priapus and a host of oriental deities.'[27] In most such cases, the pagan is placed later, rather than earlier: the Miltonic backdating is untypical. As the recent Black Athena controversy serves to remind us, cultural primogeniture seems to matter (however problematic the arguments), and for centuries Christian

20 *Peristephanon*, 2. 1–20.

21 Jauss (2005) 333.

22 Cf. §25. In his preface, Augustine too chooses Virgil as his point of departure, in the shape of the historical mission statement from *Aeneid*, 6. 851–3, which exhorts the Romans to war down the proud, but spare the conquered.

23 Momigliano (1963) 83.

24 *Praeparatio Evangelica*, 10. 10. 7 (488d).

25 *Commentaria super opera diversorum auctorum de antiquitatibus loquentium* (1498).

26 *Paradise Lost*, 1. 730–51, looking back to *Iliad*, 1. 570–94.

27 Bull (2005) 240; see further Thuillier (1960), 2. 213.

sensibilities sought to endow their religion with the patina of age, in response to pagan challenges that it lacked the true authority of antiquity.[28]

But while the Christians may have triumphed on the battlefield of history, their one-upmanship *vis-à-vis* the pagan remained precarious in other ways. From the first, engagement with the ancient classics exposed impressionable students to their power and beauty. An intriguing *concordia discors* was the outcome. For a thousand years of the Latin West, the *oeuvres* of virtually every major author, from Augustine to Aquinas, from Boethius to Dante, bear witness to the uneasy marriage of Christian faith and pagan learning, in which attraction and revulsion, desire and bad conscience, engender a wide variety of creative compromises. There were Christian intellectuals who liked to think of their handling of the pagan heritage in terms of Deuteronomy 21, which details the preliminary procedures of ritual subjection before 'going in unto' a beautiful captive woman and making her one's wife – procedures that include the shaving of her head and the paring of her nails.[29] This tale of capture and domination, the allure of beauty and the need for the domestication of alien elements, suggests something of the conflicts Christians experienced when they immersed themselves in the pagan classics. Some were unable to resist temptation, and granted more attention to the 'beautiful captive' than even they thought they should. The results could be dire: witness Jerome's nightmare of being whipped by Christ and his angels and being branded 'a Ciceronian, not a Christian', because of his devotion to classical Latinity.[30]

The premise of all such anxieties is that during the 'Christian millennium' (say, 300–1300), despite various 'renaissances' (notably the Carolingian in the eighth and ninth centuries), the temporal break with the ancients was not perceived as especially pronounced if indeed it was felt to exist at all – a continuity parallel with and informed by the felt continuity of the emergent Romance languages with Latin (§13). It is Petrarch who makes up for this oversight by distinguishing 'antiquity' ('historiae antiquae') from the more 'recent age' ('historiae novae'), and elsewhere characterizing that age as a *period between*: a 'middle age' ('medium tempus') between antiquity and a new era that is, perhaps, at hand.[31] That 'middle age' itself has been (or still is) an age of 'squalor', because it sees the decline of 'humane' learning ('studia humanitatis') and classical (meaning Ciceronian) Latinity.[32] This

[28] For the early period, see Droge (1989) and Gnilka (1984), (1993).

[29] Authors who use the topos include Origen, Jerome, and Hrabanus Maurus: de Lubac (1998) 211–24.

[30] 'Ciceronianus es, non Christianus': *Epistles*, 22. 30.

[31] *Rerum familiarium*, 6. 2 and *Epistula metrica*, 3. 33. 4–6: see §29 (and, for the paradox of Petrarch's own 'medievalism', §29 n. 37).

[32] Cf. Greer (2000), Mommsen (1942). The expression 'studia humanitatis' derives from Cicero (Rüegg 1946) and is first used, not by Petrarch himself, but by Leonardo Bruni, in connection with Petrarch, in his *Ad Petrum Paulum Histrum dialogus* (1401): Pfeiffer (1976) 15–17; cf. §4 n. 54, §16 n. 24. Likewise, the specific phrase 'media antiquitas', for 'middle age(s)', is first attested in the writings of Erasmus' pupil, Beatus Rhenanus (early XVI): Pfeiffer (1976) 84. 'Ciceronian': §§7, 29.

tripartite division of history had Christian precedents, which Petrarch audaciously reconfigured in a classicizing key.[33] A similar strategy informed his coronation as 'poet laureate' by the senate and people of Rome on the Capitol on 8 April 1341. This was Easter Day, the central date in the Christian calendar, but that year marking a double 'resurrection': of Christ (by the grace of God) and of classical-Roman antiquity (through the cultural efforts of Petrarch himself).

Petrarch never repudiates Christianity. Faith and learning operate in harmony, both in his Coronation Oration and his unfinished Latin epic *Africa*, where he invokes Christ as well as the Muses, and promises Christ to return to Christian writings once he has fulfilled his classical calling. Even so, his sublime *coup de théâtre* unquestionably marks the dawn of a new 'humanist' era, in which the pagan classics are accorded an unprecedented status of exemplary value and authority, and gradually free themselves from Christianity's ideological embrace. Meanwhile, Petrarch's sense of a new age and his commitment to a new ideal of classical learning are enforced, less flamboyantly, by his friend Boccaccio, who acclaims Dante and Petrarch himself as reviving 'Italy's lost glory': Dante by 'daring to make the Muses sing in his mother tongue', Petrarch by 'following the path of the ancients'.[34] Giotto, too, he celebrates as recreator of a figurative art that had been 'buried for centuries'.[35]

The Renaissance, thus officially inaugurated in Italy, later encompasses France and (less comprehensively) England, in rough correlation with the Latin-relatedness of the native languages in question: Italian and French, both Romance languages, direct reflexes of Latin; English, a Germanic language, but virtually hybridized by Norman French (§13). And just as the German language (from the same Germanic source as English) is only ever trivially influenced by Latin, so too the German territories are only superficially affected by Renaissance culture and ideals – a development (or non-development) with profound consequences, which become apparent in the centuries to come, when the cultural impetus shifts from Italy to France, England, and, eventually, Germany itself.

'Resurrection': Petrarch's choice of imagery was not unique. Earlier in the fourteenth century, Benvenuto Campesani had rejoiced at the 'resurrection' of Catullus, when the first manuscript of Catullus' poems was discovered in his home town of Verona; while three centuries later, Francis Bacon, confronted with the antique nudes on display in the Earl of Arundel's garden, could only exclaim: 'The resurrection!'[36] The imagery proved persistent, even after the temporal threshold asserted by Petrarch had become a historical period in its own right: 'The Middle Ages,' declared the art historian Panofsky, 'had left antiquity unburied. The Renaissance

[33] Cf. Schreiner (1987) 410–11.

[34] Letter to Iacopo Pizzinga (1371).

[35] *Decameron* (*c.* 1350), 4. 5. 6.

[36] *De resurrectione Catulli poetae Veronensis* (*c.* 1305); Bacon, 'Apothegms', 18 (in Tenison, *Baconiana*: 1679). See Blumenberg (1983) 105–6.

stood weeping at its grave and tried to resurrect its soul. Resurrected souls are intangible, but have the advantage of immortality and omnipresence. Therefore the role of classical antiquity after the Renaissance is somewhat elusive but, on the other hand, pervasive.'[37] For Renaissance interpreters of their own world, alternative models, with different messages, were available. In his meditations on Italian art, old and new, from his perspective in the mid-sixteenth century, Vasari traces the decline of ancient Rome to the turning of Fortune's wheel.[38] The implication would seem to be that a turn of the wheel *could* reinstate the former glories of Rome,[39] or – as Vasari thinks, with Michelangelo, above all, in mind ('in his own self surpassing moderns, ancients, and Nature') – already *had*.[40]

During the early modern period, perceptions of time itself undergo a transformation, from medieval personifications of Father Time (aged, bearded, and on crutches) to Time-Saturn, a muscular classicizing nude devouring his children.[41] And reconceptualization in the visual imagination soon finds its counterpart in science, with newly available data from antiquity and a broadly anti-clerical determination to search for scientific truth combining to generate new reckonings of time and new understandings of history. If Paulus Crusius, in 1578, still centres historical time on the birth of Christ, Joseph Justus Scaliger, only five years later, feels free to construct his chronology without reference to religious dogma.[42] The mechanical view of the universe that culminates in Isaac Newton's *Principia* (1687) had its roots in classical sources like Euclid and Ptolemy;[43] but the gradual secularizing of time did not end ideological struggles over the meaning and larger cultural authority of specific periods of history, and classical antiquity in particular.

Quite the contrary: a new cult of progress, along with the growth of nationalism and national pride across Europe, hugely enhances the status of modern writings in the vernacular (Newton's *Principia* is itself among the last 'great books' to be written in Latin), one outcome of which is a protracted conflict over their relative value *vis-à-vis* the Greek and Roman classics. Vasari's claims for Michelangelo prefigure a series of comparable claims for modern culture in general, literature included. The classicizing English poet Ben Jonson, writing 'To the memory of my beloved . . . Master William Shakespeare' in 1623, was bold, for his time, in suggesting that at least in comic drama ('when thy socks were on'), Shakespeare – uniquely –

37 Panofsky (1960) 113.

38 The image goes back to Boethius, *Consolatio*, 2. 1 – cf. Frakes (1988), Kiefer (1979) – but is prefigured by much earlier Greek appeals to the 'cyclical' turn of events (*kuklos*: 'circle', 'cycle', 'wheel'), as in Herodotus (n. 6 above).

39 So Bull (2005) 3.

40 Vasari, *Lives*, proem to Part 3.

41 See Cohen (2000) on illustrations in successive editions of Petrarch's *Trionfo del tempo*.

42 Crusius, *Liber de epochis seu aevis temporum et imperiorum* (1578); Scaliger, *Opus novum de emendatione temporum* (1583). Cf. Grafton (1993a).

43 In full, *Philosophiae naturalis principia mathematica* ('The Mathematical Principles of the Philosophy of Nature'): Mittelstrass (1979).

equalled his ancient counterparts (they 'leave thee alone for the comparison'). In 1687, Charles Perrault's poem on 'The Age of Louis the Great', read out before the French Academy on the occasion of the recovery of Louis XIV from surgery, was bolder still in proposing that the cultural achievements of France not only rivalled, but by now actually surpassed, the efforts of the ancients; and the fact that the long list of writers cited includes, among others, the great Molière, but – shockingly – misses out the great Racine, sums up the almost casual nature of the claim.[44]

In the years that followed, Perrault went further by aligning and comparing creative achievers and achievements from Greco-Roman and modern culture (mostly French culture) across the arts and sciences, broadly to the advantage of the moderns, in a five-part dialogue, *Ancients and Moderns in Parallel* (1688–92).[45] Like Quintilian in imperial Rome, upholding the claims of Roman writers against their Greek counterparts,[46] but less circumspect than Quintilian, Perrault now proclaims the supremacy of the moderns 'in all the arts and all the sciences', with a query, only, about 'eloquence and poetry'.[47] The concentration, in the last part of his work, on 'sciences' like astronomy and medicine, on Cartesian philosophy, and (finally and climactically) on the splendours of the palace and gardens of Versailles, all made the conclusion hard to resist. Others, though, disagreed: the primacy of the present may hold true in the sphere of science, they retorted, but the case is fundamentally different in the arts. The so-called 'quarrel' (*Querelle des anciens et des modernes*) eventually ended in a sort of truce, which the German Lessing summed up in a moment of youthful brio in 1748: 'The past has Homer to put us to shame: | The glory of our age takes Newton's name.'[48]

With hindsight, the citation of Homer here is symptomatic of a new outlook. Since Quintilian, indeed, many would have granted the unique distinction of Greek Homer over (even) Roman Virgil,[49] but Lessing's citation of Homer rather prefigures a specific shift towards Greece, and a distinctive valuation of Greek culture as a whole, that becomes more marked – especially in Germany – as the 'progressive' tendencies of the eighteenth century unfold. Among much else, these tendencies

44 On Perrault's choices, cf. Kortum (1966). Ironically, in the yet more modern ages that follow Perrault's 'modern' rejection of Racine, French perspectives on drama become more, not less, Racinocentric, from Stendhal (*Racine et Shakespeare*, 1823/5) to Barthes (*Sur Racine*, 1963).

45 *Parallèle des anciens et des modernes en ce qui regarde les arts et les sciences.*

46 Quintilian, *Institutio Oratoria*, 10. 1. 46–84 (Greek), 85–131 (Latin).

47 *Parallèle*, 4. 292–3: 'dans tous les arts et dans toutes les sciences, à la réserve de l'éloquence et de la poésie, les modernes sont de beaucoup supérieurs.'

48 'An den Herrn M. . .': 'Das Alter wird uns stets mit dem Homer beschämen, | Und unsrer Zeiten Ruhm muss Newton auf sich nehmen.' Lessing was nineteen at the time. Cf. Riedel (1976) 29–30. Among many comparable formulations, William Wotton distinguishes progressive science and aggregative art in *Reflections upon Ancient and Modern Learning* (1694). The 'quarrel' is most intense and long-lasting in France: cf. Norman (2011) and, more generally, Highet (1967) 261–92, Levine (1991), Lowenthal (1985) 74–124.

49 Quintilian, *Institutio Oratoria*, 10. 1. 85–6. In XVIII, the Homer/Virgil confrontation becomes an issue in its own right: Simonsuuri (1979), Vogt-Spira (2003), Wlosok (1990).

include a revolution in historical consciousness that impacts on the truth-value of the 'sacred history' encased in the Bible, but which also has significant repercussions for the perception of antiquity, especially its 'prehistoric' material. As the protocols of empirical certainty change, the modern notion of myth comes into view (§24). Once identified as records of events in universal history – perhaps inaccurate records ('thus they relate, | Erring'), but still records – many ancient myths are now read as imaginative tales, and writers as different as Vico, Fontenelle, and Heyne set out to explore the factors responsible for their creation (Heyne, for instance, sees Greek myth as reflecting primitive reactions to natural events).[50] In this respect, as in many others, the eighteenth century is a time of transition, constructing an intermediary 'philosophical' history between the sacred history of earlier ages and the secular historicism that soon becomes dominant.[51]

In some respects, the momentous developments of the eighteenth and early nineteenth centuries in Continental Europe and the English-speaking world took the sting out of assertions and counter-assertions about the status of classical antiquity and its works. The anti-traditional animus of the Enlightenment,[52] of romanticism and revolution, the rise of historicism and its relativistic understanding of cultures and epochs (each being 'immediate to God', in Ranke's famous formulation),[53] the development (or recognition) of 'literature' in its modern sense (§22), the invention of 'aesthetics' and 'history of art' in the modern sense (§§11, 29), the organizing of museums and art galleries on historical principles (§17), and, in general, the increasingly fashionable credo of historical progress: all these weaken the once habitual impulse to negotiate the position of the present in historical time with reference to the classical past – an impulse certainly assisted by (though not strictly dependent on) the earlier conviction that (as Racine put it) 'good sense and reason are the same in every age'.[54]

The one great exception here, though, is romanticism: not a historical movement in any politico-historical or socio-historical sense, but a time-specific nexus of ideas and expression, of undeniable complexity and importance. Within this multifarious movement, there is indeed much that looks in quite new directions (especially inwards, to the soul of the creative genius) and much that glorifies the new ideal of relativity ('lichen, moss, fern, and the richest scented flower: each blooms in its place in God's order').[55] At the same time, and paradoxically (but romanticism specializes

[50] *De causis fabularum seu mythorum veterum physicis* (1764). Cf. §24.

[51] See variously Burke (1969), Seifert (1986), Zedelmaier (2003).

[52] Despite such diverse productions as Montesquieu's *Considérations sur la cause de la grandeur des Romains et de leur décadence* (1734) and Moses Mendelssohn's *Phädon oder über die Unsterblichkeit der Seele* (1767).

[53] 'Jede Epoche ist unmittelbar zur Gott': *Über die Epochen der neueren Geschichte* (1854).

[54] 'Le bon sens et la raison . . . les mêmes dans tous les siècles': Preface to *Iphigénie* (1674).

[55] Herder, *Briefe zur Beförderung der Humanität*, 8. 107 (1796). On the radical novelty of romanticism overall, cf. Blanning (2010).

in paradoxes), one can point to a major restatement of the periodizing comparison between ancient and modern and a new, and decisive, self-definition with reference to the classical itself.

A crucial figure in these developments is the German thinker, Johann Gottfried Herder – and German ideas and experiments are at the heart of the new movement. 'The fountainhead of universal literary history', René Wellek once called him[56] – but, in Herder's thinking, literary, cultural, and national history are often hard to distinguish. As cultural historian, Herder acknowledges diversity ('Every age has its tone, its colour'), with a cyclical, rather than progressive, understanding of cultural development, which privileges origins ('origins show the nature of a thing') and values, above all, the authenticity of the original: the original as vested in a language, a culture, a nation ('the genius of a language is also the genius of the literature of the nation').[57] In these configurations, Herder acclaims the generative, and (as he hopes) regenerative, power of native 'folk' creativity, which turns out to subsume, not only the medieval romance (quite literally the immediate point of reference for the new 'romanticism'), but also the mature freshness of Homer and the Old Testament, Dante, and Shakespeare. This is the new positive, and opposed to it – the sharply defined negative – is 'the classical' ('O, that accursed word, "classical"'),[58] which tends to subsume, not antiquity as such, but Rome, and the largely Roman proclivities of the Renaissance and (above all) of neoclassicism. The target is everything that is taken to be secondary and vicarious: Rome, imitation, artificiality, and (in contemporary terms) France – but then, for Herder, contemporary Germany is deeply tainted too.

In one sense, it can seem that for Herder all creativity is timeless ('Shakespeare is Sophocles' brother'),[59] or perhaps there is an all-but-timeless cultural dynamic opposing the creative and the imitative in any age. But then again, we moderns are tied to the secondary inadequacies of our inauthentic world ('we hardly see or feel any longer: we only think and brood'),[60] as against the primary past, not least the ancient Greek past, and – perhaps – the future. It is not, then, that we can move to the hoped-for future by *copying* that past: absolutely not. We need to be *like* the Greeks in our native creativity.

From such explosive fragments (not Herder's alone, but his thoughts are both influential and representative), a generation of Romantic thinkers and writers construct the momentous opposition, 'classical' versus 'romantic' – which, by a suitably Romantic paradox, was first formally articulated by the French critic, Madame de

[56] Wellek (1955) 183.

[57] *Briefe zur Beförderung der Humanität*, 7. 88 (1796); *Zerstreute Blätter*, 2, 'Bilder und Träume', 2. 2 (1786); *Über die neuere deutsche Literatur*, 1, 'Die Sprache . . .' (1767).

[58] 'O das verwünschte Wort: Classisch!': *Über die neuere deutsche Literatur*, 3. 1. 9 (1767).

[59] *Von deutscher Art und Kunst*, 'Shakespeare' (1773).

[60] Ibid. 'Ossian' (1773).

Staël,[61] in her book *On Germany* (*De l'Allemagne*) in 1813.[62] Like, but also very unlike, the Petrarchan Renaissance, the new movement yearns to divide cultural history into two – the ancients and us – but now, almost invariably, this means the Greeks and us: hence the remarkable development whereby romanticism (whose definitive impulse is German) is bound up with German classicism, which is itself – unlike the Renaissance Germany never had – centred on Greece.

Adumbrating the difference between 'antique or classical' and modern or 'romantic' in 1816, the German critic August Wilhelm Schlegel reaches for architectural analogies: 'The Pantheon is not more different from Westminster Abbey or the church of St Stephen in Vienna than the structure of a tragedy of Sophocles from a drama of Shakespeare' – with the whole opposition summed up as 'the Grecian' as against 'the Gothic'.[63] One can hardly fail to notice that this 'Pantheon', though actually Roman, is seemingly counted as Greek, while 'Shakespeare' is actually English, but (without reference to the considerable Renaissance imprint on his work) is counted as representative Germanic ('Gothic'). These recategorizations, at all events, assume a premise of cultural discontinuity – them and us, the ancients and the Romantics – which does mean (perhaps . . .) that we are, or might one day be, a new beginning, *like them*.

Romantic hopes and laments, abundant and diverse in their attachments, are full of beginnings and awakenings. Listen to the poets. 'Bliss was it in that dawn to be alive, | But to be young was very heaven!': thus Wordsworth, on 'The French Revolution, as it Appeared to Enthusiasts', in 1809. 'The Young Captive Woman' and 'The Young Tarentine' are among the poems through which André Chenier – guillotined by the Revolutionary Tribunal in 1794, and posthumously identified by French Romantics as one of their own – achieves that honorary status, though himself more neoclassical than Romantic in his affiliations.[64] In the medieval world of Christian innocence, muses the German poet-thinker Novalis in 1799, Europe still possessed

[61] In XVIII Britain, critics anticipate the opposition by opposing 'classical' to 'Gothic': so Richard Hurd, *Letters on Chivalry and Romance* (1762). See also Eicher (1972).

[62] The publication date: the work was finished in 1810, but suppressed by Napoleon. Partly because of its German-ness (actual and perceived), romanticism at first impinges on France as a problem. The cultural allegiances of Revolutionary and Napoleonic France are still strikingly Roman, from David's paintings (§§21, 33) to Couvrai's 'anti-Catilinian' speech against Robespierre (§26) to, even, de Staël's own enthusiasms: France (1985); Parker, H. T. (1937); summary in Highet (1967) 390–9. In the poetic sphere, the most decisive manifesto of French romanticism is late (Victor Hugo's *Preface de Cromwell*, 1827), while, later still, French thinkers and writers profess uncertainty about what romanticism really is. In the first of his 'Lettres de Dupuis et Cotonet' (1835), Alfred de Musset's mouthpiece Dupuis 'recounts how Romanticism has been historical in one year, and a matter of introspective intimacy the next, only to re-emerge, shortly after, first as a system of philosophy and political economy, and then as the habit of not shaving and of wearing wide-lapelled waistcoats': Kay, Cave and Bowie (2003) 211.

[63] Opening pages of the second edition of *Vorlesungen über dramatische Kunst und Literatur* (originally lectures in 1808–9), as tr. by John Black in 1846.

[64] 'La jeune captive' and 'La jeune Tarentine', published in 1795 and 1801 respectively. On Chenier as neoclassicist, cf. e.g. Gamble (2008).

'the lovely bloom of its youth, faith, and love'.[65] 'In the youth of the world, men dance and sing': Shelley in his *Defence of Poetry* (1821). And to the Romantic mind the Greeks can seem very close to that youthful world. 'The poems of Homer . . . were the delight of infant Greece': Shelley again.[66] In Italy, the innovative sensibility of Leopardi encompasses the thought in 1822 by invoking ancient myth in terms of spring.[67] Some years earlier, an engraving by the poet-artist William Blake, around 1796, makes the point in a striking visual image. Blake at this time is captivated by the 'immense flood of Grecian light and glory which is coming on Europe';[68] in this spirit, his *Albion Rose*, or *Glad Day*, depicts a moment of triumphant fresh life, with a young man dancing towards the viewer – in a classicizing pose seemingly based on reproductions of a bronze faun recently found at Herculaneum – naked, arms outstretched, and head radiating brilliant light, a veritable Apollo in all his youthful glory [*Plate 1*].[69]

But any attempt to *recreate* the youthful creativity of those Greeks, any attempt actually to *be* 'like them', is doomed, and card-carrying Romantics, and fellow-travellers too, all know it. 'We are all Greeks', says Shelley in 1822 – but with reference to derivation, not affinity ('Our laws, our literature, our religion, our arts have their root in Greece').[70] 'We are not Greeks any more' is the frank assessment of the German painter Philipp Otto Runge in 1802.[71] And 'for us to wish to become inhabitants of Rome or Athens ourselves' – these words are Humboldt's in 1804, endorsed by Goethe – 'was, after all, only an illusion.'[72] In 1821, in Canto III of his satirical masterpiece *Don Juan*, Byron creates a poignant 'song', 'The Isles of Greece', for a modern Greek 'singer', which glances once more at the youthfulness of ancient

[65] 'Die Christenheit oder Europa'.

[66] Cf. Karl Marx's suggestion, a generation later, that ancient Greece represents 'humanity's historic childhood, its most beautiful unfolding' – but also that 'a man cannot become a child again, or he becomes childish': *Grundrisse der Kritik der politischen Ökonomie* (written, 1857–8: end of Introduction).

[67] *Alla Primavera, o delle favole antiche* ('To Spring, *or* On Ancient Fables').

[68] Letter to George Cumberland, 2 July 1800. The year before, Blake had declared that 'the purpose for which alone I live . . . is . . . to renew the lost art of the Greeks' (letter to John Trusler, 16 August 1799).

[69] See Bentley (1978) 314, 720; cf. variously Howard (1982) 117–18 and Wilton (1976) 196–8. The Apollo connection is borne out by Blake's use of the engraving to illustrate a reference in his poem *Vala* to 'the Sun dances upon the mountains': Bentley (1978) 1267. Blake's Hellenism soon waned, and by the end of his life he could only see (in Christian-mystical mode) 'the Greek and Roman Classics [as] the Antichrist' (marginalia to Thornton's *The Lord's Prayer*, 1827); cf. Howard (1982) 140.

[70] Preface to *Hellas*.

[71] 'Wir sind keine Griechen mehr': letter to his brother Daniel, February 1802 (in response to traditionalist criticisms of his *Achilles and the River Gods*, entered for the Weimar exhibition a year earlier).

[72] Goethe, *Winckelmann und sein Jahrhundert* (1805); letter from Humboldt to Goethe, 23 August 1804. Contrast, though, Goethe in 1818 ('Antik und Modern'): 'Let everyone be Greeks their own way – but let them be Greeks!' Contrast, too, Nietzsche's – post-Romantic – defiance in his later years: 'Aren't we, precisely, Greeks?' (among the closing words of the preface to *Die fröhliche Wissenschaft*, 2nd edn, 1887, repeated at the end of *Nietzsche Contra Wagner*, 1888); cf. Silk (2004c). Conversely, Wagner: §31.

Greece – but in abrasive contrast to mediocre modernity. Not only does the 'song' insist, explicitly, on the distance between past and present ('Eternal summer gilds them yet, | But all, except their sun, is set'); it gives way to a devastating put-down in the poet-narrator's own ironic voice:

> Thus sung, or would, or could, or should have sung,
> The modern Greek, in tolerable verse;
> If not like Orpheus quite, when Greece was young,
> Yet in these times he might have done much worse.[73]

But as early as 1795, in his meditation on *Naive and Sentimental Poetry*, Friedrich Schiller had already offered a prefiguration of the antithesis between classical and romantic whose very terms showed why self-conscious modernity ('sentimental') could never recapture the Greeks' creative innocence ('naive'): the 'naive' writer (like the Greeks) '*is* nature'; the 'sentimental' writer (like most of *us*) can only '*seek* nature'.[74] For Friedrich Hölderlin, a few years later, the seekings, the beginnings, the Greeks, all fuse agonisingly into an overpowering sense of loss. In Hölderlin's 'Bread and Wine' ('Brod und Wein', 1800), the images are of 'some lonely man | Thinking of distant friends and youth', but especially of 'Blessed Greece' and its holy festivals, of the ancient gods who attended their worshippers at those festivals and who may still, in some sense, 'be alive' – but 'We have come too late.'

Inklings of a mysterious synthesis between the Greek Dionysus and Christ haunt Hölderlin's poems of this period.[75] As with August Schlegel's more prosaic correlation of Romantic modernity, Shakespeare and Gothic cathedrals, the typically paradoxical co-existence of a historical sense and equations beyond the historical is apparent. So too is the perceived awkwardness of fitting Christianity into the schema, but so, above all, is the irreducible sense of distance – not distant continuity, simply distance – between ancient and modern, the Greeks and *us*.

In the wake of romanticism, and even in the 'progressive' philosophies of history that the nineteenth century is famous for (Lyotard's 'grand narratives'),[76] the normative status of classical antiquity continues to play a role. It has an exemplary status for Hegel, whose celebrated schema of the conflictual ('dialectical') progress of history is set forth in parallel with the patterns of conflict in Greek tragedy.[77]

[73] See further Silk (2009b) 381–3.

[74] *Über naive und sentimentalische Dichtung*, 1–2. Cf. Heinrich von Kleist in 1810: 'And so – said I, a trifle distractedly – should we eat once more from the Tree of Knowledge, that we may fall back into the state of innocence? Of course, he replied: that is the last chapter in the history of the world' (*Über das Marionettentheater*, closing sentences).

[75] Compare, somewhat later, the strange co-existence of Christian and pagan in Walter Pater's short stories, 'Apollo in Picardy' (1886) and 'Denys L'Auxerrois' (1893). Pater's immediate inspiration, however, is Heinrich Heine's poem, 'Die Götter im Exil' (1853).

[76] 'Grands récits': Lyotard, *La Condition postmoderne* (1979). Cf. §30.

[77] Chiefly, but not only, in his *Ästhetik* (published posthumously in 1835/42): summarily, Silk and Stern (1981) 312–26.

Even Hegel's erstwhile follower Karl Marx, who in his youthful dissertation on Epicureanism (1841) compares the 'utilitarian' age of Epicurus to his own, remains committed to a classicizing aesthetic of balance and harmony, which fuels his utopian dream of an unalienated society. He duly finds it realized in Greek art, notwithstanding the irony that, in Marxian terms, this attainment of artistic perfection coincided historically with the most primitive socio-economic system (slave labour).[78]

Throughout the later nineteenth century, and beyond, the status of the classics continues to play a significant role in debates about 'culture and anarchy' (Matthew Arnold) and the 'decline of the West' (Oswald Spengler)[79] which accompany the political enfranchisement of large underprivileged segments of the population, while various writers and thinkers of the nineteenth and earlier twentieth centuries, from Burckhardt to Horkheimer and Adorno, use periods or figures from antiquity to think through the course of history as a means of pondering problems of their own times, often in a deeply pessimistic spirit.[80]

Yet this essentially contrastive appeal to the ancient world is not the whole story. Historical perceptions and self-perceptions in the modern age, and more generally since the Renaissance, have sometimes appropriated 'the classical' in very different fashion. With the rise of the modern nation-state and the full emergence of national literatures in the vernacular, 'elective affinities' are discerned that are not always fraught with disappointment. In the years that follow the sack of Constantinople by the Turks (1453), Aeneas Sylvius Piccolomini (Pope Pius II, 1458–64) acclaims Christian Europe as a plurality of nations united not only by their religion, but also by their common roots in Greco-Roman antiquity and its values,[81] while a century earlier, and repeatedly in the centuries that follow, this plurality is boldly singularized in more chauvinistic appropriations of the ancient heritage. Petrarch and his contemporary Cola di Rienzo believe that the revival of classical learning and political ideas might coincide with the re-establishment of the *Imperium Romanum*, with Rome at the centre of a unified Italy and Europe[82] – and this, in implicit contradistinction to the conviction of an Augustine or a Dante that the Catholic Church is a continuation, on a higher level, of that Roman Empire itself;[83] or indeed to the Carolingian vision (epitomized by the very title of the 'Holy Roman Empire') of a convergence between the Church of Rome and the former imperial ideal. In a later

[78] In a given sense, Greek art is still 'a norm and an unattainable model': *Grundrisse* (n. 66 above), end of Introduction.

[79] Arnold, *Culture and Anarchy* (1869); Spengler, *Der Untergang des Abendlandes* (1918–23).

[80] See esp. Burckhardt, *Griechische Kulturgeschichte* (1898–1902); Horkheimer and Adorno, *Dialektik der Aufklärung. Philosophische Fragmente* (1947), ch. 2: 'Odysseus oder Mythos und Aufklärung'. Cf. §34.

[81] *De Europa* (1458). See generally Hay (1957).

[82] Struve (2004).

[83] After the Reformation, the relationship is acknowledged by Catholicism's opponents in different terms. 'The papacy is not other than the ghost of the deceased Roman Empire, sitting crowned upon the grave thereof': Hobbes, *Leviathan* (1651), 4. 47.

century, there is a strident nationalist tone to Joachim Du Bellay's appeal, on behalf of the emergent French poetic Pléiade, for French poetry to achieve equality with the classics by 'looting' the city of Rome and 'pillaging' the temple at Delphi (1549).[84] And if the Augustan poets of early eighteenth-century England are content to find satirical analogies in the poetry and politics of Virgil, Horace, and Ovid, Napoleonic France at the century's close is more directly attracted to the grandeur and the territorial reach of imperial Rome.

Napoleon's German neighbours, fragmented and politically feeble, were less single-minded. While a German-nationalist strand is a recurrent element in the Hellenism of Herder and his successors (it reaches its climax in the political-artistic vision of the 'new Aeschylus', composer Richard Wagner),[85] the great Goethe, with his *Italian* journeys and his *Roman* elegies (the 'German Propertius', as Schiller called him), transcends even the Greek allegiance;[86] and Weimar classicism – with Goethe and Schiller its leading lights – epitomizes the very different ideal and self-perception of Germany as a *Kulturnation* (this too was the message of Madame de Staël's essay on Germany), forging a 'religion of culture and education' (*Bildungsreligion*) from a more considered study of the classics. In fact the most explicit, and most nakedly chauvinist, of all national appeals to the classical comes from Italy in the first half of the twentieth century, when Mussolini seeks to put into practice Petrarch's and Cola di Rienzo's dream of imperial Rome revived.[87]

Meanwhile, alongside such menacing uses of antiquity, the Western world invents modernism: a highly sophisticated and often unashamedly elitist cluster of movements that encompass art and architecture, music and ballet, theatre and cinema, poetry and prose. Across this great range, classical technique, sometimes, is residually apparent – even 'the Bauhaus's machine-age aesthetic can be traced back to a neoclassical forthrightness'.[88] Classical reference, often, is unmistakable – as in the work of Picasso and Valéry, Cocteau, and Joyce. Classical allegiance, conversely, is explicit in the unusual case of T. S. Eliot ('classicist in literature': §35), but more often dismissed within a larger repudiation of the un-modern; 'an abrupt break with all tradition' was Herbert Read's formula for 'Art Now' (in a book of that name in 1933). Amidst such contradictions, modernism can be seen to articulate an acute self-consciousness about the relation of the 'modern' to the past (including the classical past) that recalls the anxieties of Schiller and his contemporaries a century before – however different the attitudes, the outcomes, or indeed the commitment

84 *Deffence et illustration de la langue françoyse*, 'Conclusion'.

85 §31 n. 68.

86 Cf. the impartiality in his (and Humboldt's) talk of Rome and Athens (p. 27 above). In the Romantic generation, a persistent strand of German thinking attaches itself to Italy, from the establishment of the 'Nazarene' brotherhood of painters in Rome in 1810 to the famous encapsulation of Goethe's own Italian yearnings in the wistful first line of Mignon's song in *Wilhelm Meisters Lehrjahre* (1794–6): 'Kennst du das Land, wo die Zitronen blühn?' Cf. Hachmeister (2002).

87 By comparison, the flirtation of Nazi Germany with ancient Greece (Losemann 1977) is peripheral.

88 Perl (2010) 597: cf. §11.

to any systematic revaluation of what Eliot, in a different spirit, refers to as 'Time present and time past'.[89] Modernist preoccupation with fragments rather than wholes, on the part of Eliot and others, is symptomatic.

In the wake of twentieth-century catastrophes and barbarisms on an unprecedented scale, grand constructions of world-historical coherence have become unfashionable,[90] and meaningful analogies between ancient civilization and the present, too. Seen through a postmodern kaleidoscope, history constantly reconfigures itself in random fashion: the normative and the subversive, the classical and the anti-canonical, appear side by side in a cheerful tumbling that resembles carnival (though carnival, too, as Bakhtin reminds us, has its classical parallels and sources: §12). Within the academy, at least, it is increasingly 'the other' of antiquity – the non-canonical, the under-privileged, the previously marginalized – that is considered a source of scholarly interest and legitimacy, whereas in some quarters the classical itself elicits suspicion, or even scorn, unless deconstructed or critiqued. For all that, the conversation with Greco-Roman antiquity continues, even if the spirit of the dialogue has often shifted from a grand-manner reading of periods and ages to a more playful dalliance with particular detail. But as Napoleon had occasion to remark, after the retreat from Moscow in 1812, and with reference to one of the most elusive of ancient aesthetic concepts: 'from the sublime to the ridiculous is only one step'.[91] And *vice versa*.

[89] The opening line of *Four Quartets*.

[90] Notwithstanding Francis Fukuyama's 'end of history' (1992) or Samuel P. Huntington's sub-Hegelian 'clash of civilizations' (1997).

[91] 'Du sublime au ridicule il n'y a qu'un pas' (quoted in De Pradt's 1815 *Histoire de l'Ambassade dans le grand-duché de Varsovie en 1812*, 6th edn, p. 215): cf. §30.

§4

Sustaining the Tradition

Classics and Education

In 1720, Antoine Coypel, history painter in the grand manner, delivered an address to the Royal Academy of Painting and Sculpture in Paris in which he expounded the requirements for practising artists, and specifically their need for a broad base of knowledge. The areas of expertise specified include various technical matters, including perspective and proportion, but it is the broadly cultural and less specifically painterly items that predominate: poetry and philosophy; history, 'sacred, profane, or fabulous'; rhetoric (because, like the orator, the painter must 'teach, please, and touch the heart'); and opening the list, and evidently a prerequisite of the list as a whole, 'a thorough acquaintance with the humanities'.[1]

Coypel's prescription is striking in that it seems to assume a direct relationship between creative outcomes and formal classical education (where else would the artist get his 'thorough acquaintance with the humanities', quite apart from full access to rhetoric or to 'fabulous' – meaning mythological – history?). That assumption is not necessarily unusual, over the centuries, even if it is not always quite so obvious. A century later, the painter Ingres can be heard proclaiming that any suggestion of an artist getting by 'without studying antiquity and the classics' is either 'madness or laziness',[2] while extensive classical learning underlies the observations (as well as the artistic practice) of leading figures, from the humanist architect

[1] 'une grande teinture des humanités': H. Jouin, *Conférences de l'académie royale de peinture et de sculpture* (1883), p. 277.

[2] Recorded by Ingres's friend the Vicomte Henri Delaborde, in his *Ingres, sa vie, ses travaux, sa doctrine* (1890), p. 138.

The Classical Tradition: Art, Literature, Thought, First Edition. Michael Silk, Ingo Gildenhard, and Rosemary Barrow.

Published 2017 by John Wiley & Sons Ltd.

Alberti in the fifteenth century to the 'peintre philosophe' Poussin in the seventeenth.[3]

But what is much more profusely attested in the published thoughts of artists is debate over the pros and cons (and after Poussin's century, increasingly the cons) of a technical upbringing centred on learning to draw from classical models. For many artists, the value of such a training had once been axiomatic, as it was for Poussin's older contemporary, Guido Reni:

> Once asked by a pupil which exemplars he drew [his] noble forms and fair faces from . . . he showed him a few common plaster heads cast from antique statues – the Niobe, the Medici Venus and others – and replied: 'These are my teachers'.[4]

From the eighteenth century onwards, such practices are increasingly called into question. Witness this, from Jean-Baptiste-Siméon Chardin to the admission jury of the Paris Academy in 1765:

> When we are seven or eight years old, a pencil is put in our hands. We start drawing from the cast . . . Our backs have long been bent over our boards, when we are put in front of a Hercules or an antique torso, and you have not been a witness to the tears that the Satyr, the Gladiator, the Venus de' Medici, the Antaeus, have caused to flow . . . After withering for days and nights . . . we are presented with living nature, and suddenly all the years gone by seem wasted.[5]

The relevance of these modes of technical training to the classical tradition is self-evident. Equally, though, they have only a tangential connection to classical education as such – in obvious contrast to the observations of Ingres or, especially, Coypel. We begin our overview of classical education with this contrast for two reasons: to make it clear that in certain respects the visual arts have their own story (§11), which means that, for the moment, it is 'literature' and 'thought' that take centre stage; but conversely to note how pervasive the demand for 'acquaintance with the humanities' was, in what can properly be called the classicizing age.

Traditions depend on a continual investment in cultural practices; and the classical tradition, however eccentric in other ways, is a case in point. Such practices are often organized by specially trained 'priests of meaning', men (they have been, usually, men) who do their work of cultivation within specific institutional contexts for specific social groups with a vested interest in sustaining their activities. Across the world's cultures, these cultivators have included Brahmans and mandarins,

[3] Alberti: §§11, 30. Poussin: cf. the observations published by his biographer, G. P. Bellori, *Le vite de' pittori, scultori, ed architetti moderni* (1672), pp. 460–2, though the actual phrase 'philosopher-painter' seems to be late-XVIII: Blunt (1967), 3. 160.

[4] Bellori, *Le vite* (1672), p. 6.

[5] Recorded by Diderot in his review of the Salon of 1765, and quoted by the brothers Goncourt, *L'art du XVIIIe siècle* (1873–4), 1. 130–1. A similar debate is still exercising the late-XIX British art world: Barrow (2007) 102–3.

rabbis and mullahs, monks and theologians, scribes and scholars, and – our special concern here – schoolmasters and planners and overseers of education.[6] And the formal cultivation of Greco-Roman antiquity, after its actual demise, is conducted largely by such men, within such institutional contexts. These contexts are realities, as much as the individuals who belong to them. And no less a reality is the fact that, within its educational contexts (and like many 'traditions', again), the classical tradition has, for long periods, been sustained by a nexus of power and knowledge, and by mechanisms of inclusion and exclusion, disenfranchisement and privilege.

From antiquity until fairly recently, an education rooted in the learning of Latin (and, at various times, Greek) and the study of the Latin classics (with or without their Greek counterparts) has served powerful segments of successive populations: top people in the court and the Church; emperors interested in imperial bureaucracies; rising nation-states concerned to unify their citizens through a prestigious and coherent cultural prospectus; empire builders bent on training an elite to rule the world.[7] And in Britain, for instance, one can easily trace the correlations, over the centuries, between a traditional, language-centred, classical education and a class system based on land and wealth, then between the weakening of the class system at large, during the twentieth century, and the displacement and attenuation of that version of classical education, in favour of the natural sciences, on the one hand, and modern languages and literatures, on the other.

The opening section of a much-loved comic history of England, first published in 1930, and epitomizing what was once known as 'public-school humour', makes explicit (with considerable self-deprecating irony) the correlation of classics and class that was already – not that the humour hints at it – fatally undermined. From its premise of shared familiarity with school-classics topoi (variously abbreviated, parodied, or inverted) to a choice acknowledgement of the norms of class/colonial superiority at the end, the passage sums up a whole era of exclusive educational provision:

> The first date in English History is 55 BC, in which year Julius Caesar (the *memorable* Roman Emperor) landed, like all other successful invaders of these islands, at Thanet. This was in the Olden Days, when the Romans were top nation on account of their classical education . . . [Having already] defeated the Ancient Britons by unfair means . . . [Caesar] set the memorable Latin sentence 'Veni, Vidi, Vici,' which the Romans, who were all very well educated, construed correctly. The Britons, however, who of course still used the old pronunciation, understanding him to have called them 'Weeny, Weedy and Weaky', lost heart and gave up the struggle, thinking that he had already divided them into Three Parts . . . The Roman Conquest was, however, a *Good Thing*, since the Britons were only natives at that time.[8]

6 Cf. Assmann and Assmann (1987) 12–13. Scholars: §16.

7 Empire builders: see e.g. Vasunia (2011).

8 W. C. Sellar and R. J. Yeatman, *1066 and All That* (1930), ch. 1. The book was published on 16 October 1930, and by December was already on its eighth printing.

Investment in classical learning as an exclusive undertaking has entailed discrimination, not only on the basis of social class, but also of gender. The remarkable, and traditionally male, activity of composing Latin verses in classical metres is paradigmatic here. Such composition has rarely been 'a mark of personal literary ambition', but rather 'a defining ability of the educated elite from the Middle Ages to the twentieth century'; and 'any woman who has left an oeuvre of Latin verse, whatever its poetic merit, was by definition occupying a space normally regarded as belonging entirely to men.'[9]

The history of classical education is thus, in part, a history of struggle between the defenders of privilege and excluded groups anxious to get a share of it. In eighteenth-century England, Samuel Johnson's accomplished friend Mrs Carter 'could make a pudding as well as translate Epictetus';[10] around 1500, Cassandra Fedele was even invited to deliver a Latin address in praise of literature, to the Doge and Senate of Venice, in which (courtesy of the humanist Giorgio Valla) she proposed to 'seek immortality' through learned study;[11] but until recent generations, formal opportunities for women to make progress in the classical domain, alongside the culinary, have been few.[12] In 1399, towards the end of the French Middle Ages, Europe's first professional woman writer, Christine de Pizan, composed a verse critique of the thirteenth-century *Romance of the Rose* and its apparent sexism (much of it introduced by the learned Jean de Meun, translator of Boethius' Latin *Consolatio* into French prose). Her response to the work was at the same time a challenge to a male monopoly on writing and learning – Latin learning – from which women in general were excluded.[13] A hundred years earlier still, in his 'Banquet', Dante is explicit in assuming that, even among the nobility, most women will know no Latin.[14] *Plus ça change* . . . In sixteenth-century France, the great humorist François Rabelais floats the whimsical thought that 'even women and girls have come to aspire to the glorious celestial manna of sound [i.e. classical] learning'.[15] His compatriot Michel de Montaigne, more soberly, notes that '*except for education and custom*, the difference between [male and female] is not great';[16] and as recently as the early twentieth century, the novelist Virginia Woolf is found lamenting her inferior instruction in the Greek language, which, she evidently supposes, prevents her from fully partaking in the ultimate cultural source of human wholeness.[17]

9 Stevenson (2005) 20–1. At the Canterbury school founded by Theodore and Hadrian, Latin verse composition was taught as early as VII (e.g. to Aldhelm): Lapidge (1979) 211.

10 Johnson's own words: G. B. Hill, *Johnsonian Miscellanies* (1897), 2. 11.

11 Robin (2000) 159–62. Other women humanists: King and Rabil (1983).

12 In modern times, Jane Harrison is the first big success-story: Beard (2000), Robinson (2002). Cf. n. 52 below.

13 Gaunt (1989), Solterer (1995).

14 *Convivio* (*c.* 1305), 1. 9.

15 Gargantua's letter to Pantagruel: *Pantagruel* (1532), ch. 8.

16 *Essais*, 3. 5 (closing sentences: our emphasis).

17 Goldhill (2002) 234; generally, Waquet (2001), Winterer (2007).

In classics teaching over the centuries, there have been striking differences between educational systems in different countries (even those as geographically close as England and Scotland);[18] likewise between different systems in any one era (since World War II, practices in the English-speaking world have diverged sharply from those in Continental Europe); likewise, also, *within* any one system in a given era (the differences between Oxford and Cambridge in the eighteenth century are a case in point).[19] Even so, over the millennium and a half of the classical tradition there has been a clear trajectory in the rationale of a classical education and the rationale of the classical within education overall. Three main phases are distinguishable: the classical as a vocational, practical, even technical guide; the classical as the basis for an elite 'humane' education; and the classical as one basis for general education, but an academic specialism among others. In terms of eras, the first corresponds roughly to the Middle Ages, but continues beyond; the second runs from the end of the fifteenth century to (depending on which culture and which level of educational provision one has in mind) somewhere around the end of the nineteenth; the third to the modern period since then. In terms of focus, the first centres on the learning of medieval or scholastic Latin, *lingua franca* of the medieval world; the second on the acquisition of classical Latin, with or without Greek; the third on exposure to Greek and Roman literature, thought, and civilization, with or without significant reference to the ancient languages – in the English-speaking world, increasingly, and at all levels, *without*.

That last development, a departure from the most venerable of educational practices, can be read in different ways – perhaps as a demographic breakthrough, with the hitherto underprivileged at last granted access to educational resources once available only to the social elite. The most striking instance here is the GI bill enacted in the USA in the wake of World War II, which rendered a university education affordable to those who had paid their dues in the armed services. For the first time, university education meant 'mass education', and institutions of higher learning had to adjust to an influx of students from families with little exposure to high culture. One of these adjustments (in line with the already established American tradition of 'great books' teaching)[20] was to teach 'classics in translation' – a practice subsequently adopted across the British educational systems too.

Alternatively, the fact of – perhaps especially the symbolism of – such delinguifying can be seen as a symptom and instrument of decline: part of the levelling down that passes for progress in the modern world. 'In the 1920s,' a Canadian scholar recalled, decades later, 'the mere thought of ancient literature in translation would have been as repellent as . . . allowing women to smoke in public – wearing trousers.'[21] Contemplating an earlier stage of this democratizing process in England,

[18] Clarke (1959) 133–59.

[19] Ibid. 61–73: in XVIII, Cambridge (but not Oxford) 'abandoned the ancient authorities and took Newton and Locke as her masters' (ibid. 68).

[20] Pioneered in 1919 at Columbia University by John Erskine under a 'General Honors' rubric.

[21] Quoted by Hall (2008c) 319.

mindful of the rise of the 'average man' in America,[22] mindful too of recent and impending provision of school-level state education on the British side of the Atlantic,[23] Matthew Arnold (himself a schools inspector, as well as literary and cultural critic) proposed a radical solution: students must continue to encounter the classical, but rather than having it mediated by reading ancient texts in English translation, their engagement with the classical could take place through the immediacy of the classics of English literature that themselves embody the classical. Above all, Arnold was exercised by the difficulty of translating poetry – especially poetry in the 'great style' – and here he looked instead to the poetry of Milton:

> The verse of the poets of Greece and Rome no translation can adequately reproduce . . . In our race are thousands of readers, presently there will be millions, who know not a word of Greek and Latin, and will never learn these languages. If this host of readers are ever to gain any sense of the power and charm of the great poets of antiquity, their way to gain it is not through translations of the ancients, but through the original poetry of Milton, who has the like power and charm, because he has the like great style.[24]

Since Arnold's day, the study of English literature in the educational systems of the English-speaking world (and likewise the study of other native literatures in other nations) has indeed assumed a prominent, and often dominant, position within what is still labelled 'the humanities'[25] – but seldom with Arnold's particular agenda in mind.

Ironically enough, Arnold's century, in England and elsewhere, is in some ways not one of attrition, as far as formal classical education is concerned, but the opposite. Here, one can point to reforms and revivals within the British public schools, which led to something of a reassertion of language-based classics for the rising bourgeoisie,[26] but especially to the new system of secondary education – the 'humanistische Gymnasium' – inaugurated in 1809/10 by Wilhelm von Humboldt in Germany. As Prussian minister of education, Humboldt had a unique opportunity to put a neo-humanist vision into practice; and though the challenge to develop a new system was created, no doubt, by external factors (a climate of revolution, a drive for modern nationhood, the separation of Church and state), and though the

[22] A development presciently read by Nietzsche, around the same time, as a mark of 'democratic' (yes-we-can) self-confidence akin to that of the Periclean Age. In ancient Athens, and now in modern America, individuals feel 'they can do just about anything': *Fröhliche Wissenschaft* (2nd edn, 1887), section 356.

[23] The Education Acts of 1870 and 1902 instituted state education at primary and secondary levels respectively.

[24] 'Milton' (in *Essays in Criticism*, second series), 1888.

[25] In restricted educational contexts, the label retains its old connection with Greek and (esp.) Latin: §16 n. 24.

[26] Or 'grammar schools', of which 'public schools' were a subsection. At the end of XVIII, Eton, even, 'was only the largest and most important of the grammar schools': Clarke (1959) 74. The distinction (eventually one of status) is originally a matter of catchment area: 'public' schools took pupils from far and wide. See generally ibid. 74–97, Stray (1998) 30–45.

choice of classics was partly pragmatic (as a convenient *rite de passage* for a new, secular, and not exclusively aristocratic, ruling class) – even so, it was still Humboldt's initiative, as 'theorist' of the 'true, new Hellenism' of his age,[27] to install the ancient languages, 'Hellenic' and Roman, too, at the centre of elite education for a century and more.[28] In re-emergent Italy, the *liceo classico* was created in 1859 on comparable lines – though without quite the same visionary aspiration – while the original model for all such outcomes was the Napoleonic *lycée* in France, instituted in 1802 and centred (in accordance with the prevailing inclinations of French classicism) on Latin. Across the four nations, these institutional developments had something of a nationalistic impetus; in the next century this was to become most marked in Italy, where the *liceo classico* was especially privileged.[29]

Against this background, the recent innovations in educational practice, throughout the English-speaking world, take on a special significance, in contrast to a reluctance to innovate elsewhere. To this day, Continental Europe, by and large, has been unable or unwilling to take the decisive step of divorcing study of the ancient world from tuition in Latin and Greek, or of providing for both – however limiting, in a mass-democratic age, a continuing association between language-based classics, on the one hand, and socially and politically conservative elites, on the other. In the French student demonstrations of the late 1960s, '"Down with Latin" became one of the reformers' rallying cries', while, 'when the Italian parliament debated keeping Latin in the middle-class *liceo* but not in the socially inferior *scuola media* in 1962–3, the argument proceeded along party lines: the Christian Democrats defended Latin and the Socialists and Communists opposed it.'[30] In Britain, with much of the old association with privilege gone (and decades after symptomatic egalitarian developments like the abolition of Greek and Latin as general entry requirements for admission to Oxford and Cambridge),[31] there are, currently, active initiatives for the teaching of classical languages in inner-city schools,[32] while in the state secondary sector the demand for Latin teachers now exceeds the supply.[33]

[27] Pfeiffer (1976) 170. Humboldt: Benner (2003), Menze (1975).

[28] Despite much criticism ('we should be raising young Germans, not young Greeks and Romans' – this, from Kaiser Wilhelm II, recalling his own traumatic experience of classical-language learning, in a speech of 4 December 1890 – Röhl 2001: 431), the humanist *Gymnasium* retained its position until reforms in the 1960s significantly reduced hours of tuition in the classical languages. Meanwhile it had become a model for educational institutions elsewhere, from Greece to the USA.

[29] Until 1969, only graduates from the *liceo classico* had access to all forms of higher education. The classicism of all these various institutions is enshrined in their names: *Gymnasium* and Italian *ginnasio* look back to educational centres in ancient Greece (*gymnasia*), as *lycée/liceo* does to Aristotle's school in the Lyceum in Athens – and as 'Academy' (intermittent designation of schools and other educational institutions in many countries) does to the site of Plato's school, in Athens again.

[30] Kallendorf (2010) 298.

[31] In 1920 (Greek) and 1960 (Latin).

[32] Notably London's Iris project; the Bronx Latin School in New York has the same rationale. The West London Free School, a 'free' state school set up in 2011 by British journalist Toby Young, is (its mission statement declares) 'a school with a classical curriculum'.

[33] Cf. Chris Arnot, 'A Classic Case of Undersupply', *The Guardian*, 5 February 2008.

Old associations, of course, linger on. In some educated versions of the British popular mind, 'classics' still means 'ruling classes'. 'Unfortunately, the UK, possibly as a legacy of our colonial past, is [*sic*] run largely by classicists': this, from a Professor of Engineering in 2009.[34] His tone of weary outrage, it may be, was influenced by the recent election of an Oxford classics graduate, Boris Johnson, as Mayor of London in 2008, and a speech the new incumbent gave at his first press conference at City Hall, where he floated the thought that promoting classical (and other) language-learning in state schools might help to divert young people from the path of crime. Reactions to that speech included a revealing headline in Britain's mass-circulation daily, *The Sun*: 'Make Yobs Learn Latin.'[35] The headline, purporting amused surprise as if to some challenge to the existing order, relies on the same association as that activating the outraged engineer.

But popular associations are based on something, and in this case on what was once, in the not-too-distant past, a pervasive fact of cultural-educational life, in Britain and elsewhere. As the Western nations industrialized and prepared for world war during the nineteenth century and the early twentieth; as new science and new technology generated motorized travel on land, sea, and air, new means of communication and new modes of creative and commercial expression (photography, telephone, skyscraper, cinema, radio); as art recentred itself, in swift succession, on realism, on impressionism, on a series of new movements all the way to cubism and beyond; as literature, on a related trajectory, recentred itself on the realist novel and symbolist poetics; as long-standing habits of thought were challenged by Darwin and Einstein, by Marx, Nietzsche, and Freud – throughout these momentous developments, formal educational institutions (German *Gymnasium*, French *lycée*, Italian *liceo*, British public school and grammar school, American high school) all kept Greek and Latin embedded firmly and prominently in their curricula. The products of such an education duly staffed the professions, administered the apparatus of the state, became propagators of the classics in schools and universities in their turn. Whatever else it may have achieved, a classical education served, not least, to consolidate the social identity of the elite; its rationale, in this sense, was to enforce, within each nation, coherence and conformity.

That said, the effect of a training in the ancient languages on the individual, especially the imaginative individual, has always been unpredictable. It is easy to point to great creative figures with, seemingly, a less than comprehensive upbringing in the classics, who nevertheless bulk large within the classical tradition as elsewhere: Shakespeare, with his 'small Latin and less Greek', is one obvious example.[36] On the other side, we have those whose classical training, at notable institutions, impacted demonstrably and decisively on their later careers: Milton and Dryden at

[34] R. G. Austin, in a letter to *The Times* (London), 26 February 2009.

[35] *The Sun*, 5 June 2008.

[36] Ben Jonson's elegy 'To the Memory of… Shakespeare' (1623); his comment assumes the perspective of the linguistically qualified. Shakespeare's classical training is (still) variously estimated: Burrow (2004).

the public schools of St Paul's and Westminster; Racine at the Jansenist abbey of Port-Royal; Nietzsche at the boarding school (also once an abbey) of Pforta.[37] But then again, as far as conformity – social, institutional, intellectual – is concerned, no-one could be much less conformist than Nietzsche in the Humboldtian nineteenth century, or indeed than Milton in the neoclassical seventeenth.

The creative role of the individual (to restate the point) is as important as the determinative force of context, and in the educational sphere as much as anywhere else. Contrary to the simplistic assumptions of some cultural historians (and the academician Coypel), it is rarely possible to identify *necessary* connections between an institutional apparatus and human outcomes. Preoccupation with the classical has not disappeared in our time, despite a widespread absence of institutional support for it. Conversely, suppose one looks back – without any knowledge of historical context – to the creative *oeuvres* of Wordsworth or Stendhal, Caspar David Friedrich or Giuseppe Verdi or David Hume: one would hardly suspect, most of the time, that all these considerable figures lived in an age when the primacy of the classical was, broadly speaking, institutionalized across the Western world.[38] Conversely again, the triumph of vernacular literature that begins with Dante's *Commedia* (completed *c.* 1318) anticipates by around six hundred years the privileged place eventually occupied by vernacular languages and literatures within the educational systems of the West.

Clearly, the characteristic possibilities in any era are influenced by institutional norms – more or less – while the opportunity for individuals to transcend, or subvert, those norms may be imponderable. Clearly again, a tradition sustained makes unforeseen applications possible which might otherwise remain un(fore)seen. Yet if, beyond these generalities, there is one stretch of time within which a direct correlation between institutions and outcomes is broadly apparent, it must be the Middle Ages and the ensuing classical age, up to (roughly) the later seventeenth century: a period when Latin, in one or other version, is the international language (§13), and, in particular, when negotiations between the pagan classics and the Christian establishment often take centre stage. The developments in this period call for a more detailed examination.

The first Christian emperor, Constantine, already realized that religious scruples should not be allowed to get in the way of a training in the classics, making sure to assign to his three sons 'the most accomplished teachers of secular learning';[39] and training in grammar and approved texts, as a means of attaining facility in correct language, written or spoken, remained an important prerequisite for members of the imperial elite.[40] After the fall of the Western Empire, virtually all Greek learning,

[37] An equally impressive series of big names within the classical tradition were pupils of the Jesuits, from Tasso to Molière to James Joyce.

[38] It is true, but not the point, that (e.g.) Wordsworth knew and admired Latin poetry (Bush 1932/3) and that some of Hume's minor essays are classically focused (cf. Baumstark 2010).

[39] Eusebius, *Vita Constantini*, 4. 51. Cf. Downey (1955) 57.

[40] See e.g. Matthews (1975), Kaster (1988).

and teaching, was confined to the Greek East, and it was left to monks and monasteries in the West to maintain the continuity of pedagogical or scholarly assimilation of classical – now meaning Latin – materials. In the sixth century, the senator Aurelius Cassiodorus established a syllabus, in his *Institutiones*, consisting of Christian and pagan texts: *divinae litterae* (Book 1) and *saeculares litterae* (Book 2). The latter he subdivided into what would become the seven liberal arts: grammar, rhetoric, dialectic, arithmetic, music, geometry, astronomy (subsequently grouped into sets of three and four, the elementary *trivium* and the advanced *quadrivium*).[41]

Given that the sacred texts of the Western Church were in Latin, the Christian establishment soon realized that it made sense to provide training for their priests in Latin grammar, and looked to canonical classical sources, in the shape of Aelius Donatus, most famous of the late-antique grammarians. Some, indeed, worried that the Latin (Vulgate) Bible itself did not always conform to the highest standards of good style.[42] And who knew how God might assess a baptism that used a semi-literate formula like *Baptizo te in nomine Patria et Filia et Spiritu sancta*?[43] Virgil of Salzburg thought the sacrament must be valid and received the support of Pope Zachary. St Boniface disagreed: suppose the Lord were a stickler for correct Latin usage, howlers like this could well consign an unfortunate child to eternal damnation.[44]

In the seventh and eighth centuries, relief for a war-torn continent came from the British Isles and the missionary zeal of Irish monks, who exported their standards of literacy and learning to England and beyond. When Charlemagne wished to corroborate his imperial sway with a cultural politics (later known as the Carolingian Renaissance), one of his most famous recruits was Alcuin of York, prolific writer of textbooks that spanned both the liberal arts and Biblical exegesis, and one of the brains behind the *Admonitio generalis* (789), which laid down stipulations for new schools as well as regulations for a new curriculum.[45] In the eleventh and twelfth centuries, these institutions evolved into the medieval universities (the first formal foundation was at Bologna in 1088),[46] in which the students could pursue more advanced studies in law, medicine, and theology, once they had mastered the

[41] The system was immortalized by a verse mnemonic: 'GRAMM loquitur, DIA vera docet, RHET verba colorat, | MUS canit, AR numerat, GEO ponderat, AST colit astra': 'Gramm(ar) talks, dia(lectic) teaches truth, rhet(oric) gives colour to words, mus(ic) sings, ar(ithmetic) counts, geo(metry) weighs [*sic*], ast(ronomy) studies the stars': Sandys (1921) 670, Stroh (2007) 138.

[42] Vulgate: §13 n. 5.

[43] Literally, 'I baptize you in the name fatherland and daughter and by the Holy Spirit': *Monumenta Germaniae Historica: Epistolae Merowingici et Karolini Aevi*, vol. 1, ed. Dümmler (1892), p. 336. Linguistic perspective: Lepschy (2009).

[44] Letter of Zachary to Boniface, *c.* 746.

[45] Bullough (2004).

[46] Other early foundations (XII/XIII) include Paris, Vicenza, Oxford, Cambridge, Arezzo, Montpellier, Salamanca, Seville. In Central Europe, several notable universities were founded in XIV, including Prague, Cracow, Vienna, Heidelberg. Some seats of higher learning existed, often on a specialist basis, long before their formal recognition: Salerno in Italy was known as a school of medicine as early as IX.

seven liberal arts.[47] These higher branches of learning, severely practical in outlook, all had classical points of reference: the teaching of law was influenced by the rediscovery of Justinian's codification in the eleventh century; medicine looked in part to Arabic and, thereby, Greek sources;[48] and the scholastic theology of the medieval universities (especially the University of Paris)[49] was strongly influenced by Aristotelian philosophy, with this particular Christian-Aristotelian synthesis receiving its definitive treatment in the *Summa theologiae* of Thomas Aquinas (completed in 1273).[50]

Over the course of the fourteenth and fifteenth centuries, medieval scholasticism, in Italy first and foremost, largely gave way to significant developments in educational practice. These included a new, classicizing anthropology, a renewed commitment to classical Latinity, a revival of Greek studies and (following the revolutionary invention of the printing press, by Gutenberg, in Germany) the first mechanical standardizing of texts and textbooks in Western history. Initially, humanist ideas on education revolved around the integration, but eventually the separation, of classical culture and Christian religion. A spate of treatises contributed to a decisive reorientation which has continued to define secondary schooling across the West up until the present day: Maffeo Vegio's *On the Education of Children and Their Moral Foundations*, Pier Paolo Vergerio's *The Character and Studies that Befit a Free-Born Youth*, Aeneas Sylvius Piccolomini's *The Education of Boys*, Battista Guarino's *A Programme of Teaching and Learning*.[51] The common element was wide reading and self-improvement for young men.[52] Leonardo Bruni summed up the new educational orientation with the phrase 'humane studies' ('studia humanitatis'), which would both 'finish' ('perficiant') and 'embellish' ('exornent') the chosen few.[53] The syllabus of the humanists (*humanistae*)[54] was broad. It included a range of classical texts, from moral philosophy to oratory, historiography, and poetry, and was designed to achieve verbal fluency and polish, as well as moral improvement

[47] Ferruolo (1998), Haskins (1972), Rashdall (1936).

[48] As early as VII, Arab scholars began to seek out and study a wide range of Greek materials, esp. scientific, medical, and philosophical prose: summary in El-Abbadi (2004) 174–81; see generally Cameron (1997) 4–18, Cotton *et al.* (2009), Gutas (1998), Makdisi (1989), Walzer (1958).

[49] Cf. n. 83 below.

[50] Aristotle was read in Latin translations – some late-antique (e.g. by Boethius), others via Arabic: summaries in Bolgar (1954) 153, 161–2, 172–3.

[51] Kallendorf (2002).

[52] And occasionally for noblewomen. Thus, Bruni's *Study of Literature* (*De studiis et litteris*, *c.* 1420? – Cox 2009: 47) is addressed to the Lady Battista Malatesta of Montefeltro. Significantly, Bruni (*De studiis*, 14–15) insists that the benefits his addressee is to draw from her education are spiritual and philosophical, and unrelated to public speaking; likewise, Fedele (p. 35 above) indicates that women should study 'literature', not for public 'honours', but for its own sake.

[53] Bruni, ibid.: cf. Grendler (1989), (1995). 'Studia humanitatis': §3 n. 32.

[54] The word 'humanist' derives from '(h)umanista', the accepted name of the early modern Italian scholar, but 'humanism' from German 'Humanismus', a back-formation coined as late as 1808 by F. J. Niethammer: Kristeller (1956) 572–4, Reynolds and Wilson (1991) 270. The modern (anti-religion) sense of 'humanist' is only distantly related: cf. §27.

and practical wisdom. But the ultimate logic of all this 'finishing' and 'embellishing' – not always laid bare by its enthusiastic promoters – was a new ideal of individual value (§8), of moral and intellectual freedom; and though the era was, and remained, centred on Latin, one factor that undoubtedly helped to stimulate the development of this ideal was access to the Greek experience as embodied in classic texts, from Homer to Plato to Plutarch and beyond.

In the medieval West, knowledge of Greek was exceptional,[55] and an institutional apparatus for its propagation non-existent. From around 1400, under the stimulus of itinerant scholars from Byzantium, the systematic teaching and learning of Greek was revived in Italy, especially in Florence and Venice, and the first steps were taken in the collection of manuscripts and the formation of libraries, some of them substantial.[56] Petrarch's desire to interact with Greek authors had been limited to having their manuscripts in his library (those of Homer and Plato were his special pride), but Boccaccio, at Petrarch's suggestion, actually learned the language.[57] Knowledge of Greek rapidly became a mark of scholarly distinction, with genealogies of tuition spreading across Europe. Thus, around the end of the fourteenth century, the Greek Manuel Chrysoloras taught the language to a series of receptive pupils, several of whom became distinguished scholars (Bruni among them). Another Greek, Georgios Hermonymos, moved to Paris in the 1470s to pass on his knowledge to Reuchlin from Germany, to Erasmus from the Low Countries, to Budé from France. The capture of Constantinople by the Ottomans in 1453 marked the end of the Eastern Roman Empire which had preserved, and in some areas developed, a version of Greco-Roman antiquity for a millennium.[58] This cataclysmic event only accelerated the migration of Greek scholars (and their manuscripts) to Italy, and thus the spread of Greek studies across the West.[59]

Printing revolutionized schooling in the classics. The availability of textbook material in print made possible a systematic approach to instruction in the language, no longer dependent on the presence of single personalities. Incongruously enough, the transposition of Greek literature from manuscript to print began with the printing of a parody of Homeric epic, the (Hellenistic?) *Battle of the Frogs and Mice* (Brescia, *c.* 1474), as a text suitable for language beginners.[60] A pioneer in the printing of teaching material was Bonaccorso Pisano, who drew on his network of acquaintances with Greek scholars to reprint the Greek grammar of Constantine

[55] For the 'exceptions' (like William of Moerbeke: §15), see Berschin (1988).

[56] The statistics are remarkable. Thus, when Giovanni Aurispa reached Venice from a trip to Constantinople in 1423, he brought with him a cargo of 238 Greek 'books': Sandys (1908), 2. 36.

[57] From Leonzio Pilato.

[58] See variously Holmes and Waring (2002), Kaldellis (2008), Mullett and Scott (1981), Wilson (1983).

[59] Along with Chrysoloras, the leading figure was Georgios Gemistos Plethon; their successors included some who became establishment figures in the West, notably Bessarion, who became a Cardinal in 1439: Wilson (1992).

[60] This had been a school text in Byzantium; to that extent, the choice of the poem for a primer reflected recent Greek practice.

Lascaris with a facing Latin translation, along with a Greek–Latin dictionary and introductory readings that included Aesop's *Fables* and a bilingual Psalter (Milan: 1476–81).[61] The first classical texts to become available in print were in Latin: this honour went to Cicero's *De Officiis* and *Paradoxa Stoicorum*, which appeared in Mainz in 1465. Initially lagging behind Latin literature, which saw print runs of all the major authors by the 1490s, the publication of Greek literature acquired new momentum when Aldus Manutius set up his press in Venice around 1495, despite the technical difficulties involved.[62] In 1500 Manutius founded an academy, designed to publish in print a 'good [meaning *classical*] author' every month. The constitution of the academy was written in Greek, and discussions in any other language were punishable.[63] A quarter of a century after *Frogs and Mice*, Manutius' systematic transposition of manuscript texts into printed editions produced the *editio princeps* of Sophocles (1502), soon followed by those of his fellow-dramatists Euripides and Aristophanes, and, in 1518, three years after his death, the first edition of Aeschylus. Other authors and genres were similarly favoured. In Thomas More's *Utopia* (1516), the traveller Raphael Hythlodaeus already carries Aldine editions in his suitcase.

Alongside changes in pedagogy and media, old institutions of learning evolved and new ones developed. Across the disciplines taught in the universities, doctrines and teaching methods inherited from the Middle Ages made way for 'new', classically inspired, ideas. Academies began to flourish, most notably one sponsored by the Medici in fifteenth-century Florence.[64] Its first head, Marsilio Ficino, authored the first complete translation of Plato into Latin (1484: the Greek *editio princeps* would not appear until 1513), and, together with his pupil Giovanni Pico della Mirandola, gave a definitive shape to an influential version of Neoplatonism, combining Christian doctrine with pagan wisdom and a search for mystical insight. Both the system of thought and the institution travelled north. In 1495, on the Florentine model, a group of German humanists including Conrad Celtis and Johann Reuchlin founded the Academia Platonica, which devoted most of its energies to the printing and dissemination of classical texts. The high status of all such ventures – even in the largely unreceptive German territories – is indicated by the contribution of Albrecht Dürer, the most notable German artist of his day, to the illumination of the Aldine editions.[65] Germany remained unreceptive, however, especially after the Reformation, itself a German movement in the first instance. Symptomatically, the representative German humanist of the age, Philipp Melanchthon, focused his energies on a new Christian humanism: 'his mind was the meeting-place of three traditions, the medieval, the humanist and the protestant'.[66] As Nietzsche was later

[61] Botley (2002).

[62] Proctor (1900).

[63] Ciccolella (2007), Lowry (1979).

[64] Renaissance Academies: Pade (2011). Florentine Academy: Hankins (1991).

[65] Though Dürer was hardly a straightforward proponent of art 'in the antique manner' (his own phrase: letter to Wilibald Pirckheimer, 1506).

[66] Bolgar (1954) 346.

to remark, on Luther and the Reformation: 'a German monk . . . *against* the Renaissance . . . Oh, those Germans, what they have cost us!'[67]

In England, and especially in France, humanist ideals took deeper root and more substantial institutional structures were soon in place. The establishment of Greek teaching posts at Oxford (1516) and Cambridge (1518),[68] and of comparable positions in the classical languages at what would become the Collège Royal in Paris (early 1530s), are significant moments. Significantly, too, both sets of appointments (especially those in Greek) aroused immediate opposition from groups suspicious of 'modern' secular learning: in England, from a party of self-styled 'Trojans';[69] in France, from the spokesmen for medieval scholasticism at the Sorbonne.[70] Within a generation, however, the humanist foundations of Paris had generated the two great poet-representatives of the French Pléiade, Pierre de Ronsard and Joachim Du Bellay, while by the 1540s Cambridge, in particular, had become a flourishing centre for the reading of Greek authors, from Sophocles to Plato, along with (in the admiring words of the scholar Roger Ascham) 'the best authors who flourished in the golden age' of Rome.[71]

For all such talk of the 'best authors', it may, with hindsight, seem revealing that the whole process of dissemination on which the new structures largely depended should have begun with the printing of a Greek grammar, a dictionary, and inconsequential bits of ancient literature (Aesop's *Fables* and the *Frogs and Mice*). Even though the premise of the new learning and the education associated with it was indeed access to classical texts, the fact is that in much educational practice the texts were studied as an aid to learning the two languages, and not *vice versa*. Sometimes this was even made into an explicit objective, especially for Latin, and especially when humanist goals were adjusted to those of the Reformation or reactions to it. For the most distinguished educational theorist of the age, the great Dutch humanist Desiderius Erasmus, writing in the second decade of the sixteenth century, ancient authors were never to be studied simply for 'unusual words' and the like, but at least deserved a second reading 'for content'.[72] By contrast, the emphasis of Calvin's teacher, the French scholar Mathurin Cordier, was summed up in the title of his Latin treatise on correct Latin, *De corrupti sermonis emendatione* ('On the Improvement of Defective Speech', 1530). For the Jesuits, 'literature was studied for the sake of composition and for no other reason'; in the official manual (*Ratio studiorum*) of 1591, an appendix 'warns the teacher against digressions into history or antiquities: his task is to teach the use of words'.[73] In England, Cardinal Wolsey's letter to the masters of Ipswich School in 1528 prescribes Latin authors on purely

[67] *Antichrist* (1888), section 61.

[68] St Paul's School had already been founded on a humanist basis, embracing Greek and Latin, by John Colet in 1509.

[69] Bolgar (1954) 313.

[70] Stevens (1950).

[71] 'Latinos . . . optimos quosque et saeculo illo aureo florentes': letter to Brondesby, 1542/3.

[72] Bolgar (1954) 339: Erasmus, *De ratione studii* (1512) (opening section).

[73] Bolgar (1954) 359.

linguistic grounds: 'of those authors who contribute much towards a pure, terse or finished conversational speech, is any wittier than Aesop or more useful than Terence?'[74]

These teaching practices continued for hundreds of years, on and off, attaining their celebrated *reductio* in the welcoming words of a nineteenth-century English headmaster to his pupils: 'Boys, this term you are to have the privilege of reading the *Oedipus Coloneus* of Sophocles, a veritable treasure-house of grammatical peculiarities.'[75] Such a *milieu* might induce (almost by accident) an interest in antiquity or a love of literature; the outcome might well be the opposite. Reviewing his own, unusual, upbringing in 1580, the 'great sage'[76] Montaigne rejoices that he did not 'leave school hating books the way most French aristocrats do.'[77]

In the Renaissance and beyond, the methods employed in the teaching of the languages themselves varied greatly, from a grammar-centred regime[78] to the learning of passages from approved authors,[79] from translation and retranslation of classical authors[80] to simultaneous translation from one ancient language into the other.[81] In some centres, like the Collegium Trilingue at Louvain (from its foundation in 1517) and Westminster School (from the seventeenth century), the teaching of the two languages went hand in hand with the teaching of Hebrew.[82] In the richly inventive narratives of Rabelais from the 1530s, the giant Gargantua, in a letter to his son Pantagruel, even acclaims the conjunction of Hebrew and the two classical languages as an organic element of Renaissance culture – printing, learning and all. In his youth (Gargantua recalls), the world was still 'dark' ('ténébreux'); that was still the bad old world of 'the Goths', whereas now –

> Now all branches of learning ['disciplines'] have been restored, all languages revived; Greek, without which it is a disgrace for anyone to call himself a man of learning ['savant'], Hebrew, Chaldean, Latin. The technique of printing, truly elegant and accurate, was invented in my time by divine inspiration.[83]

[74] Quoted by Clarke (1959) 9.

[75] Bowra (1945) 10; ascribed to Samuel Butler when Headmaster of Shrewsbury (1798–1836) by Leedham-Green (1996) 30.

[76] Screech (2003) xiii.

[77] *Essais*, 1. 26. His upbringing involved learning Latin as his first language: 'I was six years old before I knew French' (ibid.). His classical education was at the Collège de Guyenne in Bordeaux.

[78] Already criticised by Ascham, *The Schoolmaster* (1570), 1.

[79] See e.g. Woodward (1897) 45, 164, 169.

[80] Advocated by Ascham: *The Schoolmaster*, 1.

[81] Practised at Pforta: Wilamowitz (1928) 79.

[82] Esp. common in Reformation circles, where the ability to read the Bible in the original meant access to divine truth unmediated by the Catholic Church. Collegium Trilingue (where Erasmus was an important figure): de Vocht (1951). Hebrew at Westminster: Leach (1911) 513. The pioneer in the introduction of Hebrew into English schools was Archbishop Holgate (mid-XVI): Clarke (1959) 190.

[83] *Pantagruel* (1532), ch. 8. Except for 'Chaldean' (Syriac or Aramaic), the list of languages alludes to chairs founded in Paris in the early 1530s (partly at Budé's instigation), at what became the Collège Royal, against opposition from the anti-humanist, scholastic-minded, Sorbonne. The scholastics are famously satirized in Rabelais's books; in return, the Sorbonne banned them.

To a modern, and perhaps also a Renaissance, ear, the solemn appeal to inspiration, and the quaint-sounding addition of 'Chaldean' to the short list, may well seem to invest this summary of educational realities with some irony. Yet, essentially, these are still the realities.

One other notable feature of classical language teaching, in both languages, was composition, in prose and in verse. For centuries, as we have noted, Latin verse composition enjoyed a special status. An accomplishment of Renaissance poets, from Petrarch in fourteenth-century Italy, to Du Bellay in sixteenth-century France, to Milton in seventeenth-century England, composition in (meaning, usually, translation into) classical Latin, and in canonical Latin verse-forms, becomes a staple of classics teaching in England's public schools and ancient universities, and generally remains so – for boys, at least – until the last third of the twentieth century. As a specialized and sophisticated establishment practice, verse composition generated a series of arguments about its value and rationale.[84] Ridiculed by the nineteenth-century public-school reformer Thomas Arnold (father of Matthew) as 'a contemptible prettiness of the understanding', it was defended in 1911 by A. E. Housman, classical scholar and poet, not as an educational resource, in the ordinary sense, at all, but as a minor art-form ('a fine art . . . not one of the great arts, but . . . no mere handicraft either').[85] The habit of verse composition helps to explain how it could come about that some – greater – poets (notably Milton) could reach the stage of effectively transposing Latin verse phraseology into poetry in their own language (§35).[86] At the same time, Housman's defence presents a provoking unconcern that talent sufficient to sustain a 'fine art' should be devoted to what – in terms of creative usage and living communication – could only ever be a marginal activity.

A century before Housman, Coleridge had deplored 'the custom of writing Latin verses and the great importance attached to these exercises in our public schools' – adding, pointedly: 'Whatever might have been the case in the fifteenth century, when the use of the Latin tongue was so general among learned men that Erasmus is said to have forgotten his native language, yet in the present day it is not to be supposed that a youth can think in Latin.'[87] Housman's defence inhabits the age ('belongs to' seems inappropriate) soon to be graced by modernist artists, writers, and thinkers like Picasso and Stravinsky, Eliot, Joyce, and Pound, Mikhail Bakhtin, and Martin Heidegger – all deeply implicated in the classical tradition, and all in different degrees cultivating a restricted public – yet all preoccupied, in different ways, with the problematic of communication in the modern world. It is the total absence of that concern on Housman's part – his unworldly defence of verse composition, as much as the phenomenon itself – that raises questions.

[84] See e.g. Stray (1998) 68–74.

[85] Housman's Cambridge Inaugural: Ricks (1988) 298. Arnold: Clarke (1959) 79.

[86] Among the classically trained poets of Milton's era, contrast e.g. Ben Jonson: Moul (2010).

[87] *Biographia Literaria* (1817), ch. 1. Cf. Herder: 'A true poet must write in his own language' ('Ein wahrer Dichter muss in seiner Sprache schreiben'): *Über die neuere deutsche Literatur*, 3 (1767).

In Housman's time (it is hardly irrelevant to note) unworldliness is increasingly associated, in popular perception, with those tasked with the transmission of classical learning.[88] One thinks of the 'etiolated' Edward Casaubon in George Eliot's *Middlemarch* (1871–2)[89] – and then of the Bergsonian inflexibility of the classics masters depicted in popular fictions from the first half of the twentieth century: *The Blue Angel*; *Goodbye, Mr Chips*; *The Browning Version*.[90] And looking back to the mid-nineteenth century, one ponders the description of Pforta, by its Rector Kirchner in 1843, as a scholastic institution dedicated to 'the serious study of classics and other kindred subjects, divorced from all contact with the distractions of urban life':[91] a true *reductio* of the Humboldtian ideal.

In the age of Coleridge, meanwhile, the Humboldtian project itself did more than institutionalize classical education in emergent Germany. It also helped to foster a new educational focus on the study of 'the ancient world' in the round, on its history, culture, customs, structures, artefacts (§16); and classical studies in this enlarged, and newly professionalized, sense eventually becomes the international norm. By the second half of the twentieth century, university 'classics' in particular reflects this reorientation, across the Western world; and today there is probably no classical teaching anywhere, at school or university level, that is unaffected by it – while today's 'classics in translation',[92] though no part of Humboldt's vision, has paradoxically become the plausible corollary of its outcomes. Study of the ancient world in the round is more or less convertible to study 'in translation', in a way that, by definition, a language-based curriculum is not.

At the same time, language-based learning continues to epitomize a classical education; it is certainly what most of those professionally involved in education (classical or other) understand by 'Classics' with a capital 'C'; and the cachet of a 'disciplined' training in the ancient languages continues to impress beneficiaries and outside onlookers alike. However, beneficiaries, in particular, may be impressed in more than one way. Three contrasting examples from twentieth-century Britain make the point. For the literary critic F. R. Leavis in 1948, looking back, in part, to his own schooldays, the 'developed disciplines' of a classical education were an undoubted strength – but also promoted a damaging sense of 'language divorced from experience'.[93] For the anti-authoritarian George Orwell in 1947, recalling his

[88] As far as the *products* of a classical education are concerned, however, the converse is more common. Cf. the oft-quoted words of Thomas Gaisford, Dean of Christ Church, Oxford, in his Christmas Day sermon of 1831, commending 'the study of Greek literature, which not only elevates above the vulgar herd, but leads not infrequently to positions of considerable emolument': Tuckwell (1907) 124.

[89] Jenkyns (1980) 128; cf. Nuttall (2003). Casaubon: §16 n. 112.

[90] *Der blaue Engel*: film (dir. von Sternberg, 1930), based on Heinrich Mann's novel, *Professor Unrat* (1905). *Goodbye, Mr Chips*: novel by James Hilton, 1933–4, first filmed in 1939. *The Browning Version*: play by Terence Rattigan, first filmed in 1951 (dir. Anthony Asquith).

[91] 'aus dem von aller Berührung mit städtischen Zerstreuungen geschiedenen Ernst der klassischen und diesen verwandten Studien': quoted by Förster-Nietzsche (1912) 83.

[92] Often implicit in courses on 'classical studies' or 'classical civilization': cf. §15.

[93] Leavis (1948) 38–9, 134–5 (the latter passage originally part of a 1933 pamphlet, *How to Teach Reading*).

experiences at prep school, the 'discipline' encompassed not only the precision of teaching and learning, but the dismal inevitability of physical chastisement: 'I doubt whether classical education ever has been or can be successfully carried on without corporal punishment.'[94] More positive than either is the testimony of the novelist-philosopher Iris Murdoch – or the male narrator of her 1975 novel, *A Word Child*: 'I began to learn . . . An ability to write correct Latin prose began to offer me an escape from . . . the prison house, began in time to show me vistas headier and more glorious than any I had ever before known how to dream of . . . *Amo, amas, amat* was my open sesame, "Learn these verbs by Friday" the essence of my education.'[95]

In ideological terms, the now venerable practice of verse composition occupies the opposite pole from the more recent phenomenon of 'classics in translation'; but if the older, elite practice raises questions, so too does the newer, egalitarian one. At the deepest level, questions can be raised about all the world's educational practices, including, indeed, that whole cultural-educational continuum that lies between, and behind, our two poles.

In a classic (and classical-oriented) work of modernist poetry, *Hugh Selwyn Mauberley* (1920), written within a few years of Housman's refined *obiter dicta*, Ezra Pound, American poet resident in Europe, offers a sharply relevant presentation of the continuum as an agonizing cultural-existential conundrum. From the land of the 'average man' (as Matthew Arnold had called it; a 'half-savage country' is Pound's own label),[96] the American poet and his part-surrogate Mauberley find in the European heartland of the West nothing but ironies and betrayals. In the wake of World War I and profound cultural disillusion, Pound invokes, as simultaneously true ideal and false ideal, *both* the world of publicly available classics now[97] *and* the physical remains of antiquity that activated the humanist Renaissance at its outset. Pound's first target, however, is the modern age, in ironic (almost Byronic) juxtaposition to the ancient world, which for the moment means ancient Greece:

The age demanded an image
Of its accelerated grimace,
Something for the modern stage,
Not, at any rate, an Attic grace;

Not, not certainly, the obscure reveries
Of the inward gaze –

This 'inward' implies 'unworldly', perhaps, but not in Housmanic terms, because Pound's 'obscure' evidently points to the necessary complexity of cultural-intellectual advance. The critique resumes:

94 In 'Such, Such Were the Joys', an essay first published in *Partisan Review* in 1952. On Orwell, cf. Burton (2005). In earlier centuries, corporal punishment in classical education is criticised by e.g. Montaigne (*Essais*, 1. 26), following Quintilian.

95 *A Word Child*, 'Thursday (first week)'.

96 In 'E. P. Ode pour l'élection de son sépulcre', with which *Mauberley* begins.

97 Given the poem's date, there is something prescient about Pound's reading of this public availability: cf. Arnold's '*presently* . . . millions' (p. 37 above).

Better mendacities –

'Old men's lies', Pound goes on to call them: 'old lies and new infamy'; but –

Better mendacities
Than the classics in paraphrase!

This 'classics in paraphrase' is both a positive (antithetical to the lies: 'mendacities' are preferred to *even* the . . .) and a negative: 'paraphrase' is surely less authentic, and presumably more ephemeral, than 'the classics' proper.

Soon, though, Pound's focus shifts to the more direct displacement of the classical in favour of the multifarious ephemeralities of contemporary life. This is seen as sheer loss, suitably ironized:

The tea-rose tea-gown, etc.
Supplants the mousseline of Cos,
The pianola 'replaces'
Sappho's barbitos.

And the irony in the po-faced (un)punctuation and the 'etc.' of the first line, and in those inverted commas in the third line, reaches its peak with a quotation from the poet Pindar and a masterfully sardonic pun:

O bright Apollo,
τίν' ἄνδρα, τίν' ἥρωα, τίνα θεόν,[98]
What god, man, or hero
Shall I place a tin wreath upon!

That 'wreath' (in Pindar, the victor's laurel crown) and that 'tin' ('tin hat': a soldier's helmet) prepare the way for a lament for the war-dead (and more ironic allusions, this time to patriotic Latin mottoes from Horace) – the dead, who died (in a classically evocative 'myriad') *for what?*:

There died a myriad,
And of the best, among them,
For an old bitch gone in the teeth,
For a botched civilization.

Charm, smiling at the good mouth,
Quick eyes gone under earth's lid –

This 'botched civilization' (which is all we are and all we have) is botched not least, one infers, because (unlike the 'organic' world of antiquity?) it is all in bits, in

[98] *tin' andra, tin' hêrôa, tina theon* (a reshuffled version of Pindar, *Olympian*, 2. 2), 'which man, which hero, which god [shall we celebrate today]?' The diacritics in the Greek above are corrected from the version printed in editions of Pound's poem.

fragments (Pound's friend Eliot will shortly develop this same image in *The Waste Land*, as Du Bellay already had, over three centuries before)[99] – but now in a climactic, devastating move, these bits are suddenly identified with the bits of antiquity (visual and verbal) that actually inspired the Renaissance:

> For two gross of broken statues –

Statues of 'bright Apollo', among others, no doubt: statues, anyhow, that inspired Guido Reni and his age; meanwhile a 'gross' (twelve dozen: a prosaic commercial measure) is a suitably decreative measure of what purports to be creative civilization –

> For a few thousand battered books.

The whole continuum of Western culture as we know it is seen to be centred on the classical tradition; and that culture, and that tradition, with all the educational apparatus that sustained it (all the way from 'paraphrase' to the 'battered books'), has never been more harshly interrogated by one of its own.[100] Not the least impressive feature of the classical tradition is its capacity to generate questions that go beyond itself, even in stark defiance of its own rationale.

[99] Du Bellay: 'Nouveau venu . . .' (1558): §25. Eliot: §35.

[100] Unlike Adorno's anxieties about writing poetry 'after Auschwitz' (§34), Pound's critique does not, at least, seem to pass judgement on new poetry like his own. *Mauberley* is not yet itself a 'battered book' – though as a representative of the continuum, perhaps it too is not exempt.

§5

Authority and Authorities

In 1663, the newly founded Royal Society – the first and (to this day) most illustrious scientific body in the British Isles – chose a Latin motto to accompany the arms granted by Charles II: 'nullius in verba', meaning 'take nothing on trust'. The Latin phrase comes from a line of Horace, in which the poet asserts his independence of all schools of philosophy: '*nullius* addictus iurare *in verba* magistri' – '[I am] *not* bound to swear allegiance *to the words of any* master.'[1] In the new world of scientific and (soon) Enlightenment progress, authority, if it exists, has to be supported by argument and evidence. Yet while the motto proclaims this new outlook, the use of a Latin phrase, with its appeal to a canonical classical author and his own repudiation of authority, neatly illustrates the complications of any such endeavour in a classicizing age – and hints at the possible complications of allegiance to authority on the part of the classical tradition itself.

In a set of reflections 'On Schoolmasters' Learning' ('Du Pédantisme'), in 1580, Montaigne points critically to appeals to ancient authority as an established practice:

> We know how to say, 'this is what Cicero said'; 'this is how morality is for Plato'; 'these are Aristotle's *ipsissima verba*'. But what have *we* got to say? What are *our* judgements?[2]

[1] Horace, *Epistles*, 1. 1. 14.

[2] '. . . que jugeons nous?': *Essais*, 1. 25. 'On Schoolmasters' Learning' is Screech's version of the title (2003: 154). Dates for Montaigne, here and elsewhere, reflect the three-stage composition of the *Essays* (summarized ibid. xv–xvi, lviii).

The Classical Tradition: Art, Literature, Thought, First Edition. Michael Silk, Ingo Gildenhard, and Rosemary Barrow.

Published 2017 by John Wiley & Sons Ltd.

Appeals to ancient authority, of these and other kinds, are characteristic of Montaigne's age and, in an important sense, of Montaigne himself, whatever his reservations. Over and over again, exemplary material, quotations, and doctrine from ancient sources are his first point of reference. Thus, on Seneca and Plutarch: 'My book . . . is built entirely from their spoils' – and thus, more generally: 'when I give my view, it is to reveal the measure of my sight, not the measure of the thing.'[3] And like the founding fathers of the Royal Society, Montaigne appeals to, and through, ancient precedent in the very act of repudiating authority. '"This is what Zeno said" – but what do *you* say? "And Cleanthes" – but what about *you*?': the words are those of Montaigne's beloved Seneca.[4]

Compare and contrast the philosopher Berkeley in 1710:

> When a schoolman tells me *Aristotle hath said it*, all I conceive he means by it is to dispose me to embrace his opinion with the deference and submission which custom has annexed to that name.[5]

What Berkeley goes on to call, precisely, men's 'willingness to resign their judgement to authority' is, no doubt, more objectionable to him than it was – even – to Montaigne; but in the 'long' seventeenth century it is still a current practice, and in this period is repeatedly criticised by philosophical thinkers, above all. For Descartes, around 1628, we should indeed read 'the writings of the ancients', but not 'study them too closely', which merely risks transmitting 'their mistakes' to us.[6] Francis Bacon, in the same decade, is more sweeping: 'to spend too much time in studies [of classical texts] is sloth; to use them too much for ornament is affectation; to make judgment wholly by their rules is the humour of a scholar.'[7] Representatively, Bacon's *Novum organum* ('A New Organon', 1620) is a specific attempt to supersede an ancient authority, Aristotle's hugely influential logical works (the original *Organon*),[8] which had reached the high point of their influence amidst the scholasticism of the thirteenth century. Contrast, then, the uncomplicated commitment shown by Bacon's namesake, the philosopher-scientist Roger Bacon, at that time: Aristotle may not have reached the very 'limits of wisdom', but 'in authority' he is '*the* philosopher', and in philosophy carries the same weight as the Apostle Paul in divinity.[9]

It is not, of course, only thinkers who acclaim, or reject specific authorities. With Pound's 'broken statues' and 'bright Apollo' still in mind (§4), the example of the

[3] *Essais*, 2. 32 and 2. 10.

[4] *Epistulae Morales*, 33. 7. An additional significance attaches to Montaigne's regard for Seneca (and Plutarch), insofar as the 'unsystematic, open-ended form' of such 'privileged texts' is seen to 'endorse that of the *Essais* themselves': Cave (1979) 271.

[5] *A Treatise Concerning the Principles of Human Knowledge*, Introduction, 20.

[6] *Regulae ad directionem ingenii*, 3 (written *c.* 1628, published posthumously).

[7] *Essays* (1625), 50: 'Of Studies'.

[8] Bertolt Brecht's *Miniature Organum for the Theatre* (*Kleines Organon für das Theater*, 1948–53) looks back to both: §10.

[9] *Opus maius* (*c.* 1260), 2. 13 ('philosophus nominatur, in auctoritate philosophiae, sicut Paulus').

Apollo Belvedere can serve as a simple paradigm of authority in the visual sphere. Discovered, apparently, in the fifteenth century, and acclaimed by connoisseurs of art from Vasari in 1568 ('sweetness . . . severity . . . perfect grace')[10] to Winckelmann in 1755 ('the consummation of the best that nature, art, and the human mind can produce'),[11] this influential statue was a model for artists from the Renaissance (when its 'broken' parts were restored)[12] onwards. Alongside 'the Apollo', Vasari lists other recently excavated antiquities (his characterization in fact covers all these pieces), including 'the Laocoon, the Hercules, the great Belvedere torso', 'the Venus' (now known as Venus ex Balneo) and 'the Cleopatra' (Sleeping Ariadne); and the point of his list is precisely that their rediscovery has helped to make possible the 'supreme perfection' of the 'modern' style of art, beginning with Leonardo.

For artists and theorists of art in the classicizing ages, texts can be authoritative too, whether as technical guides, like Galen's medical treatises (§6) or Vitruvius' architectural manual (§30), or as a sourcebook, as Ovid's *Metamorphoses* was to become (§11) – while Ovid, among others, is also a guide for artists in the mysteries of love (§9). Overwhelmingly, though, it is writers who defer to Ovid, to Cicero, to Plutarch or Seneca, or to any of the literary texts whose authors are treated as authorities. Such deference, involving imitation and appropriation of all kinds, is characteristic of the long span from the Middle Ages to the eighteenth century, but especially of the Renaissance and the seventeenth. In 1842/3, looking back at that era, the poet Wordsworth noted that 'an importance and a sanctity were at that period attached to classical literature that extended . . . both to its spirit and form in a degree that can never be revived.'[13] Wordsworth's reflective placing captures the reality of the situation. It is not that the Western world of the 1840s has lost interest in the classical. It is rather that, in the wake of Wordsworthian and other romanticism, along with the large developments associated with, or against, it (especially the new science and the deference to 'progress'), the nature of the classical tradition has changed irrevocably. And one way of summing up the change would be to say: *before* this age, it often makes sense to discuss the classical tradition (in thought, literature, art) in terms of authorities – as the Apollo Belvedere is an ultimate point of reference for Winckelmann in the mid-eighteenth century, and as Seneca and Plutarch are for Montaigne two centuries earlier – whereas *after* this age (after the earlier nineteenth century), it rarely does. Or, more summarily still: insofar as the classical tradition implies an imperative in favour of specific authorities, one might say that, towards the end of the eighteenth century, the classical tradition starts to become optional.

[10] *Lives*, Preface to Part 3:

[11] *Gedanken über die Nachahmung der griechischen Werke in der Malerei und Bildhauerkunst*, 1 (see §29). Cf. Goethe: 'We were discussing the Apollo Belvedere yet again . . . an inexhaustible topic of conversation for artists': *Italienische Reise* (1816–17), entry for September 1787 ('Bericht'). Cf. *Figure 3* (p. 105 below).

[12] A missing right hand and left arm were restored by Montorsoli in XVI.

[13] Among notes dictated to Isabella Fenwick (Wordsworth, *Shorter Poems, 1807–20*, ed. C. H. Ketcham, 1989, p. 544): Wordsworth's specific reference here is to Milton's *Lycidas* (first published in 1638).

Qualifications are in order here. Romanticism (even without the concomitant developments) undoubtedly marks one of the decisive shifts in Western sensibility, but here, as elsewhere, precise chronologies may be misleading. In particular, relevant shifts, prefiguring the new outlook, are clearly visible from earlier in the eighteenth century.[14] Here we need only recall the way Chardin deplores the continuing practice of copying the 'antique torso' in 1765 (and this, a few years before Winckelmann's tribute to his beloved Apollo) – or ponder the significance of a first shift from Rome to Greece, in the shape of Homer's rise in esteem and Virgil's relative decline (§3) (significant, if only because it breaks the continuity of earlier allegiances) – or note the increasing willingness of critics to discount the importance of classical allegiance as such, not least with reference to Shakespeare. For Samuel Johnson, in 1765, Shakespeare's plays combine tragedy and comedy, *therefore* flout both ancient precedent and 'the rules of criticism', *and yet* emerge triumphant;[15] for Germany's first notable man of letters, Gotthold Ephraim Lessing, in 1759, 'Shakespeare is a much greater tragedian than Corneille, *even though* Corneille knew the ancients pretty well, and Shakespeare hardly knew them at all.'[16]

The fact remains: up until romanticism, classical authorities are more or less the rule; afterwards, very much the exception. Even in the twentieth century, the work of many considerable poets, in particular, is informed by a classical education or classical reading – from D'Annunzio to Rilke, from Valéry to Ted Hughes – but none of these very different writers treats classical poets as normative in the old sense; and the abandonment of that old sense is already apparent in the Romantic age. Even by comparison with a Johnson or a Lessing, that age, if it has a sense of authority at all, is liable to attach it to entities of a more diffuse kind, from wild nature to the inner self. And even where the classical (usually the Hellenic) is indeed seen as authoritative, it is again, characteristically, in such diffuse terms: Hölderlin, with his unspecific Greek yearnings (§3), is a case in point. Indeed, German Hellenists, from Hölderlin to Nietzsche, often look less to Greek authors than to the Greek experience overall for a model of exemplary existence: 'Oh those Greeks! They understood how to *live*.'[17] Sometimes, again, the general authority of the ancients is itself actually secondary to today's lack of it: in this spirit, Keats 'appeals to antiquity as a supreme fiction . . . whose imaginative rehabilitation might guarantee the authority of modern poetry.'[18] Relatedly, too, writers of this period are wont to acknowledge, as masters, great figures from the past without commitment, in the old sense. In the preface to his drama *Cromwell* (1827), Victor Hugo acclaims Homer and Greek tragedy – along with Shakespeare, Milton, Dante, and others: the roll-call signifies

[14] From earlier still, if one counts the dispute, in France and elsewhere, between 'Ancients' and 'Moderns', but the many arguments subsumed under that label are rarely focused in a relevant way. E.g. Perrault's programmatic roll-call in 1687 belittles the classicizing Racine, but champions the classicizing Molière (§3).

[15] *Preface to Shakespeare*: §22.

[16] 17. *Literaturbrief*, 16 February 1759: our emphasis. Contrast Lessing on Aristotle: p. 67 below.

[17] Preface to Nietzsche's *Die fröhliche Wissenschaft* (second edition, 1887), section 4.

[18] Aske (1985) 1.

his own high ambition and, less self-centredly, the greatness available to a new age, but hardly his (or its) deference to authority. Hugo is not alone, either, in finding the 'real definition' of the Romantic movement in *freedom* ('freedom in art, freedom in society'),[19] as against models or rules ('there are no rules or models, only the laws of nature').[20] And these and other related tendencies become more, not less, apparent in the generations that follow.

Yet even in the classicizing ages, when classical authority means classical authors,[21] there are other caveats to be made. In the first place, appeal to specific names may be misleading, because many 'authors' quoted (or excerpted or otherwise invoked) turn out to have been known to the quoter, at least in part, vicariously, because the quotation comes from elsewhere, and most probably from an anthology. Such collections were strikingly influential from the Carolingian age[22] to the Renaissance, where one particular anthology, the *Adages* of Erasmus (first published in 1500) commanded a wide and continuing readership (Rabelais, among others, 'drew on them again and again');[23] in the course of the sixteenth century, well over a hundred editions were produced. 'Plato and Homer,' observes Montaigne (later in that century), 'may be cited by those who have never set eyes on them. I too have often taken my quotations not from the originals but from somewhere else.'[24]

Then again, some classical authors turn out to be more 'classical' than others, which means more authoritative than others. To some extent, this is a matter of canonical status within a genre. To Quintilian, writing a century after Virgil, the poet of the *Aeneid* is *the* Roman epicist, in a different category to all possible rivals, from Ennius (by now, three centuries old) to Valerius Flaccus (only a generation).[25] That this judgement rests on a genuine response to the poetry in question is beyond dispute – but at the same time, Valerius, from Quintilian's standpoint, is probably too late for a serious comparison, and Ennius (revered 'like the ancient trees' in a sacred grove) certainly too early.[26] And from the Renaissance onwards, some such calculus (largely irrelevant in the Middle Ages) begins to be reapplied to Latin texts

[19] 'La liberté dans l'art, la liberté dans la société': 'Lettre-Préface' to *Poésies de feu Charles Dovalle* (1830).

[20] Preface to *Cromwell* (1827).

[21] Irrespective of the etymological link between 'author' and 'authority' (a link reinforced adventitiously in some languages, including English, by seeming association with the etymologically unrelated 'authentic'). The rhetorical force of Foucault's celebrated 1969 critique of authorial status ('Qu'est-ce qu'un auteur?': 'What is an author?') is enhanced by the connection – esp. as 'auteur' in French (unlike 'author' in English) encompasses authority figures from non-literary creative spheres, notably film directors.

[22] Summary in Bolgar (1954) 125–6, 410.

[23] Screech (1979) 10. 'When Rabelais cites the *Adagia* . . . he is citing a source which can be almost as normative as Holy Writ': ibid.

[24] In 1588: *Essais*, 3. 12.

[25] Quintilian, *Institutio Oratoria*, 10. 1. 85–90.

[26] Ibid. 88. In the visual sphere, the schematic understanding of periods of ancient art initiated by Winckelmann (§§11, 29) presents obvious parallels. Cf. §3.

in particular, and especially to the exclusion of almost anything 'late' – which in practice increasingly means starting with Plautus and Terence, from the second century BC, and stopping around the end of the first century AD, with Martial and Juvenal in verse, and Tacitus and Quintilian himself in prose.[27]

With Greek, things are less clear-cut. In and after the Renaissance, special weight is indeed often given to the surviving tragic and comic dramas of Athens from the second half of the fifth century BC (more, then, to those of Sophocles and Euripides than to those of Aeschylus)[28] and to the dialogues of Plato from the fourth, along with other texts of that time-span (mostly, likewise, Attic texts), but also to Aeschylus' contemporary Pindar (the only lyric poet to survive *in extenso*) and of course to Homer – from a much earlier period, but then, as now, regarded as the effective beginning (the *fons et origo*) of Western literature.[29] At the same time, though, the Renaissance and the neoclassical centuries too are happy to espouse the moral and historical reflections of Plutarch,[30] the wit of Lucian,[31] the playful sophistication of the Greek romances, or the Neoplatonic intricacies of the philosopher Plotinus (of various periods, but all 'late').[32] And the fact that Plutarch writes, not in 'classical' Attic, but in the Hellenistic *koine*, and the others in various gradations of revivalist Attic, is not felt to compromise their status. All these writers, of course, write in prose, and with Greek verse, it is true, a more restrictive attitude prevails, and from the first: by comparison with their prose-writing contemporaries, surviving poets, from Apollonius (third century BC) to Nonnus (fifth AD), attract relatively little attention in the Renaissance or (outside the world of professional scholarship) thereafter.[33] With or without this complication, though, the overall picture remains largely unchanged until a significant shift within German Hellenism (with Nietzsche an influential figure here) towards privileging the early-classical

[27] Apuleius (II AD) is one notable exception. For the classicizing centuries, the problem with 'early' Latin is less acute: except for the comedies of Plautus, not much survives.

[28] Correspondingly, the performance histories of (e.g.) Euripides' *Medea* and Aeschylus' *Agamemnon* show very different trajectories: Hall *et al.* (2001), Macintosh *et al.* (2005).

[29] And exceptionally, even, praised (by Eobanus Hessus, in 1540) as 'the foremost poet of all the ages' ('poetarum omnium saeculorum longe princeps'): Ford (2007) 138.

[30] Important, not only for Montaigne (see esp. 1. 25; 2. 32), but e.g. for Shakespeare (Braden 2004) and for French Enlightenment thinkers, Rousseau in particular (in *Confessions*, 1, written in the 1760s, Rousseau famously declares that it was Plutarch's heroes who inspired his own 'esprit libre et républicain').

[31] Strikingly influential in the Renaissance for writers as different as Alberti (§11) in his Latin dialogues (the *Intercenales*) and Rabelais, who translated Lucian into Latin and 'for many Frenchmen of his day' was 'the French Lucian': Screech (1979) 7.

[32] Longus' *Daphnis and Chloe*, in particular, has its creative devotees as late as Goethe ('the whole composition betokens the highest art and culture': letter to Eckermann, 20 March 1831), and Plotinus as late as Leopardi ('Dialogo di Plotino e di Porfirio', 1824).

[33] The most notable exceptions are the *Idylls* of Theocritus, founder of pastoral poetry (and a huge influence – partly, but not entirely, through Virgil – on Renaissance pastoral and, thereby, on early opera: §12), and the post-classical poems once ascribed to Anacreon: summary in Michelakis (2009) 342–6.

and the archaic against the fourth century BC or even the fifth: Aeschylus against (even) Euripides, the Presocratic philosophers against (even) Plato.[34]

In our often clamorously relativistic age, notions of 'early' and 'late' as symptoms of inadequacy are out of fashion,[35] and a tolerant indulgence towards works of all periods is the norm. In such a climate it is salutary to note that, virtually throughout our millennium and a half, the hierarchy of canonical authors is never entirely rigid, but often conceals, or even fosters, debate about particular alternatives. Nietzsche's attempt to have his contemporaries value *this* over *that*, in fact, is one of many. For Dante, Aristotle – the ancient author referred to most often across his *oeuvre* – is 'the master of them that know'.[36] For Petrarch, only a generation later, Aristotle is repeatedly found to be fallible (even if Petrarch's main target is not Aristotle himself, but the 'stupid Aristotelians').[37] The eighteenth century has its argument about Homer and Virgil. We shall encounter another such debate, in the Renaissance, about the special status of Cicero (§7).

There is, in any case, a difference between availability and esteem. Throughout the medieval West, all 'classical' Latin texts in our possession now were available somewhere – otherwise we would not possess them now – but many were not in general circulation, which is to say, were not esteemed, without significant qualification. By contrast, virtually no Greek authors were available to be read in the original – and there was virtually no-one to read them, if they had been – though some (like Aristotle or Galen) became well-known, and influential, in Latin translation. And though access to Greek texts, in Greek, was of course one of the defining features of the Renaissance, the classicism of Renaissance culture, in Italy and elsewhere, is and remains essentially Greco-Roman or simply Roman (which is as true of Renaissance art as of Renaissance literature and thought); and in particular the preeminent authority of Greek texts, *without reference to Latin*, is very limited before German Hellenism at the time of, or after, the Romantic watershed. Both the specificity and the tone of that attachment to Greece are distinctive: in Burckhardt's words, this was a *hieros gamos*, or 'holy union'[38] (and the tag neatly recalls Wordsworth's appeal to the 'sanctity' of classical writings in earlier centuries). But again, the relative authority of Greece and Rome is not always constant at any one time. While German Hellenists are busy promoting Greece, Robespierre is going to his death convinced that (as Jürgen Habermas put it) 'antique Rome was a past laden with momentary revelations'.[39]

It will be apparent both how fundamental, and yet also how complicated, issues of classical authority can in practice be. A moral essay, in letter form, by Petrarch makes the point, by addressing several of the significant complications. Like the

34 Silk and Stern (1981) 155–9.

35 Cf. §3.

36 *Inferno*, 4. 131. 'Most often', apart from the Bible: details in Toynbee (1968) 55–8.

37 *De sui et multorum ignorantia*, 4 ('stultos Aristotelicos').

38 Introduction to his *Griechische Kulturgeschichte*, published posthumously in 1898.

39 Habermas (1981) 5. Cf. §3 n. 62 and §§6, 26.

Royal Society motto, Petrarch's letter is in allusive Latin.[40] Its subject, a good man is hard to find:

> 'The good are few; their number barely matches | The gates of Thebes or the rich Nile's outlets.' 'Whose words are those?', you ask. What difference does it make? If you approve of the saying, why ask about its author? As Augustine says, whatever is true derives its trueness from the truth ['a veritate verum'] . . . These are the words of experience, which is not used to lying; and the words of truth, which is incapable of lying. But if you must know . . . the words belong to one most experienced in such matters, Juvenal, who knows mankind and its ways ['mores hominum'] from top to bottom. If you don't believe him, listen to someone else, someone whose words come from Him who not only knows mankind, but created it. So what does *he* say? 'There is none that doeth good, no, not one.' The poet says 'few', the apostle ['propheta'] 'none'; and from their different points of view ['secundum suum sensum'], each is quite right. But . . . by way of reconciling these different views, listen to Horace who, like an arbitrator, declares: 'No-one born is without faults: the best is whoever | Finds himself bothered by fewest.'

The way Petrarch deploys his classical and Biblical authorities can only be called provoking. He gives us two quotations from the pagan classics, Horace and Juvenal,[41] who, as satirists, can claim special insight into ethical matters, along with one from a Church Father (Augustine) and one from the Bible, Paul's Epistle to the Romans.[42] At the same time, he questions the notion that authority needs an author – teasing his reader, at first, by evading the obvious question, 'who said it?' Instead of blindly following a name, he points to specific sources of insight: higher truth and experience. Juvenal is an authority on ethics, not because he is an *auctor*, but because of his experience of life – while it is presumably Horace's experience of the same that even prompts the audacious thought that human wisdom can be used to reconcile the word of man and the Word of God – both of them, on their own terms, 'quite right'.

The lessons of this text are several. Even in the 'age of authority', authorities can be routinely challenged; authorities do not necessarily agree (though one is always inclined to *want* them to agree: §22); the higher truth of revealed religion of course outweighs the human truths of the classics, but, then again, there appears to be some possibility of compromise even here; and, not least, there is a significant site of authority – 'experience' – which, in centuries to come, will empower empirical science beyond all existing authorities, and perhaps help to provoke the influential Romantic shift away from existing authorities too.

Over the millennium and a half that concerns us, these various complications are visible again and again. Over that same millennium and a half, furthermore, classical authority manifests itself so diversely that in one area, in a given period,

[40] *Rerum familiarium*, 3. 15.

[41] Horace, *Satires*, 1. 3. 68–9; Juvenal, *Satires*, 13. 26–7.

[42] Augustine, *Soliloquies*, 1. 25. 27; Romans, 3. 12.

the picture may look very different from the way it looks in another. In the sections that follow, we seek to give some impression of this diversity. Classical authors have served as authorities across a wide range of cultural activity, both within and beyond the educational contexts discussed in §4. They have provided models for diverse forms and genres (§22) and essential sources for reworkings of myth (§24). More immediately, they have served as 'masters of knowledge' (§6), 'models of style' (§7), and 'beacons of morality' (§8) – all these, above all, in the classicizing centuries, from the Middle Ages to the pre-Romantic age. Yet ancient texts have also functioned as amoral guides to erotic experience (§9), and, more loosely but very strikingly, as inspiration for idiosyncratic 'special relationships' between figures from antiquity and the post-classical age (§10); and in these two very different cases, at least, the power of authority reaches well beyond the Romantic age and (in defiance of all contemporary relativisms)[43] into our own.

Given the emphasis on authors and texts in the next five sections overall, our focus here will be largely on writers and thinkers, rather than visual artists (whose own 'authorities' are mostly distinct: §11). And given that it is largely in the classicizing centuries that classical authority itself is an issue, writers and thinkers from Germany will be less prominent in these sections than elsewhere: in those centuries German literature and thought, less subject than their neighbours to Renaissance influences (§3), are implicated in the classical tradition less substantially.

[43] And of sweeping characterizations like 'the past has lost its authority' *tout court* (Arendt, 'Tradition and the Modern Age', 1968: cf. §34).

§6

Masters of Knowledge

'Re-read the books of the Greek physicians with care . . . A [veritable] chasm of knowledge is what I hope to see [in you]': Rabelais's Gargantua to his son, in advisory mode.[1] Over a large part of our millennium and a half, knowledge is fundamental to the authority of the classical, and often in the most literal sense: the ancients had the knowledge and after-comers need their writings to get at that knowledge for themselves.[2] This is most obvious with technical and scientific matters, in the medical sphere ('the books of the physicians') not least. In the eleventh and twelfth centuries, a series of translators, from Constantine the African to Burgundio of Pisa, made important treatises from the Greek medical corpus available in Latin, including some by Galen (who 'became the darling' of the medieval schools)[3] and some from the Hippocratic corpus, including the *Aphorisms*;[4] that same work was subsequently edited in Greek by Rabelais himself (the great comic writer was also an accomplished scholar and a trained doctor) and published in

1 *Pantagruel*, 8. After his 'Greek' physicians, Gargantua lists others (from the Arabs to the Cabbalists), and as an additional source of knowledge cites the Scriptures – but Greek medicine comes first.

2 'Antiquity is now used merely as a propaedeutic for thinking, speaking, and writing, but there was a time when it was the essence of worldly knowledge' – Nietzsche, notes for 'Wir Philologen' (1875): Colli and Montinari (1967–), 4. 1. 125.

3 Bolgar (1954) 235.

4 Ibid. 172–3. Various of the above were mediated through Arabic sources: ibid. 171–4. *Nachleben* of ancient medicine overall: Nutton (2010b).

The Classical Tradition: Art, Literature, Thought, First Edition. Michael Silk, Ingo Gildenhard, and Rosemary Barrow.

Published 2017 by John Wiley & Sons Ltd.

1532. Seventeen years later, in 1549, works by the same Hippocrates and Galen were prescribed as medical textbooks, across the English Channel, in the revised statutes instituted for the universities of Oxford and Cambridge.[5]

In the same spirit, a whole range of technical literature was cultivated and consulted during the Middle Ages and the Renaissance. The medieval hunger for information was satisfied partly by encyclopedic works,[6] but increasingly by primary texts, like those of Hippocrates and Galen and, along with them, the systematic grammars of Donatus and Priscian in the sphere of language,[7] the codification of Justinian in the domain of law,[8] and Latin versions of Euclid's treatises on mathematics, Ptolemy's on astronomy, and Aristotle's on natural science.[9] Not much had changed by the end of the sixteenth century, when Marlowe's learned Faustus 'in his study sits', reviewing the efficacy of Aristotle, of Galen and his 'physic', of Justinian and the 'universal study of the law' – and of 'Jerome's Bible' – before opting for 'magic' and the 'metaphysics of magicians' instead.[10] Magic and magicians apart, some of these writings retained part of their authority until recent times: Aristotle's *biologica* into the nineteenth century;[11] Euclid still later (the *Elements* remained one main basis for mathematics teaching in secondary education, from America to Italy, well into the twentieth century);[12] while Roman law (based on Justinian, among others) remains to this day a specific point of reference in the legal codes of nations as different as Turkey and Scotland.[13]

In various important instances, though, the movement from medieval to Renaissance meant a shift from the more narrowly technical to the more broadly 'humane'. This is unmistakable in the domain of poetics, where medieval scholars knew and studied Horace's *Ars Poetica* (object of an extensive commentary as early as the Carolingian age),[14] but under technical-rhetorical influence diluted its wit and wisdom into low-level compositional handbooks.[15] The rediscovery of Aristotle's *Poetics* (a work, unlike most of Aristotle's, unknown in the West until the fifteenth

5 Clarke (1959) 31.

6 Like those (in V) by Martianus Capella and (in VII: early medieval, but classical-based) by Isidore of Seville.

7 See e.g. Vineis and Maierù (1994).

8 See in summary Bolgar (1954) 144–6; more generally, Stein (1999), Vincenti (2010).

9 Though Aristotle's scientific works were banned by the Paris Council in 1210: Bolgar (1954) 172–3, 180–2. Ptolemy: Evans (2010).

10 *The Tragical History of Doctor Faustus* (completed, *c.* 1589; first published, 1604): Faustus's opening monologue, 29–91.

11 'No-one prior to Darwin has made a greater contribution to our understanding of the living world than Aristotle' – the biologist Ernst Mayr (1982: 87).

12 See Giacardi (2006), Pritchard (2003) 461–526.

13 Burdick (1938) 26–7, Mousourakis (2003) 445; cf. Stein (1963).

14 The *Tractatus Vindobonensis*, described by Brink (1971) 39 as 'a Carolingian rehash of one set of ps.-Acronian scholia'.

15 Even in a relatively sophisticated treatise like Matthew of Vendôme's *Ars versificatoria* (*c.* 1175), we find e.g. Horace's large principle that a portrayal of Achilles should follow mythological tradition (*Ars Poetica*, 120–2) converted into a narrow rule for using stock epithets (*Ars versificatoria*, 1. 44).

century)[16] transformed the tone and perspective of Renaissance debate and stimulated a new age of poetic theory[17] (as of poetic productivity, in tragedy above all). With the Horatian text now seen in a more humanistic light and widely read alongside Aristotle's ('but an interpretation of that of Aristotle': the French Jesuit René Rapin, as late as 1674),[18] we glimpse the beginnings of literary criticism in the modern sense, with a philosophical dimension and comparative points of reference across the vernacular literatures. When the process is intensified by the assimilation of the treatise *On the Sublime*, attributed to Longinus,[19] the first stage of a momentous shift is complete, from deference to the technical minutiae of ancient sources to a developing concern with larger issues of aesthetics and ethics. Fully independent critical thought, in these terms, is achieved (like much else) in the Romantic age, with Schiller and Friedrich Schlegel, Coleridge and Wordsworth; such critics allude freely to ancient theory (and practice) – but choose when to do so. Their understandings entail no allegiance to authorities as such: the classicizing imperative is left behind.[20]

An equivalent shift, at least in part, is apparent in the case of rhetoric. A training in persuasive language (spoken or written) had been a central aspect of Greek and Roman cultural activity from the fourth century BC, but it was chiefly the nuts-and-bolts rules and regulations of the rhetoric industry, and not its larger cultural ambitions, that remained alive in the medieval West. With the Renaissance, once influential sourcebooks like the *De Inventione* (by Cicero) and the *Ad Herennium* (ascribed to Cicero) were superseded in esteem by the more exploratory works of Quintilian and Cicero himself. Poggio Bracciolini's discovery of the full text of Quintilian's *Education of the Orator* in the monastery of St Gallen in 1416 is a symbolic moment: 'the whole of humanism with its manifold variations was to some extent implicit in Quintilian's conception of the perfect orator.'[21] Parts of Quintilian's lengthy treatise had been in circulation for centuries,[22] but in an age when rhetoric was strictly subservient to 'thought' (logical, theological, scholastic) the work could only be subject to ecclesiastical suspicion, both for its promotion of worldly individual achievement and, more generally, because of anxieties about the potentially immoral use of verbal skills.[23] In the reception of Cicero, too, emphasis

[16] First Latin translation (by Giorgio Valla), 1498; first printed edition (Aldine), 1508. A few blurry glimpses of the *Poetics* had reached the medieval West via Arabic sources: Copeland and Sluiter (2009) 462–3, 481–2, 670, 735, 788.

[17] Though, at first, only in the form of prescriptive works in Latin, like Vida's verse treatise on poetry (1520) and Scaliger's *Poetices libri septem* (published posthumously in 1561). Renaissance and later (re-) readings of the *Poetics*: Halliwell (1986) 286–323.

[18] *Réflexions sur la Poétique d'Aristote*, 1. 7.

[19] Only made widely known by Boileau's translation of 1674 (§30).

[20] Within literary theory, as within the classical tradition, the shift is part of a much larger transformation: summary in Silk (2012).

[21] Bolgar (1954) 346; cf. Classen (2003).

[22] Since at least XII: Bolgar (1954) 423. Cf. Russell (2001) 22.

[23] A concern from Augustine, *De Doctrina Christiana* (4. 3) onwards (with classical precedents in Plato and Cicero's *De Oratore*); cf. §21 on 'heroic' individualism.

on the technical works is replaced by a broader interest in the more wide-ranging and theoretical mode of the *De Oratore*, *Brutus*, and *Orator*.[24] Symptomatically, these three works figure prominently among the first set of printed Latin texts in 1465–9.[25] Then, three centuries later, in the generation of republicanism and revolution, the conversion of Cicero from technical expert to guide to public life is completed, when his whole political-oratorical persona – speeches and political causes, as well as rhetorical theory – acquires canonical status, in France above all; a celebrated public denunciation of Robespierre as Cicero's enemy Catiline (§26) is a typically flamboyant instance.

That revolutionary generation, however, is coincident with the first phase of the Romantic age – and to the Romantic sensibility, rhetoric is deeply suspect. If medieval Christendom had its anxieties about classical rhetoric, many Romantic writers and thinkers felt something closer to revulsion. Rhetoric for them was a prison-house of conventional rules and technical artifice, with its goal – public eloquence – trivial by comparison with the true, poetic uses of language, which must be personal and inward ('eloquence is heard,' says the youthful John Stuart Mill in 1833, 'poetry is overheard').[26] Backward-looking treatises, like Richard Whateley's *Elements of Rhetoric* (1828), would still command the attention of traditionalists (and Whateley's premises and categories would mostly have been familiar to Quintilian or even Aristotle), but rhetoric and its classic texts disappear from the intellectual mainstream until fitfully reappropriated by independent-minded theorists of language and communication, like Gérard Genette and Umberto Eco, in the later twentieth century.[27]

Remarkably enough, a first independent response to the inherited rhetorical system had been fashioned four centuries earlier. In 1536, Petrus Ramus (Pierre de la Ramée) – Huguenot convert, educational reformer and, eventually, victim of the St Bartholomew massacre in 1572 – launched his academic career with a disputation on the thesis that 'everything Aristotle said is false'.[28] He then set himself the task of reorganizing the disciplines of rhetoric and logic ('dialectic'), and duly produced a series of polemical treatises (in Latin) against the three giants of the rhetorical canon, Aristotle, Cicero, and Quintilian,[29] along with the first major work of philosophy in French (or any vernacular language), *Dialectique* (1555). Rhetoric itself he sought to reduce from 'a sort of omnibus discipline, comprising . . . grammar . . .

[24] Between IX and XIV, attested copies of the *Ad Herennium* and the *De Inventione* greatly outnumber those of the *De Oratore*: statistics in Bolgar (1954) 396.

[25] Ibid. 276.

[26] In 'What is poetry?', first published in *The Monthly Repository*, January 1833.

[27] Thus: Genette (1966), (1969), (1972); Eco (1984). Cf. (less high-profile, but earlier) Perelman and Olbrechts-Tyteca (1958) and Tuve (1947) – the latter both a historical study of Renaissance theory and a rehabilitation.

[28] *Quaecumque ab Aristotele dicta essent commentitia esse.*

[29] *Aristotelicae animadversiones* (1543); *Brutinae quaestiones* (1547); *Rhetoricae distinctiones in Quintilianum* (1549).

the art of speech . . . logic, philosophy and ethics' to its core functions of 'expression' and delivery[30] – but the outcome of his efforts was a rehabilitation of true eloquence and true reason, as much as a critique. In at least one important respect, Ramus's rhetoric, and his logic too, looked back to the scholasticism of the thirteenth century, rather than ahead to the new thinking of the seventeenth. His system still 'posited a pre-existent body of true knowledge, already complete and perfect, which required only to be uncovered and revealed'.[31] It is no coincidence that in the learned world of Reformation England, Ramist principles were influential for several generations, with some of the strictest classicists, from Sidney to Milton, finding them congenial.[32]

Ramist or otherwise, the sixteenth century is the last in which there is still an active consensus that 'the road to truth' is to be equated with 'the discovery or rediscovery of a universe whose laws were the legacies of a wiser past or the fiats of an unimpeachable God.'[33] And in these terms the period is still one in spirit with the Middle Ages. During the Christian millennium, which coincides with the first millennium of the classical tradition, the unquestioned source of authority in matters of knowledge and truth is divine revelation captured in the scriptures and mediated by the Church. Nevertheless, even beyond the technical sphere, medieval Christian thinking never dismisses pagan learning as a whole. The huge example is the central place of Aristotle (in Latin) within the imaginative scholastic synthesis of Greek philosophy and Christian theology, whose great formal exponent is Aquinas in the thirteenth century and whose supreme artistic monument is Dante's *Commedia* in the early fourteenth.[34] The most curious example of pagan-Christian reconciliation, by contrast, belongs to Renaissance Florence in the following century, when a sometimes aggressively anti-scholastic Christian Platonism acclaims the 'authority' of the esoteric doctrines of the *Corpus Hermeticum*.[35]

In this context, the *Corpus* provides a useful reminder that identifying 'the classical' is a retrospective exercise. The body of thought assembled in this strange collection represents a *mélange* of various mystical and mythical traditions: Christian, Gnostic, Pythagorean, Neoplatonic, Jewish. Of anonymous authorship, the treatises that now make up the collection belong to the imperial period, but were

30 Castor (1964) 128–9.

31 Ibid. 133.

32 Cf. Tuve (1947) 331–2. Ramism in a wider context: Fumaroli (1980).

33 Craig (1950) 3. In the previous century, one distinctive spokesman of the 'wiser past' principle was Pico della Mirandola, whose *Conclusiones* (1486) – in some ways anticipating the works of Leo Strauss (§34) – found truth in all philosophies and all religions.

34 Aquinas: Flannery (2001), Keys (2006), Wippel (2004). For Dante, Aristotle is 'master and guide of human reason' (*Convivio* 4. 6): see Boyde (1981) 36 and (on Dante's study of Aristotle) 306–7. In this era, thinkers from all three religions of the book (notably Averroes, Maimonides, Aquinas) seek to reconcile Aristotelian rationality with faith and dogma – though not all the receptions of Aristotle are reverential: witness the obscene figure of the 'mounted Aristotle' (Desmond 2006: 13–27).

35 Platonism in the Middle Ages and Renaissance: Hankins (1990), Klibansky (1981), Kristeller (1986).

put together in Byzantium. The *Corpus* presents itself as the wisdom of the mythic figure of Hermes Trismegistus ('thrice-great'), himself a conflation of the Greek messenger god and the Egyptian deity Thoth, and (by synchronistic logic) identified as a contemporary of Moses. As such, this Hermes became an ancient, alternative source of primordial wisdom, with Biblical, as well as classical, credentials, that readily caught the fancy of those unenthused by the rational outlook and orderly systems of Aristotle and the scholastics. In the great age of Renaissance rediscovery, an agent of Lorenzo de' Medici brought a copy to Italy, and Marsilio Ficino, busy at the time with a translation of Plato, was urged to give priority to the Hermetic texts.[36] They were first printed in 1463, and saw numerous reprints in the years that followed, with Giordano Bruno, among others, eager to enlist them in a quest for the ultimate truth, the *prisca theologia*.[37]

Looking back at these diverse appeals to ancient knowledge, many today are likely to see such respect for authority as one of the most alien aspects of the classical tradition as a whole. Most of us, no doubt, find it easy to accede to Lessing's formula, opposing 'Homer' to 'Newton' (§3), the artistic-creative past that will always be with us and the scientific-progressive present that in an obvious sense has transcended the past and made it redundant.[38] 'What is antiquity *now*?', is Nietzsche's question in 1875, and his immediate answer: 'It is not the treasure-chamber of all knowledge any longer.'[39] This (we tend to think) sums up the reality of the situation; and Newton – embodiment of the Royal Society in action, whose new system finally demonstrates the transience of ancient authority in the physical sciences – represents the decisive moment when knowledge (*scientia*) is shown to be for 'men of today' to pronounce on, with no looking back. For a time Newton can still be celebrated, in classicizing epigrammatic verse, as himself part of God's natural order ('Nature and Nature's laws lay hid in night. | God said, "Let Newton be!", and all was light')[40] – but the impetus of 'natural' science to override the authorities, classical or Christian, who formerly determined that order, soon puts any such union of perspectives out of reach.

That said, it is salutary to note that cases persist, where something like the knowledge of the ancients in the old sense is still respected and treated as special. Quirks apart (and one recalls that Newton himself was a devotee of Hermetic wisdom),[41]

36 See e.g. Walker (2000) 62.

37 Ebeling (2007), Yates (1964).

38 In his polemic on behalf of the French language in 1549 (§7), Du Bellay, *Deffence* (1. 10), seems to contemplate the possibility that one day we moderns will have sucked everything we can, or want, from both the 'sciences' and the 'arts' of the 'Greeks and Latins' – but here 'les Ars et Sciences' points to ancient technique and *doctrina*, rather than to ancient works of art (contrast Perrault: §3), and in any case to the prospect of the French *language* satisfying its needs thereby (§13).

39 Notes for 'Wir Philologen': Colli and Montinari (1967–), 4. 1. 145.

40 Pope, 'Epitaph: Intended for Sir Isaac Newton' (1730).

41 Westfall (1972). In more modern times, Hermetic and allied occult writings have attracted such illustrious figures as the poet Yeats: Harper (1974).

the main instances involve philosophy:[42] a notable irony, given that the fiercest critiques of authority in earlier centuries are in this very area. 'The safest general characterisation of the European philosophical tradition' – thus the philosopher A. N. Whitehead, famously, in 1929 – 'is that it consists of a series of footnotes to Plato.'[43] Unless we make an exception for his political philosophy, however,[44] Plato's continuing and contemporary presence is surely a matter of philosophical approach and questions raised, rather than answers given and 'knowledge' as such. And the same is certainly true of recent responses to most of the other philosophizing that survives from the ancient world. Even the intense engagements conducted by Martin Heidegger with Presocratic thought – Heraclitus, Parmenides, and others – could hardly be said to involve an acknowledgement of authority.[45] One may grant that Plato's master Socrates continues to exert, as he has long exerted, a notable fascination on philosophers and others,[46] but here there is no written text (Socrates wrote none), and without a text – *pace* Foucault[47] – there can be no 'authority' in the given sense.

The one ancient philosopher who *is* still referred to in a relevant spirit is Aristotle. On the eve of the Romantic revolution, Lessing still assumes the absolute authority of the *Poetics* ('as infallible ['unfehlbar'] as Euclid's *Elements*');[48] and two centuries, and more, later, this and related works continue to be cited by those investigating the logic of laughter or the effect of tragedy[49] and to be used (in the spirit of Montaigne) as a point of departure by literary theorists as different as Paul Ricoeur, Giorgio Agamben, and Northrop Frye.[50] Then again, more directly, American textbooks on screen-writing regularly 'invoke Aristotelian authority for the now canonical three-act model . . . of Hollywood film structure.'[51] The title (and

[42] Minor instances include the continuing appropriation of tips from classical *rhetorica* in manuals on memory training and handbooks for those unaccustomed to public speaking – Bovée (2003), a typical instance, subsumes both – though in such cases the ultimate classical sources are rarely acknowledged.

[43] Whitehead (1929) 39 – having already taken care to insist, however, that 'nothing rests on authority' (ibid.).

[44] Esp. for Leo Strauss, for whom various classical/classicizing thinkers remain, in effect, authorities: §34.

[45] See esp. the conversations recorded in Heidegger and Fink (1970), along with Heidegger's 1942/3 lectures on Parmenides. Cf. Most (2002a).

[46] Trapp (2007a), (2007b).

[47] See Foucault on 'discursivity' in 'What Is an Author?' ('Qu'est-ce qu'un auteur?', 1969).

[48] *Hamburgische Dramaturgie*, 101–4 (19 April 1768): contrast Lessing on Newton as modern achiever (§3).

[49] See e.g. Provine (2000) 116 ('Aristotle showed acute intuition about . . .') and Nuttall (1996) (where 'Aristotle and After' takes up about a third of the book).

[50] 'It is [Aristotle] who actually defined metaphor for the entire subsequent history of western thought': Ricoeur (1978) 3. Aristotle is one of Agamben's 'principal philosophical interlocutors': Johnson (2007) 266. 'The critical theory of genres is stuck precisely where Aristotle left it': Frye (1957) 13 – admittedly (even in mid-XX) a considerable exaggeration (cf. §22).

[51] Lowe (2000) x.

especially the subtitle) of one recent handbook speaks for itself: *Aristotle's Poetics for Screenwriters: Storytelling Secrets from the Greatest Mind in Western Civilization.*[52]

Some of this (with tragedy, for instance) is not easily distinguished from continuing awareness of the importance of Aristotle's historical contribution. More impressive, accordingly, is the confirmation that 'in several areas' – from philosophy of action to metaphysical issues of substance, essence, and natural kinds – 'his influence remains strong and alive'.[53] Against the odds, perhaps, a definitive end to this section cannot yet be written.

52 Tierno (2002); cf. Field (1994).

53 Charles (2005) 53; cf. Pozzo (2004). One might add the continuing influence of the Aristotelian tradition of 'anthropology' (§27).

§7
Models of Style

'I would have you model your style on Plato's Greek and Cicero's Latin': Rabelais's Gargantua to his son, once again.[1] In Renaissance thinking, as if by some natural conjunction, a classical authority may well be a master of knowledge and a model of style too. Thus, 'Melanchthon gives Homer and Hesiod priority among those authors "who both foster knowledge of things (*rerum scientiam*) and contribute greatly to the acquisition of eloquent discourse (*sermonis copiam*)".'[2] In a modern perspective, the difference between the two seems obvious. Whereas knowledge is, in principle, painlessly transferable across times and places, modelling *my* style of writing on *his* calls for imitation: one of the most problematic concepts of the classical tradition in Romantic and post-Romantic eyes, but one of the most characteristic procedures of the tradition, throughout all the centuries preceding.

Stylistic imitation, certainly, is no straightforward matter. Within the tradition, it involves all the intricacies of language-crossing (even when the source language is classical Latin and the host language Medieval or neo-Latin, this is true in a restricted sense), while, as Terence Cave points out, it is in one sense 'a kind of intertextual dialogue or conflict',[3] in another a mode of interpretation: 'the interpretative act' is implicit in 'a second discourse which claims to be a reconstitution of the first'.[4] And the problems it raises are far-reaching. There are issues of historical

[1] *Pantagruel*, 8.

[2] Cave (1979) 174: Melanchthon, *Praefatio in Hesiodum* (1526). On 'copia' and eloquence, cf. Cave (1979) 3–34.

[3] Ibid. 36, citing Quintilian, *Institutio Oratoria*, 10. 5. 5, 'certamen atque aemulationem'.

[4] Cave (1979) 35.

The Classical Tradition: Art, Literature, Thought, First Edition. Michael Silk, Ingo Gildenhard, and Rosemary Barrow.

Published 2017 by John Wiley & Sons Ltd.

context: the situation of a vernacular culture seeking to profit by imitation of an authoritative other is different from that of a writer imitating another within a single culture. But there are in any case problems of large theory. For a start, any purposeful talk of 'style' invites the notorious question: 'style', as opposed to *what*? The traditional opposition was with 'content' or 'subject-matter' – in Renaissance, and classical, terms, *verba* ('words') with *res* ('things')[5] – whose separation represents a piece of conceptual sorcery that threatens us with such disconcerting apparitions as word-less content and content-less style.[6] And the problem – unsolved, to this day[7] – gets worse when imitation is added to the mix. Assuming that a notional separation of *verba* and *res* is imaginable, then – Cave again – 'which should the imitator attempt to transcribe? what is the distinctive quality of a text consecrated by tradition? can this elusive factor be captured and resuscitated?'[8] And indeed, what might such a 'capture' amount to in practice? In Renaissance France, the poet Ronsard can claim that by imitating 'the very best' classical texts, he is 'imitating Nature' herself.[9] The modern reader, it may be, marvels at the paradox, and moves on. Our review of 'models of style' will yield an abundance of paradoxes, problems, complications – and we shall, at least, pause to consider some of them, before moving on.

Debates about good style already raged in antiquity – from the contest of heavyweights ('Aeschylus' and 'Euripides') in Aristophanes' *Frogs*, all the way to disputes between oratorical promoters of 'Asianism' and 'Atticism' in the Greco-Roman world, and disagreements about recommended usage between imperial-period grammarians concerned to preserve what were by now institutionalized as classical Latin and classical (Attic) Greek. Crucially, then, antiquity was already familiar with the phenomenon of a programmatic commitment to the style of an earlier period now deemed to be normative. On the Roman side, one could argue the paradox that the survival of classical Latin is to be ascribed to its early death, or (less melodramatically) to its attainment of seeming perfection in the late republic and early empire. Many informed readers have indeed supposed that it is the 'aesthetic exemplarity' of the greatest works written in Latin that turns the authors of this period, Cicero and Virgil above all, into stylistic authorities forever after.[10] The creative idiom and mode of expression developed by the most impressive writers in prose

[5] Horace, *Ars Poetica*, 311, offers one influential formulation: 'verbaque provisam rem non invita sequentur' ('once the *res* is in prospect, the *verba* will readily follow it'). On the formula in Renaissance and subsequent (XVII) usage: Howell (1946), Kessler and Maclean (2002).

[6] And/or 'degree-zero' style: Barthes (1953).

[7] The problem is widely evaded by stylisticians. Weber (1996) is a representative collection: contributors either focus on specifics or merely gesture at 'problems' and 'perplexities': so Taylor and Toolan, ibid. 87. Meanwhile, Aristotle's '*how?* versus *what?*' (*Rhetoric*, 3. 1. 2) is a better stop-gap than most. Two very different discussions are noteworthy: Gray (1969) ('style' is a non-entity, like 'ether' in premodern science) and Barthes (1984) 141–50 (originally a 1969 essay, 'Le style et son image').

[8] Cave (1979) 35.

[9] 'J'amasse, trie et choisis le plus beau | . . . j'imite la Nature': 'Hylas', 423–6 (1569).

[10] 'Die ästhetische Mustergültigkeit seiner [sc. Latin] Meisterwerke': Stroh (2007) 112.

and verse (and not merely the stage of the Latin language that their usage happens to reflect)[11] becomes a standard for later writers. There is certainly a case to be made (Eliot makes it, in part, in his essay, 'What Is a Classic?': §35) for the proposition that there is, objectively, such a thing as 'maturity of language' (which Eliot identifies with 'perfection of the common style') and that the Latin language achieves this 'maturity', precisely, in the usage of Virgil (§35).

In the case of Greek (and notwithstanding Gargantua's tip about Plato), there is no precise counterpart to this 'maturity' or its embodiment in particular writers,[12] even though the Attic Greek of fifth- and fourth-century Athens becomes the canonical standard for revival movements that aspire to recreate its perceived status, above all in the so-called Second Sophistic, several centuries later. In both the Roman and the Greek world, in any event, many texts continue to be valued (and therefore transmitted by copying) precisely because they are taken to be exemplary repositories of approved usage – and it is fair to say that, throughout this process, and for centuries afterwards, too, little distinction is made between individual creative idiom and the accidental 'stage of the language', even though in practice, as in principle, the distinction is obvious enough.

On the Greek side, most of the most obvious cases have involved the accidental – with the decisive issue, often, the use of Attic (real or revival) as against the Hellenistic *koine* or the diverse dialects of archaic Greece. It is widely assumed to have been such considerations that helped to determine the survival through Byzantium of real-Attic Aristophanes, but not *koine*-tinged Menander; of acres of fourth-century Attic oratory, but only scraps of 'dialect' lyric (the only lyric poet to survive the Byzantine system in bulk is Pindar). The Greek case, in particular, shows how readily linguistic decisions encode ideology: a return to Attic norms has tended to coincide with the desire to revive the grandeur of classical Athens in a new day and age – whether in the Second Sophistic (as an assertion of Hellenicity under Roman rule), in medieval Byzantium or Renaissance Venice, or (less comprehensively but more notoriously) in the nineteenth and twentieth centuries, for most of which the 'purified', high-status version of the modern language (*katharevousa*) competed with, and generally dominated, vernacular 'demotic' Greek for all official and public purposes.[13] Within the West, though, it is responses to classical Latin – no less ideologically fraught, but more diverse in their outcomes – that bulk much larger; and it is, accordingly, the developing problematics of Latinity that chiefly concern us here.

11 E.g. Cicero's periodic style ('idiom'), as against his tendency to avoid the indicative in indirect questions ('stage').

12 Because of the quite different history of the Greek language: the much greater time-span of its recorded literature, the cultural importance of various of its dialects, the special nature and status of Homeric Greek.

13 In the case of Modern Greek, a narrative of exceptionalist 'continuity' with classical antiquity has been at the heart of this much-debated 'language question' (seemingly resolved, since 1976, in favour of a modified demotic): see e.g. Christidis (2007), Georgakopoulou and Silk (2009). 'Language questions' more generally: §13.

Throughout late antiquity and the Middle Ages, beneficiaries of exposure to the classics faced a conflict, as we have seen, between truth and beauty, Christian ideology and pagan style. Jerome, tormented by his devotion to Cicero (§4), is just one of many of the conflicted. Others came down firmly on the side of truth. At the close of the sixth century, Pope Gregory the Great, though himself classically trained, saw fit to reject pagan Latinity outright. He pronounced it an 'indignity' that 'the words of the oracle of Heaven should be restrained by the rules of Donatus' (most famous of the late-antique grammarians), and castigated the Bishop of Vienne for teaching grammar: 'the praise of Christ cannot consort in one mouth with the praise of Jupiter.'[14] The Church soon compromised, with a canon of approved authors (*auctores*), within which the stylistic qualities of a Cicero or a Virgil were, in effect, approved. One consequence was that some of the most outstanding intellects in the Western tradition would be helped to find a distinctive voice by negotiating their own versions of the compromise – and none more programmatically and influentially than the two great poet-thinkers of the Italian Middle Ages and the Italian Renaissance, Dante and Petrarch.

In the opening Canto of Dante's *Comedy*, we meet the author, threatened by savage beasts and uncertain where to turn. Then the figure of a man appears. 'Pity me' ('Miserere di me'), cries Dante, in an idiom as evocative of Latin as of any vernacular Italian – 'whatever you may be, shadow or real man!' ('Qual che tu sii, od ombra od uomo certo').[15] The apparition denies the second of these alternatives ('Not *man*: man I *was*') without endorsing the first, and proceeds to offer elegant, periphrastic clues to who he indeed 'was'. Born in Mantua of 'Lombardic' parents, he lived in Augustan Rome 'at the time of the false and lying gods' ('Al tempo degli dei falsi e bugiardi'); and he was the 'poeta' who sang of the son of Anchises and his flight from Troy.[16] This is more information than Dante needs to conclude, with due astonishment:

Or se' tu quel Virgilio e quella fonte
  Che spande di parlar sì largo fiume?[17]

Then you must be that Virgil and that spring
That spreads so wide a stream of eloquence?

And he adds:

O degli altri poeti onore e lume,
  Vagliami il lungo studio e il grande amore,
  Che m' ha fatto cercar lo tuo volume.
Tu se' lo mio maestro e il mio autore;

[14] Cubberley (1920) 68.
[15] *Inferno*, 1. 65–6.
[16] Ibid. 67–75.
[17] Ibid. 79–80.

Tu se' solo colui da cui io tolsi
Lo bello stile che m' ha fatto onore.[18]

O light and honour of all other poets,
May my long study and my great love for you,
That made me search your work, come to my aid.
You are my master and my author(ity);
To you and you alone I owe
The lovely style that has brought honour to me.

Dante's homage to Virgil may seem unqualified, but it comes with a double twist. The first concerns the accident of birth. Virgil lived too early to partake of divine revelation, and, while Dante proclaims his debt to his predecessor for his own 'lovely style', *his* Virgil is frank in acknowledging that he belonged to an age innocent of Christian truth (here, at least, content and style are quite distinct). The urgent need, therefore, is for a passing of the torch: the world requires a Christian *Aeneid* and a Virgil for modern times. A drama of succession thus unfolds: Dante expresses gratitude to Virgil for furnishing him with the means of expression necessary to surpass the pagan classics, while Virgil, master of a bygone age, steps aside for Dante to take his place. The casting of the main personae in the two underworld journeys provides a clue to the agenda. In Virgil, it is the Sibyl who serves as guide to Aeneas; in Dante, Virgil takes on the role of the Sibyl himself, while the Christian poet doubles as author of the text (like Virgil) and questing hero within the text (like Virgil's Aeneas). Dante thus assumes the positions of both his predecessor and his predecessor's protagonist, while assigning to his stylistic mentor the voice of decentred prophecy.

The personnel, language, and imagery of Dante's poem reinforce the symbolism of succession. Much in Dante's underworld looks familiar, based as it is on *Aeneid* 6. But Virgil's trappings reappear in Christian guise. The Charon we meet in Canto 3, while clearly modelled on his counterpart in Virgil, has become a demon of Christian theology;[19] and, in the same Canto, Virgil's plangent simile of fallen leaves and the generations of humankind is re-employed (stylistic imitation in action),[20] but with its doctrinal content radically altered. For Virgil, as for other ancient authors (the comparison is a topos that goes back to Homer),[21] the image sums up the problematic of human endeavour in the face of mortality; Dante uses it, rather, to show that human nature is vitiated by sin, and therefore that the torments of the underworld are logical and just, as Christian doctrine requires.

The second twist is less obvious. The author of the vernacular *Commedia* (*c.* 1306–*c.* 1318) is also author of an unfinished Latin treatise defending vernacular poetry, *De vulgari eloquentia* (*c.* 1303–4); and for this vernacular poet, the figure of

18 Ibid. 82–7.
19 *Inferno*, 3. 82–111 (esp. 109): *Aeneid*, 6. 295–416.
20 *Inferno*, 3. 112–17: *Aeneid*, 6. 305–14.
21 *Iliad*, 6. 145–9.

Virgil made eloquent in Dante's native Italian, but praised as the fountainhead of his style, constitutes a poignant paradox. In the opening section of the treatise, Dante distinguishes between Latin – acquired laboriously (if at all) through formal instruction – and vernacular speech, and argues, on several grounds, for the superiority of the latter: the vernacular is used by everyone; it is primary; and it is natural, whereas Latin is the product of 'artifice' ('artificialis').[22] In this light, the encounter between Dante and Virgil in the *Inferno* marks a historical watershed. Dante acknowledges the medieval deference to classical *auctores* with a gracious bow to Virgil, above all.[23] But in the end, the pagan poet-authorities (*even* Virgil) are relics of the past, superseded both ideologically and linguistically (though whether also *stylistically* is not so clear): a society of dead poets that Dante leaves behind in Hell or, at best, in Limbo.[24]

But, as a German saying would have it, those wrongly reckoned to be dead live longer. While Dante's *Comedy* marks a decisive stage in the evolution of the vernaculars towards literary languages in their own right (§13), the rise of humanist Latin, only two generations later, affirms another law of Western literary history: the eternal return of the classic(al) masters. The defining figure, who generates both the revival (or reinvention) of the ancient *auctores* and yet also the further development of vernacular literature, is Petrarch (§29). In his 'elderly correspondence' (*Epistolae seniles*, 1350s/1360s), Petrarch recalls his first encounter with Cicero years earlier. Young as he was, he hardly understood what Cicero was saying, yet he was instantly smitten by the sheer beauty of his language; in comparison, any other mode of expression now struck him as harsh and dissonant.[25] His devotion became total, rivalling that of Jerome, and like his august predecessor he had to pay dearly for his love affair with Cicero's classical Latinity. In his case, though, it was not Christ in a nightmare who meted out punishment, but his worldly father, in a more hands-on fashion. Envisaging a profitable career in the law for the talented young man, Petrarch's father watched his immersion in the world of antiquity with dismay,[26] and took (as he supposed) decisive action, making a funeral pyre of Petrarch's treasured library of pagan classics. Only two *codices* did he deign to rescue from the flames at the desperate pleading of his son: a copy of Virgil, for recreational purposes; and a volume containing the 'Ciceronian' rhetorical treatise,

[22] *De vulgari eloquentia*, 1. 1. In Medieval/Renaissance Latin, 'artificialis' tends to have positive connotations of acquired skill or culture; here it is close to 'artificial' in the familiar modern sense. Latin and the vernaculars: §13.

[23] Virgil later (*Inferno*, 4. 85–90) introduces Dante to Homer, Horace, Ovid, and Lucan, and, later still, cedes his role as guide to the supposed Christian convert Statius (who presents himself in *Purgatorio* 21). Cf. generally Barolini (1984), Brownlee (1993).

[24] At *Inferno*, 25. 94–9, Dante claims to outdo Lucan and Ovid (here, in the depiction of gruesome metamorphosis). At *Purgatorio*, 27. 126–42, Virgil's final gesture is to acclaim Dante as his superior.

[25] *Epistolae seniles*, 16. 1: cf. Leonhardt (2005).

[26] There are parallels, four centuries later, with Goethe and *his* father, who had him study law at Leipzig, when Goethe himself yearned for a classical training, under Heyne, at Göttingen: *Dichtung und Wahrheit* (1811–33), 6.

Ad Herennium – this, evidently, on practical grounds (instruction in rhetoric would be useful for an aspiring lawyer).[27]

For Petrarch, this generational strife within the family mirrored a world-historical conflict of Hegelian proportions: on the one side, a desperate and narrow-minded scholasticism, that had outlived its hold on the imagination; on the other, a bright and progressive future, paradoxically characterized by a return to the Greco-Roman past. This new vision entailed (negatively) a rejection of both the scholastic Medieval Latin and the functional attitude to Latinity that had prevailed for centuries and (positively) an aesthetic affirmation of the classical, in literary idiom above all.[28] Soon, the books his father had used to fuel his classical bonfire would take centre stage in humanist circles, and every humanist schoolboy would be 'supposed to speak, write, and think as if he were an integrated member of the same speech community as Cicero and Virgil'.[29] But though in principle a stylistic affair, the turn towards humanist Latin was bound to be more than stylistic. The revival of a classicizing mode of writing encouraged a new mode of thought, poised somewhere between *studia humanitatis* and Christian piety, between republican Florence and the papacy of Rome. As Fubini and others have argued, 'a pure and simple restoration of the ancient culture was unimaginable for a humanist of the fifteenth century without taking Christian and ecclesiastical traditions into account'[30] – even if at times it might seem that the goal entailed a simple shift, from one allegiance (theological) to another (aesthetic).

The fifteenth and early sixteenth centuries saw the rise of stylistic imitation at its most specific, in the shape of Ciceronianism, which elevated Ciceronian usage in particular to the benchmark of pure and eloquent Latin. Much as Greek grammarians and lexicographers of the Second Sophistic had fetishized the use of vocabulary and idioms by Plato or Demosthenes, maybe five centuries earlier than their own day, the new Ciceronians (looking back about three times as far) proscribed the use of any Latin word not found in the *oeuvre* of their model, and overenthusiastic humanists at the papal court even began to rewrite the Latin of the Church Fathers and the traditional liturgy in a classical idiom, to the point of turning God into Jupiter and nuns into Vestal Virgins.[31] Pope Gregory would have turned in his grave. But extreme Ciceronianism soon began to wane, ridiculed by scholars like Erasmus,[32] whose *Ciceronianus* (1528) recommended an altogether more pragmatic and flexible attitude towards Latin usage. Erasmus pointed out, correctly, that Cicero himself

[27] *Epistolae seniles*, 16. 1.

[28] Medieval versus classical Latin: §13.

[29] Moss (2003) 5.

[30] Fubini (2003) 44.

[31] See Erasmus, *Ciceronianus* (1528). A milder version of a related procedure is the Romanizing of Greek gods (etc.) in classicizing literature as late as XVIII: Pope's *Iliad* has 'Jove' for 'Zeus' (etc.) (cf. §24).

[32] As Lucian ridiculed Atticism in the days of the Second Sophistic, notably in his *Lexiphanes* and *Pseudologista*.

had introduced many neologisms into Latin, and argued that it was precisely by innovation, as well as imitation, that one became a true Ciceronian.[33] Several decades earlier, though, another scholar, Politian, had already formulated a simpler and more unanswerable riposte to the new fashion: 'Someone objects, "you don't write like Cicero." So what? I'm not Cicero.'[34]

All such preoccupations in any case became academic, when the onset of the Reformation helped to change the priorities of the Roman curia.[35] In the long history of the classical tradition, the Ciceronians' devotion to a single author's mode of expression is probably unique; and arguably it is the distinctive circumstances of Renaissance Italy – the initiatory role of Italian and Italians in the Renaissance and the special relationships between emergent Italian, the Latin language, and the Church of Rome (§13) – that made it, not only possible, but a matter of such urgency. Thereafter, we find echoes of the Italian debates, but no real equivalents to them. Admiration for Cicero's Latin itself survived across the West in the educational domain, but Ciceronian idiom resurfaced more significantly in vernacular contexts, especially in England and France. In Augustan England, Alexander Pope invokes 'that easy Ciceronian style, | So Latin, yet so English all the while'.[36] In revolutionary France, amidst a host of other Latinizings and Romanizings, imitation of Cicero's oratorical style helps to shape, or complicate, political exchange.[37] But even such cases lack the single-minded specificity, as well as the larger rationale, of the earlier Italian example.

In this connection, another complication needs to be acknowledged and another distinction made. In *The Schoolmaster* (1570), the Englishman Roger Ascham (formerly tutor, himself, to the princess who later became Queen Elizabeth I) reviews the several kinds of imitation, one of which aims 'to follow for learning of tongues and sciences the best authors'; and at this point Ascham notes 'a great controversy, whether one or many are to be followed; and, if one, who is that one, Seneca or Cicero, Sallust or Caesar; and so forth in Greek and Latin.'[38] Here, though, what we have in effect – more modestly – is stylistic models for *genres* (oratory, historiography 'and so forth'). More modestly and less problematically, too: genre, certainly in the classicizing ages, carries with it enough of a sense of subject-matter, if not to eliminate the *verba*/*res* complication, then at least to limit its scope.

[33] On these Italian debates: McLaughlin (1995). On related arguments in France (culminating in Dolet's *De imitatione Ciceroniana*, 1535): Cave (1979) 39–55.

[34] Letter to Paolo Cortesi (a Ciceronian: 1480s).

[35] In respect of stylistic authority, the symbolic point of 'onset' is Luther's German translation of the Bible (1522–34).

[36] 'Epilogue to the Satires', 1. 73–4 (1738). Arguably, though, 'easy Ciceronian' points to the intimacy of the orator's epistolary writings (esp. *Ad Atticum*), as much as to his oratorical works themselves: cf. Eden (2012).

[37] See succinctly Ridley (2006) 74–8 and generally Krause-Tastet (1999), Négrel and Sermain (2002). 'Latinizings and Romanizings': Highet (1967) 396–9.

[38] *The Schoolmaster*, 1, 'Imitatio'.

And this version of imitation is common enough. An instructive case is Du Bellay's *Vindication and Ennobling of the French Language* (*La deffence et illustration de la langue françoyse*, 1549). This momentous proclamation – 'located between a living but unconsecrated language and a consecrated but dead culture'[39] – is *both* a rallying-cry on behalf of the French language *and* a polemical manifesto for the classicism of the French poetic Pléiade[40] *and* a theoretical statement that assumes imitation as a central condition for the development of a language.[41] Appealing to classical precedents, Du Bellay notes that Cicero and Virgil 'enriched their language' by 'imitating the Greek authors'. French writers, then, must do the same with 'the good Greek and Roman authors'. In poetry, this means that the epigrammatist should study Martial; the elegist, Ovid, Tibullus, and Propertius; the satirist, Horace; and the composer of 'rustic eclogues' (meaning pastoral poetry), Theocritus and Virgil. It is striking, no doubt, that, for all the talk of 'the good Greek and Roman authors', Greek writers (like Theocritus here) hardly figure. More to the point is that it is the *generic* imitation of Roman (and occasionally Greek) poetry that is the premise throughout.[42]

In the Renaissance and the neoclassical generations that follow, this kind of genre talk abounds. Sometimes, it can shade off into personal preferences that seem almost to reinstate the principle of a single model of style, but sooner or later the generic principle reasserts itself. One example from English letters can suffice. Over the second half of the seventeenth century, the poet Dryden's prefaces and postscripts repeatedly invoke the names of Ovid and Virgil as exemplars of stylistic 'beauties' and 'elegant turns'; in the previous century, Virgil in particular (Dryden affirms) had been, in this sense, Spenser's model in the *Faerie Queene* and Tasso's in his sonnets;[43] and Virgil, too, is named (in Dantean mode) as 'my master' in the preface to one of Dryden's own poems.[44] Among much else, though, Dryden is a preeminent satirist (and Virgil, he fancies, might even have made a decent satirist himself)[45] – but, needless to say, Dryden's actual satirical writing has as its models

[39] Cave (1979) 70.

[40] The imitative classicism of 'la Pléiade' is inscribed in its name, with its (learned) allusion to the ancient name of a group of (learned) poets (in fact, tragic poets) in Alexandrian Greece. But though first used to designate the new 'constellation' of poets by Ronsard himself, in passing, in 1556 ('À Christophe de Choiseul, son ancien amy', 37–8), the label is only institutionalized later. Ronsard's own designation was 'la brigade' (see ibid. and the opening of 'Le Voyage d' Hercueil', 1549): Lèbegue (1966).

[41] For the conjunction of interests, compare (but also contrast) George Puttenham's *Art of English Poesy* (1589), esp. 1. 2 ('That there may be an art of our English poesy, as well as there is of the Latin and Greek') and 3. 4-5 ('Of Language'/'Of Style').

[42] *Deffence*, 1. 7; 2. 3–4. In 2. 3 Du Bellay adds, alongside the 'good Greek and Roman authors', 'even the Italian, Spanish and others' – but, apart from passing references to the likes of Petrarch (2. 4) and Ariosto (2. 5), nothing much comes of this ecumenical gesture in the event. Genres: §22.

[43] Near the end of 'A Discourse Concerning the Original and Progress of Satire' (1693): Watson (1962), 2. 150–1.

[44] In Dryden's 'Account' of *Annus Mirabilis* (1667).

[45] 'A Discourse': Watson (1962), 2. 131.

the Roman satirists proper, Horace and Juvenal ('I owe more to Horace for my instruction, and more to Juvenal for my pleasure').[46] What we have here, then, is a particular, complicated, but – in the end – unmistakable case of generic authority.

After the classicizing ages, and especially after the great Romantic shift, such appeals to generic authority are hardly found. If anything, echoes of idiosyncratic stylistic allegiance, though infrequent enough themselves, are more common. Tennyson – some have thought – writes like Virgil.[47] Nietzsche, in his late phase, claims a special indebtedness to the style(s) of Horace and Sallust.[48] And – beyond our remit – Homer, above all, has a special significance (stylistic, among much else) for the poets of modern Greece, from Kalvos to Seferis.[49] But the whole situation has changed. For the English-speaking world, representatively, Eliot sums it up: 'Incidentally we do not believe that a good English prose style can be modelled upon Cicero, or Tacitus, or Thucydides.'[50] No: and the very notion of 'models of style' now seems as remote as the notion of style itself, when pressed, seems intractable.

46 Ibid. 2. 127.

47 'The most Vergilian of English poets': Tucker (1983) 17; likewise, Joseph (1992) 137. Cf. §35.

48 Götzendämmerung (1888), 'Was ich den Alten verdanke', 1 ('nach römischem Stil'): cf. Silk (2004c) 588–90.

49 Ricks (1989).

50 'Euripides and Professor Murray', in *The Sacred Wood* (1920).

§8

Beacons of Morality

In 1518, the English humanist John Colet, Dean of St Paul's, admirer of Erasmus and Ficino, and also collaborator with William Lily, doyen of Latin grammarians in England, laid down the statutes for St Paul's School.[1] The boys were to read 'good literature, both Latin and Greek', and the 'good authors' were 'specially' to include 'Christian authors', from Erasmus all the way back to Augustine, but authors whose language was not 'distained' or 'poisoned' by unclassical 'corruption'. Seemingly correlating linguistic impropriety with deficient ethical standards, Colet denounced the false and proclaimed the true:

> I say that filthiness and all such abusion which the later blind world brought in, which more rather may be called *blotterature* than *litterature*, I utterly abbanish and exclude out of this school, and charge the masters that they teach all way that is the best and instruct the children in Greek and Latin in reading unto them such authors that hath with wisdom joined the pure chaste eloquence.[2]

[1] The work widely known as 'Lily's Grammar' went through numerous versions before and after Lily's death in 1522; a 1540 version was institutionalized as the standard manual for teaching Latin in England by Henry VIII in 1542. Reflecting contributions, in earlier versions, by Colet, Erasmus, and (esp.) Lily himself, the book was published as *Brevissima institutio seu ratio grammatices cognoscendae* and *A Short Introduction of Grammar* under the names of Lily and Colet in 1549.

[2] Quoted from Clarke (1959) 5, but with our italics, and with the spelling largely modernized (we have left the –tt– of 'litterature' to match Colet's 'blotterature').

The Classical Tradition: Art, Literature, Thought, First Edition. Michael Silk, Ingo Gildenhard, and Rosemary Barrow.

Published 2017 by John Wiley & Sons Ltd.

'Wisdom' and 'pure chaste eloquence': this conjunction recalls Quintilian's classic formula for the orator ('a good man, skilled in speaking'),[3] but the anxieties that inspired these thoughts of a Christian-compatible syllabus – thoughts apparently ignored in practice[4] – are, broadly, more characteristic of the medieval world, between the age of Quintilian and the age of Colet himself.

In the *Dialogus super auctores* by Conrad of Hirsau (*c.* 1100–30), a pedagogical colloquy about the pitfalls and benefits of an education in the pagan classics, the earnest pupil asks his teacher: 'Why should a young recruit in Christ's army subject his impressionable mind to the writings of Ovid?' While willing to concede that Ovid's texts contain occasional nuggets, the pupil worries that these are buried in filth: anyone seeking them out will surely soil himself. In his reply, the teacher praises the good sense of the student and concedes – with reference to scriptural chapter and verse[5] – that the 'idol-worshipping' *Metamorphoses*, in which all manner of substances undergo all manner of heretical transformations, falls foul of Christian teaching; but he goes on to suggest that Ovid did grasp some aspects of divine truth and that the pious reader can draw important lessons from the peculiar mixture of blindness and insight on display in the poem.

Whereas Colet's statutes seem to evade the issue (perhaps in deference to a defensive religious establishment in England), Conrad's exchange better illustrates the creative hermeneutics that characterize the engagement with pagan materials in the ages of dominant Christianity. The interpretative strategies whereby Christian writers find truth in falsehood (or nuggets in filth) include moral allegory, rationalization in the tradition of Euhemerus, and the discourse and practice of astrology – those diverse practices to which Jean Seznec has more generally ascribed 'the survival of the pagan gods' in his study of the mythological tradition.[6] Ovid's *Metamorphoses* plays a key role in each.[7]

Conrad's 'dialogue' itself stands in a tradition of exegesis that dates back to late antiquity, when grammarians and critics begin to assist readers by composing introductions to canonical works of literature, the so-called *accessus ad auctores*. These can be grouped into various types, with different emphases. What medievalists call the 'Type B' or Servian introduction has its origins in the fourth-century commentary by Servius on Virgil's *Aeneid*. 'Type B' tends to provide summary information under a set of headings: biography (*vita poetae*), title (*titulus operis*), genre (*qualitas carminis*), project (*intentio scribentis*), scale (*numerus librorum*), organization (*ordo librorum*), and perceived significance (*explanatio*). In the twelfth century, however,

[3] *Institutio Oratoria*, 12. 1. 1, 'vir bonus, dicendi peritus', ascribed by Quintilian to Cato the Elder.

[4] Clarke (1959) 6.

[5] Romans, 1. 18–23.

[6] Seznec (1953): see §24.

[7] See e.g. the Vulgate Commentary (*c.* 1250), the anonymous *Ovide Moralisé* (*c.* 1320), and Pierre Bersuire's *Ovidius Moralizatus* (*c.* 1340: §24 n. 34). Cf., from the Carolingian age, Theodulf of Orléans, 'De libris quos legere solebam': Chance (1994) 129–39.

a different type ('Type C') comes to prominence, which goes back to late-antique commentaries on Aristotle. This places more emphasis on didactic concerns, aiming, in particular, to show the ethical relevance of the author under discussion. If and when securely identified, by such means, as a source of moral improvement, classical authors could duly take their place within the Christian scheme of things; and 'the success of the "Type C" prologue was probably due in large measure to the fact that it enhanced the prestige of secular literature (mainly the work of pagan philosophers and poets) within the standard frameworks of knowledge as defined in the twelfth century.'[8] The premise is that some readers, at least, were *looking for* ways to reclaim the forbidden texts.

In the Renaissance, moral readings of the classics become more widespread, but both the mode and the spirit of the exegesis have changed. Humanists value the ancient authors for their articulated insights into the human condition (§27), perhaps on the basis of transferable philosophical maxims, but often with specific reference to the sustained arguments of moralizing thinkers from the ancient world. Contrary to some popular modern stereotypes, very little Renaissance thinking is secular thinking, but, conversely, classical-derived ideals relating to the individual, the social, or the political sphere now acquire an impetus of their own. One representative concern is the values of friendship – summed up in a 'Portrait of Two Friends' (*c.* 1521–4) by the painter Jacopo Pontormo, which depicts one of the 'friends' displaying a sheet of paper inscribed with a passage from Cicero's *De Amicitia*, the definitive treatise 'On Friendship',[9] and one that made an early impact (it had its first vernacular translation in 1418).[10] Friendship, too, was the designated theme of the *Certame Coronario*, a competition held in Florence, in 1441, to promote new poetry – while the humanist Leon Battista Alberti, who chose the topic, himself expatiated on it in Book 4 of his dialogue, *Della famiglia*, completed around the same time.

Distinctive, and potentially more disturbing, was advice to those in power – the so-called mirror of princes – a genre with medieval precedents (like Aquinas' *De regimine principum*)[11] and good classical models (like Seneca's *De Clementia*),[12] but also now the context for a controversial masterpiece in the shape of Machiavelli's *The Prince* (*Il Principe*, written in 1513, and first published in 1532: §31). When, for instance, Machiavelli explains that a ruler must learn 'how not to be good', he would have been understood, in antiquity, by Thucydides, as he will certainly be understood, in a later century, by Nietzsche – but the reaction of the Colets of the time

[8] Minnis and Scott (1988) 13; cf. generally Quain (1945).

[9] *De Amicitia*, 22: 'amicitia res plurimas continet . . .' ('friendship embraces so many things . . .').

[10] By Premierfait, into French.

[11] Seemingly unfinished by Aquinas on the death of its dedicatee, the king of Cyprus, in 1267 and finished subsequently by Tolomeo of Lucca: Mohr (1974).

[12] But also (less 'good') the corpus of fake letters ascribed to the legendary tyrant Phalaris, a figure known to the Middle Ages and prominent in the Quattrocento: Hinz (2001) 161–228. The fake was exposed by Bentley: §16.

(as of the Vatican establishment in due course) will have been less understanding.[13] Among the more bland alternatives to Machiavelli's realism was a treatise by the leading French scholar, Guillaume Budé; his *Instruction for a Prince* (*Le livre de l'institution du prince*) was presented to Francis I in 1519. On much safer ground, in flagging up (with Plutarch's help) the moral lessons of great lives, from Alexander to Pompey to Hercules, Budé's work– by the very variety and ambiguity of its models – still points to the potential pitfalls of the genre as a whole.[14]

More characteristic, and less threatening to the established order, was a series of Christian-humanist moralizings in Latin. Their authors included Quintilian's rediscoverer, Poggio Bracciolini, who pondered the instability of human affairs in a series of essays (from *The Unhappiness of Princes* to *Marriage in Old Age*), and used a mixture of Stoicism and Christianity to recommend that human existence be faced with equanimity.[15] Valla's *On Pleasure* explored the value of ancient philosophical thought in a similar vein, albeit with a celebration of sensual, rather than spiritual, delights. In a meticulously schematic treatment of competing moral authorities, the work presents a dialogue between Catone Sacco, who endorses a Stoic view of the highest good, and Vegio, who puts forward the Epicurean alternative. Then, in the third dialogue, the Franciscan Antonio da Rho elaborates a 'Christian Epicurean' position, arguing for the identity of 'true pleasure' ('vera voluptas') and 'the love of God' ('caritas'), in effect equating redemption with the pleasures of Paradise.

Classical moralists continue to provoke admiration for centuries, though less frequently (according to the now familiar trajectory) from the late eighteenth century onwards. For Montaigne in 1580, Seneca's 'virtue' is 'pure' and 'steadfast';[16] for Frederick the Great in 1780, Cicero's *De Officiis* is 'the best book on morality';[17] and even in the twenty-first century, we find a digest version of Seneca's philosophy (entitled *Seneca for Managers*) acclaimed as one of the 'five greatest advice books of all time'.[18]

Meanwhile, though, among successive generations of thinkers and writers (and artists, too), many find Greek and Roman moralizing less and less to their taste (and the very vocabulary of 'moralizing' becomes, often, pejorative). In some cases, this is one element in a larger, sceptical argument about the Western ethical belief-system

[13] In ch. 15; compare the approximation to 'might is right' at Thucydides, 5. 105. 2 (and contrast the ideal of virtuous rulers in texts like Plato's *Republic* and Xenophon's *Cyropaedia*: cf. §26). 'Thucydides and, maybe, Machiavelli's Prince are most closely related to me through the unconditional will not to fool oneself and see reason in *reality*': Nietzsche, *Götzendämmerung* (1888), 'Was ich den Alten verdanke', 2 (cf. §31). Machiavelli's works were put on the Vatican's Index of Forbidden Books in 1559 (§9).

[14] Budé and Francis: McNeil (1975). Hercules: §21.

[15] Kajanto (1989), (1994).

[16] *Essais*, 2. 32 ('vertu', 'nette', 'ferme').

[17] 'Le meilleur ouvrage de morale, qu'on ait écrit et qu'on écrira': *De la littérature allemande*, 55. Cf. van der Zande (1998) 75–94.

[18] Dale Dauten, 'The Corporate Curmudgeon', *Arizona Daily Star*, Business Section, 10 January 2003; Annas (2006).

as such ('the Sea of Faith | Was once, too, at the full . . .');[19] and here there is no more strident repudiation than that by Nietzsche, who, especially in his last productive years, sees Christian morality as the great negative force in Western history, and the moral impetus of Socrates and Plato (the supreme 'proto-Christian')[20] as its prefiguration. For Nietzsche, these two Hellenic (or anti-Hellenic) thinkers are 'symptoms of decline' and 'tools of Greek disintegration'; Socrates' 'bizarre equation', 'reason = virtue = happiness', goes against 'all the instincts of the earlier Greeks'; 'from Plato onwards', Greek philosophy turns 'pathologically' moralistic; Socrates was 'a misunderstanding', and 'the entire morality of improvement (Christian morality included) has been a misunderstanding'.[21]

In the modern age, there have indeed been those who insist that (in the words of the painter Paillot de Montabert, David's pupil) the whole spectrum of artistic experience, from ancient Greece to contemporary France, is, or should be, 'an eminently moral concern';[22] and, against the tide, idiosyncratic thinkers like Tolstoy and Simone Weil succeed in reclaiming even the *Iliad* for Christian ideals, by seeing in it the triumph of compassion (Weil) or of 'religious perceptions' that can be spoken of in the same breath as the brotherhood of man (Tolstoy);[23] but, from the nineteenth century onwards, if and when the moral quality of specific ancient writings is singled out for commendation, it is much more likely to be on grounds, not of moral goodness as such, but of comprehensive vision. It is partly on such grounds that the mythic trajectories of Homer and Greek tragedy come to hold a special appeal for twentieth-century writers in an era of moral crisis[24] – Joyce's *Ulysses* (1922) and Sartre's *Flies* (*Les mouches*, 1943) are two of many instances – while in the previous century Matthew Arnold pinpoints the achievement of his most admired Greek tragedian precisely in such terms: Sophocles ('be his | My special thanks') 'saw life steadily, and saw it whole'.[25] On such grounds, too, T. S. Eliot will eventually acclaim Virgil, but Dante ahead of Virgil.[26] But then again, earlier in his career, and in the wake of a generation of avant-garde variations on the theme that 'all art is immoral' (Wilde, 1891)[27] or, conversely, 'nothing is immoral' (the Futurists, in 1910),[28] it comes as no surprise to find this same Eliot acclaiming ancient amoralism in the shape of Petronius' *Satyricon*: 'we think more highly of Petronius than our grandfathers did'[29] – this in 1920 (and one reflects that, two years on, a morally

[19] Matthew Arnold, 'Dover Beach' (published in 1867).

[20] *Götzendämmerung*, 'Was ich den Alten verdanke', 2 ('präexistent-christlich').

[21] Ibid. 'Das Problem des Sokrates', 2, 4, 10, 11. Compare the argument of Williams (1993) that Homer and Greek tragedy offer an alternative ethical framework to the Christian-Kantian.

[22] *L'artistaire. Livre des principales initiations des beaux-arts* (1855), section 30.

[23] Weil, 'L'Iliade ou le poème de la force' (1940); Tolstoy, *What is Art?* (1898), ch. 9.

[24] Cf. §24.

[25] 'To a Friend', 1849.

[26] 'Virgil and the Christian World' (1951): §35.

[27] *Intentions*, 'The Critic as Artist', 2.

[28] 'Futurist Painting: Technical Manifesto', by Boccioni and others.

[29] 'Euripides and Professor Murray', in *The Sacred Wood*.

disturbing passage from the *Satyricon* duly forms the epigraph of Eliot's *Waste Land*).[30]

A necessary precondition of all these modern reversals and revisions is the formation of the – modern – sense of human individuality, whose roots, ironically enough, lie in the age of Renaissance moralism itself. Western understandings of individual integrity and development, and *therefore* of individual choice without deference to authority, are hard to imagine without early modern 'self-fashioning': 'we continue to see in the Renaissance the shaping of crucial aspects of our sense of self'.[31] This momentous development is epitomized, on one level, by masterpieces of individualizing art like Raphael's portrait of Pope Julius II (1513), which (according to Vasari) embodied such 'truth' and exerted so powerful a presence that 'everyone who saw it trembled as if the Pope were standing there in person'.[32] It is summed up, more generally, in a series of essays from the previous century on human value. Giannozzo Manetti's *Human Dignity and Excellence*, Giovanni Pico della Mirandola's *Discourse on Human Dignity*:[33] such titles speak for themselves.

But whatever challenges to traditional moral understandings this new 'self-fashioning' held in store, and however revisionary the attitudes to ancient moral (or amoral) texts might eventually become, it remains the case that, throughout the Renaissance itself, classicizing thinkers repeatedly appeal to ancient authority on moral grounds. And if the potentiality of the human individual is acknowledged as a part of such appeals, the acknowledgement is commonly accompanied by an insistence, not on the scope of that potentiality as such, but on its necessary limits: moralizing warnings, rather than celebrations, are the norm. Representative here is Philip Sidney's neo-Aristotelian formula for tragedy, in his *Apology for Poetry* (1595):

> the high and excellent tragedy . . . that maketh kings fear to be tyrants, and tyrants manifest their tyrannical humours; that, with stirring the affects of admiration and commiseration, teacheth the uncertainty of the world, and upon how weak foundations gilden roofs are builded.

'*Admiration* and commiseration' gives Aristotle's 'pity and *fear*' a celebratory nudge, but 'uncertainty' and 'weak foundations' redirect the argument in the opposite direction, and away from Aristotle altogether.[34] As if by way of assuring the reader, nevertheless, both of the classical pedigree of this stern doctrine, and of the moral

30 *Satyricon*, 48: '. . . *apothanein thelô*' ('. . . I want to die').

31 Greenblatt (1980) 174. The notion of expanded individualism that we identify with 'the hero' is likewise a Renaissance construction: §21.

32 Vasari, *Lives*, 3, 'Raphael'. The painting (now in the National Gallery, London) was first displayed in the nave of Santa Maria del Popolo in Rome.

33 *De dignitate et excellentia hominis* (written in 1452, but not published till 1532); *Oratio de dignitate hominis* (1486). Cf. §27.

34 Aristotle: *Poetics* 6 (and *passim*). 'Admiration' (i.e. 'wonder') is prominent in the *Poetics* (and hence in Renaissance thinking: Minsaas 2001), but not as one of the two 'affects' (pity and fear) programmatically 'stirred'.

propriety of the classical, cautionary citations from Seneca and Plutarch duly follow.[35]

A few years before the publication of Sidney's treatise, however, an extraordinary run of conceits by the young Shakespeare contrive to subvert, and even ridicule, any supposition that recourse to the classics is likely to be morally improving *per se*. In *Titus Andronicus* (*c*. 1590?), Ovid's *Metamorphoses*, first of all, is presented as a 'rapist's manual'.[36] An explicit point of reference for Shakespeare's play is the sad tale of Philomela, body ravished and tongue cut out by Tereus, but able to denounce her assailant by sewing the story of his crime into a cloth.[37] Going one better, Shakespeare's Demetrius and Chiron – acting, in concert , as a 'craftier Tereus',[38] at the prompting of Aaron the Moor – duly violate their victim, Lavinia, and not only cut out her tongue but also hack off her hands, to prevent her from imitating her mythological counterpart. These students have clearly profited from their Ovidian training, and in a moment of metaliterary *grand guignol*, it is Ovid himself who is called upon to reveal the deed. With her mutilated arms, Lavinia flicks through a copy of the *Metamorphoses*, eventually stopping at the Tereus episode, and thereby making her dreadful mistreatment known.

Later in this disturbing drama, Shakespeare's youthful meditations on morality and the classics acquire a yet sharper edge when Titus, Lavinia's father, sends the guilty pair a bundle of weapons wrapped in a scroll with a Latin message:

DEMETRIUS What's here? A scroll, and written round about?
Let's see:
[*reads*] *Integer vitae, scelerisque purus,*
Non eget Mauri iaculis, nec arcu.
CHIRON O, 'tis a verse in Horace, I know it well:
I read it in the grammar long ago.[39]

Chiron is quite right: the quotation consists of the opening two lines of Horace, *Odes*, 1. 22: 'Whose life's upright and free from crime | Needs no Moor's javelins or bow'. But it is also apparent that despite his training in Latin (the reference is to Lily's Grammar, 'the standard text-book', in which 'the quotation occurs twice'),[40] he is oblivious to the ethical element in Horace's poem, which negotiates a space between moral earnestness and carefree existence in love. In contrast to Chiron, dim-witted as well as morally obtuse, Aaron, the scheming malcontent (and literally a Moor), instantly understands that the message is 'barbed':[41]

[35] Seneca, *Oedipus*, 705–6; Plutarch, *Life of Pelopidas*.

[36] Maslen (2000) 16. With the following discussion, cf. Bate (1993) 101-17.

[37] Ovid, *Metamorphoses*, 6. 401–674: *Titus Andronicus*, 2. 3. 36–43. On the myth and its (re)uses: §24.

[38] Ibid. 2. 4. 41.

[39] Ibid. 4. 2. 18–23.

[40] Bate (1995) 220. 'Mauris' (adjective, 'Moorish') in modern editions of Horace, but 'Mauri' (noun in the genitive) in Shakespeare, following Lily's Grammar (n. 1 above).

[41] James (1991) 132.

AARON Ay, just – a verse in Horace, right, you have it.
[*aside*] Now what a thing it is to be an ass.
Here's no sound jest! The old man hath found their guilt,
And sends them weapons wrapped about with lines
That wound beyond their feeling to the quick.[42]

If Chiron is both cruel and stupid, Aaron is cruel and knowing (and, throughout this uncomfortable play, an amoral mouthpiece for the exposure of moral hypocrisy) – but it does not occur to Aaron, any more than to Chiron, to ponder, or even acknowledge, the ethical affirmation in Horace's words.

Ovid's shocking tale of rape, it would seem, provides no cautionary lesson, but only useful tips for the self-indulgent, while the moral philosophy articulated in Horace's poem can simply be ignored. But worse is to come. In the final *coup de grâce*, Titus, before his own death, makes a formal appeal to classical precedent – this time to a story made famous by Livy – to justify killing the mutilated innocent, his own daughter:

TITUS My lord the emperor, resolve me this:
Was it well done of rash Virginius
To slay his daughter with his own right hand
Because she was enforced, stained and deflowered?
SATURNINUS It was, Andronicus.
TITUS Your reason, mighty lord?
SATURNINUS Because the girl should not survive her shame,
And by her presence still renew his sorrows.[43]

There are very different views on the merit (and indeed the authorship) of Shakespeare's play.[44] But the classics as 'beacons of morality' . . . What can hardly be in doubt – in the age, still, of classicizing moralism – is the vivid, even lurid, quality of this play's successive challenges to any complacent belief in *that* ideal. Ezra Pound, we note, is by no means the first to use the classical tradition to challenge its own presuppositions.

[42] *Titus Andronicus*, 4. 2. 24–8.

[43] Ibid. 5. 3. 35–41: Livy 3. 48 – but in Livy and also (*pace* various commentators on Shakespeare) in the other ancient source, Florus 1. 17. 24, Virginius' daughter is not actually yet 'deflowered'. A comparable killing, based on the same sources, figures in Vittorio Alfieri's Roman tragedy, *Virginia* (1777–81).

[44] Representatively: 'one of the stupidest and most uninspired plays ever written, a play in which it is incredible that Shakespeare had any hand at all' (Eliot, 'Seneca in Elizabethan Translation', 1927). Authorship: Vickers (2002) 148–243.

§9

Love Guides

Livy, of course, seldom unbends; but Horace and (especially) Ovid, along with various other ancient sources, canonical and uncanonical, have much to say on the subject of love and (especially) sex; and much of what they do say is sharply at variance with the 'heteronormative reproductive imperative' of Judaeo-Christian culture.[1] From that standpoint, classical antiquity might well be taken to be a realm of polymorphous perversity, visited by a long succession of impressionable travellers, from members of medieval religious communities to Michel Foucault – with ancient myth in particular, and its Ovidian versions not least, a repository of every desire under the sun, from bestiality (Pasiphaë) to pederasty (Orpheus the sodomite),[2] from obsessive self-love (Narcissus) to lesbian passion (Iphis),[3] from sexual violence (Tereus and many others) to incest (Myrrha) and agalmatophilia (Pygmalion).[4] Small wonder that ancient erotica should have acquired authoritative status in later centuries. If any Renaissance collector ever tried to find manuscript evidence to vindicate a Byzantine encyclopedia's bold identification of Astyanassa (Helen's legendary maid) as inventor of the sex manual,[5] he was surely disappointed. But

[1] Desmond and Sheingorn (2003) 100.

[2] Bein (1990).

[3] Cf. Simons (1994).

[4] See Gross (1992).

[5] *Suda* ('Suidas'), A 4261, which credits the lady with a treatise 'On the Positions of Intercourse' (*Peri skhêmatôn sunousiastikôn*).

The Classical Tradition: Art, Literature, Thought, First Edition. Michael Silk, Ingo Gildenhard, and Rosemary Barrow.

Published 2017 by John Wiley & Sons Ltd.

there was always Ovid's *Ars Amatoria*, which was a special point of reference then, as indeed it had already become in the Middle Ages.[6]

A notable case in point is a twelfth-century Latin poem on a gathering of nuns at the 'Council of Remiremont'.[7] The subject is love: a Lady Cardinal ('cardinalis domina') presides over the deliberations, which quickly turn into a formal debate on the relative merits of the knight ('miles') and the clerk ('clericus') as lovers. Representatives of the two factions of ladies praise their candidates and belittle the opposition. Finally a vote is taken, and the nuns come down in favour of the clerk, notwithstanding their weak-minded ('quod stulte promittitur') vows of celibacy.

What we have here is a medieval variant on Ovid's idea that Jupiter tolerates perjury in love.[8] The author stresses that during the entire council no appeal was made to holy writ. Rather, experience counted. In her youth, for instance, Sibilia, the door-keeper, had followed Amor's commandment to become a soldier of Love ('miles Veneris': an outrageous misprision of 'soldier of Christ'), and she had taken up her calling without too much resistance ('quicquid Amor iusserat, non invita fecerat'). But what makes the poem so striking in the context of authorities is the explicit way the nuns incorporate Ovidian chapter and verse into their heterodox scriptures. Their opening ceremony includes a reading from the *Ars Amatoria* itself:

Intromissis omnibus virginum agminibus,
lecta sunt in medium, quasi Evangelium,
praecepta Ovidii, doctoris egregii.

Lectrix tam propitii fuit Evangelii
Eva de Danubrio, potens in officio
artis amatoriae, ut affirmant aliae.[9]

With all the maidens' delegations present,
Commandments from their great instructor, Ovid,
Were read out in their midst, as fits a Gospel.

The reader of this most propitious Gospel
Was Eve of Deneuvre, expert in performing
The art of love (as vouched for by the others).

Nuns were not the only ones to get excited by pagan love poets. Montaigne cites their physiological observations at some length;[10] and, a century before Montaigne, there was many a classicizing skeleton in the closet of Aeneas Sylvius Piccolomini, which started to rattle once he became Pope Pius II in 1458. In a later age, Goethe caused a certain scandal by reviving elegiac love *à la* Propertius in his *Roman Elegies* (*Römische Elegien*, 1795), but nothing to match Piccolomini's *In Cynthiam*. In these

6 Hexter (1986), Minnis (2001).
7 *Concilium Romarici Montis*: Dronke (1968) 229–31.
8 *Ars Amatoria*, 1. 633.
9 *Concilium*, 25–30.
10 *Essais*, 3. 5.

Latin verses, later repudiated, the future pontiff recreates Propertius' erotic-elegiac mode (flagged by the name of his fictive mistress), along with a team of pagan divinities obsessed with sex. At times the sauciness of Piccolomini's imagination outclasses his ancient models, as when he writes (this time *à la* Ovid) in the persona of an adulterous girl, looking for action round the clock and trying to persuade her fancy man, who prefers the cover of darkness, to visit while her spouse is away at work. Under marital law, the nights belong to her husband; it occurs to her to wonder whether her lover is disinclined to come during daylight hours because of scruples about full-frontal nudity ('forsitan et totus nudusque viderier horres?').[11]

All this, though, is tame by comparison with some Renaissance erotica, which take their inspiration from the ancient collection of priapic verses (*Priapea*)[12] and combine their literary allegiance with visual display. Pietro Aretino's *Lewd Sonnets* (*Sonetti lussuriosi*, 1524) are salacious verbalizations of classicizing woodcuts by Giulio Romano, which enhance the coarseness of contemporary pornography with polished classical allusion. Tonal clashes between mythological apparatus and down-to-earth rutting are part of the point: 'Mars, you clumsy fool, this is no way to get on up a lady. Venus can't just be fucked in such a blind hurry, with no finesse.' 'I am not Mars, I am Ercole Rangone, and it's you I'm fucking, Angela Greca.'[13] When Shakespeare rejects the world of 'false compare', by contrast, mythological formula makes way for an ardently felt realism: 'I grant I never saw a goddess go; | My mistress when she walks treads on the ground.'[14] By which point, even if a classical presence can still be felt (*per contrarium*), specific authorities are no longer in view.

Visual material leaving little to the imagination supplemented the verbal. Giulio's drawings (*I modi*, 'The Positions') were themselves based in part on depictions of the sexual act on surviving medallions from ancient Rome (so-called *spintriae*),[15] which no doubt circulated among select antiquarian groups. On a grander scale, pagan divinities and classical carnality were displayed in Federico II Gonzaga's mannerist pleasure-palace in Mantua, the Palazzo Te (1525–34), designed and decorated with extraordinary frescoes by Giulio Romano once again.[16] Here the artist's sources ranged from canonical classical texts and Roman wall paintings and sculptures[17] to free invention. Thus the Camera del Sole treats its viewers to an (un-author-ized?) 'anal perspective' of Helios and his horses, whereas the Sala della Psiche, based partly

11 'Puella in amatorem': *Carmina*, 1. 66b. The configuration recalls the ancient adultery mime.

12 Parker (1988) lists eight editions from XV alone; another was issued with the authority of the Aldine Press in 1517.

13 *Sonetti*, 1. 12: 'Marte malatestissimo poltrone! | Così sotto una donna non si reca, | E non si fotte Venere al a ceca, | Con assai furia, e poca discretione. | Io non son Marte, io son Hercol Rangone, | E fotto voi che sete Angela Greca.'

14 Sonnet 130.

15 Talvacchia (1999) 49–70.

16 Belluzzi (1989), Cox-Rearick (2000).

17 Vinti (1995).

Figure 1 Giulio Romano, 'Jupiter and Olympias'. Source: Mantua, Palazzo Te. © 2013. Photo: Scala, Florence.

on Apuleius' *Metamorphoses*,[18] features the magnificent wedding banquet of Psyche and Amor (Cupid). Other frescoes illustrate the transformative powers of passion that reduce humans, or even gods, to animals. Jupiter (in Ovidian fashion) we see partly changed into a snake, though still sporting a truly divine erection aimed at Olympias, mother of Alexander (opposite a lusty senior, calmly – like an inverted Leda? – sodomizing a swan) [*Figure 1*].[19]

Less exuberant, but no less radical in their challenge to Judaeo-Christian norms are the diverse responses to Plato's *Symposium*, a distinctive text among the surviving Greek 'guides' to the erotic. While this most literary of dialogues identifies a philosophical goal of spiritual, sublimated 'love', beyond the human, it also assumes a conventional norm of same-sex male desire[20] – but in terms of unequal relationships between older and younger man (or 'boy'), which, to the modern mind,

[18] And partly on Colonna's recent allegory (below, p. 96): Arasse (1985).

[19] Ovid is involved more directly in La Sala di Ovidio, where landscape designs alternate with depictions of Apollo, Pan and Minerva, Orpheus, Marsyas, the Judgement of Paris, and Bacchus and Ariadne. Giulio's erotic 'transformations' are echoed, and inverted, in Pound's 'Coitus' (in *Lustra*, 1916): 'The gilded phalloi of the crocuses', 'naught of dead gods', 'O Giulio Romano' (editions of Pound print 'phaloi').

[20] Except for the heterosexual-centred speech by Aristophanes.

suggest pederasty rather than homosexuality as generally understood.[21] In the Renaissance, and beyond, some readers responded to the philosophical ideal: Ficino's *De amore* (1469) offers both an interpretation and a re-enactment of Plato's text;[22] and in 1818, the poet Shelley translates the dialogue into English, and uses it as a central point of reference, that same year, in his typically high-minded *Discourse of the Manners of the Ancients Relative to the Subject of Love*.[23]

Whereas the practice of direct appeals to specific ancient authorities generally weakens in, and after, the Romantic generation, the late development of any clearly-defined homosexual culture, or subculture, across the West ensures that relevant texts from the classical world retain a special status well beyond that period. At the turn of the twentieth century, for instance, André Gide's *Amyntas* (1904) and *Corydon* (1911) are suitably coded evocations of the boy-loving rustics of Virgilian and other ancient pastoral.[24] In that same era, though, it is certainly the *Symposium*, once again, that exerts a more definitive influence. In late Victorian and Edwardian England, following the publication of Benjamin Jowett's translation (1871), which made the text more widely accessible,[25] and in the wake of far-reaching developments in the new German 'science' of sexology,[26] Plato's dialogue becomes an inspirational point of reference for the articulation of male homosexual identity.[27] In *A Problem in Greek Ethics* (1883), the essayist and critic John Addington Symonds, a pupil of Jowett, reads the *Symposium* (along with a related Platonic dialogue, the *Phaedrus*) as a vision of an ideal pederasty, which subsequently, in *A Problem in Modern Ethics* (1891), he reapplied to modern sexuality itself. In E. M. Forster's novel *Maurice* (written in 1913/14, but not published till 1971), Maurice and Clive begin their (unconsummated) love affair after the former reads the *Symposium* during his summer vacation from Oxford.[28]

A generation earlier, in the comic opera *Patience* (1881), W. S. Gilbert had identified the 'high aesthetic' preference for 'An attachment *à la* Plato | For a bashful young potato',[29] which the supreme aesthete, Oscar Wilde, duly sanctified at his trial for 'gross indecency' in 1895. In his impassioned speech from the dock, Wilde acclaimed 'the Love that dare not speak its name', referring specifically to 'such a great affection of an elder for a younger man as there was between David and Jonathan, such as Plato made the very basis of his philosophy'.[30]

21 Winckelmann's response to Greek sculpture is comparable: §29.

22 Devereux (1975), Leitgeb (2004). Contrast Hölderlin's response: Leitgeb (2003).

23 Holmes (1980).

24 'Virgil's songs are pure, except that horrid one | Beginning with *Formosum pastor Corydon*': Byron, *Don Juan*, 2. 45 (with reference to Virgil, *Eclogue*, 2).

25 Jowett was Regius Professor of Greek at Oxford, where Greek studies acquired something of the status of a 'homosexual code': Dowling (1994).

26 Matzner (2010).

27 Blanshard (2007).

28 While Clive could not forget 'his emotion at first reading the *Phaedrus*': *Maurice*, ch. 12.

29 Gilbert and Sullivan, *Patience*, Act I (Bunthorne's song).

30 Cf. Ellman (1988) 435.

But the capacity of Greek homoerotic literature to exercise authority was not confined to the male domain. Alongside Plato, there was also Sappho, iconic poet of seventh-century BC Lesbos. For the modernist post-aesthete Ezra Pound, 'Sappho's barbitos' symbolizes true art (*Mauberley*, 1920: §4); for the poet Leopardi, in the Romantic generation, her agonizing 'last song' evokes the freedom of death;[31] but for many others in the post-Romantic years, Sappho is, rather, the prototypical lover of women. This is the premise of innumerable allusions and several focused depictions – in paintings (like Simeon Solomon's watercolour, *Sappho and Erinna in a Garden in Mytilene*, 1864); in novels (Rachilde's *Monsieur Vénus*, 1884);[32] above all, in Sappho's own medium of poetry (Baudelaire's 'Lesbos', 1850; Swinburne's 'Masque of Queen Bersabe' and 'Anactoria', 1866). Pound, too, acknowledged this Sappho, configuring her woman-love into a four-word 'fragment', a triumphantly imagist poem of 1916, 'Papyrus':

> Spring. . . .
> Too long. . . .
> Gongula. . . .

'Gongula' – or, by more normal transliteration rules, 'Gongyla' – is indeed one of the women who inhabit Sappho's poems and prospectively (like Anactoria and others) her love-life.[33]

Until the rediscovery of some of Sappho's lost work, from 1898 onwards,[34] only a few fragments of her poetry were known; there was not much text to respond to, though ample scope for imaginative (re)construction.[35] The new finds stimulated not only Pound's 'Papyrus', but a series of poetic imitations by Pound's protegée

[31] 'L'ultimo canto di Saffo' (published in 1824).

[32] 'Rachilde': the pen-name of Marguerite Eymery.

[33] 'Papyrus' (existing discussions fail to make clear) follows a compositional technique for which Pound is famous/notorious, on a larger scale, in poems like *Homage to Sextus Propertius* (1934), where words in another language (there, Latin; in 'Papyrus', Greek) are subjected to creative 'mistranslation'. 'Papyrus' (from the collection *Lustra*, and a few poems away from 'Coitus', n. 19 above) is such a 'mistranslation' of lines 2–4 of Sappho, fr. 95 Page/Voigt, a 16-line fragment on parchment (P. Berol. 5006: not strictly 'papyrus'), first published in 1907. Only the opening letters of the three lines survive, which read (in transliteration) as: *êr' a* . . . | *dêrat* . . . | *Gongula* . . . The first sequence probably marks the beginning of a question, but *looks like* something to do with *êr*, 'spring'; the second is unintelligible, but *looks like* something to do with *dêr-/dār-*, 'too long'; the third *looks like*, and is, the woman's name. In the later, less fragmentary, part of the Greek fragment, Sappho voices a despairing 'longing to die'; and 'it is an obvious . . . conjecture that it was unsatisfied love for Gongyla which was the cause of Sappho's despair' (Page 1955: 86). Wittily, and poignantly, Pound has translated the frustrating incompleteness of the Greek into the frustrated incompleteness of the poet's love-life – as well as into the self-conscious incompleteness of modernist aesthetics.

[34] Published chiefly in *Oxyrhynchus Papyri*, beginning with vol. 1 (1898), edited by B. P. Grenfell and A. S. Hunt (the two scholars commemorated in Tony Harrison's play, *The Trackers of Oxyrhynchus*, 1988).

[35] See variously Dejean (1989), Gubar (1996), Prins (1999).

(herself 'a Sapphic fragment'), H. D.[36] Meanwhile, the most lurid of the 'imaginative' responses was Pierre Louÿs's volume of poems, *Les chansons de Bilitis* (1894), which traces the life of the fictional 'Bilitis' from her initiation into the pleasures of lesbian love by Sappho to a career as a courtesan in Cyprus. Louÿs presented his volume (dedicated to André Gide) as a translation of poems by one of Sappho's pupils, recently excavated from Sappho's tomb; it was actually a *mélange* of free compositions, epigrams from the *Greek Anthology*, and sequences based on surviving bits of Sappho herself. The collection prompted a caustic scholarly debunking by Wilamowitz in 1896, seemingly motivated by his earnest conviction that Sappho, though literally a Lesbian, had not been, as vulgarly supposed, a lesbian as well.[37] More creatively, the collection also prompted a 'work of pure sensuous charm', in the form of three songs by Debussy.[38]

Both in this modern era, and much earlier too, the scope of texts with a sexual content to acquire authority in the public arena was drastically limited by censorship and bowdlerization; the classics might be inherently authoritative – though their modern imitations much less so – but either could still fall foul of institutional morality. Among the ancient exemplars, Plato's *Symposium* had its philosophical credentials to redeem it;[39] and Sappho's poetry – even after the new finds – barely existed anyway. Other texts, with more complete or more explicit sexual reference, from Petronius' *Satyricon* to Aristophanes' *Lysistrata*, were not so fortunate. The precedent was set in Renaissance Florence, when Savonarola consigned to the flames the works of Ovid (along with, supposedly, those of Boccaccio and Dante) in the notorious 'Bonfire of the Vanities' (1497). In the cold climate of the Council of Trent (1545–63), censorship in Catholic Europe intensified. Pope Paul IV had the distinction of presiding over both the invention of the fig leaf, as a way of concealing the sexual presence of classicizing statuary (from 1557), and the establishment of the Index of Forbidden Books (*Index Librorum Prohibitorum*, 1559), whose early victims included Aretino and Rabelais (as well as Machiavelli and Erasmus).[40] In the 'classical age' that follows, many of the writings of French authors, in particular, can be

[36] The American poet Hilda Doolittle, whose career ended with a series of posthumously published novels (*HERmione*, among others) on lesbian themes, but 'all began with the Greek fragments' (her own words, in *End to Torment*, 1979: entry for 23 April 1958). 'Pound . . . introduced [her] to the literary world in 1913 as a Sapphic fragment, with her name abbreviated into the elliptical letters H. D., the embodiment of an "Imagist" aesthetic inspired by Sappho's Greek': Prins (1999) 4–5. See further Rohrbach (1996).

[37] In *Göttinger Gelehrte Anzeigen*: Wilamowitz (1913) 63–78. The scholarly evidence for lesbian Sappho is carefully reviewed, *contra* Wilamowitz, by Page (1955) 140–6, along with a graceful tribute to the superior insight of John Addington Symonds: ibid. 140–2.

[38] Lockspeiser (1962) 175. The songs, *Chansons de Bilitis*, were composed in 1897–8.

[39] Though still discreetly bowdlerized at times. In Britain, Shelley's only precursor as translator of the text, Floyer Sydenham, in 1759, 'disguised the dialogue's homoerotic atmosphere by manipulations (e.g. adolescent boyfriends of older men become "mistresses")': Halliwell (2000) 376.

[40] Grendler (1988) 45.

seen to constitute challenges to, or compromises with, repressive orthodoxy, from the sophisticated heights of Molière to the low titillations of a verse anthology like 'The Parnassus of Satyric Poets' (*Le Parnasse des poètes satyriques*, 1622).[41]

Punitive censorship was not confined to the feverish atmosphere of the Counter-Reformation. Enlightenment England, though heir to Chaucer's *Canterbury Tales* and Shakespeare's 'country matters',[42] demonstrated the perils of publishing sexually explicit material in the first British obscenity trial, in 1727,[43] when Edmund Curll was convicted (eventually under the common law offence of 'disturbing the King's peace') after publishing an English version of the Abbé du Prat's pornographic novel, *Vénus dans le cloître* (1683).[44] The title is not without significance: French pornographic writings often staked a claim to legitimacy under the guise of classical myth.[45]

To avoid entanglement with the law, meanwhile, and also, sometimes, to 'protect' the innocent reader, it was a regular practice in the eighteenth and nineteenth centuries for translators of sexually explicit classics to excerpt their originals or tone them down.[46] Here the English (or English-speaking) experience is representative, both before and after the Obscene Publications Act of 1857 transformed the sale of 'obscene' literature from a common law misdemeanour to a statutory offence (the Federal Anti-Obscenity Act of 1873 had a similar rationale in the USA). A complete English translation of Petronius' *Satyricon* by John Addison was published in 1736, but Bohn's Classical Library translation of 1854 (by Walter Kelly) excluded sexual details or left them in Latin.[47] In 1902 Charles Carrington issued

[41] See Jeanneret (2003) and cf. Crawford (2010).

[42] *Hamlet*, 3. 2. 111.

[43] In Britain censorship applied also to the staging of plays with even remotely sexual connotations; as late as 1910, Sophocles' *Oedipus Rex* was banned on such grounds: Macintosh (1995).

[44] Translated (by Robert Samber) as *Venus in the Cloister: or, The Nun in her Smock*. Curll is notorious for his efforts in this area: recently uncovered evidence suggests that in 1714 he silently added 'a collection of pornographic verses about dildos', under the title 'The Cabinet of Love', to an edition of *The Works of the Earls of Rochester and Roscommon*: *The Times* (London), 4 February 2011, p. 11. Cf. Baines and Rogers (2007).

[45] Goulemot (1994) 96. 'The Cabinet of Love' (n. 44 above) included a poem entitled 'The Delights of Venus'. In this era erotica might also be authorized by more prosaic sources. In 1684, for instance, an English-language pregnancy guide and sex manual was marketed as *Aristotle's Masterpiece*. Loosely appealing to the philosopher's interest in biological functions in (e.g.) *Generation of Animals*, the 'masterpiece' maintained a covert existence for centuries.

[46] A famous case of 'protection' is Charles and Mary Lamb's *Tales from Shakespeare* (1807), 'submitted to the young reader as an introduction to the study of Shakespeare' (Preface), but in effect aiming to replace it.

[47] More inventive solutions were found for the 'English' translations in the Loeb Classical Library (established by Heinemann publishers in 1912). The Loeb Catullus (1913: translations by F. W. Cornish and W. H. D. Rouse) merely cut out or paraphrased rude bits (e.g. Catullus 16 and 37); but the Loeb Martial (1919: W. C. A. Ker), responded to poems irredeemably focused on sex by putting them into Italian (e.g. 2. 51, 61, 62, 84). The logic of this practice (anyone who can read Italian is beyond redemption anyway?) was never explained. Cf. generally Roberts (2008).

the first unexpurgated English translation for over a century, falsely attributing it to Oscar Wilde.[48] Its foreword was headed, warningly, 'On the Danger of Issuing the Present Translation', and, as the publisher was also a major supplier of pornography, the reader was left in no doubt about the risqué nature of the text.[49] Carrington also commissioned an English translation of Apuleius' *Golden Ass* from Richard Burton which was never published: readers in search of an English version had to make do with Adlington's (*c.* 1566) or else with Walter Pater's other-worldly 'Story of Cupid and Psyche' (in *Marius the Epicurean*, 1885) or William Morris's staid reworking of the same excerpt (in *The Earthly Paradise*, 1868–70). The English experience was far from unique. In Germany, sixteenth-century readers had a full Apuleius translation (by Johann Sieder, 1538), whereas by the nineteenth century only expurgated or selective versions were available.[50]

In 1896, Leonard Smithers, a British publisher on the same circuit as Carrington, issued a prose version of Aristophanes' *Lysistrata*, plausibly advertised as the first 'wholly translated' English version and subsequently identified as the work of Samuel Smith. The frankness of Smith's prose contrasted sharply with the rollicking English of the then (and perhaps still) best-known English translator of Aristophanes, B. B. Rogers, whose *Lysistrata* had appeared in 1878. Though Rogers's model, W. S. Gilbert, himself admired and even aspired to emulate Aristophanes,[51] there is little doubt that Smith's version of (say) *Lysistrata*, 124, 'Well, we must abstain from – Penis', is vastly closer to the Aristophanic, both in letter and spirit, than Rogers's demure euphemism, 'We must abstain – each – from the joys of Love.'[52] As Robin Sowerby notes: 'Smith regarded the play as a "Rabelaisian protest" against the Peloponnesian War during which it had been written. The *Lysistrata* of 1896 may be regarded as a Rabelaisian protest against Victorian values.'[53]

Smith's 'Rabelaisian' English was accompanied (and Aristophanes' bawdy humour matched) by Aubrey Beardsley's now celebrated illustrations of masturbating women and ithyphallic men. Beardsley's phallic images, in particular, raised another set of censorship issues beyond the textual sphere. In ancient culture, the phallus was a symbolic object with meanings beyond the sexual, ranging from the regenerative to the apotropaic. For Beardsley, though, the phallic imagery (whose specifics he derived from Pompeian artefacts and Greek vase paintings) carried a purely erotic message; and eroticism, likewise, was what most archaeologists and art collectors of his day read into the ancient versions of such images. For museums

48 Boroughs (1995), Mackie (2004).

49 In 1934 proceedings under the 1857 Act were taken against Fortune Press, London, for (among other books) a reissue of Carrington's Petronius: Craig (1962) 92–3.

50 By Johann Christian Elster (1854), Otto Siebert (1889), and others.

51 He was 'The English Aristophanes' by the time of his death: Sichel (1911).

52 *aphektea toinun estin hêmin tou peous*: example cited by Sowerby (2000) 369.

53 Ibid. In Rabelais himself, there is little trace of Aristophanes (Plattard 1910: 175), though plenty of other Greek authors (including Plato's *Symposium*, in the opening sentence of the prologue to *Gargantua*).

with classical holdings, therefore, and especially for the great public collections that grew in size and importance during the nineteenth century, such material raised awkward questions about display. The response of the Naples Archaeological Museum to Pompeian 'obscenities' was to create a *gabinetto segreto* in 1819 to house all objects deemed unsuitable for the general public.[54] In the late eighteenth century, Richard Payne-Knight had made a pioneering use of Pompeian material to examine the religious implications of the ancient phallus, but his privately published *Account of the Remains of the Worship of Priapus* (1786) was itself condemned for indecency.[55] Naples' 'secret room' was only opened to the general public in 2000, and then with a warning alerting visitors to its contents. In the same vein, the British Museum originally used a closed space (or 'secretum') to house sexual material (actual or supposed), but, since the 1930s, the items in question have been subsumed within the general collection.[56] In recent years, certainly, attitudes have changed. In 1999 the museum acquired (for £1.8 million) the Warren Cup, a sexually-explicit homoerotic silver Roman skyphos, and in 2006 devoted a special exhibition to its display; today it remains one of the museum's most popular exhibits.

The moral tolerance, verging on relativism, that is so characteristic of official cultures across the modern West, clearly has its limits: ancient pederasty, in particular, has no sanctioned counterpart in our world. At the same time, sexual identity is widely considered a cultural construct; and the relative freedom currently accorded to what was hitherto categorized as sexual deviance, and to open sexual expression in general, has meant that the ancient embodiments of such expression have much less of a distinctive ('authoritative') force. To a contemporary sensibility, equally, sublimations of the erotic from earlier centuries can seem disconcertingly indirect. Many of us will feel free to relish Giulio Romano's sexual depictions in the Palazzo Te without embarrassment, but may find it harder to relate to Francesco Colonna's *Hypnerotomachia Poliphili* ('Poliphile's Dream of the Strife of Love'), an allegorical romance (published with woodcuts by Aldus Manutius in 1499), wherein Poliphile's quest for lost love, in a dream-world of his own making, is co-ordinated by the goddesses Venus and Diana. The work deserves attention, indeed, on several counts. It was the first non-classical text to be printed by Manutius; it represents a remarkable experiment in Latinate Italian; and it is the first sustained erotic fantasy in Western literature.

But the gulf between a modern sensibility and the culture that created both Poliphile and the Palazzo Te is wide. We inhabit a Western world that has learnt to digest Freudian notions of infant sexuality and the frankness of Lawrence's *Lady Chatterley*,[57] Foucault's interrogations of sexuality, ancient and modern, and a welter

[54] The collection was, however, published as vol. 8 of Louis Barré's series on Pompeii and Herculaneum: García y García and Jacobelli (2001).

[55] Funnell (1982).

[56] Cf. Gaimster (2000).

[57] *Lady Chatterley's Lover*: first published – in Italy – in 1928; banned in the English-speaking world until the successful outcome of a celebrated obscenity trial in 1960.

of sexual imagery in visual media, commercial and other (the aestheticized male nudes of Robert Mapplethorpe's photography come to mind). Amidst such norms, it is easy to forget the distinctive impact that classical erotica could and did make even a hundred years ago – though Mapplethorpe, for one, clearly assumes 'the forms and ethos of classical sculpture',[58] and Lawrence explicitly invoked 'the creative portrayals of the sexual impulse that we have in . . . the Greek vase-paintings or some Pompeian art'.[59] We do well to bear in mind, whatever else, that, until very recently, open sexuality, whether celebrated or condemned, was rarely perceived as something 'modern', but quite the opposite. In this spirit, Byron sees his Juan and Haidée as 'a group that's quite antique, | Half-naked, loving, natural, and Greek.'[60]

Amidst the profusion of today's explicit sexuality, nonetheless, the authority of specific ancient exemplars still occasionally resurfaces. The spirit of Remiremont, even – witness this, from the British daily newspaper *The Guardian*, in 2007: 'How to be a Latin lover: forget all those modern guides to dating. If you want to find a partner, the ancient Romans can tell you all you need to know . . . Charlotte Higgins explains what we can learn from Ovid's *Ars Amatoria*'.[61]

[58] Talvacchia (2010) 771. See further Celant *et al.* (2004).

[59] 'Pornography and Obscenity' (1929).

[60] *Don Juan*, 2. 194. On the possible Greek 'group' alluded to (Cupid and Psyche in the Uffizi?), cf. Larrabee (1943) 167.

[61] *The Guardian*, 25 September 2007, G2 Feature, p. 4.

§10

Special Relationships

We are looking to make sense of the myriads of diverse instances that make up the classical tradition, but looking to make sense easily slips into looking *for* correlations and patterns, historical or other. In the context of 'authorities', in particular, we note that some instances can only be read as randomly idiosyncratic.

Take the English poet Christopher Logue, who died in 2011. Logue's early work, published in the 1950s and 1960s, subsumes a variety of themes, forms, and influences, with no particular connection to the classical tradition (despite a stage play of 1960, *Antigone*) and no easily definable orientation, except a certain willingness to accommodate the prosaic and an intermittent engagement with earlier poets, mostly modernists, or at least mod*ern*:

> So do you agree with them
> Spender, and Barker, and Auden?
> And you, my newly married master, Eliot[1]

From the early 1960s, however, Logue largely, and increasingly, confined himself to one thing: a poetic 'account' of Homer's *Iliad*, in successive publications, from *Patrocleia* (1962) to *Cold Calls* (2005). Widely acclaimed as a powerful, if profoundly eccentric, equivalent to the Homeric text, these versions now served to associate Logue with the modernist Pound, both in idiom and in conception (Pound's equally eccentric *Homage to Sextus Propertius* of 1934 is one model for both). Representatively, the following lines from *Kings* (1991) recall Pound in their 'imagist' precision

[1] 'To My Fellow Artists' (1959).

The Classical Tradition: Art, Literature, Thought, First Edition. Michael Silk, Ingo Gildenhard, and Rosemary Barrow.

Published 2017 by John Wiley & Sons Ltd.

and concision, their ellipses and stage directions, and (not least) the boldly anachronistic connections over gulfs of time that serve perhaps to modernize, perhaps to detemporalize, their antique original. This is Logue's version of the critical moment in *Iliad* 1 when Agamemnon (the speaker of the opening lines) demands a substitute for the concubine that religious protocol obliges him to relinquish:

'. . . as the loss of an allotted she
Diminishes my honour and my state,
Before the army leaves the common sand
Its captain lords will find, among their own,
Another such for me.'

Low ceiling. Sticky air.
Our stillness like the stillness
In Atlantis as the big wave came,
The brim-ful basins of abandoned docks,
Or Christmas morning by the sea.

Until Achilles said . . .[2]

That the local usage here – from the quaintly objectifying 'she' to the sudden conceit of 'Christmas morning' – is more Pound than Homer is apparent,[3] but not the point. The point is that for four decades Logue's poetic efforts were concentrated on this accommodation with Homer. And remarkable as the accommodation was, no less remarkable is that Logue's commitment to his Homeric project had no adequate 'explanation' in terms of contemporary fashion or ideology or external determinants in his world, any more than it did in his own previous work. Given the Poundian affinities of his Homerizing, one might propose that Logue was using Homer to find a Poundian self, but, given also that there is nothing that connects Pound definitively with Homer,[4] the proposition explains nothing, either. Simply, Logue had, or developed, a special relationship with Homer's poem.

Such special relationships – those as specific and clear-cut as Logue's with Homer – have been few. Many ancient authors, of course, have had some large significance for this or that subsequent user, but often because those ancient authors had a

[2] From *Kings*, 1: compare *Iliad*, 1. 118–21. Logue's 'anachronisms': cf. §17 n. 93.

[3] Cf. e.g. this, from Pound's *Canto* II: 'Seal . . . , | Sleek head, daughter of Lir, eyes of Picasso | Under black fir hood, lithe daughter of Ocean; | . . . Ear, ear for the sea-surge, murmur of old men's voices: | "Let her go back to the ships, | Back among Grecian faces . . . | Moves, yes she moves like a goddess | And she has the face of a god and the voice of Schoeney's daughters"' [our points of omission]. Compare the early appraisal of Logue's work by Carne-Ross (1962).

[4] Alongside *Homage to Sextus Propertius*, from the Latin, Pound produced two full-length 'translations' from the Greek, but both from Sophocles (*The Women of Trachis*, published in 1955, and *Electra*, 1989). In his critical writings, he discusses 'Early Translators of Homer' in 1918–20 (Pound 1954: 249–75) and duly recommends the Homeric epics (e.g. 'How to Read', 1927–8: ibid. 38) – but alongside Confucius and Ovid, Flaubert and Provençal song. The most significant point of connection, esp. for Logue, is probably the Homeric (though Odyssean) 'translation' that the *Cantos* begin with (*Canto* I: 'And then went down to the ship . . .').

special significance for their age – as Virgil and Aristotle did for the Middle Ages, or Cicero and Ovid for the Renaissance, or (to take a different and obviously relevant example) Homer himself did for many poets of the Romantic-revolutionary age: for Shelley (reads and rereads Homer),[5] for Alfieri (founds a chivalric 'Order of Homer'),[6] for Victor Hugo (sees Homer, and the epic, as definitive for all antiquity),[7] for Schiller (makes Homeric poetry paradigmatic of the great 'naive'),[8] for Keats ('a new planet').[9]

Alternatively, and yet more commonly, relationships are generic. Montaigne, as moralist-essayist, looks back to the moralizing reflections of Seneca and Plutarch;[10] Racine, as classicizing tragedian, to Euripides;[11] Milton, as epic poet, to Homer and Virgil;[12] Schopenhauer, as philosopher, to Plato;[13] Aretino, as pornographic poet, to the pornographic-poetic *Priapea* (§9); Dryden, as satirist, to Juvenal and Horace (§7); Petrarch as (*especially* as) letter-writer to Cicero.[14] Other cases, again, that might at first look idiosyncratic have a kind of generic rationale. Why does Dante choose Virgil as guide at the outset of his *Commedia* (§7)? Why not Aristotle, whose philosophy underlies the late-medieval synthesis of which Dante himself is so consummate an expositor? In formulaic terms: partly because Virgil, too, is an immensely significant figure in this age, but specifically because Dante as poet of Roman Christianity needs a pagan Roman guide to the underworld, as Virgil (with *Aeneid* 6) is ideally placed to be, and yet one who is close to Christianity, as Virgil, in the Middle Ages, is also taken to be. Revealingly, by comparison with the huge presence of Virgil in the *Commedia*, there is no significant Virgilian presence – literally, stylistically, or otherwise – in Dante's lyric output (the *Rime*).[15]

Logue-like special relationships are few, but no less significant for that. By way of modest relief (or challenge?) to seekers after patterns and correlations, it can safely be said that such relationships are only characteristic of the post-Romantic

[5] A volume of Homer was 'continually in his hand', according to his friend T. J. Hogg, in his *Life of Percy Bysshe Shelley* (1858), vol. 2, ch. 11.

[6] 'Childishly proud of having almost overcome the difficulty of Greek, I invent the Order of Homer and *autokheir* [with my own hand] confer a knighthood on myself': part of the heading to the thirty-first, and final, chapter of Alfieri's *Memoirs* (*Vita*, 1804).

[7] 'The Muse of the ancients was purely epic': Preface to *Cromwell* (1827).

[8] *Über naive und sentimentalische Dichtung* (1795–6).

[9] 'On First Looking into Chapman's Homer' (1816): §15.

[10] See esp. 1. 25 and 2. 32 (§5). In one sense, Montaigne's *Essays* have no generic precedent: their title is novel (*Essais*: 'trials', 'experiments'), and the 'autobiographical' relation of work and author famously innovative too. At the same time, they do look back, not least, to the reflective 'essays' (usually called moral treatises, *vel sim.*) of Seneca and Plutarch.

[11] The primary source for his *Andromaque* (1667), *Iphigénie* 1674), *Phèdre* (1677). See e.g. Allen (1982), France (1982), Goodkin (1991).

[12] See e.g. Martindale (1986): §35.

[13] See e.g. Hein (1966), Neeley (2000).

[14] As also to Seneca: cf. Eden (2012) 52. See further §29.

[15] Dante's Virgil: Foster (1977) 156–253. Medieval Virgil: Comparetti (1997). Dante and Aristotle: §6 n. 34.

age, and – broadly and collectively – assume the disjointed condition of eclectic modernity, within which individual inclinations have, in effect, free rein. Logue-like, though less extreme, cases are T. S. Eliot's attachment to Virgil ('our classic, the classic of all Europe': §35), and Brecht's (*per contra . . .*) to Aristotle's *Poetics* (§18). The most extreme case of all, perhaps, belongs to the world of art – to the painter de Chirico and his lone obsession with the figure of Ariadne (§24) – though Nietzsche's with Dionysus runs it close.[16] In both these cases, of course, no ancient 'author' in the ordinary sense is involved.[17] Even so, it is once again the modern, post-Romantic age that provides the context, and the stimulus, for such idiosyncratic preoccupations.

[16] See variously Baeumer (1976), Figal (2008), Jaggard (2004), Kaufmann (1974) 32–3, 410–11. Nietzsche's 'relationship' with Dionysus is almost matched by his lifelong preoccupation (but, this time, largely agonistic) with another non-authorial authority, Socrates: Dannhauser (1974), Schmidt (1969), Silk (2007c).

[17] One might compare Petrarch's obsession with his Laura (cf. §29), both in his Latin poetry and the vernacular *Trionfi*, but esp. in the *Canzoniere*. There, Laura is repeatedly identified with the Daphne of Ovid's *Metamorphoses*, alternately human and a laurel tree. However, she also far transcends this Daphne (cf. Foster 1982: 131). Among much else, 'Laura' is metamorphosed (by sound) into 'l'aura' ('the breeze'), as (by situation) into an ideal 'hidden beauty' ('una chiusa bellezza': *Canzoniere*, 105) and an ideal, if painful, 'sacred' inspiration ('l'aura mia sacra': ibid. 356); and while a 'relationship' with *Metamorphoses* (or with Ovid in general) is, in this era, unremarkable, Petrarch's 'special' relationship is in any case with the figure herself (both present and 'timeless' – Foster 1982: 72) and the ideals she embodies.

§11

The Visual Arts
Contexts and Connections

Within the long history of Western art and architecture, textual authorities from ancient Greece and Rome certainly count for something (Vitruvius is a striking case: §30), but overall they have only a limited and occasional significance. By contrast, deference to visual models can claim a privileged position, at least from the Renaissance onwards. Until the Renaissance, though, the classical tradition in the visual sphere is more a tale of evolution than of imitation, of survivals rather than revivals. In particular, and more markedly even than in the realms of literature and thought, the advent of Christianity represents a bridge between classical and medieval as much as a boundary, because what emerges from the sixth century AD onwards is a hybrid culture that combines pagan and Christian belief systems, social practices, and visual forms. There is an unmistakable kinship between the basilical and central designs of Roman imperial architecture and Justinian's monument to the 'divine wisdom' of Christ (Hagia Sophia) in Constantinople (537), as there is between that great work and innumerable church buildings thereafter. So there is, equally, between imperial Roman portraiture in the fourth century and Christian depictions on the Ravenna mosaics in the sixth – and then those in the paintings of Duccio and Simone Martini in the early fourteenth.

More directly, Romanesque architecture from the tenth to the thirteenth centuries not only maintains the Roman rounded arch, but literally incorporates Roman columns and capitals into church interiors and porticos. More strikingly still, pagan Roman sarcophagi serve as church altars or fonts or are reused for burials.[1]

[1] On the wider contexts of such reuse, cf. Greenhalgh (2009).

The Classical Tradition: Art, Literature, Thought, First Edition. Michael Silk, Ingo Gildenhard, and Rosemary Barrow.

Published 2017 by John Wiley & Sons Ltd.

Charlemagne's tomb at Aachen contains a Roman sarcophagus decorated with the myth of Proserpina and Pluto; and the example is representative in another sense too. Just as textual versions of pagan myths are subjected to Christianizing interpretations, visual renderings are assigned new meanings to suit their new context and purpose.

In the Middle Ages, ancient objects that were not reused were often destroyed or melted down, but many small items (cameos, engraved gems, coins) survived intact, as did various architectural monuments and individual statues, particularly in the city of Rome.[2] Travel guides for pilgrims to the Holy City, like the *Marvels of Rome* attributed to 'Master Gregorius' (mid-twelfth century), list architectural and sculptural antiquities as sites of interest. A notable instance is the bronze equestrian statue of Marcus Aurelius which still stood, *in situ*, in front of the Lateran palace in the twelfth century, only to be moved to the Capitoline Hill in the sixteenth.[3] This over-life-size bronze (for centuries assumed to be a representation of Constantine) would in due course inspire a series of equestrian ruler-portraits, from the ninth-century statuette (identified as Charlemagne) in the Metz Cathedral Treasure to Richard Westmacott's two monuments to George III, in Hanoverian England, a thousand years later.

If, in the visual domain as in others, the markers between late antiquity and the Middle Ages are elusive, so too – here, above all – the beginnings of the Renaissance cannot be understood in terms of an epiphanic moment when a lost classical legacy was abruptly reclaimed; there is no counterpart in the visual arts, indeed, to the symbolic event of Petrarch's laurel coronation in 1341 (§3). Rather, the beginning of the early modern period is a transitional phase which shares important characteristics with the eras before and after – and this, despite the fact that the new classicizing presents obvious contrasts with the Gothic art and architecture that dominates Europe in the thirteenth and fourteenth centuries. Dante's contemporary, Giotto, is widely regarded as the father of Italian Renaissance painting; at the same time, his subjects (like Dante's own) lie entirely within the range of late-medieval Christendom, and his specific links with northern Gothic art are clear. About a century after Giotto's mature work, however, Lorenzo Ghiberti's north doors on the Cathedral Baptistery in Florence (1403–24) represent a textbook example of transition:[4] Gothic doors, but with classicizing Roman portrait busts looking out of the roundels on the frame.[5]

Renaissance Italy continues the practice of putting Roman artefacts to practical use, while also cultivating a new respect for classical authority, whereby artists and architects self-consciously and systematically defer to classical examples. As early as 1260, Nicola Pisano's carved marble pulpit for the Baptistery in Pisa Cathedral appropriates pagan iconography, with the mythological Hercules symbolizing the

2 Greenhalgh (1989); cf. §25.

3 Haskell and Penny (1981): no. 55.

4 A less well-known, and less spectacular, precursor to his 'Gates of Paradise' of 1425–52 (Michelangelo's description, according to Vasari, *Lives*, 2, 'Ghiberti').

5 Radke (2007).

Figure 2 Nicola Pisano, pulpit detail (Hercules), Baptistery, Pisa Cathedral. Source: © 2013. Photo: Scala, Florence.

Christian virtue of fortitude [*Figure 2*]. Pisano, however, has looked to sarcophagi in the Pisan Campo Santo, whereas his successors are soon able to draw on a larger and more varied body of sculptural prototypes.

Major rebuilding projects in fifteenth-century Rome uncovered quantities of classical statuary. These were the finds that, as Vasari proclaimed,[6] helped to shape the whole course of Italian Renaissance art, all the way up to the 'modern' magnificence of Raphael and Michelangelo – though the finds themselves consisted mostly of Roman copies and adaptations of Classical or Hellenistic Greek sculptures. 'Although no one knew it at the time, the Renaissance was essentially' – thus Malcolm Bull, with pardonable exaggeration – 'a revival of a revival: the Hellenistic revival in Roman art that lasted from the first century [BC] to the second [AD].'[7] The irony of the situation was not appreciated for centuries.[8]

6 *Lives*, Preface to Part 3.

7 Bull (2005) 372.

8 XIX scholarship reassessed many high-status 'Greek' sculptures – like the Apollo Belvedere, venerated since the Renaissance and acclaimed by Winckelmann as a paradigm of high-classical Greek art (cf. §§5, 29), but now seen to be made of Italian marble and duly downgraded to the status of a Roman copy of a III BC Greek original. See Haskell and Penny (1981): no. 8.

Figure 3 Marcantonio Raimondi, engraving of the Apollo Belvedere (early sixteenth century). Source: New York, Metropolitan Museum of Art. Engraving, 11 7/16 × 6 3/8 inches (29.1 × 16.2 cm). The Elisha Whittelsey Collection, The Elisha Whittelsey Fund, 1949. Acc.n.: 49.97.114. © 2013. Image copyright The Metropolitan Museum of Art/Art Resource/Scala, Florence.

Initially, new finds were housed on papal premises, but soon aristocratic families throughout Italy were amassing rival collections.[9] Display was an essential component of collection: Pope Julius II's Belvedere sculpture court was constructed behind the Vatican palace in 1503 to display a set of pieces that included the Apollo Belvedere,[10] the Belvedere torso, and the Laocoon. These and other sculpures were made accessible to scholars and artists, and disseminated through plaster casts, sketchbooks, and, eventually, printed engravings [*Figure 3*]. Statues of naked figures presented the unclothed human body as an idealized form of existence. As such, they confronted an unsuspecting public with a new cultural outlook – both

[9] Rediscovery and collection of classical statuary: Waywell (1992), Christian (2010); cf. §17. Discovery and ownership of significant sculptures: Haskell and Penny (1981). Renaissance reception of lesser-known pieces: Bober and Rubinstein (1986).

[10] To this day, many ancient statues are identified by their Renaissance provenance in the form of names designating their original location (Apollo Belvedere) or ownership (Medici Venus).

a challenge and an opportunity – that was to have an incalculable influence on the mode and spirit of representational art, in painting no less than in sculpture, for centuries (§§27, 33). The Laocoon, meanwhile, rapidly acquired a special significance of its own.[11] Rediscovered in 1506, immediately hailed as a masterpiece and connected with Pliny's Rhodian sculptors and Virgil's *Aeneid*,[12] the group depicts the Trojan priest and his two sons strangled by sea serpents. In the throes of an agonizing death, with body taut, sinews visible, and muscles bulging, the Laocoon presented artists, and viewers, with a classic image of heroic endeavour, a human form stretched to its extreme. Yet even with such a classic image, disseminating might mean re-imagining. The group is soon depicted, for instance, on a maiolica dish by Francesco Xanto Avelli da Rovigo (humanist, ceramicist, and poet), clothed, as well as restored [*Plate 2*].

For sculptural figures rediscovered in a fragmentary state (Pound's 'broken statues'), restoration was routine (§17). Fragmentation was a guarantee of authenticity, but restoration promised aesthetic enhancement. Its goal was not fidelity to original form but an enhancement of 'grace' (*grazia*); the restored outstretched arm of Laocoon, for instance, was not intended to reinstate its original position but rather to satisfy a desire for aesthetic harmony.[13] The fragmented Belvedere torso, meanwhile, was felt to possess sufficient artistic 'grace' in the movement of its extreme muscularity to make modern additions unnecessary.[14] In this way, both the 'whole' Laocoon and the incomplete Belvedere torso take their place in the Renaissance imagination with a constructed identity that remains fixed for successive generations.

By the High Renaissance, the idealized nude human figure is a major new focus for both sculptor and painter, but, here and elsewhere, pagan and Christian continue to co-exist. The phenomenon familiar in classicizing literature from works like Milton's *Paradise Lost* – classical form, Christian content – is yet more characteristic of the visual arts. 'Botticelli's Venus,' said Kenneth Clark, 'dissolves into his image of the Virgin Mary.'[15] The heavily-developed musculature in the figures of Michelangelo's Sistine Chapel ceiling (completed in 1512) is directly indebted to Greco-Roman sculpture, but in the service of an all-embracing Christian narrative.[16] In architecture above all, though, the Christianizing of the classical that marks the earlier

[11] Cf. Christian (2010) 163, Curren (2012) 39–43.

[12] Textual authority of a kind, then: Pliny, *Natural History*, 36. 37; Virgil, *Aeneid*, 2. 199–231.

[13] See Haskell and Penny (1981), no. 52, for an outline of the restoration. In 1960 a new restoration changed the position of the arm from outstretched to bent.

[14] As with other 'satisfying' fragments: cf. Barkan (1999). By XVIII, Cavaceppi (sculptor-restorer and friend of Winckelmann: §17) is insisting on restorative accuracy (cf. p. 237 below), but the tradition of interpretative restoration continues until early XIX.

[15] Clark (1969) 107–8. The best part of two centuries later, Bernini's super- (or supra-) erotic sculpture of *The Ecstasy of St Teresa* (completed in 1652) is seen by one shocked contemporary as having 'dragged Teresa down' and turned that 'pure virgin' into 'a Venus, not only prostrated, but prostituted': Lavin (1980) 121.

[16] Cf. Howard (2003) 48–9.

phases of the tradition is reversed. Innumerable architectural borrowings, from the fifteenth century onwards, point towards this new goal. The Hadrianic Pantheon in Rome, used as a Christian church from the seventh century, is an inspiration for Brunelleschi's Florentine Duomo, completed in 1436 (§20). The architectural practice of Leon Battista Alberti – drawing on the remains of ancient Roman buildings, but also the writings of Vitruvius (§30) – likewise combines Roman form with Christian function. An early work, the Malatesta Temple or Church of San Francesco in Rimini, completed in the 1450s, incorporates a facade modelled on triumphal arches (notably the nearby Arch of Augustus) and Roman aqueducts. The range of classicizing styles that defines St Peter's Basilica in Rome – from the work of Bramante and Michelangelo in the early sixteenth century to Bernini's flamboyant contributions a century later – sums up an era in which, in Italy above all, the connection of Christian and classical (beyond any consideration of specific detail) is axiomatic.

Meanwhile, in the sixteenth-century Veneto, Andrea Palladio uses pagan religious precedent to revolutionize the design of aristocratic houses. Organized in the form of a centralized block raised on an elevated podium, Palladian country villas look back to Hadrian's villa at Tivoli, as well as to texts of Vitruvius and Pliny (here, as with Alberti, ancient textual authority certainly matters), but a significant point of reference is Roman temple architecture (§30). After the publication of his *Four Books of Architecture* in 1570, Palladio's designs are emulated across Europe and duly inspire the British architectural styles of Inigo Jones and (through Jones) Christopher Wren – whose eventual, iconic design for St Paul's Cathedral in London (completed in 1710)[17] represents yet another of the many triumphs of the pagan-Christian synthesis, in the long line of classicizing church buildings, from the Renaissance to the modern age.

Up until the Renaissance, art and architecture are seen as practical skills[18] and their creators – like, broadly, their counterparts in classical antiquity – as craftsmen. They are organized into guilds and, whatever their individual reputations, have only a peripheral role in the intellectual and cultural circles of their day and no claim to be regarded as significant players on the intellectual or cultural stage. By the time of Vasari in the mid-sixteenth century, a profound shift is apparent. For Vasari, the majestic development of Italian art begins with the two culture heroes, Cimabue and Giotto,[19] whose formative significance is acclaimed at length. In the fourteenth century, by contrast, the same two painters had been cited by Dante, almost casually – as emblems, not of heroic stature or cultural growth, but of human pride and its transience:

[17] St Paul's: §20. Earlier plans included the 'Warrant' design of 1675, which gestured significantly towards Gothic. Palladian tradition: §30.

[18] E.g. in Hugh of St Victor's *Didascalion* (XII), 2. 22, architecture is one of the 'mechanical arts', along with agriculture and hunting: van Eck (1998) 286–7.

[19] See e.g. the final sentences of the sections on the two artists in *Lives*, Part 1, where Giotto, in particular, is a 'great man'. Cf. Stack (2000) 163–76.

In painting, Cimabue thought
He held the field; now all they shout
's *Giotto*; the other's fame is lost to sight.[20]

One of the ideals generated by the Renaissance is that of the 'universal man', whose breadth of interests and activities now can, and in celebrated cases conspicuously does, extend to visual culture. If the most celebrated instance is Leonardo da Vinci, the earlier case of Leon Battista Alberti is, in the present context, more revealing.[21] Practising architect, humanist scholar, and prolific author in both Latin and Italian, Alberti encompasses an extraordinary range of literary genres, from biography to love poetry, from a dialogue (in Italian) *On the Family*[22] to a treatise on painting (in both Latin, *De pictura*, and Italian, *Della pittura*: 1435–6),[23] and subsequent Latin treatises on sculpture (*De statua*, 1446–7) and architecture itself (*De re aedificatoria*, 1446–52).[24] The treatise on painting, in particular, marks a notable point of departure. 'It broke with the Middle Ages' and 'prepared the way for the art, the artist, and the patron of the Renaissance'.[25] The Italian version discusses contemporary art and ancient practice, addressing itself (without any formal dedication) to Alberti's fellow artists – Brunelleschi and Donatello, among others. By contrast, the Latin version, suitably informed with classical learning, is dedicated to the humanist patron Gianfrancesco Gonzaga of Mantua; and 'in addressing the patron [Alberti] is already indicating the death of the guild system'.[26] Between them, the two versions sum up the earlier gulf between high culture and the artistic practitioner, while working powerfully to help bridge it. Meanwhile, the *De re aedificatoria* has its own significance. In this lengthy treatise (ten books in all), a practitioner presents his thoughts on his own medium in authoritative (Latin) form for the attention of the educated elite.[27] This too is a profound innovation:[28] the

20 *Purgatorio*, 11. 94–6.

21 Alberti is already acclaimed in such terms by Burckhardt, *Die Kultur der Renaissance in Italien* (1860), Part 2. Alberti generally: Gadol (1969), Grafton (2000), Grayson (1998).

22 *Della famiglia* (1433–40), a blend of Aristotle, Xenophon, Cicero, and personal experience.

23 The relative datings of the *De pictura* and the *Della pittura* are disputed: Grafton (2000) 71, Sinisgalli (2011) 3–16.

24 Not irrelevantly, Renaissance architects are often 'artists' of other kinds too: so already Giotto, and likewise Bramante, Raphael, Michelangelo.

25 Spencer (1966) 11. But the individual patronage that plays such an important role in Renaissance culture itself develops out of a well-established courtly system of commissions: Price (1996), and other essays in Wilkins and Wilkins (1996).

26 Spencer (1966) 29: an overstatement (privileging 'great men', rather than institutions), but the right way round.

27 In 1485, after Alberti's death, the *De re aedificatoria* was printed along with a dedicatory letter (by Politian) to Lorenzo de' Medici. The manuscript version had been dedicated to Leonello d'Este, Marquis of Ferrara.

28 Cf. Hart and Hicks (1998). Earlier statements, like the painter Cennino Cennini's *Libro dell' arte* (c. 1400?), are limited in scope and sophistication.

thoughts of a practising artist are seen to inform the mainstream of Western 'thought' itself.[29]

The same transitional role is apparent in a quite different sphere of Alberti's activity. Among his many distinctions is to have devised a manageable way of classicizing the design of the private house (less grand, but, in retrospect, more influential than Palladio's, in the next century):[30]

> Brunelleschi's idea had been to introduce the . . . columns, pediments and cornices which he had copied from Roman ruins . . . The problem . . . was to find a compromise between the traditional house, with walls and windows, and the classical forms . . . Alberti . . . found the solution . . . [For the] Florentine merchant Rucellai, he designed an ordinary three-storeyed building . . . [but] used classical forms for the decoration of the façade. Instead of building columns or half-columns, he covered the house with a network of flat pilasters and entablatures which suggest a classical order without changing the structure of the building. . . . [He] 'translated' a Gothic design into classical forms.[31]

Alberti, in effect, was doing for architecture what the humanists had been doing with Renaissance Latin, promoting the idiom of classical usage – and this very analogy occurs to Alberti's admirers at the time. 'Ancient building . . . compares to modern [i.e. 'Gothic'] as [ancient to modern] in literature', where 'after several centuries, prose has once again become eloquent' under the influence of 'Cicero and Virgil': thus Alberti's fellow-architect Filarete[32] – and the new facade of the Rucellai Palace is precisely one of Filarete's examples of a revived architectural 'eloquence'.[33]

Alberti's century initiates the integration of the visual arts and artists into high culture, and within a hundred years of his death, in 1472, the process – in Italy, at least – is effectively complete. The new status of the artist shows itself in a variety of ways. Artists now are patronized by the same great aristocratic families – the Medici and others – that patronize the leading humanist scholars; they belong to the same circles as the most esteemed writers; they may indeed be esteemed as writers themselves, and (like Alberti) well beyond the sphere of art theory. Titian

[29] In the prologue, Alberti makes clear that the architect must command 'the highest and noblest disciplines' (symptomatically, the form of his treatise shows the influence of ancient rhetorical theory: Biermann 1997, van Eck 1998). Comparison with the situation in antiquity is instructive. Few texts by practising artists or architects are attested; most of those few must have been limited technical treatises for fellow artists (like Polyclitus' lost *Canon*); a work like the (extant) *De Architectura* of Vitruvius (addressed to Augustus) is exceptional (cf. §30).

[30] Far more so, if one assesses the residue of 'classical ornament' on, not just grand-manner architecture, but much domestic building, in Britain, for instance, well into XX.

[31] Gombrich (1995) 249–50.

[32] Antonio di Piero Averlino, author of an influential *Trattato di architettura* (*c.* 1460–4), itself a witness to the new world of artist and patron: the treatise is dedicated in one manuscript (the Codex Magliabechiano) to Piero de' Medici.

[33] *Trattato*, 8.

belongs to Aretino's circle in Venice; Vasari's 'divine' Michelangelo is also a considerable poet; the dedication of one of the most widely-known and influential prose works of the Italian Renaissance, Castiglione's *Book of the Courtier* (1528),[34] acclaims the author's artist friend Raphael, along with Michelangelo too. The age of 'the artist' in the modern sense has arrived; and with the establishment of the first Academy of Art, in Florence, in 1563, the artist is formally institutionalized – as an individual who possesses, not merely functional expertise, but privileged understanding, and is recognised as a communicator of that understanding at the highest level: an innovator who transcends taught skills.

As an index of the place of visual art in high culture overall, and as a determinative factor in the artist's new status, the development of the artist-patron relationship has an unmistakable significance. But the establishment of private, alongside religious, patronage has more practical consequences too. Among much else, it facilitates the artistic exploration of pagan myth (§24), with all its emphasis on human agency and potentiality, alongside the characteristic limitation of the human in Christian religion. In the fifteenth century, Christian and classical had come together, under the influence of Neoplatonic philosophy, in the mythic allegory of Botticelli's *Primavera* (itself a Medici family commission, *c.* 1478). Increasingly, mythological subjects now attract an eroticized treatment of the human form, with luscious nudes – representing pagan deities – sanctioned by their high-art classicizing associations.[35] But if it is ancient sculpture that provides the model for a new aesthetic focus on the idealized nude, it is textual sources from which the mythological subject matter derives,[36] with ancient literature and art thus co-operating to shape the ambitions of successive phases of artistic classicism. In particular, Ovid's *Metamorphoses* (the acknowledged compendium of 'all the stories' of 'all the poets and other ancient writers'),[37] becomes a virtual handbook for artists, with even the intractable (and, in Christian terms, subversive) subject of pagan metamorphosis itself attempted in Antonio Pollaiuolo's painting *Apollo and Daphne* (1470–80) and fully realized, arguably, in a sculpture of the same name by Bernini in 1625.[38]

In the post-Renaissance visual world, Italy remains one, but now only one, centre of innovative classicizing. The sharply original work of the Italian architect-sculptor Bernini encapsulates the new energy of seventeenth-century Baroque,[39] amidst new tensions between normative classicism and creative art. In the paintings of

[34] *Il libro del cortegiano*: translated into Spanish in 1534, French in 1537, English in 1561, Latin in 1588.

[35] See generally Bull (2005), Seznec (1953).

[36] E.g. 'the fact that the Laocoon was universally admired did not make his story a popular subject for artists': Bull (2005) 12. From all the centuries of Western classicizing, Reid (1993) lists only drawings by Filippino Lippi, Jusepe de Ribera, Pietro da Cortona, and Raymond de La Fage; a fresco design by Giulio Romano; a painting by El Greco; and a few sculptural adaptations.

[37] Barthélemy Aneau, preface to his translation (with Clement Marot) of *Les trois premiers livres de la Metamorphose d'Ovide*, 1556.

[38] Metamorphosis: Barkan (1986), Buxton (2009) 1–18; cf. §27.

[39] Baroque responses to classical material: Rowland (2006).

Caravaggio, theatrical emotion and naturalism co-exist – his *Bacchus* (1595–7) combines conventional Greco-Roman iconography of the wine-god with the professional model's dirty finger-nails and sun-tanned face – as they do, rather differently, in the voluptuous nudes of the Flemish painter Rubens, whose work reflects both the Northern Renaissance style and the artist's own outlook as scholar and collector of antiquities. Critical of Caravaggio's naturalism, art theorist Giovan Pietro Bellori insisted on order, harmony, and proportion as the true classical ideals. For Bellori, under the influence of the Neoplatonic aesthetic of Plotinus, the 'highest and eternal intellect' had fashioned the supreme archetypes of multifarious nature, the 'Ideas', out of his own being, as the 'perfection of natural beauty', and the artists of antiquity had looked beyond nature to the superior 'Idea' itself.[40] Against Caravaggio ('too natural in painting likenesses'),[41] Bellori acclaimed the French painter Poussin, whose landscapes and figurative works were characterized by cool colour, simplicity in composition, and minimal movement.

Poussin's achievement represents the new status of France as custodian-in-chief of the visual legacy of antiquity. In response to the establishment of civic academies of art during the Italian Renaissance, the French Royal Academy of Painting and Sculpture was founded, on a national basis, in 1648, to set standards for artistic production and to initiate a system of training for art students based on copying from casts of ancient sculptures. The type of work the Academy promoted is exemplified by a large history painting, *The Tent of Darius* (1660–1), by its first director, Charles Le Brun, in which Alexander's sympathetic treatment of his defeated enemy's wife proclaims his heroic nobility. Throughout the neoclassical eighteenth century, France maintains its position as spiritual home of the classical tradition in such moralizing terms, with subjects from Roman history particularly favoured for their didactic potential and (like classical sculptures in Renaissance Italy) often disseminated across the visual media. Le Brun's painting itself was duly reproduced as a tapestry by the Manufacture des Gobelins, a Flemish company based in Paris [*Figure 4*], which then generated further replications.

Meanwhile, in contradistinction to Bellori's 'Ideas', a new interest in the material realities of antiquity becomes apparent. In French painting, a growing preoccupation with archaeological authenticity, prompted by the rediscovery of ancient Herculaneum in 1738 and Pompeii ten years later, encouraged the use of Romanizing costumes and settings. British interest in material antiquity was stimulated by the Grand Tour, when aristocratic travellers took the opportunity to amass their own collections of ancient art (and then to house them in suitably classicizing villas based on Italian models).[42] Like their Roman predecessors, modern collectors now commissioned copies when demand for originals outgrew supply. Copying had always been central to the Renaissance aesthetic – within a few years of the

[40] Preface to *Le vite de' pittori, scultori e architetti moderni* (1672), from a lecture, 'L'idea del pittore, dello scultore, e dell'architetto', given in Rome in 1664.

[41] Ibid.

[42] See variously Coltman (2006), Watkin (2000).

Figure 4 Flemish tapestry after Charles Le Brun, *The Tent of Darius*. Source: The Getty Research Institute, Los Angeles (97.P.7).

rediscovery of the Laocoon, the architect Bramante had even arranged for a formal competition between leading sculptors to copy the statue – but now a significant market opened for both high-end and popular reproductions. In the 1760s, Robert Adam's ante-room at Syon House (in what is now west London) included architectural decoration of gilded-gesso copies (reduced in size) of twelve well-known statues, with the grand entrance hall sporting four full-size versions of the most admired statues in Italian collections (Laocoon, Dying Gaul, Apollo Belvedere, Antinous).[43] In Italy itself, around the same time, the Doccia factory produced glazed earthenware copies of the Laocoon, while in nineteenth-century England the Minton factory's inexpensive Parian-ware statuettes of classical sculptures found a ready market among the burgeoning middle class.

In art, as elsewhere, the era of revolution and romanticism marks a profound shift away from the continuities operative since the Renaissance. The distinctive authority of the classical archetypes, and the time-honoured practice of learning by copying them, are no longer assumed as universal norms; and within the classical tradition itself, the primacy of Rome – or of the effectively undifferentiated Greco-Roman – gives way to the new preoccupation with Greece. Nevertheless, the overall picture is far from tidy. In France, Jacques-Louis David, who more than any other translates revolutionary and then Napoleonic ideals into pictorial form, looks back to Rome in idiom, as often in subject matter too (§§21, 33) – just as, in the emblematic architecture of the newly independent United States, it is Rome that inspires

43 Huntington (1968) 255–60.

the original design (as well as the name) of the Capitol.[44] In Britain the monumental classicizing architecture of the first half of the nineteenth century is sometimes Greek in conception (looking to models from the fifth and fourth centuries BC). Robert Smirke's designs for the restructured British Museum quote Greek temple architecture (rectangular structure fronted by grand Ionic portico: 1823–48), as does H. W. Inwood's St Pancras Church (caryatids and all: 1822). Conversely, other public buildings are essentially Roman (St George's Hall, Liverpool: R. L. Elmes, 1839) or eclectically diverse (Taylorian Institution, Oxford: C. R. Cockerell, 1845).[45] In architecture, moreover, the nineteenth-century Gothic revival (most prolific in Britain and the USA) represents, arguably, a more straightforward victory for anti-classicizing medievalism than any counterpart in the literary sphere, for all the prominence of the 'Gothic' novel and medievalizing romance. In Victorian England, above all, monumental Gothic, epitomized by Charles Barry's Parliament buildings (1839–52), represents an uncompromising affirmation of the non-classical past.

At the same time, the sense of a new response to the ancient world itself is unmistakable, with the very eclecticism of its visual embodiments (which increases exponentially as the nineteenth century wears on) a prime symptom of a new, authority-free age – or an age that feels free to read, and assign, authority at its own discretion. Here, as elsewhere, the eighteenth century can claim a decisive transitional role. If this is the century in which the copying of classical models comes under serious attack – we recall Chardin's critique, in 1765 (§4) – it is also the century in which the German art historian, Johann Joachim Winckelmann (§29), publishes his *History of the Art of Antiquity* (*Geschichte der Kunst des Alterthums*, 1764). In the 1750s, Winckelmann had already acclaimed the Greeks, and imitation too, in his *Reflections on the Imitation of Greek Works in Painting and Sculpture*.[46] Now, his *History* gives a huge momentum to the emerging shift of interest towards Greece, underwriting it with a pioneering chronology of ancient sculptural types. Celebrated statues as well as recent discoveries are given a new context by his schema. Once again the Laocoon is admired and scrutinized: Winckelmann ponders its seemingly paradoxical combination of beauty and pain, and (in his wake) Lessing's essay *Laokoon* (1766) uses the statue to challenge a long-standing theoretical alignment of painting and poetry, summed up in the Horatian formula *ut pictura poesis*,[47] which was axiomatic in Renaissance thought.[48]

The irony of Winckelmann's reverence for Greek art is well known. Both the date and the provenance of the Laocoon remain unresolved (Roman copy of a Hellenistic

[44] Original design by William Thornton (1793), with the dominant feature a dome based on the Pantheon. The current dome (Thomas U. Walter, 1855–66) recalls, rather, Wren's St Paul's. Domes: §20.

[45] The new Romanizing: Salmon (2000).

[46] *Gedanken über die Nachahmung der griechischen Werke in Malerei und Bildhauerkunst* (1755), 1: 'the only way to become great . . . is by imitating the ancients'.

[47] 'As painting, so poetry': Horace, *Ars Poetica*, 361.

[48] On the formula: Lee (1967), Markiewicz (1987). Enlightenment responses to the Laocoon: Brilliant (2000). The legacy of 'ut pictura poesis', arguably, continues today: Barolsky (2011).

original or early imperial Greco-Roman pastiche?),[49] but in any case Winckelmann's Hellenism and his classification of Hellenic art in general are based – like Renaissance 'receptions' of Greek art in earlier centuries – on a knowledge of Roman copies alone. Whatever the rhetoric of artists and their spokesmen (and from early in the fifteenth century, Alberti and others invoke the sacred names of Greek artists like Zeuxis),[50] up until the closing years of the eighteenth century the reception of ancient art is almost entirely dependent on Roman examples. Now, though, a number of factors combine to put Greece centre-stage: the new current of German Hellenism, fed by Winckelmann's studies; the expedition to Athens by James (nicknamed 'Athenian') Stuart and Nicholas Revett in 1751–3, during which surviving works of classical architecture are measured, recorded, and subsequently made publicly available in a four-volume *Antiquities of Athens* (1762–1816);[51] and the accident that, after revolutionary upheavals, much of Europe is occupied by Napoleon's armies, and travellers and archaeologists likewise find Greece, though still under Ottoman rule, an attractive site for exploration.

For centuries, awareness of Greece as a physical and visual actuality had been as attenuated in the West as knowledge of the Greek language in the medieval centuries.[52] The impact of awareness now is considerable. Enthusiasm for Greek independence is one by-product (an inspiration for creative figures as different as the painter Eugène Delacroix and the poets Byron and Hugo); the 'Greek revival' in architecture is another, for which, in the English-speaking world above all, Stuart and Revett's meticulous documentation of Greek sites provides a direct stimulus.[53] And if much of the notable 'revivalist' classicizing takes place, not surprisingly, in 'Hellenic' Germany – from Langhans's Brandenburg Gate (1789–91) to Schinkel's Altes Museum (1828–30) (both in Berlin) – it is in Britain that Hellenic ideal and visual reality converge most sharply.

In 1816, the Elgin marbles (consisting of the Athenian Parthenon frieze, metopes, and pedimental sculptures) were bought by the British Museum, where they were installed as models for creative emulation. Eulogized by artists like West and Canova, Flaxman and Fuseli, these ancient sculptures were hailed by Keats's friend, Benjamin Haydon, as heralding a new age in British art.[54] In the event, it was not until the 1860s that a classical revival was established within British art, sanctioned by the Royal Academy of Arts (founded in 1768). By this time, though, eclecticism,

[49] The irony would be greater, were there any truth in the suggestion that the Laocoon we have is actually the work of Michelangelo: Catterson (2005).

[50] 'Zeuxis, most eminent of ancient painters': Alberti, *On Painting*, 2.

[51] 'Greece was the great mistress of the arts, and Rome . . . no more than her disciple': Preface to *The Antiquities of Athens*, 1 (1762).

[52] Eisner (1993).

[53] Soros (2006).

[54] 'I felt the future, I foretold that they [the marbles] would prove themselves the finest things on earth, that they would overturn the false beau-ideal, where nature was nothing, and would establish the true beau-ideal, of which nature alone is the basis': *Life of Benjamin Robert Haydon*, ed. T. Taylor (1853), ch. 6 (entry for 1808). Influence of the marbles on contemporary art: Gurstein (2002).

even within classicizing circles, was not the exception but the rule; accordingly, artists felt free to look impartially to Greek sculptural models or to the Renaissance and *its* inspirations. Representatively, Frederic Leighton's statue *Athlete Wrestling with a Python* (1874–7) does not (unlike some of Leighton's work) emulate the restrained elegance of the Elgin marbles but rather the vivid movement and high drama of the Laocoon.[55] But (to invoke Pound's *Mauberley* once again) 'the age demanded' something less deferential altogether. For the avant-garde – realists, impressionists, and their various successors – all such art could only seem 'academic' in the limiting sense, and its ancient sources, even, questionable. Some continuities are still apparent: 'much of Cézanne's work tells us of his long obsession with the ideal landscape through its prior realizations in Romano-Campanian painting and in the work of Poussin, whose canvases Cézanne studied in the Louvre.'[56] More generally, discontinuity is the norm. 'The big mistake,' said Paul Gauguin in a letter of 1897, 'is the Greek – never mind how beautiful it is.'[57]

The twentieth century, with all its new experiments and rejections, marks the final break with the many versions of institutional classicism current across the Western world for five centuries and more. Anti-academic sentiment disdained the high-art traditions inherited from the Renaissance; machine-age architects eschewed the conventions of classical design and, especially, of classicizing ornament; and modernist movements increasingly challenged all figurative and representational modes of expression, not least those associated with the idealized human body and its classical-sculptural archetypes (§27). Even so, with leading artists like Pablo Picasso ready to acclaim 'the art of the Greeks' as 'more alive today than . . . ever',[58] antiquity – generally, indeed, Greek antiquity – continued to stimulate new aesthetic forms. Paradoxically, perhaps, liberation from prescriptive classical norms made it possible for artists, and eventually architects too, to look back to the forms (and the contents) of antiquity without a sense of compromise, artistic or ideological.

In the 1920s and 1930s, Freudian-influenced Surrealist paintings by Dali, Magritte and Ernst use classical myth to explore psychological truth,[59] while, a decade later, American abstract expressionists Pollock, Rothko, Gottlieb, and Newman turn to myth (as also to the classical-derived 'sublime') to contemplate universal issues of existence beyond time and place.[60] Picasso himself explores a distinctive range of mythic archetypes through the recurrent bull and minotaur imagery of his *Vollard Suite* etchings (1930–7) and the political masterpiece *Guernica* (1937). Earlier in the century, excavations of Cretan-Minoan civilization by the British

[55] Victorian classical revival: Barrow (2007).

[56] Kubler (1962) 51; cf. Berthold (1958).

[57] 'La grosse erreur, c'est le Grec, si beau qu'il soit': letter to Georges Daniel de Monfreid, written in Tahiti, October 1897.

[58] 'Picasso Speaks' (interview with Marius de Zayas), in *The Arts* (New York), May 1923.

[59] Chadwick (1980).

[60] Cf. (with special reference to Rothko) Polcari (1988). 'Sublime': §30.

archaeologist, Arthur Evans, had brought the myth of Minos to popular consciousness,[61] while the later nineteenth century had already responded to the rediscovery of pre-classical non-naturalistic art forms in Bronze Age Greece by Schliemann (§16) and others, along with the excavation of abundant archaic statuary on the Athenian Acropolis. Artistic interest in the visual culture of earlier Greece now merged with an appropriation of Oceanic and African art forms to produce a primitivism articulated by Picasso, among others.[62] Beyond the realm of acknowledged high art, meanwhile, Art Deco, the trans-national consumer-oriented design movement of the 1920s and 1930s, combined formal echoes of the classical with technological modernity and decorative motifs from world cultures – African, Meso-American, Chinese[63] – to create a uniquely coherent visual grammar across a range of mass-produced artefacts, from fashion to furnishings to poster design, along with one-off triumphs of commercial architecture. The Empire State Building in New York, for instance (architects, Shreve, Lamb, and Harmon: 1931), retains the imprint of a classical structure, along with specific classical-derived features in its detail.[64]

With functionalist designs seemingly the preferred ideal for a machine age, closer approximations to grand-manner classicism in architecture increasingly became the preserve of totalitarian regimes. The austere sub-Roman grandiosity of Albert Speer's German Pavilion for the World Exhibition in Paris (1937), representatively, affirmed monumental scale at the expense of ornament (a tacit gesture to functionalist principle), but also of any rapport between individual human viewer and undifferentiated power inscribed in stone.[65] Hardly emboldened by such ruthless appeals to the classical, innovative traditionalism ran its course. With a certain symbolic appropriateness, work on Edwin Lutyens's design for Liverpool Catholic Cathedral – described by John Summerson as 'the latest and supreme attempt to embrace Rome, Byzantium, the Romanesque and the Renaissance in one triumphal and triumphant synthesis'[66] – stopped in 1941 and was later abandoned. Summerson himself felt able to argue for the 'classical parentage' of the 'Modern Movement' as a whole, seeing in Behrens's AEG Turbine Erection Hall (Berlin, 1908) 'a neo-classical

[61] Ziolkowski (2008).

[62] Cf. Noble (1991).

[63] Cf. Striner (1990).

[64] 'For instance, the upper vertical corners of the stone-faced tower are chamfered and curved slightly inward, introducing a purely visual refinement reminiscent of entasis in a classical Greek column': Siry (2008) 192. The tower itself was 'reportedly' (ibid. 193) inspired by the Romanesque cathedral at Autun. American Deco architecture at its most flamboyant has only a tenuous connection with the classical; William Van Alen's Chrysler Building in New York (1930), with its 'Aztec pinnacle' (as the poet Charles Tomlinson put it: 'All Afternoon', 1984), is a case in point. However, some 'non-classsical' configurations favoured by Deco architects actually have classical/classicizing precedents – like the stepped-pyramid steeple of Hawksmoor's St George's Church in Bloomsbury, London (1716–31), itself inspired by Pliny's description of the Mausoleum at Halicarnassus (*Natural History*, 36. 31).

[65] Compare/contrast Fascist architecture in Rome (§25).

[66] Summerson (1990) 256.

building . . . with all the stylistic signs and symbols left out or changed' and a kind of classicizing (even 'Renaissance') spirit in the Modulor system of Le Corbusier[67] – though such non-allusive 'classicism' is unlikely to impinge on most observers as part of the classical 'tradition'.

In today's art world, however, and in Britain not least, artists have both found a new use for, and have simultaneously mounted a further challenge to, traditional classical norms. One notable development involves the use of racially aware reworkings of cultural stereotypes to question Western ideals of beauty and their Greco-Roman sculptural basis.[68] The title of Chris Ofili's *Afrodizzia* (1996) adroitly plays on the names of a 1970s African-American hairstyle, an erotic stimulant, and the Greek goddess of beauty and love. With its collage, glitter, map-pins, and elephant dung, Ofili's work challenges both conventional art media and the venerable association of female desirability with the form of the nude sculptural Venus. Very differently, environmental artists have used archaeological remains to invite an aesthetic reconsideration of classical artefacts,[69] and (differently again) some contemporary art incorporates, not just the classical antique, but also the classical tradition, into its new aesthetic forms. In 2007 the Henry Moore Institute's exhibition 'Towards a New Laocoon' displayed sculptures by British artists, including Tony Cragg, Richard Deacon, and Eduardo Paolozzi, which presented a series of non-figurative reinterpretations of the iconic statue,[70] while Calum Colvin's photographic collage, *Brief Encounter* (1990), references, not the Laocoon itself, but Leighton's *Athlete Wrestling with a Python*, now struggling with electrical cables and superimposed over a Greek bronze and the Venus de Milo [*Plate 3*].[71]

In a comparable spirit, postmodern architecture, reacting against the austere functionality of the modernist International Style, has come to embrace classicizing detail among its eclectic borrowings from different histories and cultures.[72] Charles Moore's Piazza d'Italia in New Orleans (1976–9) combines 'ancient' and ultramodern, with its neon lighting and Ionic capitals of stainless steel. In Rome, Paolo Portoghesi's Islamic Mosque (1974–95) brings together Eastern and Western elements, making special appeal to Rome's own distinctive architectural history, from antiquity to the Baroque.[73] Yet whatever the seeming randomness of such eclectic allusions, the contemporaneity of the classical here is arguably no more (and no less) surprising than the Roman presence in the Christian Hagia Sophia (or indeed in the Islamic mosque that it too later became, under Ottoman rule).

67 Summerson (1964) 43–6; cf. Levin (2007). Modulor system: §30.

68 Cf. Dyer (1997) on the cultural construction of whiteness in artistic and popular-cultural forms.

69 Renfrew (2003).

70 Curtis *et al.* (2007).

71 The struggling, along with the erotic associations of the (incomplete) Venus, are given additional significance by the allusion in Colvin's title to the British film *Brief Encounter* (1945: dir. David Lean), a celebrated tale of doomed (and unconsummated) love.

72 Cf. Galinsky (1992), Levin (2007).

73 Cf. §25.

If one can still speak of establishments and norms in today's multifarious visual culture, works like Ofili's *Afrodizzia*, Colvin's *Brief Encounter*, and Moore's Piazza d'Italia suggest resistance to them, on different levels and in different degrees, as much as conformity. In a long perspective, the Christian-classical hybridizing that inaugurates the classical tradition in the visual arts, though remote from today's experiments in its detail, is not dissimilar in its momentum. The history of the tradition in the visual domain is an intricate story of survival and rediscovery, of reuse and (occasionally) abuse, of scholarship, patronage, collection, and display, of connections and disconnections with the 'separate' worlds of literature and ideas – but, not least, of the artistic appropriation (in Aachen, New Orleans, wherever) that presents classical continuities as a challenge as well as an affirmation.

§12

Popular Culture and Its Problematics

If the classical tradition, for most of its history, is bound up with authorities and canonical practice, 'the classical tradition in popular culture' at once seems problematic. How can antique themes, forms, or allusions function in a frame of reference where (as many think) the very notions of authority and the canonical are alien, and where tradition itself, perhaps, is a marginal concern?

The problem is best approached in the perspective of modern debates surrounding the categorization of culture. In the newly industrialized nineteenth century, anxieties about the growth of mass entertainment are marked by rigid classifications of cultural production and consumption into 'high' and 'low'. This oppositional value is expressed forcefully in 1869 by Matthew Arnold, for whom 'culture' represents 'the best knowledge and thought of the time', and 'anarchy' the anti-cultural outcome of the 'raw and unkindled masses'.[1] In the twentieth century, Marxist-inspired Frankfurt School theorists Theodor Adorno and Max Horkheimer restate these classifications for a new era of economic and cultural expansion, critiquing the mass production of culture in terms of negative commodification, standardization, and passive consumption.[2] From the late 1950s, conversely, French structuralism shifts the emphasis from judgement to societal assumptions, while Roland Barthes, as cultural theorist, helps to make even the unblest world of post-war consumer society a subject of serious intellectual enquiry in its own right.[3]

1 *Culture and Anarchy*, 1 ('Sweetness and light').
2 Adorno and Horkheimer (1972).
3 *Mythologies* (1957).

The Classical Tradition: Art, Literature, Thought, First Edition. Michael Silk, Ingo Gildenhard, and Rosemary Barrow.

Published 2017 by John Wiley & Sons Ltd.

Then, in the years that follow, the influential Birmingham Centre for Contemporary Cultural Studies, under the directorship of Richard Hoggart and, later, Stuart Hall, comes to affirm an ideal of popular culture as creative consumption, with consumers seen, potentially or actually, as active producers of meaning.[4]

In the wake of these developments, 'high' and 'low' have been widely read as terms of contrasting milieux rather than contrasting quality, while from the 1980s onwards Cultural Studies (an expanding academic field, in the English-speaking world at least) has tended to challenge any social model based on cultural polarity, and a more general climate of postmodernism has promoted scepticism about cultural categories of value altogether. The high/low distinction has thus been treated as a matter of taste, rather than cultural production,[5] while bold (but unconvincing) theoretical claims have been made in favour of a 'popular aesthetic' that foregrounds content, as against an elite ('pure') aesthetic centred on form.[6] One might note, rather, that, in many ages, at least some 'elite' culture is accessed and appreciated by the socially underprivileged, and at least some 'popular' culture consumed by elites. The irreducible datum would seem to be the broad contrast of elite and non- (or 'sub'-) elite cultural *contexts* down the ages, whether before or after the emergence of mass culture. In this perspective: popular culture is, first and foremost, 'the culture of the non-elite',[7] irrespective of its period, its characteristics, or its value; today's mass media (cinema, television, advertising, internet) are significant vehicles of popular cultural expression, as are various older sources of (non-elite) fiction and performance; and within any of these, reworkings and other outcomes of ancient material can be identified as recognisable contributions to the classical tradition across the Western world.

In these debates, however, academic discussion of popular culture has tended to focus overwhelmingly on industrialized or post-industrial societies, and discussion of the classical within popular culture likewise. The upshot is that attempts, by classical scholars in particular, to come to terms with the relationships between the classical and the post-classical in the popular domain may or may not acknowledge the 'older sources' just cited (often not), but in any case tend to concentrate on popular modernity and its distinctive *consciousness* of the classical past, as evinced through reuse of classical subjects. We take issue with this emphasis, and with its premise. While accepting the importance of such reuse, we would insist on a major qualification. In the arena of popular culture, as in various others (from language to law), there have been important *continuations* ('reflexes') of the classical, especially, though not only, in pre-industrial Europe, and these have no less right to be counted as embodiments of the classical tradition than receptions as ordinarily

[4] Hoggart (1957); Hall (1980), (1981); contrast Hoggart (2004) on the paradoxes of meaning in an era of mass communication.

[5] Cohen (1999).

[6] Bourdieu (1979) 33–6.

[7] Burke (2009) xiii, 7–15 – *pace* those who equate popular culture with mass culture (like Bell 1989: 1459–84) and those who draw a sharp distinction between them (like Ginzburg 1976).

understood. The 'older sources', indeed, have a much more pervasive significance than is often allowed.

In the first place, medieval and early modern 'folk culture', and, above all, what Mikhail Bakhtin has taught recent generations to identify as the culture of 'carnival', can be seen to have subsumed survivals from antiquity among its miscellaneous inversions and travesties, rituals, and masquerades.[8] Within such modes of collective social activity, there is little or no sign of any individual consciousness at work (such creativity is essentially anonymous)[9] and no reworking of any classical models as such – and yet here, as with so much else in the medieval and early modern West, a complex negotiation between pagan and Christian is implicit. Bakhtin himself placed particular emphasis on the co-existence of Christian context and counter-Christian ritual, while tracing the roots of carnival back to 'the Roman Saturnalia'[10] – whose usage indeed prefigures attested 'comic' misappropriations of high-status costumes and insignia and the crownings and symbolic killings of a mock king.[11] Furthermore, the utopian affinities of the Saturnalia and its nostalgia for a golden age of abundance are transmitted into early-modern Europe in the legends of Cockaigne, as in the practices of Shrovetide feasting.[12]

Reaching a climax on Shrove Tuesday or Mardi Gras, immediately before the beginning of Lent, carnival celebrations were characterized by indulgence and disorder. The popular spectacles foregrounded the irregular and the informal, whereas royal and aristocratic pageantry of the same period adhered to strict hierarchical codes of behaviour. Yet a degree of interaction existed between the two worlds. Spectacular Renaissance festivities sponsored by elite patrons included weddings and bridal entries into a city,[13] with rituals that combined pagan and Christian, great

[8] Overview: Burke (2009) 255–86. Carnival culture was strongest in Italy, France, and Spain (ibid. 271), and, for obvious reasons, survivals of 'classical' ritual and custom likewise. Outside the 'Latin' territories, though, carnival culture could still be strikingly classicizing. 'In Nuremberg in the late fifteenth and early sixteenth centuries, carnival plays (*Fastnachtspiele*) portrayed Apollo, Aristotle, Caesar, Fabius and Lucretia: one was titled *The History of the Roman Empire*. In seventeenth-century London the annual Lord Mayor's Show introduced (among other classical figures) Astraea, Apollo, Mercury, Neptune, Orpheus, Scylla and Charybdis, Thetis and Ulysses': Burke (2010a) 766. But in Germany, in particular, these (and other) popular-cultural manifestations with classical connections are more restricted: cf. n. 56 below.

[9] A well-attested phenomenon, even in the modern age – witness (e.g.) the soldiers' songs sung by the British Army on the western front in World War I, consisting of dozens of (mostly sardonic) new lyrics for hymn tunes and popular melodies. 'Like mediaeval ballads, these songs are anonymous, and even the method of their composition is a mystery': thus Brophy and Partridge (1965) 15 – despite the fact that their compilation of material and reminiscences began in the late 1920s (ibid. 11–12), when over a million soldiers survived to tell the tale.

[10] Bakhtin (1968) 6–8. Such relationships were already apparent to learned observers in XVI/XVII: Burke (2009) 291–2. Erasmus, for instance, saw 'traces of ancient paganism' ('veteris paganismi vestigia') in the Siena carnival: 'Supputatio errorum in censuris Bedae' (1527).

[11] Bristol (1989) 34.

[12] Ibid. 88–9.

[13] Bull (2005) 43–7. Such bridal rituals can themselves be linked with ancient festivals, as duly noted by Marco Antonio Altieri, *Li nuptiali* (early XVI).

artists and light entertainment, refined classical imagery and 'broad' popular elements – with the choice of classical imagery itself calculated to appeal to the less educated, as well as to those versed in ancient myth. Such spectacles were often private courtly events, yet even these sometimes evoked, or in turn influenced, the popular carnival:

> When in 1479 Eleanora of Aragon, the bride of Ercole d'Este, stopped in Rome on the way to Ferrara, the entertainment consisted not only of the traditional mystery plays, but pantomimes[14] featuring Orpheus and the animals, Perseus and Andromeda, Bacchus and Ariadne, Ceres, and the education of Achilles. For the wedding of Isabella of Aragon to his nephew [1489], Ludovico Sforza employed Leonardo to design sets for a spectacle that involved the planetary deities, the Seven Virtues, and the Three Graces; the following year, Leonardo worked on the production of a comedy about Jupiter and Danae for the marriage of Anna Sforza and Alfonso d'Este. In Venice, mythological pantomimes featured at patrician weddings, and classical elements played an increasingly important role in the carnival from the 1520s.[15]

This kind of interplay between popular and elite is no isolated phenomenon.[16] In the development of the European novel, from Boccaccio to Cervantes and beyond, a significant contribution is made both by the sophisticated ancient 'novels' (or 'romances') of an Apuleius or a Heliodorus and by more popular works like the *Alexander Romance*.[17] In the history of comic drama, such interplay is apparent again. In the modern world, sophisticated comic-dramatic practice, from Chekhov to Tom Stoppard, runs parallel to a familiar (and in the English-speaking world, ubiquitous) range of popular forms, on stage, on radio, on television, and on film, from the sitcom to musical comedy (with a few creative figures, like Woody Allen and Stephen Sondheim, straddling the sophisticated/popular divide). Ultimately, both traditions derive in large part from the Greek 'New Comedy' of Menander (and others), via Plautus and Terence in Rome and a welter of more-or-less sophisticated imitations (and reflexes) between the Renaissance and the seventeenth century – with the sophisticated imitations epitomized by Shakespeare and by Molière. But if Molière's comedy is informed, also, by a strain of sharp satire, itself

[14] Generally: short dramatic performances, without words, centred on gesture, movement, tableau, and dance. See generally Heller (2010) and cf. n. 59 below.

[15] Bull (2005) 44.

[16] Beyond any reference to early modernity or the classical tradition, Russian Formalist theory went so far as to make the influence of popular on elite both a *desideratum* and a 'law' of literary history (first formulated by Shklovsky in *Literatura i kinematograf*, 1923). 'This "law", which became known as "canonization of the junior branch", posited that periodically, in order to renew itself, literature should draw on motifs and devices of subliterary genres': Erlich (1973) 633.

[17] The *Romance* (traditionally misascribed to Callisthenes) had a huge circulation, in different versions and translations, in medieval Europe: 'The storie of Alisaundre is so comune | That every wight that hath discrecioun | Hath herd somewhat or al of his fortune' (Chaucer, *The Monk's Tale*, 641–3). However, it is an exaggeration to suggest that 'the roots of Western popular literature lie in ancient Greece': Hansen (1998) vii. On the 'medieval Alexander': Cary (1956); cf. Centanni (2010). On the influence of Heliodorus and others: Doody (1996) 175–300; cf. e.g. Beaton (2007) 229–31.

inspired partly by ancient sources,[18] Shakespeare's is enriched by a carnival-related ('festive') element. Ancient comic drama itself had its 'popular' aspect. Plautus in particular hybridized *his* Menander with the native Italian traditions of popular performance that modern scholarship associates with the 'Atellan farce' (*fabula Atellana*) – whence (seemingly) Plautus' inspiration for song and (perhaps) word-play and coarse humour, along with his amplification of the 'trickster slave' (*servus callidus*). And between Plautus and our era of sitcoms and musical comedies, there have been notable instances of convergence between 'low' and 'high', popular and elite.

In Elizabethan-Jacobean England, Shakespearean drama (and not only comedy) is a prime example. In this era, theatrical performance attracts socially diverse audiences;[19] the status of actors (mid-way between servants and independent professionals) defies easy categorization;[20] and printed text and oral tradition meet on various levels. It is obvious that wily servants like Tranio in *The Taming of the Shrew* (*c.* 1594) and Puck in *A Midsummer Night's Dream* (*c.* 1596) declare the lineage of Plautus' slaves,[21] but 'popular' figuration in a sophisticated context is presented more decisively by Shakespeare's clowns and fools in the 'serious' plays. Figures like the graveside clowns in *Hamlet* (*c.* 1601) and the fool in *Lear* (*c.* 1605) embody aspects of the 'comic' inversion of the 'serious' *status quo* characteristic of the carnival tradition, all the way back to the Saturnalia of old, with or without specifiable derivation from particular ancient forms, literate or other.[22] Especially significant is the fool-like behaviour of 'serious' characters, including Lear himself, on 'this great stage of fools', and the 'mad' clowning of Hamlet ('it is but foolery'):[23] direct incursions of Bakhtin's carnival spirit into the most high-serious of tragic situations. Conversely, the celebrated moment when King Harry disowns his former play-fellow Falstaff –

> I know thee not, old man. Fall to thy prayers.
> How ill white hairs becomes a fool and jester[24] –

represents a reassertion of the high serious, but, by the stark poignancy of the moment, also affirms the significance of carnival 'folly' for Shakespearean high seriousness itself.

If the popular traditions associated with carnival are important for Shakespeare, their importance is paradigmatic, as Bakhtin suggested, for Rabelais. 'Festive laughter', as Bakhtin conceived of it, is centred on 'the grotesque body', whose 'most

[18] See e.g. Kasparek (1977), but, on Molière and the popular tradition, also p. 129 below.

[19] But commonly excluding the very poor and the very rich: Astington (2001) 111–12.

[20] Henderson (2007).

[21] Cf. Anderson (2005) and (generally) Miola (1994), Riehle (2004).

[22] Details much contested: see variously Barber (1959), Beadle (2004), Gillespie and Rhodes (2006), Thomson (2004), Twycross and Carpenter (2002), Weimann (1978), Wiles (1987).

[23] *King Lear*, 4. 5. 179; *Hamlet*, 5. 2. 161.

[24] *2 Henry IV*, 5. 4. 47–8.

masterful literary expression' (in Stephen Greenblatt's words) is in Rabelais's *Gargantua and Pantagruel*. Following, but also qualifying, Bakhtin, Greenblatt encapsulates the Rabelaisian carnival-grotesque in the comic novel's scatological account of the giant Gargantua's birth, where gigantic infant and gigantic 'foul-smelling excrescences' are all but indistinguishable, and where 'an exuberant parody of classical legends of the birth of heroes' (from Bacchus to Castor and Pollux) is itself almost indistinguishable from mockery of 'the miraculous nativity at the heart of Christianity itself'.[25]

Though quick to identify the anti-clerical in Rabelais's comic creation, Bakhtin himself played down the significance of the 'classical legends', and effectively equated Rabelais's reuse of carnival culture with that culture itself. This is surely an oversimplification. As Greenblatt, again, insists, Rabelais's elusive comic novel is 'not carnival, but the brilliant aesthetic representation of carnival motifs; not the communal laughter of a largely illiterate populace, but the highly crafted classicizing of a supremely literate individual.' Furthermore, the Rabelaisian 'representation' is, arguably, a sophisticated treatment, not of some venerated popular tradition, but of a tradition under threat. In Rabelais's lifetime, 'carnivalesque recreations had come under increasingly effective attack . . . from clerical authorities [and] social reformers',[26] as part of a reaction against (and withdrawal from) popular culture which takes effect, across Europe, between the sixteenth and eighteeth centuries.[27] It would then be precisely the success of this reaction that explains the novel phenomenon of high-cultural enthusiasm for 'the people' and the popular in the Romantic age of Herder and Wordsworth: 'in 1500 [educated men] despised the common people, but shared their culture. By 1800 their descendants had ceased to participate spontaneously in popular culture, but . . . were in the process of rediscovering it.'[28]

In Rabelais, as in Shakespeare, such a dissociation has not taken effect, as it has in (say) Racine or some of the English Augustans. In Rabelais's case, perhaps (Greenblatt, once more), the 'festive representations derive at least some of their intensity from this new agonistic situation: not carnival in its recurrent, cyclical struggle with Lent, but the carnivalesque threatened in its very existence' by 'a literary, social and religious world hardening in its commitment to order, discipline and decorum.'[29] But, surely more important (and a necessary qualification to such revisionist readings themselves), Rabelais's conjunction of the sophisticated classical and the popular-cultural, distinctive and even extraordinary though it is, is also paradigmatic of diverse convergences and cross-overs in the centuries that follow.

At the risk of seeming now to suggest that such cross-overs represent the norm (an overstatement, no doubt, though a suggestive one), we can point to striking

[25] *Gargantua*, 3–6: Greenblatt (1990) 64–6. Such *scatologica* assume e.g. 'the mock mass, in which excrement was used in place of incense' (ibid.).

[26] Ibid. 67–8.

[27] Burke (2009) 289–334, 366–81.

[28] Ibid. 386. Cf. (in the sphere of language) pp. 160–1 below.

[29] Greenblatt (1990) 68.

examples in, for instance, the history of opera, specifically Italian opera – and particularly striking, because for many, in today's world, opera (Italian or other) is the very epitome of high culture. The origins of opera, on the face of it, are clearly 'high'. The operatic form arises from a cluster of learned, classicizing experiments – musical and dramatic – in late-sixteenth-century Italy, which give rise also to the pastoral tragicomedy, made famous by Battista Guarini's *Faithful Shepherd* (*Il pastor fido*, published in 1589).[30] Opera itself was pioneered in Florence by the musician Jacopo Peri and the poet Ottavio Rinuccini, under the influence of the Florentine salon known as the *Camerata*, as an attempt to recreate an equivalent to ancient tragedy, which was widely, if erroneously, taken to have been an essentially musical form. The now familiar alternations of song (aria) and melodized speech (recitative) – corresponding, supposedly, to the dynamic alternations within the ancient dramas – were the outcome. As Rinuccini declared in the dedication of the first publicly performed opera, *Euridice*, in 1600: 'It is generally imagined that the tragedies of the Greeks and Romans were entirely sung; but this noble kind of singing had not till now been revived.'[31]

The contexts of the early operas, like their Greco-Roman mythological contents, were also undeniably elite. Peri and Rinuccini's *Euridice* enjoyed royal patronage (that first 1600 performance took place at the wedding of Henri IV of France to Maria de' Medici at the Pitti Palace); their collaboration had begun with *Dafne* (the earliest attested opera of all), which was first staged privately (in 1598), then performed at the Medici court, before the Duke of Parma, in 1604; a few years later, Monteverdi, the first operatic composer of lasting repute, embarked on his career with *Orfeo* (1607) and *Arianna* (1608), both classical-subject pieces and both premièred under the auspices of the Gonzaga court in Mantua. And yet even such sophisticated and socially exclusive developments had their links with the popular domain through the *intermedi* – distinctive elements in the world of spectacle and classical imagery sketched above.[32]

30 The paradoxically un-classical outcome of another such experiment in this period was the invention of the permanent indoor theatre, as a site for classical or classicizing drama. The oldest surviving instance is the Teatro Olimpico in Vicenza (designed by Palladio and Vincenzo Scamozzi); the inaugural production (in 1585) was of Sophocles' *Oedipus Tyrannus*, in an Italian translation by Orsatto Giustiniani, with incidental music by the Venetian Andrea Gabrieli.

31 Tr. by Charles Burney, *A General History of Music* (2nd edn, 1789), 4. 1. The claim assumes both that the lyrical parts of tragedy were sung (as, in Greece at least, they were) and that spoken (iambic) dialogue was also sung – this, ultimately, on the basis of problematic evidence like Ps.-Plutarch, *De Musica* 1141a, ch. 28 ('they say Archilochus [in VII BC Greece] . . . had some iambics spoken with instrumental accompaniment, and some sung, and that later the [Greek] tragic poets followed this procedure') and misunderstood evidence like Aristoxenus, *Elementa Harmonica*, 1. 18 (on the 'melody' of Greek speech: *logôdes ti melos*). The Florentine experiment was dismissed by the young Nietzsche in 1872 as the artificial concoction of 'cultivated Renaissance man' (*The Birth of Tragedy*, 19). Nietzsche shared the belief in the originary musicality of Greek tragedy, but on quite different grounds: Silk and Stern (1981) 137–41, 239–51.

32 *Intermedi* and early opera: Kimbell (1991) 19–93.

The *intermedi* were short, staged musical 'interludes' interpolated between the acts of Italian plays and operas from the sixteenth to the eighteenth centuries.[33] Their repertoire extended from the refined spectacular to the popular grotesque, and the refined and the grotesque might indeed be co-present, especially in the earlier history of the form, where 'its essence was to be found in . . . pantomimic dancing', and where 'impresarios did not flinch from mixing together the most incongruous ingredients – "buffoons and tumblers . . . mythological evocations and moral and political allegory".'[34] Representatively, a performance of Terence's *Andria* at the d'Este court in Ferrara in 1491 featured '*intermedi* involving nymphs and savages';[35] and such undemanding amusements were preferred to the high-classical dramas they accompanied by even the learned Isabella d'Este herself.[36] Reflecting its popular affinities, the *intermedio* remained essentially light-hearted and especially suitable as an accompaniment to comedy,[37] but more specifically: 'the coarser and more farcical elements never quite vanished from the *intermedi* and in due course this strain becomes one of the sources of Italian comic opera.'[38] And yet the *intermedi* had also been one of the influences on the embryonic Florentine opera itself; and indeed, a few years before their collaborations on *Dafne* and *Euridice*, Peri and Rinuccini were both involved in one of the most celebrated *intermedi* of all, an allegorical extravaganza staged at the Uffizi Palace in Florence in 1589, in honour of Ferdinando de' Medici's marriage to Princess Christine of Lorraine.

The popular affinities of opera were realized more directly in seventeenth-century Venice, with the opening of the first public opera house (the Teatro San Cassiano) in 1637, and the staging of performances to the paying public during carnival season.[39] The association with carnival, symbolizing the appeal of opera across the social spectrum, spread to other Italian cities and lasted for centuries. At the height of its popularity in nineteenth-century Italy, the opera calendar was divided into spring, autumn, and carnival seasons. Beginning on St Stephen's Day (26 December) and lasting until Lent, the opening and closing of carnival season saw the most spectacular performances.[40]

As a performative genre, Italian opera continued to proclaim its popular pretensions – at the same time, intriguingly, as its links with the classical past – well into

[33] The term *intermedio* is first attested thus in Niccolò da Correggio's *Cefalo* (1487): Pirrotta (1969) 66.

[34] Kimbell (1991) 21, quoting Pirrotta (1969) 72.

[35] Lockwood (1984) 312.

[36] Kimbell (1991) 19. Classically educated in her youth, Isabella became a noted patron of the arts; her beneficiaries and circle of contacts included Leonardo and Titian, Bembo, Ariosto, and Castiglione.

[37] In a theoretical defence of his tragicomic experiment, Guarini protests: 'Comedy has become so tedious and is so little valued that if she is not accompanied by the wonders of the interludes [here, *intermezzi*], no-one today can stand her' (*Il pastor fido e il compendio della poesia tragicomica*, 1601). On the relation between *intermedi* and *intermezzi*: Kimbell (1991) 295–7.

[38] Ibid. 21.

[39] Rosand (1991).

[40] Kimbell (1991) 428.

the twentieth century, through the complex reception of its nineteenth-century master, Giuseppe Verdi. In Italy, in his own day, Verdi's operas, from *Nabucco* (first performed in 1842) to *Falstaff* (1893), famously acquired the status of the 'national-popular narrative' (Gramsci's expression)[41] enjoyed in other Western countries by the novel. For the poet D'Annunzio, Nietzscheanizing champion of ancient hierarchies, Verdi, on his death in 1901, could be acclaimed as a 'bard' ('aedo') in the tradition of Homer.[42] In the Fascist decades that soon followed, however, Verdi was appropriated, rather, as a unifier of ancient past and 'national-popular' present, above all through spectacular open-air productions like (most famously) a 1938 *Aida* at the Baths of Caracalla in Rome. It was no coincidence that such spectacles should have been located in Rome and in an ancient setting; here, wrote an American reviewer, 'one breathes the atmosphere of an illustrious, remote antiquity'.[43] But within Fascist ideology itself, such productions, more pointedly, were a demonstration that 'operatic theatre' ('il teatro lirico') had become 'popular theatre' ('teatro popolare') 'in the richest and widest sense'.[44]

Yet another form of Italian public entertainment which crossed the barriers within early modern society was the *commedia dell'arte*, a largely improvised, pantomimic, and often coarse counterpart to the formal, scripted, classicizing *commedia erudita* that looked back directly to the Plautine and Terentian texts. Characterized by formulaic plots and stereotyped figures, often masked, the *commedia dell'arte* took shape in sixteenth-century Italy; by the eighteenth century it had spread across Europe; and the itinerant players who performed it were welcomed in town squares and aristocratic houses alike. Where formal comedy was essentially a cultivated imitation of classical Latinity, the *commedia dell'arte* too could claim to have roots in antiquity, but (like carnival) by direct descent from the popular forms of ancient Italy, the farce and the pantomime.[45]

From its stock characters, especially its comic servants (*Zanni*), the *commedia* generated other forms of popular entertainment. Punch and Judy puppet shows were first recorded in England by Samuel Pepys in 1662; by the nineteenth century, they had become a symbol of class defiance, with Mr Punch both a violent clown and an irreverent, subversive figure, who disrespects marriage and religion, and defies the policeman and the hangman.[46] Punch (along with other European

41 Gramsci (1975) 125–32. Beyond Italy, across Europe and America, XIX opera 'was *simultaneously* popular and elite . . . it was attended both by large numbers of people who . . . experienced it in the context of their normal everyday culture *and* by smaller socially and economically elite groups who derived . . . social confirmation from it': Levine (1998) 86.

42 'In morte di Giuseppe Verdi', 1903.

43 *New York Times*, 14 August 1938.

44 Corsi (1939) 312. The D'Annunzian 'Homer' and the nationalist-ideological 'popular' were neatly combined in the Fascist period by Cornelio Di Marzio, who acclaimed Verdi as 'the mythical Homer . . . an epic and a people': Di Marzio (1941) 7. In XIX, Wagner's 'festival' drama had a similar aspiration: §31.

45 Richards and Richards (1990) 11–15. Origins and development of the *commedia*: Bourqui (1999), Nicoll (1931) 214–349, Richards and Richards (1990).

46 Leach (1985).

variants) derives directly, both in form and name, from one of the stock figures of the *commedia*, Pulcinella, who can be traced back, in turn, to the Plautine *servus callidus* (or its Atellan prototype), the trickster slave bent on serving his master, but also on manipulating events to his own advantage.

The very prominence of servants in the *commedia* recalls Plautus, and their formulaic nature does too. The Plautine slave, cunning but ultimately loyal, seems to underlie the familiar types of 'Columbine' and 'Harlequin' – Columbina (clever female servant) and Arlecchino (mischievous man-servant) – along with Pedrolino (loyal and trusty). In the seventeenth and eighteenth centuries, Pedrolino gives rise to a new performance type, Pierrot. First attested with the Italian comedians in Paris,[47] Pierrot – white face, loose hat, soft white clothing – discards any remaining coarse features to become a sensitive ('sentimental') figure in the literature and art of eighteenth-century France – from Marivaux's *Arlequin poli par l'amour* (1720) and Florian's *Le bon ménage* (1782) to the paintings of Antoine Watteau and Jean-Honoré Fragonard.[48]

In nineteenth-century France, Pierrot modulates further into a poetic, suffering lover, thanks to his portrayal in the Parisian *Théâtre des Funambules* by the mime artist Jean-Gaspard Debureau, whose performances won the admiration of such notable literary figures as Heine, Gautier, and Baudelaire; the subsequent outcome was a lingering fascination with Pierrot among Decadent circles in the last decades of the century,[49] along with a memorable cinematic evocation at the end of World War II.[50] In late-Victorian Britain, more prosaically, 'pierrot shows' became a fixture in the light-entertainment world (usually as a seaside entertainment) and remained so for decades. In one late, and noteworthy, reuse of the figure in a political context, theatre director Joan Littlewood dressed the players of her anti-establishment musical satire, *Oh, What a Lovely War!* (1963), in Pierrot costumes, ironically investing the grim arithmetic of World War I slaughter with the innocence of the seaside show – but something, still, of the stylized subversiveness of the *commedia dell'arte* and its antique sources.

In the curious history of the *commedia* and its progeny, cross-overs between popular and high are characteristic. It is clear, furthermore, that not only was the *commedia* itself formalized in the same era as opera and pastoral tragicomedy, but that significant links existed between all these different forms. Early opera was often

[47] The earliest depiction is of the player Giuseppe Giratoni, in an engraving of the 1670s.

[48] In XVIII, coincidentally, sophisticated interest in the *commedia* partly reflects a new interest in artistic improvisation, which in turn feeds into the Romantic cult of spontaneity, but equally into unexpected new connections with antiquity. 'Classical scholars, travel writers and novelists all joined the fray over whether the improvvisatore was or was not the modern incarnation of the ancient rhapsode': Esterhammer (2008) 59.

[49] One example in England was Ernest Dowson's verse play, *Pierrot of the Minute* (1897), illustrated by Beardsley (in whose own work Pierrot is a recurrent figure). History of Pierrot: Storey (1978).

[50] The Debureau figure, 'Baptiste' (played by Jean-Louis Barrault), has a central role in Marcel Carné's 1945 film, *Les Enfants du Paradis*.

set in an pastoral-idyllic world, where 'music was natural';[51] it was disseminated across Italy, and Europe, by travelling companies modelled on the *commedia* troupes. At the Medici wedding at the Uffizi Palace in 1589, *commedia dell'arte* and its more formal, humanistic cousin, *commedia erudita*, were performed in parallel on the same stage on different nights, with the proto-operatic *intermedi* staged betweeen the acts.[52] In Venice, Andrea Calmo's *Egloghe pastorali* (1553) combined a bucolic subject with farcical comedy and 'prototypes of *commedia dell'arte* masks'; in Ferrara, Torquato Tasso's pastoral drama *Aminta* was performed (for the Ferrarese court) by a *commedia* troupe in 1573.[53] It comes as less of a surprise, then, to find, down the centuries, the *commedia* exerting influence on the 'high' comedy of, even, Molière[54] – as on the refined, dream-like pictorial world of Watteau's *fêtes galantes*, which bring together images of leisured aristocrats, classical statuary, pipe-playing rustics, and *commedia*, or *commedia*-derived, performance.[55]

After industrialization, popular performance, at its most informal in its earlier association with carnival festivities, has a more organized character – and most amply in Britain, where the industrial revolution begins, and then in the USA.[56] In the wake of its own massive industrialization after the Civil War, America eventually becomes the popular-cultural capital of the world; by the end of World War I, American dominance in popular music and dance is unmistakable, as (thanks to Hollywood) it soon becomes in popular film. In theatrical entertainment, however, this dominance is less clear-cut – and perhaps partly because it is in the theatrical sphere that European, and especially British, institutions had already developed their own popular forms, generations before. Among these forms, in any event, classical-related entertainments figure prominently.

In Paris, where the Pierrot mimes of Debureau and his successors maintained an echo of ancient performance, the *opéras-bouffes* of Jacques Offenbach established a more direct classical connection. Formally trained at the Paris Conservatoire and,

51 The words of the Florentine music-theorist Giovanni Battista Doni: *Trattato della musica scenica* (1635), ch. 6. That reading of the idyllic, along with opera itself, was savaged by Nietzsche (n. 31 above).

52 Andrews (1999) 287–8.

53 Ibid. 295–6.

54 Esp. on his minor characters: see generally Jolibert (1999), Wadsworth (1987). Molière himself is associated with a new set of artistic hybrids: his *Psyché* (1671), a 'tragedy-ballet' (composed in collaboration with Corneille, Quinault, and Lully), contributed to the development of French opera, while his *Les fâcheux* ('The Bores', 1661) was an experiment in spectacular 'comedy-ballet'.

55 Cf. Crow (1985) 45–74.

56 By contrast, classicizing at the popular level, throughout the industrial age, seems to be most limited in Germany (cf. n. 8 above), where 'popular' overwhelmingly means 'German-folk', as already in the influential collections of folk-songs (Brentano and von Arnim, *Des Knaben Wunderhorn*: 1806–8) and folk-tales (the brothers Grimm, *Kinder- und Hausmärchen*: from 1812). Counter-instances include examples of anti-classicizing, like the ballad on the Battle of the Teutoburg Forest ('Als die Römer frech geworden') by Joseph Viktor von Scheffel (1847), commemorating the German victory over the Romans by Arminius ('Hermann'), a significant figure in German consciousness since the early modern period.

for a time, *chef d'orchestre* at the eminently respectable Comédie-Française,[57] Offenbach pioneered a more subversive mode of musical comedy. His first full-length operetta, *Orpheus in the Underworld* (*Orphée aux invers*, 1858), was a burlesque treatment of the Orpheus myth, which for good measure parodied a range of classical-related idioms, from the stylized performance poses of the Comédie-Française to the 'poetic' emotion of high opera (Gluck, among others).[58] Along with Orpheus' humiliation as violinist-composer, Eurydice's metamorphosis into a Bacchante, a parade of party-goers in togas (based on Gustave Doré's iconic illustrations of Dante's Virgil), and a rousing *galop infernal* (can-can) as send-off – all this made for a truly carnivalesque inversion of high-cultural norms. Offenbach's subsequent work included other classical-subject pieces (*Daphnis et Chloé*, 1860; *La belle Hélène*, 1864), but, overall, developed the operetta form rather than the classical connection.

In Britain, theatre figured prominently among the earliest sites (and sights) of mass entertainment in the newly industrialized era. Here we meet new categories of classical reception, which, like Offenbach's *Orphée*, appropriate earlier receptions along with aspects of antiquity itself. In early-Victorian London, a significant figure was the English-born antiquarian and playwright-librettist J. R. Planché, an influence on W. S. Gilbert's comic opera and a notable contributor to the development of the distinctive British pantomime.[59] Among his other achievements, Planché brought classical burlesque to the popular stage in the form of musical extravaganzas on mythological subjects which targeted classical texts and (like Offenbach's operetta again) elite classicism too. In this spirit, *Telemachus, or The Island of Calypso* (1834) travestied Homer's *Odyssey* and Fénelon's still current novella, *The Adventures of Telemachus*.[60]

In the age of Planché and Offenbach, *tableaux vivants*, or 'living pictures', appeared on the British music-hall circuit in the form of actresses posing in imitation of Academic classical-subject paintings. The genre maintained its appeal for decades. In the 1890s, *tableaux* were given top billing by London's Palace Theatre of Varieties and, for a time, were among the most successful acts to be produced on the

[57] Founded by Louis XIV in 1680, and thus the world's longest-established theatre company, the Comédie-Française was initially associated with the classic (XVII) French repertoire, and (despite many changes and contestations) has retained its establishment status ever since.

[58] E.g. the operetta quotes snatches of the aria 'Che farò senza Euridice?', from Gluck's *Orfeo ed Euridice* (1762), 3. 1.

[59] Pantomime was an established popular entertainment on the London stage by early XVIII, and by mid-XIX approximated to its modern form: light-hearted enactments of, usually, nursery stories, sometimes in light verse (Planché's speciality), with stock roles (comedian, transvestite dame, principal 'boy') and a seasonal connection with Christmas. In its earlier incarnation, however, its repertoire included a loosely 'classical' *mélange* of spectacle, myth, mimetic dance, and Harlequin mime (while its authors included such notable literary figures as Lewis Theobald). Even in that earlier form, though, pantomime had only a tenuous connection with the ancient popular form of the same name – which, conversely, seems to have been one of the sources of the modern ballet: Hall (2008b).

[60] *Les aventures de Télémaque, fils d' Ulysse* (1699). Planché: Hall (1999).

late-Victorian popular stage.[61] By the turn of the century, however, *tableaux* had given way to *poses plastiques*, or 'living statues', whose success culminated in a 1906 performance of 'La Milo' at the London Pavilion, in which an actress wore long black gloves against a black background to imitate the armless effect of the Venus de Milo. In large part, the popularity of these shows was undoubtedly due to the illusion of female nudity created by tight-fitting body stockings (fleshings),[62] and around the same period the classicizing male body, too, began to exert a similar sort of appeal, at the onset of the 'physical culture' movement of body-building. The pioneer of the movement and the notable performer who turned the fashion into popular art was the German, Eugen Sandow. Professional strong-man and weight-lifter, Sandow went on to make a successful career out of a stage show that toured Europe and America, where spectators flocked to see him pose as Greco-Roman statues (muscles and all) like the Farnese Hercules and the Dying Gaul.[63] When appropriate, Sandow sported a high-Renaissance fig-leaf, thus himself evoking earlier classicism, as well as ancient archetypes.

Yet another example of theatrical classicizing was the toga play or Roman-subject melodrama, characterized by sensational plot lines and spectacular staging. Toga plays too attracted large audiences across Britain and the USA.[64] Many adapted story lines from well-known historical novels – Lew Wallace's *Ben-Hur* (1880), Henryk Sienkiewicz's *Quo Vadis?* (1896) – along with historically-authentic sets and costumes from Academic history painting. This is a particularly clear example of a pervasive tendency in the classicizing entertainments of this era (and, equally, the novels that some of them rely on). These various works are produced in a culture within which knowledge of the classical world is associated primarily with an elite educational system; for non-elite groups without access to traditional modes of education or transmission, classical reference is at least as likely to be mediated through earlier receptions as taken directly from an original source.[65]

The most commercially successful toga play was *The Sign of the Cross* (1895), written by British actor-manager Wilson Barrett and focused on the violent interaction of paganism and Christianity under the Roman empire. Its popularity, though, was due to its sensational staging of Christian persecution rather than to any exploration of religious conflict. In the same vein, the Theatre Royal's 1902 *Ben-Hur* relied on pageantry and the spectacle produced by a panorama of Jerusalem, the interior of a Roman slave galley, and a chariot race with twenty-two horses. In America, the popularity of spectacle generated another wave of Roman-inspired

61 Barrow (2010).

62 Victorian popular theatre favoured eroticized display of the female body: Davis (1991).

63 Wyke (1997b).

64 Barrow (2010).

65 Hence, such 'receptions' are not always receptions *of antiquity* in any strict sense: cf. Goldhill (2007a) 263–4 on the Coen brothers' 2000 film, *O Brother, Where Art Thou?* At the opposite pole, the specific allusions in (say) Pope's *Dunciad* (1743) or the studied deviations from classical norms in XVI mannerist art (cf. Shearman 1967) assume a classically informed readership/viewership.

entertainment in Barnum and Bailey's circus shows and Kiralfy's extravaganzas, *The Fall of Babylon* and *Nero, or The Fall of Rome*, while, on New York's Coney Island, James Pain's firework display, set against a painted backdrop and stage set, recreated the eruption of Vesuvius and the destruction of Pompeii.[66]

As popular entertainment, Victorian spectacle can be read as a cultural form positioned against high art, and especially against 'serious' theatre and its growing interest in Greek drama[67] – with each offering contrasting modes of expression and audience demographics; the same might be said of the *commedia dell'arte* and the *commedia erudita* of an earlier age. By way of qualification, though, recent studies have shown that in the nineteenth-century entertainment industry, in Britain at least, cultural categories were not fixed and audience class boundaries were readily breached. In particular, London's West End venues were patronized by a socially varied clientele 'ranging from almost the bottom of the social scale to the very top'.[68] A similar capacity to appeal to a wide audience demographic was apparent in twentieth-century culture, where encounters with the classical world were often (as they are often, still) mediated through cinematic presentations. Spectacular display and sensational treatment of Roman themes are transposed directly into early cinema, which, like the toga play, draws freely on historical novels. Edward Bulwer Lytton's *The Last Days of Pompeii* (1834) was made into an Italian short in 1908 and a feature-length film (directed by Mario Caserini) in 1913. Hollywood imitated silent Italian cinema for historical features like D. W. Griffith's *Intolerance* (1916), whose 'Fall of Babylon' sequence looked back to constructions of Roman decadence favoured in popular performance. Then, in Hollywood's 'golden era', classical themes continued to provide compelling subjects, as with Cecil B. DeMille's adaptation of Barrett's *The Sign of the Cross* (1932).

In this same era, the first great age of the Hollywood musical can claim a measure of continuity with the classical. From the 1890s, theatrical musical comedy in England and (increasingly) America supplanted burlesque and operetta as the dominant popular musical-theatrical form, with plots[69] endlessly reworking the ancient New Comedy formula: a quest for love (usually in the boy-meets/loses/finds-girl sequence), a coherent social setting, a set of more-or-less sympathetic central characters, an action propelled (in the tradition of Shakespearean comedy and its ancient sources) by coincidences and misunderstandings – *and* song and dance, which had been a constituent part of Greek New Comedy, though not of most of its derivatives. The transference of the musical to the cinema offered opportunities for what might reasonably be seen as an intuitive reconstitution of classical stylization. Thus the

[66] Malamud (2001), Yablon (2007). The ultimate prototype of Pain's spectaculars – but more aristocratic than popular – was the late-XVIII European fashion for artificial volcanoes (the most famous, at Wörlitz, belonged to Prince Leopold Friedrich Franz von Anhalt-Dessau): Brodey (2008) 125–8.

[67] Cf. Macintosh (1997), (2008a).

[68] Kennedy (2004) 21; cf. Nield (2004) 94–5.

[69] I.e. those *with* plots; many musicals, on screen and esp. on stage, were looser assemblages ('revues') without continuous action.

archetypal Hollywood musical (and representative commercial hit) of the 1930s, *Top Hat* (1935), combines a recognisably comedy-of-errors romantic plot with some strikingly classicizing Art Deco sets (overseen by Van Nest Polglase) and the meticulous precision of Irving Berlin's music and the dancing of Ginger Rogers and Fred Astaire. On stage (but also on screen) a generation later, the musical-dramatic experiments of American composer-lyricist Stephen Sondheim – themselves intermittently attached to classical-subject material[70] – represent yet another cross-over, with Sondheim's successsive attempts to convert musical comedy into something altogether more 'high'.[71]

The 1950s and 1960s heyday of Hollywood epic cinema was defined by big budgets, large casts, exotic locations, and dramatic historical stories, in a suitably heroic attempt to divert audiences away from the new medium of television. Familiar narratives – *Quo Vadis?* (1951) and *Ben-Hur* (1959) – co-existed with new retellings of Roman history, like *Cleopatra* (1963), which looked back to Shakespeare, and *Spartacus* (1960), based on Howard Fast's Marxian novel of 1951. Elaborate sets and costumes assured the viewer of historical verisimilitude, although – as Barthes's essay on Mankiewicz's *Julius Caesar* (1953) points out – the visual signifiers of Roman-ness do not necessarily derive from ancient sources at all.[72] In Britain, meanwhile, the classical was appropriated, rather, as comedy, notably in the bawdy innuendo of the low-budget films *Carry on Cleo* (1964) and *Up Pompeii* (1971), which not only travesty ancient Rome, but parody the high expenditure and pseudo-authenticities of their Hollywood predecessors. *Up Pompeii* (both the film and an earlier BBC TV series) was also noteworthy for its prominent use of a figure ('Lurcio') closely modelled on the Plautine trickster slave. Versions of this Plautine figure – masterful, but, in social terms, precisely not a 'master' – have now graced a wide range of popular fictions in the English-speaking world, from P. G. Wodehouse's 'gentleman's gentleman' Jeeves to Sondheim's Pseudolus in the Broadway musical, *A Funny Thing Happened on the Way to the Forum*.[73]

On the screen, mythological Greece has figured too. It was the subject of 1950s Italian *peplum* B-movies, which starred professional bodybuilders, *à la* Sandow, often in the role of Hercules/Heracles. By contrast, Hollywood's *Jason and the Argonauts* (1963) and *Clash of the Titans* (1981) converted myth into fantasy, with much use of special effects, while, in televisual culture, myth became science-fiction in the two American cult series of the 1990s, *Hercules: The Legendary Journeys* and *Xena:*

[70] From *A Funny Thing Happened on the Way to the Forum* (1962; film version, 1966) to an adaptation of Aristophanes' *Frogs* (2004) (on which: Gamel 2007).

[71] E.g. *Pacific Overtures* (1976) used conventions derived from Japanese *kabuki* theatre to dramatize the opening of Japan to the West.

[72] 'The Romans in Films' in Barthes (1957) identifies the fringed hairstyles of the male characters as a distinctively cinematic creation of Roman identity.

[73] Jeeves first appeared (with his ineffectual young master Bertie Wooster) in *The Man with Two Left Feet* (1917). Sondheim: n. 70 above. These and many other English-language 'servile' figures are apolitical. Contrast the truculently anti-aristocratic Figaro in Beaumarchais's *Le mariage de Figaro* (1784).

Warrior Princess. The more recent resurgence of the Hollywood epic, signalled by the box-office success of *Gladiator* in 2000, followed by *Troy* (2004), *Alexander* (2004), and *300* (2007), relies on the familiar treatment of classical subjects as authenticating spectacle, but now enhanced by digital imaging and computer graphics. Yet again, though, antiquity is mediated through a mixture of original source and earlier reception: *Gladiator*'s director, Ridley Scott, cited paintings by nineteenth-century Academic artists Jean-Léon Gérôme and Lawrence Alma-Tadema as particular inspirations.[74]

As mainstream entertainment, television series and Hollywood movies fit squarely into the category of popular culture, but art cinema and its classicizing films – Cocteau's *Orphée* (1950), Godard's *Le mépris* (1963), Pasolini's *Medea* (1969), Fellini's *Satyricon* (1969), Jarman's *Sebastiane* (1976) – cannot be so easily categorized. On any reading, art cinema's aesthetic-intellectual agenda – though deployed in the same medium as the Hollywood blockbuster – is 'high'; and the cinematic outcomes certainly attract a different audience. Like their more popular counterparts, though, art films reference both antique sources and later receptions: Jarman invokes St Ambrose from late antiquity and Guido Reni from the Baroque; Fellini looks back to Petronius and Pompeian art, but also to earlier cinematic representations of Roman decadence.

Despite its high profile in our own time, cinema has no monopoly on the popular reception of classical subjects. Historical fiction – from the Greek-inspired novels of Mary Renault to Lindsey Davis's Roman detective series – has put imaginative re-creations of antiquity on the best-selling lists,[75] while Robert Harris's *Pompeii* (2003) received scholarly commendation for its author's extensive research. Vulcanology, Roman engineering, Latin texts, and Pompeian archaeology are among his points of reference, but (once again) Harris also evokes earlier incarnations of Pompeii – with the climactic eruption of Vesuvius recalling sensational recreations by Lytton, Pain, and early cinema. Casual allusions in other popular forms follow the same trajectory. The tradition of reference to the iconic Venus de Milo – once prominent in the world of *poses plastiques* – is revived in the lyrics of American popular song: 'Venus de Milo was noted for her charms. | Strictly between us, | You're cuter than Venus, | And what's more, you've got arms'.[76] The reference is loosely to antiquity (where 'Venus' exercised her 'charms'), but more specifically to the statue's familiar 'modern' condition (armless).

The scope of popular culture has always been wide and, arguably, has got wider, across the Western world, with each successive challenge – democratizing,

[74] See variously (cinema): Blanshard and Shahabudin (2011), Joshel *et al.* (2001), Paul (2013), Theodorakopoulos (2010), Winkler (2001), Wyke (1997a); and (cinema and television) Renger and Solomon (2012).

[75] Graphic fiction, too, deserves a mention, esp. the internationally popular *Astérix* (Goscinny and Uderzo), set in Caesar's Gaul and first published as a French comic in 1959: Braden (2010), Hull (2010).

[76] 'Love Is Just Around the Corner', words by Leo Robin, 1934; introduced by Bing Crosby in that year; successfully revived by the Four Freshmen in 1956.

mass-producing, consumerizing, globalizing, digitizing[77] – to traditional hierarchies, social and cultural. Deco art (§11), at its commercial peak in the late 1920s and earlier 1930s, makes the point. The more or less recognisable derivatives of ancient sculptural forms that defined many Art Deco ornaments, as well as the countless variations on classical (among other) patterning that figured profusely in the architectural stylization of skyscrapers, cinemas, airports, and factories, belonged to a universal design language that transcended barriers of education and class. One of the most familiar 'classical' revivals of the last hundred (plus) years makes the point in a different way. Baron Pierre de Coubertin founded the modern Olympic Games – first formally institutionalized in Athens, in 1896 – as 'the restoration of an idea that is two thousand years old'. 'The Olympism of ancient Hellas,' he declared, 'has re-emerged'.[78] And it was an integral part of his vision of 're-emergence' that the 'Olympist' performers should be cultivated 'gentlemen' (therefore, of course, amateurs – and male), and their public likewise: 'games for the élite: an élite of contestants . . . an élite of spectators.'[79] The socio-cultural realities of the contestants in today's Olympics, and of the mass public that follows them, especially on television, are very different. The Games remain – or, rather, have become – elite in respect of athletic professionalism; in every other respect, they exercise 'popular' appeal, across the social spectrum, world-wide.

The long history of cross-overs and convergences does not, indeed, entitle us to play down the differences between popular and elite in general, or popular and elite uses of antiquity in particular. Likewise, while still insisting on their 'popular-classical' kinship, we should certainly acknowledge the distinction between continuations (survivals, 'reflexes'), as in carnival and the *commedia dell'arte*, and receptions (direct or indirect), in fiction, film, and elsewhere. The popular receptions assume the same complex intertextuality as their elite cultural counterparts and, like them, draw on a diverse but still recognisable range of sources. For such receptions (but *not* for popular reflexes, as such), the fact of recognition itself is of prime significance. It is the privileged position accorded to the classical that makes its multiple receptions possible, both in high culture and the popular domain, and (underpinning that privilege) the canonical status of Greek and Roman texts and art objects on which the recognisability of the classical depends. It is no coincidence, though, that so many of the popular receptions involve subversion in the form of parody or burlesque. These are modes of response that (unlike the expansive 'intertextuality' of critical theory)[80] require at least some general sense of the

[77] In the sphere of digital entertainments, there is now a well-established subgenre of classical-subject video games: Lowe (2009). Cf. §17 n. 81.

[78] Quoted in Young (1984) 67.

[79] Ibid. 57. The much-discussed discrepancy (ibid. *passim*) between Coubertin's assumptions about antiquity and the less tidy realities of ancient athletics is another matter.

[80] In Kristeva's foundational understanding of intertextuality, *all* literature (or art) is equally and substantively intertextual: 'every text is the absorption and transformation of other texts' (Kristeva 1969: 146).

primary reference, but also some sense that the reference point is *worth* referring to and *worth* subverting – because fashionable, or established and canonical, or both.

Meanwhile, though, the repeated evidence of interaction between elite and popular, high and low, indicates that the relationship between the categories – in terms of provenance, properties, and value – even if, indeed, broadly contrastive and oppositional, is not necessarily one of incompatible opposites. It is *not* a given that popular receptions of antiquity (or popular reflexes of antiquity, either) are at odds with elite art, literature, thought, as such. This is one of those cases where today's theoretical debates can surely profit from the perspective of the classical tradition and its distinctive developments.

§13

Languages and Language

Our special concern is with the classical tradition in Italy, France, Germany, and the English-speaking world. Accordingly, we are concerned with the relationships between the four languages, Italian, French, German, and English, and the languages of classical antiquity. However, given the huge presence of Medieval and Renaissance Latin in the cultural history of the West, the 'classical' languages with which our four are, in different degrees, bound up cannot be restricted to antiquity, in the strict sense. Conversely: given both this huge presence and the special relationship to Latin (classical and post-classical) of Italian, French, and (less directly) English too, Latin-centred developments will be prominent in this section, but their Greek equivalents, for once, much less.

In this connection we note that, while – from the standpoint of Western classical education, or indeed of Roman antiquity – 'the classical languages' comprise a unity, there is no underlying entity referable to that label. There is, rather, a connection by privilege of two independent languages, first in the Western empire (but much less in the Greek-speaking East), then again, on more or less the same terrain, in and after the Renaissance. In historical-linguistic terms – within the Indo-European language family – Greek and Latin have no special relationship: they share certain archaic traits, especially in grammar, chiefly because both are attested early, whereas many branches of the family (Germanic, for instance) are not attested until much later, giving them far longer to lose their inherited archaisms.

The distinctive trajectories in the development of our four languages, along with the special status of Latin in successive phases of Western culture,[1] constitute a

[1] Overviews of Italian: Migliorini and Griffith (1984), Serianni and Trifone (1993–4). French: Chaurand (1999), Tritter (1999). German: Bach (1970). English, Hogg *et al.* (1992–2001), Mugglestone (2006). Medieval Latin: Mantello and Rigg (1996). Neo-Latin, Ijsewijn (1990). See also Herman (1990), Solodow (2010).

The Classical Tradition: Art, Literature, Thought, First Edition. Michael Silk, Ingo Gildenhard, and Rosemary Barrow.

Published 2017 by John Wiley & Sons Ltd.

central aspect of the classical tradition. The significance of Latin in, especially, Medieval and Renaissance Europe is widely discussed and well understood; it figures in all accounts of the tradition in these periods. The development of the vernaculars, though, is not always given significant acknowledgement in this connection, and in recent treatments is often elided altogether. There are two reasons for this: a shift across the humanities away from language;[2] and the reluctance, among classically trained champions of the classical tradition above all, to consider reflexes, along with receptions – even when (as is the case with language) reflexes, of Latin in particular, are important facts of cultural history in their own right and important factors in the development of literature and thought.

In the Roman empire, at the start of the Christian millennium, Latin and Greek are privileged, not only as native languages of the two heartlands of that world, but as instruments of practical communication across the empire, and as the acknowledged culture languages of civilized humanity. All other contact languages are marginalized, whether themselves culture-languages (like, say, Egyptian) or not – like the Celtic languages or the Germanic. The Celtic languages were once spoken over much of Europe, including large parts of the empire; Germanic speakers lived largely outside the imperial provinces until, in a rapid series of migrations, several of their disparate tribes overran the western territories in the fifth and early sixth centuries, only to adopt the vernacular Latin of various of these territories in due course. That 'vernacular Latin', traditionally known as 'Vulgar Latin', the language (in whatever versions) of the uneducated masses, had been marginalized too. It had no status and no formal expression. We know it from aberrant spellings in inscriptions or aberrant usages in late-antique documents, from Pompeian graffiti, from partial representations in Plautine comedy and Petronian satire, from forbidden forms listed by Roman grammarians[3] – and, at one remove, from the Romance languages, which are its (more or less) direct descendants.[4]

[2] Notwithstanding the growth of scientific linguistics and a preoccupation with *meta*-linguistic issues in much recent philosophy. Cf. p. 187 below.

[3] Also from broad indications, in late antiquity and soon after, of discrepancies between standard and vernacular Latin – like Augustine's preference for 'popular' over 'grammatical' usage ('melius est reprehendant nos grammatici quam non intellegant populi': *Enarratio in Psalmum 138*, 20) and St Columban's contrast of 'Latin' ('Latine') and 'your mode of speech' ('vestrae idiomate linguae') in a letter to the Italian Pope Boniface IV, in 613 (*pace* e.g. Frank-Job 2003: 22). In classical antiquity, conversely, Quintilian distinguishes 'grammatical' from 'Latin' ('grammatice'/ 'Latine'): *Institutio Oratoria*, 1. 6. 27.

[4] 'More or less': summary of discrepancies between Vulgar Latin (VL) and Romance in Posner (1996) 98–103. The notion of VL, current for over a century (von Ettmayer 1916: 2. 1. 231–80), has been challenged as too tidy. It tends to imply a simple opposition between a monolithic 'high' (represented by most classical Latin texts) and a monolithic 'low' – whereas, at either end of the spectrum, 'Latin, like any natural language, was an amalgam of varieties, not [a] homogeneous monolith': Lodge (1993) 35; further, Clackson and Horrocks (2007) 227–302. The objection reflects good sociolinguistic principle, but is perverse in practice: the truth is this way round; and given that most of the variabilities have disappeared, and that nothing (except linguistic clumsiness) is gained by talking of (e.g.) 'varieties of sub-elite Latin' (ibid.), the choice lies between simplification and silence. *Pace* Clackson and Horrocks (2007) 231, VL is still accepted by linguistic specialists (with the appropriate qualification about varieties): e.g. Adams (2003) xxii, 765; Baldi (2002) 29; Herman (2000), with Wright's comments on p. ix.

After the collapse of the Western empire, vernaculars were marginalized, under new circumstances, by a new form of Latin, once again. While the spiritual significance of Greek and Hebrew for Western Christendom lent both a notional high status (however few the individuals who knew any of either), effective authority was vested in the third 'sacred' language: the language of the Vulgate Bible, the official medium of the Church,[5] and the language of continuity with the lapsed *Imperium Romanum*. However, this Latin – 'Medieval Latin' – though itself a spectrum of different versions, and essentially a written medium, was seldom, if ever, a close match for the Latin of the surviving classical texts. It was and remained a 'cultural artefact',[6] and no-one's first language, but compared with the language of Roman antiquity, its structures were simpler, its syntax, idioms, and lexicon in part new, and its detail open to influence from the specific vernacular habits of the user. In particular, its features were assimilated to at least some of the characteristics of the emergent Romance with which it co-existed for centuries in a kind of equilibrium, for as long as the various versions of emergent Romance were perceived as merely 'corrupt' versions of Latin itself.[7]

By the end of the first millennium AD, large parts of the former Roman empire in the West were thus, in effect, diglossic. The official, cross-national *lingua franca* of the educated was (Medieval) Latin.[8] In what had once been, approximately, Roman Italia, Hispania, and Gallia, the unofficial proto-national vernaculars were the various reflexes of Vulgar Latin.[9] Unregulated and largely unrecognised, these vernaculars were by now early versions of what would become the recognised languages of Western Europe: Italian, Spanish, French. All of these will have existed in and alongside multiple dialectal forms, some of which would themselves one day attain a distinct status (Portuguese, Catalan, Occitan),[10] while in due course others would give way to the pressures of standardization from the dominant versions. The now well-known Romance vernaculars must have been distinct already – though the details and datings are disputed[11] – but their official emergence was undoubtedly delayed (and modern interpretation complicated) both by the dominant position

5 The Vulgate was begun by Jerome in late IV and completed in/around VIII; Latin was also the language of the Church Fathers, saints' lives, the liturgy, theological exegesis and doctrine.

6 Clackson and Horrocks (2007) 302.

7 Though Wright's contention (1982) that, until the Carolingian reforms, Medieval Latin and Romance *only* differed as written versus spoken codes of 'the same' language is hardly credible.

8 The expression 'lingua franca' is itself medieval. It originally signified a hybridized Italian employed in the Levant, but, in effect, meant 'European language' – assuming the earlier (Islamic etc.) equation of 'Franks' with '(Catholic) Europeans', from the experience of the Crusades (led initially by, among others, French nobles who claimed descent from Charlemagne).

9 Influenced, variously, by the languages of their conquerors. French, most obviously, took words from Frankish.

10 The last best represented, in literary terms, by Provençal. Reflexes of VL in other areas of former Roman territory include Romanian (now spoken in – roughly – what once was Roman Dacia, but perhaps the outcome of migrations of proto-Romance speakers from the former Roman provinces of Moesia and Illyricum).

11 Though Latin was differentiated, regionally, from an early date: Adams (2007).

of Medieval Latin and by the more or less perceptible continuities between each and Latin itself.[12] 'Official emergence', we suggest, should be measured not least by written literary production; and in this period, certainly, evidence for any such vernacular literature is thin in the extreme.

In this same period, Germany – here as elsewhere – was different. In the latter part of the first millennium, the prestige language was indeed Latin. This was the language of the Carolingian court,[13] and the court took its Latin seriously: it was part of the Carolingian project to 'reform' it by nudging it closer to ancient norms, but hardly to champion the German dialects, for literary purposes or any other.[14] Even so, a perceived need to communicate with a wider public generates a notable instance of self-conscious vernacular-Christian poetry as early as the ninth century, in the shape of Otfrid von Weissenburg's *Gospel Book* (*Evangelienbuch*). Anticipating Dante's great experiment in the promotion of native Italian by several hundred years, this poem (also the earliest surviving German work of any significance to use the new, and non-classical, feature of rhymed verse) proclaims at the outset the propriety of disseminating the Christian message in the language of the people ('Of Christ we sung, in our own tongue').[15]

By the end of the twelfth century, writing in German is the norm. To the decades around 1200 belong a diversity of works, some essentially 'native', others influenced, directly or indirectly, by the classics. Surviving works include: the *Nibelungenlied* (retelling inherited pagan myth); Wolfram von Eschenbach's *Parzival* (doing the same for the Christian-Celtic Grail legend); the lyrics of Walther von der Vogelweide; Albrecht von Halberstadt's *Metamorphosen* (based on Ovid); and Heinrich von Veldeke's *Eneide* – a verse narrative (based partly on the Old French adaptation of Virgil's *Aeneid*, the *Roman d'Eneas*) which combined the tale of Virgil's Trojan hero with a celebration of the birth of Christ under Augustan Rome, and a reading of Augustus himself as precursor of Frederick I (Barbarossa), Holy Roman Emperor (1155–90). With its majestic linkages, this last work sums up the new authority of the German language in its own domain – in the very act of acknowledging the authority of antiquity (pagan and Christian) on the literary-intellectual level. With or without reliance on Latin tradition, though, and notwithstanding lexical borrowings from Latin,[16] the status of the German language is now established reality. As an assertion of linguistic authority, Luther's Bible translations, three centuries later, represent – irrespective of their new and momentous theological (and political)

[12] The end-of-millennium situation of emergent Modern Greek is comparable. An archaizing version of the Greek language, Byzantine Greek (roughly equivalent to Medieval Latin in the West), coexisted with the vernacular descendant(s) of the *koine*, which eventually (as vernaculars usually do) supplanted it, albeit in modified form, as the standard language (§7 n. 13).

[13] The Carolingians 'asserted their legitimacy by continuing to legislate in Latin'; 'the sacred language was also the language of imperial power': Smith (2005) 37–8.

[14] E.g. the vernacular alliterative poem *Muspilli* (?IX) survives in one fragmentary version, written in the spaces of a work of Latin theology. Carolingian language reforms: Edelstein (1965).

[15] 'Wir Kriste sungun | in unsera zungun': 1. 1. 125.

[16] See n. 36 below.

significance – the logical culmination of such earlier developments; and the respect of the learned for classical Latin, in Luther's age and beyond, has limited significance. Latinate vocabulary indeed augments the language of learned and academic usage; there are even apparent cases of grammatical borrowing; but the essential continuity of German is unaffected.[17]

The course of the English language, and of English literature in relation to it, is different again, though for a time both run parallel to developments in Germany. During the fifth and sixth centuries, most of the former Roman province of Britannia is settled by Germanic-speaking invaders, whose various dialects supplant both the native 'British' (Celtic) dialects (hereafter restricted to the 'fringe' areas of Cornwall, Wales, and Scotland)[18] and the Latin that was once the elite language of the former province. Unlike Germany, then (where Germanic dialects, in effect, survived intact), or Italy, Spain, and France (where the Germanic invaders adopted local versions of Vulgar Latin), England was settled by Germanic invaders whose languages (collectively, 'Old English') were imposed on the native population. In the process, whatever Vulgar Latin had once existed disappeared, along with more formal versions.[19]

The subsequent history of Old English up to the Norman Conquest is a story of complex accommodations of closely related dialects, further accommodations with the versions of Scandinavian Germanic introduced by Viking settlers (largely in the ninth century), and – meanwhile – the reintroduction of Latin, in the form of Medieval Latin, in the wake of the Roman mission of St Augustine in 597. At the end of the first millennium, therefore, the situation in England is akin to that in Germany: the native language (versions of Old English) is Germanic; the high-status *lingua franca* for ecclesiastical and some other educated use is Medieval Latin;[20] and the divide is reflected in a diversity of literary production, from the pagan epic *Beowulf* (written down around the end of the tenth century, but largely composed centuries before) to Bede's *History of Christianity in England* (finished in 731) and Caedmon's *Hymn* (seventh century). Of these: *Beowulf* is in Old English and (notwithstanding the family relationship with, say, Homeric epic) is independent of the

[17] In the humanist period, a new tendency (now standard) to relocate the verb in subordinate clauses to clause-final position is arguably the result of Latin influence: Bach (1970) 286–7, Berić-Djukić (1988). From XVI, German grammars 'translate' German facts into Latin-style declensions etc. (cf. Tavoni *et al.* 1998: 42–3), but the facts are essentially independent of the presentation (though cf. p. 159 below). Latin influence: further, n. 36 below.

[18] Along with Brittany in north-western France, where many displaced 'British' (Celtic) speakers resettled. Celtic-speaking Ireland remained outside the sphere of Germanic penetration (except for Viking incursions, from late VIII), as it had remained outside the Roman empire – albeit, paradoxically, a haven for Latin learning after the fall of the empire itself (§4).

[19] For the British historian Gildas (mid-VI), Latin is still 'lingua nostra', 'our language': *De excidio Britanniae*, 23. Thereafter, such a claim is inconceivable.

[20] Rather differently, Smith (2005) 36: 'Latin and Old English complemented each other as languages of power and authority. Tenth- and early eleventh-century kings and their counsellors legislated in Old English but heard Mass in Latin.' Note, however, the influence of Latin-derived rhetoric on Old English *poetry*: Steen (2008).

classical world; Bede's *History*, like all his known work, is in Latin (*Historia ecclesiastica gentis Anglorum*); Caedmon's Christian poem exists both in vernacular versions and in Latin (the latter quoted by Bede himself).

With the conquest of England by Romance-speaking Normans in the eleventh century, everything changes: 'the Norman invasion . . . was the most important event ever to occur in the outer history of the English language.'[21] For three centuries or so, Norman French is the official language of the country, and for most of this time the effective language of the court, the law, and the upper reaches of the Church. In Church circles the written language remains Latin – but then, the language in which Latin is taught is French;[22] and the cultural authority of the French linguistic presence in England is summed up by the fact that significant works of French literature are apparently composed for its Norman-French speakers (however small their numbers).[23]

By the end of the thirteenth century, native English has begun to reassert itself. Around this time, Robert of Gloucester writes a verse chronicle – in English – praising the ordinary people for their stubborn adherence to their native tongue;[24] by the mid-fourteenth century, John Cornwall, Fellow of Stapledon Hall (now Exeter College) in Oxford lets his pupils construe their Latin in English, not French;[25] in 1362, in the notoriously conservative sphere of the law, English becomes the official language for legal proceedings; and in 1399 the new king, Henry IV, becomes the first monarch since the Conquest to be a native speaker of English. By the late fourteenth century, too, 'English' is coming to mean a new, standardized form of the language, centred on the London dialect,[26] which duly presents itself as something approaching the established norm when printing crosses the Channel a hundred years later.

Yet if, by the end of the fourteenth century, Norman French had effectively disappeared as a spoken language in England, its impact on English itself had been huge. Thanks to the Conquest and its aftermath, the language that now resurfaces is, and will remain, effectively a Germanic-Romance hybrid.[27] In morphology, grammar, and 'grammatical terms' (articles, particles, conjunctions, pronouns), English remains the Germanic language it had been[28] (albeit much simplified morphologically). Lexically, though, English has now absorbed and assimilated large quantities

[21] Millward (1996) 142.

[22] Ibid. 143–4.

[23] Short (1992) 229–49.

[24] *The Metrical Chronicle of Robert of Gloucester*, ed. W. A. Wright (1887), 2. 544 ('lowe men holdeth to engliss').

[25] Rothwell (1968).

[26] Cf. Schaefer (2006).

[27] I.e. impressionistically as opposed to genetically: to a native speaker, impressions outweigh the genetics that are rightly the concern of comparative linguists.

[28] Despite e.g. the spread of French-derived prefixes (like *re*-) and suffixes (like -*able*) onto native lexemes (*re*do, do*able*).

of French loanwords (overwhelmingly of Latin origin), both during the period of initial Norman supremacy and then again in the thirteenth and fourteenth centuries.[29] The impact of the shift is hard to overestimate. It is not just the vocabulary of officialdom that gains general currency ('*Members* of *Parliament* and other *government officers* all *pay taxes* to the *state*').[30] French borrowings penetrate to the deep levels of everyday usage: 'learn some *table manners*'; '*finish* your *dinner*'; '*fresh fruit* and *flowers* at the right *price*'; '*poor people* never get a *second chance*'; 'little and *large*'; '*peace* and *quiet*'; 'true or *false*'; 'stop *cry*ing and don't *touch* your *face*'; 'your *aunt* looks *nice*, but she's *trouble*'; 'I'm *real*ly sorry, but we can't *remember* the *address*'; '*just* ar*ound* the *corner*'; '*use* your *common sense*'; 'what's his *collar size*?'; 'get *moving*'; '*sure* thing'.

In the literary output of late medieval England, the new linguistic accommodation is as marked as a new scope and authority in the literature itself. The *oeuvre* of the poet John Gower – who composes significant works in French (*Le mirour de l'omme*) and Latin (*Vox clamantis*), as well as English ('The Lover's Confession')[31] – indicates an age of transition, but overall the rise of English is unmistakable. To the fourteenth century belongs an impressive range of texts in English, from the Wycliffe Bible and Langland's alliterative *Piers Plowman* to Chaucer's *Troilus and Criseyde* and *The Canterbury Tales*. And if Wycliffe and Langland often recall the Germanic strengths of Old English, Chaucer's more cosmopolitan sophistications epitomize the now distinctive hybridity of the language, just as their narratives look impartially to native traditions, to the emergent literatures of France and Italy, and to the Latin classics beyond. His *Troilus* adapts Boccaccio's *Filostrato*, itself a reworking of a Latin version of the twelfth-century *Roman de Troie* by Benoît de Sainte-Maure. His *Canterbury Tales* rework (besides Boccaccio) such diverse sources as Nicholas Trivet's Anglo-Norman Chronicle (*The Man of Law's Tale*), Dante's *Paradiso* (the invocation to the Virgin in *The Second Nun's Tale*), and Ovid's *Metamorphoses* (*The Manciple's Tale*) – while in *The Physician's Tale* he tells the same story of Virginia, killed by her father to protect her honour, that Shakespeare alludes to in *Titus Andronicus* (§8), derived ultimately from Livy but, in this version, directly from the *Roman de la rose*. In Chaucer's account ('There was, as telleth Titus Livius, | A knight that callèd was Virginius'), French-derived vocabulary serves to give classical reference a Romance, therefore suitably Latin-related, texture. Take the description of Virginia and her virtues:

In hir ne lakkèd no *condicioun*,
That is to *preyse*, as by *discrecioun*.

[29] Some of the later borrowings are from the now prestigious French of Paris and the Île-de-France – see variously Millward (1996) 198–201, Rothwell (2001) 539–59 – but these must still have been mediated by Anglo-French speakers in the first instance.

[30] French-derived items, here and in the examples that follow, in italics.

[31] But with Latin title, *Confessio amantis* – signifying a desire to assert classical authority still: Pearsall (1987). All these works belong to the last three decades of XIV.

As wel in goost as body *chast* was she;
For which she *flourèd* in *virginitee*,
With alle *humilitee* and *abstinence*,
With alle *attemperaunce* and *pacience*,
With *mesure* eek of bering and *array*.
Discreet she was in answering alway;
Though she were wys as Pallas, dar I seyn,
Hir *facound* eek ful wommanly and *pleyn*,
No *countrefeted termes* hadde she
To seme wys.[32]

With or without minor semantic or other adjustment, all but one of these French-derived borrowings survive today (whereas at least two of the 'native' Germanic lexemes do not);[33] the representative modernness of Chaucer's vocabulary is evident.

For some educated users of the language at the time, the now established hybridity was a problem. It still was a century later, when Caxton acknowledged the concern provoked by 'curyous termes' that exceeded the linguistic competence of the common people.[34] Much earlier evidence comes from the monk Ranulph Higden in his Latin *Polychronicon* (*c*. 1327), later translated into English by John Trevisa in the 1380s. Here, the original modes of speech in England (all derived, we learn, from peoples from 'Germania') are said to be under threat. Thanks to population mixtures with Danes and then Normans, 'the language of the country has been corrupted'. The irony that the English version of this claim itself contains three loanwords from French – 'the *contray longage* is *apayr*ed' – seems to have been lost on the translator.[35]

A second irony here is that in due course such hybridity is widely seen as a strength of the language, especially once the Romancifying process reaches a further stage. This comes in the sixteenth and seventeenth centuries in the form of large numbers of more or less learned borrowings from (largely) Latin, designed to meet the perceived needs of Renaissance culture and not least to create equivalents for

[32] *Physician's Tale*, 41–52: 'In her there lacked no condition worthy of praise by (one of) sound judgement. She was chaste in mind as well as body; thus she flourished in virginity with all humility and abstinence, with all temperance and patience, also with moderation in demeanour and dress. She was always discreet in conversation; though, I dare say, she was wise as Pallas, her speech was also quite womanly and plain; she had no (range of) factitious expressions so as to seem wise.' Romance loanwords and classical reference go hand in hand a century earlier in the opening lines of the northern English poem, *Cursor mundi*: 'Man yhernes *rimes* forto here | And *romans* red on *manere* sere – | Of Alisaundur the *conquerour*, | Of Iuly Cesar the *emparour*' ('One likes to hear poems and native-language narratives read in various ways . . .').

[33] The non-survivor on the Romance side is *facound*, 'eloquence' < OF (Old French) *faconde* < Latin *facundia*, compared with (on the Germanic) *ne*, 'not', and *eek*, 'also' (while *goost* ['ghost'] is now obsolete in the sense 'mind').

[34] Prologue to *Eneydos* (1490).

[35] *Contray* < OF *contree* < VL *contrata* (*regio*); *longage* < OF *langage* < VL *lingua* + *-aticum*; *apayr* ['appair'; cf. modern 'impair'] < OF *empeirer* < VL *impeiorare*. Cf. Corrie (2006) 94–5 (but missing the irony).

items featuring in translations from the classics.[36] The new Latinisms include a range of now familiar words, from *expect* and *joke* to *exaggerate* and *industrial*. Like their Latin counterparts, most such items are polysyllabic (*joke* is untypical), in contrast to the increasingly monosyllabic appearance of Germanic English[37] – while the now established French borrowings vary (as our examples suggest) from the Germanic-sounding short (*touch, move, nice, poor*) to the Latinate-sounding long (*patience, virginity*). Many of the Latinate novelties do not survive,[38] but those many that do (we would suggest) owe much of their subsequent acceptance to a sense of the continuity, including the large measure of *syllabic* continuity, between new Latinisms and now established French.[39] And educated English-speakers who now take pride in the hybridity of the language are liable to cite, precisely, its new syllabic range as a strength. An early example is *The Excellencie of the English Tongue* (c. 1595) by Richard Carew, who combats criticisms of the new English by noting, in general, that his countrymen have simply followed the Greeks and Romans in borrowing words from 'either necessitie or convenience' and, in particular, that the new syllabic range makes for a distinctive aesthetic: 'the long words that we borrow, being intermingled with the short of our owne store, make up a perfect harmonie.'[40]

[36] Cf. §15. With the flood of Latin/Romance borrowings into English, contrast the situation in German, where medieval loans into the basic vocabulary come in a slow drip. Among the examples (in modern form): Old High German period, loans shared with other Germanic languages, like *Tisch*, 'dish' (Latin *discus*), *Wall*, 'wall' (*vallum*), but also more specific loans, like *Fenster*, 'window' (*fenestra*), *Pforte*, 'door' (*porta*), *schreiben*, 'write' (*scribere*). Representative later borrowings include (XII), via French, *falsch*, 'false' (*falsus*), *Person* (retaining French word-final accentuation), 'person' (*persona*); XIV/XV, early humanistic, *Fabel*, 'story' (*fabula*), *studieren*, 'study' (*studere*: the German form contains one of the most significant bits of French influence on German, the verbal suffix *–ieren* < French *-ier*, soon added to native stems, as in *halbieren*, 'halve', *stolzieren*, 'strut'). In the generations that follow, conversely, many Latinate (or Greco-Roman) terms enter the lexicon of learning – items like *Advokat* ('lawyer') < Latin 'advocatus', *Medizin* ('medicine') < 'medicina', *Philosophie, Logik, Akademie, Gymnasium*: Bach (1970) 284–5, Polenz (2000) 21. By XVIII, intellectual prose often clusters loanwords. The opening proposition of Herder's first collection of *Fragmente* (1767) is almost as Latinate in his German (for all his preoccupation with Germanness) as its equivalent English (Latin-derived items in italics): 'Der *Genius* der Sprache ist also auch der *Genius* von der *Litteratur* einer *Nation*' ('The *genius* of a *language* is also the *genius* of the *literature* of a *nation*').

[37] Esp. after the widespread loss of inflectional word-endings in Middle English.

[38] Early examples include many of the 'aureate' coinages ('half-chongyd Latyn') by the poet-translator John Lydgate (*c*. 1370–1449): Smith (2006) 124–5.

[39] Pragmatic evidence for this sense of continuity can be found in XVI arguments about Latinate 'inkhorn' terms (below, p. 147). The alternatives offered to such terms by their opponents are not randomly Germanic/French in origin, but heavily Germanic – like Spenser's *spill* (for *perish*), Cheke's *moond* (for *lunatic*), *biword* (for *parable*), Recorde's *threlike* (for *equilateral*), Lever's *endsay* (for *conclusion*), *saywhat* (for *definition*). As with these examples (taken from Millward 1996: 230), it is often the case that the Latinism survives, unlike the Germanicism.

[40] In the 1614 edition of William Camden's *Remains Concerning Britain*, to which Carew's essay was attached: Dunn (1984) 41, 43. Carew was responding to Richard Verstegan's *Restitution of Decayed Intelligence in Antiquities* (1605). Verstegan acknowledged that the English 'delight in strange language-borrowing' (ibid. 206), but applauded, instead, 'words of monosyllable' (ibid. 189) – though willing to use the polysyllabic word *monosyllable* itself. Among later vindications of English hybridity is one by German philologist Jakob Grimm in a speech of 1851 ('a surprisingly intimate alliance of . . . the Germanic and Romance'): Silk (2009a) 9.

The several centuries of French and Latin borrowings not only affected the perceived 'harmonie' of English: they enriched the language with an apparatus of lexical doublets. English now possessed (and possesses) an unusual range of part-synonyms, distinct tonally, even if not otherwise: thus (Romance/Germanic), 'commence'/'begin', 'present'/'gift', 'terrible'/'awful', 'author'/'writer', 'just'/'right', 'people'/'folk', 'necessity'/'need', 'concerning'/'about', 'flower'/'bloom'. More remarkably, the new Latinizing yielded sets of comparable doublets (often semantically differentiated) with earlier French derivatives: thus (Latinized/French), 'probe'/'prove', 'regal'/'royal', 'pallid'/'pale', 'floral'/'flowery', 'fragile'/'frail'. And these multiple developments have momentous implications for the literary language. Among much else, Renaissance and later translations from Latin are able to exercise a degree of verbal continuity with a classical original, and thereby affirm a sense of cultural continuity too. This is summed up by the first line of Dryden's *Aeneid* (1697), with its simple but audible echoes of Virgil's vocabulary, meticulously located in the first and last words:

> *Arms* and the man I sing, who, forced by *fate* . . .
>
> *arma* virumque cano, Troiae qui primus ab oris
> Italiam *fato* profugus . . .[41]

Then again, the composite nature of the English lexicon, and the feeling (still strong today) that Latinate vocabulary is broadly different in tone from – more elevated, or alternatively more formal, than – 'native' words (which by the early modern period effectively includes the older French borrowings), makes possible some of the most decisive moments in the history of the literary language. There is a much-cited instance in Shakespeare's *Macbeth*, 2. 2 (Latinisms italicized):

> Will all great *Neptune's ocean* wash this blood
> Clean from my hands? No, this my hand will rather
> The *multitudinous* seas *incarnadine*,
> Making the green one red.

Macbeth is made to articulate the horror ('blood' on his 'hands') in native Germanic, but the remote hope ('Neptune's ocean') in Latinate-classical, before the horror spreads to the Latinate itself ('multitudinous', 'incarnadine'), then is restated in native terms again ('making . . . red') – with the contrasting syllabic dimensions of the two sets of words integral to the sequential effect as a whole.[42] *Multitudinous* and *incarnadine*: in Shakespeare's age, such learned Latinisms are contemptuously

[41] More abrasively, Milton's version of Horace, *Odes*, 1. 5, begins, 'What slender youth, bedewed with *liquid odours*', for Horace's 'liquidis . . . odoribus'. Cf. §35. Dryden's proto-Augustan English is significantly Latinate too (though less abrasively): 'Poetry requires ornament, and that is not to be had from our old Teuton monosyllables' ('Dedication of the *Aeneis*', 1697).

[42] A rather different reading of these lines and associated issues: Haynes (2003) 40–73.

designated 'inkhorn' terms,[43] without reference to their constructive and creative use in passages like this. By contrast, there is nothing of the inkhorn about Dryden's 'arms' and 'fate' – because they are not recent borrowings, but also because, though Latin-derived (via French), they conveniently uphold the 'native' tendency towards the monosyllabic.

We have given special prominence to English and its developments for several reasons: because their complications and the debates associated with them are distinctive, as is their importance for the trajectory of English poetry (§35); because all of these are the easiest to expound *in* English; and because (by comparison with German, in particular) the additional Romance factor gives these developments a special relevance to the classical tradition. As we look again now at French and Italian, some elements of the story will seem familiar. The one big difference is the more intimate relation between the two Romance languages and Latin (Medieval or Classical) and, in the first instance, the tension between them and Latin, which may be said *both* to have retarded their emergence *and* to have provided them with special creative opportunities.

This emergence, at least, might be supposed to have taken place in an ideology-free zone, remote from issues and debates, below the level of consciousness. This is not exactly the case. Even without consideration of the 'sub-elite' status of Vulgar Latin, it is beyond dispute that, for centuries after the first acknowledgement of Romance, its cultural and social inferiority – in all its versions – is a given. Dante's bold defence of the vernacular in the *De vulgari eloquentia* (*c.* 1303–4) is no rhetorical exercise: vernacular literature is stigmatized as 'barbaric' in at least one Latin text of the same period,[44] and similar scorn is still recorded much later.[45] That 'first acknowledgement' itself is generally agreed to belong to the age of Charlemagne, and specifically to Canon 17 of the Council of Tours (813), whose Latin text calls on the clergy to preach 'in the informal Roman(ce) language' ('rusticam romanam linguam') or else 'in German' ('thiotiscam'), 'so that everyone can understand what is being said more easily'. The declaration not only implies that 'Romance' is now distinct from Latin (and, in its distinctness, on a par with German),[46] but allows the

[43] 'Borrowings of other languages, such . . . as smell of the inkhorn': George Gascoigne ('Certayn Notes of Instruction Concerning the Making of Verse', 1575). For their opponents, inkhorn terms are pedantic; for their supporters, welcome alternatives to mundane vulgarity. Cf. the caricature at Shakespeare's *Love's Labour's Lost*, 5. 1, where Armado impresses the pedant Holofernes with his '*posteriors of the day*, which the rude multitude call the afternoon'. To Holofernes the locution is 'liable, congruent and measurable for *the afternoon*'. After this, and more, Holofernes turns to the humble constable, Dull, noting that 'Thou hast spoken no word all this while'; and Dull, 'Nor understood none neither, sir.'

[44] 'Barbarico' ('hiatu') is used thus – seemingly of French – in an anonymous late-XIII Latin poem: Novati (1905) 298.

[45] Cf. below, pp. 151, 156.

[46] The text actually speaks of 'translating' into 'Romance' and 'German', though Wright (1982) 120–1 and (2002) 142–3 attempts to resist this obvious interpretation of the Latin verb 'transferre' in the interests of arguing for the continuity of Romance and Latin throughout the era. The argument is reasonable, the resistance perverse.

supposition that – as one might in any case infer from the innovatory nature of French, on the phonetic and morphological levels – it is very likely French that *was* the first version of Romance to be clearly distinct.[47]

These surmises are confirmed by another ninth-century text, the Strasbourg Oaths of 842, the earliest document in any Romance language. The narrative frame of this text is in Latin, enclosing 'oaths' in 'teudisca lingua' (German) and 'romana lingua' (Romance), with the latter recognisably a kind of Old French,[48] despite what appear to be archaizing spellings. In a much later age of political contestation between Germany and France, the circumstances of the emergence of French in a Frankish-Germanic-Carolingian context, and, by association, even the name 'French' itself, occasioned some discomfort: 'German spirit in a French form is exactly what the word *français* so precisely expresses, with its German root and Latin suffix' (thus Gaston Paris in 1884).[49] By the end of the first millennium, at all events, our evidence suggests that not only is French distinct from Latin, but that French Romance is distinct from Italian Romance, and that from Latin, too. The Latin epitaph on Gregory V (who died in 999) reports that this Pope, whose native tongue was German ('lingua Teutonicus'), preached in three other languages ('eloquio triplici'): French ('Francisca [voce]'), vernacular Italian ('vulgari [voce]'), and Latin ('voce Latina').[50] Among the scanty and often problematic documents of this period, the earliest candidates for recognisable Old Italian are indeed tenth-century: the 'Veronese riddle' (*c.* 900) and legal texts from the archive at Monte Cassino (960–3).

As yet, though, and for some time to come, the Romance vernaculars are regarded as (literally) substandard: as the informal language of the uneducated and illiterate (*lingua rustica*), of the common people (*vulgaris*), of the laity (*laica*).[51] Latin, by contrast, is the language of education, culture, and the ecclesiastical apparatus; the language of writing and grammatical rules; the ideal language as opposed to all

[47] One consequence of the Carolingian reforms to Latin usage must have been to widen the perceptible distance between Latin and Romance (esp. French Romance?), with the effect that the autonomous existence of the vernacular was harder to ignore: Ricard (1989) 17–19, Wright (1982) 104–44.

[48] Compare e.g. *cadhuna cosa*, 'everything' (< VL 'cata una(m) causa(m)'), with modern French *chaque chose* (and for the suffix cf. *chacune*).

[49] In his journal *Romania* (1884) 626. The preoccupation still surfaces. In his meta-literary narrative collage, *Les ombres errantes* (*The Wandering Shadows*, 2002), novelist Pascal Quignard recalls the beginnings of 'French' history at Soissons in 486, when (as recorded in Gregory of Tours, *Liber historiae Francorum*) the Franks, under Clovis, defeat Syagrius, last Roman overlord of what will eventually become France, and, in the wake of victory, ban the use of Latin – while Quignard's title itself looks back to Syagrius' enigmatic last words, 'où sont les ombres?' ('where have the shadows gone?'). Ten years later (496), Clovis converts to Christianity and the Franks adopt Latin as their official medium: classical languages are more durable than shadows.

[50] Cf. Wright (2002) 205–6.

[51] The vernacular is 'lingua laica' in (e.g.) the *Doctrinale* (*c.* 1199) by the Norman Frenchman Alexander de Villa Dei: Vineis and Maierù (1994) 182.

actualized versions (not least, of course, the actual vernaculars themselves).[52] Hence the sometime use of *grammatica* – originally 'grammar', but already defined by Alcuin, in the late eighth century, as 'guardian of correct speech and writing'[53] – to designate 'correct' Latin itself. And it is not until Dante that there is any sign of sufficient interest in the Romance vernaculars collectively to acknowledge their relationship.[54]

If the growth of written literature is a fair indicator of the growing prestige of a vernacular language, this is doubly true for the Romance vernaculars, competing with Latin as they were. And just as French is seemingly the first Romance language to emerge, so French literature is first to challenge the supremacy of written Latin on its own ground. Initially, vernacular literature centres on Christian material, as Medieval Latin had and would continue to. From northern France we have a verse life of St Alexis (*c.* 1050) and, from the south, and belonging to a later date in the eleventh century, a Provençal narrative, also in verse, known as the Clermont-Ferrand *Passion*. By the end of the century, however, new verse genres are on the rise, catering to more secular interests and aspirations: narrative epics subsumed under the name *chansons de geste* ('deed songs'), of which the *Chanson de Roland* (*c.* 1100) is the best known; and Provençal lyric, art-form of the troubadours. The first-known troubadour, and the first lyric poet since antiquity known to have written in a vernacular, is William IX of Aquitaine (died, 1127). His language, the Provençal *langue d'oc*, can claim to be the first vernacular culture-language in the medieval West; it is duly acclaimed as such by Dante.[55]

Over the next hundred years, Provençal lyric not only flourishes in its own lands, but is disseminated abroad, especially across northern Italy. In Medieval Latin, comparable lyric writing had existed since at least the 'Cambridge Songs' of the eleventh century.[56] That must rank as a remarkable development – encompassing the expression of 'natural' personal feeling within the artificial and supposedly fixed language of the Western world – and 'natural' and 'artificial' here evoke, not so much the as yet alien dynamic of romanticism, as Dante's great insight that the vernacular, in contrast precisely to Latin, is primary and 'natural to us'.[57] In these terms, the troubadours' logic in appropriating 'personal' lyric for the vernacular is surely premised on a recognition that 'natural' feeling belongs in 'natural' language,[58] and,

[52] Cf. Cucchi (1983) 65. References to Italian in X Latin texts call it 'our common [vernacular] language' ('nostrae vulgaris linguae', in a letter of Gonzone of Novara in 965; cf. the 'vulgaris' in the Gregory epitaph, above), 'the native language' ('voce nativa': the panegyric of Berengarius in 915), 'Roman(ce)' ('lingua romana': Widukind), 'informal speech' ('rusticis verbis': cod. Cassin. 451): examples from Migliorini and Griffith (1984) 42. The name 'Italian' itself is not thus used until XIII (e.g. by Brunetto Latini, in the – French – form 'Ytalien').

[53] *Dialogus Franconis et Saxonis de octo partibus orationis* ('custos recte loquendi et scribendi').

[54] *De vulgari eloquentia*, 1. 8–10, groups, in effect, Spanish, Catalan, French, Occitan, Italian.

[55] Ibid. 1. 10.

[56] Dronke (1968) 271–81.

[57] *De vulgari eloquentia*, 1. 1 (§7). Cf. *Convivio*, 1. 12. 5, 'a man's own vernacular is closest to him.'

[58] Notwithstanding the conventionality of the actual songs.

as such, the appropriation represents a distinctive challenge to the scope of Latin on this newly fashionable ground. Even here, though, the sense of Latin's centrality is still strong. In William's poem 'In the Sweetness of this New Season', the birds sing 'Each *in its Latin* ['en lor lati'] | To the tune of this new song.'[59] Latin remains the unchallengeable point of reference, at the very moment of innovative vernacular usage – and one reflects that the Provençal verb that engenders the name 'troubadour' (*trobar*, 'invent') derives from a term of ancient rhetorical theory, the Latin *tropus*, 'trope', thus neatly acknowledging the authority of classical rhetoric and its legacy of stylistic finesse.

From the twelfth century, the dialects of northern France come to the fore: Norman French (now a significant presence in England) and, soon, the French of the Île-de-France and Paris; and by the thirteenth, the latter, for straightforward political reasons, begins to acquire normative status. In the northern *langue d'oïl*, as in the southern *langue d'oc*,[60] the influence of Latin – both the language and, often inseparably, its cultural connections – is strong. The new literature in northern France is open to the assimilation of Latin vocabulary, as all French texts are seen to have been, from the outset;[61] and these new texts are rich in Latin-related (including Greco-Roman-related) reference. Such reference is already apparent in the twelfth century, where alongside such 'modern' narratives, of history or legend, as the *Chanson de Roland* (on Charlemagne), we find 'tales of antiquity', like the *Roman d'Eneas* and the *Roman de Troie* (both *c.* 1160), which are essentially adaptations of Virgil's *Aeneid*.[62] The titles of these and other 'romans antiques' are instructive. As with the *rustica romana lingua* identified by the Council of Tours in the ninth century, 'roman' (but here as a noun) signifies a work in vernacular French and, only by additional connotation, a story or 'romance' – the sense that attaches to the word hereafter in French (and thence in German too).

The progress of written French is rapid, both within and beyond the literary sphere (from 1254, French is even used in royal documents), and in the thirteenth century prose literature emerges alongside verse. Early examples, from the opening decades of the century, include two anonymous treatments of Roman history, a so-called *History of Antiquity up to Caesar* (*Histoire ancienne jusqu'à César*) and *The Deeds of the Romans* (*Li fet des Romains*), the latter a widely read celebration of Julius Caesar that was translated into Italian. The high-cultural status of French, now even in prose, is indicated by the appearance, in French itself, of an influential 'Thesaurus' (*Li livres dou tresor*, *c.* 1267) by the Florentine, Brunetto Latini,[63] which

[59] *Ab la dolchor del temps novel.*

[60] The two dialectal groups are still labelled thus – by the respective words for 'yes' – as they were by Dante (*De vulgari eloquentia*, 1. 8).

[61] Early examples in Ricard (1989) 33–4.

[62] The opening of Jean Bodel's poem 'The Saxons' (*Les Saisnes*, *c.* 1200) lists tales of France and tales of antiquity ('Rome') as two types of current narrative, alongside a third, less impressive type (tales of Britain).

[63] Likewise the Venetian Marco Polo has his autobiographical *Divisament dou monde* written in French in 1298.

acclaims the language as both 'delightful' ('delitable') and 'universal' ('commune à toutes gens').[64] Compare this, from a thirteenth-century Norwegian encyclopaedia: 'should you wish to be perfect in knowledge, learn all languages, but especially Latin and French, because these are the ones most widely in use.'[65]

Not all French literature of the later Middle Ages has any special Latin affinities: there is not much Latinizing, for instance, in the realist projections of Villon's *Testament* in 1461 (he 'sings of things as they are', said Ezra Pound).[66] Meanwhile, though, the relation between French literature and Latinity takes on a new dimension when humanist scholarship spreads from Italy in the later fourteenth century. And from the fourteenth to the sixteenth, learned Latin influence on the French language becomes a significant fact in its development, yielding neologisms (often abstract, from *évidence* to *régularité*), Latinate idioms, and reshapings of inherited vocabulary, whereby (for instance) inherited *esmer* ('value') makes way for *estimer* (Latin *aestimare*), *leün* ('vegetable') for *légume* (*legumen*), and, appropriately enough, *antif* ('ancient') for *antique* (*antiquus*).[67] Like classical models for works of literature, the ancient word-shape, along with, no doubt, the transparent etymology, is felt to be an imperative.[68] New Latinisms are often the work of translators. As early as the second half of the fourteenth century, Nicholas Oresme successfully introduces a wealth of lexical items, both Latinate and Latinized Greek, from 'abréviation' to 'artificiel', from 'démocracie' to 'économie'.[69] In the sixteenth, by which time French is the official language of a politically united France, one still encounters claims in favour of the primacy of Latin over 'corrupt' French,[70] but Du Bellay's argument that, by imitation of the classics, French can and will finally supplant the ancient languages is both more representative and more influential.[71] By the turn of the seventeenth, Jean Vauquelin de la Fresnaye can declare that 'our language' has indeed now overtaken 'the very finest'.[72]

If one contemplates the dominance of Italian language and culture in the Renaissance, the slow emergence of Italian, in the wake of French, may well seem remarkable – but far more remarkable is the trajectory of Italian after that emergence, and, in particular, the swiftness of its rise, from murky beginnings in the

[64] *Li livres*, 1. 1. 1.

[65] *Speculum Regale*: Nyrop (1899–1930), 1. 34.

[66] *Le testament* (1910): Pound (1952) 171.

[67] Examples from Ricard (1989) 76–9. The high point of Latinate usage, penetrating deep into syntax and idiom, comes in XVI: ibid. 81–99. See generally Cave and Castor (1984).

[68] 'The issue, again and again, is whether to . . . legitimize contemporary and . . . vernacular uses of language, or . . . to "monumentalize" language . . . and . . . keep the traces of history intact, including the supposed etymological transparency of words': Georgakopoulou (2009) xviii (on the long history of language contestation in Greece).

[69] Though the details are disputed: Babbitt (1985) 10. Oresme translated works of Aristotle (from the Latin), among others: cf. §15 and (on the word 'democracy') §26.

[70] So e.g. Charles de Bouvelles, *De differentia vulgarium linguarum et gallici sermonis varietate* (1533).

[71] In *Deffence* (1549), esp. 1. 3; 1. 8; 2, 'Conclusion'. Contrast Jacques Peletier's *Art poétique* (1555): writers should cultivate the innate virtues of French, not the idiosyncrasies of the classical languages.

[72] *L'art poétique* (1605), 1056 ('la plus brave').

tenth century, to the first signs of significant literature in the late twelfth (verse) and mid-thirteenth (prose),[73] to its high status in the fourteenth – which is more obviously the work of one huge creative figure (Dante) than with any comparable case in Western literature since Homer.[74] Why the retardation of Italian? Insofar as such questions admit of an answer, one factor is surely the peculiarly close relation between emergent Italian and Medieval Latin. Awareness of this relation is clear: a letter of 965 refers to 'our vernacular language which is close to Latin':[75] three centuries later, Dante's *De vulgari eloquentia* makes it explicit that, among the Romance languages, whose kinship he proclaims, 'the language of the Italians' seems to 'rest more on' Latin.[76]

Appropriately enough, most of the salient facts of early Italian linguistic, and literary-linguistic, history are acknowledged by Dante himself, in the *De vulgari eloquentia* or elsewhere:[77] the recentness of Italian literature;[78] the established status of French as (not least) the language of literary prose;[79] the priority of Provençal lyric within Romance poetry;[80] the rise, in the thirteenth century, of Sicilian lyric, with its distinctive poetic idiom[81] – reflecting both Provençal and Latin precedents, and in turn a major influence on the style of Dante's own lyric poetry, the 'sweet new style' ('dolce stil novo');[82] and, first and last, the cluster of language issues that centre on the status of Italian and its relation to Latin, some of which will resonate for centuries to come.

These issues include the wider kinship of the Romance tongues with each other and with Latin[83] (it is surely both the fact and the perception of this kinship that facilitate the successive transitions from Provençal to Sicilian to Dante's own modified Tuscan) and (not that he quite acknowledges *this*) the massive, yet still selective, re-Latinizing of Italian, of which his own usage is representative. Then there is the view of language – language *tout court* – as a problem, insofar as the world's diverse

[73] Respectively, in polyglot poems by the Provençal poet Raimbautz de Vaqueiras and a rhetorical treatise in Latin and Italian (*Parlamenta et epistole*) by Guido Faba. XII/XIII Italian: Casapullo (1999).

[74] And a more decisive case, too, given the collective aspect of Homeric poetry and Dante's creativity in more than one range of poetry (lyric, alongside the *Commedia*) and in intellectual prose as well.

[75] Gonzone of Novara (n. 52 above): 'nostrae vulgaris linguae quae latinitati vicina est'.

[76] Or, in his terms, on 'grammar' ('gram(m)atica'), in *De vulgari eloquentia*, 1. 10, 'magis videtur initi gramatice' – where the phrase 'in(n)iti gram(m)atic(a)e' presumably implies the use of the verb found at (e.g.) Pliny, *Natural History*, 16. 127 (trees 'innituntur' on their roots). However, Dante's text is difficult (and 'videtur' is conjectural for MSS 'videntur'): Grayson (1965) 54–76, esp. 61–4. In any event, Dante's association of Italian and Latin is doubtless assisted by the fact that Tuscan (of which *his* Italian is a modified form) was 'the most archaic of the Italian peninsular dialects and therefore closer to Latin': Cremona (1965) 159.

[77] See generally Mazzocco (1993).

[78] *Vita Nuova*, 25; *Convivio*, 1. 10.

[79] *De vulgari eloquentia*, 1. 10.

[80] Ibid.

[81] Ibid. 1. 12.

[82] Dante's own phrase at *Purgatorio*, 24. 57.

[83] *De vulgari eloquentia*, 1. 4–7.

tongues are taken to be degenerated from a primordial original (at which point the Biblical tale of Babel is invoked);[84] but then again, more positively, the contestation between Latin and the vernacular.[85] And the positive here is that, alongside the case for the superiority of the 'incorruptible' art-language,[86] there is the case Dante makes for the proposition that vernacular language is both original and 'natural'(§7).[87]

But not only this: Dante argues that the vernacular can itself achieve the stability of an art-language;[88] that it can be developed as a vehicle for the highest ideas;[89] and that, above all, a common version of the Italian dialects is desirable and attainable, and will yield an 'illustrious Italian language'[90] – and here Dante is both describing his own great project and (with this conception of the *vulgare illustre*)[91] demarcating 'the language question' in terms of Italian identity, as it will be debated beyond his own age. And it is entirely in keeping with this complex understanding of language as such, and art-languages in particular, that in the *Commedia* Latin poetry is seen as 'dead poetry', which will 'rise again' in vernacular form; that great authors of that 'dead poetry', like Lucan and Ovid, must themselves make an appearance but 'be silent'; and that the greatest of those poets, Virgil, is both Dante's indispensable guide and, beyond a certain point, a guide no more, who disappears, in silence again.[92] There are profound truths here on the linguistic and literary-linguistic levels, as on the level of existential theology: as early as the *Vita Nuova* (his first book, from the 1290s), Dante announces that God has spoken to him – first, 'obscurely', in Latin, but then in Italian.[93]

Dante's unique status as emancipator of the Italian language – by his arguments in its favour, by his development of intellectual prose, by his poetic achievement – is, intermittently, acknowledged by Petrarch and Boccaccio, in his wake. For Boccaccio in 1371, in a rewriting of terms anticipated by Dante himself, his great forerunner had demonstrated that the vernacular was more than a vernacular: neither simply a language of the common people ('vulgar') nor simply informal ('rustic').[94] For

[84] Ibid. This is a standard view of language(s) in the Middle Ages (and beyond): Fyler (2007).

[85] Strictly speaking, between 'grammatica' and the vernacular. In *De vulgari eloquentia*, 1. 1, 'grammatica' is not a one-to-one equivalent of Latin, but the unchanging 'secondary' mode of language which 'other' peoples, too, are said to have (including 'the Greeks') – but for practical purposes the only 'grammatica' Dante is concerned with is indeed Latin. Latin itself he sees not so much as the source of the Romance vernaculars (though cf. *De vulgari eloquentia*, 1. 8), rather as a conventionalized and anciently regulated version of them (cf. *Vita Nuova*, 25).

[86] *Convivio*, 1. 5. 7–15. 'Art-language': cf. p. 74 above.

[87] *De vulgari eloquentia*, 1. 1.

[88] *Convivio*, 1. 13.

[89] Ibid. 1. 10.

[90] *De vulgari eloquentia*, 1. 11–19; 2. 1.

[91] Dante's (Latin) phrase at *De vulgari eloquentia*, 1. 18, and elsewhere – 'a kind of abstraction, a linguistic ideal': Cremona (1965) 159.

[92] *Purgatorio*, 1. 7 ('ma qui la morta poesì resurga'); *Inferno*, 25. 94, 97 ('Taccia Lucano . . . | Taccia . . . Ovidio'); *Purgatorio*, 27. 124–42 (Virgil's last words) and 30. 49–57 (his disappearance).

[93] 'In parole volgari': *Vita Nuova*, 12.

[94] In a letter to Iacopo Pizzinga.

Petrarch, around the same time, looking back at 'eloquence in our vernacular', Dante had been 'our leader'.[95] At the same time, Petrarch's exemplary use of Latin for most of his work, along with a notoriously equivocal attitude towards enhancing the vernacular at all, as Dante had (and as he himself did in his lyric poetry), precipitates a temporary shift in attitudes among the learned (Boccaccio included): 'Italian intellectuals for a century after Petrarch's death channelled their efforts into perfecting Latin rather than Italian.'[96]

For all that, the contest between the two languages could never be the same again. The more prosaic correlative of Dante's understanding of the way Italian might be said to 'rest on' Latin is the abundant evidence of Latin influence on the developing vernacular at all levels. In this, of course, Italian was not alone. We have noted the phenomenon of Latin borrowings, and reborrowings, and then the restoration of Latin word-shapes, in Romancified English as in Romance French. For French and Italian, it has been estimated that between the later Middle Ages and the sixteenth century around 30 per cent of their vocabulary is borrowed, or reborrowed, from Latin.[97] In Italian, the influence of formal Latin on vernacular writings reaches a peak in the humanistic circles of the fifteenth century, where 'in some texts we have the impression of an Italian grammatical framework carrying an almost entirely Latin vocabulary'[98] – but the felt affinities of Latin and Italian, not least in word-shapes and word-rhythms, had long since made the incorporation of Latin loanwords a natural (*sic*) practice for Dante and his successors, and made it easy in turn for many such Latinisms to pass into normal usage, whether under literary influence or not.

Among the numerous Latin loanwords to establish themselves in this period are items as diverse as *esistenza* ('existence') and *esattore* ('tax-collector'), *indigente* ('poor') and *invitto* ('invincible').[99] Dante's own Latinisms include both the Biblical and the classical, and are often used 'to lend solemnity to a speech attributed to one of the protagonists', as, for instance, *cive* (Latin *civis*, 'citizen') appears 'only in lofty discourses' by Beatrice, Charles Martel, and St Peter[100] – and in the first case, aptly, in the context of the 'new Rome' of Christ. In his Italian lyrics, Petrarch Latinizes Italian forms in even the most basic words: *condutto* for *condotto* (Latin *conductus*, 'led'); *belli* (*occhi*) for *begli* ('lovely (eyes)', Latin *belli*); Italian *buono* and Latinized *bono* (Latin *bonus*, 'good') in a single line.[101] In his *Decameron*, from the 1350s, Boccaccio proposes to write 'in the Florentine vernacular' – but he too Latinizes to the extent of (for instance) favouring a sentence-final position for the verb.[102]

[95] *Rerum senilium*, 5. 2: 'dux nostri eloquii vulgaris'. Cf. §29.

[96] McLaughlin (1996) 226.

[97] Posner (1996) 150–1.

[98] Migliorini and Griffith (1984) 192.

[99] Examples, ibid. 152.

[100] Ibid. 127: *Purgatorio*, 32. 101-2, *Paradiso*, 8. 116 and 24. 43.

[101] *Trionfo della fama*, 1. 126: examples from Migliorini and Griffith (1984) 135.

[102] 'In fiorentin volgare' (*Decameron*, Day Four, Introduction). Language of the three writers overall: Manni (2003).

The three great *trecentisti* have a momentous legacy both within and beyond Italy, as models for poetry and (in Boccaccio's case) literary prose.[103] Within Italy itself, they establish Tuscan Italian (with whatever modifications and expansions) as a high-culture language inferior to none and the prime candidate for a national language for Italy as a whole. Yet what Dante in particular inaugurates is an era of debate about language. As early as 1332 the Paduan Antonio da Tempo closes his treatise on verse forms by acclaiming the special status of Tuscan ('more suitable for literature than any other language') – even though he says it in Latin;[104] as late as the 1860s and 1870s, the elderly novelist Manzoni and the philologist Ascoli are still arguing about the status of Tuscan, or Florentine, new or old, literary or collective, as the basis of an Italian standard.[105] The established dictum that today's standard Italian is 'largely based upon a literary version of the Tuscan variety'[106] is both true – and conceals a long history of complications and contestations.

In the fifteenth century, debate centres, still, on the status of vernacular Italian as against Latin; and the paradox of Petrarchan humanism – that one of the great enablers of Italian literature should also play a central role in diverting attention back to Latin – helps to explain why. At the same time, *this* dispute becomes inextricably bound up with the arguments about *which* Latin (Medieval, Classical, Ciceronian, whatever: §7) and, above all, *which* vernacular – which soon becomes *the* 'language question'.[107] For the polymath Alberti, around 1440, the aim is to elevate the (Tuscan) vernacular 'by grafting onto it Latin vocabulary and syntax'.[108] For Mario Equicola in the early sixteenth century, Latinity remains the criterion – 'I only observe the rules of Tuscan insofar as they conform to Latin' ('non observo le regule del toscano se non tanto quanto al latino son conforme') – and the Latinate Italian used here bears out the claim.[109] In his *Book of the Courtier* (1528), Castiglione espouses a version of the vernacular that is 'Italian, collective ['comune'], copious and varied' – but then prefers Latinizing forms like *populo* to Tuscan *popolo*.[110] According to the grammarian Gian Francesco Fortunio in 1516, Italian

[103] The status of XIV Italian literature internationally is summed up by the influence of Petrarch's *Canzoniere* on the England of Sidney, Shakespeare, and Donne, and by the way literary manifestoes from Du Bellay's *Deffence* to Milton's Preface to *Samson Agonistes* cite 'the Ancients and Italians' (Milton's phrase: §22) on a par.

[104] *Summa artis rithimici vulgaris dictaminis*: 'lingua tusca magis apta est ad literam sive literaturam quam aliae linguae.'

[105] Migliorini and Griffith (1984) 413–19.

[106] Trask (2000) 175. Correlatively, the 'Italian' composites of Dante and others do not correspond precisely to any 'spoken version'.

[107] Prototype of 'language questions' in many Western speech communities, from Greek to Czech. On the language question(s) in Italy, see variously Grayson (1960); Serianni and Trifone (1993–4), vol. 2; Tavoni (1984); Vitale (1978).

[108] Tavoni *et al.* (1998) 30, summarizing Alberti's *Grammatica della lingua toscana*.

[109] *De natura de amore* (*c.* 1505–8), Dedication.

[110] *Il libro del cortegiano*, 1. 11; 1. 39.

had become a 'transfused' version of Latin;[111] in the eyes of the humanist Celio Calcagnini, all Italian – language and literature – remained 'foul' and 'barbaric'.[112] The influential positions of the Venetian Pietro Bembo in the same generation – that Latin should be pure Ciceronian, but that modern literature should be in the Italian of Boccaccio and Petrarch[113] – represented a suitably paradoxical compromise, while, in the wake of Bembo's arguments, the Paduan Sperone Speroni made a case for the legitimacy of all vernaculars, in a dialogue that would be a notable influence on Du Bellay's claims for French a few years later.[114]

Amidst these arguments, 'Latin and Italian were in constant symbiosis'[115] – or at least constant tension. The influence of Latin usage, certainly, was now huge, especially when the result of learned imitation. 'It was agreed that authors could borrow from Latin models; this had consequences that were slight for Italian morphology, important for Italian syntax and very important for Italian vocabulary.'[116] Literary experiments often followed the trajectory of the language debates. Ariosto's epic *Orlando Furioso* converted a medieval subject into a modern masterpiece, with help from Dante, Virgil, and his immediate predecessor, Boiardo. The poem was first published in 1516, then republished in revised form in 1521 and again, more substantially, in 1532. In its earlier form, the work contained extensive Latinizing – which was significantly reduced, under the influence of Bembo, in the final version.

In Bembo's century, meanwhile, Latin itself retained much of its establishment status. The Index of 1559 forbade the unauthorized printing, reading, or possession of an Italian Bible; and as late as 1573 the *Accademia Papinianea* of Turin was founded on the basis of exclusive communication in Latin. The prototypes of Shakespeare's pedantic Latinizer Holofernes were Italian, and the Latinizing pedant was a stock character in Renaissance comedy.[117] In 1589, the Florentine *Accademia della Crusca* (soon to produce a dictionary of Italian) still felt it necessary to confront the question whether the Tuscan language had sufficient intellectual capacity to 'encompass the sciences'.[118]

By the end of the sixteenth century, at all events, our four languages (irrespective of continuing issues in Italy) are all fully established in their own territories, with clear literary pedigrees. Earlier in the century, an instructive corroboration of their collective status is provided by Rabelais. In one of his grand encounters, Pantagruel meets the learned Panurge, who speaks to him in a series of languages, real and fabricated.[119] In order, the languages are: German, nonsense, Italian, English, Basque,

[111] 'La latina lingua . . . fu in questa che noi volgar chiamiamo trasfusa': Preface to *Regole grammaticali della volgar lingua*.

[112] 'Foedissima barbaries', in a letter of 1532 ('On Imitation') to Giraldi.

[113] In *De imitatione* (1512) and *Prose della volgar lingua* (1525).

[114] *Dialogo delle lingue* (published in 1542).

[115] Migliorini and Griffith (1984) 163.

[116] Ibid. 211; see further ibid. 177–94, 236–50.

[117] As in Francesco Belo's *Il pedante* (1529). Holofernes: n. 43 above.

[118] Migliorini and Griffith (1984) 203.

[119] *Pantagruel*, 9.

nonsense again, Dutch, Spanish, Danish, Hebrew, classical Greek, more nonsense, Latin, then finally French. If one discounts the several sequences of nonsense, the list begins with German, Italian, and English, then shifts to the exotic or outlying (Basque, Dutch, Spanish (!), Danish), then to the three special languages, Hebrew, Greek, Latin (classical, sacred, or both), before coming to rest on French in the end.[120] Our four frame the whole.

If one takes stock of the four languages in the centuries that follow, there are some clear common trends. First and foremost is the steady displacement of Latin in the worlds of literature and thought. Latin retains its status as a medium of high-intellectual communication for some while, but beyond the seventeenth century a case like Newton's *Principia mathematica* (1687) – new thought, and still in Latin – is seldom found.[121] Yet if, by the modern age, most of its authority has been ceded to the vernaculars, *they* have all in varying degrees now absorbed Latin vocabulary, idiom, and rhetorical structures. The paradox has aptly been likened to the process immortalized by Horace, whereby Rome conquered Greece and was conquered in turn by Greek culture: 'vernaculars overthrew the dominance of Latin only by subjugating themselves to its terms.'[122]

This same paradox is apparent in other important areas of common ground. One notable case is the movement towards language standardization – or rather (since English and French, in particular, might be said to have more or less standard forms already established),[123] towards the institutionalization of formal procedures for such standardizing. Language standardizing is commonly bound up with issues of national identity.[124] Separate nations can and do share virtually identical languages (Germany and Austria, Britain and the USA);[125] and nation-states (or 'empires' in earlier centuries) can be multilingual (from the Austro-Hungarian empire to

[120] Of these, the only ones Pantagruel or his companions understand, or even identify, apart fom French, are Hebrew and Greek – though the Danish passage prompts talk of 'Gothic' (not a compliment), while the Latin elicits no direct comment.

[121] The use of Latin for intellectual exposition lasts longest within classical studies. In the 1841 preface to his commentary on Pindar, J. W. Donaldson defends his decision to write 'in a vernacular form', adding: 'the question, whether commentaries on classical authors should be written in Latin or in English, is by no means finally settled' (p. xviii).

[122] Waswo (1987) 137: Horace, *Epistles*, 2. 1. 156–7.

[123] 'More or less': with French, there long remained a gap between official *francien* and the local *patois*. According to the abbé Grégoire in 1794, 12,000,000 of the 28,000,000 inhabitants of France had no command of French proper (their primary allegiance was to the *patois*, or Occitan, Breton, or Basque): *Rapport sur la nécessité et les moyens d'anéantir les patois et d'universaliser l'usage de la langue française*.

[124] See e.g. Ayres-Bennett and Jones (2007), Edwards (2009), Grimm *et al.* (2003). The maxim that 'a language is a dialect that has an army and a navy' (attributed to Max Weinreich: Mazrui 1997) has great force. 'Language' and 'dialect' are not distinguishable by technical linguistic criteria.

[125] The words of the American spelling reformer Noah Webster, in 1789, are revealing: 'Let us then seize the present moment, and establish a *national language* [*sc.* by distinctive orthography: his italics], as well as a national government': Appendix to *Dissertations on the English Language*.

modern China). But in all nations of a certain level of sophistication the push towards a single standard language has always been strong – and, with it, the desire of ruling groups to use the language to enforce national identity. The connection between the continuing language question and the late date of political unification in Italy (1861) is obvious.[126]

The mechanisms of institutionalization for our languages are various. Chief among them are dictionaries, grammars, and regulations for agreed orthography,[127] and in Italy and France, in particular, the activation of these mechanisms centres on the work of the great Academies. The Florentine *Accademia della Crusca*, founded in 1582, dedicated itself to the task of language purification and produced the first version of its *Vocabolario*, a pioneering dictionary of (largely) Florentine Italian, in 1612, with the most influential version a third edition of 1691.[128] The *Académie Française* was formally approved as a national institution in 1635, under the sponsorship of Richelieu. Statute 26 ambitiously promised to compose 'a dictionary, a grammar, a rhetoric and a poetics'. In the event, no grammar appeared until 1932,[129] but the first aspiration was met by Richelet's *Dictionnaire de l'Académie Françoise* in 1694, with the explicit commitment of making 'a living language' into something 'fixed'.[130] The overall aim, then, was to institutionalize definitive uniformity – to which end, an official list of authors of approved usage had been produced some decades earlier.[131] As a final confirmation of national-linguistic identity, and the autonomy of the national language, the whole enterprise constitutes an impressive achievement. At the same time, its *modus operandi* is totally dependent, still, on classical paradigms. The lexicographical premises of the *Dictionnaire* are those of earlier, Renaissance dictionaries of the ancient languages;[132] its (and their) ultimate

[126] German unification (under Prussian leadership, in 1871) comes even later – but Germany had for centuries had a stronger basis for cultural unity, thanks, not least, to Luther's choice of Saxon High German for his Bible ('ich rede nach der sechsischen Cantzeley': *Tischreden*, 1566, ch. 70). 'The publication, at approximately the same time, of Luther's translation of the New Testament (1522) and of Bembo's *Prose* (1525) gives an indication of the different destinies [of the two languages]': Tavoni *et al.* (1998) 15.

[127] See Considine (2008), Tavoni *et al.* (1998) 2–108. Early landmarks: Alberti, *Grammatica della lingua toscana* (*c.* 1440); Fortunio, *Regole grammaticali della volgar lingua* (1516); Dubois, *In linguam gallicam isagwge* [*sic*] (1521: in Latin); Laurentius Albertus, *Teutsch Grammatick* (1573: also in Latin); Bullokar, *Bref Grammar for English* (1586).

[128] In Germany, language societies (*Sprachgesellschaften*) were set up on the Florentine model. In England, the Royal Society (founded in 1662), though primarily focused on natural science, had a strong initial concern with language (cf. below, p. 159); the diarist John Evelyn's proposals to the Society called for 'a lexicon or collection of all . . . English words' (letter to Peter Wyche, 20 June 1665).

[129] Though a Port-Royal *Grammaire* by Lancelot and Arnauld appeared in 1660.

[130] Dedication to the 1694 edition.

[131] In 1638: P. Pellisson-Fontanier, *Relation contenant l'histoire de l'Académie Françoise* (1653), part 3. Among the notable omissions on the approved list was Rabelais.

[132] E.g. Robert Estienne's dictionary of Latin (*Dictionarium, seu latinae linguae thesaurus*, 1531), and his son Henri's dictionary of Greek (*Thesaurus graecae linguae*, 1572).

model is the Atticist inventories of approved Greek usage under the Roman empire; while the ideal of a 'fixed' language points unmistakably to the status of Latin as the unchangeable Other, against which the developing vernaculars, French and the rest, had struggled to establish their authority for centuries.

If the French commitment to definitive regularization is extreme, it is also representative. Standardizing processes in early modern Europe do more than fix on a particular speech version as normative. Their common aim is to regulate and regularize that version, and to do so on the model of the language long seen as the paradigm of rules and regulation, Latin. And insofar as the new regulators are *changing* their own languages (as they always must be, if only by selection), this is necessarily change from the top down[133] – socially and (in their view) aesthetically, intellectually, and morally (the French Academicians early on decided that the *Dictionnaire* should exclude vulgarities) – on the model of exclusive, elite Latin, again. In sum: in their regularization, the new vernaculars were converging towards the classical languages, as their earlier versions had once converged in their deference, then resistance, to Medieval Latin, with the new vernacular authority itself modelled on the authority once given uniquely to Latin (Medieval or otherwise) itself.

Convergences of quite different kinds, or on quite different levels, are apparent too. In the seventeenth century, the rise of modern science is widely associated with a call for 'clear' or 'plain' language in vernacular usage, and most articulately in England and France. If the *clarté* famously espoused by Descartes in his *Discourse on Method* is primarily a matter of 'clarity' of thought and method itself,[134] the implications for language are spelled out in England by John Wilkins (soon to be a central figure in the Royal Society) and (as prescript for presentations to the Society) by Thomas Sprat. Thus Wilkins in 1646: 'It must be plain and natural, not being darkened with the affectation of scholastical harshness or rhetorical flourishes . . . The greatest learning is to be seen in the greatest plainness.'[135] And Sprat in 1667, on the need 'to reject all the amplifications, disgressions and swellings of style' in favour of 'a close, naked, natural way of speaking; positive expressions; clear senses; a native easiness: bringing all things as near the mathematical plainness as they can, and preferring the language of artisans, countrymen and merchants before that of wits or scholars.'[136]

133 As sociolinguists insist, language change is normally bottom-up: Milroy (1992).

134 *Discours de la méthode* (1637). However, Cartesian *clarté* also evokes a distinctively French claim, most insistent in the neoclassical age, that linguistic transparency is not just desirable ('whatever has been conceived clearly can be stated clearly': Boileau, *L'art poétique*, 1674, 1. 154), but characteristic of French usage *per se*: 'anything unclear is un-French' ('ce qui n'est pas clair n'est pas françois'), Rivarol, 'De l'universalité de la langue françoise' (1784). In general terms, this fetishizing of clarity looks back to classical rhetoric and poetics, where clear expression is one of Quintilian's four prerequisites for prose style (*Institutio Oratoria*, 8. 1–2) and one of Aristotle's two requirements for poetic *lexis* (*Poetics*, 22: n. 137 below).

135 *Ecclesiastes*: cf. Jones (1970) 196–7. Wilkins's 'it' is actually the language of *preaching*.

136 In Sprat's *History of the Royal Society*, 2. 20: variously, Jones (1970) 204, Vickers (1985).

In the Romantic age, a new common theme – superficially similar, but among *littérateurs*, this time – is the quest to rediscover the 'language of the people' and make it the basis of poetic usage in particular. 'In particular', because since Aristotle it had broadly been an expectation and a theoretical requirement that poetic language should not only be 'clear' but also 'elevated';[137] and except in 'low' genres like comedy and satire, verse writing broadly satisfies the expectation throughout post-Aristotelian antiquity, the Christian millennium,[138] and the classicizing centuries up to and including (not least) the eighteenth. Perceived exceptions to the 'rule' prompt unease or outright condemnation, especially in the neoclassical age. Notorious examples are French criticisms of Homer's similes, in the late seventeenth and early eighteenth centuries (Ajax like 'an ass'? Scamander and 'pig fat'?!),[139] and a few decades later, Samuel Johnson's distaste for Macbeth's 'vulgar' locutions ('for who, without some relaxation of his gravity, can hear of the avengers of guilt *peeping through a blanket*?').[140]

Later in the eighteenth century (and by way of tacit vindication for Dante's insights), the immediacy of 'natural' language increasingly becomes, on the contrary, a specific value and a goal. Herder's reflections on originary speech and primal 'folk' poetry (like Ossian's) are followed by Wordsworth's manifesto on behalf of 'a selection of language really used by men', in explicit opposition to 'what is usually called poetic diction'; more elusively, by Victor Hugo's ideal of 'liberalism in literature', which (for poetry) subsumes 'verse that is by turns poetical and practical'; and more marginally, in Italy, by the opposition of a Pietro Borsieri to literary style determined by 'phrase and convention'.[141] In the post-Romantic world of realist literary prose, deference to the 'natural' is taken to a new level (and the *natural*ism of Zola is among the contexts in which explicit appeal to 'the language of the people'

[137] Or, as Aristotle originally put it, 'clear but *not low*' (*mê tapeinê*): *Poetics*, 22 (cf. §35). His *Rhetoric* (3. 2. 1–5) extends the principle to prose, which (subject to appropriateness) *may* even allow 'ordinary usage' (3. 2. 5). According to Roger Ascham in 1545, 'he that will write well in any tongue must follow the counsel of Aristotle, to speak as the common people do': 'To All Gentlemen and Yeomen of England', preface to *Toxophilus*. Aristotle would not have approved the simplification.

[138] One reason why Dante's *Comedy* (whose range of diction is exceptionally wide) is so called: cf. his Epistle to Cangrande della Scala (*c.* 1316); further, §22 n. 40.

[139] *Iliad*, 11. 556–65 and 21. 361–5. On the French critiques: Costil (1943), Hepp (1968). Cf. (with an additional Popean perspective) Mason (1972) 61–112.

[140] In *The Rambler* 168 (1751) on *Macbeth*, 1. 5. 49–53. In modern editions the words are ascribed to Lady Macbeth, which would hardly have assuaged the critic's indignation ('these imperfections of diction . . . will strike a solitary academic less forcibly than a modish lady'). It is part of Johnson's point that language has changed since Shakespeare's day – but (as 'imperfections' shows) for the better.

[141] Herder, *Abhandlung über den Ursprung der Sprache* (1772) and (on Ossian) *Von deutscher Art und Kunst* (1773); Wordsworth, 1802 Preface to *Lyrical Ballads* (Brett and Jones 1965: 244, 251) (cf. §35); Hugo, prefaces to *Hernani* (1830) and *Cromwell* (1827); Borsieri, in the (short-lived) journal, *Il conciliatore* (27 December 1818: 'quello stile fraseggiato e convenzionale'). In post-Wordsworthian England, 'the language of the people' is often converted to 'Saxon' (broadly under the influence of XIX philological understandings), as e.g. by the poet Hopkins: Milroy (1977) 33–98.

is made)[142] – but this whole momentous shift in sensibility and usage is engendered, in the first place, by reaction to the classical and its 'rules'.

Then again, there have also been divergences between the languages – from the prolongation into the nineteenth century of the language question in Italy to the formidable traditions of intellectual German prose style[143] to the continuing obsession with language purity (including unremitting hostility to any anglification of the French language) by the *Académie Française*. That last development reflects the phenomenon of fluctuations in linguistic authority (and often, inseparably, in literary or literary-intellectual authority), which presents itself as a distinguishing feature in its own right. The long-standing primacy of Medieval Latin was challenged by French, then – from the late Middle Ages to the end of the mid-sixteenth century – French by Italian. The French response, when it came, was hardly associated with hostility to Italian or a reassertion of the achievements of medieval France. Quite the contrary: for the Pléiade, above all – for Ronsard's practice, as well as Du Bellay's theory – Petrarch is a model on a par with any ancient, while medieval French, with all its works, is almost as unsavoury as Medieval Latin had been to Petrarch himself.[144] That deference to Italian and that sense of its equivalence to Latin and Greek had long co-existed in France; in 1410, the translator Laurent de Premierfait produces a French version of Cicero's *De Amicitia*, a favourite Italian-Renaissance classic (§8), and then, a few years later, a version of Boccaccio's *Decameron* (1414). The French rivalry was rather with Latin itself. In Du Bellay's *Deffence*, Latin is something to emulate, but then transcend, while the French-dominated contest of ancients and moderns a century later subsumes the final stage of 'a struggle between Latin, the international language, and French, which, having ceased to be a dialect, was now asserting itself as a culture-language'.[145]

Given the success of that 'assertion' in the seventeenth century and beyond, and the undeniable (if subsequently belittled) stature of French in the Middle Ages, it can fairly be claimed that the French language has actually been an international medium, on and off, for significant stretches of the last thousand years. From the seventeenth century to the nineteenth (and beyond), French was the preferred

[142] 'La langue du peuple': in the preface Zola added to his novel *L'Assommoir* (1877). Novelists across the West had long since made moves in this direction. Manzoni's *I promessi sposi* (1827) seeks to refound written Italian on spoken (Florentine) models, in the face of a gap between the two so wide that conventional literary Italian struck him as almost a dead language (letter to Claude Fauriel, 9 February 1806). By comparison with Herder or Wordsworth, though, Zola and Manzoni are struggling against the tide: in the modern age, 'the language of the people' resonates most strongly (as slogan and reality) among German and English speakers.

[143] Fortified by arguments, like that of Leibniz in *Ermahnung an die Teutsche* (c. 1680), that German is specially suited to philosophy.

[144] Du Bellay, *Deffence*, 2. 2; 2. 4; 2. 11 (but contrast commendation for the old 'romances' and 'chronicles' in 2. 5–6).

[145] Highet (1967) 644.

linguistic medium for upper-class discourse across the West (and beyond),[146] while the tally of literary works written in French by writers whose first language was *not* French is remarkable. Just as the Englishman, John Gower, and the Italian, Brunetto Latini, wrote in French in the Middle Ages, so too, in more recent times, one can cite a string of works from the *Théodicée* of Leibniz (1710) to Oscar Wilde's *Salomé* (1892), while in the twentieth century French was the medium for writings of international importance by (among others) the Romanians Tristan Tzara and Eugène Ionesco, the Spanish artist Pablo Picasso, and the Irishman Samuel Beckett.[147]

In 1784, Antoine de Rivarol lectured in Berlin 'On the Universality of the French Language',[148] to the approval of the elderly Frederick the Great of Prussia (who himself had recently written a study of German literature in French).[149] As so often, though, the late eighteenth century is to be seen as a time of transition – in this case, a time of competing nationalisms and linguistic identities,[150] as well as dreams of 'universality'. It is in this century that the English language begins its massive rise towards world dominance, assisted by literary achievement, but also by imperial conquest and the new potential of an independent United States of America. Late in the seventeenth century, the French critic René Rapin is said to have learnt English specially to read the work of Dryden.[151] A century later, and four years before Rivarol's thoughts on the universality of French, the American John Adams, Founding Father and President-to-be, declared:

> English is destined to be in the next and succeeding centuries more generally the language of the world than Latin was in the last or French is in the present age. The reason of this is obvious, because the increasing population in America and their universal connection and correspondence with all nations will, aided by the influence of England in the world, whether great or small, force their language into general use.[152]

The prophetic clarity of Adams's words is as striking as his historical sense.

In view of the largely successful democratizing of Western languages, even in their literary forms, it is ironic that one of the most conspicuous of all their shared tendencies in and since the nineteenth century has been a new and extensive expansion of classical-derived – and now usually Greek-derived – vocabulary to satisfy

[146] Even in increasingly nationalist-minded Germany. As late as 1862, Bismarck, then Prussian ambassador to Russia, sent reports to the Prussian Foreign Office in French.

[147] T. S. Eliot, early in his career, contemplated writing predominantly in French: *Paris Review Interviews* (1963) 85.

[148] Above, n. 134. In 1782 the Berlin Academy had offered a prize for the best essay on this subject.

[149] *De la littérature allemande* (1780).

[150] Informed, or complicated, by the rise of historical linguistics. Note e.g. the case of the 'Romantic Aryans': Figueira (2002) 27–49.

[151] According to Dryden's friend, Charles Blount: Epistle Dedicatory of Dryden's *Religio Laici* (1683).

[152] Letter to Congress, 5 September 1780.

the changing needs of external civilization (though also the self-sufficiency of a new technically-minded scientific elite).[153] From the start of the industrial age, the world's languages, including our four, expand in response to new science, new technologies, new concepts, with a flood of Greek-based loans and coinages. The response of English-speakers to this drastic change to the linguistic landscape is instructive. For the linguistically sensitive, issues of assimilation and non-assimilability arise, as they had with non-native terms centuries before. To a mind and ear schooled in traditional English (which by now subsumes much Latinate English), the new range of vocabulary can be disturbingly alien, in individual shape as well as in connotations of techno-modernity itself:

> *Microscopic anatomy* of *ephemerides*,
> Power-house stacks, girder-ribs, . . .
> . . . are not bred
> Flesh of our flesh, being unrelated
> Experientially.[154]

The popular-cultural response, as it can fairly be called, is quite different. Such vocables are either ignored, and left to specialists, or (if they designate what are felt to be significant items or aspects of modern life) are assimilated (Greek-based terms, but also Latin-) by conversion into that most English of word-shapes, the monosyllable. The alienated youth who refuses to be *dissed* ('disrespected'); the secretary who sends a *fax* ('facsimile reproduction'); the readers of *ads* ('advertisements') that promise *porn* ('pornography'): these (and many others) are all reflecting and sustaining the monosyllabic tendency of English – especially 'Saxon' English – that developed in the Middle Ages. Likewise their predecessors, over the last two centuries, who reacted to earlier tides of Latin- or Greek-derived polysyllables (often reflective of new technology in their times) by shortening 'bicycle' to *bike*, 'aeroplane' to *plane*, 'telephone' to *phone*, 'refrigerator' to *fridge*, 'mathematics' to *math*(*s*), 'gymnasium' to *gym*, 'influenza' to *flu*, 'omnibus' to *bus*, 'perambulator' to *pram*.[155]

More ironic still is a modern reclassicizing of language on the grand scale. Among the wide variety of utopian experiments practised on the Western world in the post-industrial age is a set of newly-invented 'international auxiliary languages'. Several hundred of these are on record, most of them favouring self-evidently international word-stocks, chiefly Latin-based, or Greek-based, or both – and all of them conceived on the model of the international language that Latin once was. The IAL movement actually begins in the mid-seventeenth century, precisely at the time

[153] Cf. Millward (1996) 325–7.

[154] 'The Thyrsus Retipped' (1931), by a minor modernist poet, Ronald Bottrall, now chiefly remembered for a favourable notice by Leavis (1932) 202, where the lines are quoted: italics ours.

[155] A special – and undiscussed? – form of what linguists call 'clipping': Durkin (2009) 116–17. Some such shortenings are surprisingly early (e.g. *fan* for 'fanatic', attested in XVII and revived in late-XIX).

when the international authority of Latin is being subjected to its final challenge,[156] but it is the later outcomes that are the more substantial.

The best known of the new languages is the largely Latin-based Esperanto, invented by a Polish ophthalmist, Ludwik Zamenhof, in 1887. The most coherent is probably Interlingua, originally called Latino Sine Flexione ('Latin Without Inflexions': as the name indicates, entirely Latin-based), brain-child of the Italian mathematician, Giuseppe Peano, in 1903. The most revealing, for our purpose, is Interglossa, invented by an English biologist, Lancelot Hogben, in World War II, during 'empty hours of fire-watching in Aberdeen'.[157] Like Zamenhof and Peano, then (and like most of the seventeenth-century pioneers), Hogben was a scientist, and the scientistic temper of his enterprise is obvious from the uncompromising subtitle of his primer, when published in 1943: *Interglossa: A Draft of an Auxiliary for a Democratic World Order, Being an Attempt to Apply Semantic Principles to Language Design*. The language itself is based on internationally familiar elements – which, as the new name suggests (Latin *inter* meets Greek *glossa*), are almost entirely Latin or, more often, Greek. Regarding the logic of these choices, Hogben was explicit: 'during the past two centuries, science has created a world-wide technical vocabulary', partly Latin-based, partly based on Greek, but – 'a truly international vocabulary must be the offspring of technology, and technology increasingly turns to Greek rather than to Latin for new material. Of the many who know that *micro-* means small, few know that *parvus* means the same.'[158] As a hard-headed 'democrat', meanwhile, Hogben was contemptuous of the traditions of elite classical education that had engendered his international vocabulary in the first place: 'in England school education is the last bulwark of caste privilege'.[159] The paradoxes and ideological intricacies associated with the classical tradition have rarely been more piquant.

In the face of such innocent optimism about language and its possibilities, we should also acknowledge its opposite. Within Western thought, there is a powerful tradition of mature pessimism about the limits of language, even from some highly distinguished users of language themselves. If many writers, from Aristophanes to Rabelais to Shakespeare to Joyce, have used creative literature to celebrate the seeming limitlessness of extra-ordinary language, an equal number have expressed anxieties.[160] In our own age, we meet one set of doubts in Beckett, in Célan, in Eliot's *Four Quartets* ('the intolerable wrestle | With words and meanings');[161]another in Adorno's oft-quoted rejection of poetry after the Holocaust;[162] philosophical versions

156 Overview: Eco (1995). Besides lesser-known figures like Wilkins (above, p. 159), the movement attracted great intellects like Descartes and Leibniz.

157 Hogben (1943) 7.

158 Ibid. 12–13.

159 In Bodmer (1944) 11.

160 Cf. Steiner (1967) 30–74.

161 'East Coker', II; on these three writers, cf. Wolosky (1995).

162 But cf. p. 402 below.

in Derrida's insistence on the infinite regress of linguistic signification (*différance*) and Wittgenstein's reflections on meaning and word;[163] something different again in the uncomfortable implications of Raymond Queneau's *Exercices de style* (1947), which tells 'the same' story in ninety-nine different ways.[164] In earlier centuries, we have the mystical conviction that language is inadequate to confront the highest truths,[165] not to mention the myth of Babel, with all its cautionary implications.

This whole pessimistic tradition contrasts not only with science-centred optimism, but equally with the belief in linguistic transparency that so characterizes the neoclassical age, especially in France, and behind it, the assurance of the practical efficacy of language that is the premise of ancient rhetoric. Yet if linguistic pessimism, in its many guises, is in this sense a cumulative critique of the classical tradition,[166] let us recall that its earliest consequential formulation itself belongs to the ancient world: the statement in Plato's Seventh Letter of the 'inherent weakness of language'[167] (and Plato, of course, remains one of rhetoric's most articulate opponents). It is more than a banal generalization to conclude that, one way and another, today's Western languages – with all the paradoxes they embody and the debates they reflect – are as much a part of the classical tradition as ever.

[163] Both in *Philosophical Investigations* of 1953 ('family resemblances') and earlier in the *Tractatus* of 1921: 'whereof one cannot speak, thereof one must be silent' (Last Proposition); 'The limits of my language mean the limits of my world' (5. 6).

[164] Margolin (1971) compares Queneau's *Exercices* with what Cave (1979) 24 calls Erasmus's 'virtuoso display' of creative synonymy in *De copia*, 1. 33. Cf. also Steiner (1998) 336–8 on Hermann Broch's lyrical-prose meditations in *Der Tod des Vergil* (1945) and its English translation by Untermeyer (*The Death of Virgil*, 1945).

[165] E.g. Dante, *Paradiso*, 33. 55–7 ('seeing was much more than speech can show'). Cf. Moses' despair at his own inarticulacy in Schoenberg's *Moses und Aron* (1930–2) ('O Wort, du Wort, das mir fehlt': the final words of Act II).

[166] *Pace* attempts to read back Derridean pessimism into Renaissance texts: thus Lynch (1998) makes Montaigne 'a premodern poststructuralist' (85) and credits the Renaissance as a whole with 'an emerging skeptical view of language as entirely [*sic*] arbitrary and slippery' (84). Note rather the 'copiousness' of an Erasmus: n. 164 above.

[167] 342e (along with the argument of 341b–343a as a whole).

§14
Modes of Engagement

We have shown, already, how the classics and the classical have engendered reflexes and responses of many different kinds, on many different levels. It would be a challenging task to attempt a list of *all* the kinds, on *all* the levels. In this section, more modestly, we offer a selective review of active responses – *engagements* – partly to provide an additional perspective for our earlier discussions, partly to acknowledge some identifiable 'modes of engagement' which, for one reason or another, we shall not be confronting in any detail, partly to introduce the three sections that follow, each dealing with an important 'mode' which, in the context of this book, does call for separate treatment.

Everyone who encounters the classics or the classical belongs to at least one (sometimes more than one) of five categories. There are practical users; there are students; there are scholars; and there are what one might distinguish as travellers and tourists. Users vary from (among our earlier examples) the medievals who incorporate Roman architectural features into church interiors (§11) to the triumphant heirs of that French culture envisaged by Du Bellay which absorbs its classical models *and* gets beyond them (§§7, 13). For practical users, and often for students too, any encounter with things Roman or Greek has a specific aim. By contrast, tourists, travellers, and scholars, broadly speaking, are (in the Kantian sense) disinterested. Broadly speaking: the physician-humorist Rabelais, scrutinizing an ancient Greek medical text (§6), is essentially a user, as is James 'Athenian' Stuart, measuring ancient Greek monuments in the eighteenth century (§11). Both seek to learn specific lessons from the ancients; their modern counterparts – researchers in the

The Classical Tradition: Art, Literature, Thought, First Edition. Michael Silk, Ingo Gildenhard, and Rosemary Barrow.

Published 2017 by John Wiley & Sons Ltd.

field – are unlikely to have any such practical agenda. Correspondingly, the classical holdings in libraries and museums – those great resources of scholarship and learning – may once have had a significant practical rationale, as materials for the practitioner,[1] but they now cater to scholars and students as a matter of course, to travellers and tourists randomly, to practical users hardly at all. At the same time, such collections do not arise spontaneously; and those who assembled them in the first place are 'users' of a very specific kind.

Travellers and tourists: we mean the terms, and the distinction, figuratively,[2] but literally as well.[3] Tourists, as opposed to travellers, are routinely despised by aficionados of high culture, because tourist (ad)ventures tend to be shorter, and their high-cultural content slighter or less informed, but also because they are to a significant degree pre-arranged: tours are guided, holidays packaged. 'The traveller sees what he sees,' said G. K. Chesterton, 'the tripper' – as tourists in the modern sense were once known – 'sees what he has come to see.'[4] And the sights the tripper-tourist has come to see are (probably) predictable, even compulsive, and (maybe) are consumed as such:

> Behold then Mr Septimus Dodge returning to Dodge-town victorious. Not crowned with laurel, it is true, but wreathed in lists of things he has seen and sucked dry. Seen and sucked dry, you know: Venus de Milo, the Rhine, or the Coliseum: swallowed like so many clams, and left the shells.[5]

In this respect, the eighteenth-century 'gentlemen amateurs and the merely curious'[6] who make the Grand Tour are, as the name suggests, generally a version, however lofty, of the despised tourist of more modern times. Though their responses are various, and often studious, their visits are programmed. James Boswell's résumé is indicative:

> I have almost finished my tour of Italy. I have viewed with enthusiasm classical sites and the remains of the grandeur of the ancient Romans. I have made a thorough study of architecture, statues and paintings.[7]

Yet there is surely nothing to despise in the Boswellian tourist, any more than there is in the forays into the classical of the touristic reader – unless, indeed, the forays

[1] Libraries, and in particular their classical holdings, were esp. important for users, before the rise of modern science: Cavallo *et al.* (1989), Chartier (1994), Grafton (1993b), (1997).

[2] With various precedents, scholarly and other: cf. Keats, p. 168 below, and van den Abbeele (1992).

[3] Literal touring and travelling, in a classical perspective: Elsner (2010).

[4] *Autobiography* (1936), ch. 15.

[5] D. H. Lawrence, *Studies in Classic American Literature* (1923), ch. 4 ('Fenimore Cooper's White Novels'). For Lawrence's generation, the classical sites of old Europe are a characteristic tourist target, and visitors from the new America the typical tourists.

[6] Hornsby (2000b) 3.

[7] Letter to Rousseau, 11 May 1765.

are motivated essentially by a sense of duty ('a classic is something that everybody wants to have read and nobody wants to read': Mark Twain).[8]

The traveller, in any event, is different. Since the Romantic age, above all, antiquity has been somewhere preeminently to travel *to*, with literal travel itself even acquiring some connotative link with the antique: 'I met a traveller from [*where else but*?] an antique land . . .'[9] But though travel may acquire its own compulsive character ('I cannot rest from travel', says Tennyson's Ulysses),[10] it is essentially unpredictable ('It *may be* that the gulfs will wash us down: | It *may be* we shall touch the Happy Isles').[11] As such, it is conducive to new perspectives, in a way that touring is probably not ('all experience is an arch wherethrough | Gleams that untravelled world . . .').[12] Travellers are more open to profound experience. The poet Keats, 'On First Looking Into Chapman's Homer' (1816), is explicit: he has already 'travell'd in the realms of gold', but his new encounter with Chapman has shown him unforeseen new worlds ('a new planet', even) (§15). The poet Rilke, confronted by the power of an 'Archaic Torso of Apollo', is more explicit still. His confrontation is interactive: 'you' have seen the statue, but there is no *place* (no part of the powerful statue) that does not 'see you'; 'you', therefore, 'must change your life'.[13]

Touring may, of course, lead to life-changing travel too. A momentous visit to Italy in 1786–8 allowed Goethe to experience the statues *he* had only read about in Winckelmann. The Apollo Belvedere took him 'out of reality';[14] the outcome overall was a kind of personal 'rebirth'.[15] More literally life-changing: Byron's Grand Tour (1809–11) took him out of the Grand Tourist's comfort zone to Albania and then Greece, where personal and political investment in the embryonic nation eventually led to a hero's death in 1824.

Grand Tourists, of course, belong to a certain social class, and the presumption of 'grandeur' characterizes the self-understanding of that class as much as it defines the 'touring' itself. It makes no sense to ignore the larger enabling conditions and wider contexts in which these and other modes of engagement have taken effect. And if scholars, travellers, tourists (even grand ones), are disinterested, in their responses to antiquity, the same cannot be said of Lord Elgin's relationship with the Parthenon marbles that culminated in their removal from Athens to London (§§11, 17). Goethe's visits to the antiquities in Rome are very different from those of Jean Du Bellay. The latter (uncle of Joachim and bishop of Paris, then Cardinal) owned

8 After-dinner speech in 1900: Paine (1912) 1120 (*sic*).

9 Shelley, 'Ozymandias' (1818) – where, however, the exotic name points not to classical antiquity, but to ancient Egypt.

10 'Ulysses' (1833), 6: §35.

11 Ibid. 62–3: our italics.

12 Ibid. 18–20.

13 'Archaïscher Torso Apollos' (1908): 'denn da ist keine Stelle, | die dich nicht sieht. Du musst dein Leben ändern.'

14 'Hinausgerückt aus der Wirklichkeit': *Italienische Reise* (1816–17), entry for 9 November 1786.

15 'Wiedergeburt': ibid. 3 December 1786.

an estate near the Baths of Diocletian and made repeated visits, many spent organizing excavations, the finds from which were sent back to France, chiefly to enhance the royal collection of Francis I at Fontainebleau (§17).

On one of his visits, in 1534, Du Bellay was accompanied by Rabelais, then his private physician, who involved himself in the excavations, but also, more disinterestedly, in the study of the topography of the ancient city (the outcome, later that year, was Rabelais's revision of Bartolomeo Marliani's *Antiquae Romae topographia*). This alliance of a committed user and a more-or-less innocent scholar-viewer is representative. Collections that make possible the most disinterested viewings have generally been assembled by dint of money and power, and sometimes under an explicitly imperialist agenda (§§16, 17).

At the same time, the possibility of viewing material objects depends both on their location and on the viewer's circumstances. Texts can be copied and (especially after the invention of printing) raise only limited questions of access; art-objects (unless in the modern sense of Benjamin's 'mechanical reproduction')[16] exist uniquely in one place, which may or may not be accessible to a would-be viewer. Aristocrats and patricians like Byron and Goethe can, literally, travel to view antiquities *in situ*. A humbler 'traveller' like Keats can reach the world of Homer in his head and heart; he can visit the Elgin marbles in London; Italy, he only visits for his fading health. An engagement with the classical may be implicated in issues of politics and power; it may be innocent; more untidily, it may be both.

A quite different variable is one that all students of reception should constantly have in mind. When we ponder an artist's, writer's, thinker's, encounters with the ancient world – with *that* statue, with *this* version of a myth, with *those* political ideas, with *these* aspects of antiquity and *those* earlier receptions inextricably – we cannot assume that there is any convenient formula for any such encounter, or its outcomes. In particular, one cannot assess the spirit of an engagement on the basis of some objective category of receptions. Take, as a single case-study, the phenomenon of Latin quotations.

In *An Audience at Agrippa's* (1875), Victorian classical-subject painter Lawrence Alma-Tadema adds a historically accurate dedication (partially visible) to the plinth of a statue of Augustus; in his *Spring* (1894), the seemingly innocent jollity of a Roman festival procession is qualified by a banner (again partly hidden in the crowd) with Priapic verses – not crude verses, but verses which, once identified, are suggestive of raw sexuality. In the one painting, the Latin functions to assure the viewer of the archaeological authenticity of the depiction; in the other, it invites a sophisticated reappraisal of the scene and its implications, on the part of the knowledgeable interpreter.[17]

The first words of Prudentio, the pedant, in Francesco Belo's Italian comedy of that name (*Il Pedante*, 1529), are a Virgilian quotation, in untranslated Latin, about

[16] 'The Work of Art in the Age of Mechanical Reproduction' ('Das Kunstwerk im Zeitalter seiner technischen Reproduzierbarkeit', 1936).

[17] Barrow (2001) 82–5, 151–2.

love;[18] the theme of the quotation is relevant to the amorous interest of the play, but the simple function of the quotation is to pinpoint the stereotypical pedantry of the speaker at the outset. At the final climax of Christopher Marlowe's *Doctor Faustus* (written around 1589), the agonized Faustus, with 'but one bare hour to live', invokes a line from Ovid's *Amores*, again in untranslated Latin, 'Run slowly, slowly, horses of the night!'[19] The original context of the words does add a certain irony;[20] and the aptness of a *Latin* quotation here does befit a 'hero' (§21) who now despairingly regrets his earlier decision to turn his back on orderly learning in favour of his fatal pact with the Devil[21] – but the chief point of *this* quotation is the plain meaning of the Latin words themselves.

In 1850, in a Parliamentary debate on the Don Pacifico affair,[22] the British Foreign Secretary, Lord Palmerston, used an attested Latin formula, 'I am a Roman citizen', to evoke majestic images of Roman antiquity, from Cicero to the Vulgate account of St Paul:[23]

> as the Roman, in days of old, held himself free from indignity, when he could say *Civis Romanus sum*; so also a British subject, in whatever land he may be, shall feel confident that the watchful eye and the strong arm of England will protect him against injustice and wrong.

The same formula was invoked in June 1963 by President Kennedy in West Berlin:

> Two thousand years ago the proudest boast was 'civis Romanus sum'. Today, in the world of freedom, the proudest boast is 'Ich bin ein Berliner' ['I am a Berliner'] . . . All free men, wherever they may live, are citizens of Berlin.

The spirit of the two uses, as well as their context, is significantly different. Palmerston, addressing an educated gathering, is drawing together the specifics of a classical catch-phrase and the connotations of high-cultural reference to amplify an esoteric individual case into a point of high principle. Kennedy (with the Berlin Wall and the still beleagured status of the 'free' city in mind) is appealing to a looser sense of the Latin (though, with a modern mass audience, it may seem surprising that he should be alluding to it at all) to provide a foil for a huge symbolic declaration at an already huge symbolic event.

By using the title *Noli Me Tangere* ('Touch Me Not') – Jesus' words, again in the Vulgate, to Mary Magdalene after the resurrection[24] – a succession of artists

[18] Act I: 'omnia vincit amor, et nos cedamus amori', 'Love overcomes everything: let us, too, give in to love' (Virgil, *Eclogues*, 10. 69).

[19] *Doctor Faustus*, 5. 2: 'o lente lente currite, noctis equi' (*Amores*, 1. 13. 40).

[20] In Ovid, the words are those of a lover, keen to prolong his pleasure.

[21] Faustus' opening monologue (in 1. 1) contains half a dozen different Latin quotations.

[22] Britain had sent a naval squadron to exact compensation from Greece on behalf of a Gibraltar-born (therefore technically British) Portuguese-Jewish merchant, David Pacifico, whose house in Athens had been destroyed in an anti-Semitic riot.

[23] Cicero, *In Verrem*, 2. 5. 162; Acts, 22. 27.

[24] John 20. 17.

(notably Titian, *c.* 1514) identify the subject of a painting for its viewers in a Latin-centred Christian age. In a later phase of that same age, Poussin's *The Arcadian Shepherds* (*Les Bergers d'Arcadie*, *c.* 1640), features a tableau of idealized countryfolk grouped around a tomb inscribed with the famously evocative Latin words, 'Et in Arcadia Ego' [*Plate 4*]. Famously evocative, but also famously elusive. Though many critics – including Erwin Panofsky, in successive versions of a notable essay[25] – have attempted to delimit 'the' meaning of the phrase in context, the Latin words (first attested in two other Arcadian Shepherd paintings, by Guercino, *c.* 1620, then again by Poussin, 1627) flatly defy such exegesis. Their compressed and elliptical phrasing allows a whole series of alternative interpretations: 'I too in Arcadia . . .' or 'Even I in Arcadia . . .' or '*Even* [or *also*] in Arcadia, I . . .' – and '. . . am' or '. . . still am' or (in effect) '. . . lived and died' or '. . . now (being dead) am' (all these with a human subject) – or (with Death as subject?) '. . . am here'. 'I' (but who or what?) am connected with *this* (or *any*?) 'Arcadia', but precisely *how*? The informed viewer registers a general connection of 'Arcadia' with the Virgilian-based tradition of an ideal pastoral world, as also the general relevance of mortality (suggested both by the tomb and by the association with Guercino's more death-ful depiction),[26] as well as the general connection, in this period, of epitaphs with Latin.[27] Beyond that, even the *precise* point of having a Latin inscription (*as if* alluding to some ancient source?) remains elusive. The overall elusiveness, even, is part of the point overall? The open-endedness of the tag is summed up, indeed, by subsequent allusions – such as the almost triumphal (and far from death-ful) way that Goethe uses it as epigraph to his *Italian Journey*, but now in exclamatory German ('Auch ich in Arkadien!').

An inscription on the tomb of the architect, Christopher Wren, in St Paul's Cathedral, assumes not that its readers can catch an allusion to a quotation, but that they can both translate a new bit of Latin and appreciate a mild irony: 'Lector, si monumentum requiris, circumspice' ('Reader, if you are searching for a/his memorial, look around you'). The motto used on US coinage since the late eighteenth century,[28] *e pluribus unum* ('out of many [states or peoples], one'), is sufficiently familiar to pop up in casual usage in American popular culture, from the film *The Wizard of Oz* to the animated TV sitcom, *The Simpsons*[29] – but its classical source is both *recherché* and irrelevant.[30] The motto of the Canadian Air Force, *sic itur ad astra* ('this is the way to the stars'), is an apt, if flattering, quotation in terms of its

[25] Panofsky (1936), (1955); cf. Marin (1995). See further Carrier (1993) 29–35, 145–74.

[26] Guercino's is a *memento mori* painting, with the shepherds looking at a skull.

[27] Cf. McFarlane (1986).

[28] Also on the 1782 design for the Great Seal of the United States.

[29] In the film (1939), the Wizard himself refers to 'the land of *e pluribus unum*', while 'E Pluribus Wiggum' was the parodic title of an episode of *The Simpsons* (January 2008) about a Presidential election.

[30] Ps.-Virgil, *Moretum*, 104, 'color est e pluribus unus' ('the many colours [of a ground garlic and herb mixture] blend into one').

overt content, but not so much flattering as hyperbolic, in respect of its original context.[31]

In many of these cases, the use of Latin is premised, in some degree, on the continuing notion that Latin is the language of eternity ('Dr Johnson said the inscription should have been in Latin, as everything intended to be universal and permanent should be').[32] There are also cases where that premise seems to be the main point, beyond any consideration of the content, let alone the original context – from the portentous epitaph on the grave of Carl Jung ('vocatus atque non vocatus, deus aderit': 'God will be here, whether called upon or not')[33] to the sublimely incongruous words that frame the head of Hollywood's MGM lion (*ars gratia artis*: 'art for art's sake').[34]

Across the many and varied manifestations of the classical tradition, diversity of engagement is the norm. Appeals to authority can operate on very different levels: think of the very different significance of Plato for the scholars and translators in Ficino's Florence, for the young men in Forster's *Maurice* (§9) – and for the Buddhist-nihilist Neoplatonism of the German thinker Schopenhauer.[35] Chains of classicizing allusion are especially liable to involve responses of diverse kinds: the effect of the Baroque reference in Portoghesi's Islamic Mosque in Rome (§11) has little in common with the impact of Italian Baroque (on the modern sight-seer, *or* on early bystanders) *in situ*. Performance – one of the topics we shall not be confronting in its own right here[36] – offers textbook examples. Modern stagings of Aristophanic comedy, for instance, cover the spectrum from scholarly reconstruction to (in our figurative sense) touristic fun.[37] And diversity of encounter and response is richly evident in three large and significant modes of engagement to which we now give separate treatment: looking at the past (§17), 'scientific' scholarship (§16), and, first, translation (§15).

[31] Virgil, *Aeneid*, 9. 641, the words of Apollo (in heaven) to Aeneas' son Ascanius/Iulus (in battle, on earth), with special reference to the young man's destiny, as ancestor of the 'divine' Caesars ('deos', 642), in centuries to come.

[32] Boswell, *The Journal of a Tour to the Hebrides with Samuel Johnson* (1785): entry for 5 September 1773. A generation later, in *Du Pape* (1819), 1. 20, Joseph de Maistre makes a related point *apropos* Wren's epitaph, contrasting its memorializing idiom with the ephemeral 'chattering' (his word is 'bavarder') of the vernacular.

[33] The same inscription stood above the door of Jung's house (along with the grave, in Kusnacht, Switzerland); the quotation is from Erasmus, *Adagia*, 2. 3. 32. Other doors offer more personalized mottoes. 'Si non oscillas, noli tintinnare' ('If you don't swing, don't ring', in *ad hoc* Latin) is said to be carved above the entrance to Hugh Hefner's Playboy Mansion in Chicago.

[34] Seemingly a Latin translation of Théophile Gautier's slogan (in the preface to *Mademoiselle de Maupin*, 1835), 'l'art pour l'art' (itself prefigured in Victor Cousin's 1818 Sorbonne lectures, 'Du vrai, du beau et du bien').

[35] Schopenhauer and Plato: §10 n. 13.

[36] But one that has attracted much attention, esp. in connection with Greek tragedy, in recent years: Flashar (1997), Goldhill (2007b), Macintosh (2008a).

[37] Hall and Wrigley (2007).

§15

Translation

Translation has its analogies in the visual domain,[1] as also in the diffuse realm of cultural practice,[2] but it concerns us as a specific phenomenon of language, involving a conversion from one tongue into another. And for us what matters is not practical communication between co-existing speech communities, but engagement with texts from another culture. In recent years, translation (of both kinds) has given rise to a new academic specialism: 'translation studies'. Over the centuries, more broadly, translation (largely of the second kind) has generated a remarkable diversity of claims, often urgent in tone, which should exercise anyone concerned with the theory, the practice, or the history of the phenomenon.[3]

Much of the claiming has focused on the relation between translations and their originals. The stock question (inescapably significant for literary texts) is: should translators attempt to render their originals as 'literally' as possible, or not? should they aspire to translate 'word for word', or in paraphrase? The alternatives were already formulated in these terms by Cicero, who opposes a 'word for word' rendering to one that concentrates on preserving the spirit and sense ('the

[1] 'The metaphor of translation has been used commonly since the late eighteenth century to describe both the activity and the end result of painting': Hanoosh (1986) 22.

[2] Steiner (1998) 437 identifies 'culture' as 'the translation and rewording of previous meaning' and proposes (ibid. xii) that translation itself is 'formally and pragmatically implicit in *every* act of communication' (italics his).

[3] Variously: Delisle and Woodsworth (1995), Kelly (1979), Lianeri and Zajko (2008). As these and other overviews make clear, many of the categories and preoccupations of translation studies long predate it. 'Much of what we are saying has been said already, albeit in a different kind of [*sc.* without much] jargon': Lefevere (1992) xiv.

The Classical Tradition: Art, Literature, Thought, First Edition. Michael Silk, Ingo Gildenhard, and Rosemary Barrow.

Published 2017 by John Wiley & Sons Ltd.

overall character and force') of the original.[4] In 1680, John Dryden added a third possibility, 'imitation' – 'where the translator (if now he has not lost that name) assumes the liberty, not only to vary from the words and sense, but to forsake them both as he sees occasion; and taking only some general hints from the original, to run division on the ground-work, as he pleases.'[5] His examples of this 'imitation' include Cowley's versions of Pindar (1656);[6] a generation later, he might perhaps have added Pope's *Iliad* (1720). The other alternatives, Dryden distinguishes as 'paraphrase' (where 'words are not so strictly followed as . . . sense') and 'metaphrase' ('word by word and line by line': his paradigm for that, Ben Jonson's version of Horace's *Ars Poetica*, 1640). Paraphrase is his preferred option.[7]

In practice, few translations stick to consistent metaphrase or consistent paraphrase or, indeed, consistent imitation, in any systematic way, but an impression of the extremes may be helpful. This is *Iliad*, 12. 322–8, in Lang, Leaf, and Myers's largely metaphrastic prose (1882). Sarpedon's rallying-call to Glaucus:

> Ah, friend, if once escaped from this battle we were for ever to be ageless and immortal, neither would I fight myself in the foremost ranks, nor would I send thee into the war that giveth men renown, but now – for assuredly ten thousand fates of death do every way beset us, and these no mortal may escape nor avoid – now let us go forward, whether we shall give glory to other men, or others to us.

And this is 'the same' passage, in Pope's part-paraphrase, part-imitation, a century and a half earlier (1720):

> Could all our care elude the gloomy grave,
> Which claims no less the fearful than the brave,
> For lust of fame I should not vainly dare
> In fighting fields, nor urge thy soul to war.
> But since, alas! ignoble age must come,
> Disease, and death's inexorable doom,
> The life which others pay, let us bestow,
> And give to fame what we to nature owe;
> Brave though we fall, and honour'd if we live,
> Or let us glory gain, or glory give.

'A pretty poem,' said the scholar Richard Bentley, 'but you must not call it Homer.'[8] The quip is both tiresome and illuminating. Pope's couplets read, as they are

[4] *De Optimo Genere Oratorum*, 14: 'verbum pro verbo', as against 'genus omne verborum vimque servare'. Cf. Jerome, *Epistles*, 57. 5.

[5] Dryden's preface to his translation of *Ovid's Epistles*.

[6] In Cowley's own words (preface to his *Pindaric Odes*): 'I have . . . taken, left out and added what I please; nor make it so much my aim to let the reader know precisely what he spoke as what was his way and manner of speaking.'

[7] Explicitly so in the preface. Cf. O'Sullivan (1980) and (rather differently) Silk (2007b) 287–8.

[8] Quoted by J. Hawkins, in his edition of *The Works of Samuel Johnson* (1787), 4. 126. The exact form of the quotation is open to doubt (Hopkins 2010a: 253), and the story may be apocryphal anyway (Levine 1984). Bentley and Pope: cf. §16.

designed to read, like English Augustan poetry: like Pope's own, in fact. And like Pope's own, they proclaim, with great lucidity, coherence, and mature eloquence, the antitheses (both formal and ethical) and the seeming stabilities of the neoclassical age. In the process, the elusive concreteness of Homeric idiom and vision (still residually apparent in Lang, Leaf, and Myers: 'escaped from this battle') disappears in favour of concentrated abstractions, which are themselves the tokens of the stabilities of Pope's world: 'lust of fame', 'ignoble age', 'inexorable doom', 'nature'.[9] There is great gain, and there is loss; and the two are not easy to disentangle. But – central to the gain – 'Pope has at least the merit of translating Homer into *something*.'[10]

In the translation theory of Lawrence Venuti, in our own day, Dryden's metaphrase and paraphrase, the two familiar alternatives,[11] are distinguished on ideological grounds. Translation approximating to metaphrase is taken to have a positive potential, precisely because of its point-by-point deference to its source. Any such 'foreignizing' allows alien features of the original idiom their (on this argument) due recognition (as in Lang, Leaf, and Myers's 'ten thousand fates of death' and their long parenthesis, 'for . . . avoid'). A freer mode of translation tends to be 'domesticating', by accommodating itself to the norms of the translator's language and culture (as in Pope's more fluent syntax and his majestic Augustanism, 'death's inexorable doom'); as such, it is seen (in postcolonial fashion) to imply an imperial master's attitude towards a colonial subject.[12] The positive logic of foreignizing was first proposed in 1813 by the German theologian, and translator of Plato, Friedrich Schleiermacher, who, in comparable terms (but in a pre-colonialist spirit), favoured the cultivation of a linguistic idiom 'bent towards a foreign likeness',[13] as a means of doing justice to the thought of his author. Unlike Venuti's argument, however, Schleiermacher's has a specific internal rationale: a distinctive relevance to the translating of, precisely, *thought*, like Plato's (and, in Schleiermacher's own philosophy, language is coextensive with thought).

The foreignizing of Lang, Leaf, and Myers involves recourse to archaism ('thee', 'giveth', 'beset'), in evident reflection of the antiquity, the remoteness, and perhaps also the perceived dignity, of their Homeric source. More often, though, archaizing is associated with domesticating. In such cases, it is as if the translator feels the need of 'a natural habitat for the alien presence', which can be *present*-ed, paradoxically, as 'a part of one's own tradition temporarily mislaid'.[14] Here belong such celebrated instances as the English (King James) Bible (1611) and, two centuries later, the German Shakespeare: 'the German reader of the Wieland–Schlegel–Tieck

[9] Cf. Silk (2004b) 40–61. Compare/contrast the reading of Pope's *Iliad* in Hopkins (2010a) 293–310.

[10] Ezra Pound in 1918 (his italics): Pound (1954) 250.

[11] The third, imitation, is generally sidelined (as by Venuti) or run together with paraphrase.

[12] See e.g. Venuti (2008).

[13] *Über die verschiedenen Methoden des Übersetzens*: 'zu einer fremden Ähnlichkeit hinübergebogen'. German translator-theorists: Kitzbichler *et al.* (2009).

[14] Steiner (1998) 365.

Shakespeare experiences the flattering impression of looking back on something entirely his own. The remoteness is that of his own historical past.'[15]

With or without archaizing, domestication is a familiar procedure, and often an explicit goal, presented as necessary and appropriate. In this spirit, Luther, in 1530, defended the Germanizing ('Verdeutschung') in *his* Bible, against earlier German versions, based on the Vulgate,[16] and, more explicitly still, John Denham, in 1656, the Englishness of his Virgil translation: 'If Virgil must needs speak English, it were fit he should speak it not only as a man of this nation, but as a man of this age.'[17] Few translators of note have practised the converse, and fewer still have produced any articulate account of their practice. Exceptions include Chateaubriand, in 1836, in defence of his anglicizing French Milton, replete with Miltonic syntax and 'calques' of Milton's Latinate lexicon;[18] Nabokov, in 1955, on translating Pushkin ('the clumsiest literal translation is a thousand times more useful than the prettiest paraphrase');[19] and – of special relevance to us – Hölderlin, whose version of sixteen odes of Pindar, in 1800 (or the years following),[20] was conceived of as a 'gymnastic exercise' for the German language, the hoped-for outcome of which would be a new embodiment, in German, of 'foreign modes' and 'foreign beauty and power.'[21] Later in the century, Nietzsche was to draw a striking contrast between the now established German tradition of translating – both 'antiquarian', as he saw it, and historicizing – and the bolder French inclination ('in the age of Corneille, and even the Revolution') to 'take possession of Roman antiquity'. That, he compared, in turn, to the way the Romans themselves once treated their Greek predecessors; for them, 'translation was a form of conquest.'[22] Nietzsche's frame of reference is suggestive. Hölderlin's claims (like his practice) are bold, even extreme, yet also representative of a new age of historical awareness.

15 Ibid. One remarkable experiment in this vein comes from Emile Littré (politician, editor of the Hippocratic corpus, lexicographer of the French language), who translated Dante's 'Inferno' into medieval French ('L'Enfer mis en vieux langage François') in 1879.

16 Luther, *Ein Sendbrief vom Dolmetschen*.

17 'The Destruction of Troy: An Essay upon the Second Book of Virgil's *Aeneis*.' Denham's formulation was copied, without acknowledgement, by Dryden on Virgil and others in 1685, on Juvenal in 1692, on Virgil in 1697: Watson (1962), 2. 19, 154, 247.

18 In the *Remarques* prefacing his *Paradise Lost* (*Le Paradis perdu*): 'J'ai calqué le poème de Milton à la vitre'.

19 Nabokov (1955) 496.

20 Dating: Benn (1962) 9–24. In the early 1800s, Hölderlin translated Sophocles' *Oedipus Tyrannus* and *Antigone* in the same spirit.

21 Letter to Neuffer, July 1794: 'das Übersetzen ist eine heilsame Gymnastik für die Sprache. Sie wird hübsch geschmeidig, wenn sie sich so nach fremder Schönheit und Grösse, oft auch nach fremden Launen bequemen muss.'

22 'Die Franzosen . . . bemächtigten sich des römischen Alterthums'; 'man eroberte damals, wenn man übersetzte': *Die fröhliche Wissenschaft* ('Gay Science', 1882), 2. 83. The contrast is already in Herder: 'Homer must come to France as a captive, and dress according to their fashion . . . We poor Germans . . . like to see him the way he is' (*Fragmente*, 'Zwote Sammlung', 1767: 'Von der griechischen Literatur in Deutschland').

What should a translation of a classic text do *for* (as opposed to *to*) its original? It can give access to it: 'The ultimate value of a translation lies in its power to ease our way into an original' – so Anthony Burgess in 1992.[23] It can shed light on it: 'Tis good to have translations, because they serve as a comment' – John Selden, as reported in 1689.[24] There is 'criticism by translation' (which Ezra Pound ascribed to Dante).[25] And, less specifiably, translation can complement and 'continue' its original (Walter Benjamin).[26]

The chances of success on any of these fronts are materially affected by whether readers of a translation can, or do, read the original. In many eras (including our own), translation into English, and certainly translation from the classics, is likely to be, not a supplement to its original, but a replacement for it. We recall Arnold's caveat ('the verse of the poets of Greece and Rome no translation can adequately convey') and his suggestion that 'the original poetry of Milton', instead, might inform the 'millions' who 'know not a word of Greek and Latin, and will never learn these languages' (§4).

Whether a reader is able to judge the relation of translation to original or not, the contingent facts of language and culture are unavoidable complications for any translator. Differences between languages ensure that even the most literalizing translation must differ from its original in a variety of ways, large and small, from the historical resonance of given usages to individual word-shapes; and in classic texts the complexity and precision of verbal properties resists all homology. It follows that any translation of such a text customarily falls below its original. The translator of great poetry, in particular, 'can never recreate it in its full perfection': the observation of Cervantes, in his *Don Quixote*[27] (a work itself translated into English, French, and Italian within a dozen years of its completion in 1612). Rendered into French, Heine's German poetry (the poet agreed) was 'stuffed moonlight'.[28] The alternative possibility, that – in principle, and occasionally in practice – a translation can surpass its original,[29] has provoked some curious reactions, from righteous indignation ('A translator is to be like his author,' declared Dr Johnson: 'it is not his business to excel him')[30] to paradox ('the original is unfaithful to the translation': Borges)[31] to self-contradiction: alongside his literalist tendencies,

23 *A Mouthful of Art*, 1, ch. 11.

24 *Table Talk*, ch. 29.

25 'Date Line' (1934): Pound (1954) 74.

26 'Die Aufgabe des Übersetzers' (1923).

27 1. 6 (words spoken by the priest).

28 'Stuffed with straw', as in taxidermy: 'clair de lune empaillé' – from Heine's (French) preface to his *Poèmes et légendes*, vol. 1 (dated June 1855). The image was not Heine's own ('comme a dit une méchante personne qui se moquait de mes poésies traduites').

29 Translations of the Greek New Testament – and not only, but not least, the English Bible versions, from the Wycliffe to the King James – must be prime candidates here.

30 *Life of Dryden* (1781): Hill (1905), 1. 423.

31 Jorge Luis Borges, 'On a Translation by Henley' (1943), on William Beckford's Gothic novel *Vathek*, written in French in 1782 ('in three days and two nights') but translated into more felicitous English (by Samuel Henley) and published, in translation (in 1786), before the first publication of the French original (in 1787).

Hölderlin, perhaps uniquely, proclaimed the right to 'correct' or 'improve' ('verbessern') an original.[32]

The more familiar view, reflective of the inevitable discrepancies, is that adequate translation is not just hard to attain, but simply unattainable, above all with poetry at the highest level. 'An impossible task,' Humboldt called it (though himself a translator of great poetry);[33] 'poetry,' said Robert Frost, 'is what is lost in translation';[34] and Dante, 'nothing harmonized by the bond of the Muses can be translated from its own language into another without shattering all its sweetness and harmony.'[35] In Dante's Italy, this pessimistic view soon generated a proverb equating 'translators' with 'traitors' – *traduttore, traditore* – a paronomasia sufficiently attenuated in any possible English version for Roman Jakobson, with some ingenuity, to cite the discrepancy itself as a paradigm of the limitations of translation in the face of creative language.[36] Most eloquent, perhaps, is the warning of the poet Shelley – also himself a translator – that the very notion of translating poetry is mere 'vanity': 'it were as wise to cast a violet into a crucible, that you might discover the formal principle of its colour and odour, as to seek to transfuse from one language into another the creations of a poet.'[37]

More pragmatically – more responsibly, one might argue – Goethe insisted on the value of translation for cultural transmission: 'Say what you like about the inadequacy of translation: it remains one of the most important and worthwhile undertakings among all the categories of human experience.'[38] Here, Goethe is opposing not only the pessimistic judgements of a Dante or a Humboldt about the prospects of successfully recuperating an original, but also a fashionable suspicion of the effects of translation on the recuperating culture itself. The hopes of a Hölderlin for the spread of 'foreign modes' are the fears of many others; and the kind of purist anxieties we have discussed as features of the developing European vernaculars (§13) have often been aroused by translation. 'The great pest of speech is frequency of translation,' said Dr Johnson – this, precisely on the grounds that a language at large is influenced by linguistic features transferred, however temporarily, from outside (by surreptitious 'foreignizing,' in fact): 'no book was ever turned

32 In this case, a Sophoclean original: letter to Wilmans, 28 September 1803.

33 Letter to A. W. Schlegel, 23 July 1796. Humboldt translated, most notably, Aeschylus' *Agamemnon* (1816).

34 Quoted in Untermeyer (1964) 18.

35 *Convivio*, 1. 7.

36 Jakobson (1959) 238.

37 *Defence of Poetry* (1821). Among other works, Shelley translated Plato's *Symposium* (1818: §9), seven *Homeric Hymns* (*c.* 1817) and parts of Goethe's *Faust* (1822): Webb (1976). Like Pope, Dryden, and Marlowe (translator of Ovid's *Amores*, 1597), Shelley thus belongs to a distinguished group of 'original' poets who are also translators. More recent examples include: Yeats (esp. his version of Sophocles' *Oedipus at Colonus*, published in 1934: Silk 2010); Valéry (Virgil's *Eclogues* – 'Bucoliques' – written under German occupation and published in 1956); Quasimodo (Ovid's *Metamorphoses*, 1966); Ted Hughes (notably his *Oresteia*, 1999: see Silk 1999a and discussions in Rees 2009).

38 '. . . eins der wichtigsten und würdigsten Geschäffte in dem allgemeinen Weltwesen': letter to Carlyle, 20 July 1827.

from one language into another, without imparting something of its native idiom.'[39] In France, the Pléiade had pondered the question, two centuries before. For Du Bellay, in 1549, imitation – of the ancients – was necessary and desirable, whereas literary translation, in any strict sense, was an 'unprofitable' and even 'pernicious' practice,[40] which could hinder expression of the distinctive genius (the 'naïf', or the 'je ne sais quoi') of the French language in a brave new world of national languages and literatures.[41] For Denham, pondering the pros and cons of translation a century later, in the context of his own rendering of Virgil, the danger was both that 'the grace of Latin will be lost by being turned into English words' and that 'the grace of the English' might be endangered too, 'by being turned into the Latin phrase.'[42] In Goethe's Germany, Herder expressed a related anxiety more forcefully: valuable as translations might be for the formation of a language, 'there are greater benefits for the language in protecting itself against *all* translation' – because, once translated into another tongue or once affected by translation from another tongue, it would lose its innocence and forfeit its integrity.[43]

Against all such doubts, Goethe's insistence on translation as a positive force – and Hölderlin's too – assumes that translation can have, ideally should have, what T. S. Eliot called a 'vitalizing effect' on the culture it augments by its presence. Eliot used the phrase, in 1920, in a critique of Gilbert Murray's Swinburnian renderings of Euripides: 'Greek poetry will never have the slightest vitalizing effect upon English poetry if it can only appear masquerading as a vulgar debasement of the eminently personal idiom of Swinburne.'[44] Vitalizing effect: this is among the primary functions of translation, and it is this primacy that the political correctness of a Venuti tends to obscure. The single thing that matters most about any literary or intellectual text is what it can do for the culture it speaks to; and the single thing that matters most about a *translation* of such a text is not whether it domesticates or foreignizes (significant though that indeed is), but what it can do for its new culture. A foreignizing translation lacking in force or felicity will do nothing for it; nor indeed will any such domesticating translation; but successful foreignizing (experience suggests) is harder – *even* harder, *much* harder – to attain.[45]

39 Preface to *A Dictionary of the English Language* (1755).

40 *Contra* (e.g.) Thomas Sebillet, *Art poétique françoys* (1548).

41 *Deffence*, 1. 6: see Castor (1964) 65–6, 80–2, and generally Norton (1984). In a later age, this recommendation is reversed. Emile Deschamps, collaborator of the young Victor Hugo, proclaims that 'the time for imitations is over: we must create or translate' (in the preface to his *Etudes françaises et étrangères*, 1828 – one of various Romantic manifestoes that, ironically, look back favourably to the Pléiade poets themselves).

42 'The Destruction of Troy' (n. 17 above).

43 'So sehr man Ursache hat, Übersetzungen zur Bildung der Sprache anzupreisen: so hat doch die Sprache grössere Vorzüge, die sich vor aller Übersetzung bewahret' (it is implicit in 'aller' that translation both ways is in question): *Fragmente*, 'Erste Sammlung' (2nd edn, 1768), 'Die Bildung einer Sprache'. Herder's translation theory: Costazza (2007).

44 'Euripides and Professor Murray': *The Sacred Wood*.

45 Cf. Croce (1922) 68, 73. Creative foreignizing: cf. also Carne-Ross (1989), Hopkins (2010a) 307–8.

In 1877, the challenge of translating Aeschylus' *Agamemnon* provoked the poet Robert Browning (widely known for experiments with idiomatic English) to attempt a literalizing 'transcription'; his aim was to make 'the very turn of each phrase . . . as Greek . . . as English will bear'.[46] The outcome can only be called bizarre. This is part of the Herald's account of the storm that wrecked the Achaean fleet:[47]

For, ships against each other Threkian breezes
Shattered: and these, butted at in a fury
By storm and typhoon, with surge rain-resounding, –
Off they went, vanished, thro' a bad herd's whirling.
. . .
And now – of them if anyone is breathing –
They talk of us as having perished: why not?
And we – that they the same fate have imagine.

One notes the pleasing simplicity of the 'why not' (in line with Browning's normal light touch); the 'expressive' sound-patterns in the first four lines ('ships/shattered', 'shattered/butted', 'rain/resounding', 'bad/herd', 'herd/whirl': highly Aeschylean, in passages of action, though not, as it happens, in this passage); the hit-and-miss 'transcription' of the imagery ('butted', interesting; 'herd', incomprehensible); and the imponderable Latinate-Miltonic feel of the inversions ('of them if anyone', 'we . . . imagine').[48] The point is that these words impinge (if at all) as *English* words with *English* associations. The whole thing, in fact, is no more 'Greek' than Pope's Homer – just less English. The vitalizing potential of *this* Browning version is nil, and the poet knew it (it had been a 'fruitless adventure', he later acknowledged).[49]

The fact is that, in such a case, foreign literalisms have to work as *real* English (or whatever the second language), however *un*-English, in the ordinary sense, they may ostensibly be. And what – for reference – might real English look like in such a connection? Can one imagine Aeschylean-poetic strength – powerful imagery, charged sound and rhythm, intense play of words and connotations – in coherent but distinctive English, commensurate with Aeschylus' coherent and distinctive Greek? As it happens, yes: all this calls to mind the poetry of Browning's greater (though then unknown) contemporary, G. M. Hopkins.[50] Listen to the storm from 'The Wreck of the Deutschland' (composed a year before Browning's *Agamemnon*, in 1876):

Hope had grown grey hairs,
Hope had mourning on,

[46] In the introduction to his translation, *The Agamemnon of Aeschylus*, p. v.

[47] Corresponding to Aeschylus, *Agamemnon*, 654–73; Browning's punctuation throughout.

[48] Latinate-Miltonic: §35.

[49] Introduction, p. v; cf. Benitez (2004). Pound, though an admirer of Browning, was frank in his criticism: 'Translators of Greek' (1919), in Pound (1954) 267–70.

[50] Classically trained at Oxford, Hopkins was briefly Professor of Greek at University College Dublin. His Aeschylean affinities were first noted by Stanford (1941).

Trenched with tears, carved with cares,
Hope was twelve hours gone;
And frightful a nightfall folded rueful a day
Nor rescue, only rocket and lightship, shone,
And lives at last were washing away:
To the shrouds they took, – they shook in the hurling and horrible airs.

Here – besides the rhythm, the sound, the imagery – one notes the almost eerie life given to Hopkins's empathetic summary by the felicitous dislocations, 'frightful a nightfall', 'rueful a day'. Aeschylean poetry is not dissimilar in kind.

Meanwhile, Housman's celebrated parody ('Fragment of a Greek Tragedy') –

O suitably attired in leather boots
Head of a traveller, wherefore seeking whom
Whence by what way how purposed art thou come
To this well-nightingaled vicinity? –

asks to be read as a parody of literalizing English translations of the Greek tragedians, at least as much as of Greek tragedy itself; and its original date (1883)[51] allows the thought that Browning's 'fruitless adventure', six years earlier, helped to provoke it. The conclusion, in any event, must be that in translation, just as much as in 'original' writing, the quality of the writing is, inevitably, decisive. It is only the random genius of a Hölderlin (greater poet than Hopkins, or Browning) that can even contemplate the possibility that a radically foreignizing translation can also be vitalizing – as Hölderlin's clearly did vitalize his own creative endeavours, if nothing else.[52]

In any event: Goethe and Eliot are right. The positive importance of translation for cultural development is beyond doubt, and on a variety of levels. In a helpful sketch, Gilbert Highet distinguished four distinct ways a culture stands to gain:[53] transmission of thought and ideas; enrichment of its language (*pace* Du Bellay *et al.*); stylistic enrichment of the literary language – which may seem insignificant, by comparison, until one recalls cases like the Italian invention of blank verse,[54] by imitation of ancient 'stichic' metres, and the consequential, and momentous, development of blank-verse 'iambics' (themselves pioneered in a translation from the classics) in English poetry;[55] and last but not least, the stimulus to new creativity

[51] See Ricks (1988) 499–500.

[52] Louth (1998). Cf. Eliot's formula for Pound (in 1928), 'the translator is giving the original through himself, and finding himself through the original': introduction to Pound's *Selected Poems* (1959).

[53] Highet (1967) 104–13.

[54] Usually ascribed to Gian Giorgio Trissino's 'endecasillabi sciolti' in his pioneering tragedy, *Sofonisba* (composed in 1515).

[55] *Aeneid* 4, translated ('*and drawne into a straunge meter*') by Henry Howard, Earl of Surrey (*c.* 1540, but first published, with the quoted phrase in the title, in 1554). Cf. Hardison (1986).

(Eliot's point). And these four ways sum up the distinctive significance of translations from the classics down the ages.[56]

In our terms, translation represents a 'mode of engagement' of surpassing importance. Translation, quite simply, has been coextensive with, and substantially constitutive of, the classical tradition, over most of its long span. In terms of 'stimulus to new creativity', above all, this is unmistakable. 'A great age of literature,' Ezra Pound suggests, 'is perhaps always a great age of translations, or follows it';[57] and nowhere is this more apparent than with translations from the classics – whether the 'great age' we have in mind is the Renaissance (with its wealth of translations from Greek into Latin, and from both into the vernaculars),[58] or the neoclassical age of Pope's Homer in England,[59] or the Romantic age in Germany, which produced not only a German Shakespeare, but the numerous German translations of (largely) Greek texts by Hölderlin and Schleiermacher, Humboldt, Wieland, and Voss.[60]

Shakespeare – the English Shakespeare – is an impressive witness to the truth of Pound's dictum. Shakespeare's direct sources of inspiration include Thomas North's version of Plutarch's *Lives* (1579) – without which the Roman plays (above all, *Antony and Cleopatra*, *c.* 1607) could hardly exist – and Arthur Golding's translation of Ovid's *Metamorphoses* (1567). Golding's Ovid informs a wide range of Shakespeare's work, dramatic and other, from *Venus and Adonis* (1593) to *The Tempest* (*c.* 1611), and underlies a diversity of particular detail. It was demonstrated, a century ago,[61] that most of Shakespeare's mythological allusions depend on Ovid (which mostly means, depend on Golding), and it is easy to point to specifiable debts. 'Or go thou like Sir Actaeon, he,' says Shakespeare's Pistol, 'With Ringwood at thy heels' – recalling Ovid's account of Actaeon and his hounds, but specifically in Golding's version, where the dogs' Greek names become English names, and the last of them, 'Hylactor', becomes 'Ringwood'.[62] It is still a matter of dispute whether Shakespeare accessed Ovid only in Golding's translation, or in the original Latin as well – to the point where one critic has suggested that translator and playwright are engaged in a joint task of 'translating Ovid into a common Elizabethan idiom' and that Golding's version offers 'a Shakespearean reading of Ovid'.[63]

[56] The only comparable phenomenon is translations of the Bible, from the Septuagint and Vulgate to the vernacular versions. See Ackroyd *et al.* (1963–70).

[57] 'Notes on Elizabethan Classicists' (1917): Pound (1954) 232.

[58] Data and overviews: Bolgar (1954) 506–41, Botley (2004), Kristeller *et al.* (1960–2003), Lockwood (1918).

[59] See esp. Hopkins (2010a).

[60] Berman (1984). Voss translated, among much else, the *Odyssey* (1781) and *Iliad* (1793); Wieland, a range from Lucian (1788–9) to Cicero's letters (1808–12). The age also produced notable rewritings of classical works, like Goethe's *Iphigenie auf Tauris* (1787) and Kleist's *Amphitryon* (1806).

[61] By Root (1903).

[62] *Merry Wives of Windsor*, 2. 1. 113–14; Ovid, *Metamorphoses*, 3. 224; Golding, 3. 270. 'Hylactor' is actually 'Barker' (Greek *hulaktein*, 'bark'), but is in effect re-etymologized by Golding as from Greek *hulê*, 'wood'.

[63] Brower (1971) 121. See further Bate (1993), Taylor (2000).

The claims of translation to a place of honour in our 'Overview' are clear – even without the neat rhetorical knots with which some literary and cultural critics have attached translation to the class*ic* as a matter of definition: as in Maurice Blanchot's argument that the classic is constituted by its continual retranslation; or Walter Benjamin's proposal (which underlies Blanchot's) that classic status assumes 'translatability'; or Frank Kermode's suggestion that the classic is to translation as permanence to change, the timeless to the temporal – with the two attuned, Heraclitus-fashion, as opposite tensions.[64]

The story of translation in the Western world (as also of translation theory, embedded or explicit) runs in parallel with the story of languages and literatures set out in §13; and like the developing literatures, translation has involved a disparate traffic of modes and ideas across linguistic boundaries and between (as also within) distinguishable cultural traditions. In the case of the classical tradition, the special status of translation reflects the distinctive bilingual outlook of ancient Rome, the outcome of Rome's fashioning its literature on Greek models. Whereas the Greeks themselves remained 'proudly monolingual', as Momigliano put it, [65] confident that only they possessed truly human (or at least truly intelligible) speech, the Romans turned to translation as a straightforward means of expanding their linguistic and cultural horizons – in intriguing synchrony with the expansion of their military might[66] – and may even be said to have invented the very notion of 'a classic' in the process of first translating from the Greek in the third century BC, when Livius Andronicus (half-Greek in name, and maybe in fact too) turns the *Odyssey* into Latin. Since that moment, at all events, 'translation has been at the heart of literary culture in Europe'.[67]

Over the course of the tradition, translation has played a range of roles, from the pivotal to the peripheral, and not only with translations from Latin or Greek into the vernaculars. In the Middle Ages there are translations from Greek or Latin into non-European languages (for instance, from Greek into Arabic),[68] as from non-European Arabic into Latin.[69] In the Renaissance, there are not only numerous translations from Greek into Latin, but a few from Latin into – ancient – Greek.[70] There have been, of course, translations from the vernaculars into Latin or Greek, especially, but not only, as a teaching tool.[71] And then there are translations of

[64] Blanchot (1971); Benjamin (1923: n. 26 above); Kermode (1975).

[65] Momigliano (1980) 162: 'I Greci rimasero orgogliosamente monoglotti.'

[66] The Greeks, as so often, are the great exception. 'Oh, those Greeks! . . . They turn our aesthetics upside down!': Nietzsche, *The Birth of Tragedy*, 7.

[67] France and Gillespie (2008) vii, who, however, date the 'moment' to the time of Cicero.

[68] Esp. after the rise of the 'Abbâsid dynasty and the foundation of Baghdad in 762: Gutas (1998).

[69] Tamani (1992).

[70] Quaint examples: Elizabethan translations of Virgil into Greek (by Daniel Halsworth and George Etherege): Binns (1990) 216. Quainter still: the translation (in XVII) of parts of the Old Testament into Homeric Greek by James Duport.

[71] In Britain, the practice remains alive, not only in educational contexts (§§4, 16), but as a fringe phenomenon more widely: witness commercially available publications like *Harrius Potter et Philosophi Lapis* and *Winnie Ille Pu*.

translations, where a vernacular version of a Greek or Latin text is retranslated into another vernacular. Some famous versions are cases in point. For instance, North's Plutarch (1579) is itself a translation of the French version by Jacques Amyot (1559). In his *Iliad* (1611), George Chapman broadly followed the literalizing Latin version by the French poet Jean de Sponde (1583), itself a revision of an earlier Latin version by Andreas Divus (1537), and was criticised for so doing by (in Chapman's words) 'a certain envious wind-fucker'.[72] For his translation of *Iliad* 1 (1700), Dryden drew on existing translations in four languages (including Chapman's in English) to assist his work.[73] And for his version of the *Aeneid* (1490), William Caxton used an earlier version by 'some noble clerke of fraunce' (who had based his own text on Boccaccio as well as Virgil), not without some anxiety about his ability to do justice to the 'fayr and honest termes and wordes in frenshe'.[74]

Some authors have translated their own work, especially in the multilingual culture of early modern Europe: we recall the way Alberti wrote his treatise on painting in both Italian and Latin in the 1430s (§11). Any such duplication is likely to cater to different reading publics, while in some cases it also carries significant implications for distribution and censorship. Thomas Hobbes first penned *De cive* in Latin (1641), before publishing it a decade later in an English translation, entitled *Philosophical Rudiments Concerning Government and Society*.[75] That English version appeared in the same year (1651) as the English text of *Leviathan* was published in London, while in 1668 a Latin translation of *Leviathan* itself came out in Amsterdam, facilitating its dissemination across Europe, and helping to stimulate political thought on the Continent, at a time when England had returned to monarchical rule.

Against the grain of much recent translation theory, which assumes interchange between two languages or two cultures only, even this brief survey shows that in the context of the classical tradition, at least, translators are often 'struggling between *several* languages . . . and . . . cultural frameworks.'[76]

Translations may in any case differ sharply in function and purpose. At the opposite end of the spectrum to the literary experiments of a Hölderlin or a Browning are the severely practical concerns of the Middle Ages, where translating is primarily a matter of knowledge transfer: Highet's 'transmission of thought and ideas' in its most basic form. Here belongs the now exotic-seeming traffic from Greek to Arabic and, later, from Arabic (including texts previously translated from

[72] Preface to the 1611 edition. Andreas Divus' Latin was also Ezra Pound's source for his version of Odysseus' descent to the Underworld (*Odyssey* 11) in *Canto* I (published in 1925, but composed years earlier): cf. Pound (1954) 259–64.

[73] Hopkins (2010a) 19. Compare/contrast, more recently, Yeats's versions of Sophocles' Oedipus plays (essentially rewritings of Jebb's literal English): Macintosh (2008b), Silk (2010).

[74] Caxton's *Eneydos,* 'Englisht from the French *Livre des Eneydes*'. The 'noble clerke' was Guillaume Le Roy, whose work was published in 1483.

[75] The actual authorship of the translation is disputed: Malcolm (1998).

[76] Lambert (2008) 2.

the Greek) to Latin (sometimes via Hebrew). This latter process begins towards the end of the eleventh century and peters out in the second half of the sixteenth, when textual authority as a source of scientific knowledge starts to wane.[77] Notable figures in this story include Constantine the African, active in eleventh-century Italy as translator of Hippocratic material (both from Arabic sources and directly from the Greek); Gerard of Cremona, who practised his craft in twelfth-century Toledo, and translated (from the Arabic) several of Aristotle's scientific works; and Adelard of Bath, who authored the first virtually complete translation of Euclid's *Elements*.[78] Translation tended to take place in the contact zones of Spain, Italy, and Sicily, but had significant reverberations in intellectual centres across the Latin West. 'From translation, all science had its offspring': the apt words of Italian philosopher Giordano Bruno, around the end of the sixteenth century.[79]

The revival of translation from the Greek, which reached its peak in the Renaissance, begins in the later Middle Ages. The dominant figure here is the Flemish Dominican, William of Moerbeke, who, in or around the 1260s, elected to put into Latin – or to revise existing Latin translations of – all the available works of Aristotle, translating (or revising) directly from (or against) the Greek. Scholarly legend, most likely faulty, has it that he did so at the request of Thomas Aquinas,[80] but whatever the truth of that, part of the motivation will have been doubts about the authenticity of existing translations based on Arabic sources. In any event, William's repertoire is characteristic of his age: besides Aristotle, he translated Proclus, Hippocrates, Galen, and Archimedes – theology, natural science, medicine, and mathematics. Artistic appeal was not his prime concern. He was praised for the literalness of his versions, on the premise of deference to ancient authority, which called for *verbatim* translation and wide dissemination. In that same spirit, some such works were subsequently put into the vernacular. Thus Aristotle's *Ethics* was translated from the Latin into Italian (by Brunetto Latini?) in 1290, and into French (by Nicholas Oresme) around 1375.

In England, the story begins much earlier with a programme of translation initiated by King Alfred towards the end of the ninth century. Alfred sponsored, and himself contributed to, English versions of a range of texts, from Boethius' *Consolation of Philosophy* to Orosius' *World History*.[81] His approach to translation, unlike William's, seems to have been characterized by royal liberties with the source text, by significant additions and hermeneutic adventures, to the point that Dryden's 'imitation' might well seem the appropriate label for his work. His Boethius, for instance, is effectively a 'reinterpretation of the neoplatonic philosophy of Boethius

77 Burnett (2005); cf. §6.

78 See generally Goyens *et al.* (2008), Hamesse and Fattori (1990).

79 Recorded (in this English form) by John Florio, in the preface to his English version of Montaigne's *Essais* (published in 1603).

80 Cf. Torrell (2005) 174–7; generally, Brams (1997).

81 Waite (2000) 1.

in the light of the teachings of Augustine and Gregory'.[82] Aptly enough, Alfred is the first to elevate the status of the translator by detecting, in the translating process, an analogy with the role of Christ as mediator between God and Man.[83]

Like Alfred in England, Notker the German helped to promote a vernacular literary culture a century later by fusing commentary, paraphrase, and translation, from Christian and classical sources. One notable outcome was a commentary on (again) Boethius' *Consolation*, which Notker combined with a partial translation of the text into Old High German.[84] Other works rendered by this prolific scholar (a schoolmaster-monk at St Gallen) included Aristotle's *Categories* and Latin treatises on logic and rhetoric used in the medieval classroom. In a letter to Bishop Hugo around 1015, he even floated the idea of translating school texts like Terence's *Andria* and Virgil's *Eclogues*. Notker was fully aware of the limited linguistic resources at his disposal in German; at the same time, he seems to have appreciated that producing vernacular texts in the service of exegesis threatened to disturb the existing Latin world-order.[85]

A millennium later, there is a surprising analogy between Notker's project and the now common use of translations as a medium of classical education in schools and universities in the English-speaking world.[86] Or rather, this analogy will seem most surprising to scholarly purists, for whom translations, in any such context, are suspect features of the contemporary scene, or else to those (publishers, above all) who convince themselves that each new Homer (etc.) is a gain for the human spirit, on a par with Pope (etc.).

The many English Homers of recent years – those of Lattimore (1950s and '60s) and Fagles (1990s), the Loeb and the World's Classics, and numerous others – represent invaluable teaching aids, conveniences for scholarly reference, and straightforward examples of Highet's 'transmission of thought and ideas'. For these purposes, all such 'functional' translations constitute an eminently respectable genre.[87] Only a few of the English versions produced in this vein have any literary distinction: William Arrowsmith's brilliant rendering of Petronius (1959); Guy Lee's almost Hölderlin-like attempt to translate Horace's *Odes* into syllabic equivalents of the original quantitative metres (1998).[88] A few others are discussible as phenomena – like E. V. Rieu's Penguin *Odyssey* (1946), which, by domesticating Homer into a boys' adventure story,[89] achieved a readable prose sufficiently engaging to become (until overtaken by the unexpurgated *Lady Chatterley's Lover*, in the 1960s) the

[82] Bately (2000) 20.

[83] In the preface to his version of Boethius' *Consolation*: Harbus (2007) 723–4.

[84] Schröbler (1953).

[85] Copeland (1991) 107; cf. Ellis (1989). Compare the case of Otfrid (§13).

[86] Ideally, 'classics *through* translation', rather than '*in* translation': cf. Parker (2001).

[87] 'Functional' is Martindale's helpful term (contrasting with 'aesthetic'): Martindale (2008) 104.

[88] Lee's Horace: Silk (1999b).

[89] E.g. : 'you an only son, the apple of your mother's eye; and King Odysseus dead and gone, far from his home in foreign parts . . . the moment your back is turned those fellows will be plotting mischief against you' (Eurycleia to Telemachus: *Odyssey*, 2. 365–9).

best-selling paperback in British publishing history.[90] In 1972, H. A. Mason produced a critically sensitive demonstration of the literary limitations of functional translation in the shape of various modern Homers (Lattimore's among them) – in the context, aptly, of a critical defence of Pope's Homer as a plausible 'guide' to Homer in the original ('To Homer Through Pope').[91] Nothing has changed since.[92]

And yet, and yet . . . the broad educational gain represented by this range of translation is unaffected: nothing has changed there, either. And bearing in mind its contribution to the current vibrancy of classical studies in the English-speaking world, one can only marvel at the hostility that the whole phenomenon has provoked. In the 1946 issue of the American *Journal of Higher Education*, Herbert Newell Couch reported that 'Mr. Whitehead protests against the mood that he has observed in the presence of scholars whenever a translation is mentioned; their emotional reaction is that of decent people in the presence of a disgusting instance of moral turpitude.'[93] Couch compared scholarly responses to the spread of classical translation in 1940s America to trench warfare, with stubborn educators 'fighting to the end' over 'each inch of ground', which was only yielded after 'bloody resistance'.[94] With due irony, the editors of the journal put next to Couch's contribution a piece entitled 'Veterans' Education in the Universities: Forcing Flexibility and Change on Administrators and Teachers', which explored the sea-change in American higher education in the wake of World War II and the GI bill (§4), when a 'horde of veterans' descended on the campuses, in search of intellectual enlightenment without benefit of linguistic training. British academia experienced similar battles several decades later; the prejudice against translation 'still blighted the lives of undergraduates reading Literae Humaniores at Oxford as late as the 1980s'.[95]

Behind the hostility to translation among some of the classically trained, politically sensitive observers may well detect self-interest. If, even today, knowledge of Latin and Greek constitutes a medium of access to two privileged cultures and, therefore, a form of symbolic capital in polite society, the 'vulgarization' of the classical texts and their mass dissemination in vernacular versions can indeed be perceived as a threat – not unlike the threat of counterfeit money that undermines the value of a currency. Alternatively, the anxiety can be seen as more disinterested, conditioned by a sense of loss that classics as an academic discipline should have ceased to be primarily literary (and no primarily literary discipline is sustainable without a concentration on language) – and should have become, instead, a more broadly based, though intellectually sophisticated, cultural-historical studies.[96]

[90] Hall (2008c) 330. *Lady Chatterley*: §9.

[91] Mason (1972) 179–206; cf. Hopkins (2010a) 294–8. Ben Jonson's distinction between poets and poetasters comes to mind (*The Poetaster*, 1601/2); cf. Moul (2006).

[92] Cf. Silk (1997) on Fagles's *Odyssey* and Lombardo's *Iliad*.

[93] Couch (1946) 357.

[94] Ibid. 352.

[95] Hall (2008b) 319.

[96] In the English-speaking world, that shift is observable across all the formerly literary disciplines, including English itself: cf. pp. 138 above and 220 below (Said and de Man).

If analogies suggest themselves between the rationale of translation in Notker's day and our own, there are clear contrasts with the pattern that becomes apparent towards the end of the medieval period in Romance-speaking France and Italy and part-Romancified England. Here, the educational functions of translation are less pronounced or less distinct, and though inevitably produced within learned circles, translation tends to cater to wider interests. More specifically, the co-existence of emerging vernaculars and contrasting types of Latinity (classical and scholastic, literary and administrative, pagan and Christian) generates a range of linguistic registers, embedded in complex discourses of authority and exegesis. Literary production in these contexts seldom fits neatly into modern categories. Original composition, marginal commentary, translation, and paraphrase merge into one another, as in the fourteenth-century French 'poem', *Ovid Moralized* (*Ovide moralisé*), a work several times the length of Ovid's *Metamorphoses*, which is its main, but not its only, source. Textual materials in any case cross and re-cross linguistic boundaries. A typical case is the *Roman de Troie*, composed in the French vernacular by Benoît de Sainte Maure around 1160. Around 1287, the Sicilian Guido delle Colonne produces a Latin prose translation, entitled 'The History of the Sack of Troy' (*Historia destructionis Troiae*). A series of vernacular (re)translations and adaptations of both texts follows, including John Lydgate's *Troy Book* (*c.* 1420) and Raoul Lefèvre's *Recueil des histoires de Troie* (1464), Caxton's translation of which becomes the first book printed in English (1474).[97] Representatively, though, Benoît's composition, which transposes material from two late-Latin sources ('Dares' and 'Dictys'), is itself presented by its author, in his prologue, as a 'translation': 'a history ['estoire'] which I shall put into Romance ['en romanz metre'], from the Latin where I found it, so that those who cannot understand the letter ['la letre'] can enjoy the story.'[98] In a multilingual setting, meanwhile, such switches from Latin to vernacular are matched by a pattern of translation *into* Latin, for as long as Latin retains its status as an international language of elite communication.[99]

A new era begins with the 'interlinear' Latin translations of the *Iliad* and *Odyssey* that Petrarch commissioned from the Greek monk Pilatus in 1360. Translation now begins to serve the cause of humanist learning, and in the course of the humanist age virtually the entire corpus of classical Greek literature is translated into Latin or one or more of the vernaculars, and the Latin corpus into the vernaculars likewise. Renaissance choices of texts for translation can still follow Christian imperatives: in sixteenth-century England, for instance, the Greek texts initially selected for Latin translation are mostly from the Church Fathers.[100] Conversely, classical Latin texts are translated into French at an early date: in the first decades of the fifteenth century, Laurent de Premierfait's versions of Ciceronian and Senecan

[97] Data in Scherer (1964) xiii–xvi, 224–6.

[98] *Roman de Troie*, 34–9: Warren (1990). Medieval and later terminologies of 'translating': Goldin Folena (1991).

[99] Cf. Burke (2007).

[100] Binns (1978) 148.

prose; around 1380, anonymous versions of Lucan, Sallust, and Suetonius; and as early as 1352, a translation of Livy by Petrarch's friend, Pierre Bersuire. Then again, Leonardo Bruni's versions of Aristotle's *Ethics* (1416) and *Politics* (1435–7) are early testimony to the humanist inclination to naturalize suitable texts on the Greek side too.

The rationale of Renaissance choices becomes more obvious when we compare the number of published vernacular translations of a model author like Seneca with those of an essentially technical source like Vitruvius' *De Architectura*. Vitruvius' treatise was disseminated, in Latin, after the first printed edition of 1486, but up to 1600 existed in only a very few translations: one in German (by Rivius in 1548); one in French (by Martin in 1572);[101] none in English; and four in Italian (by Cesariano, 1521; Caporali, 1536; Barbaro, 1556; and in abridged form, by Rusconi, 1590). Compare and contrast the pattern of translation for Seneca, whose first printed editions (of the moral essays, epistles, and tragedies) came out in the 1470s and 1480s. Several of the essays and epistles had already been translated into French by Premierfait, around 1408; individual works began to appear in English from 1547 (Whytinton), in German from 1507 (Hoeltzel), in Italian (the complete epistles, by Manilio) in 1492. The complete tragedies were translated into Italian in 1497 (by Evangelista Fossa) and French (by Grognet) in 1534, with individual plays translated into English (by Heywood and others) from 1559. Various other translations of individual Senecan works, or sets of works, were produced in the four languages during the fifteenth and sixteenth centuries.[102] The special interest in Vitruvius in sixteenth-century Italy reflects the perceived relevance of Vitruvian principles for Italian architects and designers during this period (§30); that apart, the difference between the general currency of a 'humane' author and a technical repository is unmistakable.

It is in humanist circles that modern translation theory makes its appearance – on the basis of ancient doctrine (notably Cicero's and Jerome's),[103] and in step with the recuperation of important texts by Cicero, among others. Following some occasional remarks by Coluccio Salutati, Leonardo Bruni's 'How to Translate' (*De interpretatione recta*, c. 1426) offers a comprehensive restatement of Ciceronian principles that justifies talk of this treatise as 'the earliest written document of modern translation'.[104] A new investment in the authority of classical literature called for the same sort of respect as was routinely granted to the sacred scriptures; accordingly, Bruni demands fidelity and accuracy here too. In a very un-medieval climate, the practice of a medieval translator like William of Moerbeke is now enshrined in theory.

[101] There was also an extract in a 1539 French translation of Diego de Sagredo's (Spanish) *Medidas del Romano* (1526: the first book on architecture published in any vernacular language outside Italian).

[102] Lists for Seneca: Bolgar (1954) 534–7.

[103] See n. 4 above.

[104] Morini (2006) 8–10. Cicero's *De Oratore*, *Brutus*, and *Orator* were rediscovered in 1421, not long before Bruni's treatise.

The humanist concern for fidelity eventually manifests itself as a demand for strict scholarly accuracy. A nice instance involves Henri Estienne's edition of Thucydides in the mid-sixteenth century, by which time bilingual editions were not uncommon, and knowledge of Greek and the availability of Greek texts made a careful checking of translation against original possible. Estienne's edition (1564) contained the Greek original, the Greek scholia, and a revised version of Valla's pioneering Latin translation of 1452 – which itself had enjoyed the distinction of being translated into French by Bishop Seyssel of Marseilles in 1527. In Estienne's Latin preface, both of these predecessors are subjected to zealous criticism. Citing a passage from Thucydides, followed by Valla's Latin, Seyssel's French, the scholar's own re-translation of Seyssel's French into Latin, and his own Latin translation of the Greek, an indignant Estienne uncovers a chain of errors: Valla had been led astray by 'nonsense' ('ariolatio'), which Seyssel had simply 'duplicated'.[105] In all innocence, meanwhile, Thomas Nicolls had based his English translation of Thucydides (1550) on Seyssel, prompting Thomas Hobbes (who went on to translate Thucydides into English in 1629, but directly from the Greek) to appeal to the now established *bon mot*: so far, the great historian had not been translated into English, but only traduced.[106]

During the Renaissance, the spread of vernacular versions of the classics impacts on whole areas of Western thought and perception. In the sphere of literary theory, for example, sixteenth-century translations (Italian and other) of Horace's *Ars Poetica* and Aristotle's *Poetics*[107] give these works a status for the educated public that is only challenged by the appearance of another translation, Boileau's Longinus (1674), which brings 'the sublime', in turn, to public notice (§30). More generally, the scale of translation from the classics helps to generate, or to colour, a range of new issues, from the linguistic preoccupations of Du Bellay and others[108] to anxieties about moral propriety (§9). The moral issue prompted some to suspect that certain texts might be better left (in Gibbon's phrase) 'in the obscurity of a learned language'.[109] This consideration led to a body of apologetic literature, typified by the

[105] Thucydides, 8. 96. 5: Boone (2000), Dionisotti (1995). Valla himself famously criticised earlier translations, notably Jerome's New Testament: *Adnotationes in Novum Testamentum* (1444: first publication overseen by Erasmus, 1505).

[106] Schlatter (1945).

[107] The *Ars Poetica* was translated into Italian by Dolce (1536), French by Peletier (1541), English by Drant (1567); there were Italian versions of the *Poetics* by Segni (1549), Castelvetro (1570), Piccolomini (1572): cf. §22.

[108] Between 1475 and 1540, over 300 texts were translated into French, including around 100 from classical authors: Chavy (1981). In Italy, by contrast, Speroni's *Dialogo delle lingue* (1530s) – itself, a prime source for Du Bellay (§13) – focused on the more fundamental language question and was *followed*, in the 1540s and 1550s, by a notable increase in translation into vernacular prose.

[109] In *Memoirs of My Life* (1796), ch. 8, Gibbon wrote: 'My English text [*sc.* in *History of the Decline and Fall*] is chaste, and all licentious passages are left in the obscurity of a learned language' (often misquoted as 'decent obscurity', following a parody in the *Anti-Jacobin*, 1797–8). In *The Decline and Fall* itself (1776–88: 2. 40), Gibbon had written, of Theodora, 'her murmurs, her pleasures and her arts must be veiled in the obscurity of a learned language.'

'Epistle' that Golding prefixed to his translation of the *Metamorphoses* (1567). Treating Ovid's poem essentially as disguised allegory ('a dark philosophy of turned shapes'), this document has been taken as 'evidence that Ovid was for the Renaissance as for the Middle Ages a highly moral author'.[110] It is, rather, evidence that Golding was anxious to turn him into one, given that the text lends itself to a diversity of amoral and immoral readings, as Shakespeare among others was soon to show (§8).

By the mid-sixteenth century, translation – like vernacular literature in general – has established itself as a medium in which to proclaim and propagate national identity. The humanist Gavin Douglas composed his version of Virgil's *Aeneid* (*c.* 1513) 'in the langage of Scottis natioun', adding a vernacular scholarly apparatus by way of enforcing its superiority to English adaptations by Chaucer and Caxton, at whose treatment of Virgil he 'spittit for dispyte'.[111] If the Scots 'langage' lacked the lexical range and perfection of Latin, it could still hold its own as a national and literary language against its English rival – just as Douglas's appropriation of Aeneas as ancestor of the kings of Scotland served to challenge the lineage that the English insisted on tracing back to Brutus.[112]

Implicit in such constructions is the notion of translation as a geographical movement of empire (*translatio imperii*) and learning (*translatio studii*) from East to West.[113] The notion helps to inform Nietzsche's view of French, and Roman, appropriation as 'a form of conquest'.[114] It is also implicit in Du Bellay's proposal that French writers should use imitation (but *not* direct 'translation') to 'march' on Rome and appropriate its treasures, as the Romans had once done to the Greeks.[115] The 'Brigade' – Ronsard's original name for the stellar Pléiade[116] – coincidentally evokes the militaristic connotations of this project.

In the century after Douglas and Du Bellay, John Dryden's verse epistle, 'To the Earl of Roscommon, On his Excellent Essay on Translated Verse' (1684), applies this same notion to the triumph of English letters. One of the most accomplished and influential of all translators in English literary history,[117] with his own distinctively expansive understanding of 'translation' (all the way from metaphrase to imitation), Dryden uses the conceit to construe cultural history as, literally, a history of translation, tracing a teleological vector from ancient Greece to contemporary England. In his own verse 'Essay', earlier that year, Roscommon had acclaimed the cultural benefits of translation for France –

110 Brower (1971) 127.

111 In his prologue to Book 1: Canitz (1996). Douglas makes a point of saying that, unlike Caxton's, *his* Virgil is based on the original.

112 Singerman (1986) 270–6.

113 Worstbrock (1965); cf. Gumpert (2001) 123–42 and §25. In XIV, Oresme suggested that Charlemagne initiated the *translatio* northwards; Petrarch disagreed: McNeil (1975) 33.

114 Above, p. 176.

115 *Deffence*, 'Conclusion'.

116 §7 n. 40.

117 Cf. Hopkins (2010a) 113–249.

There (cultivated by a royal hand)
Learning grew fast, and spread, and blest the land;
The choicest books that Rome or Greece have known
Her excellent translators made their own[118] –

before adding, with patriotic pride:

But now we show the world a nobler way,
And in translated verse do more than they.[119]

Britain above France: as a broad-brush characterization of translations from the classics, this makes some sense. Seventeenth-century French versions (from Benoît Bauduyn's Senecan tragedies in 1629 to Madame Dacier's *Iliad* in 1699) are fewer in number and no doubt slighter in quality than their English counterparts,[120] or indeed than their counterparts in sixteenth-century France (the century of Seyssel, Amyot, Peletier, and even versions of Virgil and Ovid by Du Bellay himself). Still, this is a bold claim, insofar as France, under Louis XIV, was currently at a cultural peak – with that great sun-god monarch himself seen not only as a conquering Alexander, but as a new Augustus, inspirer of the arts.[121] As if prompted by such contemporary mythologies across the Channel, but now himself mythologizing in yet bolder terms, Dryden reconfigures the relationship between the rival kingdoms as the final act of a truly heroic drama. From uncertain origins in Egypt or the Near East, the arts and sciences grew through their 'translation' from East to West. The first translators (*pace* Momigliano) were the Greeks, then came the Romans:

Nor stopped translation there; for conquering Rome
With Grecian spoils brought Grecian numbers home.

Here, Dryden translates – that is, *imitates* – the famous lines from Horace's *Epistle to Augustus*:

Graecia capta ferum victorem cepit et artes
intulit agresti Latio; sic horridus ille
defluxit numerus Saturnius, et grave virus
munditiae pepulere.[122]

Slave Greece enslaved her own crude lord, and pressed
Her arts on uncouth Latium. Thus was that coarse
Saturnian metre drained, and its dull dregs
Flushed out by refinement.

118 Cf. ibid. 123–5.
119 'Essay', 31–4, 39–40.
120 See generally Hayes (2009).
121 Burke (1992).
122 *Epistles*, 2. 1. 156–9. Horace's paradox is a favourite point of reference within the classical tradition: cf. §13 (p. 157 with n. 122).

The reciprocal imperialism that is the main point of the Horatian passage is suppressed; and, with subtle economy, Dryden collapses the Horatian distinction between the general ('arts') and the particular (the triumph of Greek metres, including hexameters like Horace's own, over native Saturnians). In Dryden's version, the emphasis on metre ('numbers') has become exclusive, in line with the theme of his 'Epistle' as a whole. This particular *translatio* is thus clearly marked as only the first stage of a yet more momentous process. After the debasement of 'verse to rhyme' in the barbarous Middle Ages, Britain in the new Caroline age represents the culmination of a process of cultural revival, whereby *translatio imperii* is effected from Italy (Dante and Petrarch) to France – and

> Britain, last,
> In manly sweetness all the rest surpassed.
> The wit of Greece, the gravity of Rome,
> Appear exalted in the British loom;
> The Muses' empire is restored again,
> In Charles his reign, and by Roscommon's pen –

so that Britain can be said to have finally reconciled worldly dominion (the restored monarchy of Charles II) and (neo)classical taste (Roscommon) in the restored 'empire' of the Muses.[123]

Where translation is at the forefront of cultural activity, competition also arises between translations. Such rivalries are especially acute if alternative renderings of a classic text are seen to represent contrasting eras, and modes, of writing. A case in point is the long-running contest – pursued for the most part retrospectively, and by proxies – between two Homers (especially two *Iliads*), Pope's, from England's Augustan age, and the earlier version by George Chapman. Despite their dates, Chapman's *Iliad* (1611) and *Odyssey* (1615) – the first complete translation of Homer into any vernacular – are widely regarded as 'Elizabethan' in spirit.[124] Chapman's *Iliad*, in particular, composed in ballad-like 'fourteeners',[125] is as different from Pope as Pope is from the Victorian metaphrases of Lang, Leaf, and Myers. This is Chapman's version of Sarpedon's words to Glaucus:[126]

> O friend, if keeping back
> Would keep back age from us, and death, and that we might not wrack
> In this life's human sea at all, but that deferring now
> We shunned death ever, nor would I half this vain valour show,
> Nor glorify a folly so, to wish thee to advance;
> But since we must go, though not here, and that beside the chance
> Proposed now . . .

123 'To the Earl of Roscommon', 7–8, 24–9.

124 Only Chapman's first publication of *Seven Books of the Iliads* [*sic*] *of Homer* (1598) was literally Elizabethan.

125 Cf. Matthew Arnold, *On Translating Homer* (1861), lecture II.

126 Above, pp. 174–5.

In *On Translating Homer* (1861), Matthew Arnold cites this passage (alongside Pope's version) and reasonably points to Chapman's 'freshness' and 'vigour', but also to the insistently 'fanciful' (and 'Elizabethan') impulse of his 'thought': the impulse that adds 'wrack | In this life's human sea' to the 'plainness' of Homer's Greek.[127] Whether 'plain' is quite right as a characterization of Homeric poetry may be doubted; no-one, though, can doubt the 'Elizabethan' feel of the added phrase. For Arnold, nonetheless, Chapman has strengths – not least in simple narrative – that Pope (despite his 'prodigious talent') does not.[128]

More sympathetic to Chapman than Arnold had been, and less (*even* less) sympathetic to Pope, Ezra Pound nevertheless echoes, indeed amplifies, Arnold's reservations about the 'Elizabethan' poet-translator: 'Chapman remains the best English "Homer", marred though he may be by excess of added ornament, and rather more marred by parentheses and inversions, to the point of being hard to read in many places.' And Pound adds: 'Pope is easier reading, and, out of fashion though he is [this, in 1920], he has at least' – and now the dictum we quoted earlier – 'he has at least the merit of translating Homer into *something*.'[129]

For our present purposes, the obvious applicability of Pound's characterization of Chapman to our specimen passage (not cited by Pound) is less important than his casual remark about Pope: 'out of fashion'. If Pope was out of fashion for Pound's generation, that was in large part due to Chapman, and to Keats, and his fellow-Romantics, on Chapman. It was they who restored the once-admired Chapman to a position of esteem. Even before its full publication, Chapman's 'inchoate Homer' had been acclaimed;[130] to the seventeenth-century poets Sheffield and Waller (so Dryden reports), Chapman's Homer was – still – the source of 'incredible pleasure and extreme transport'; but to Dryden's more exact taste, Chapman had 'thrown [Homer] down as low as harsh numbers, improper English and a monstrous length of verse [the 'fourteeners'] could carry him.'[131] Dryden's own version of *Iliad* 1 (1700) gave a powerful impression of what a neoclassical alternative might look like, which Pope's *Iliad* (completed in 1720) effectively brought to fruition. In his own preface, Pope praised Dryden, but – ironically – found him too dependent on Chapman. Chapman himself he praised for his 'daring fiery spirit', though not for his 'fustian' English.

Pope's *Iliad* rapidly acquired canonical status. Despite Bentley's caveat, it set new standards of taste, displacing all existing versions of Homer – until the Romantic revolt against the neoclassical. For Johnson, in his *Life of Pope* (1781), it was 'a performance which no age or nation can pretend to equal',[132] and certainly

127 Lecture I.

128 Ibid.

129 Viz, into Augustan English. For Pound, 'the nadir of Homeric translation' is 'Leaf–Lang prose': 'Translators of Greek: Early Translators of Homer', in Pound (1954) 249–50.

130 By Francis Meres, in 'A Comparative Discourse of our English Poets with the Greek, Latin and Italian Poets', in his *Palladis Tamia: Wit's Treasury* (1598).

131 Preface to *Examen Poeticum* (1693): Watson (1962), 2. 167.

132 Hill (1905), 3. 236.

incomparably superior to Chapman – which, however, Johnson acknowledged as one of Pope's sources: 'With Chapman, whose work, though now totally neglected, seems to have been popular almost to the end of the last [*sc.* seventeenth] century, he had very frequent consultations, and perhaps never translated any passage till he had read his version, which indeed he has been sometimes suspected of using instead of the original.'[133]

Even with Dryden's rejection of Chapman, and Johnson's veneration of Pope, the tone of these discussions is measured enough. All that changes in the Romantic age. Romantic dissatisfaction with neoclassicism – epitomized by Wordsworth's Preface to *Lyrical Ballads* (1800/1802) – subsumes a particular discomfort with its conventional 'poetic diction', seen as a barrier to engagement with 'real life'. In this light, Pope's *Iliad*, inevitably, comes to seem problematic.[134] One representative moment in Pope's version was his treatment of the 'moon' simile at the end of *Iliad* 8:

> The troops exulting sat in order round,
> And beaming fires illumined all the ground.
> As when the moon, refulgent lamp of night,
> O'er heaven's pure azure spreads his sacred light,
> When not a breath disturbs the deep serene,
> And not a cloud o'ercasts the solemn scene.[135]

Within a few years, the passage became a punch-ball. Coleridge lectured on 'Mr Pope's . . . translation of Homer, which I do not stand alone in regarding as the main source of our pseudo-poetic diction', and singled out the 'absurd' diction (and 'sense') of the 'moon' passage, as against the 'just and happy' imagery of the Homeric original.[136] 'That gorgeous misrepresentation of the exquisite moon-light picture in Homer', Keats's friend, Leigh Hunt, called it in 1814;[137] and in his *Essay Supplementary to the Preface* (1815), Wordworth likewise condemned its falsity to 'the phenomena of nature'. In a letter to Hunt later that year, Byron defended the description as 'appropriate'[138] – but, among the leading Romantics, Byron's was a lone voice.[139]

Two years later (1817), in one of the most famous of all engagements with the classics, the young Keats reported the impact of 'First Looking into Chapman's Homer'. With all the power of a momentous original, Chapman's translation

133 Ibid. 115.

134 Though between (e.g.) 1770 and 1830, Pope's *Iliad* and *Odyssey* were reprinted dozens of times, and Chapman's not at all: Young (2003) 205–30.

135 Corresponding to *Iliad*, 8. 553–8.

136 *Biographia Literaria*, 2 (published in 1817, but referring back to lectures given several years earlier).

137 'Notes on the Feast of the Poets', in *The Feast of the Poets*, p. 35. Hunt translated the simile himself in *The Examiner*, 16 June 1816.

138 September–October 1815.

139 Romantic responses to the neoclassical are complex and sometimes contradictory (Wordsworth himself echoes Pope's 'moon' passage in his 'A Night-Piece', composed in 1798) – but the contrast of attitudes and styles remains.

impinges on this receptive 'traveller' as both a new world and a world of remote antiquity – with the remoteness, however, Elizabethan as much as classical-antique:

Much have I travell'd in the realms of gold,
And many goodly states and kingdoms seen;
Round many western islands have I been
Which bards in fealty to Apollo hold.
Oft of one wide expanse had I been told
That deep-brow'd Homer ruled as his demesne:
Yet did I never breathe its pure serene
Till I heard Chapman speak out loud and bold:
Then felt I like some watcher of the skies
When a new planet swims into his ken;
Or like stout Cortez, when with eagle eyes
He stared at the Pacific – and all his men
Look'd at each other with a wild surmise –
Silent, upon a peak in Darien.

The poet casts himself as an Odyssean wanderer, who has 'travelled' the world of poetry without ever encountering Homer, until he 'looked into' – or actually *heard* – the words of Chapman. The stimulus for the sonnet was a visit to his friend and mentor Charles Cowden Clarke, who read him Chapman's version of Ulysses' shipwreck in *Odyssey* 5.[140] Hunt, for one, was warm in praise both of Chapman and Keats: 'Chapman certainly stands upon no ceremony. He blows as rough a blast as Achilles could have desired to hear . . . Mr Keats's epithets of "loud and bold" showed that he understood him perfectly.'[141] But besides bearing witness to a special moment of inspiration, Keats's sonnet acts out an unexpected polemic, with a silence and an endorsement. In acclaiming Chapman, Keats elides his familiarity with Pope's Homer, a monument of artistic neoclassicism, yet also, now, a symbol of the social order and aesthetic decorum of the Tory establishment.[142]

Finding 'serenity' in the run-away lines of Chapman, rather than the heroic couplets of Pope, directly challenged accepted standards of taste; and the point is made sharper by the wording of the line, 'Yet did I never breathe its pure serene'. This turns out to be a revision of something clumsier, and weaker, 'Yet could I never judge what men could mean'. The earlier version containing that line was published on 1 December 1816 in Leigh Hunt's radical weekly, *The Examiner*; the later, not long afterwards, in Keats's first collection (*Poems*, 1817). And coyly, and perhaps under Hunt's influence, the new version contrives to evoke Pope's now notorious 'moon' simile: 'When not a breath disturbs the deep serene'. *That* line, among others,

[140] Clarke and Clarke (1878) 130.

[141] In *Lord Byron and Some of His Contemporaries* (2nd edn, 1828), 1. 412.

[142] Cf. Amarasinghe (1962). For Keats's knowledge of Pope's Homer, see his letters to Haydon, 10–11 May 1817, and his brother Tom, 3 August 1818 (where he quotes from Pope's *Odyssey*).

Hunt himself had recently stigmatized as one of Pope's 'cuckoo-song verses, half up and half down', with reference to the supposedly monotonous Popean verse-shape.[143] And Keats's willingness to align himself with Hunt's anti-Popery would duly earn him notoriety as a member of the 'Cockney School of Poetry' at the hands of the Tory classicists who wrote for *Blackwood's Edinburgh Magazine*.[144]

Keats, though, elevates Chapman not only above Pope, but even, in effect, above Homer, an impression enforced by his surprising choice of historical reference. A generation later, Tennyson suggested that Keats was confused in alluding to Cortés (who conquered the Aztec empire), rather than Balboa (the first European to 'stare at' the Pacific).[145] But Keats, arguably, knew what he was doing: the logic of the sonnet, in which the secondary (the translation) seems to usurp the place of the original, calls for Cortés, the after-comer, who usurps the place of Balboa and eclipses his name. The choice of this sixteenth-century conquistador enacts what the 'Elizabethan' Chapman, by his translation, is felt to have done to Homer[146] – and Cortés (a generation before the Elizabethans) and Chapman (a decade or so after) evoke that great age of discovery and creativity between them.

Ironically enough, Chapman himself thought of Homer rather differently, imagining an encounter with Homer's ghost and a relationship of succession ('thou didst english me'), more like Dante's with Virgil.[147] Ironically, too, Keats, Chapman, and Pope had one thing in common: a modest (in Keats's case, negligible) knowledge of ancient Greek.[148] The point was lost on the *Blackwood's* reviewers; Keats, they declared, simply, 'knows Homer only from Chapman'. And the deeper significance of his espousal of the 'Elizabethan' was lost on them too. Keats's rejection of neoclassicism was the corollary of an implicit endorsement of *English* idiom, which – as he would eventually make clear – he located in earlier usage: in Shakespeare (rather than Milton), in Chaucer, and (at one remove, and bizarrely, indeed) in Chatterton.[149] For the hostile reviewers, by contrast, Keats and the rest of the supposed 'Cockney School' were 'uneducated and flimsy striplings', and lacked 'learning enough to distinguish between the written language of Englishmen and the spoken jargon of Cockneys'. It is true that the diction and inversion in lines like 'Which bards in fealty to Apollo hold' actually does nothing to evoke English usage before

143 In 'Notes on The Feast of the Poets', pp. 27–35.

144 Article 'No. 4', by 'Z' (presumed to be John Gibson Lockhart and John Wilson), August 1818: Kandl (2001) 1–3. Most reviews were more favourable: Redpath (1973). Keats had in any case invited adverse criticism by an ill-judged tirade, opposing 'high imagination' to 'Boileau' and the 'musty laws' of Popean classicism, in 'Sleep and Poetry' (163–4, 206, 195), in the 1817 *Poems*. That poem incidentally suggests 'how thoroughly Pope was identified in this period with modern French rather than ancient classical ideas about poetry': Chandler (1984) 494. Keats and 'the culture of dissent': Roe (1997).

145 In Palgrave's *Golden Treasury* (1861): Kandl (2001) 18 n. 5.

146 Cf. Watkins (1989) 26–31.

147 Chapman, *The Tears of Peace* (1609), l. 85. The conceit is as old as Ennius, in *Annals* 1. Dante: §7.

148 On Chapman, cf. Fay (1952) 107–8.

149 See his letters to George and Georgiana Keats (21 September 1819), Reynolds (21 September 1819), Fanny Brawne (August 1820). Cf. Newey (1994). Keats and Milton: §35.

the age of Pope (the youthful Keats was not practised enough to contemplate *that* kind of enactment), but the reviewers' critique is no less feeble for that. So too their sneering response to the classicizing, large and small, itself: 'From his prototype Hunt, John Keats has acquired a sort of vague idea that the Greeks were a most tasteful people, and that no mythology can be so finely adapted for the purposes of poetry as theirs.'

With this one poem, and its celebration of a 'new' translation, the young poet had contrived to challenge cherished doctrines of neoclassicism and – by sidelining, not just Pope, but the Greek Homer – the deference (canonized by Renaissance humanism) to classical language-learning too. With his endorsement of a translation, he had seemingly scorned the authority of the original and the pretensions of those who considered knowledge of Greek a prerequisite of taste.[150] But over and above such ephemera (who, after all, now knows or cares about the *Blackwood's* reviewers, except when studying Keats?), he had also brought into sharp focus the truly emancipatory power of translation[151] – had demonstrated, in fact, that the 'courier of the spirit' (as Pushkin called the translator)[152] can indeed create engagements with antiquity of the most compelling kind. The distinctive significance of translation is richly apparent.

[150] Cf. Levinson (1988) 11–15.
[151] Cf. Hall (2008c) 334.
[152] Quoted by Steiner (1998) 262.

§16
Science and Sensibility

The 'developed disciplines'[1] that constitute the modern version of 'the classics' subsume not only processes of precise language learning, but also the research techniques associated with systematic scholarship and the 'scientific' treatment of research materials – techniques to a large extent developed within classical scholarship itself. We have touched on these developments already (§4). We offer now a closer consideration of the phenomenon of scholarly research, and the 'scientific' study of antiquity in particular, as a distinctive mode of engagement with the ancient world, as an impressive source of knowledge of that world, and as a site of conflict with responses to antiquity beyond the reach of 'science'. And the inverted commas that proliferate here and hereafter ('scare-quotes', in contemporary academic slang) duly acknowledge that neutral reporting of this conflict is not an option.[2]

In the modern academy, study of the ancient world covers a well-established set of subject areas, from archaeology, art, and material culture to cultural, social, and political history, from religion to philosophy, from linguistics to the textual and literary studies most closely associated with the venerable label, 'philology'. And today's scholars may well approach their areas from any one of a range of contemporary perspectives – from feminism to reception-aesthetics – that have, on the face of it, little in common with science. Yet (we suggest) the issues that arise most

[1] Leavis's phrase: §4.

[2] Complementary, and alternative, perspectives to ours: Clark (2006), Harpham (2009), Ziolkowski (1990), and *Arion* (cf. p. 211 below), *passim*.

The Classical Tradition: Art, Literature, Thought, First Edition. Michael Silk, Ingo Gildenhard, and Rosemary Barrow.

Published 2017 by John Wiley & Sons Ltd.

acutely with the aspiration to scientific scholarship also arise with scholarly research as such.

Classical scholarship as 'scientific', therefore prospectively methodical, systematic, 'objective', and not directly concerned with assessing the merits or demerits (aesthetic, moral, spiritual, cultural, political) of its objects of study: that perspective first came to the fore in the sphere of textual studies, or 'classical philology' in the traditional sense. Within both classical studies and the classical tradition, however, scientific method (without scare-quotes) is also a reality in other areas: in linguistics (witness our own discussion of language in §13) and again in archaeology. And the development of archaeology is peculiarly revealing of the relationships between the more and the less scientific aspects of a discipline, as also between the discipline itself and wider engagements with the ancient world.[3]

By the middle of the nineteenth century, archaeology is recognised as a systematic field of learning, with its own protocols and procedures, clearly distinct from amateur collecting and art appreciation. In the philological arena, Germany takes the lead, and so it does here too; it is in the 1850s that German universities institute Chairs of Archaeology, soon followed by their opposite numbers in Italy, with their British and French counterparts following suit in the 1880s. Antiquarian interest in classical artefacts was already a defining feature of the Renaissance – witness a figure like Ciriaco de' Pizzicolli from Ancona, in the fifteenth century, traveller, art-collector, and student of inscriptions: 'the Schliemann of his time'.[4] And the beginnings of a scientific approach to the object are apparent as early as the seventeenth century, in the work of men like Raffaello Fabretti from Urbino, director of the archives at Rome and author of precise studies of Roman aqueducts (1680) and Trajan's Column (1683), or Poussin's spokesman, Giovanni Pietro Bellori, who produces a 'Capitoline Plan' of Rome (1673) and a compendium of Roman art in his *Admiranda Romanorum antiquitatum vestigia* (1693).[5] However, as that title indicates ('*Impressive* Remains of Roman Antiquities') – and as Bellori's connections with contemporary art might, in any case, lead one to expect – such validation of ancients objects, effectively on a par with ancient texts,[6] is bound up, still, with what will shortly be called 'aesthetic' appreciation.

A century after Fabretti and Bellori, growing awareness of the academic importance of material antiquity is apparent in Winckelmann's pioneering histories of ancient art, in the first comprehensive study of ancient coinage by Joseph Eckhel,[7] and in the establishment (in 1767) of the first educational cast collection in the university library at Göttingen. Even now, though, archaeological excavation – soon to be at the centre of the developed scientific discipline – is still the province of

3 General history of archaeology: Ceram (1967), Schnapp (1996).

4 Sandys (1908), 2. 39.

5 The more famous Raphael (Sanzio) began a systematic study of ancient Rome much earlier (letter to Pope Leo X, 1519): cf. §25.

6 Cf. Schnapp (1996) 179–81.

7 *Doctrina numorum veterum* (1792–8).

art-*lovers*: 'amateurs', in the etymological sense. At a time when royal or governmental interest in excavations has hardly begun, amateur patronage plays a major role in funding digs. The Hyperborean Society (subsequently transformed into the German Archaeological Institute, in 1828) is founded by German scholars in Rome, and sponsors important publications, including volumes of 'unpublished monuments' (*Monumenti Inediti*, 1826). In Britain it is art-'lovers' again, in the shape of the Society of Dilettanti (founded in 1732), that fund Stuart and Revett's *Antiquities of Athens* (1762–1816) and *Ionian Antiquities* (1769–1814), and then C. R. Cockerell's excavations in Aegina in 1811 and Bassae the following year.

When national museums or their governments do begin to fund excavations, their primary motivation is acquisition – less of knowledge than of prestige finds and tokens of cultural and political domination. In an age still preoccupied with the primal and the originary, new excavations are favoured in sites of renowned antiquity, across and beyond the former heartlands of the classical world, from Egypt to the Near East to the Greek, or once Greek, areas of the Eastern Mediterranean. The British Museum finances expeditions to Greek Asia Minor at Lycia, Halicarnassus, Cnidus, Priene, and Ephesus; the newly unified German state provides the finance for Ernst Curtius's excavations of Olympia in the 1870s; France funds digs on the Acropolis in the 1850s and, later in the century, at Delos and Delphi. Under a nationalist agenda, archaeology flourishes, and foreign schools become important presences abroad; between 1846 and 1886, French, German, American, and British institutes are set up in Greece.[8]

In the following decades, the national-ideological rationale of practical archaeology becomes more marked still, most obviously under the expansive totalitarian regimes of the inter-war years. Across the territory known to the Romans as Germania, but also elsewhere, Nazi archaeology is dedicated to the demonstration of Germanic superiority,[9] while excavations conducted by Fascist Italy in North Africa and Italy itself serve the cause of validating connections between ancient and modern Rome.[10] And yet even such activity may proceed under the banner of enlarging knowledge and may be executed according to now-established professional norms of excavation, recording, publication, and conservation.[11]

The case of Herculaneum and Pompeii sums up the association, in all its shifting detail, of archaeological science and national agenda. Since their rediscovery in the

[8] Wittenburg (2010).

[9] Harke (2002).

[10] Cf. §25 and Dyson (2006).

[11] Cf. Perry (2001–2). In the internationalist post-war era, excavation rights may be negotiated between national or supranational bodies. In the 1970s, the UNESCO Carthage project brought together teams from Tunisia, Europe, and America under the common aim of preservation. The Roman Forum has a distinctive history of international intervention. First excavated in the 1770s (labour provided by convict chain-gangs), it was earmarked by Napoleon for a major site clearance (Ridley 1992), but had to wait till the end of XIX for Italian, German, and British teams to begin systematic digging. In 2003 the Italian Ministry of Culture approved a collaborative archaeological excavation between the American Institute for Roman Culture and the Universities of Oxford and Stanford; meanwhile the Municipality of Rome runs its own Forum project.

eighteenth century, these important sites were effectively under Italian control. Initially sponsored by the young king of Naples,[12] excavation began in 1738 and was designed to uncover *objets d'art* for the royal collection. Under the military engineer Roque Joachim de Alcubierre, the techniques employed were haphazard and destructive. Tunnels were cut over sixty feet deep through anything that happened to lie in the way; detachable items, from metal artefacts to impressive frescoes, were removed; much else was destroyed, by accident or design; only with the engagement of Swiss architect Karl Weber, in 1749, was the site and its artefacts documented.[13] Yet it was not until the 1860s that systematic excavations began under the directorship of Giuseppe Fiorelli[14] – in the wake of Italian political unification. Fiorelli focused his efforts on preservation, instituted a new system of recording, and insisted on a careful survey of the site before digging began. His excavation methods were scrupulous: individual strata were removed gradually, and the contents of each layer and their depth from the surface noted. New finds were published, and Fiorelli's documentation included a map of excavations which divided the town of Pompeii into *regiones* and *insulae*, a system that was to form the basis for Pompeian topography up to the present day.

During this age of professionalization and national sponsorship, however, one name stands out as a gigantic exception to all the new rules: Heinrich Schliemann.[15] Self-taught and self-funded for his momentous excavations at Hisarlik, site of ancient Troy, in the 1870s, Schliemann seems to inhabit an earlier age of amateur treasure-hunting – evincing, at the same time, the purest Romantic veneration for the originary. Accused of dubious excavation practices, inaccurate dating, and even forging artefacts, Schliemann did, nevertheless, expose an unfamiliar Bronze Age Greece through his finds at Troy, and thereafter at Mycenae, Orchomenos, and Tiryns. Subsequent work at Troy under Wilhelm Dörpfeld, along with the discovery of 'pre-Hellenic' tombs at Spata and Menidi in Attica and Vaphio in Laconia, confirmed the historicity of a Mycenaean civilization distinct from the familiar classical past. In the 1890s, excavations on the Greek islands by the Greek archaeologist, Christos Tsountas, further revealed a Cycladic culture visibly different from anything on the mainland, while from 1900 Arthur Evans's discoveries at Knossos in Crete indicated that Mycenaean civilization itself had its roots in the earlier culture of Minoan Crete.

This demonstration of the Mycenaean and pre-Mycenaean basis of the classical helped to give an entirely new shape to historical understandings of the Greek world[16] – and yet it all began with Schliemann's 'unscientific' archaeological methods and his Romantic motivation for pursuing them. The excavator of Troy was driven

[12] Charles of Bourbon (subsequently Charles III of Spain).

[13] History of Pompeian excavation: Cooley (2003), Harris (2007), Parslow (1995).

[14] Castiglione Morelli (1999).

[15] Bibliography: Runnels (2007).

[16] Understandings further reshaped by the demonstration (by Ventris and Chadwick in the 1950s) that the language of the Mycenaeans (preserved on Linear B tablets first unearthed by Evans in Crete) was Greek.

by a combination of self-heroization and belief in primal artistic truth, accessible across the ages. Specifically, his excavations arose directly from a semi-mystical conviction that the tales embodied in the Homeric poems – the *Iliad* in particular – communicated authentic history; and an early intimation of this special status of Homeric communication came (on his own testimony) from a chance encounter in the grocer's shop in Germany where, as a young man, he worked as an apprentice and where, one evening, he heard a clergyman's son recite Homer – 'and though I could not understand a syllable, the melodious sound of the words made a deep impression on me.'[17] Schliemann's personal investment in his own discoveries was summed up, in later life, by his 'Homeric' mansion in Athens (inscribed with the name *ILIOU MELATHRON*)[18] and (rather as the composer Wagner called two of his children Isolde and Siegfried) his Iliadic-sounding offspring, Andromache and Agamemnon.

Quite different, but no less revealing of the tensions between a scientific discipline and the non-scientific impulses of its practitioners, were the responses to some of the new finds. The discovery of the Cycladic culture, for instance, might be an undeniable archaeological achievement – but for the future Director of the Munich Glyptothek, German archaeologist Paul Wolters, in 1891, a life-size Cycladic marble found on the island of Amorgos was nothing more than a 'repulsively ugly head.'[19]

The claims of philological scholarship to scientific status predate those of its archaeological counterpart by a couple of generations. Unlike archaeology, however, classical philology was already millennia old and was, and is, privileged (or burdened) by an additional claim to centrality within the classical tradition itself. For some, the transmission and correction of Greek and Latin texts is the defining narrative of the tradition as a whole,[20] and a narrative with a suitably heroic cast of characters. The individuals who made it possible for us, even today, to read at least some of the *ipsissima verba* of classical authors were copyists or 'scribes', who soon attracted learned co-workers: scholars, or philologists. For centuries scribes and scholars co-existed in symbiotic harmony: if weary-eyed (or over-inventive) scribes introduced mistakes in the process of copying, eagle-eyed scholars could spend a lifetime spotting and correcting them; and if scribes ensured the availability of the texts, scholars could endow them with meaning.[21] In most histories of classical scholarship, this story begins in Hellenistic Alexandria and continues today; and the iconic figures of the tale are the great commentators and textual critics who (as some have supposed) form a 'free, world-encompassing, intellectual community across the millennia.'[22] But any such evocation of a trans-historical mission, however

17 Meyer (1969) 14.

18 Quasi-Homeric Greek for 'Hall of Troy' (based on usages like *Priamoio melathron*, 'Priam's hall', at *Iliad*, 2. 414)

19 Renfrew (2003) 51.

20 So e.g. Reynolds (1983) xiii–xiv.

21 See generally Reynolds and Wilson (1991).

22 Pfeiffer (1961) 21: 'über die Jahrtausende hin eine freie, die Welt umfassende geistige Gemeinschaft.'

uplifting (and, in its own terms, legitimate), tends to play down significant fissures in the relation between classical scholarship and the tradition overall. The invention of printing has to count as one such caesura, if only because it ultimately put the scribes out of business; but another, of overriding importance, is the rise of modern 'scientific' research.

For historians of classical scholarship, from the pious (like Sandys) to the critical (like Nietzsche), classical philology became a modern discipline on 8 April 1777, when Friedrich August Wolf enrolled himself at the University of Halle under the unorthodox title of *studiosus philologiae*, 'student of philology'.[23] Once appointed to a Chair in the following decade, Wolf renamed his subject *Altertumswissenschaft*, 'the scientific study of antiquity'; possible alternatives, such as the unscientific-sounding *literae humaniores*, were dismissed ('bad Latin – and what's with the comparative?').[24]

Arguably, Wolf's reputation as founding father of modern philological studies does an injustice to important premodern precursors. Quite apart from such notable eighteenth-century figures as the Englishman Richard Bentley (Pope's *bête noire*: §15), Renaissance humanists had already used their philological skills not only to naturalize true classics but also to expose false idols. An early case in point involved 'The Donation of Constantine', a medieval document of unknown authorship, purporting to be the work of Constantine the Great, and recording his donation of the Lateran Palace (and, with it, control of Rome and the Western Roman Empire) to Pope Silvester. Long used as evidence to bolster papal claims to worldly power, the *Constitutum Constantini* was exposed as an anachronistic forgery by Lorenzo Valla, who committed himself to the task in the name of truth, justice, and God (albeit in defiance of the Church).[25] Other victims of philological debunking included the *Corpus Hermeticum*, hailed by heretical enthusiasts as 'the Bible of original Christianity' and a prime source of primeval wisdom, but exposed by the Swiss Huguenot scholar Isaac Casaubon, in 1614, as a collection of texts assembled in the first centuries of the Christian era.[26]

Yet Wolf indeed represents the start of an era. His most inflential work was the Latin treatise that invented 'the Homeric question' in its modern form, the *Prolegomena ad Homerum* of 1795,[27] where Wolf offered a new kind of 'Homer' and a new kind of methodical scholarship, based partly on a study of the Homeric scholia

[23] Sandys (1908), 3. 51. Nietzsche, 'Wir Philologen' (n. 45 below): Colli and Montinari (1967–), 4. 1. 90. Wolf was not actually the first so to enrol: Schröder (1913) 168.

[24] Gürtler (1831–5), 1. 11. The phrase *literae humaniores* looks back to Petrarchan usage: cf. Pfeiffer (1976) 15–17 and §3 n. 32. Originally it identified study of the classics as the 'more human(e) studies', in contradistinction to divinity (and, by implication, to technical subjects like law and medicine); it was subsequently used to designate university courses, notably at Oxford (from 1800). At the oldest Scottish universities, St Andrews, Glasgow, and Aberdeen (all founded in XV), 'Latin' was called 'Humanity' until recently.

[25] 'causa veritatis, causa iustitiae, causa Dei': Bowersock (2007), section 5.

[26] Cf. §6 and Grafton (1983a) 78–93.

[27] *Prolegomena to Homer*: Grafton, Most and Zetzel (1985).

and devoted to 'the first history of a text in antiquity'.[28] He proposed that the two great Homeric epics must have been composed before, therefore without, the use of writing; that transmission by oral reciters must have resulted in many adjustments to the earlier compositions; and that in their known form, the epics must be the product of later compilations of once independent poems, which were further adjusted and 'edited' in the process. There was indeed a 'Homer', original author of most of the component parts of the new wholes. And the new wholes *were* wholes: Wolf freely acknowledged the overall creative unity of the two epics – but insisted that this unity could not be the work of 'Homer' himself.

Fundamental to this argument is the distinction between a historical and an anachronistic reading of sources. The distinction was not invented by Wolf; it is implicit in the philological endeavours of Valla and his fellow humanists. But in the age of Herder and historicism, it acquires a deeper significance as, in effect, an opposition between correct (prospectively) and incorrect (necessarily). Belief in a single privileged meaning – *historical meaning* – is made determinative.

The impact of Wolf's arguments was profound, both in the scholarly field and in the republic of letters beyond. Initially, the *Prolegomena* was attacked by scholars across Europe.[29] In Germany, some of the leading *littérateurs* responded with suspicion or outright hostility – among them, the poets Klopstock, Schiller, and Wieland, and the poet-translator Voss. But Goethe, at first, was equivocal; Humboldt and the brothers Schlegel (August and Friedrich) were positive; and Herder offered the back-handed compliment of claiming crucial parts of the argument as his own.[30]

Why the outrage? – and why the strength of response at all? The obvious, and conventional, answer is the culture-shock produced by Wolf's new orientation, away from the work of art and towards the presumed history of its composition, along, indeed, with a shift towards 'history' in general (as befitted a new 'science of antiquity'). Yet this is not the whole story. *History* (or composition) versus *art*? Yes, but also *origins* versus *outcomes*, and *impersonal* origins versus *authorial* authenticity – and as that reformulation serves to suggest, a significant part, both of Wolf's novelty and of the challenge his work presented, lay in his unacknowledged appeal to, but *also* denial of, a crucial nexus of imperatives from his own Romantic era. Wolf had a new tale to tell: an influential tale of origins and of more-or-less spontaneous creativity ('Homer') – and all this, in accord with the aesthetic and other preoccupations of the age.[31] Conversely: though Wolf never denied the artistic achievement

28 Ibid. 15.

29 Overview: Sandys (1908), 3. 57–8.

30 Ibid.

31 Cf. §3. On 'origins' cf. Harpham (2009) 54: 'philology has bequeathed to modern scholarship the conviction that things are explained when their origins have been identified.' Indeed – though the 'conviction' (along with the primacy of 'spontaneous creativity') is not the invention of philology (or of Wolf): §3. Nor was Wolf's scientific method entirely his philological invention; it was partly indebted to the methodology of theological Bible Studies: Grafton, Most and Zetzel (1985) 18–26.

of the epics (the *Odyssey*, in particular, remained, for him, 'the most outstanding monument of the Greek genius'),[32] his two- or three-stage reconstruction of the compositional process detached that achievement from the 'original' author, and thereby challenged the most sacred tenet of Romantic aesthetics, the irreducible authority of that primal-authorial source (§3). To make matters worse, he had performed this operation on the unsurpassably primal poetry of the unsurpassably primal Greeks. Romantic readers in awe of the 'one Homer' could only be shocked. And it was no compensation that Wolf himself – again, as a child of his Romantic age – fully acknowledged his embarrassment at 'the scepticism' that had 'robbed him of belief' in that same 'one Homer'.[33]

In Wolf's Germany, as the responses to his book indicate, academic research and creative writing are still very much in communication. Within a generation, that relationship largely disappears.[34] Following its own new rationale, but operating now within a small, coherent, specialist community, scholarship expands, and nowhere more representatively than in the study of Homer itself. Over the next century and a half, Wolf's numerous successors – mostly German and, in more recent discussion, collectively styled 'analysts' – produce a series of alternative exposures of the supposed traces, within the two epics, of different versions of the epics themselves, with much talk of 'editing' and 'interpolating' and (in a revealingly archaeological spirit) successive 'layers' of composition. The fact that the analysts were eventually challenged in their own scholarly terms,[35] and the largely separate fact that the whole 'Homeric question' is now widely taken to have been transformed (or, as some propose, eliminated) by comparative studies of oral-improvisatory epic, from the 1920s onwards[36] – these undoubted facts are almost by the way. Simply: the progress of scholarship, in the wake of Wolf's *Prolegomena*, ensures that, in Germany in particular, scholarly and other engagements with the poetry of Homer (especially engagements by cultivated 'tourists' or 'travellers') operate on different planes, almost without reference to one another.

Here, then, is yet another contributory factor – for the classical tradition, above all – to that momentous divide in Western cultural life between the earlier classicizing centuries and everything that comes after the Romantic generation. Wolf had invented what is now taken for granted: the paradigm of an autonomous academic subject, advanced by systematic research and marked out as a new field of practice.[37] Here truly begins the age of modern 'theoretical man', as Nietzsche called it, and the

[32] 'Praeclarissimo monumento Graeci ingenii': Wolf, *Prolegomena*, ch. 41. Even so, Wolf envisages 'restoring Homer's work to the genuine, pure form that first poured forth from his divine lips' ('divino eius ore'): ibid. ch. 2.

[33] Jebb's paraphrase of Wolf's afterthoughts: Sandys (1908), 3. 57.

[34] Cf., from a Nietzschean perspective, Silk and Stern (1981) 9–14, 21–4.

[35] By 'unitarians' – mostly outside Germany itself, though latterly by German scholars like Wolfgang Schadewaldt (*Iliasstudien*, 1938).

[36] First and foremost through the work of the American scholar, Milman Parry. Overview: Fowler (2004) 171–87, 220–32, 324–43.

[37] In effect, a new social subsystem: Gildenhard (2003) 173–9.

commitment to an ever-growing 'pyramid of knowledge', all on the premise that 'knowledge' (in Bacon's celebrated dictum) 'is power', and even (Nietzsche again) 'the power of a panacea', with error as 'the evil *par excellence*'.[38] In more prosaic terms, here begins the modern knowledge industry, whose remit today extends across the sciences (and 'sciences'), and the whole range of humanities too.[39]

Within the study of the classics itself, engagements with the surviving remains of ancient Greece and Rome (but also the lost traces of the ancient world) could now take place in frames and settings newly defined by institutional, professional, and 'disciplinized' requirements.[40] And the juggernaut of research engendered transformations on the human level too. Early-modern polyhistors made way for specialized assemblers and assessors of evidence and, beyond the textual sphere, antiquarians and connoisseurs left the stage to ancient historians and the new breed of specialist archaeologists.[41] And in the process, Romantic visions of the primal and the originary – such as had informed the responses of the great German Hellenists of Wolf's age, and still, residually, informed his own – these, too, gave way to scholarly concern with the (re)construction of precise historicity and original 'historical' meaning, within a broadly-based understanding of antiquity in all its aspects.

These transformations did not take place in a single convulsive movement across the Western nations. Germany, and Prussia in particular, led the way,[42] and by the mid-nineteenth century the contrast between organized academic practice there and elsewhere was marked. Roman historian Theodor Mommsen, for one, became so irritated by the backwardness of some of his Italian counterparts that he threatened to dish up the Neapolitan antiquarian Gervasio as a delicacy ('piatto squisito') in the pages of the *Bullettino di Napoli*: 'I have to eat one of them, or else I eat myself.'[43]

Since Mommsen's time, the knowledge industry has come to dominate the intellectual life of the Western world, from the 'hard' sciences to the least 'hard' of the

[38] With this commitment to knowledge more decisive than even the rise of free-thinking philosophy and natural science in XVII. Nietzsche, *The Birth of Tragedy* (1872), 15; Bacon, *Meditationes sacrae* (1597), 'Of Heresies' ('et ipsa scientia potestas est').

[39] In the earlier years of this process, modern minds sometimes thought of philology as representative of modernity at its best. In 1848 the French thinker Ernest Renan equates it with 'the modern spirit', identified in turn with 'rationalism, criticism, liberalism': *L'Avenir de la science*, ch. 8.

[40] Cf. Most (2002b).

[41] Cf. Grafton (1983b) 159–92. On the 'transition from amateur to professional' in the sphere of art appreciation: Fisher (1975) 590–1, Howard (1992), Jenkins (1992); cf. Jarvis (1995). In some areas – e.g. institutional realities – systematic research begins as early as the Renaissance, as with Budé's *De asse* (1515) or the lesser-known Carlo Sigonio's *De occidentali imperio* (1578).

[42] A significant part was played by Humboldt, who envisaged the new University of Berlin, in particular, as a 'community of scholars', devoted less to teaching than to 'knowledge', which duly became 'a model for the universities of Europe': Lloyd-Jones (1982) 69. Contrast the spirit of Humboldt's other great project, the humanistic Gymnasium at the secondary level (§§4, 27).

[43] Wickert (1964) 310–11: 'ich muss einen fressen, sonst fress' ich mich.' Mommsen was Professor of Ancient History in Berlin (1858–1903). Cf. Ceccarelli (2006) 93.

humanities, but its relation to the classical tradition, and to the classical itself, remains complex and fraught with tension. The now established premises of academic research on Greco-Roman antiquity, with the privilege they grant to historical meaning (and the sometimes monumental effort involved in unearthing it), the reading practices widely employed to generate the required knowledge, and, above all, the non-evaluative, or even anti-evaluative, attitude towards empirical data (including once canonical texts): all this is hard to reconcile with most of the modes of engagement, and in particular the concern for values, that have energized the classical tradition and its creative figures down the centuries.[44] Nietzsche, again, aptly notes the gulf between 'poet-philologists' like Goethe and Leopardi and 'scholar-philologists':[45] between learned but creative 'users', 'travellers', or 'tourists', in our terms, and scholars pure and simple.

The large issues at stake here are summed up by the attitudes of two of the most illustrious of all standard-bearers of 'pure' classical scholarship, German and English: Wilamowitz and Housman, both immensely impressive figures within their respective scholarly traditions, the one Professor of Greek in Berlin, the other Professor of Latin in London, then Cambridge.[46] Wilamowitz's career began in striking and symptomatic fashion with a fierce critique of Nietzsche's first book, *The Birth of Tragedy*, in 1872. Nietzsche at the time was Professor of Classical Philology in Basel, but that first book distanced itself sharply from the world of the 'scholar-philologist', by seeking, among much else, to reintegrate the worlds of learned discourse (in respect of the study of Greek tragedy) and contemporary art and cultural life (in the shape of Wagnerian music-drama).[47] In 1928 the now elderly Wilamowitz – who had rushed into print to condemn Nietzsche's book over fifty years before – looked back at that *cause célèbre* and his sense of outrage at the time: 'the violence done to historical fact and all philological method was clear as daylight, and drove me to fight for my imperilled science.'[48]

[44] Within the humanities in general, academic research necessarily raises comparable questions, *mutatis mutandis*.

[45] 'Philologen-Poeten' and 'Philologen-Gelehrten': this, in a series of notes for a projected book, 'Wir Philologen' ('We Philologists'), written in 1875: Colli and Montinari (1967–), 4. 1. 120. Nietzsche also notes the 'discrepancy between the philologists and the ancients' they study (meaning especially the 'great individuals' of early and classical Greece: ibid. 97, 102, 119). *That* contrast, Yeats dramatized – with reference to the poetry of Catullus – in 'The Scholars' (1915): 'respectable bald heads | Edit and annotate the lines | That young men, tossing on their beds, | Rhymed out . . . ' Auden spoke up for the bald heads: 'Edit indeed. Thank God they do. If it had not been for scholars working themselves blind copying and collating manuscripts, how many poems would be unavailable, including those of Catullus?': (1963) 43. This confuses scribes (who ensured survival by copying) and scholars (who edit and annotate).

[46] Assessments of the two, as scholars: Calder *et al.* (1985); Brink (1986) 150–98, Butterfield and Stray (2009).

[47] Silk and Stern (1981) 15–61 and *passim*; cf. §31.

[48] 'Die Vergewaltigung der historischen Tatsachen und aller philologischen Methode lag offen zutage und trieb mich zum Kampfe für meine bedrohte Wissenschaft': Wilamowitz (1928) 129; cf. Silk and Stern (1981) 90–131.

No less symptomatic was Wilamowitz's distaste for the actual word 'classical' – the word that, above all others, affirms value as the ultimate rationale of the classical tradition and the classics, behind it. In a letter, late in life, he wrote: 'I have never seen any point in the word "classical", which I loathe, so I don't expect anyone else to see one either.'[49] And throughout his career, Wilamowitz disavowed all attempts to make use of any but 'historical' perspectives in the interpretation of the ancient world and its products. Indeed, he made a virtue of his disavowal. His reading of Greek tragedy and its theosphere, for instance, was (he proclaimed) 'unaffected by the anthropologists or theologians of today'; what sustained him here was 'not the self-confidence of modern wisdom, least of all my own, but a loving submission to the old beliefs.'[50]

The most enthusiastic defender of Wilamowitz might find it hard to grant him any adequate awareness of the logic or the limits of historicizing research – but also (*therefore*?) any conspicuous success in avoiding 'modern wisdom' in the event. Hugh Lloyd-Jones noted a prime example of the great man failing in his historicist duty:

> In 1891, a year after the première of Ibsen's *Hedda Gabler*, he wrote this of Phaedra in his commentary upon Euripides' *Hippolytus*. 'No vulgar woman – she is altogether the high society lady, knows and does her duty; she has a husband and children, relations and a social position, and knows how to render all these the regard she owes them. But she has no inner relationship to husband or children, let alone to any other object. Her life lacks the blessing of work, and she is too intelligent to be content with idleness and empty social activity . . . So she is ripe for passion. Suddenly she encounters in her stepson a being who astonishes her just because she cannot understand him.' It is easy now to see that this description is far more relevant to Ibsenian heroines like Nora, Rebecca West or Hedda Gabler than to Phaedra; Euripides took no interest in Phaedra's disposition or her social situation, only in her passion.[51]

For all that, it was Wilamowitz, in a lecture of 1908, who captured the paradoxical aspiration at the heart of historical hermeneutics in a memorable image that looks back to Homer's Odysseus and his mission to interrogate the dead in the underworld:[52]

> The tradition is dead: it is our task to revive the life that is past. We know that ghosts only speak when they have tasted blood; and the spirits we summon demand the blood of our hearts. We give it to them gladly. But if they then respond to our questions,

[49] Calder (1983) 261: 'Ich habe mit dem Wort "klassisch", das mir ein Greuel ist, nie etwas anfangen können'. Compare/contrast Herder (§3).

[50] Wilamowitz (1895) 1. xvi.

[51] Lloyd-Jones (1982) 200, following Reinhardt (1960) 236. The specific influence of *Hedda Gabler* is questionable (Calder 1985: 92), but the point stands.

[52] Albeit an image seemingly borrowed from Nietzsche (!): Silk and Stern (1981) 102. 'The desire to speak with the dead' unites old and new historicists; Greenblatt (1988) 1 identifies it as the driving force of his research, but without reference to Odysseus.

> something of us has entered into them, something alien, that must be cast out again, cast out in the name of truth.[53]

A. E. Housman, from the same generation, had a related stance, though his slogans were rather different. His credo is summed up by his words to a friend and former colleague in a letter of 1916. Housman devoted many years to the production of a major edition of a minor Latin poet, Manilius: 'minor', maybe, and not (say) an Aeschylus – but: 'If you prefer Aeschylus to Manilius you are no true scholar; you must be deeply tainted with literature, as indeed I always suspected that you were.'[54] A joke, as the tone (and the friendship) indicates – but no joke.[55] What Housman said to a friend, in private, he had already said, more forcefully, in public: 'Literature is so alien from science that the literary temper in himself is a peril against which the scholar must stand on guard. The aim of science is the discovery of truth, while the aim of literature is the production of pleasure.'[56]

The fact that Housman was himself a minor poet, like (though in specifics very unlike) his Manilius, adds a strange twist to his case history, but it is no less a fact that in public, professional, and even private life, this poet-philologist notoriously 'kept the two gifts as separate as possible'.[57] He believed, indeed, that 'textual criticism is a science', yet 'also an art';[58] also that (almost in Nietzschean vein) 'the great critics of the classical literatures . . . are such men as Lessing or Goethe or Matthew Arnold, scholars no doubt, but not scholars of minute or profound learning';[59] *but* also that literary criticism must be, in itself, entirely separate from classical (or other) scholarship, because 'scholarship . . . is itself a department . . . not of literature but of science',[60] so that a Professor of Latin, like himself, was under no obligation to be a spokesman for the cultural or other value of the Latin classics, either to fellow-scholars or students or a wider public ('that a scholar should appreciate literature is good for his own pleasure and profit, but it is none of his business to communicate that appreciation to his audience').[61] And of the relation between his

[53] 'Die Überlieferung ist tot: unsere Aufgabe ist es, das vergangene Leben zu erwecken. Wir wissen es, daß die Schatten erst reden, wenn sie Blut getrunken haben . . .': Wilamowitz (1926), 2. 245; our version borrows in part from Gilbert Murray: (1908) 25. The title of Lloyd-Jones (1982) derives from Wilamowitz's phrase: cf. ibid. 200.

[54] Letter to Arthur Platt, 6 April 1916. The first volume of Housman's *Manilius* was published in 1903, the last in 1930.

[55] Platt was also a scholar Housman respected sufficiently to write a graceful tribute, on his behalf, in 1927, three years after Platt's death (Ricks 1988: 344–8, 507), which he wrote 'in the interests of scholarship and literature' (ibid. 507). Ironies: Housman once acknowledged, 'my favourite Greek poet is Aeschylus' (in a letter of 1933: ibid. 469), and (in a letter of 1924: ibid. 464), 'I adjure you not to waste your time on Manilius . . . My interest in him is purely technical.'

[56] Cambridge inaugural lecture of 1911: ibid. 305.

[57] Brink (1986) 160. The separation in Housman is a premise of Tom Stoppard's play, *The Invention of Love* (1997).

[58] Ricks (1988) 325; cf. Housman's thoughts on verse composition (§4).

[59] Ibid. 269.

[60] Ibid. 302.

[61] Ibid. 303.

own scholarly proficiency and his poetry, the most he could say was: 'I suppose that my classical training has been of some use to me in furnishing good models, and making me fastidious, and telling me what to leave out' – but, more pointedly: 'no doubt I have been unconsciously influenced [in my poetry] by the Greeks and Latins, but I was surprised when critics spoke of my poetry as "classical". Its chief sources of which I am conscious are Shakespeare's songs, the Scottish Border ballads and Heine.'[62] More pointedly still, the converse thought that his own poetic creativity might somehow have impacted on his scholarship seems not to have crossed his mind. Like Wilamowitz (whatever their other differences), Housman saw his calling as compartmental; and the portentous significance of the fact that the scholarly ambiences of Germany and Britain could create leading figures with such views is unmistakable.

In point of fact, neither Wilamowitz nor Housman were wholly typical of their national scholarly traditions. In Germany, indeed, Wilamowitz's own dominant position within the subject helped to engender a significant 'humanist' reaction, led in the first instance by his successor at Berlin, Werner Jaeger.[63] In the English-speaking world, the situation had long been more variable, with the focus on historical meaning to the exclusion of any other (epitomized by Wilamowitz's remark on Greek religion) always less relentless than in Germany, and Housman's professed unconcern with value less predictable, likewise. By the second and third quarters of the twentieth century, shelves could easily be filled with works of scholarship animated by a 'preference' (*pace* Housman) for major works of literature and the concomitant determination to explain *why* they might deserve to be thought of as major. The more striking examples range from Marxist spokesmen of Aeschylus and Lucretius from the British Isles[64] to the scholar-critics who wrote, in truly humanistic vein, for the American journal *Arion* – a publication programmatically subtitled 'A Quarterly Journal of Classical Culture' (and latterly 'A Journal of Humanities and the Classics') – which (among much else) published a first complete English translation of Nietzsche's subversive reflections on philology.[65]

No less significant: in textual scholarship across the English-speaking world, and extending back to at least the middle of the nineteenth century, there is a more pervasive, if often more diffuse, sense of the 'English' tradition of 'principled' criticism (as Christopher Ricks has called it) that runs 'from Johnson to Leavis' (and beyond),[66] with the 150-year gap between Johnson and Leavis occupied, pre-eminently, by Matthew Arnold – for whom 'poetry' was 'at bottom a criticism

[62] Ibid. 455 (a letter of 1903) and 469 (a letter of 1933).

[63] See Flashar (1995), and cf. §27.

[64] Aeschylus: George Thomson, *Aeschylus and Athens* (1941). Lucretius: Benjamin Farrington, writing for 'the anxious contemporary mind, Christian or Marxist' (1967: 149), acclaimed Lucretius (author of 'the greatest philosophical poem in the world', 1967: 136) in a series of publications, from *Science and Politics in the Ancient World* (1939) to *The Faith of Epicurus* (1967). Thomson was English, Farrington Irish.

[65] 'We Philologists' (n. 45 above), tr. by the chief founding father of the journal, William Arrowsmith: *Arion* n.s. 1 (1973–4) 279–380. The journal began life in 1962.

[66] Ricks (2002) 243.

of life';[67] whose definition of criticism was 'a disinterested endeavour to learn and propagate the best that is known and thought in the world';[68] whose proselytizing attitude was applauded by Housman himself;[69] and whose own *On Translating Homer* (1861/2), as a characterization of Homeric poetry as much as a study of translations, has figured prominently in English-language scholarly discussion of Homer ever since.

Even in the heartland of philological scholarship – the edition with commentary – this presence of the 'principled' critic can be felt. Two examples from the Victorian era make the point: commentaries on Sophocles by the Hellenist, R. C. Jebb, and on Lucretius by the Latinist, H. A. J. Munro. The introduction to Jebb's commentary on the *Oedipus Tyrannus* is representative.[70] It begins with the ringing declaration that the play 'is in one sense the masterpiece of Attic Tragedy',[71] then, by way of justifying the claim, assesses the play's use of its sources and its plot and characters, before turning to 'other plays on the subject' by Seneca, Corneille, Dryden, and Voltaire,[72] and finally to 'recent revivals' of the *Oedipus* at Harvard and the Théâtre Français, as testimony to the 'meaning and power' of Greek tragedy and its continuing 'virtue for the modern world'.[73] Much might be said about the literary sophistication, or unsophistication, of Jebb's treatment of his author,[74] and especially its modernity or non-modernity. What cannot be denied is his commitment to the value of the Sophoclean text and to the relevance of the classical tradition for the scholar concerned to reinterpret that text.

Munro's *Lucretius* tells a similar story, albeit the indicators are more scattered.[75] The long introduction with which Munro prefaces his notes on the poem is full of literary-critical judgements on the *De Rerum Natura* and its place in Latin literature, and equally full of reference to literature thereafter. Munro's enthusiasm for the Epicurean poet-philosopher spills over into his judgements on Epicurean moments in others; we are, for instance, to 'contrast the varied graces and exuberant beauty of Virgil, when he is pleased to assume the garb of an epicurean, with the leaden dulness and tedious obscurity of the stoic Manilius' (Housman, take note?).[76] The commentator is prepared to take the poem seriously as poetry and, in the same breath, to relate it to modern science seriously. Thus on the Epicurean theory of images in Book 4: '[Lucretius] wrestles with [the theory's] gigantic difficulties and

[67] *Essays in Criticism, Second Series* (1888), 'Wordsworth'.

[68] *Essays in Criticism, First Series* (1865), 'The Function of Criticism at the Present Time'.

[69] 'He spent a lifetime trying to teach his countrymen how to use their minds': Ricks (1988) 276.

[70] Here cited from the first edition (1883).

[71] Ibid. xiii.

[72] Ibid. xxxv–xlix.

[73] Ibid. xlix–lii.

[74] Cf. Easterling (2004) 7–30.

[75] Citations from the fourth edition (1886). Assessment of Munro: Brink (1986) 141–3.

[76] Munro (1886), 2. 6. Privately, Housman would have agreed: cf. n. 55 above. Housman in any case paid Munro a glowing tribute in 1911: 'In his *Lucretius* he produced a work more compact of excellence than any edition of any classic which has ever been produced in England' (Ricks 1988: 299).

often overcomes them with singular power, energy and controversial address. And in truth the most obvious objections to this doctrine of images apply almost as strongly to the Newtonian theory of the emission of light which . . . so long maintained its ground.'[77] A brief survey of modern responses to Lucretius runs from 'the Italian scholars of the fifteenth century' to Milton and Dryden, Voltaire and Sainte-Beuve and Goethe.[78] In his commentary, Munro goes on to cite 'imitations' by Molière and by Milton,[79] versions of the 'pathetic fallacy' in Shakespeare and George Herbert,[80] comments by Wordsworth and Wordsworthian parallels.[81] All in all, one is less than surprised to find that it was his encounter with Munro's first edition of 1864 that inspired Tennyson to compose his remarkable poem 'Lucretius' in 1868 – remarkable in its own right (§35), and remarkable too in that Munro himself (sent an advance copy by the poet) pronounced it suitably 'Lucretian'.[82]

In Munro, and in Jebb too, there is indeed little sense of the *challenge* of modern literature – it is not like reading Matthew Arnold on Heine, or Flaubert, or Tolstoy – let alone any awareness of the literary avant-garde (a Mallarmé or a Strindberg); there is a kind of passivity in the literary judgements, as there is in the participation in a wider culture; but it is, still, participation. Yet for Munro, as for Jebb, this participation goes hand in hand with the utmost respect for (and *active* engagement with) the most 'scientific' achievements of German, and other, philology in their modern age. Both editors include substantial discussions of the technical histories of their texts, and of the modern scholars who peopled them; and that most pure, or austere, of modern philological practices, the collation and comparison of manuscripts, in pursuit of their stemmatic relationship, is scrupulously represented.[83] Munro's acclaim of 'the masterly work of Lachmann' – Karl Lachmann, younger contemporary of Wolf and stemmatologist supreme – is, again, representative.[84]

Further qualifications are in order. Housman's austere devotion to pure, compartmental scholarship is exceptional, even by German standards. From time to time, even Wilamowitz chose to gesture to the achievements of the 'poet-philologists',[85] just as, for a period of his life, he was 'eager to make Greece intelligible . . . to the general

[77] Munro (1886), 2. 7.

[78] Ibid. 2. 20; on Goethe ('greatest of German critics'), see also 2. 8.

[79] E.g. ibid. 2. 278 and 345 (on Lucretius, 4. 1160 and 5. 1256).

[80] Ibid. 2. 297 (on Lucretius, 5. 226).

[81] E.g. ibid. 2. 348–9 (on Lucretius, 5. 1378 and 1387).

[82] Ricks (1987), 2. 707–8. Later in Tennyson's life, Jebb too was in dialogue with the poet. In 1886 he advised Tennyson on the Greek source material for his 'Demeter and Persephone' (published in 1889), and was duly acknowledged in some dedicatory verses, 'To Professor Jebb, with the Following Poem': ibid. 3. 162–3.

[83] Munro (1886), 1. 1–38; Jebb (1883) liii–lxiii.

[84] Munro (1886), 1. vii (from the 1864 dedication to B. H. Kennedy). Lachmann: Timpanaro (2005).

[85] Thus, a review of 'modern criticism of tragedy' in vol. 1. of his *Herakles* (Wilamowitz 1895: 221–58), though mostly concerned with textual critics, includes positive words on Ronsard and Montaigne (ibid. 224–5), Lessing and Goethe (ibid. 233–5).

reader' through the medium of verse translations of Greek tragedy.[86] Conversely, admiration for pure scholarship (represented in this case by the work of the Englishman Richard Bentley, in an earlier century) could be expressed by so unlikely a figure as the poet Wordsworth. Witness this, in 1837, on Bentley's treatise, *Dissertation upon the Epistles of Phalaris* (1699):[87] 'a work of which the English nation may be proud as long as acute intellect, and vigorous powers, and profound scholarship shall be esteemed in the world.'[88] But then again, Bentley's more characteristic scholarly activity was the correction of perceived errors in literary texts, where his own, decidedly literal, taste determined the erroneous, and where editorial zeal was applied not only to the verbal subtleties of Latin poetry, but also to those of a modern classic, Milton's *Paradise Lost*; and against Wordsworth's praise of his countryman's work on Phalaris, one should set Pope's gleeful satire, a century earlier, on Bentley's emendations. Addressing the goddess 'Dulness', Pope announces Bentley as:

> Thy mighty scholiast, whose unweary'd pains
> Made Horace dull, and humbled Milton's strains.

And Bentley is presented as uncompromising in his devotion to the goddess:

> Turn what they will to verse, their toil is vain,
> Critics like me shall make it prose again.[89]

In one sense, though, Pope's satire represents a positive for the scholar. In this pre-Wolfian age, as, still, for Wolf himself (and, just about, for the ageing Wordsworth), a classical scholar is a public figure, hence open to public praise – or blame.

And one last, sharply relevant qualification: Wordsworth's nationalistic pride in Bentley is oddly prophetic of a later tendency on the part of English(-speaking) scholarship to acknowledge, but also distance itself from, the German tradition, where (it is suggested) the notion of 'science' is taken too literally, or its spirit misunderstood. Housman again (in 1911): 'For the past hundred years the study of the classics has had its centre in Germany' – but 'the superiority which Germany now retains in classical scholarship is not one of quality but of quantity.' In Germany, classical studies are 'far more completely and efficiently organised' – but depend on an overvaluing of 'method', to the extent that 'while the English fault is to confuse

[86] Lloyd-Jones (1982) 200.

[87] The date of the final revised edition; the first edition appeared in 1697.

[88] Letter to Alexander Dyce, 23 December 1837. Gibbon, likewise, thought Bentley 'tremendous': Pfeiffer (1976) 162. By contrast, Swift attacked Bentley on Phalaris in *The Battle of the Books* (1697) and elsewhere.

[89] *The Dunciad*, 4. 211–14 (1742). Housman criticised Bentley on Milton in similar terms, in 1892: Bentley emended 'whenever Milton's poetry failed to come up to [his] prosaic notions of what poetry ought to be' (Ricks 1988: 267). Coincidentally, Pope also put into Bentley's mouth an anticipation of Housman's scholarly allegiance: 'For me, what Virgil, Pliny may deny | Manilius or Solinus may supply' (*Dunciad*, 4. 225–6).

[classical scholarship] with literature, the German fault is to pretend that it is mathematics.'[90]

Perhaps the most extreme case of such distancing belongs to a British Homeric scholar, the 'unitarian' T. W. Allen. In the preface to his *Homer: The Origins and the Transmission* (1924), Allen offers a strikingly critical characterization of scholarship in his time. The first problem, we learn, is that across the range of 'classical philology', and in Homeric studies in particular, a mass of secondary 'literature' has displaced the classical texts it purports to illuminate.[91] Philology, it seems, has lost its way: 'with whatever refraction and inaccuracy classical and mediaeval mentality present to us the ancient world, the image produced by modern philological method is more distorted.' Specifically, Allen accuses modern philology of betraying the humanity of the humanities: 'the repulsive jargon in which ancient history and literary criticism are conveyed, the narrow outlook, low vision and ignorance of human nature and the human mind – its working and possibilities – have turned classical philology into ridicule.'[92]

In case any reader should be uncertain about the target of this critique (though Housman, for one, would have made the right inference from the allusion to 'method'), Allen is explicit: 'since classical philology for the last century has been essentially the product of one nation, the blame for this state of things cannot but be laid at the door of the Germans'; their 'merits and services in the collection and arrangement of material, and their capacity for soul-destroying and sometimes futile labour', cannot be denied, but what Allen does deny is their capacity 'to recapture a world three thousand years away'.[93]

It is apparent that, for all his scorn for 'method', Allen is not challenging scientific (or 'scientific') research itself. And (as his talk of 'recapturing' lost worlds indicates) he is not challenging the primacy of historical meaning. Rather: in his view, realization of these goals has actually been hindered by Wolf and his many successors in German Homeric scholarship; and in this spirit he cites, with approval, a comment by his fellow-unitarian, the American J. A. Scott: 'Wolf, Lachmann, Kirckhoff,[94] Wilamowitz, and a long list of famous names have done much to convince the world that German erudition is blind and stupid.'[95]

90 Ricks (1988) 308–9.

91 It 'has long since buried the originals': Allen (1924) 5. One notes a remarkable coincidence of thought, and time, with a line of Ezra Pound's *Canto* XIV (first published in *A Draft of XVI Cantos* in 1925): 'obscuring the texts with philology'.

92 Allen (1924) 6.

93 Ibid. 6–7. Allen had held such views for years: see e.g. his comment on 'the edifice erected by the German critics' in (1908) 72. Despite his own caveats about German 'method', Housman had no time for such nationalistic dismissals: 'I do not know which cuts the worse figure: a German scholar encouraging his countrymen to believe that "wir Deutsche" have nothing to learn from foreigners, or an Englishman demonstrating the unity of Homer by sneers at "Teutonic professors"': Ricks (1988) 328 (a lecture of 1921).

94 Adolf Kirckhoff, author of *Die Homerische Odyssee und ihre Entstehung* (1879).

95 Allen (1924) 7: Scott (1921) 152.

In assessing Allen's position, we should note that some British scholars of this period are explicit in promoting the cultural ('humanistic') role of their discipline – in opposition not only to the compartmental science of the Germans, but to the perceived austerity of their own British predecessors. Jebb is an early example. Writing in 1899, he suggests that, in the course of the century now nearing its end, 'the humanistic studies' have 'gradually been . . . brought more and more into the general current of intellectual and literary interests.'[96] By contrast, some American scholars (though not Scott) saw the issue as two-sided, acknowledging this British 'humanism' but also respectful of a now established tradition of influence from Germany.[97] In 1908, Francis W. Kelsey envisioned a distinctively American best-of-both-worlds:

> From our kindred across the sea we have the tradition of the classics as humanities, that they should be read primarily to be enjoyed, and for their refining influence . . . But side by side with this humane ideal we have the scientific, introduced from the German university . . . Herein lies the opportunity, the call of American classical scholarship, that it blend together into one both the humane ideal and the scientific, and thus create a new type, which shall be as strong in sympathy and appreciation as it is broad, exact and thorough.[98]

Unlike Jebb and Kelsey, whose pronouncements are sufficiently direct, Allen, for his part, shows a certain reticence – not indeed in criticising the Germans, but in spelling out the logic of his positive alternative. One would hardly gather from his preface that he was himself a devoted palaeographer and editor of Homer and Homerica.[99] More to the point, one would hardly gather the ultimate ground for his distaste for German philology, from Wolf to Wilamowitz, which he leaves to be inferred from passing comments in the course of the book. Yes, the Germans are 'analysts', while Allen is a 'unitarian'; but the underlying point is that the whole tradition of German analysis, in his view, denies the artistic and cultural significance of its object – unlike, by implication, the kind of ('British') scholarship Allen himself is practising. Hence, for instance, this, on the *Odyssey*: 'Blass's acknowledgement of the merits of the work artistically is for a German remarkable.'[100] For Allen, then, the ultimate rationale of Homeric scholarship is indeed the *value* of the Homeric poems – the 'humane ideal', in Kelsey's phrase – and Allen's underlying complaint against 'the Germans' is their pursuit of scientific scholarship without reference to this concern.[101]

[96] Jebb (1899) 34.

[97] German influence: cf. Calder (1966), Röhrs (1995).

[98] Kelsey (1908) 384. American attitudes in this period: Winterer (2002) 152–78.

[99] Latterly as author of a three-volume edition of the *Iliad*: *Homeri Ilias* (1931).

[100] Allen (1924) 201.

[101] More unexpectedly, Allen also criticises philology as *not* properly scientific, because not properly progressive: 'the real sciences advance in lines . . . Philology . . . ever and anon returns to the point it started from. Herein it resembles religion' (ibid. 109).

Value: irrespective of Allen, and whether one thinks *he* ever does right by the Homeric poems,[102] this indeed is surely the nub of the problem – and the problem is not in itself solved by the admirable aspirations of a Kelsey or a Jebb. However productive in their own terms, scholarly reading practices are problematic if and insofar as they promote a mind-set for which value is irrelevant (where both a scholar's own mind-set and the mind-set of the scholar's readers are in question): this is what Housman, with his refusal to 'prefer', fails to see. And the quest for historical meaning is problematic (if and insofar as . . .), likewise: this is what Wilamowitz fails to see ('the historical view,' Wilamowitz opined in 1900, stepping out boldly into the minefield, 'has replaced the aesthetic').[103] That latter problem, one might argue, and perhaps the former too, is minimized in practice by a Jebb, in his *Sophocles* (or a Munro, in his *Lucretius*) – but then it is arguable that even Jebb's whole-hearted reviews of what would now be called reception history, or performance history, hardly affects his own reading of 'the' meaning of Sophocles in any material way.

But where do all these arguments, and counter-arguments, leave *us*? First of all, it is beyond dispute (*pace* Allen) that scholarly research in Germany and elsewhere, over the last two hundred years, has changed our understanding of antiquity, and in particular has revolutionized, not only our information levels, but our understanding of the *ancient* understandings (uses, significations, meanings) of ancient words, concepts, mentalities, practices, texts, and artefacts; and that this constitutes a huge, cumulative achievement of classical scholarship, in its own terms, across the whole spectrum of ancient culture and society. At the same time, the scholarly achievement has created a series of paradoxes that need to be acknowledged too.

The doctrine of historical meaning, for a start, is as dominant as ever, within classical studies and elsewhere;[104] and the awareness, on which it is premised, that texts, artefacts, and events did not necessarily mean to earlier ages what they mean to 'us'[105] has led to a huge investment of time and energy in teasing out, as accurately as possible, those earlier meanings – despite the fact that earlier meanings are prospectively, and precisely, no longer the meanings that matter most (to 'us') now.

[102] His positive comments on Homer are 'principled' (as with Jebb and Munro) but few and uneventful: see e.g. a passing comparison of 'Homer and his disciples [*sic*]' to 'Shakespeare and Ben Jonson' and a broad, neoclassicizing assessment of 'Homer at his best, or at what has always been considered his best', pursuing 'the portraiture of character or ethos by means of rhetoric': Allen (1924) 175, 179.

[103] Quoted by Paulsen (1919–21), 2. 742.

[104] With or without an additional ideological framework (structuralist, New Historicist, whatever). In general, such frameworks affect the questions posed and the idiom of the answers given, not the quest for historical meaning itself. The practical outcomes of reception theory are comparable, but one historical meaning is usually replaced by a multiplicity (cf. the 'radical philology' proposed by Gurd 2005, who sets out 'to assess the realities involved in the multiple productions of a classical text': ibid. x).

[105] Scare-quotes here, because there is not and never has been a *homogeneous* 'us': see e.g. Fish (1980).

More urgent, for our purposes: within the protocols of modern research, the status of cultural artefacts (especially texts and artworks) differs markedly from those they have had for most participants in the classical tradition – be they 'users', 'travellers', or 'tourists', or even, in many periods, students or scholars too. Rather than repositories of beauty or enlightenment, enhancements of experience, or sources of inspiration,[106] they are primarily data: objects of research for the generation of a specific type of knowledge. A prime instance of this phenomenon involves the changes that came to define editorial practice in the nineteenth century, once Lachmann and others had established that a sound edition of an ancient text requires reconstruction of the history of its transmission. That task calls for the systematic perusal of surviving manuscripts for discrepancies, errors, and inconsistencies – on the (correct) premise that such formal differences have a special importance in establishing how the transmission hangs together. But to read versions of the same work again and again on the lookout for lapses is (to say the least) a distinctive kind of engagement with antiquity. This counter-intuitive privileging of error over truth, which Anthony Grafton has identified as a key methodological principle in such research,[107] seems only in the most contorted sense to acknowledge the human(e) value of the ancient authors, let alone the authoritative status those authors once had. In fact, insofar as the classical tradition reposes on the transmission of Greek and Latin texts, modern philology sets itself the task of *undoing* it – in the sense of perceiving that transmission as a story of decline and fall, of slowly accumulated blemishes that now serve as the rungs of the proverbial ladder up to the archetype, to be cast aside once the goal has been reached.

Above all, though, the modern knowledge industry operates according to its own imperatives, which differ sharply from those that created the tradition in the first place. Its remit is comprehensive and indiscriminate. As the doyen of nineteenth-century cultural historians, Hermann Usener, put it: 'the true philologist must be a knight without fear.'[108] Not only must scholars like Housman be prepared to tackle any text, however rebarbative. Researchers in general are asked to accept that each scrap of evidence has in principle the same status – and to apply themselves with the same self-denying enthusiasm to the scrutiny of the Elgin Marbles and bits of broken pot, to Homer's *Iliad* and a shopping list on a papyrus fragment from Hellenistic Egypt.

By contrast, the classical is (or tends towards) the canonical. It is by definition selective: whatever is not good enough falls by the wayside. Moreover, the classical entails, in some sense, a prospect of permanence, if not timelessness (§17), whereas the very essence of research is the challenging of accepted certainties through continual reinvestigation: in the knowledge industry the truths of today are the errors

[106] Here, we note the inadequacy of formulae for 'the humane' like Kelsey's (p. 216 above). 'Enjoyment' and 'refining influence': not wrong, just inadequate. Cf. §27.

[107] Grafton (1983b).

[108] *Rektoratsrede*, 'Philologie und Geschichtswissenschaft' (1882): Usener (1907) 28.

of tomorrow.[109] Yes, as Petrarch and Winckelmann, Nietzsche and Arnold, and a hundred others, have helped us to see, 'the' canon is not (or should never be regarded as) something fixed, but as something itself open to debate: the ideal (in Arnold's words) is 'not a having and a resting, but a growing and a becoming', and Arnold's own vision of 'the best that is known and thought' needs to be understood in this light.[110] But even so, the logic of the classical is to endow certain authors and objects with normative value, whereas research, while on one level anything but value-free, is required to be indifferent to such values and norms. It operates according to a different set of priorities, not indeed necessarily constant, but defined and redefined by the demands of theories, methods, and empirical plausibility, beyond the reach of Arnold's 'best'.

Furthermore, research assumes a commitment to the investigation of what has perished no less than what survives *now*. Travellers and others may well have special feelings for ruins (§17) – but ruins have survived. Lost texts, destroyed art-works, ideas that once animated an age, but then vanished: for the researcher, these are a legitimate concern, their reconstruction even a holy grail; for most of those who represent the classical tradition, in its many modes and phases, their loss is an occasion for melancholy, perhaps, but as an instance of universal mutability, like the unrecorded visions of Keats's 'savages':

> pity these have not
> Trac'd upon vellum or wild Indian leaf
> The shadows of melodious utterance,
> But bare of laurel they live, dream and die.[111]

It is tempting, all in all, to identify a rigid opposition – between historical research and orientation in the present, between scholarship and significance, between historicism and humanism, between dry-as-dust philologists devoted to the production of knowledge for its own sake and artists, educators, and cultural critics who keep the tradition alive within society at large. In this spirit, Nietzsche warns his professional colleagues of the danger of mockery as 'philological moles', who, as George Eliot wrote of her character Edward Casaubon, in *Middlemarch* (1874), have become 'indifferent to sunlight' in the quest for buried knowledge.[112]

[109] Cf. Max Weber: 'Jeder von uns dagegen in der Wissenschaft weiss, dass das, was er gearbeitet hat, in 10, 20, 50 Jahren veraltet ist. Das ist das Schicksal, ja: das ist der *Sinn* der Arbeit der Wissenschaft' (Winckelmann 1988: 592).

[110] *Culture and Anarchy* (1869), 1, and n. 68 above.

[111] 'The Fall of Hyperion' (1819), 1. 4–7.

[112] Nietzsche's inaugural lecture at Basel ('Homer and Classical Philology', 1869): Colli and Montinari (1967–), 2. 1. 250–1. George Eliot's fictitious *Edward* Casaubon (whose goal was 'the key to all mythologies') recalls the historical Isaac Casaubon (p. 204 above), as does the scholarly narrator ('Casaubon') of Umberto Eco's 1988 novel, *Il pendolo di Foucault* (*Foucault's Pendulum*).

Fortunately for classical studies as an academic discipline, the opposition is too simple, as the case histories of Jebb and Munro already testify. Going back still further, we should also acknowledge that Wolf's own original understanding of philology as the 'application of a defined methodology to a limited field of evidence' was qualified by the requirement that this 'empirical practice' would 'prepare the way for the consideration of questions of meaning and value' – which, however, 'would be achieved by other means'.[113] Rather differently, it might be argued that the meticulous and methodical habits fostered by philology are a valuable corrective to the bad habits of (post)modern response. Precisely such an argument, indeed, has been mounted in recent years by such notable representatives of (post)modernity as Paul de Man and Edward Said.[114] And a first version of the argument was advanced – after his withdrawal from the philological arena – by Nietzsche himself:

> philology now is more desirable than ever. ..in an age . . . of haste . . . intent on 'getting things done' . . . it teaches us to read *properly* – that is, slowly, profoundly, with respect but still circumspect, with thoughts in reserve, with the doors ajar, with delicate fingers and eyes.[115]

But in any case the interface between 'research' and 'the classical tradition' defies the logic of the either/or: it is more interesting and more complex. In the first place, the tradition in all its facets is itself the object of scholarly investigation (as in the present study). And more profoundly: in the wake of revisionary epistemologies since the heyday of historicism in the nineteenth century, and despite the continuing attachment to historical meaning, the boundaries between ancient past, classical tradition, and our own moment in time are now seen to be fluid, not fixed. We now think we understand that our access to Greco-Roman antiquity is necessarily mediated in some degree through the innumerable responses that make up the tradition, which is therefore part of our antiquity, and part of us.

For a Wilamowitz, oppressed by the thought that our blood can only make the old ghosts speak at the cost of an alien presence, the task is to exorcise the present in the attempt to understand the past. But not only is complete exorcism unachievable (it would require a place to stand unaffected by historical contingency and outside time). It is, surely, undesirable: it would falsify classical studies, by denying the force of its own history, and would simply impoverish the understanding of

[113] Paraphrase by Harpham (2009) 36.

[114] See ibid. 34–40.

[115] In the 1886 preface (section 5) to *Morgenröte* ('Dawn', 1881); Nietzsche gave up his Chair, and all philological activity, in 1879. Here he adds, 'I wasn't a philologist for nothing: perhaps I still am one' (ibid.). Revealingly, perhaps, this erstwhile interrogator of 'philological moles' now describes himself (in the first sentence of the preface) as a 'subterranean' – but in the sense of 'digging, mining, undermining'. On the complexities of Nietzsche's attitudes to philology: variously, Porter (2000), Schrift (1990) 144–68.

antiquity by finally separating it from the innumerable readings (not least, creative readings) which offer immediate comparison with 'ours'. And comparison is crucial. As André Malraux once noted, in a related context: 'We can only apprehend ['sentir'] through comparison. Someone who knows *Andromaque* or *Phèdre* will get a better sense of the French genius by reading *A Midsummer Night's Dream* than all Racine's other tragedies.'[116]

More pointedly still: such comparisons change meanings, and especially when the points of comparison represent stages in a perceived continuum. In this sense 'the past', as T. S. Eliot declared in a classic argument, can be 'altered by the present':[117] Homer's epics look different (*are* different) in the light of Virgil's, and Homer's and Virgil's in the light of Milton's – and all these, in turn, in the light of the great problematic of modern poetry, to which Eliot's own poetry contributes greatly (§35).

Finally, let us remember that it is not only on philology that scientific method has made its impact. We do well to ponder, in particular, the lessons suggested by the history of archaeology. One lesson is the disconnect between outcomes and motivations. We may recall how easy it is to point to cases (and not just the notorious case of Schliemann) where the motivations behind advances are far removed from the disinterested pursuit of historicity. (The case of Wolf, and his Romantic-ideological assumptions, is not dissimilar in principle, though less obvious in practice.)[118] Does this mean that the historical meanings thrown up by classical studies lose status? Perhaps, rather, they gain in status – in the sense that they are no longer compromised by association with the scientific (or Housmanic) compartmentalism that may, as a matter of fact, have been instrumental in their finding.

A quite different point: the history of archaeology shows how readily scientific method and a wider cultural presence can co-exist. Unlike philological researches, which – now – rarely have any direct impact beyond the academy,[119] archaeological finds often have precisely such an impact, and (again) not just in exceptional cases like Schliemann's Troy. The success with which Schliemann publicized his finds, however, is indicative (he used the medium of newspaper reports, books, lecture tours), and in his wake archaeology (classical and other) has had no difficulty keeping its place in the public domain. Today, major finds are still regularly recorded by the press; archaeology is the focus of an increasing number of internet websites and blogs; and television programming in many countries runs the subject on

[116] 'La peinture de Galanis', in an exhibition catalogue (1922).

[117] 'Tradition and the Individual Talent': *The Sacred Wood* (1920). Whatever ceases to be 'altered by the present' is effectively dead.

[118] An additional motivation behind Wolfian scholarship – and many other investigations across the humanities *and* the sciences – is what Nietzsche characterized as 'solving riddles': 'Wir Philologen', Colli and Montinari (1967–), 4. 1. 99 [3 (31)]. British classical scholars featured prominently among the riddle-solvers who cracked the German Enigma codes at Bletchley Park in World War II.

[119] In the modern age, public impact is rare and short-lived, even with major events like the decipherment of Linear B in the 1950s (itself probably impinging as an archaeological event, in any case).

terrestrial and cable networks, from Channel 4's *Time Team*, in Britain, and Gisela Graichen's *Schliemanns Erben* on ZDF, in Germany,[120] to the American-based History Channel's *Secrets of Archaeology* – in all of which the archaeologist projects herself as popular adventurer and detective, as well as informed guardian of the past.[121] In the archaeological field, public taste is as attuned to a – selective – response to scholarly research as it is in the sphere of the natural sciences (from cosmology to genetics).

But value and the problem of confronting (or not confronting) value: *this* remains a constant in all versions of the scientific, cosmological or genetic, archaeological or philological. Challengingly, Nietzsche proposed that 'we make it our job to understand our own age better by means of antiquity',[122] and that the study of ancient culture *must* therefore concentrate on its distinctive and irreplaceable achievements (which for him included its capacity to create achievers).[123] This is, indeed, an insistence on the value of the 'classical' that is implicit in the very word. Yet within today's classical studies, confronting value – if not, indeed, taboo, as it was for Housman – still sits awkwardly with the academic pursuit of historical meanings and objective truths.[124] In the professional arena, it is widely regarded as bad manners (akin to discriminating against the disabled) even to voice the thought that Manilius *is* only a minor poet[125] or that – *pace* modernist primitivists (§11), and even if it was a German archaeologist who said so – Cycladic heads may well be 'repulsively ugly'.

Most important of all: the will to reshape the discipline beyond mere toleration of such opinions to the constructive pursuit of judgements and their implications,[126] in the spirit of Nietzsche or Matthew Arnold (or indeed of Petrarch or Winckelmann): this, certainly, remains to be rediscovered. Close engagement with the classical tradition and *its* close engagements with value (Nietzsche's, and the rest): this, perhaps, is the prerequisite here – and the more so, because these engagements (unlike so many academic researches) continue to have a living and evolving presence beyond the academy.

We write at a time when academic classical studies is actually less compartmental, and more open to outside influence, than at any time since the Renaissance. Its

[120] The title of the series ('Schliemann's Heirs') needs no commentary.

[121] Contrast the critique in Holtorf (2008) of archaeology's current academic/societal role.

[122] Colli and Montinari (1967), 4. 1. 107. Nietzsche adds: 'this is the antithesis of philology' (ibid.). 'Wilamowitz asked, "What can we do for philology?"; Nietzsche preferred to ask, "What can philology do for us?"': Lloyd-Jones (1982) 178.

[123] E.g. Colli and Montinari (1967–), 4. 1. 119.

[124] Though yet more awkwardly with postmodern evasions of value *tout court*.

[125] In practice, 'scientific' egalitarianism converges with misplaced neo-humanist reverence. Cf. Pound in 1917 ('Notes on Elizabethan Classicists'): 'there is no discrimination in classical studies. The student is told that all the classics are excellent' (Pound 1954: 239).

[126] In Dr Johnson's words, 'improve opinion into knowledge': *Rambler* 92 (1751). Which is not exactly 'knowledge' in the sense of *scientia*/*Wissen*(*schaft*).

spokespersons, equally, are, in principle, in a favoured position to influence the wider world in turn, and not least by the reminder that they are the custodians of value in a special sense.[127] Value is not, indeed, unique to them, but it is, perhaps, uniquely built into the fundamental identity of their subject, as it is into the long chains of response to antiquity (and the knots and the loose ends, as well as the chains), which they are – again, in principle – well placed to study and promote. Engage, *re*engage, with value, then – not so much for the sake of 'imperilled science' as for the advancement of our collective sensibility. Advance science, and the angels (one imagines) nod in approval. Advance sensibility, and the angels surely sing.

[127] Though some of the 'outside influence' itself points away from 'value' in this sense, e.g. the considerable influence of modern anthropology, most notable (*pace* Wilamowitz, p. 209 above) in the sphere of myth and religious practice (cf. §24).

§17

Looking at the Past

Edward Gibbon's *Decline and Fall of the Roman Empire* was published over a period of twelve years, from 1776 to 1788. According to one of its author's several accounts, the work was set in train by a compendious visual stimulus, years before, in the form of a chance encounter with a conflated Roman present and past:

> It was at Rome on the 15th of October, 1764, as I sat musing amidst the ruins of the Capitol, while the bare-footed friars were singing vespers in the Temple of Jupiter, that the idea of writing the decline and fall of the city first started to my mind.[1]

Two generations or so after Gibbon's inspirational moment, J. M. W. Turner exhibited his *Modern Rome: Campo Vaccino* at the Royal Academy (1839) [*Plate 5*]. Prompted by its title, as well as its compositional dynamics, viewers of Turner's painting no doubt look to the middle distance, where a bright but hazy assemblage of buildings catches the eye,[2] stretching from what would seem to be the Baroque dome of Santi Luca e Martina[3] to the husk of the Colosseum and the scattered ruins of the Forum.[4] Closer to the viewer, and literally overshadowing that bright haze, is a more modest ruin, consisting of two columns and their broken entablature – a

1 'Memoir E' in Murray (1897) 302. Gibbon's 'several accounts': Craddock (1984).

2 'A magical fusion of sunlight, mist and haze which seems more alive than anything else in the scene': Powell (2003) 196.

3 1635–64: Pietro da Cortona.

4 Turner adjusts the topography for compositional reasons: Powell (1987) 167.

The Classical Tradition: Art, Literature, Thought, First Edition. Michael Silk, Ingo Gildenhard, and Rosemary Barrow.

Published 2017 by John Wiley & Sons Ltd.

relic of the Temple of Vespasian. The eye that registers this less defined fragment of antiquity now, perhaps, identifies, at the foot of the ruin and extending across the canvas, all in shadow, small figures of peasants and their goats: anonymous representatives of the life of today, though not especially 'modern' in the expected sense.

In *Modern Rome*, Turner invites us to see *what*? His canvas was exhibited along with a matching, pendant painting, *Ancient Rome: Agrippina Landing with the Ashes of Germanicus*; the year before, likewise, Samuel Palmer had exhibited *A View of Ancient Rome* and *A View of Modern Rome during Carnival*; and that same year, Turner himself had shown another matching pair, *Ancient Italy: Ovid Banished from Rome* and *Modern Rome: The Pifferari*. This seeming fashion for visual comparison between Rome old and new was also a common feature of guide books to Rome at the time.[5] On its first showing, meanwhile, Turner's painting was informed by two Byronic verses printed in the exhibition catalogue, 'The moon is up, and yet it is not night; | The sun as yet divides the day with her.'[6] In *Modern Rome*, suggests one commentator, the ancient and the later buildings are 'knit harmoniously into one fabric', with an implication of continuity enforced by the verses: 'the sun which set on Agrippina's city still sheds its light on present-day Rome, even in its ruined state.'[7] For another interpreter, the quotation, in particular, helps to suggest that 'modern Rome, as a moral emblem for the contemporary world, exists in a kind of eternal twilight that evokes its past grandeur as well as its subsequent decline and current decay.'[8]

Both these rather different readings clearly have some force (reluctant as one may be to jump to sweeping conclusions about 'moral emblems' or 'current decay'), but *Modern Rome*, as a powerful image in its own right, can claim a deeper significance for the way that Turner, and we in his wake, look at the classical past. Our question again: Turner invites us to see *what*? Ancient Rome as a constituent part of 'modern' Rome? 'Modern' Rome as inextricably – and poignantly – ancient? The relationship between ancient and modern as not so much 'harmonious' as problematic, or at least imponderable (just think of the 'modern' goats)? At all events, in looking *for* this modern Rome, we find ourselves looking *at* the past, but of course the past as it *is* in the present – and then a past, and a present, configured in an affecting but elusive composition of shadow and light, with all the possible connotations of such a configuration.

This painting by Turner and, equally, that evocative moment of inspiration recorded by Gibbon work as only visual images of, or from, the past can. Is that a fair statement? Is there something about the visual past and its literal presence that makes 'looking *at* the past' distinctive and special – by comparison with any engagement with the thoughts or words of the past? More precisely: could there be said

[5] Cf. Powell (1987) 167, Thomas (2008) 89.

[6] Byronic, but not strictly Byron's: the verses simplify a sequence in *Childe Harold's Pilgrimage*, 4. 27 (1818).

[7] Nicholson (1990) 123.

[8] Thomas (2008) 90.

to be something special about looking at the classical past that facilitates a concentrating and a bringing into focus of the experience of the classical? We suggest that there is.

Part of the point, no doubt, is the stronger presence associated with visual experience, with *looking* as such – an experiential primacy noted by visual artists ('sight alone produces an instantaneous impulse': Gauguin),[9] but also by thinkers from Aristotle (for whom 'before the eyes' is the same as actualizing)[10] to many of today's psychologists and neuroscientists, who take it as axiomatic that 'vision is our dominant sense', along with theorists of visual culture, who affirm that 'we live in a visual world'.[11] Also relevant is the immediacy of the 'actual present' in which the visible past is experienced, as opposed to the 'duration' it underwent to get to that present.[12] And relevant, too, is surely the sheer visible *pastness* of artefacts and physical materials from a past age – pastness visible if only (though not only) because of inevitable wear and tear. Words on an ancient papyrus or a medieval manuscript are unmistakably of the past, too, being themselves physically part of physical materials from the past. Words as such, 'in the original' or in translation, are much more readily de-antiquified by the mind.

There seem to be constants here, beyond the many variables between different eras,[13] and all the varying attitudes to the past on the part of those living in these eras. Certainly that sheer pastness of ancient artefacts and other materials does seem to have impinged as evident fact throughout all the periods that are our concern: a pastness that impinges with distinctive force, especially if experienced in a sudden sensory encounter. Consider, for instance, Virgil's famous vignette of country life, after years of civil war and now of peace,

> scilicet et tempus veniet, cum finibus illis
> agricola incurvo terram molitus aratro
> exesa inveniet scabra robigine pila,
> aut gravibus rastris galeas pulsabit inanis,
> grandiaque effossis mirabitur ossa sepulcris[14] –

[9] 'Notes synthétiques' (*c.* 1888).

[10] *Rhetoric*, 3. 11. 2, *pro ommatôn energounta*. This is in the rhetorical context of imaginary 'seeing', but elsewhere Aristotle makes it clear that 'like so many philosophers, for example the British empiricists, he tends to take perception, and especially sight, as the paradigm of mental processes': Norman (1979) 95.

[11] Opening gestures by (respectively) Wade and Swanston (2001) ix, Howells (2003) 1. The primacy of vision is accepted even by recent theorists who insist on its hybridity (e.g. Pallasmaa 2011: 596, on 'the unconscious tactile perception concealed in vision').

[12] The phrases, though not quite the argument, derive from Fer (2000) 71.

[13] Including the possibility that sensory processes may themselves be subject to change in different ages or cultures: Smith, M. M. (2007).

[14] *Georgics*, 1. 493–7: 'Yes, and a time will come when in those lands | A farmer labouring at the soil with his bent plough | Will come upon spears consumed by scabby rust, | Or hit empty helmets with his weighted hoe, | And wonder at giant bones in their upturned graves.' The discussion at this point draws on Silk (2007a) 225–6.

or Dryden's elongated version, in his translation of 1697,

Then after length of time, the lab'ring swains
Who turn the turfs of those unhappy plains
Shall rusty piles from the plough'd furrows take,
And over empty helmets pass the rake,
Amaz'd at antique titles on the stones
And mighty relics of gigantic bones –

or Wordsworth's allusion to the Virgil, the Dryden, or both, in his sonnet, 'Roman Antiquities Discovered at Bishopstone, Herefordshire' (1835), which ends with an innocent's emotional reaction to the discovery of a hoard of coins, and the impact on him of one particular image, of Romulus, Remus, and the she-wolf:

Or a fierce impress issues with its foil
Of tenderness – the wolf, whose suckling twins
The unlettered ploughboy pities when he wins
The casual treasure from the furrowed soil.

There are differences, of course, between the human responses evoked by Virgil (or Dryden) and Wordsworth – but there is something irreducibly in common as well: a sense of the immediacy of the physical, visual, past-in-the-present, in both passages dramatized as an abrupt presence, almost a revelation, for Virgil's solitary farmer (or the plural 'swains' in Dryden's version) and equally for Wordsworth's unsuspecting ploughboy.

Wordsworth's ploughboy is 'unlettered'; so too, perhaps, is Virgil's 'amaz'd' farmer. More cultivated, no doubt, are those collectors of 'casual treasure' who have been prominent figures in long periods of the classical tradition, as in antiquity itself. Collecting, though not of course exclusive to the classical tradition, is widely associated with it. Indeed, among the many cultures in recorded history, this very distinctive phenomenon seems to be peculiarly associated with a subset of those with *a* classical tradition. In George Kubler's words: 'A long tradition of collecting and connoisseurship appears only among the Chinese, Japanese and European peoples.'[15]

Collecting caters to a variety of motivations. Elsner and Cardinal cite 'desire and nostalgia, saving and loss, the urge to erect a permanent complete system against the destructiveness of time.'[16] In addition, though, in any 'object-centred' society[17] a clear rationale of acquisition is that art and artefacts claim both economic worth and a 'visible cultural value'.[18] As a mode of engagement with the ancient world, collecting has much to tell us about reactions to the visual presence of antiquity and antiquities. The responses we find here do not, indeed, necessarily maximize or

[15] Kubler (1962) 44.
[16] Elsner and Cardinal (1994) 1.
[17] Cannon-Brookes (1992) 500–1.
[18] Cf. Pomian (1990) 7–44.

even facilitate the force of that presence. Sooner or later, however, this force asserts itself.

The conferment of cultural status from the acquisition of visual objects has a long history. Homeric heroes already acquire, and exchange, treasures 'as symbolic wealth or prestige wealth',[19] but, in the Western world, collecting such items on a systematic basis only begins with the Roman conquest of Greek lands in the second century BC, when art works are treated as the spoils of war, to be owned and displayed by triumphant generals (as, later, by the emperor) as symbols of rank. In the Christian Middle Ages, collecting is mostly confined to the Church, whose many works of religious art, inherited or newly commissioned, are generally on public display. Large-scale private collecting first resumes in fifteenth-century Italy with the papal accumulation, and then aristocratic acquisition, of newly-rediscovered antiquities – at which point it becomes apparent how significant (along with all other motives for collecting) the realizable monetary value of ancient artefacts may be too. While Lorenzo de' Medici collected a wide variety of sculptures and other objects,[20] his most prized possession was the Tazza Farnese, a sardonyx-agate carved bowl esteemed for its provenance (traceable back to Emperor Frederick II), its material, its workmanship – and, not least, its convenient size.[21] In the turbulent world of Renaissance Florence, a hardstone vase that could easily be transported and exchanged for cash was worth more than, say, a larger-than-life sculpture (also in Lorenzo's possession) of the flayed Marsyas. In sixteenth-century Venice, likewise, the Grimani collection's highly-valued antique cameos constituted 'important investments on a par with precious gemstones or fine jewellery: a readily portable form of wealth, easily liquified'.[22]

The fashion for collecting soon spreads across Europe, among royal families and leading aristocrats – from the English Earl of Arundel to Ludwig I of Bavaria, from Francis I of France to Queen Christina of Sweden – and it is not until the eighteenth century (as so often, the century of transition) that any fundamental change occurs. In a new climate, political and ideological, there is now a momentous shift from private collection to public institution, with the first major public museums established in the form of national collections: Florence's Uffizi Gallery (1737), London's British Museum (1753), Vienna's Albertina (1781). Existing reasons for assembling prized objects are not replaced or displaced, so much as augmented, partly by an imperative of national possession and display, but also, in the age of Enlightenment values, by an ideal of democratic education. 'By instituting a system of public exhibitions,' declared the painter David in 1799, we enable 'the people' to 'share in the wealth of genius; it will educate itself in the arts'[23] – a principle endlessly repeated

[19] Finley (1956) 70.

[20] Not the only notable Medici collector: cf. Gáldy (2009) on Cosimo I.

[21] Fusco and Corti (2006) 130.

[22] Perry (1993) 271. Renaissance collections: cf. Christian (2010).

[23] 'Le tableau des Sabines', a pamphlet written by David to accompany the display of *The Sabine Women*; 'the people', in this instance, were to be admitted for a small fee.

in that age and thereafter: 'the Louvre,' said Cézanne in 1905, 'is the book from which we learn to read.'[24]

Collection as education for 'the people' is something new.[25] Collection as national self-assertion was already familiar. In the early modern world, it was a prominent feature of sixteenth-century France. At Fontainebleau, Francis I created – in the words of the nineteenth-century historian Jules Michelet – a 'French Italy' ('une Italie française'),[26] importing from the homeland of the Renaissance, on an unheard-of scale, books and manuscripts, sculptures and paintings, and artists too, to oversee and execute the decoration of the palace and the exquisite display of the new collection in it. Such notable figures as Rosso Fiorentino, Benvenuto Cellini, and Francesco Primaticcio ensured that the project became a reality – but a reality only made possible by French coffers on the premise that art objects have a recognised financial value: they can be bought by collectors, and the collection is a display of wealth as much as of art. With symbolic aptness, perhaps, Primaticcio's fresco of *Danae* (*c*. 1543), one of the most prominent new features of the palace, has the shower of gold, with which his imperial majesty Jupiter comes to take possession of the Danae of the title, depicted as a shower of gold coins.[27]

Seemingly remote from such endeavours is the high-minded Enlightenment project, the 'democratization of treasure' and the development of the museum as 'the first teaching machine',[28] whereby display becomes less a matter of aesthetic composition for the delight of the few, such as Italian artists had created at Fontainebleau, and more a matter of the systematic and informative presentation of discrete objects to the public at large. The shifting relations between a nationalist agenda and the new Enlightenment values are neatly illustrated by the history of the Louvre.[29] In 1793 the French revolutionary government nationalized Louis XVI's collection and a public museum was established in the Louvre palace. The collection and public display of art objects were powerful political symbols, as they were again when the revolutionary government made way for the autocracy of Napoleon, and cultural ownership took on a national-imperial dimension, reminiscent of ancient Rome. After Napoleon's conquest of Italy in the 1790s, an official programme of confiscation had art-works once again taken from Italian collections (this time without benefit of purchase) – with antiquities from the Vatican museums, including the Laocoon, the Apollo Belvedere, and the Belvedere torso, installed in the Louvre after a procession though the streets of Paris akin to a Roman triumph:

[24] Letter to Emile Bernard (undated), where Cézanne's acquiescence in the principle is the more striking because he goes on to insist that 'we must not be satisfied with . . . the beautiful formulae of our illustrious predecessors'.

[25] Despite David's attempt, in 'Le tableau des Sabines', to convince himself (with appeal to the 'scholar-abbot', Jean-Jacques Barthélemy) that 'the practice of public exhibitions' was current in ancient Greece.

[26] *Histoire de France au seizième siècle. Réforme*, ch. 19 (1855).

[27] On 'venal' versions of the Danae myth, cf. Kahr (1978) 46.

[28] Fisher (1975) 589–90.

[29] Louvre: McClellan (1994); cf. generally Duncan (1995).

'presence' in a very special sense. No less implicated in the process of imperial acquisition was the removal of the Elgin marbles (from 1801 to 1812), to be displayed in London, as the great glory of the British Museum, from 1816: the legality of Lord Elgin's purchase rested on the ambiguous wording of an Italian translation of a firman granted by the Turkish authorities in Istanbul.[30]

With the restoration of the Bourbon monarchy in France, from 1814, all prominent antique sculptures were returned; conversely, the Elgin marbles were to stay in their new home. Meanwhile, though, Romantic and historicist veneration for origins had begun to generate a new awareness of the issues at stake in collection and display as such. If collecting meant detaching objects from their original homes and reassembling them in new juxtapositions elsewhere, what was its justification? Could the past be meaningfully looked at in this way? – where 'meaning' is, for the first time, referred to holistic response, and not merely intellectual understanding (including, now, historical understanding) or even aesthetic value.[31] Objects on view, in this museum or that, once belonged to a particular context. Implicit in the very act of re- (or dis-) location (it begins to be surmised) is a portentous new treatment of the relocated object as a separable 'work of art'. In 1951, in a later age, this composite anxiety is magisterially summed up by André Malraux:

> A Romanesque crucifix was not originally a sculpture, or Cimabue's *Madonna* a painting. Even Phidias' Pallas Athena was not, originally, a statue. Museums . . . have imposed on the viewer a wholly new attitude towards the work of art . . . The museum isolates the work from the 'profane' world and makes it foregather with works that are its competitors or its opposites.[32]

Early in the previous century, Malraux's compatriot Chateaubriand had already condemned (among much else) Napoleon's assemblages of looted antiquity in the Louvre, in something of this same spirit.[33]

For at least one vocal spokesman of Romantic sensibility, the offence was yet worse. As philhellene, as responsive traveller, as Romantic contemplator, Byron was

[30] Elgin/Parthenon marbles controversy: Greenfield (2007) 41–96, St. Clair (1967). Notable cases of dubious acquisition include two at the end of XIX: the shipping of the Pergamon finds (including the Great Altar) to Berlin (see Kunze 1991, Marchand 1996); and the acquisition by the American consul in Cyprus, Louis Palma di Cesnola, of a large collection of illicitly excavated antiquities, which were purchased by the newly-opened Metropolitan Museum in New York and the Boston Museum of Fine Arts: Dyson (1998) 130–2. Despite cultural property laws and a 1970 UNESCO convention, the trade continues (Cuno 2008, Vassallo 2007). The Getty Museum has recently been the focus of related allegations: Felch and Frammolino (2011), Waxman (2008) 279–367.

[31] Even upholders of the educational ideal might have their doubts. 'The sight of these masterpieces will help to form scholars, perhaps – men like Winckelmann – but artists, no!': David, on the stolen Italian treasures, in 1798 (Etienne Delécluze, *Louis David, son école et son temps*, 1855, ch. 7).

[32] The opening words of Malraux's *Les voix du silence*: cf. Marinetti (p. 232 with n. 42 below). On Malraux's argument: Allan (2003).

[33] *Le génie du Christianisme* (1802).

appalled by the removal of the Elgin marbles to London, finding it peculiarly offensive that disconnected ancient monuments should be reduced to serving the casual viewing pleasure of the disconnected masses. In 'The Curse of Minerva' (1811), at a time when the marbles were now on show in Britain, though not yet in the British Museum, Byron poured scorn on their public display, as provoking crude gawping ('While brawny brutes in stupid wonder stare, | And marvel at his lordship's "stone shop" there') or irrelevant titillation ('While many a languid maid, with longing sigh, | On giant statues casts the curious eye').[34] Elsewhere, Byron denounces 'all the mutilated blocks of art'[35] – with anger at the violence of their deracination mingled with contempt for the monetary connotations attached to the displaced objects ('shop').[36] More profound, though, is a sense of sorrow here at the reduction of powerful symbolic monuments to purely aesthetic status ('blocks of art'), correlative to the perceived trivialization of actual response ('stupid wonder', 'curious eye').[37]

Not all Romantics felt the same,[38] but it is no surprise to find the integrity of visual presence affirmed – albeit as corollary of a negative critique – in a Romantic age. More surprising, perhaps, is a comparable, but more explicit, affirmation, a century later, by Umberto Boccioni, Carlo Carrà, and the other signatories to the Futurist manifestoes of the 1910s: an affirmation the more striking because associated with glorification of the contemporary (subsuming the past, only when that past was, itself, contemporary). On the negative side, the Futurists are quick to denounce museum culture:

> We will struggle with all our might against the fanatical, irresponsible, and snobbish worship ['religione'] of the past, which is fostered by the pernicious existence of museums . . . Living art draws its life from the environment around it. Our forefathers took the stuff of their art from the religious atmosphere that loomed over their souls ['incombeva sulle anime loro']; in the same way, we must be inspired by the tangible miracles of contemporary life.[39]

More positively, the Futurists proclaim for their own art a dynamic that insists on immediacy of response. This is the implication of the often quoted, but sometimes misrepresented, slogan that Futurism will 'put the spectator at the centre of the picture',[40] the premise of which is the assurance that '*painting* and *sensation* are two inseparable words', allied to the insistence that the 'new epoch of painting' is one in

[34] Lines 181–2, 185–6.

[35] *English Bards and Scotch Reviewers* (1809), 1032.

[36] Likewise, in *English Bards and Scotch Reviewers*, 1031, the 'grand saloons' of Elgin and his like, where the works are on show, become 'a general mart'.

[37] Cf. Eliot, 'The Love Song of J. Alfred Prufrock' (1917): 'In the room the women come and go | Talking of Michelangelo.'

[38] Contrast (e.g.) Keats's 'On Seeing the Elgin Marbles' (p. 236 below).

[39] *Manifesto of the Futurist Painters* (1910).

[40] *Futurist Painting: Technical Manifesto* (1910).

which 'the public' must forget its 'intellectual culture' and 'deliver itself up' to the work of art, 'heart and soul'.[41] The situation and the temper of the Futurists are very different from Byron's, or from Malraux's, and, unlike both, what these revolutionaries are 'looking at' is not, in their eyes, 'the past' at all. That only makes their celebration of visual presence, and their conviction that the whole official apparatus of collection and display militates against it, the more noteworthy.[42]

Museum culture and 'intellectual culture': one does not have to be a follower of Futurism to see the link. The commitment of museums to their educational project has lost nothing in impetus over time: quite the contrary. In their role as public repositories of culture, museums present ancient artefacts, among others, as aesthetic objects, but in a context of information and orderly presentation calculated to make them tools for understanding Greek and Roman life. The premise here is that their viewers want to learn, and a possible corollary is that (unlike Byron's 'brutes' or 'maids') they possess a basis for learning already. This in turn carries social implications. Bourdieu and Darbel's study of European museum and gallery visitors in the 1960s concluded that cultural receptivity correlated directly with educational status: most visitors were highly educated, and 40 per cent had studied Latin, 'a telling indication of a cultivated background'.[43] Today's museum industry, by contrast, seeks to attract large audiences, and wide audience demographics, through marketing strategies, communication campaigns, focus groups, merchandising, and branding[44] – with the blockbuster exhibition a favourite means of achieving its ends. The British Museum's 2008 blockbuster, 'Hadrian: Empire and Conflict', attracted a quarter of a million visitors over four months;[45] exhibits included a newly-excavated colossus of Hadrian from Turkey; classic pieces came from museums in Paris and Rome; and merchandise on sale included stationery, T-shirts, tea-towels, olive oil, and a plaster version of a statue of Antinous. 'Democratization of treasure' for a receptive public remains the goal, however sceptical some might feel about the means.[46]

Yet such displays tend to conceal as much as they enlighten. In organizing and presenting their materials, museums seek to extend knowledge – but knowledge of a very selective kind. They do not generally point their visitors to the economic

[41] *The Exhibitors to the Public* (from the English version of the catalogue for the first international exhibition of Futurist painting, 1912).

[42] Elsewhere: 'Museums: cemeteries! . . . Identical, frankly, in the insidious promiscuity of so many bodies, without any knowledge of one another' (Marinetti's 'Fondazione e Manifesto del Futurismo', published in *Le Figaro*, 20 February 1909).

[43] Bourdieu and Darbel (1991) 15; cf. the larger analysis of culturalism and power relations in Bourdieu (1979).

[44] Cf. Scott (2000).

[45] Figures from the British Museum website ('Museum news'), 2009. The Museum's 2013 Pompeii exhibition, under way as this book is going to press, is predicted to attract one and a half million visitors – and has already led to an upsurge of tourists to southern Italy: Conal Urquhart, *The Observer*, 13 April 2013.

[46] Cf. Haskell (2000).

value of their artefacts, or to the often questionable background to their acquisition.[47] Thanks to continuing campaigns for the return of the Elgin marbles to Athens, many museum-goers will know something of the circumstances behind their presence in London, but few will know anything, for instance, about the almost industrial scale on which antiquities from the city of Rome crossed national frontiers in the century preceding.

Eighteenth-century Italy was the centre of a booming antiquities market in which the lure of foreign export taxes encouraged a slackening of laws governing the sale of antiquities.[48] An impoverished Italian nobility made use of European money to divest itself of family property, and thus the Giustiani collection was sold to Britain, the Chigi to Poland, the Odescalchi to Spain. In their quest for antiquities, Renaissance collectors had employed a host of personal and political connections, and devised flexible systems of payment (in 1506 Pope Julius II allowed the seller of the Laocoon an annual income for life from the tolls of a custom house),[49] but now professional dealers dominated the market. A commercial impetus commodified antiquity, and in Britain, above all, the Grand Tourist's cultural reference points of classical texts and archaeological ruins generated a list of tangible 'must-have' items to be bought, restored, and displayed in Palladian-style country houses at home (§11). British expatriate artist Thomas Jenkins, chief supplier of ancient objects from Italy in the second half of the eighteenth century, was the agent for Charles Townley, who amassed a large collection of restored Roman copies of Greek sculptures bought by the British Museum in 1805 after Townley's death.[50] Jenkins benefited from an arrangement with Pope Clement XIV, who was seeking pieces for his own collection in the Pio-Clementino Museum in Rome. One of Townley's most celebrated marbles, excavated in Hadrian's villa at Tivoli and identified as a copy of Myron's Discobolus, was only allowed an export licence because another version was found on the same site and claimed for the papal museum.[51] However one estimates the efficacy of the 'visual presence' of items displayed in today's museums, it is often undeniable that a tortuous history has made that presence a reality.

Like the history of collecting, the story of changing attitudes to artistic restoration has lessons for us, especially in the light of shifts in attitude towards its effective antipode, the ruin. The two – ruin and restoration – are often discussed in separate terms and separate contexts,[52] and indeed responses to the two have distinct histories to a large extent. For our purposes, the interconnections are significant too.

[47] By contrast, a 1991 exhibition of antiquities at the Ashmolean Museum in Oxford did confront these issues: cf. Beard and Henderson (1994).

[48] From XV, a series of papal edicts aimed at controlling the excavation and export of antiquities, but enforcement proved difficult: Ridley (1992) 12–46.

[49] Fusco and Corti (2006) 180.

[50] Cook (1985).

[51] Coltman (2009) 97–100.

[52] Connected by e.g. Lowenthal (1985) (rich in material, but also minor slips). Ruins: generally, Woodward (2001). Restoration: Conti (2007).

Turner's *Modern Rome* foregrounds an ancient ruin, and ruins are distinctive tokens of the past. The visible, tangible monuments of Rome (a representative, but also a special case: §25) have made the city a magnet for visitors, from medieval pilgrims to modern tourists. Much of what is visible there, and much of what has been visible there since successive devastations in late antiquity and the earlier Middle Ages, is a ruined antiquity – collapsed column drums, fallen capitals, missing entablature – as in Turner's depiction. For an eighth-century commentator, 'Rome, you lie in ruins ('male Roma ruis') already seemed an appropriate description;[53] for Petrarch, in or soon after his first visit in 1337 (§29), the once great city was one great ruin ('una ruina'), prompting remembrance of 'time past' ('tempo andato').[54]

Ruins make the pastness of the past immediate as nothing else can. The effect of seeing them can be shocking, as Cicero long ago recorded, on 'suddenly catching sight of the ruins of Corinth'.[55] The straightforward reason is that visible decay is one of the ways we comprehend time. The decay of historic artefacts, whether buildings or smaller objects, is caused by natural agents, from 'ordinary' climatic processes to more irregular events, like earthquakes and floods, but also by human intervention: fire, war, pollution, vandalism, theft, and simple reuse. It follows that, in Kubler's words, 'an unmistakable erosion wears down the contours' of every token of the past;[56] and with the 'erosion' the pastness is 'unmistakable' too.

Specific attitudes to ruins have varied over time. Petrarch and the humanists who followed him responded positively to the visible remains of antiquity, but despite, not because of, their ruined state. This attitude persisted for centuries: 'Antiquity I unfainedly honour,' declared the clergyman George Hakewill in 1627, 'but why should I be bound to reverence the rust and refuse . . . thereof?'[57] 'We are pleased in looking upon the ruins of a Roman amphitheatre or a triumphal arch, though time have defaced its beauty': the cosmologist Thomas Burnet in 1690.[58] As early as the 1490s, conversely, the association between antiquities and visible weathering was sufficiently positive for Lorenzo de' Medici (according to Vasari) to persuade the young Michelangelo to make the surface of a newly-sculpted marble Cupid 'look old', so as to sell it for a higher price, 'as an antique';[59] and Vasari also attests that, early in the next century, the Duke of Urbino had the architect Girolamo Genga 'build him a house in the form and appearance of a ruin'.[60] Quite differently, Renaissance architects commonly saw through, or behind, an ancient ruin to the

53 *Versus Romae*, 2. Cf. §25.

54 *Canzoniere*, 53. 31–5. Petrarch's 'looking' subsumes imagining, with Rome's ruins an 'illustration, iconographique et monumentale, d'un corpus de lectures': Blanc (1986) 153.

55 *Tusculan Disputations*, 3. 22. 53 ('Corinthi subito aspectae parietinae'). Cf., again, the effect on Petrarch of first seeing Rome: *Familiares*, 2. 14 (§29).

56 Kubler (1962) 46.

57 *Apology or Declaration of the Power and Providence of God*, 5. 2.

58 *An Answer to the Late Exceptions Made by Mr Erasmus Warren against The Theory of the Earth*, ch. 2.

59 Vasari, *Lives*, 3, 'Michelangelo'.

60 Seemingly in 1510: *Lives*, 3, 'Girolamo and Bartolomeo Genga'.

architectural whole it once had been, of which an undamaged imitation was their goal: in the ruins of Rome, Alberti and Brunelleschi found 'the guide and standard of all new buildings.'[61] Correlatively, restoration of sculptural art, in particular, was often the norm, or even the ideal. Vasari again: 'antiquities thus restored assuredly have more grace than . . . mutilated trunks . . . [or other] . . . damaged and defective forms.'[62]

In Vasari's century and the next, though, the characteristic response to ruins (at least on the part of the cultivated traveller)[63] was a more or less melancholy awareness of mutability. 'In the face of such mutations of time, I could hardly hold my tears back', wrote Aernout van Buchel, a Dutch visitor to the Colosseum, in the 1580s,[64] while over the next hundred years, such painters as Claude, Poussin, and Salvator Rosa used images of ruins in imaginary landscapes to convert a comparable, if less emotive, response into a now familiar aesthetic. Among eighteenth-century artists, from Canaletto to Piranesi, ruins (real or imaginary) often figure in much the same vein;[65] and for the Enlightenment theorist Diderot in 1767 the lesson of ruins is still, explicitly, that 'all things are annihilated, all things perish; only time endures.'[66] In 1558 Du Bellay had already given such responses a classic poetic form in his 'Antiquities of Rome' (§25).

For eighteenth-century connoisseurs, ruins carrying these melancholy messages are, at the same time, felt to instantiate the picturesque, both on the canvas and (in Germany and England, in particular) in new creations – artificial ruins – on the ground. Artificial ruins grace the parks of German princes and the landscaped gardens of English country houses. At Painshill, Cobham, in Surrey, Charles Hamilton's gardens included a ruined 'Roman' mausoleum (1750s) – apt emblem of the transience of life – consisting of triumphal arch, funerary urns, inscriptions, and a sarcophagus that incorporated actual Roman fragments imported from Italy;[67] and the fashion duly received its formal, Germanic seal of intellectual approval from the philosopher and landscape architect, Christian Hirschfeld, in his 'theory of gardening' (*Theorie der Gartenkunst*, 1779–80).

And yet this set of attitudes to the ruin, pervasive as it is, is strikingly compartmental. For the neoclassical mind, as for the Renaissance architect, the visible remains of antiquity, however fragmented, still inspire new, complete, buildings and

[61] Rykwert (1955) v.

[62] Vasari, *Lives*, 3, 'Lorenzetto and Boccacino.'

[63] As opposed to anyone (cultivated or not) who lived nearby: Cicero (n. 55 above) makes the distinction clear.

[64] *Iter Italicum* (1587): cf. Mortier (1974) 43.

[65] Compare (e.g.) Canaletto's *Capriccio with Classical Ruins and Buildings* (1750s) with Piranesi's views of Greek temples at Paestum (1770s). Sometimes, though, the dominant point of interest is 'architectural highlights': Giovanni Paolo Pannini's *Ancient Roman Monuments* (1735) compresses a variety of ruins into an 'entirely fictitious topography', as he 'tries to display as many famous monuments as he can': Zucker (1961) 122.

[66] Diderot, 'Le salon de 1767.'

[67] Coffin (1994) 48. Artificial ruins: Zimmermann (1989).

monuments, and continue to do so in the age of Greek Revival architecture and interior design, in self-conscious imitation of classical styles. In this age, too, antique statuary is still routinely restored, while, symptomatically, in the work of a neoclassical painter like David, 'antique structures' are commonly depicted as 'newly built or in perfect repair', and 'not even [the] ruins are crumbling'.[68]

With the shift towards Romantic sensibility, melancholy feeling – now the almost automatic concomitant of ruins, as seen by painters, visitors, viewers – takes on a new dimension. The 'natural' aspect of ruin becomes a positive, and, in a typically Romantic paradox, the ruin itself yields a kind of existential victory. 'It is time alone which meliorates the ruin, which gives it perfect beauty, and brings it to a state of nature': thus the travel-writer William Gilpin in 1786.[69] 'A noble wreck in ruinous perfection!': thus Byron's Manfred, contemplating the Colosseum by moonlight (1817).[70] The two appeals to 'perfection' neatly demarcate the new sense of value attached to the antique ruin (and one reflects that it was Byron who provided the catalogue quotation for Turner's *Modern Rome* – and that 'ruinous perfection' is an element in Turner's vision, as well). In 'On Seeing the Elgin Marbles' (1817), Keats too records, not only his un-Byronic rapture at the sight of the marbles in their museum setting, but also (more Byronically) his 'most dizzy pain, | That mingles Grecian grandeur with the rude | Wasting of old time' – the whole sight amounting to 'a shadow of a magnitude'. Where the classical ruin inspired the neoclassical viewer to reflect on transience, but build anew, it beckons the Romantic eye to a self-sufficient inwardness.

Romantic poets, and many others, may be moved by the spectacle of material decay, but such reactions tend to divert attention from the investment in conservation over the centuries. David Karmon argues that it was not by chance that ancient monuments survived the fifteenth-century rebuilding of Rome; some credit must go to Renaissance popes who initiated programmes of routine maintenance and repair.[71] However, the ideal of systematic conservation only emerges during the Enlightenment,[72] when for the first time restoration begins to acquire a privileged status – but with much dispute about how and when to restore, and many compromises as a result. Of these none is more piquant than the fate of the Acropolis in Athens, after the Elgin marbles had been removed. In the wake of international recognition of Greek independence in 1830, the Acropolis was cleared of its Turkish settlements, and a haphazard reconstruction of the north side of the Parthenon set in train; fallen blocks were re-sited, but without any proper determination of their original position; the rest of the site, meanwhile, was redesigned as a picturesque ruin.[73] Responses to ancient statuary, however, might engender compromises of a different kind; the American sculptor William Rimmer, for instance, produced a

68 Lowenthal (1985) 144.

69 *Observations, Relative Chiefly to Picturesque Beauty, Made in the Year 1772*, 1. 67–8.

70 *Manfred*, 3. 4. 28. Cf. §25.

71 Karmon (2011). Contrast notorious cases like the pillaging of the Pantheon (§25).

72 Choay (2001), Jokilehto (1999).

73 Loukaki (2008) 206–7.

bronze *Dying Centaur* (1869) without arms, in imitation of an unrestored ancient original – a practice subsequently favoured by Rodin.[74]

In today's world of museum culture and historical-scholarly norms, reconstruction follows a coherent agenda of conservation, whose aim is to protect and prevent deterioration by controlling environments, as well as by activating restoration and repair. Contemporary etiquette allows restorations only where any new additions are both integrated and yet distinguishable, and only where an original can be restored with some (historical) legitimacy.[75] Under these conditions, the nineteenth-century treatment of the Parthenon would be inconceivable, and so too a case like the 'restoration' of Townley's Discobolus. In the early 1790s the marble figure was reconstituted by Carlo Albacini, pupil of Bartolomeo Cavaceppi, with the head in a historically incorrect position, a pose so familiar to visitors to the British Museum that it remains unchanged to this day.

But it is not only in restoration of antiquities that (historical) accuracy has come to the fore. Accuracy, along with completeness and elegance, was actually what Cavaceppi claimed for his sculptural restorations, geared to the demands of the Grand Tour of his day;[76] and accuracy now shapes artistic taste, and steers the visual imagination, more widely. David's *The Sabine Women* (1799), so the artist declared, embodied a determination 'to represent the *mores* of antiquity with such exactitude that the Greeks and Romans, had they seen my work, would not have found me a stranger to those customs'.[77] In Victorian England, 'such exactitude' was equally a *desideratum* for Alma-Tadema's pictorial re-creations of ancient Rome (researched from the artist's extensive collection of archaeological photographs);[78] in the 1920s, for the 'complete' concrete replica of the Parthenon in Nashville, Tennessee, which features pedimental sculptural casts from the British Museum and supplements these with descriptions by Pausanias;[79] and in the post-war years, for the reconstruction of the Herculaneum Villa of the Papyri in the Getty Villa in Malibu (based on the partially excavated site and data extracted from Vitruvius).[80] In the age of the Getty, such precise re-creation and re-enactment, striving for accurate detail in costume and setting, governs the way our generation sees the classical past in reconstructions devised by television producers and the heritage industry. Meticulous detail is taken to offer an assurance of historical authenticity, which is assumed

[74] As (e.g.) in the notorious *Iris, Messenger of the Gods* (*c.* 1890). Cf. below, p. 400 with n. 31.

[75] See the 1964 Charter of Venice (Second International Congress of Architects and Technicians of Historic Monuments) and, generally, Feilden (1982).

[76] Barberini and Gaspari (1994). Cavaceppi: above, p. 106 n. 14.

[77] 'Le tableau des Sabines' (n. 23 above).

[78] Barrow (2001) 30. Such re-creative practice presupposes XIX historicist concern for the ordinary life, and ordinary objects, of antiquity, reflected equally in historical genre painting and the historical novel: Bann (1984).

[79] Lowenthal (1985) 291–2.

[80] The Getty Villa, erected in 1974 and renovated in 2006, houses the Getty Museum's collection of antiquities.

to guarantee an appropriate sense of past presence, in turn.[81] And 'a vivid user experience' remains the goal of experiments in 'authentic' re-creation that bring together modern technology and museum resources, in the classical sphere and elsewhere.[82]

Not surprisingly, the authentic 'reality' aspired to by all such reconstructions and re-creations has provoked critiques from postmodern theory.[83] For Fredric Jameson, visual manufacture can only achieve a 'vitiated historicity';[84] for Jean Baudrillard, only a 'simulacrum' of the past, with imitation making way for 'hyper-reality'.[85] In the Getty, Umberto Eco found the juxtaposition of recreated Roman villa and original classical art-objects self-defeating, even on its own terms: 'The public, flung from the realer-than-real reconstruction to the authentic, could lose its bearings and consider the exterior real and the interior a great assemblage of modern copies.'[86] Conversely, we might reflect that negotiation between the rival presences of original and copy has been an issue from the moment that Roman collectors first commissioned versions of Greek sculptures. Is the British Museum's sale of a plaster rendering of the Roman Antinous, on display in its 'Hadrian' exhibition, so different from the replication of multiple versions of an original Greek Discobolus at Hadrian's villa, when Roman antiquity was a present fact?

The impulse to restore, and to re-create, and the demand for authenticity associated with both, would hardly exist if visual antiquity was not, as it is, felt to be special. On a deeper level, though, it remains ruined antiquity that best demonstrates the force of that feeling. Here, preeminently, is an apprehension of the past *now*, of the past-in-present. And at this point we would argue that even if, over the centuries, there have been many different responses to the ruin, the intensity of the enthusiasm for ruins that reaches its peak with the Romantics is surely peculiar to visual experience. That same generation indeed cultivates the composition of new literary 'fragments'; but there has never been any corresponding relish for the mutilated state of a Sappho poem or a Presocratic philosopher's fragmentary argument.[87]

[81] Often now with the aid of computer modelling from archaeological data to produce 3-D reconstructions of ancient monuments; such techniques have become common in museums, television, film, video games, children's books, and graphic novels: Earl (2005). 'Simulations' might be a better name for all such 'reconstructions': cf. Hobley, cited by James (1997) 22.

[82] Lucey-Roper (2006); cf. Hooper-Greenhill (1999), Parry (2008).

[83] From the 1960s, any 'effect of reality' (Barthes 1968) is subjected to critique.

[84] Gunn (2006) 119: Jameson (1991) 1–54.

[85] Baudrillard (1981).

[86] Eco (1986) 32.

[87] What Prins (1999) 3 calls 'the Romantic aesthetic of fragmentation' (*apropos* Sappho) is quite distinct from attitudes to physical ruin. When (e.g.) Francis Jeffrey observes that 'the taste for fragments, we suspect, has become very general' (*Edinburgh Review* 21: July 1813), he is referring to newly composed literary 'fragments', like Byron's 'The Giaour: A Fragment of a Turkish Tale'. The representative theoretical text here is a 1798 fragment, on fragments, by Friedrich Schlegel: 'A fragment, like a miniature work of art, has to be wholly isolated from the world around it and be complete, like a hedgehog' ('*Athenaeum* Fragments', 206) – a formula for a literary project (perhaps analogous to the *artificial* ruin), not a comment on badly preserved bits of old literature.

The former may have inspired a *jeu d'esprit* from Ezra Pound (§9), and the latter a quest, as for the holy grail, on the part of Heidegger (§6), but neither the existential philosopher nor (even) the imagist poet commend the mutilation as such. No-one will protest if a Housman succeeds in restoring a damaged line of Catullus; many, since the eighteenth century in particular, have deplored the restoration of material objects precisely because (as William Morris succinctly put it) it destroys 'the appearance of antiquity'.[88] With words or thoughts, simply, that issue does not arise. For some aestheticians of our own era, as (almost) for Gilpin or Byron, a ruin is seen as a 'special work of art' and 'a new whole';[89] no-one, again, has seriously thought to say this of (say) the corrupt text of Aeschylus' *Agamemnon*; and it is symptomatic that the negative terminology of textual 'corruption' goes effectively unchallenged.

We can take this line of argument further. Implicit in the apprehension of the past-in-present is a sense of enhanced simultaneity, which manifests itself as something distinctively beyond ordinary apprehending. An instructive point of reference here is Penelope Corfield's recent reflections on 'time and the shape of history'. Meditating on continuity and change, Corfield proposes that the relation between the two is a paradoxical relation, not of opposition, but of mutual dependence;[90] and in this connection she cites a sculpture by the Italian Futurist Boccioni – that same Boccioni who raised his voice against the 'worship of the past' and the 'pernicious existence of museums'. Boccioni's *Unique Forms of Continuity in Space* (1913), Corfield suggests, is a work that fuses 'classical drapery with three-dimensional cubism' and, as such, presents a demonstration of 'continuity striding through space and time' [*Plate* 6].[91]

The classical tradition as a whole – like other traditions – is premised on just such a commitment to 'continuity with the past'.[92] But *this* tradition, in a special sense, continually re-enacts a commitment to past-in-present simultaneity, as a value affirmed through all the diversities of time, including the diversities of its own re-enactments. And the affirmation is most specific in the most immediate of its re-enactments, in the visual domain;[93] Turner's *Modern Rome* makes this hauntingly clear. With antique ruins, and the way we respond to them in mind, Salvatore

88 'Restoration' (1877) – in this case, with reference to old buildings.

89 Hetzler (1988) 51 and Fisher (1975) 597, respectively.

90 Corfield (2007) 46.

91 Ibid. 45.

92 Hobsbawm and Ranger's phrase (1983: 1), *apropos* XIX 'constructed traditions'.

93 Where 're-enactment' subsumes the ever-changing condition of the ruin and responses to it. Outside the visual, miniature equivalents to such immediacy come from moments of cross-temporal dislocation in poetry. Consider again Logue's version of *Iliad* 1: 'Low ceiling. Sticky air. | Our stillness like the stillness | In Atlantis as the big wave came, | The brimful basins of abandoned docks, | Or Christmas morning by the sea' (§10). Logue's technique here, though distantly evocative of the jumps of time and perspective in the Homeric simile, is akin to cinematic match-cutting in its consecutive abruptness.

Settis goes so far as to see in them a visual symbol of 'absence' and 'presence', death and rebirth.[94] Keats, contemplating his 'Grecian Urn', with its 'bold lover', its 'mysterious priest', its 'men or gods', goes further: 'Thou, silent form, dost tease us out of thought | As doth eternity.'[95] With or without its distinctively Romantic accent, that conceit neatly dramatizes the paradoxical power of the classical visual past to far exceed the seeming limitations of its 'silence'.[96]

[94] Settis (2006) 74–7. Contrast the kind of intellectual co-presence posited by Bettini (2001) 7: the classical text is a 'common language' whereby 'we share Vergil with Dante, with St Augustine, and with the emperor Augustus'.

[95] 'Ode on a Grecian Urn' (composed in 1819).

[96] Coincidentally or not, the stanza from Byron's *Childe Harold* that Turner associates with his *Modern Rome* (p. 225 above) contains a relatable line: 'When the Day joins the past Eternity.' Cf. Wittgenstein: 'If we understand eternity to mean not infinite temporal duration but timelessness, eternal life belongs to one who lives in the present': *Tractatus Logico-Philosophicus* (1921), 6. 4311.

§18

The Classical Tradition – and the Rest

Our readers may be wondering: is there any part of Western experience that does *not*, in our view, somehow belong to the classical tradition? Granted that some of our examples of belonging (like Dante's Virgil) are seen to belong more straightforwardly than others (like the pierrots in *Oh, What a Lovely War!*) – even so, we seem to feel justified in detecting relevance almost everywhere.

Well, so we do. We see this as part of our brief: to reassess Western experience, both in part and in whole, from its classical perspective. And a wide range of phenomena reveal something of their essential significance only in this perspective, not least by contrast between the more obviously relevant and the less: the distinctive trajectories of our four languages provide unmistakable examples. And it is a necessary corollary that we seek not only to contrast the more and the less on an *ad hoc* basis, but to connect them in a single narrative. Such inclusive procedures are familiar within modern study of the Renaissance and the medieval age before it, but much less so elsewhere: damagingly so, we would have to say.

More generally, of course, what is likely to raise questions about *our* practice is our flouting of the compartmental tendency of modern scholarship in general – compartmentalization that is as problematic as it is, in the short term, enabling – and, within the more obviously classical-related sphere, our interest in relationships that are wider and larger (and deeper?) than individual 'receptions'. We take the opportunity to reiterate that much of what concerns us is not intelligently discussible in terms of 'reception' at all.

The Classical Tradition: Art, Literature, Thought, First Edition. Michael Silk, Ingo Gildenhard, and Rosemary Barrow.

Published 2017 by John Wiley & Sons Ltd.

For all that, we too accept that not everything comes within our remit. In the first place, some developments of Western art, literature, thought, are so remote from any classical point of reference that it makes no sense to subsume them within the classical tradition – even if it may still make important sense to contrast them with it. On a holistic view, all Western art, literature, thought, indeed 'belongs to' the tradition insofar as none of it would be as it is without the classical, at some stage, behind it; but in atomistic terms, most science fiction, or the 'drip and slash' paintings of Jackson Pollock, or the categories of contemporary genetics, are, in their different ways, so remote from the tradition that only an all-embracing discussion like ours would even bring the (non-) relationship into view.

Even so, remoteness itself is sometimes less than straightforward. Take a distinctively modern work like the Brecht–Weill *Threepenny Opera* (*Die Dreigroschenoper*), which delighted huge audiences in Weimar Germany and beyond, from its Berlin premiere in 1928 onwards. The work impressed those audiences as, by turns, entertaining and abrasive, accessible and avant-garde, politically engaged and almost casually amoral.[1] It appropriated material from such diverse sources as Villon and Kipling. In its demotic affiliations, its anti-representational styles of acting and production, its musical idiom, it flaunted defiance of a high-art Wagnerian ideal. The musical idiom itself is an exuberant amalgam of elements from cabaret and operetta, Mahler and Stravinsky and jazz. In its plot, its characters, and (broadly) its situations, the piece is a twentieth-century reworking of an eighteenth-century mutant 'ballad opera', *The Beggar's Opera* (1728) by John Gay: a satire on eighteenth-century English society, now transposed to Victorian London. What could have less to do with the classical tradition, as generally understood?

And yet, this work does evoke the tradition, in ways large and small. We have a song lyric that inverts and subverts the lyric norm of undying love 'undivided by quarrels', celebrated by poets like Horace,[2] with the laconic thought: 'Love endures, or doesn't, | Here or some place else.'[3] We have a grotesquely contrived 'happy ending' that inverts and subverts the characteristic dénouements of grand opera and, behind them, of Greek tragedy, along with the stable 'dramatic illusion' that both forms assume:

Dear audience, we've reached the point
Where Mr Macheath'll be strung up,
Because in all of Christendom
Nothing ever comes for free.
But just so none of you suppose
We go along with that ourselves,

[1] 'Amoral', as originally presented: Brecht subsequently adjusted both text and production to reflect his shift in commitment to Marxism.

[2] *Odes*, 1. 13. 18–20, 'nec malis | divulsus querimoniis | . . . amor'.

[3] 'Die Liebe dauert oder dauert nicht, | An dem oder jenem Ort': Act 2 (Macheath).

Mr Macheath *won't* be strung up:
Instead, we've come up with a different ending.[4]

That is, we have here an anti-opera (and not just an eccentric opera), which does belong with the classical tradition in the precise sense that a negative belongs with its positive – and, as a response to a form invented as a re-creation of Greek tragedy, and as the flagrant opposite of the music-drama of the 'new Aeschylus' in particular,[5] it inaugurates Brecht's own protracted *agon* with Greek drama (or his generalized understanding of Greek drama), soon to be summed up by his successive theoretical critiques of 'Aristotelian theatre'.[6] Then again, as a twentieth-century 'imitation' of *The Beggar's Opera*, this anti-opera invites a placing against that earlier composition, which was not only a satire on contemporary England, but also a parody of 'serious' (Italian) opera, that much nearer the classical source.

As a paradigm of evolutionary distance which nevertheless confronts, and therefore recalls, a distant classical etymon, *The Threepenny Opera* might be thought to be a special case. And it is obvious enough that the further a culture develops, the more liable it is to lose, or diffuse, any sense of its original – in this case, classical – foundations. Yet even this is not necessarily so, because cultural developments are not always linear. A striking case in point, from more recent times, is postmodern theory, a major strand of contemporary thought developed from French philosophy, which, in its French heartland at least, has shown itself remarkably willing to concern itself with ancient Greek perspectives. One need only think of Derrida's engagement with Plato, or Lyotard's interest in the Greek sophists, or his appropriation of the venerable category of 'the sublime'.[7]

More fundamentally, though, some components of Western experience were never part of the classical tradition in the first place: the German language, and the English language in its pre-Norman form; the 'native' mythology and much of the cultural production associated with those languages; and, above all, Judaeo-Christianity, with its monotheism, its Bible, and its dominant – New Testament – doctrines of redemption and sin. From the first, Christianity accommodates itself to classical norms and forms – from the verbalizing of Biblical chapter and verse in Greek and Latin to the appropriation of pagan philosophy, from the establishment

[4] 'Verehrtes Publikum, wir sind so weit | Und Herr Macheath wird aufgehängt | Denn in der ganzen Christenheit | Da wird dem Menschen nichts geschenkt. | Damit ihr aber nun nicht denkt | Das wird von uns auch mitgemacht, | Wird Herr Macheath nicht aufgehängt. | Sondern wir haben uns einen anderen Schluss ausgedacht' (where the sudden abandonment of regular rhythm, albeit still within rhyme, enforces the subversive message of the last line). The inverted end follows, but sharpens, Gay's ('The catastrophe is manifestly wrong, for an opera must end happily': *Beggar's Opera*, 3. 16), with some help from Molière's *Tartuffe* (1664/9), where, as in Brecht, it is the monarch who intervenes to change the ending.

[5] Wagner: §31.

[6] Summarily, Silk (2001).

[7] Derrida: Leonard (2010). Lyotard: see Crome (2004) (sophists) and §30 (sublime).

of the Church of Rome as institutional successor of the Roman Empire to the development of Christian art and architecture from late-Roman models. And across a broad spectrum of individual and social experience, from education (§4) to myth (§24), it could indeed be said that Christendom is an enabling factor that helps to make given versions of the tradition possible. Nevertheless, however intertwined in practice, Christian and pagan-classical are distinguishable and distinct in principle, and of course often in conflict, throughout the Christian millennium and beyond.

Two very different nineteenth-century theorizations of Western culture agree in representing the relationship as one of sharp contrast. For Matthew Arnold, in *Culture and Anarchy* (1869), 'Hebraism' and 'Hellenism' are alternative ideals, outlooks, and cultural embodiments: 'the uppermost idea with Hellenism is to see things as they really are; the uppermost idea with Hebraism' – which, in Arnold's view is maintained and developed in Christianity, old and new – 'is conduct and obedience.'[8] Compare and contrast the formulae of Nietzsche's last writings, in 1888, where the opposition is more profound, perhaps, and certainly more violent. In *The Antichrist*, Nietzsche opposes Greek, but also Roman, wholeness and 'yes-saying' to Christian inwardness and 'no-saying', and sees in that 'no-saying' both the subversion of ancient Rome and (through the Reformation and its aftermath) a rebuff to the Renaissance: Christian morality and Christian 'decadence' undid the *Imperium Romanum*, while 'the German monk, Luther' set himself '*against* the Renaissance'; on both counts, 'Christianity has cheated us out of the harvest of ancient culture.'[9] And in the final words of Nietzsche's last book of all, the autobiographical *Ecce Homo*, the opposition is luridly mythologized as 'Dionysus against the Crucified'.

Fortunately, it is not our job to identify the causal chains that have determined the precise course of Western cultural history; but it is safe to say that out of the conflicts between the classical and the Christian have emerged some of the determinative features of our Western world,[10] including modern science, which is among the outcomes of the secularizing individualism of early modern Europe, but, in its momentum and its specifics, unrelatable, unless superficially, to the classicizing of that or any later age.[11] One might, indeed, relate science to Arnold's Hellenism ('seeing things as they really are'), in dynamic opposition to the 'Hebraic' insistence on authority ('obedience', in Arnold's terms) – but this, once again, is a thesis of ultimate relationships, of little expository value. The actual distancing of 'modern' science from classical authority in the seventeenth century is no doubt a more representative fact.

Suppose, though, we approach the whole question of relationship from the standpoints of the contemporary Western world, rather than from those of past history. On this basis, we might cite two diffuse tendencies of recent times as even more alien to 'the classical' than either Christianity or science. The first is the

[8] *Culture and Anarchy*, ch. 4. Arnold, Hebraism, Hellenism: §30.

[9] *Antichrist*, chs. 58, 61 (Nietzsche's emphasis), 60. Cf. Silk (2004c).

[10] Cf. Leo Strauss on 'Athens' and 'Jerusalem' (§34).

[11] 'Superficially', as with the 'classical' basis of scientific vocabulary (§13).

increasingly fragmented, but also global, perspectives of Western culture. The classical tradition, on any reading, is European at the outset and Western, through and through; but from at least as early as the later eighteenth century, artists, writers, and thinkers from within the Western world have sought to extend their frame of reference beyond the inherited classical or Biblical or (indeed) scientific, embracing (instead or as well) a wide range of other experience as valid and even paradigmatic. Romantic enthusiasm for the 'Indian wisdom' embodied in the Sanskrit language or the Buddhist scriptures; the primitivism of Gauguin (looking to Tahiti) or Henry Moore (to Mayan sculpture); the archaeological uncovering of ancient Near Eastern cultures and the anthropological and other scholarly study of indigenous traditions across the globe; the incorporation of African rhythms (and more) into the Western mind-set (or ear-set), in response to the world-wide diffusion of jazz and its simpler popular derivatives; the first faltering attempts to incorporate Islam into a Western world-view (if only by journalistic acknowledgement of the 'three Abrahamic faiths'): within Western cultural experience, all these developments (and others) are challenges, on different levels, to the absolutism of that experience as understood in the Christian millennium or the classicizing centuries that follow it.[12] A few, indeed, of the individual figures who have contributed to these movements have also been direct contributors to the classical tradition, like Friedrich Schlegel, who first proclaimed the 'wisdom of the Indians' (*Die Sprache und Weisheit der Indier*) in 1808. The fact remains that all such developments imply alternative points of reference or (insofar as the notion can still be said to have meaning) of cultural authority.

'Insofar as the notion can still be said to have meaning': yet more alien to the classical tradition, and in part a response to awareness of cultural alternatives, has been the rise – most marked, again, since the later eighteenth century – of what might be called the *tabula rasa* principle. Does the Western world seek to build on its past? Any such building will keep it in some relation to the tradition that has so informed its past. Or would it rather try, somehow, to start again, with a clean slate? Any such attempt will work in the opposite direction, as a long series of projects and proposals, cultural and intellectual, confirm. This, indeed, is one of the characteristic cultural modes of our age. Examples stretch from the sublime to the ridiculous, from the well-intentioned to the perverse: from Rousseau's proclamation of childhood and 'savage' innocence to the hippydom of the 1960s; from socialism to naturism; from the deconstructive arguments of Marx, Nietzsche, and Freud (all classically informed) to the anti-Enlightenment relativism (literally uninformed?) that prefers museum displays to be unfettered by chronological arrangement or hierarchical preference, let alone aesthetic criteria; from the Romantic ideal of artistic originality to the uncritical faith in human ingenuity that converts technological innovation into a crypto-moral imperative.

[12] We distinguish here Western appropriations of the non-Western from non-Western critiques or rejections, or indeed appropriations, of the Western, which are not our direct concern (§1).

The deep causes of the *tabula rasa* principle lie partly, no doubt, outside the classical tradition in any meaningful sense: in the Reformation, or the rise of capitalism, or both. But there is also a case for saying that the impulse to 'start again' was, early on, nurtured from within the tradition itself, in the debate of 'ancients and moderns' in the seventeenth century. In this connection, Molière's *Misanthrope* (*Le Misanthrope*, 1666) is a document worth pondering.

Formally in the tradition of Terentian comedy, Molière's play presents us with a contrasting pair of friends, the idealist Alceste and the worldly Philinte. However, their considerable Terentian inheritance (which extends from their Greek-sounding names to their attempts to find favour with their lady-loves) is matched by a wholly new preoccupation with the limitations, as well as the satisfactions, of contemporary behaviour in a (neo)classical world. Alceste, the 'misanthrope' of the title, is an extreme figure, in the tradition, again, of comic figures like Terence's 'self-tormentor'.[13] More precisely, Alceste is subject to a two-fold, contradictory extremity. He is obsessed with the flirtatious, and frankly unsuitable, Célimène, but more fundamentally is driven by an uncompromising commitment to sincerity in human dealings which prompts him (in Philinte's words) to 'change the world' and (in his own) to 'confront the human race',[14] while, in his 'hatred for all mankind', he is willing to entertain thoughts of escape and solitude.[15] Both extremities (and not just the fact of extremity) have familiar classical precedents: on the one side, Alceste exudes all the extravagance of a love-sick shepherd in a pastoral,[16] whereas his misanthropy recalls the ancient figure of Timon,[17] who, 'in loathing for the wickedness of men', abandoned human society altogether.[18]

In a memorable early scene, Alceste combines the two extremities in a telling literary exchange. For all the world like a Wordsworth *avant la lettre*, he dismisses as affected the conventional classicizing figures of a rival's love-sonnet (addressed to the suitably pastoral-sounding 'Phyllis'), and proclaims the virtues of truth, nature, and simplicity that he finds in an old folk song;[19] but as Rousseau, philosophical spokesman of such values, was later to complain,[20] in this play it is not the quest for simplicity and truth that is vindicated by events, but the conformist realism ('one must live in the world') of Philinte:[21] where Philinte, seemingly, gets

[13] In the play of that name (*Heauton Timoroumenos*). The centring of a play on such a character type is a practice taken over from Greek New Comedy: Menander's *Bad-Tempered Man* (*Dyskolos*), not known in Molière's age, is representative. History of the misanthrope figure: Sullivan (1992). For Jauss (1983), questionably, Molière's *Misanthrope* bypasses character 'types' altogether.

[14] 'Le monde par vos soins ne se changera pas'; 'mon dessein | Est de rompre en visière à tout le genre humain' (1. 1).

[15] 'Je hais tous les hommes'; 'De fuir dans un désert l'approche des humains' (1. 1).

[16] Cf. Hall (1984) 178–222.

[17] Ibid. 187.

[18] Aristophanes, *Lysistrata*, 813–15 – though Molière will have known the figure primarily through Lucian's *Timon*.

[19] 'Ce style figuré'; 'la vérité', 'la nature'; 'une vieille chanson' (1. 2).

[20] *Lettre à M. d'Alembert sur les spectacles* (1758).

[21] 'Il faut parmi le monde' (1. 1).

his woman in the end, Alceste's beloved Célimène, though willing to marry him, refuses to leave society to follow him into his solitude.[22] And yet Alceste – as other characters agree – remains an honourable figure worthy of respect.[23] As such, the trajectory of the play seems all too cynically Terentian. Compare, for instance, the disturbing 'resolution' of Terence's *Eunuch*, where a calculated rape is condoned, and the courtesan Thais, far and away the most substantial (and honourable) figure in the drama, is required to share her favours between her true lover, Phaedria, and the rich buffoon, Thraso.

But if Molière's play recalls the worldly accommodations of classical precedent, that only serves, in retrospect, to draw attention to the radical alternative – simplicity and truth – and to the seeming implication that the classical tradition, with all its sophisticated modes and manners, is a prime obstacle to that alternative. This is hardly (one hastens to say) Molière's 'message'; but then if (as one of his characters declares, in classicizing terms, in an earlier play) 'the business of comedy is to represent the faults of all men in general, and those of our time in particular',[24] it is the classicizing premise itself that invites the anti-classical conclusion. Or (reading *this* 'message' more broadly) we are allowed to infer that the free-thinking fostered by classical experience threatens to undermine – as it *did* go on to undermine – classicism itself.

The contestation of 'ancients and moderns', of which Molière's *Misanthrope* might be said to subsume an early, and elusive, version,[25] is strikingly different from the earlier contest between Renaissance humanists and the scholastics. There, both sides belong straightforwardly, though in different degrees, to the classical tradition, but the more classical is the more 'modern'. In the new debate, the classical presents itself as the establishment, and – by the time of Rousseau and his many successors – is seen as problematic, not so much because he or they are necessarily reluctant to look 'back' to the classical (his Romantic successors are strikingly eager to look 'back' to the 'natural' Hellenic, behind the perceived artifice of the establishment Roman), but because there are now seen to be choices, and one of the choices is to stop looking 'back' altogether.

In this sense, Molière's play offers a working model of the way that (in Eagleton's phrase) creative art uncovers the 'fault lines' of a dominant ideology.[26] In effect, Alceste's aspirations, and his negative critique of his own world, anticipate anti-establishment Romanticism – not French Romanticism specifically, but, more

22 5. 4.

23 'Un homme . . . de mérité et d'honneur' (5. 4: Arsinoe).

24 Brécourt in *L'Impromptu de Versailles* (1663), scene 4. Cf. Molière's 1669 preface to *Tartuffe*: 'If the purpose of comedy is to correct men's vices . . .' ('Si l'emploi de la comédie est de corriger les vices des hommes . . .'). The proposition derives from late-antique sources, notably Donatus (?), *De Comoedia* ('from [comedy] one learns what is practical in life and what, on the other hand, to avoid').

25 Cf. Jauss (1983) 311: 'In matters of theory [Molière] was an "ancient" . . . in matters of practice he was a "modern".'

26 See e.g. Eagleton (1976) 180–1 (on Dickens), and in a comparable spirit (on *Le Misanthrope*) cf. Jauss (1983) 315–20.

generally, that characteristic Romantic combination of 'starting again' and '*back* to nature' (Alceste's choice is an 'old' folk song). In the two centuries since the Romantic divide, the purest *tabula rasa* movements have in fact sought to 'start again' without any sense of 'back' at all. Alongside the examples cited above, one thinks of twentieth-century movements like Functionalism in architecture or logical positivism in philosophy or the New Criticism in literary study, all seeking to free themselves of traditional points of reference (not least, classical-traditional reference) in their different spheres.

All of which brings us back to our earlier proposition. The classical tradition is both so integrally and diffusely relevant to Western culture that much cultural development that seems unrelated to it is either implicated in it, even if (like Christianity) ultimately independent of it, or else arises, in significant part, out of it, even in reaction to it. If our readers only take away one large thought from our book, they could do worse than take away this one.[27] They will find it, in any event, a premise, or a subtext, of the investigations in the remaining parts of the book, where a cross-section of more specific categories of the tradition is submitted to critical review.

[27] This 'large thought' invites the question: *why* has the tradition been so influential? The very pervasiveness of the tradition must make any single answer imponderable – but among the pointers to a possible answer we would include our discussions of myth (§24) and Vitruvianism and the sublime (§30).

Part II
Archetypes

§19

Preface

In Part II we discuss 'the dome' (§20), 'the hero' (§21), and 'word-genres' (§22). Question: what do these three disparate presences in Western culture – visual, conceptual, verbal – have in common? Answer: they all have origins in classical antiquity and complex histories thereafter; in the classicizing ages their ancient forms have direct legacies; and they all survive today – they are all active presences today – without, usually, any direct reference to, or direct dependence on, their ancient forms. The relationship with antiquity (the relevance to the classical tradition) is still apparent to anyone knowledgeable enough and interested enough to explore it, but it is, now certainly, a relationship of specific instantiations to an archetype. Reception of ancient forms or instances may be involved (especially in the classicizing ages), or then again may not (especially in our modern age) – though even in the classicizing ages themselves, it may well make more sense to discuss given examples under some other rubric than 'reception'. This is especially clear in the case of the hero.

With the hero, it is also clear that, over time, traditional premises are subjected to challenge (witness the modern concepts of mass heroics and the anti-hero), alongside, still, an instantiation of the ancient form. The dome, in this respect, represents a less complicated reality, though one complicated, quite differently, by changing material factors. Word-genres lie somewhere between the two, though here there is the yet more profound complication that it is not the individual genres of antiquity, but broader categories (even as broad as 'literature' itself), that maintain a presence and truly instantiate the archetype.

The Classical Tradition: Art, Literature, Thought, First Edition. Michael Silk, Ingo Gildenhard, and Rosemary Barrow.

Published 2017 by John Wiley & Sons Ltd.

Various other presences that we examine elsewhere under other headings might be examined under this one: political categories like democracy, for instance (§26). There, though, explicit connections with ancient experience continue to influence debate, in a way that hardly arises with our three.

'Archetype': we use the term, not specifically in a Jungian sense, and not, indeed, because we wish to appeal to a Jungian 'collective unconscious', but because the term aptly suggests a notion of 'universals', even if (as will always be the case) the presences in question are far from universal in their cultural specificity.

§20
The Dome

Life like a dome of many-coloured glass
Stains the white radiance of eternity,
Until death tramples it to fragments.[1]

Shelley's expansive image points nicely to the status of the dome in Western thinking as symbol of earthly aspiration, between the human individual, looking up, and the cosmic firmament whose shape it purports to echo. No less, Shelley's lofty tone serves to efface the hard material facts – innovations in building technology and structural engineering – that made the dome possible, first in ancient Rome, then in the Renaissance and later ages. Within the classical tradition, material culture has a story all its own.

From the Duomo in Florence to the Panthéon in Paris, from Washington's Capitol Dome to London's Millennium Dome,[2] large, hollow hemispheres are a familiar shape, and often a dominating presence, in the townscapes of the Western world. Traces of arch and vault structures have been recovered from Hellenistic Greece, but the arch, the barrel vault, and the dome as we know them are essentially Roman developments that have enabled architects, then and thereafter, to cover vast interior spaces with unsupported semi-circular ceilings in a (literally and figuratively) uplifting fashion. In the Middle Ages, barrel vaults are used functionally in cellars, crypts, and long hallways, and from the early Christian period domes

1 Shelley, 'Adonais' (1821), stanza 52.
2 Cf. n. 38 below.

The Classical Tradition: Art, Literature, Thought, First Edition. Michael Silk, Ingo Gildenhard, and Rosemary Barrow.

Published 2017 by John Wiley & Sons Ltd.

are characteristic of Byzantine (as also of Islamic) architecture, but it is not until fifteenth-century Italy that the dome begins its distinguished career as a defining feature of Western architecture.[3]

The largest dome to survive intact from antiquity is the Pantheon, Hadrian's temple to 'all the gods', which consists of a circular drum surmounted by a hemispherical dome spanning 142 feet.[4] Converted into a Christian church in the seventh century, the Pantheon remained a token of Roman architectural achievement, along with various ruined structures that still display the remains of domed roofs within the city of Rome: the Basilica of Maxentius, the Temple of Minerva Medica, the Baths of Caracalla, the Tomb of the Gordians. In the Renaissance imagination, accordingly, vault construction was so characteristic of the classical past that Raphael's *The School of Athens* (1510–11) is situated, not in the open-air grove of Plato's Academy, but under a coffered barrel-vaulted interior 'which evoked classical antiquity for Raphael's generation as nothing else could'.[5]

While Raphael's vaults seem to lead to an open drum, as if in acknowledgement of Roman ruins,[6] the Pantheon's dome had remained intact: a tribute to its mode of construction. Its rotunda was constructed with the aid of concrete. It was built up in horizontal concrete rings, with each layer poured into wooden coffers. Thick drum walls helped to support lighter masonry towards the top; rings of coffers filled with concrete could then serve as multiple intersecting arches in the finished building. But whereas the Pantheon was reinforced with concrete, smaller post-classical domes, like Palladio's San Giorgio Maggiore in Venice (designed in the 1560s), were constructed of ordinary masonry, held together by compressive force and friction.[7] Nevertheless, with concrete no longer a core element within Renaissance building technique, vault construction posed problems: nearly twenty years before the design of San Giorgio Maggiore, the collapse of the ceiling vault in the Library at Piazza San Marco even led to the imprisonment of Jacopo Sansovino, its architect.[8]

Larger structures, like Brunelleschi's Santa Maria del Fiore in Florence (1420–36) [*Figure 5*], posed an even more significant challenge. Brunelleschi designed an octagonal double-walled dome, made of bricks locked in a herringbone pattern (characteristic of Imperial Roman and then Byzantine building) and linked together with brick ribs and metal chains.[9] The dome, resting on a drum and not on the roof itself, allowed for a construction process free from external centring. Besides its

[3] Counting (e.g.) the domed Basilica of San Marco in Venice (IX) as Byzantine, therefore 'Eastern' (as in idiom, as well as political orientation, it was).

[4] Pantheon and its influence: MacDonald (1976).

[5] Liberman (1997) 75.

[6] And of St Peter's Basilica, begun in 1506 and now under construction.

[7] Beltramini and Burns (2009) 172–5, Boucher (1998) 182–94, Cooper (1991), Damerini (1956), Piana (2009).

[8] Beltramini and Burns (2009) 12.

[9] Mainstone (1977).

Figure 5 Filippo Brunelleschi, Santa Maria del Fiore, Florence. Source: © 2013. Photo Ann Ronan/Heritage Images/Scala, Florence.

decorative advantages, the lantern or cupola summit – a feature of many Renaissance domes thereafter – served the practical purpose of admitting light. The outcome was an acclaimed masterpiece: in a modern perspective, 'a symbol of Renaissance ambition, technical achievement, and intellectual imagination'.[10] In that ambitious Renaissance world itself, Vasari saw Brunelleschi's cathedral as, simply, 'the greatest, tallest and most beautiful building ever constructed in modern times, or in antiquity, even'; it 'challenges the heavens', he declared, and noting that 'lightning strikes it every day', he added: 'the heavens are envious.'[11]

After Brunelleschi, large-scale domes were built with inner and outer shells. The most famous of all, St Peter's Basilica in Rome, was first conceived by Bramante in 1503 and brought to completion by Michelangelo in 1590. Around 1502, Bramante had already designed the Tempietto of San Pietro in Montorio, a small, circular structure with a domed roof based on a Greek *tholos* temple. For the significantly

[10] Adams (1983) 513.

[11] Vasari, *Lives*, Part 2, 'Filippo Brunelleschi'. Brunelleschi's dome: Di Pasquale (2002), Fanelli and Fanelli (2004), King (2000), Saalman (1980).

larger project of St Peter's, Bramante (or, in the event, Michelangelo) linked his two shells with masonry ribs and supported the dome with four large piers.[12] In late-seventeenth-century London, Christopher Wren designed St Paul's Cathedral, likewise, around a large central dome. Here a triple, rather than double, dome consists of a conical brick middle shell, carrying most of the weight, with a smaller dome of the cathedral interior inside, and, outside, a larger, more hemispherical dome made of wood, covered in lead.[13] In the following century, in Paris, Wren's dome served as a model for Jacques-Germain Soufflot's Panthéon – built as a church dedicated to Ste Geneviève and begun in 1756.

In places of worship, many post-classical domes, like the Pantheon dome of old, had an important function as a visual and spiritual evocation of the celestial, with representations of the heavens on vaulted or domed ceilings attested in both pagan and Christian contexts:[14] 'a starlit or a moonlit dome', as the poet Yeats put it.[15] But the ancient Roman dome was not restricted to sacral space. It was also located in sites of display, leisure, and commemoration: the domed octagonal dining room of Nero's Domus Aurea, the centralized vaulted room of the Baths of Caracalla, the semi-domed serapeum in Hadrian's Tivoli villa, the domed rotunda mausoleum of the Tomb of the Gordians. The dome, therefore, might be felt to connote power, wealth, or simply pleasure,[16] and in this spirit Renaissance villas adopted the dome as a sign of their owner's economic and cultural status. Palladio's Villa Rotonda near Vicenza (begun in 1567), centred on a Pantheonic dome rising from a circular hall, was designed as the retirement home of a wealthy cleric.[17] The most famous dome in English poetry, Coleridge's in 'Kubla Khan' (1816), was likewise the epitome of worldly status and leisured existence –

> In Xanadu did Kubla Khan
> A stately pleasure-dome decree –

with residual religious associations transposed:

> Weave a circle round him thrice,
> And close your eyes with holy dread,
> For he on honey-dew hath fed
> And drunk the milk of Paradise.

[12] Bramante's design for St Peter's: Bentivoglio *et al.* (2001), Betts (1993), Licht (1985).

[13] Wren's dome: Campbell (2008), Downes (1994).

[14] Lehmann (1945).

[15] 'Byzantium' (1932). Such phraseology is esp. common in the Romantic age, but commonly reapplied to a more-or-less secularized firmament: thus Shelley acclaimed 'the blue dome of air' ('The Cloud', 1820) and Dorothy Wordsworth 'the dome of the sky' ('Grasmere Journal', 27 July 1800). Baudelaire's anti-Romantic sensibility acknowledged the connection rather differently, with 'the sky's splenetic dome' ('Chacun sa Chimère', 1862: 'la coupole splenétique du ciel').

[16] Cf. Grabar (1990).

[17] Beltramini and Burns (2009) 364–5, Chastel and Cevese (1990), Isermeyer (1967).

In the wake of Palladio's 'well-proportioned' designs,[18] a domed rotunda with temple-form facade, now recalling Renaissance Italy as much as ancient Rome, became a common feature of domestic architecture in neoclassical England. William Kent's Palladian country house for Lord Burlington at Chiswick (1717) references the Villa Rotonda with its octagonal-domed saloon. Nicholas Hawksmoor's mausoleum at Castle Howard (1742), with a Doric colonnade encircling a cella capped with drum and dome, derives rather from Bramante's Tempietto. Conversely, Robert Adam evoked Roman architecture with the spectacular barrel-vaulted library ceiling in his remodelled Kenwood House in Hampstead (1779) and again in his designs for Luton Hoo in Bedfordshire (1767), the latter based on the Arch of Constantine and the dome of the Pantheon.[19] Long since, a feature of Byzantine and thence Russian church architecture beyond the Western world, the dome now exerted a Western-classical influence eastwards into the Russian empire. Towards the end of the eighteenth century, under the patronage of Catherine II, Russian neoclassicism, like its British counterpart, looked to Italian and Roman examples.[20] At Pavlovsk, Scottish architect Charles Cameron designed a Palladian villa that recalled the Villa Rotonda's central dome, sided with porticoes (1781–6),[21] while Giacomo Quarenghi's semi-circular Great Hall at the Alexander Palace near St Petersburg looked more directly to Roman bath structures (1792–6).[22]

Across Europe and America, secular public architecture began to assimilate the dome across a wide range of new contexts. Jacques Gondouin's anatomy theatre in the Parisian École de Médecine (1775) was erected as a half Pantheon, while Karl Schinkel's Altes Museum in Berlin (1828) included an interior Pantheonic entrance hall invisible from the outside. The main structure of Thomas Jefferson's Library at the University of Virginia is a domed rotunda (1836), as is Sydney Smirke's British Museum Reading Room (1856), which, like many other Victorian buildings, utilized cast-iron frames and added copper roofing. The dome of the circular wheat market of Halle au Blé in Paris was constructed in timber (1763) and rebuilt, over forty years later, in cast iron.[23]

Effected and perfected without the use of concrete, post-classical dome structures derived from classical-architectural forms but not Roman building methods. Roman concrete – a mixture of sand, lime, and volcanic ash or pozzolan – facilitated arch, barrel-vault, and dome construction to become a defining feature of public building projects, and, from the first century BC to the end of empire, concrete-enforced vaulted structures enabled water supplies, glorified gods and generals, and

[18] 'Some well-proportioned dome': Pope, *Essay on Criticism* (1711), 2. 47. Palladio and his influence: Boucher (1998), Harris (1994), Mitrovic (2004), Rykwert (1999); cf. §30.

[19] English Palladianism: Crook (1972), Worsley (1995). Chiswick: Harris (1994). Castle Howard: Hart (2007). Kenwood and Luton Hoo: King (1991), Rykwert and Rykwert (1985).

[20] Burns (2003).

[21] Shvidkovsky (1996).

[22] Beltramini and Burns (2009) 380–1.

[23] Wiebenson (1973).

beautified imperial palaces. The course of concrete application in Rome can be charted from the few surviving architectural manuals: Vitruvius, writing at the end of the first century BC, advises that concrete only be used for cisterns, whereas Faventinus' treatise on building (fourth century AD) seems to take it for granted that concrete is a core building material. Yet, only a century later, Palladius hardly refers to the use of concrete at all, with the clear implication that this versatile material is already falling out of favour for major projects.[24]

Traditional accounts of cement-making assume that the practice disappears from architectural construction after the fall of Rome and only revives in the eighteenth century. During the Middle Ages, certainly, admiration of the Pantheon was qualified by a 'belief that it owed its existence to . . . demons',[25] rather than to building technology, but the assumption that all knowledge of concrete was lost has been challenged. It is likely, rather, that 'tacit' knowledge and techniques were handed down by generations of artisan builders who ensured that practical understanding survived on a small scale.[26]

Then again, Renaissance respect for classical authority surely makes it improbable that interested readers could or would overlook references to concrete in now familiar Latin sources. Vitruvius and Pliny, after all, not only describe its durable and hydraulic properties, but also identify the specific location of pozzolan in the neighbourhoods surrounding Mount Vesuvius;[27] and even if no precise formula for the mixture of lime, sand, pumice, and ash survived, these texts still offered architectural theorists a sense of the general process of cement-making. Palladio in fact cites Vitruvius' description of the use of pozzolan in mortar, 'which immediately cements in the water, and makes buildings very strong',[28] and offers a recipe for lime mortar for use in wall and vault construction and water-proofing buildings.[29] In the fifteenth century, Alberti had pointed out that dome creation could be managed with arches and rings on the principle of compressive force without the use of centring. Clearly aware of Roman techniques, he notes that 'in antiquity many architects exploited the inherent strength of this structure' by filling in the vault 'rather hastily, by just pouring in a cement mix'.[30] He adds that, for his own preferred building method, 'I would much rather that, during the construction of the vault, care is taken to ensure that the rings are not too infrequent and that they are connected one above another, and so too the arches side by side, with the same technique as is used to bond stones together in the wall'.[31] Perhaps, then, the use of concrete was not so much lost as rejected. From Alberti one might infer that the

24 See Plommer (1973) 17–25.

25 Buddensieg (1971) 260.

26 Hence, in XVII, the use of hydraulic cement in the French Canal du Midi: Mukerji (2006).

27 Vitruvius, 2. 6. 1; Pliny, *Natural History*, 35. 167

28 *Four Books of Architecture*, 1. 4–6 (as tr. by Ware, 1738).

29 Ibid. 1. 5–6.

30 *De re aedificatoria* (1452), 3. 14.

31 Ibid.

Roman technique of pouring concrete into wooden coffers, layer by layer, was thought of as slapdash, and the method of assembling masonry bonded with lime mortar in a set pattern as more satisfactory.

Whereas some Renaissance architects – Bramante, Giuliano da Sangallo, Giovanni da Udine – did attempt to find the recipe for Roman concrete, it was indeed not until the eighteenth century that the 'rediscovery' of the Roman cement formula (credited to Antoine-Joseph Loriot and Polycarpe de La Faye in France and Bry Higgins, James Parker, and John Smeaton in Britain) began to revolutionize the building industry.[32] Loriot's cement was in fact only a mixture of sand, brick dust, and lime, while La Faye researched Roman accounts of the use of lime in the preparation of mortars that were already known to Alberti, Palladio, and others. Higgins issued a patent for hydraulic cement for exterior plastering use, and (more innovatively) Parker for a naturally-occurring hydraulic cement made from a combination of clay and limestone burnt to a high temperature. It was Smeaton, though, commissioned to rebuild Eddystone Lighthouse in Cornwall, who combined burnt limestone with pozzolan from Civitavecchia to produce the first high-quality hydraulic cement since the fall of ancient Rome. In 1824, Portland cement, destined to become the most familiar type of all, was patented by Joseph Aspdin. For a time, Aspdin's cement was used primarily in port, dock, and marine construction and, though one of the earliest concrete buildings in Britain (in 1870) was a Portland-based private house (Thomas Wonnacott's Fernlands villa in Chertsey, which duly included a domed tower), it was not taken up on a large scale by the domestic market until the twentieth century.[33]

Typical cement, water, and pumice mixes had a high resistance to compressive stresses, but tension caused by bending could result in cracking and separation of the concrete. By the second half of the nineteenth century, the development of reinforced concrete incorporating metals with high strength in tension offered architects a less brittle material. Now, at last, Roman-style vaults and domes could be erected that were resistant to compression and tension.[34] The dome of Max Berg's 1913 Centennial Hall in Breslau, made of reinforced concrete, steel, and glass, served as an important reference-point for new structures. Important architectural projects in reinforced concrete were carried out in France by Auguste Perret and Eugène Freyssinet. Perret designed reinforced-concrete barrel vaults in the Esders Factory (1919), the Olivier-Mètra Studios in Paris (1925), and a rotunda and flattened dome in the entrance hall of the Musée des Travaux Publics (1938),[35] while barrel vaults of thin pleated concrete featured in Freyssinet's hangars at Orly airport (1921–3).

32 Loriot, *Mémoire sur une découverte dans l'art de bâtir* (1774); La Faye, *Recherches sur la préparation que les Romains donnoient à la chaux* (1777); Higgins, *Experiments and Observations Made With the View of Improving the Art of Composing and Applying Calcareous Cements and of Preparing Quicklime* (1780); Smeaton, *An Account of the Eddystone Light-House and Rocks* (1824).

33 British cement industry: Francis (1977).

34 History of concrete: Elliott (1994), Idorn (1997).

35 Perret: Gargiani (1994).

As materials became lighter, domes became thinner. In the 1930s, Spanish architect and engineer Eduardo Torroja designed a thin-shell roof for Algeciras Market Hall, spanning 150 feet with a dome only 3½ inches thick. In Italy, Pier Luigi Nervi also experimented with thin 'eggshell' domes of pre-stressed concrete, using layers of fine steel mesh sprayed with cement mortar, in the small Cinema Augusteo in Naples (1926–7) and the much grander Palazzetto dello Sport in Rome (1958).[36] In the wake of Nervi's acclaimed constructions, reinforced concrete domes became a familiar feature of American sports stadia, from the 1960s Houston Astrodome to Atlanta's Georgia Dome in the 1990s. With the use of fabric membranes, more recently, the transparent dome came into being, creating a play of light by day, but a barrier against darkness at night. One spectacular example is the Izumo Dome in Japan, constructed in 1992 out of wood, concrete, and PTFE-coated glass-fibre fabric, and achieving a height of 49 metres and an impressive diameter of 143 metres.[37]

London's controversial Millennium Dome,[38] designed by Richard Rogers, was opened as an exhibition and show space in 2000. Its status, as a flamboyant symbol of populist-governmental display, was apparent from the first. In the words of one political commentator, 'the Dome was intended to be New Labour's Xanadu, and Tony Blair its Kubla Khan.'[39] It has now been rebranded as the O2 arena, hosting music concerts, sports events, and (with adventitious 'Roman' reference) spectacles including the live-action 'Chariot Race' from *Ben-Hur*, staged in 2009. Like the Millennium Dome, the huge concrete vault of the Parisian Centre National des Industries et des Techniques, built in 1958, was designed as an exhibition hall, but has recently been remodelled as a multi-purpose complex, with a hotel, office space, and shopping centre. In today's consumer culture, a shopping facility might indeed seem an appropriate use for the great spaces that modern light-weight domes can cover, and in a neat combination of contemporary function and overt classicizing gesture, the postmodern Forum shopping arcade in Caesars Palace, Las Vegas [*Figure 6*] – a 1966 extravaganza of mosaic floors, animatronic statues, fountains and fish tanks – is encased in a dome, decorated to represent the sky, and designed to show the sky's shifting appearance from dusk to dawn during the arcade's opening hours. While the structure itself derives from Roman examples, the novelty ceiling also calls to mind Roman precedent in the shape of the main banquet hall of Nero's Domus Aurea, which (according to Suetonius) 'was circular and revolved constantly, day and night, like the heavens'.[40]

[36] Italian use of concrete: Iori (2001). Nervi: Iori (2009).

[37] Fabric membranes: Robbin (1996). Izumo Dome: Ishii (1999) 250–5.

[38] Dome in name and general appearance, but not strictly a dome in the traditional sense, insofar as the Teflon-coated glass-fibre roof is not self-supporting, but rests on steel masts in the manner of a tent.

[39] Rawnsley (2001) 326.

[40] Suetonius, *Nero*, 31. Excavations at the site of Nero's palace have revealed an octagonal dining hall in the form of a large-scale domed rotunda.

Figure 6 Forum shopping arcade in Caesars Palace, Las Vegas. Source: photo by Dr Shelley Hales.

Classically-inspired vaults and domes have spread far beyond the West to the global architectural arena. A dome was an integral part of Edwin Lutyens's grand design (1912/13) for the Viceroy's House (now the Rashtrapati Bhavan) in New Delhi. The National Museum in Singapore, likewise designed (as the Raffles Library and Museum) under colonial rule in 1887, was a Palladian structure centred around a domed rotunda roofed with zinc tiles and stained glass panels. The redevelopment of the building in 2006 imitated its original design with the construction of another rotunda at the rear, made up of contemporary materials in the form of an outer drum of glass and an inner drum of wire mesh. In Japan, Arata Isozaki's Fujimi Country Club (1975) playfully twists a barrel vault to resemble a question mark. The interrogation point, representing a golf ball, asks, 'why do the Japanese play golf?'[41] – while also prompting larger questions about the place of the classical tradition in non-Western cultures.

Pantheonic cathedrals and churches, Renaissance palaces and English country houses, American shopping malls and a Japanese country club: their common feature is a shape; a sense of its ancestry has long given way to other connotations. Yet this most distinctive feature of Western, and now world, architecture still retains,

41 Jencks (2002) 101.

in its diverse uses and its associations of opulence and awe, more than a trace of the meanings it had in ancient Rome, while its complicated practical history and its formal perfection combine to produce a paradoxical evocation of the ideal and the all-too-human at one and the same time. Like the classical tradition as a whole, perhaps, it seems to lay claim to a peculiarly worldly innocence: 'Ah, these children's voices, singing under the dome!'[42]

[42] Verlaine, 'Parsifal' (1886): 'Et, ô ces voix d'enfants chantant dans la coupole!' Eliot quotes the line in *The Waste Land*, 202, in the all-too-worldly context of Mrs Porter.

§21

The Hero

One among many: larger than life: raised above his peers by exceptional deeds: driven to challenge the norms of his world: free to choose and free to act: 'he took hold and let go, he chose and was able'.[1] Versions and variants of 'the hero' exist in a wide variety of contexts: Machiavelli's Prince and Nietzsche's 'superman' (*Übermensch*); Shakespeare's 'great ones' and Carlyle's 'great men';[2] the named achievers celebrated in Tasso's 'heroic sonnets' and the unnamed 'great man' to whose memory Beethoven's Third Symphony, the 'Eroica' (1803–4), is dedicated;[3] David's depiction (1800/01) of Napoleon at the Saint Bernard Pass, complete with windswept drapery, rearing charger, and evocative inscriptions that served to bracket the new Consul with Charlemagne and Hannibal.[4]

[1] Rilke, *Duino Elegy*, 6 (1922): 'er ergriff und liess aus, wählte und konnte'.

[2] *Hamlet*, 3. 1, 'madness in great ones'; Carlyle, *On Heroes, Hero-Worship and the Heroic in History* (1841), I: 'The history of the world is but the biography of great men'. In that last formula, the hero, as substantive archetype, intersects with biography as – another – archetypal form. Biographies have been a significant reality in Western literature from Plutarch's *Lives* to medieval saints' lives to majestic compilations like the (*Oxford*) *Dictionary of National Biography* in contemporary Britain: cf. Woolf (2010).

[3] 'Sinfonia eroica composta per festeggiare il sovvenire di un grand' uomo', originally alluding to Napoleon, eventually to Prince Lobkowitz.

[4] There were in fact five versions of 'the' depiction; the first (now in the Château de Malmaison) was completed around 1801. 'Bonaparte est mon héros', said David in 1797/8: Delécluze, *Louis David, son école et son temps* (1855), ch. 7.

The Classical Tradition: Art, Literature, Thought, First Edition. Michael Silk, Ingo Gildenhard, and Rosemary Barrow.

Published 2017 by John Wiley & Sons Ltd.

Effectively a Renaissance conception, or rather reconstitution, the hero is product of Renaissance individualism (§8),[5] allied to humanist admiration for the man of action,[6] but constructed initially from Roman materials – Livy's early Roman achievers,[7] Cicero and Quintilian's consummate orator, the passionate self-expressive figures of Senecan tragedy[8] – with some help (on the Greek side) from Plutarch's *Lives*, from Aristotle's thoughts on the victims of tragic misfortune,[9] and from a long-standing association of the term 'heroic' with epic poetry in the tradition of Homer.[10] The Homeric paradigm, more generally, is significant. Not all Homer's heroes are equally 'heroic', but they are all men of action; and in ancestry, as in achievement, beings like his Achilles bridge the gulf between human and divine. Like the actors within Greek myth in general, Homer's are mostly descendants of a divinity and bestride the human stage accordingly: Achilles himself is a sea-nymph's son and a river-god's adversary.[11] For later ages, such beings continue to suggest the possibility of an exceptional existence ('those the ancients called "heroes" humanity venerates as gods', said Ficino),[12] or, at least, of an ideal freedom. 'I alone am king of me,' says Dryden's Almanzor: 'I am as free as nature first made man.'[13]

The heroes of Greek myth present a long history of receptions (§24) – largely in Roman guise. The demigod-hero Hercules (Greek Heracles) has a strikingly varied

[5] Medieval 'greatness' tends to champion, not challenge, society's norms. On late-medieval French playing-cards, four great figures feature as kings (Waith 1975: 233) – the Christian Charlemagne (hearts), the Old Testament David (spades), and the appropriated pagans, Caesar (diamonds) and Alexander (clubs). These four represent pre-eminent kingly achievement, rather than heroic self-assertion. Cf. the examples in Curtius (1953) 167–82.

[6] As in Petrarch's *De viris illustribus* (published posthumously in 1379) and Cristoforo Landino's *De vita activa et contemplativa* (*c.* 1473).

[7] Renaissance humanists 'sought for heroes, so that in their writings we find Livy valued above Tacitus': Bolgar (1954) 281.

[8] Cf. Eliot, 'Shakespeare and the Stoicism of Seneca' (1927): 'there is, in some of the great tragedies of Shakespeare, a new attitude. It is not the attitude of Seneca, but is derived from Seneca . . . it is modern, and it culminates . . . in Nietzsche . . . It is the attitude of self-dramatization assumed by some of Shakespeare's heroes at moments of tragic intensity'.

[9] *Poetics*, 13.

[10] So already in antiquity: [Demosthenes], 60. 9. By the early Middle Ages, epic poetry is regularly called heroic poetry. See e.g. Isidore, *Etymologiae*, 1. 39. 9, on *carmen heroicum* ('heroic poetry/song'): 'in it the affairs and deeds of brave men are narrated; for men are called heroes when raised aloft, so to speak, and worthy of heaven on account of their wisdom and bravery.' So too in the Renaissance: e.g. Tasso, *Discorsi del poema eroico*, 1594. Meanwhile, 'epic' metres often likewise attract the label (again from antiquity onwards: Plato, *Laws*, 958e; Aristotle, *Poetics*, 24) – though with its eventual application to pairs of rhyming iambics in English poetry (the 'heroic couplet'), any connection with 'heroic' epic (let alone with 'heroism') has gone.

[11] *Iliad* 21. Beyond mythic literature, Greek hero-cult institutionalizes worship of the superhuman dead, Achilles among them (worshipped thus from Elis in the Peloponnese to Olbia on the Black Sea).

[12] *Theologia Platonica*, 14. 8 (1469–74).

[13] *The Conquest of Granada*, I (1670), 1. 206–7. The emphasis on personal freedom of action recalls Milton's Satan: 'Here at least | We shall be free' (*Paradise Lost*, 1. 258–9).

legacy.[14] The tale of Hercules at the crossroads, between the paths of virtue and vice,[15] was readily adapted to Christian allegory, and became a popular subject for the early modern age. In an unlikely pairing, the superhuman pagan came to be associated with the Biblical figure of David: Dante matches Hercules' victory over Antaeus with the young Nazarite's over Goliath,[16] while a statue of Hercules was planned as a pendant for Michelangelo's *David* (1501–4) in the Florentine Piazza della Signoria. Pictorial treatments of Hercules' choice by Dürer (*c.* 1498) and Annibale Carracci (1596) ally moral decision with heroic action: in both depictions, heroism is – literally – embodied in a muscular nude torso,[17] a physical necessity for Hercules' labours and famously displayed in the ancient Farnese Hercules, which flaunts the hero's bulging biceps even though his body is at rest.

In literary representations, Hercules' superhuman strength is a marker of hypermasculinity: 'this Herculean Roman', says Cleopatra of her 'man of men' Antony.[18] In the world of politics, Hercules' physical and moral qualities are invoked in the self-fashioning of royal and aristocratic families from the Este[19] to the Habsburgs.[20] Protean in his adaptability, this hero is an emblem in the sixteenth-century French court[21] and a symbol of revolution for a later age.[22] A recognisable figure even today, he enters the popular media – where heroes are now 'most accessible, frequently encountered, and publicly approved'[23] – in Italian *peplum* B-movies,[24] and more recently has starred in a Disney film and his own television series.[25]

Such a tally of receptions illustrates the way that retelling, and reapplying, myths keeps ancient heroes alive in the post-classical world. But whether its instantiations are linked directly with the classical world or not (and connections and disconnections are frequently blurred), the heroic archetype can claim a deeper significance for Western culture as – above all – mode and model of masculine identity.

Like other such heroes, Hercules is identified first and foremost by his physicality. 'Heroes think with their hands', said Fielding.[26] The *Iliad*, though not given to lengthy character descriptions, stresses its great warriors' size, with Agamemnon and

14 Literary incarnations: Galinsky (1972), (2010); Waith (1962).

15 *Locus classicus*: Xenophon, *Memorabilia*, 2. 1. 21–34.

16 *De monarchia*, 2. 10.

17 Panofsky (1930).

18 Shakespeare, *Antony and Cleopatra*, 1. 3. 84; 1. 5. 71.

19 The aptly-named Ercole d'Este claimed descent from the hero. Further: Bull (2005) 91.

20 Emperor Charles V equated his imperial exploits with Hercules' labours across the globe – 'not just in geographical terms but in virtue, valour, and fame': ibid. 92.

21 Henri IV, in particular, used Herculean imagery as heroic self-advertising: Dickerman and Walker (1996).

22 French republicans reclaimed Herculean imagery for seals, festivals, and statuary – following American models, such as a medal struck for Benjamin Franklin: Hunt (1983).

23 Donald (2001) 170.

24 First in *Le Fatiche di Ercole* (1958), starring American body-builder Steve Reeves.

25 The only Greek hero to have 'a significant impact on modern popular culture': Nisbet (2008) 46.

26 *Joseph Andrews* (1742), 3. 10.

Ajax distinguished by height, Odysseus by broad shoulders and chest.[27] In the wake of Polyclitus' Doryphoros (the ultimate warrior-athlete), visual representations of heroic masculinity feature impressive physiques that signal authority and strength of purpose. Over life-size, the Doryphoros (fifth-century BC) and its successors, from the first-century AD Prima Porta Augustus to the third-century bronze portrait statue of Trebonianus Gallus, equate heroism with superhuman dimensions. In the same spirit, Richard Westmacott's *Achilles* in London's Hyde Park (1814–22), a monument to the battlefield triumphs of the Duke of Wellington, stands eighteen feet tall and Canova's nude portrait statue of *Napoleon as Mars the Peacemaker* in Apsley House (1806) at just over eleven, while even Michelangelo's *David* is only one foot shorter than Westmacott's *Achilles*. 'Of stature tall and straightly fashioned, | Like his desire': so Marlowe conceived of his heroic Tamburlaine.[28]

Michelangelo's iconic image represents a giant-killing boy as a muscular man. The question arises how far brawn alone designates heroic status. Is an ideal man more than the sum of his body parts? A memorable line from the Hollywood western *High Noon* (1952) insists that 'it takes more than big broad shoulders to make a man.' The film follows the struggles of a town's long-time sheriff, played by an ageing Gary Cooper, who (like Hercules of old) is faced with a choice, but (very unlike Hercules) a choice on his wedding-day between new-found domesticity and a violent past – the latter, thanks to the return of a vengeful gang-leader he had once sent to prison. The film's theme song foregrounds the inevitable show-down between the sheriff and his old adversary:

> The noonday train will bring Frank Miller.
> If I'm a man I must be brave
> And I must face that deadly killer
> Or lie a coward, a craven coward,
> Or lie a coward in my grave.[29]

One recalls Hector's parting declaration to his wife Andromache, when she (like the sheriff's wife) begs her husband not to fight:

> But I should feel
> Dread shame amongst Troy's men, and women too,
> If like a coward I sneak out of battle.[30]

As against *High Noon*'s conflict of love and duty, it is usually physical conflict that defines the western and, overall, heroic identity itself. If big broad shoulders alone do not make a man, willingness to prove oneself in combat does. The western's

27 Among the Achaean ranks, these three figures catch Priam's eye: *Iliad*, 3. 166–229.

28 *Tamburlaine*, Part I (1590), 2. 1. 7–8.

29 Lyrics by Ned Washington.

30 *Iliad*, 6. 441–3.

gunfight conforms to widespread concepts of violence and honour (with an ultimate point of reference in Homer, once again), within which a mark of manhood is the individual's participation in acts of violence against a recognised enemy. In Turner's *Ulysses Deriding Polyphemus* (1829), the hero can only declare his identity to the rising sun once he has faced down the foe; more directly, Shakespeare's Lady Macbeth challenges her husband's qualms about killing Duncan by asking him, 'Are you a man?'[31] In antiquity, status as well as gender informs the construction of martial masculinity, on the premise that a named hero who fights on the battlefield must be of noble birth. Greek ideals of an elite warrior caste are echoed within medieval chivalry and Renaissance rituals of aristocratic duelling. By the nineteenth century, the duel has become a bourgeois activity,[32] to be replaced in the twentieth by working-class street gangs;[33] but though no longer associated with a ruling class, such aggression remains firmly linked to male behaviour, positioning individuals within a hierarchical order that assumes and emphasises gender difference.[34] More generally, violence in today's world is still largely seen as a masculine trait[35] – albeit now in negative terms, unless sanctioned by the state.

Violence is legitimized first and foremost through warfare. Until recently seen as an exclusively male activity (Amazonian warfare is the proverbial exception), war offers unrivalled opportunities for the display of individual courage, strength, and action.[36] The privileging of military prowess, indeed, is not confined to eras of expansive individuality or to contexts of obvious self-assertion: witness the epic narratives of medieval Europe, from *Beowulf* and the *Chanson de Roland* to the codification of Arthurian legend in Malory's *Morte Darthur*; or, very differently, Shakespeare's *Hamlet*, a play notoriously coloured by inaction, which nevertheless concludes with the prince's endorsement of Fortinbras, who arrives to claim the throne of Denmark by force – by which endorsement the association between martial prowess and elite status is implicitly endorsed too.[37]

The same association has long been encapsulated iconographically in equestrian portraits of military commanders and warrior-kings. Just as the cavalry on the

31 *Macbeth*, 3. 4. 57.

32 Spierenburg (1998).

33 Interestingly, Walter Hill's cult film, *The Warriors* (1979), recalls Homer's *Odyssey* and Xenophon's *Anabasis* in representing a New York gang's journey across the city.

34 Hatty (2000).

35 Though recent theorists of masculinity tend to see socialization as a more important determinant than biology: Edwards (2006) 44–63.

36 Followed – at some distance – by sport (esp. contact sport), which in modern media-speak abounds in 'heroes'. There is a partial analogue to the heroic warrior in the champion boxer, most obviously in the self-mythologized stance of the great heavyweight Muhammad Ali: 'Better far that I should go | Standing here against the foe. | . . . Better call on death to come | Than to die another dumb | Looted victim in the slum' ('Freedom', composed by Ali in the 1960s/1970s, and quoted by Bockris 1998: 31). 'Foe': war language is appropriated by sport, as sporting metaphor is by war films (Donald 2001). The analogy goes back to the *Iliad* (e.g. 22. 157–66).

37 Cf. Wells (2000) 65–9.

ancient Parthenon frieze are identified as elite members of the Athenian citizen body, post-classical martial imagery distinguishes between ordinary foot soldiers and those who can claim the privilege (and expense) of maintaining a horse. From the fifteenth century onwards, the equestrian portrait is a common mode of heroizing commemoration for royal and aristocratic subjects.[38] Deriving physically from the Roman bronze of Marcus Aurelius[39] and spiritually from later ideals of chivalric knighthood, this tradition of portraiture equates social with physical elevation and reads mastery over a horse as both an aristocratic right and a masculine skill required for battle.[40] The horse is often shown rearing forward to allow it to be controlled by its rider: examples include Pietro Tacca's monument to Philip IV (1634–40) and David's equestrian Napoleon. In Van Dyck's portrait of Charles I in London's National Gallery (1637–8), the sheer size of the horse emphasises the king's impressive horsemanship; dressed in armour and holding a commander's baton, Charles is military leader as well as monarch. By the Victorian age, horse and rider are so evocative of heroic stature that even military defeat is celebrated in this idiom: witness Henry Payne's *Lord Cardigan, Charge of the Light Brigade* (1884), where the Crimean War commander boldly gallops headlong 'into the valley of Death'.[41]

The use of cavalry, and, along with it, the association of war and individual combat, were superannuated by World War I. Machine guns and trench warfare transformed battle from a personal quest for glory to anonymous mass conflict. A new generation of artists including Weimar, Vorticist, and Futurist painters – Otto Dix, George Grosz, Wyndham Lewis, Paul Nash, Gino Severini, C. R. W. Nevinson, Fernand Léger – depicted the inglorious, impersonal nature of modern war. Here, even a rare evocation of classical precedent may be deceptive. John Singer Sargent's *Gassed* (1919) presents a line of figures on a platform in the shape of a Greek frieze – yet this is no uplifting procession of named worthies, but a stumbling line of blinded anonymous soldiers. Unlike painting, though, World War I poetry, famous indeed for its projections of futility and pity, still sometimes clings to reassuring heroic paradigms in the classical mould.[42] Patrick Shaw-Stewart's 'I Saw A Man This Morning', written at Gallipoli (1915), recalls a decisive moment in the

[38] History of the equestrian portrait: Janson (1967). The first free-standing equestrian bronze since antiquity, Donatello's *Gattamelata* (1448–50), depicts a captain of the Venetian republic, but such imagery became so associated with aristocratic grandiosity that, when Thomas Jefferson commissioned an equestrian portrait of George Washington from Jean-Antoine Houdon, he insisted it be no more than life-size, befitting republican virtue: Schwartz (1988) 668–9.

[39] Marcus Aurelius' gesture of extended right arm with downward palm is also imitated in (e.g.) Pope Paul III's tomb effigy (1552) and Titian's portrait of Doge Francesco Venier (1554–5): Mezzatesta (1984) 620–1.

[40] Cf. Schwartz (1988).

[41] Association with military catastrophe is no barrier to heroization. Cases in point include Roland and Siegfried, from medieval epic to Wagner's *Ring* cycle (§31) and subsequent Nazi fantasia: cf. Murdoch (1996) 121.

[42] British instances: Vandiver (2008), (2010).

Iliad when Achilles' return to battle is signalled by his war-cry: 'Stand in the trench, Achilles, | Flame-capped, and shout for me.' Just as the Athenian army once drew courage from the sanctuary of Heracles before the battle of Marathon, Shaw-Stewart's poem invokes an ancient hero as a model of bravery in the face of death. On the German side, correspondingly, 'Leonidas' (1916), by Joachim von der Goltz, is a call to re-enact noble self-sacrifice in the image of the Spartan three hundred.

More broadly, this sombre mass conflict fostered a notion of heroes *en masse*. An almost Homeric 'objectivity' allowed a select few – Ernst Jünger, for one – to find, even in the 'gruesome' slaughter on the Somme, a 'heroic, grand impression.'[43] Then again, populist rhetoric construed the numberless traumatized survivors of these encounters in comparable terms. 'What is our task?', was the question posed by British Prime Minister, David Lloyd George, at the end of the Great War – and his answer: 'To make Britain a fit country for heroes to live in.'[44] Such appropriations – in Britain, too – go back at least to the eighteenth century:

Some talk of Alexander, and some of Hercules,
Of Hector and Lysander, and such great names as these;
But of all the world's great heroes, there's none that can compare
. . . to the British Grenadiers.[45]

This marching song invokes a quartet of 'great names' from ancient Greece,[46] and thus acknowledges traditional heroics in the very act of acclaiming something quite different. The assembled Grenadiers, like Lloyd George's dispossessed millions, are the spiritual descendants, not of Homer's great names (Hector and the rest), but of the anonymous fighting men who, every so often, are given a voice in the *Iliad*: 'evil war and the dread din of battle: here we go again.'[47]

Mass heroics aside, it is often death in battle, rather than survival, that completes the individual hero's profile: 'Lasting doesn't concern him.'[48] In the *Iliad* the loss of young life is mourned, but still acclaimed as a potential source of glory (Hector's farewell to his wife is representative, here too), and the conjunction of attitudes lives on. In Ford Madox Ford's *The Good Soldier* (1915), the narrator John Dowell says of Edward Ashburnham (the good soldier of the novel's title), 'it would have done him a great deal of good to get killed.'[49] The comment reflects, not the spite of a

43 'Grausig', 'heroischer, grossartiger Eindruck': in Jünger's war-diary entry for 3 July 1916 (*Kriegstagebuch. 1914–1918*, first published in 2010).

44 Speech at Wolverhampton, November 1918 (commonly misquoted as 'a land fit for heroes').

45 'The British Grenadiers' (anon.): words first printed *c.* 1750: Kidson (1901) 315. More recently: 'Its heroes are not demigods but ordinary people' – the voice-over near the beginning of *The Guns of Navarone* (1961), a (largely) British World War II film, set in Greece.

46 Though Lysander (Spartan general, memorialized by Xenophon) is there less by right than for the rhyme.

47 *Iliad*, 4. 81–3.

48 'Dauern | ficht ihn nicht an': Rilke, *Duino Elegy*, 6.

49 *The Good Soldier: A Tale of Passion*, Part III, ch. 5.

cuckolded husband, but the pointlessness of Edward's post-military life (it ends in suicide), along with a sense (perhaps unpalatable, when spelled out) that anything approaching a heroic death acquires a kind of aestheticized innocence: 'the hero,' says Rilke (who does spell it out), 'is oddly close to those that died young.'[50] Death in battle at the peak of youthful masculinity has long been a familiar motif in art and literature, summed up by Northumberland's reaction, in *Macbeth*, to the news that his young son has died 'like a man':

> Had I as many sons as I have hairs,
> I would not wish them to a fairer death.[51]

Such 'fair deaths' are immortalized visually by Poussin's *Death of Germanicus* (1627–8) and by an impressive tradition of History Painting thereafter. David, in particular, favours death scenes of heroic males, presenting an array of types from the warrior in *Andromache Mourning Hector* (1783) and the philosopher in *The Death of Socrates* (1787)[52] to, more surprisingly, the radical journalist in *The Death of Marat* (1793) [*Figure 7*]. Shown murdered in his bath, wearing a vinegar-soaked turban used to relieve skin-complaints, the assassinated writer in David's stark depiction might seem to evoke a later age of documentary realism. But as Baudelaire noted, in this painting the over-weight and middle-aged Marat is transfigured: death has 'kissed him with loving lips', and in death he can 'challenge Apollo'.[53] If the fair flesh of Homer's dead Hector was once protected, and thus honoured, by the gods, it is the act of death itself that elevates David's Marat.

Revolutionary France sought heroic paradigms from early Roman history alongside Greek myth. Robespierre's rhetoric aligns himself with the Gracchi (all the way up to a premonition of his untimely death),[54] while David depicts the brothers who laid down their lives for the good of Rome (*The Oath of the Horatii*, 1784), and the father who ordered the execution of his anti-republican sons (*Brutus*, 1789), as instances of exemplary sacrifice. In Britain, with or without Roman models, Victorian discourses of empire, from political speeches to boys' adventure stories, glorify manliness in the service of country and honour in the face of death.[55] Henry Havelock's role in the suppression of the Indian Mutiny (1857–8) and George Gordon's campaigns against Sudanese rebels in the 1880s made them national heroes,[56] and the conformation is nicely captured in G. W. Joy's *General Gordon's Last Stand*

[50] 'Wunderlich nah ist der Held doch den jugendlich Toten': *Duino Elegy*, 6.

[51] 5. 11. 14–15.

[52] Effectively equating moral with martial courage: Mainz (2007) 252.

[53] 'Le musée classique du Bazar Bonne-Nouvelle' (1846): cf. Vaughan and Weston (2000) 1.

[54] Cf. Vance (1997) 24–5.

[55] Victorian school magazines listed the military achievements of old boys, with death the ultimate honour for school, queen, and country: Tosh (2005) 200. 'In the face of death': contrast Freud's claim that 'the secret of heroism' is the survival of the 'primeval' conviction that 'nothing can happen to me': 'Thoughts for Our Time on War and Death' ('Zeitgemässes über Krieg und Tod', 2: 1915).

[56] Havelock: Dawson (1994) 79–154.

Figure 7 Jacques-Louis David, *The Death of Marat*. Source: Brussels, Musees Royaux des Beaux-Arts. Oil on canvas, 65 × 50 1/2 inches (165 × 128.3 cm). © 2013. Photo: Scala, Florence.

(*c*. 1893), where Gordon, beset by Mahdists, displays all the indefatigability of an English gentleman (or a noble Roman) in his prime.

Many images of the heroic conform to a pattern whereby life in an intensely physical environment is dominated not only by fighting but by sex. 'Love's an heroic passion', says Dryden's Isabella,[57] while 'the hero', in Rilke's vision, 'storms through the stations of love'.[58] The hero's human interactions are largely homosocial, and (with few exceptions: contrast Homer's Odysseus with Tennyson's Ulysses)[59] he negates the domestic in favour of an existence unfettered by personal (as by spatial) boundaries.[60] Yet he is still an object of female desire – and here the paradigm, certainly, is the Homeric Odysseus, admired not only by his faithful Penelope, but

[57] *The Conquest of Granada*, II (1671), 1. 1. 145.

[58] 'Denn hinstürmte der Held durch Aufenthalte der Liebe': *Duino Elegy*, 6.

[59] Tennyson's Ulysses: §35.

[60] Strikingly true of cinematic westerns, as of ancient epics: Day (2008), Myrsiades (2007).

by the innocent Nausicaa and the passionate Calypso. The pattern is evoked, across the centuries, in works as different as the anonymous *Roman d'Enéas* (*c.* 1155) and Bertolt Brecht's expressionist play *Baal* (1918).

Perhaps it is the aura of power or simply the very danger and instability of the heroic existence that makes it sexually attractive. As Estelle tells her lover's wife, Serafina, in Tennessee Williams's *The Rose Tattoo* (1950): 'A man that's wild is hard for a woman to hold, huh? But if he was tame – would the woman want to hold him?'[61] The theme is far from new. It is the premise of the disconcertingly modern-sounding question put to Marlowe's Zenocrate, when she falls for Tamburlaine: 'How can you fancy one that looks so fierce?'[62] But, without doubt, the bad-boy hero is an especially familiar figure in recent drama and fiction. In another Williams play, *A Streetcar Named Desire* (1947), Stanley Kowalski is aggressive, angry, and brutish, but his appeal – embodied in the young Marlon Brando's macho posturing, first on Broadway, then in Hollywood – is unmistakable.[63] As Shakespeare's Mariana says of her faithless lover Angelo, who has committed both sexual exploitation and murder:

> They say best men are moulded out of faults,
> And, for the most, become much more the better
> For being a little bad.[64]

If a lover's misbehaviour can be excused, in effect, by appeal to heroic convention, it is clear that heroism more generally can be constructed from decidedly negative material. In ancient Greece, madmen, murderers, and rapists – Ajax, Heracles, Theseus – were favoured with hero cults; and as Jonathan Richardson noted in England's Augustan age, 'savage cruelties' are prominent among the deeds of such various worthies as 'Achilles, Ulysses, Aeneas, Orlando, Godfrey etc.'[65] A distinctive case is Milton's magnificent, but cautionary, portrayal of Satan (influenced by Homer's Achilles) in *Paradise Lost* (1667). For the Romantic age, most notoriously for William Blake, Milton's Satan could be read as a positive figure (§35), whatever the necessary qualifications; for Hazlitt, indeed (effectively without the qualifications), 'Satan is' – simply – 'the most heroic subject that ever was chosen for a poem.'[66] Less extreme is the long line of dark, melancholic male figures – perhaps with a troubled past, perhaps pursuing some lonely quest – inaugurated by Byron's *Childe Harold's Pilgrimage* (1812) and *The Corsair* (1814), and thereafter a striking

[61] 1. 1.

[62] *Tamburlaine*, Part I, 3. 2. 40 (Agydas speaking). Zenocrate's reply stresses Tamburlaine's other qualities, however.

[63] Brando as Stanley: Cohan (1997) 241–52.

[64] *Measure for Measure*, 5. 1. 436–8.

[65] *Explanatory Notes and Remarks on Milton's Paradise Lost* (1734): 'Orlando', in Ariosto's *Orlando Furioso* (1516–32); 'Godfrey' ('Goffredo'), in Tasso's *Gerusalemme Liberata* (1581).

[66] *On Shakespeare and Milton*, Lecture III (1818). Cf. n. 13 above.

presence in Anglo-American fiction, from the Brontë sisters' Heathcliff and Rochester to Hemingway's Jake Barnes.[67]

The versions of the heroic profile delineated here comprise a set of closely related types. There are other distinctive brands, including types constructed in opposition or reaction to these. In the early modern period, we meet strenuous attempts to accommodate secular heroics to Christian ethics. The age in which the Englishman Roger Ascham can dismiss Malory's *Morte Darthur* as a tale of 'open man-slaughter and bold bawdry',[68] and the Spaniard Baltasar Gracián can find heroic distinction 'not in fighting, but in governing',[69] is an age that also takes pleasure in moralizing compositions like Gian Giorgio Trissino's *Sofonisba* (1515) and Madeleine de Scudéry's voluminous *Artamène, or Cyrus the Great* (1649–53): works not centred on imperfect 'men of honour', but on men who keep 'the strict rules of moral virtue'. The contrast belongs to Dryden, and his essay 'Of Heroic Plays' (prefixed to *his* 'heroic play', *The Conquest of Granada*, 1672), where Homer's Achilles exemplifies the all-too-human hero – who is more to Dryden's own taste.[70]

Then there are the specifically anti-heroic figures who dominate many works of fiction and drama, from Arthur Miller's Willy Loman all the way back to Cervantes' Don Quixote and Marlowe's Faustus.[71] Of piquant relevance here is the case of Tolstoy's *War and Peace* (1862–9). That novel, whose subject, as well as scale, recalls the Iliadic tradition, contains a set of positive, but not fully heroized, figures (including even Prince Andrey), and then a specifically de-heroized Napoleon – with 'the charger-mounted hero of David's painting . . . turned into a fat gelding, wriggling with pleasure as his grooms give him the body-brush.'[72]

A quite different issue that arises from some such cases is the relation – or, often, verbal confusion – between a legendary (or comparable) achiever and the focal character of a specific narrative or (originally) drama. The word 'hero' has an untidy history. In ancient Greek usage, *hêrôs* (singular) and *hêrôes* (plural) are largely restricted to the semi-divine figures of myth and cult, including the many 'heroes' of Homer.[73] In Rome, by Cicero's time, the naturalized term 'heros' can be used of illustrious men of the past (like Plato) or indeed the present (like Brutus).[74] By the

[67] Emily Bronte, *Wuthering Heights*, and Charlotte Bronte, *Jane Eyre* (both 1847); Hemingway, *The Sun Also Rises* (1926). Hemingway's male figures: Fantina (2005). The Byronic type (Thorslev 1962) has points of contact with the Timonic, as in Molière's *Misanthrope* (§18).

[68] With the latter glossed as 'foulest adulteries': *The Schoolmaster*, I (1570).

[69] Dedication to his treatise, 'The Hero' (*El héroe*, 1637).

[70] Though, late in life, Dryden dismisses such heroes as 'athletic brutes': Dedication to *Fables* (1700).

[71] Miller, *Death of a Salesman* (1949); *Don Quixote* (1605–12); *Doctor Faustus* (first produced *c.* 1589) – with whose anti-hero contrast the redeemed everyman of Goethe's *Faust* (1790–1831).

[72] Kelly (2000) 592.

[73] Though soon applied to historic individuals institutionalized as gods, like the Spartan Brasidas (Thucydides, 5. 11).

[74] Cicero, *De Republica*, 3. 8, and *Ad Atticum*, 14. 6. 1.

end of the sixteenth century, learned usage across the Western languages has established derivatives of the Greco-Roman term in the secularized Ciceronian sense, though generally with a quasi-Homeric application to warrior heroes: 'valour in arms has earned the name of "hero"' (Ronsard).[75] Meanwhile, Italian literary theorizing formulates the concept – more or less on Aristotelian authority – of the single focal character of a tragic drama;[76] and a century later (seemingly in France and England, in the first instance), that focal figure comes to be called 'the hero': Bajazet, says Racine in 1672, 'is the hero of my tragedy',[77] and Dryden, likewise, refers to 'the chief character or hero in a tragedy', in 1679.[78]

By the early eighteenth century, confusion or conflation of the great achiever and the focal figure is common. Addison, discussing *Paradise Lost*, provides an early example: it is wrong to think 'that the devil was in reality Milton's hero'; if anyone, 'it is certainly the Messiah'.[79] Such confusion is largely gratuitous. Great achievers and focal figures certainly overlap, especially in the form of what E. M. Waith identified as the 'Herculean hero' – staple of many English dramas from Marlowe's *Tamburlaine* to Dryden's *All For Love*, and defined by Waith himself as 'a warrior of great stature who is guilty of striking departures from the morality of the society in which he lives'.[80] Yet often, and not least at the Greek fountainhead, the difference is obvious. Take the title figure of Sophocles' *Oedipus Rex*. This Oedipus is a huge presence, but not physically. He asserts himself and crosses boundaries – or proves to have done so in the past – but despite his scuffles with Tiresias and Creon, neither cavalier behaviour nor martial confrontation is central to his persona. He has a woman (horrifically), but no heroic amours. He 'makes a mistake', in the sense of Aristotle's *hamartia*, but hardly possesses any relevant 'flaw' (a rereading of Aristotle's term that commends itself to the Renaissance).[81]

And our heroic profile: where is it today? In recent years, feminism and gender studies have helped to promote an understanding of maleness that identifies multiple

[75] 'Priere a la Fortune' (1573), 156–7: 'la vertu par armes s'est acquise | Le nom d'heros'. Similarly: Tasso, 'invitti eroi' ('indomitable heroes'), *Gerusalemme liberata* (1581), 1. 52; Shakespeare, 'Noble heroes, my sword and yours are kin', *All's Well* (c. 1602), 2. 1. 38. The eymologically unrelated German 'Held' is used likewise.

[76] 'More or less': Aristotle, *Poetics*, 13.

[77] *Bajazet*, second preface: 'c'est lui qui est le héros de ma tragédie.' So already Racine's letter to Louis XIV attached to *Alexandre le Grand* (1665) ('mon héros').

[78] 'The Grounds of Criticism in Tragedy', prefixed to *Troilus and Cressida* (1679) (as already in 'Defence of the Epilogue', 1673); cf. Silk (2004a) 255 n. 30. In earlier Italian theory, this focal figure is referred to with locutions like 'una persona' ('one person'); e.g. Castelvetro, *Poetica* (1576).

[79] *The Spectator*, 9 February 1712, criticising Dryden's preface to the *Aeneis* (1697). One quaint case of confusion in a Yeats anecdote quoted by Ezra Pound in *ABC of Reading* (1934): 'A plain sailor man took a notion to study Latin, and his teacher tried him with Virgil; after many lessons he asked him something about the hero. Said the sailor: "What hero?" Said the teacher: "What hero, why, Aeneas, the hero." Said the sailor: "Ach, a hero, him a hero? Bigob, I t'ought he waz a priest."'

[80] Waith (1962) 11.

[81] Bremer (1969) 65–98. *Hamartia*: *Poetics*, 13.

and fluid masculinities rather than one heroic ideal; and the traditional heroic image rarely features in the more sophisticated art and literature of the contemporary West. Indeed, negotiations between heroic masculinity and the sensitivity and gender-awareness ascribed to the 'new man' have contributed to a perceived 'crisis' in masculinity,[82] where the hero figure 'largely defines the masculinity to which many Western men aspire', but which 'just as thoroughly defines their inevitable failure'.[83]

That said, the heroic paradigm survives. In the popular-cultural modes of film, television, and computer games, it is ubiquitous. On a larger canvas, few individuals have been more fervently heroized in their own age than the revolutionary Che Guevara[84] – man of action, *par excellence*, and also celebrated womanizer, among much else. And on a more collective level, at moments of exceptional stress or risk, society still finds reassurance in behaviour that recalls the male-heroic ideal – and, though not quite on the basis of the mass heroism championed by Lloyd George, on suitably demotic terms. After 9/11, media focus on the masculine courage and self-sacrifice displayed by New York fire-fighters and police officers repeatedly equated these 'real American heroes' with their traditional counterparts.[85] It may be true that not 'all the things that belong to Troy' have contemporary relevance, but – seemingly against the odds – the heroic imperatives retain their force.

82 See e.g. Whitehead (2002) 47–59.

83 Boon (2005) 304.

84 And not just by impressionable students. To Graham Greene, 'he represented the idea of gallantry, chivalry and adventure'; to Jean-Paul Sartre, he was 'the most complete man of his age'; to Frantz Fanon, 'the world symbol of the possibilities of one man': Kunzle (1997) 19.

85 See Connor (2010).

§22
Word-Genres

In the course of his influential manual, *On Letter-Writing*, Erasmus declares:

> The [ancient] rhetoricians, generally speaking, acknowledge three classes of subject [for a speech]: persuasive, panegyric and judicial. Letter-forms, generally speaking, belong to these three types.[1]

The first proposition is uncontroversial, except that it tidies up a long and complicated history of ancient rhetorical theory and reduces a variety of labels, usages, and understandings to one particular version. What Erasmus calls 'persuasive' speaking is usually called 'deliberative' oratory, within the realm of practical politics;[2] his 'panegyric' refers to 'epideictic' or 'display' speeches (generally given over to praising or blaming), beyond the practical sphere; 'judicial' speeches (also known as 'forensic') belong to the lawcourts. The second proposition, which applies the three categories from speeches to letters, has no ancient precedent: this, seemingly, is Erasmus' own idea.[3]

Erasmus' way of making his case has a representative significance. He assumes that the categories of ancient oratory and theory are fundamental; in articulating

[1] 'rhetorum plerisque tria causarum genera placuerunt, suasorium, encomiasticon et iudiciale. ad haec tanquam ad fontes pleraeque literarum formae referuntur': *De conscribendis epistolis* (first full edition, 1522), section headed 'Tres omnium generum fontes'. 'Influential': cf. Mack (2002) 24–5, 81, 280.

[2] Erasmus' 'suasorium' points to 'suasoriae', fictitious deliberative speeches.

[3] In medieval theory, rhetorical principles are applied to letter-writing (*ars dictaminis*), from Alberic of Monte Cassino's *Breviarium de dictamine* (*c.* 1080) to Lawrence of Aquilegia's *Practica sive usus dictaminis* (*c.* 1300) (see Murphy 1974: 203–66), but without any correlation with oratorical types.

The Classical Tradition: Art, Literature, Thought, First Edition. Michael Silk, Ingo Gildenhard, and Rosemary Barrow.

Published 2017 by John Wiley & Sons Ltd.

them, he avoids any impression of disagreements or loose ends between different ancient theorists; notwithstanding this deference to ancient theory, he feels free to extend its application, even radically; and, all in all, he effaces his procedures, and his own originality, so comprehensively that his reader has no sense of an argument to ponder, but only of doctrine – supposedly ancient doctrine – to accept.

There is nothing unusual here. This mode of generic theorizing is to be found everywhere, not just in Erasmian or other humanist circles, but – more or less – over the whole classicizing epoch, from the Middle Ages to the eighteenth century, when (here as elsewhere) things begin to change. Compare Dante's appeal to Horace to help support the stylistic argument for the unexpected title of his *Commedia*. 'Comedy', Dante reflects, is a distinctive kind of 'poetic narrative', stylistically low, and therein distinct from tragedy, as it is distinct also from 'other kinds of poetic narrative, like pastoral, elegy, satire and votive song, as we can see from Horace in the *Art of Poetry*'.[4] In point of fact, the designation of these forms as 'narrative' ('narratio') is wholly alien to ancient theory, including Horace's *Ars Poetica* (where, in any case, there is as much emphasis on the tonal overlap between the dramatic genres as on the contrast,[5] and where 'pastoral', in particular, is never mentioned). Or compare the way that, from the mid-sixteenth century to the end of the seventeenth, the literary theorizings of Aristotle and Horace are treated as one continuous theory[6] (with Horace as Aristotle's 'chief interpreter'),[7] and, again, as one authoritative presentation of the norms or 'laws' of literary composition: norms and laws which even the most innovative experiments (Italian pastoral tragicomedy is a case in point) are expected to obey.[8]

Contrast, therefore, in the final phase of the truly classicizing age, Samuel Johnson's more pragmatic response to literary innovation, in his *Preface to Shakespeare* (1765). The manifest hybridity of Shakespearean drama – especially the use of 'comic' elements in tragedy – had been a stumbling-block for earlier critics. Milton, for instance, had castigated 'the poet's error of intermixing comic stuff with tragic sadness and gravity, or introducing trivial and vulgar persons'.[9] Confronting the problem head-on, Johnson meditates: Shakespeare's plays 'are not in the rigorous and critical sense either tragedies or comedies, but compositions of a distinct kind, exhibiting the real state of sublunary nature, which partakes of good and evil, joy and sorrow.' And then: 'that this is a practice contrary to the rules of criticism will be readily allowed.' But now the new pragmatism asserts itself: 'there is always an appeal open from criticism to nature.' But what is this 'nature'? Johnson continues: 'the end of writing is to instruct; the end of poetry is to instruct by pleasing. That

[4] *Epistle to Can Grande*, 10.

[5] See esp. 73–98.

[6] 'Mid-sixteenth': Herrick (1946).

[7] Rapin, *Réflexions sur la Poétique d'Aristote* (1674), 1. 7.

[8] See notably Battista Guarini's defence of his *Pastor fido* (1590) in his *Compendio della poesia tragicomica* (1601).

[9] Below, p. 284; Shakespeare is not named, but the reference is unmistakable.

the mingled drama may convey all the instruction of tragedy and comedy cannot be denied, because it includes both . . . and approaches nearer than either to the appearance of life'. Remarkably, what Johnson is doing is 'using one classical principle to trump another': the Horatian version of the rhetorical doctrine of the orator's functions, whereby poetry (even comic poetry) aspires to combine instruction and pleasure, is somehow aligned with 'the appearance of life', thus effectively with 'nature' and, as such, 'seen to transcend even generic propriety'.[10]

Johnson is one of the last considerable representatives of the pre-Romantic outlook – yet his willingness to override the supposed fixities of the inherited generic system is profoundly symptomatic of the brave new world now coming into view.[11] In earlier centuries, it is almost always assumed that, across the range of literature, prose or verse, the ancient categories are permanent realities, articulated in ancient theory, embodied in ancient practice, and fundamental both for the production and the criticism of new compositions, now or hereafter[12] – as fundamental, in fact, as the individual authorities, from Cicero and Horace to Aristotle and the Greek tragedians, whose general authority they share. For this set of assumptions to be maintained, large historical complications have to be elided: not only the kind of variable labelling and usage that Erasmus ignores, but also more fundamental variations between ancient theory and practice and, not least, between the basis of the genres in earlier Greece and in later Greece and Rome. In archaic and classical Greece, most genres are determined primarily by context (like the lawcourt as context for 'judicial' speeches); thereafter, mostly by form (like the fixed metre and other conventions of Greco-Roman epic) – with context and form, no doubt, the main alternative determinants of genre in any culture.[13] Ironically enough, such complications are hardly more of a concern to Johnson and the next generation than to his more classicizing predecessors. Until his age, at all events, the assumptions persist; thereafter, they are felt to be untenable.

'Across the range of literature, prose or verse': with or without special reference to Johnson's age, or any age before it, this phrase conceals a yet more fundamental problematic, much discussed in recent decades, and much bedevilled too. A few definitions of 'literature' (or similar) can serve to suggest the terms of the ongoing debate:

(*a*) 'If we recognise "fictionality" . . . as the distinguishing trait of literature, we think thus of literature in terms of Homer, Dante, Shakespeare, Balzac, Keats, rather than Cicero or Montaigne, Bossuet or Emerson.'[14]

[10] Silk (2012) 846: Horace, *Ars Poetica*, 343.

[11] Recent criticism (e.g. Clingham and Smallwood 2009) likes to see Johnson as *sui generis*: cf. §3 on period labels.

[12] In the Middle Ages, Biblical precedent is also invoked – sometimes very directly, e.g. for the requisite norms of the sermon.

[13] Context: cf. Silk (2013).

[14] Wellek and Warren (1963) 26.

(*b*) 'I will be using "literature" and "verbal art" interchangeably in this book.'[15]
(*c*) 'Literature is essentially different from ordinary language use.'[16]
(*d*) 'Autonomous verbal structure.'[17]
(*e*) 'We . . . [call] "literary" . . . any text that implicitly or explicitly signifies its own rhetorical mode.'[18]
(*f*) 'Utterances that are regarded for one reason or another as worthy in their own right of preservation and as aesthetically valuable.'[19]
(*g*) 'A text is literary because it is recognised as such at a certain moment, under certain conditions.'[20]
(*h*) 'Texts do not organize themselves into the "literary" and the "non-literary". They are so organized only by the operations of criticism upon them.'[21]

This sequence – which represents neither a chronological nor any other progression – begins with the suggestion that literature is identifiable through its fictionality (*a*) or its special language (*b*) (*c*), or else its self-containedness, either in terms of the formal coherence of the literary work (*d*) or of its supposedly elusive relation to external signification and its consequent tendency to 'self-referentiality' (*e*); the focus then switches to the conventional status of the identification, whether that identification is based on perceived value (*f*) or not necessarily (*g*) (*h*). The sequence extends, then, all the way from the identification of significant features to an insistence that 'literature' is a construct.

Let us agree that all these propositions have something to be said for them – but also against them. Proposition (*a*), for instance, makes it hard to identify didactic poetry as literature – poetry like Virgil's *Georgics* ('the best poem by the best poet')[22] – whereas (*b*) and (*c*) leave it unclear why most novels should be recognised as such. Proposition (*f*) seems to preclude the possibility of flawed or trivial literature, though, among others, all reviewers of new compositions find the notion indispensable. Proposition (*h*) loses something of its seeming force when one reflects that, for instance, shapes do not 'organize themselves' into geometrical figures (or otherwise) either; and in fact very few things 'organize themselves' into anything. And so on.

What is agreed on all sides is that the kinds of writing especially cultivated or admired (both actually and in retrospect) vary from age to age. We associate fifth-century Athens with tragedy, fourth-century Athens with oratory and philosophy.

[15] Fabb (1997) 14.
[16] Toolan (1990) 3 (citing, rather than endorsing, this position).
[17] Frye (1957) 74.
[18] De Man (1971) 136.
[19] Robins (1989) 417.
[20] Pierre Macherey in Kavanagh and Lewis (1982) 50.
[21] Bennett (1979) 7.
[22] Dryden's phrase, in the Dedication to his translation of the *Georgics* (1697). Likewise Montaigne: 'the most perfect achievement in poetry' (*Essais*, 2. 10).

The Romantic generation tended to privilege lyric poetry; ours, prose fiction. And it is widely accepted that the general sense of what counts as central to literature varies correspondingly: from poetry in earlier Greece, to poetry and 'rhetorical prose' for centuries thereafter, to poetry and non-technical prose – in effect, (*a*) + (*b*) (*c*) – in our own day. Some forms, more specifically, are indeed treated as literature in some eras, but not in others. Between the Middle Ages and the seventeenth century, on and off, sermons, speeches, and (as Erasmus indicates) letters are all discussed in what one can only call literary terms; today, even striking examples (Rilke's letters, Martin Luther King's speeches) are on the margins. And here, there is, again, a general recognition that, as so often, the eighteenth century is a time of change, in which literature and understandings of literature begin to take on their now familiar shape; and certainly the modern use of the word 'literature' (and Continental equivalents) dates from this time.[23]

Less widely acknowledged, but indisputable in fact: there is sufficient continuity in different ages between effective understandings of literature (as we now call it) to confound the blunt relativism of some of today's theorists. In the *Poetics*, Aristotle groups together all 'fictional' writings, whether in verse (dramatic or other) or prose (his term for 'fiction' is *mimesis*, 'representation', and his examples of prose representation include Plato's dialogues). He does exclude non-fictional didactic verse (like the *Georgics*; his example is the cosmological verse of Empedocles), and then also historiography (his example is Herodotus)[24] – but the evident fact that in the case of poetry/verse he is explicitly challenging an orthodoxy,[25] and in the case of poetry/history implicitly offering a novel definition, indicates that, for a less innovative sensibility of that age, *all* these forms do or might seem to belong together.

From the Italian fourteenth century, compare Boccaccio's implicit association of poetry ('poesis') with fiction ('fabulae': 'stories', like Boccaccio's own) – and then of Dante and Virgil (including the *Georgics*) with 'philosophical' and 'theological' works (including Biblical texts, among others).[26]

Or compare the critical responses in seventeenth-century France to the emergent novel. In the wake of experiments in fictional prose that reach an early peak with Madame de Lafayette's *La Princesse de Clèves* (1678), men of letters ponder the application of Aristotle's precepts for epic poetry to the new form ('epic in prose', according to the abbé d'Aubignac in 1657).[27] A century earlier, the Italian Giraldi had already pronounced the novel dramatic in structure but epic in external form, and his own creative output, reflecting these associations, included both a pioneering

[23] Wellek (1970); cf. Williams (1976) 183–8. Likewise 'art': §17 (Malraux), cf. p. 351 below.

[24] *Poetics*, 1 and 9.

[25] 'People [wrongly] attach the name "poetry" to metre' (*Poetics*, 1).

[26] *Genealogy of the Pagan Gods* (*Genealogia deorum gentilium*, begun in 1363?), 14. 7, 9–10, 12–13. 'Poesis': cf. Fowler (1982) 9.

[27] 'Epopées en prose': see d'Aubignac, *La pratique du théâtre*, 2. 7 (1715 edn). In the preface to *Joseph Andrews* (1742), Fielding uses the phrase 'a comic epic poem in prose'.

'classical' tragedy and a collection of *novelle*.[28] In the French seventeenth century, likewise, 'dramatists wrote novels, novelists wrote dramas, and critics wrote both' (d'Aubignac among them).[29]

Or again, at the dawn of the Romantic age, compare Friedrich Schlegel's laconic citation of the 'dominant' forms of literature in ancient Greece, Rome, and the modern world: tragedy, satire, and 'Roman' – with that last term covering both the *romance* of medieval Europe and the *novel* of more recent times.[30]

A broad understanding, in fact, that poetry and fiction (including dramatic fiction) belong together is common to many Western perceptions since the end of antiquity, as in antiquity itself. And this understanding is partly a matter of reception of antiquity, but chiefly of a cultural-intellectual congruence that serves to give the ancient understandings an archetypal status. In these terms, the association of poetry and narrative fiction as the effective heartland of literature is itself a *donnée* of the classical tradition.

The most significant departure from this association – and another *donnée* of the tradition – is to be found in the foregrounding of 'artistic' or 'literary' prose (fictional or otherwise) and the association of *that*, in turn, with poetry. Erasmus' assimilation of letters to speeches belongs here, though the further reference to poetic 'art' is not explicit in his case. That reference is fully explicit, however, in innumerable rhetorical handbooks, neoclassical, Renaissance, medieval, ancient. One *locus classicus* here is Quintilian's roll-call of approved genres and authors – approved, that is, for the 'education of the orator' – which covers poets (from Homer to Horace), historians (Thucydides to Livy), philosophers (Plato to Seneca), and, of course, orators too (Demosthenes, Cicero, and others),[31] with technical prose, in particular, conspicuous by its absence.[32] The same association of thought is implicit in modern critical acknowledgement of a wide range of prose forms – from political slogans to critical essays themselves – as actually or potentially 'literary', especially when emphasis is put on the 'poetic' quality of the language used.[33] Such acknowledgement tends to make little or no reference to ancient precedent, but once again the ancient archetype – the alternative 'rhetorical' archetype – remains an operative reality.

In effect, then, our 'literature' is indeed the modern instantiation of an ancient archetype. But if 'genre' implies a specifiable context, or at least a specifiable form,

[28] *Discorso intorno al comporre dei romanzi* (1554); *Orbecche* (1541); *Hecatommithi* (1565).

[29] Warshaw (1920) 277.

[30] *Fragmente zur Litteratur und Poesie* (1797), 1. 32: 'Drei herrschende Dichtarten. 1) *Tragödie* bei den Griechen. 2) *Satire* bei den Römern. 3) *Roman* bei den Modernen.'

[31] *Institutio Oratoria*, 10. 1. 46–131.

[32] So too, as a distinct category, prose fiction, i.e. the 'ancient novel'. Throughout antiquity, this range of writing is denied critical acknowledgement, though recent scholarship plausibly associates it with the rhetorical tradition, and though (conversely) ancient 'novels' are seen to be among the precursors of the modern novel (§12 n. 17).

[33] See e.g. Jakobson (1960) 357, on the 'poetics' of 'I like Ike', and Said (1979) 184–5, on the question, 'is the essay a text?'.

'literature' is hardly a word-*genre* in itself;[34] and on closer inspection the fate of the various ancient genres – genres proper – is seen to present a rather different picture. In the sphere of prose, many of the individual genres have simply disappeared without trace, not least the oratorical types that Erasmus and the classicizing centuries scrutinize so respectfully – or if a practical equivalent does survive (as 'judicial speeches' survive in the modern lawcourt), it is outside both the common understanding and the plausible delineation of 'literature'. But under whatever name, the phenomenon of 'literary prose' still exists, as it did in antiquity, albeit with somewhat different constituents. If oratory has effectively ceased to be counted as 'literary', the modern world has, as the ancient world had, the 'broad genre' of prose fiction: 'the novel' – ubiquitous in the modern age and a reality, if a more marginal reality, in antiquity.[35] Likewise, for instance, the broad category of 'philosophy' survives, albeit it neither was, nor is, strictly a genre, again. Philosophy in antiquity took many forms – Heraclitean aphorisms, Platonic dialogues, Aristotelian treatises, Lucretian didactic poetry – as does philosophy in the modern experience: compare the range from Nietzsche's prose-poetic *Zarathustra* to Wittgenstein's aphoristic *Investigations*, from Derridean word-play to the plainest of plain prose that characterizes 'Anglo-Saxon' philosophizing.

With poetry, the situation is much the same. The broad category of 'poetry' itself, of course, remains, though in practice equated now with 'lyric poetry' – yet another surviving broad category, whose numerous ancient forms, once again, have no counterparts today ('epinician', 'epithalamium', 'paean').[36] In today's world of words, more generally, the ancient poetic types (or some of them) still have their reflexes, but it makes little sense to claim an archetypal status for any one of them. The continuing sense that an 'epic' is big (and full of heroes?) and an 'epigram' short and succinct; the continuing critical appeal to (say) 'idyllic' moments and 'elegiac' notes in texts old and new; even the relation of 'tragedy' to 'comedy', which many, in the wake of Aristotle, continue to read as a fundamental opposition[37] – all of these attest in some degree to the modern currency of the ancient types, but this currency is strictly on modernity's terms. For a start, all the terms cited here formerly designated verse types, but now (as befits an age of prose) this is not necessarily, or not definitively, so (*hence* the modern equation of poetry with 'lyric', which, alone of these terms, still designates verse). Unless the focus is on the likes of Shakespeare, Racine, Molière, or of course their ancient predecessors, 'tragedy' and 'comedy' will be applied, almost invariably, to prose forms, and not even, necessarily, to prose drama. 'An epigram', likewise, probably means a *bon mot*, again in prose, by a stylist like Wilde. Modern allusion to 'an epic' is more likely to involve reference to a Hollywood blockbuster than to a poem like *Paradise Lost*. The 'elegiac'

34 *Pace* Fowler (1982) 1–19.

35 'Broad genres': Hirsch (1967) 110–11, 150–1. Novel: n. 32 above.

36 All contextually determined. Lyric: Silk (2009b).

37 'Two modes of imitation . . . intended to promote different ends by contrary means' (Johnson, *Preface to Shakespeare*): cf. Aristotle, *Poetics*, 5; *contra*, Silk (2000) 52–97.

and the 'idyllic', too, will most likely be identified in contexts remote from their original denotation – which is already the case in the Romantic era and the generation that follows. Witness, for instance, Tennyson's *Idylls of the King* (1859); these Arthurian narratives are indeed in verse, but have only the most tenuous connection to the ancient idyll.[38] Witness, again, the way Schiller, in 1795, uses both 'elegiac' and 'idyllic' to convey broad tendencies in modern writing and response.[39] In retrospect, Dante's designation of his great work as a 'comedy' prefigures all such shifting usage.[40]

But Dante (and, more broadly, the medieval age) apart, there is a decisive difference between the expectations aroused by all such terms in pre-modern writing and today. For writers and readers from the Renaissance to (as usual) the earlier eighteenth century, classical paradigms are definitive. Today, even if, exceptionally, instantiations of 'the idyllic' or (even) 'the comic' are located in a text relatable to their ancient counterparts, they enjoy no privileged status on that account. 'The comic', in itself, is indeed a prime candidate for a true universal. Within and beyond the West, all cultures, past and present, surely recognise and cultivate 'the art of laughter', in one or other generic context – but this, precisely, makes the point. 'The comic' is broader than a genre, and not necessarily even embodied in words – hence, of course, the paradoxical coherence of comic theory, from Aristotle (on comic drama) to Baudelaire (on 'the comic in the plastic arts'), from Bakhtin (on 'carnival humour') to Freud (on 'the joke').[41] Prose or verse, the striking fact is that the more specific the genre, the less likely it is to prove itself a universal, in archetypal relation to an ancient equivalent; but the broader the category, the more likely: lyric poetry, the novel, comedy (or 'the comic'), philosophy, literature itself. Where the labels attached to more specific ancient forms survive (from 'epigram' to 'comedy', again), our age does not understand, or only randomly understands, those labels in ancient-compatible terms. And in prose, where most creative activity now takes place, active word-genres today range from new cultural realities ('blogs')[42] to *ad hoc* classifications of present and past experience ('prison literature');[43] neither relate to ancient forms at all.

[38] *Pace* Pattison (1979) 15–39. The 'idyll' is an essentially modern construct (Rosenmeyer 1969: 8–9, 287–8), while the ancient *eidullion* is not even an established genre, but one name for the diverse 'miniatures' of Theocritus and others.

[39] *Über naive und sentimentalische Dichtung* (*Die Horen*, 12).

[40] The designation itself assumes both stylistic level and dramatic trajectory ('happy ending'): see §13 n. 138 and (e.g.) Silk (2000) 58–9.

[41] Aristotle, *Poetics*, 2–5; Baudelaire, 'De l'essence du rire' (1855); Bakhtin, *Rabelais and His World* (Russian original first published in 1965); Freud, *Jokes and Their Relation to the Unconscious* (German original, 1905).

[42] Genres and 'cultural realities': Frow (2006), Silk (2013).

[43] Notwithstanding the resistance of modern theory to the idea that genre ever involves 'classifying': see theorists as different as Derrida (1980) and Fowler (1982) 3. Unlike both blogs and the Greco-Roman genres, these modern quasi-generic classifications are generally based on content, with no formal or contextual basis.

By contrast, the classicizing ages understand the genres strictly in their classical instantiations, or in new instantiations modelled on them – and privilege the latter precisely in contradistinction to those outcomes that seemingly lack a classical pedigree. And if there is a significant exception, it is probably that the forms developed so impressively by the Italian Trecento acquire a 'classical' status too.[44] Take lyric poetry. For Du Bellay, poet-spokesman of French usage in 1549, 'odes or lyrical verses' are the positive, in explicit contrast to 'the rondels, ballades, virelays, chants royal, songs and other such spices as do corrupt the taste of our tongue'. And 'odes or lyrical verses' are approved, only if they conform to the formal specificity of the types within the classical canon or (as notably with the Petrarchan sonnet) their 'modern' Italian equivalents.[45] Like Erasmus with oratorical and epistolary prose, writers and readers assume the determinacy of classical types, actual or (as with Erasmus' epistolary forms) notional. And (as with Erasmus, implicitly, once again) this determinacy is felt to characterize ancient theory and practice as a continuum, from which a norm of generic 'decorum' is derived that validates, or invalidates, all contemporary innovation.

Consider more closely that anti-Shakespearean statement by Milton: 'Of That Sort of Dramatic Poem Called Tragedy', prefaced to *Samson Agonistes* (1671) and designed to vindicate his own decision to compose a tragedy. In this short manifesto, Milton appeals to ancient practice ('Aeschylus, Sophocles and Euripides, the three tragic poets unequalled yet by any, and the best rule to all who endeavour to write tragedy'); he looks for moral(izing) support in ancient theory (Aristotle), along with sundry Roman and Christian precedents (from 'Augustus Caesar' to Seneca to the medieval *Christus Patiens*); and he makes a point of invoking the more recent practice of 'the Italians', on a par with that of 'the ancients'. All this on one side; and on the other, 'the poet's error of intermixing comic stuff with tragic sadness and gravity' – which is dismissed as alien to classical precedent (one reflects that the critic had not read his Euripides with due care and attention), whereas Milton's own use of a chorus and other antique elements is a simple corollary of his determination to reproduce the 'generic repertoire' of the tragic drama of ancient Greece.[46]

One reflects, too, that a rigid generic position like Milton's not only denies the possible value of innovative hybrids, from Shakespeare to opera (§12). It also seems to allow the thought that value does attach to any embodiment of an approved genre. A glance at (say) the embarrassing sequence of verse tragedies by otherwise notable English poets of the nineteenth century should suffice to expose the absurdity of the idea.

But how different from Milton's is the attitude of even the most philhellenic of tragic theorists and practitioners in the post-classicizing age. Friedrich Schiller's play, *The Bride of Messina* (*Die Braut von Messina*, 1803), is a remarkable experiment:

[44] Cf. §13 n. 103.

[45] Du Bellay, *Deffence*, 2. 4.

[46] 'Generic repertoire': Fowler (1982) 55–74, Silk (2000) 67–9.

a verse drama set (more or less) in the Christian Middle Ages,[47] and – to quote Schiller's own subtitle – 'A Tragedy with Choruses' ('Ein Trauerspiel mit Chören'): chorus*es* (plural), because within the play 'the chorus' is mostly two rival groups. And why does Schiller include a chorus (or choruses)? The answer is surprisingly elusive – yet no-one could accuse the playwright of not having thought about it. Not only does he foreground the chorus in his subtitle; his preface to the play is an essay devoted precisely to 'The Use of a Chorus in Tragedy' ('Über den Gebrauch des Chors in der Tragödie').

In this revealing document, Schiller seeks both to acknowledge the rationale of the chorus in Attic drama and to explain its use in his 'modern' tragedy. In his phrasing, though, the two endeavours become oddly confused: he speaks of 'the chorus of Greek tragedy as I have employed it here'.[48] And this is especially odd, because he represents the Greek chorus as one thing and his own as another. The Greek chorus was 'a tool of nature' ('ein natürliches Organ') and 'an essential accompaniment' ('eine notwendige Begleitung') to a kind of drama centred on gods, heroes, and kings – whereas for the modern playwright (for *himself*), the chorus is a 'tool of art' ('Kunstorgan'): 'a single ideal person' ('eine einzige ideale Person'), whose lyrical 'freedom' to articulate large perspectives on the action can provide 'a living wall' against the temptations of modern practice – especially the temptations of naturalistic practice – which Schiller is anxious to resist.[49]

It is no surprise that Schiller's play, and especially its chorus, was and is widely regarded as a problematic experiment.[50] For Hegel, some years later, the experiment doubtless summed up what he saw as inconclusive debate, both 'about the significance of the Greek chorus' itself and about 'whether it can or should be introduced into modern tragedy'.[51] For us, reviewing the post-classical relevance of the classical word-genres, Schiller's experiment epitomizes their ambiguous status at the dawn of the modern age – an age obsessed by its own historical relativity and yet also by deceptive glimpses of the universal amidst a universe of choices.

[47] The play is set in medieval Sicily, and intermittently reflects its Islamic aspect – but also freely uses Greco-Roman imagery (Furies, oracles etc.): cf. Silk (1999c) 211.

[48] 'Der Chor des griechischen Trauerspiels, so wie ich ihn hier gebraucht habe'.

[49] Eliot's *Murder in the Cathedral* (1935), with several chorus-like groups in another Christian-medieval setting, uses XX avant-garde features (like the murderers' address to the audience) to anti-naturalize more stridently.

[50] Cf. Sergl (1998), Silk (1999c) 205–12.

[51] In his lectures of the 1820s: *Ästhetik*, 3. 3. 3. 3 (*sic*), 'Die Arten der dramatischen Poesie und deren historische Hauptmomente.' Cf. Silk (1999c) 207–8 n. 25.

Part III

The Imaginary

§23
Preface

There are realities and then there are 'realities'. In Part III we confront one of the large implications of that proposition under the heading of 'the imaginary'. In a long perspective, investment in the explanatory power of the imaginary is a recent phenomenon, associated with theoretical developments in the cultural sciences over the last two generations. For centuries, 'imaginary' was the subsidiary opposite of 'real' or 'true' ('false sorrow's eye | . . . for things true weeps things imaginary').[1] *The* imaginary has appreciated in critical value with the emergence of constructivist epistemologies according to which all cultural entities, from gender to literary texts, owe their meaning to acts of the human imagination. In a neat enactment of the Derridean logic of the supplement, it is now commonplace to identify the imaginary foundations of social realities, and to explore the role of symbolic activity (linguistic and other) in the constitution and operation of socio-political groups, institutions, and cultural forms.

The imaginary began its rise to critical prominence by assuming a significant role in specific systems of thought. Notable examples are Sartre's 'phenomenological psychology of the imagination', Lacan's post-Freudian analysis of the ego, and Cornelius Castoriadis's Marxian theory of society, within which the imaginary

[1] Shakespeare, *Richard II*, 2. 2. 26–7. In linguistic terms, 'imaginary' is the marked term, 'real'/'true' the unmarked.

The Classical Tradition: Art, Literature, Thought, First Edition. Michael Silk, Ingo Gildenhard, and Rosemary Barrow.

Published 2017 by John Wiley & Sons Ltd.

functions as a more flexible and potent alternative to ideology.[2] In more recent years, though, the term has graduated to the status of a cultural category in its own right. While it retains its affiliations with a range of theoretical stances, it is often employed – and this is how we are employing it here – as a free-standing term, which aims to capture something important about the way human beings negotiate or construe the world. Indeed, it is precisely its capacity to accommodate insights from a variety of theories – from the social constructivism of John Searle to Wolfgang Iser's reader-response approaches to literature – that makes the imaginary good to think with.[3]

The imaginary, then, if not yet a mainstream entity, is widely invoked by literary critics, philosophers, and indeed students of the classical tradition.[4] Unlike 'culture', for instance, it focuses attention on 'the ways people imagine their . . . existence . . ., the expectations that are normally met, and the deeper normative notions and images that underlie these expectations'.[5] And as such, the imaginary foregrounds the fluid transitions between different modes of creative world-making.

'Creative': we use the word advisedly, at a time when some of Darwin's successors are happy to overstate the significance of our being 'firmly ensconced within the chimpanzee family'.[6] Perhaps the definitive difference between us humans and our closest relatives in the animal kingdom is precisely 'our capacity to live in an imagined world'.[7] Whatever 'culture' our animal cousins may be presumed to have, there remains, indeed, a *world* of difference between that and human achievement in socio-political practice, in art and *the* arts, in literature and thought.

Within the overall cultural imaginary of the West, the classical tradition is a significant presence. Alongside Judaeo-Christian religion and the 'modern' values and shared understandings associated with the Enlightenment, capitalism, or scientific rationality, Greco-Roman antiquity constitutes a third source of norms and values, images and ideas, ways of thinking and figures of thought, through which Western cultures make sense of their existence. Various of the topics that we have presented from other standpoints, from 'morality' (§8) to 'word-genres' (§22), could, certainly, also be approached from this one. In the sections that follow, however, we offer four representative soundings that aim to bring into focus the ways an imaginary works, as well as the specifics under consideration.[8] First comes

[2] Sartre, *L'imaginaire: Psychologie phénoménologique de l'imagination* (1940); Lacan, *Le séminaire, Livre II: Le moi dans la théorie de Freud et dans la technique de la psychanalyse* (1977); Castoriadis, *L'institution imaginaire de la societé* (1975). A more extended genealogy might include early-modern authors who stress the world-making powers of the imagination, like Montaigne (with his 'De la force de l'imagination': *Essais*, 1. 21), or of language, like Vico (*Scienza nuova*, 1725/44).

[3] Searle (1996), whose title looks back to Berger and Luckmann (1967); Iser (1991).

[4] E.g. Shepard and Powell (2004).

[5] Excerpted from Charles Taylor's definition of the 'social imaginary': Taylor (2004) 23.

[6] Dunbar (2007) 38.

[7] Cf. Dunbar ibid.

[8] Compare and contrast our comment on archetypes in §19.

myth: not myth as story, so much as myth as mode of thought (though the two are hard to separate in the end), and myth as hermeneutic challenge, too (§24). Next, we turn our attention to 'the city', in the distinctive shape of Rome (§25), and to 'forms of government' (§26): real and imagined, both. Then finally, with 'the order of things' (§27), we reflect on understandings of 'our' place in what is conventionally, and not inappropriately, called 'the great scheme of things', with special reference to what it is to be human.

§24
Myth

Like so many modern categories and concepts, 'myth' – meaning a traditionally based story of gods or heroes, or equivalent – is a product of the later eighteenth and early nineteenth centuries. A notable part in its formation is played by the German classical scholar, Christian Gottlob Heyne, in a series of Latin essays that promote a specialized usage of the Latinized Greek 'mythus' in preference to the Latin 'fabula' (usual word for a 'story' of gods, heroes, or anything). Heyne's neologistic usage recognises that the (un-Latinized) Greek word 'muthos' could signify a narrative 'account', without any necessary implication of its truth or falsehood, and presumes that the Greek myths originally arose as responses to life by people with 'no other means of expressing their understandings'.[1] From the first, modern mythological debates have Greek myth, and its place within the imaginary, firmly in view.

Yet these debates have never properly come to terms with two peculiarities of 'Greek' myth, well-known though they both are: first, its appropriation by the Romans, so comprehensively that for many centuries Greek myth and Greco-Roman approximations are hardly distinguished; and second, the phenomenon that, within the Western imaginary, the mythological mode (Greek or Greco-Roman) has been exceptionally productive. In painting and sculpture, poetry and drama, opera and

1 'animi sensus quomodo aliter exponerent, non habebant', in 'De origine et causis fabularum [*sic*] Homericarum' (1777); cf. Most (1999) 37–8 and, generally, Horstmann (1979). 'Muth-' derivatives had long been in use in (e.g.) French ('De la theologie mythique, c'est à dire fabuleuse': the chapter heading to Gentian Hervet's 1570 translation of Augustine's *City of God*, 6. 6), but only in the wake of Heyne's usage (a back-formation?) do vernacular 'mythe', 'mythos', 'mito', 'myth', come into use.

The Classical Tradition: Art, Literature, Thought, First Edition. Michael Silk, Ingo Gildenhard, and Rosemary Barrow.

Published 2017 by John Wiley & Sons Ltd.

film, classical myth has been a favourite source of material;[2] in everyday experience, and in popular culture, it is a common point of reference, too. In the twentieth century, the ancient cast of gods and heroes provides names for Freud's *Oedipus* complex and NASA's *Apollo* space missions; for sports equipment (*Nike*: goddess of victory) and chocolate bars (the *Mars* bar, aid to 'work, rest and play': compare Ares/Mars in *Odyssey* 8); for the *Pluto* project to supply oil, under the English Channel, to the allied forces after D-Day ('Pluto', both god of the underworld and acronym of 'pipe-line under the ocean'); for the EU in the figure of *Europa*; for a whimsically-minded German travel agency (*Ikarus*)[3] – while, in the English-speaking world in particular, it continues to feed popular narratives of various kinds, from Marie Phillips's *Gods Behaving Badly* (where Aphrodite is a phone-sex operative and Apollo a TV psychic)[4] to heroic-mythic films like *Jason and the Argonauts*[5] to J. K. Rowling's *Harry Potter* series (where, more obliquely, *Minerva* McGonagall teaches 'transfiguration' at Hogwarts School of Witchcraft and Wizardry).[6]

One can hardly exaggerate the range and diversity of post-classical usage, across the cultural spectrum: Bernini's *Apollo and Daphne* and the medieval *Roman d'Enéas*; Purcell's *Dido and Aeneas*, Goethe's *Iphigenia*, Offenbach's *Orpheus in the Underworld*; the sixteenth-century illustrations of Ovid's *Metamorphoses* by German engraver Virgil Solis and, from Italy in the same century, the emblem books of the jurist Andrea Alciato;[7] James Joyce's *Ulysses* and Tennyson's 'Ulysses'; Shakespeare's 'Venus and Adonis' and Titian's several paintings of that pair – and then all those allusive usages from Freud to Harry Potter. But is there anything in common here, beyond the evocation of classical myth itself?

Negatively, at least, there is one thing. All post-classical uses of 'Greek' myth have, prospectively, a different significance – for their authors, as for their audiences – from that which the myths themselves once had in ancient Greece. Paul Veyne's memorable question, 'did the Greeks believe in their myths?',[8] may be open to more than one answer, on more than one level, but there is no doubt that *their* myths, like the gods and heroes who figure in them, were for centuries associated with 'belief', as also, and no less fundamentally, with religious practice, in a way that hardly arises in later, Western usage. Nietzsche may (eventually) identify himself with the 'Dionysus' he has spent much of his adult life invoking (§18), and Keats may come close to constructing a private religion based on ancient sources,[9] but even for Nietzsche and Keats ancient myth is something 'good to think with', rather

[2] Long lists in Reid (1993) (though inevitably incomplete, and not including film).

[3] Examples partly from Seidensticker (2003) 154–5. 'A Mars a day helps you work, rest and play' was an advertising slogan in use from 1959. Europa: Guthmüller (1997), Morales (2007) 5–18, Renger and Issler (2009).

[4] Novel, 2007; film, 2012.

[5] Film, 1963; television mini-series, 2000.

[6] Novels, 1997–2007; films, 2001–11.

[7] Emblem books: Visser (2005).

[8] Veyne: *Les grecs ont-ils cru à leurs mythes? Essai sur l'imagination constituante* (1983).

[9] Aske (1985) 3.

than an instantiation of religious belief (let alone practice). The extent to which Roman appropriations of Greek myth (or, indeed, latter-day Greek uses of Greek myth) already presume a 'thinking-with', divorced from belief (as from practice), is a separate question. What is beyond dispute is that, in ancient Greece, Dionysus, Oedipus, and all the other gods and heroes are, in the first instance, 'real' gods and 'real' heroes, whereas within the classical tradition they are something else; and here at least, their intermittent Romanizing (for 'Mars', read Ares; for 'Ulysses', read Odysseus; indeed, for 'Dionysus', read Dionysos)[10] sums up the non-'reality' of the mythological apparatus in this sense.

In one long phase of the tradition, however, the issue of belief has been profoundly relevant. During, and beyond, the Christian millennium, the religious premises of the entire mythological system impinge on the Church, not as the harmless and colourful residue of a dying world, but as a living threat to the one true faith.

Ironically, it was largely educational considerations that ensured the continuing presence of pagan myth in the early Christian world. This rival theology, with these pagan divinities, constituted one of the most intractable aspects of the inherited classical culture. Though militant Christianity could, and did, discontinue pagan cult practices and destroy the objects and sites associated with pagan worship, terms of 'fair use' had to be established for the mythic material that characterized so many acknowledged classics of the educational canon[11] – even if there were Church Fathers who wanted no truck with such toxic subject matter at all, seeing the myths as the product of 'eavesdropping' demons, bent on perverting divine revelation.[12]

But in coming to terms with the mythic heritage, Christian usage could draw on ancient traditions of thought in which myth was already identified as a problem or at least a hermeneutic challenge. From as early as the Presocratic philosophers, 'literal' understandings of myths as records of history or supernatural reality prompt feelings of disquiet, which ancient commentators address by rereading traditional tales, or their literary or artistic variants, in line with new standards of ontology and ethics. In broad terms, both they and their post-classical successors incline towards Plato's understanding of myth as equivocal between falsehood and truth, therefore problematic, yet not necessarily beneath consideration.[13] For Christian exegetes, however, more specific prototypes were closer to hand: Palaephatus' rationalizing interpretation of myth as an empirically plausible historical core, wrapped up in marvellous embellishments; Euhemerus' novelistic depiction of Olympian deities as humans who become objects of worship, but not actual immortals, after death; and the Stoic *allegoresis* of poetry, which converts, for instance, the

[10] This, in English usage. Our four languages vary in the degree of Romanizing (and from one age to another).

[11] Fiedrowicz (2000), Gnilka (1984), (1993).

[12] Allen (1970) 3.

[13] Cf. Murray (1999).

battle of the gods in *Iliad* 22 into a clash of natural forces. Christendom duly co-opts these strategies, but also supplements them with typological techniques honed in scriptural exegesis (notably the reinterpretation of the Jewish Bible as the Christian Old Testament). Thus, in Palaephatean fashion, the 'fiction' of Jupiter impregnating Danae in the form of a golden shower now yielded a historical figure who used gold to bribe his way into a princess's bedchamber,[14] while in typological mode the fourteenth-century *Ovide moralisé* (§8) contrived to find edifying aspects of the story of Christ in virtually all the tales in Ovid's epic.

Resourceful commentary in these various traditions thus enabled Christian culture to assign a meaningful place in its encyclopedia of knowledge to an otherwise recalcitrant set of materials. Greco-Roman myth could now make an acceptable contribution to history, cosmology, and, not least, practical ethics – the latter, often, through allegorical personification of abstract concepts, like the Vice and Virtue that Hercules chooses between (§21).[15] And such rereadings help to create the easy familiarity with myth that underwrites the astonishing profusion of early modern artistic creativity in mythic literature and art. Not that all *this* literature and art conforms to acceptable Christian requirements: far from it. If – even – Titian's paintings of Danae might be subordinated to a Christian reading, it is not apparent how the sensual magnificence of his *Bacchus and Ariadne* could be.[16] In early modern Europe, Titian and many others use myth with unmistakable zest to celebrate or explore worldly satisfactions, not least those associated with violence, power, and sex. Even so, explicit moral didacticism still crops up in unlikely places: Golding's preface to his translation of the *Metamorphoses* is representative here (§15). And no less representative, but now of the ironies of the ongoing pagan/Christian relationship, is the early publication history of the *Ovide moralisé*. Composed around 1320, this massive text was first printed in Bruges by Colard Mansion in 1484, then republished a few years later by Antoine Vérard in Paris – under the title, 'The Poets' Bible' (*La Bible des poëtes*, 1493).

But in any case, not everyone approved the Christianizing of pagan myth. When allegorizers of the *Metamorphoses* read the laurel as code for Mary, and Apollo for Christ, Luther, for one, dismissed their exegetical manoeuvres as mumbo-jumbo ('I loathe allegories').[17] And from time to time, others – creative writers, even – deplore the mythological habit itself, sometimes on grounds of cliché, but also for reasons of religious indecorum. In seventeenth-century England, the poet Carew, acclaiming the myth-denying ordinance of his fellow-poet, the cleric John Donne, lately dead –

[14] Danae: cf. §§17, 33. Ovid already gives a quasi-Palaephatean account of the myth: *Amores*, 3. 8 (cf. Horace, *Odes*, 3. 16. 1–11).

[15] See generally Barkan (1986), Seznec (1953).

[16] Notwithstanding affinities between (esp.) Ariadne's pose and the Virgin's in Annunciation scenes: Rosand (2004) 42, 291–2.

[17] 'Ego itaque odi allegorias': *Commentary on Genesis*, 30 (1543).

> . . . lamented the imminent return of 'the goodly exil'd traine | Of gods and goddesses' which had been 'banish'd' during the 'just' poetic 'raigne' of John Donne. After Donne's death, Carew feared, 'The silenc'd tales o'th'Metamorphoses' would return to 'stuff' the lines of English poetry and 'swell the windy page' of English poets' work.[18]

But the mythological habit was deeply entrenched. In the same poem in which he commends Donne and dismisses the pagan 'gods and goddesses', Carew himself invokes 'The Muses' garden' and Donne's 'Promethean breath', and finally (getting it both ways) pronounces Donne 'Apollo's first, at last the true God's priest.'

Enlightenment writers are less equivocal in their scorn. David Hume in 1739: 'We have been so much accustomed to the names of Mars, Jupiter, Venus, that . . . the constant repetition of these ideas makes them enter into the mind with facility and prevail upon the fancy without influencing the judgement' (*not* good to think with, then).[19] For the abbé Pluche, the same year, Jupiter and the rest were 'nothing more than puppets, only fit for a miraculous appearance on a string, to keep children amused',[20] while in 1724 his compatriot Fontenelle dismissed the entire mythological apparatus as 'a mass of chimeras, day-dreams, and absurdities'.[21] For Samuel Johnson, in 1781, there was nothing to be gained from the 'puerilities of obsolete mythology', given that 'the heathen deities can no longer gain attention'.[22] And a few years later, in the first flush of the Romantic age, poetic-mythic conceits are the poet Coleridge's particular target. In 'The Nightingale' (1798), Coleridge calls up, only to dismiss, the mythic aetiology of the songbird:

> And hark! the nightingale begins its song
> 'Most musical, most melancholy' bird!
> A melancholy bird? Oh! idle thought!
> In nature there is nothing melancholy.

The author of the 'idle thought' was Milton,[23] but even Milton's authority is not enough to justify it. The problem, for Coleridge, is that such conceits – this one, derived from the Philomela myth – still have currency among the impressionable young, because

> . . . youths and maidens most poetical,
> Who lose the deepening twilights of the spring
> In ball-rooms and hot theatres, they still,
> Full of meek sympathy, must heave their sighs
> O'er Philomela's pity-pleading strains.

[18] Hopkins (2010) 2–3: Carew, 'Elegy upon the Death of the Dean of Paul's, Dr John Donne' (1633).

[19] *A Treatise of Human Nature*, 1. 3. 10.

[20] *Histoire du ciel*, 2. 4.

[21] *De l'origine des fables*.

[22] *Life of Gray* (where the 'mythology' – in Gray's 'The Bard' – is actually Celtic) and *Life of Pope*: Hill (1905), 3. 439, 233.

[23] 'Il Penseroso' (1631).

In Romantic parlance, the opposition of 'nature' to 'poetical' (let alone the association of 'poetical' with the superficiality of 'ball-rooms' and 'hot theatres') is damning. Mythic allusion, it seems, can only misrepresent – even if Coleridge's anti-classicizing polemic ends up (like Carew's) bearing a strong resemblance to the familiar mythic-allusive mode itself.[24]

It is obvious enough why pagan myth in a non-pagan environment – Christian, Enlightenment, even Romantic – might cause offence, or at least indifference; less obvious why it should have commended itself so much more generally, *and still does*. The unanswered question – do the disparate usages of different ages have anything in common? – thus translates itself into another: is there something about classical myth as a whole that explains, and counts as a positive reason for, its reuse as a whole?

In pondering the question, we need to take into account, not only the profusion of reuse, but the way that some myths have given rise to sets of reuses: 'Antigones'; 'Masks of Dionysus'; 'Helen of Troy: From Homer to Hollywood'.[25] With Coleridge's 'most poetical' (and Milton's 'most melancholy') in mind, let us consider the tale of Procne, Philomela, and Tereus.

Homer already alludes to the nightingale story in *Odyssey* 19, but its significant instantiation was in Sophocles' *Tereus*: the mother (Procne) who kills her child (Itys) and serves him up as a meal to his father (Tereus, king of Thrace), in revenge for the rape and mutilation that Tereus inflicted on her sister (Philomela): an appalling cycle of events, only brought to an end when the gods intervene and turn the three survivors into birds – hoopoe, swallow, nightingale. (Tereus is the hoopoe, but tradition is divided on which sister becomes the nightingale and which the swallow: an entirely typical instance of variation within 'the same' myth.) Sophocles' tragedy did not survive into the Middle Ages long enough to be recovered in the Renaissance, but through Ovid's version in *Metamorphoses* 6, the myth becomes canonical. Many authors (though few artists)[26] have reworked this tale of violence and transfiguration (with Philomela generally the nightingale), from Chrétien de Troyes (*Philomena et Progne*, *c.* 1160) to Christoph Ransmayr (*Die letzte Welt*: 'The Last World', 1988), while one favourite setting has remained the stage. A series of dramatists, indeed, have engaged, not just with the story and its characters, or even just with Ovid, but with the violence itself, in a kind of ongoing dialogue.[27]

With some assistance from the gruesome behaviour of Atreus in Seneca's *Thyestes*, Ovid's narrative inspires a suitably macabre Latin tragedy by the eighteen-year-old

[24] Coleridge had already composed a less nuanced critique in 'To the Nightingale' (1794): 'Philomel! . . . How many wretched bards address thy name'.

[25] The titles of Steiner (1984); Carpenter and Faraone (1993); Maguire (2009).

[26] Notably, Rubens ('Banquet of Tereus', 1636–8) and Picasso (etching of 'Tereus and Philomela': illustration to Ovid's *Metamorphoses*, 1930): Reid (1993) 895–8.

[27] Cf. Gildenhard and Zissos (2007). Other treatments include Chaucer's *Legend of Good Women* (1380s), a lost opera (*Philomèle*) by Charpentier (1690), and poems by Goethe ('Philomele', 1782) and Matthew Arnold ('Philomela', 1853).

Gregorio Correr ('besides Seneca,' said Piccolomini, 'we have no Latin tragedians except Correr').[28] Correr's *Progne* (1428) revives classical notions of criminal insanity (*furor*), unspeakable outrage (*nefas*), and yet more unspeakable revenge, and anticipates the more-than-Ovidian horror of Shakespeare's *Titus Andronicus* (§8), as if in a contest of 'competitive mutilation'.[29] Various poets, meanwhile, dwell rather on the pain, hidden but not obliterated by the transfigurations: 'The small slain body, the flowerlike face' – 'The voice of the child's blood crying yet' (the plangent conclusion of Swinburne's 'Itylus', 1866).[30] Different again is Timberlake Wertenbaker's *The Love of the Nightingale* (1989), which rereads the two sisters as victims of patriarchal violence – a striking appeal to contemporary values, but no less a continuation of the implicit dialogue with the playwright's predecessors.[31]

Seneca aside, one implication of any such set of versions is that writers (as also artists) acknowledge the identity and integrity of a myth in the very act of rewriting it. Whatever the variations, it remains 'the' myth of Procne and Philomela – a perceptual reality that is equally a feature of ancient mythology itself and a premise of modern scholarly treatments of such 'classical receptions'. And one senses that *this* 'reality', though no answer to our large question, is relevant to it.

An answer might perhaps have been expected from the mythographers, in their unending quest for a comprehensive account of mythic lore. The mythographic tradition has a long history. Like reinterpretations of myth, mythographic compilations begin in antiquity, with handbooks like Apollodorus' *Library* and Hyginus' *Tales* (*Fabulae*), while Ovid's *Metamorphoses* represents the triumphant conversion of mythography into consummate art. Medieval compilations cover the same spectrum, from the study guide to the literary work.[32] To the first category belong the works of the three so-called Vatican mythographers (tenth to twelfth century AD?)[33] and Bersuire's *Ovidius moralizatus*;[34] and if Boccaccio's encyclopedic *Genealogy of the Pagan Gods* (still under revision at the time of his death in 1374) tends the same way, his cautionary tales of 'Famous Women' (*De claris mulieribus*, *c.* 1370) and Christine de Pizan's proto-feminist vernacular response, the 'City of Women' (*Cité des dames*, 1405), are, once again, significant works of art. So too is Pizan's

28 *De liberorum educatione* (1450).

29 Barkan's formulation: (1986) 244. Cf. Sarah Kane's play *Cleansed* (1998) (again on a seemingly unrelated subject), where the (male) protagonist not only suffers amputation of his tongue (as in Ovid) and his hands (as in Shakespeare), but also his feet, to prevent any expression of homosexual identity by dancing.

30 'Itylus': Louis (1999).

31 Cf. recuperations of Medea by Tony Harrison, *Medea: A Sex-War Opera* (1985), and Christa Wolf, *Medea: Stimmen* (1996): Bartel and Simon (2010). Wertenbaker: Brown (2004).

32 Cf. Chance (1994), (2000).

33 Overview: Pepin (2008) 1–12. These 'mythographic' compilations include material we would classify as historical: thus, inspired by *Aeneid* 6, the first has an entry on Augustus' nephew Marcellus, prompting the second to cite the Marcellus who won the *spolia opima* in 222 BC.

34 The *Ovidius moralizatus*, or *De fabulis poetarum* (distinct from, but partly dependent on, the anonymous *Ovide moralisé*), was added as book 15 to Bersuire's *Reductorium morale* (*c.* 1340): cf. §8 n. 7.

Epistre Othea, a didactic letter that the goddess Othea, newly added to the pantheon of pagan divinities, addresses to Hector, to instruct the adolescent hero in chivalric codes through the *allegoresis* of classical myths,[35] shored up with quotations from the Bible.

Whatever their differences, these medieval works agree in assuming a learned readership. From the sixteenth century, mythography takes on a popularizing role.[36] Natale Conti's 'Mythologies' (*Mythologiae*, 1567) soon establishes itself, both in its original Latin and especially in vernacular translations, as a standard work of reference for a wider public, and Vincenzo Cartari's 'Images of the Gods of the Ancients' (*Le Imagini de i dei de gli antichi*, 1556), also much translated, likewise. Yet though Cartari becomes something of a sourcebook for practising artists, and Conti for aspiring poets,[37] their ambition is limited to expounding the myths, or their characters, rather than pondering their continuing appeal: it is sufficient that antiquity transmits the myths and that their own culture defers to antiquity. Conti, indeed, has thoughts of his own. Perhaps in imitation of one of his classical sources, pseudo-Plutarch's *On Rivers*, which he had earlier translated into Latin, he is not above a learned game of inventing sources himself.[38] But reflection on later reworkings is no part of his endeavours.

The mythographic tradition continues into the modern age, not least in response to developments in education and the desire to make the classics and the classical more universally accessible. Notable examples include (in 1950s Britain) Robert Graves's *Greek Myths* and (in nineteenth-century America) *Bulfinch's Mythology*, which made a concerted effort to present both medieval legends and ancient myths (mostly from Virgil and Ovid) in terms suitable for mass consumption: 'myths', in fact, 'for the millions'.[39] Bulfinch's purpose was to entertain as well as instruct, but especially to facilitate comprehension of otherwise obscure allusions to mythological plots and personnel in art, literature, and social discourse more generally. A more recent, Bulfinch-inspired compilation proposes that, 'to this day, no one in the West who is unfamiliar with Greek myths can seriously claim to be an educated person'.[40] The claim is unassailable, and, if anything, more so in our day – five centuries after Conti and Cartari – than even in theirs: we have so much more literature and art that looks back to the myths to take account of. And yet the question remains: *why* – and why *still* – do literature and art look back to them at all?

At the risk, now, of seeming to mount a self-consciously doomed Socratic search ('continuing my quest, I then turned to . . .'),[41] we note that modern mythological

35 Myths largely derived from Ovid, via the *Ovide moralisé*: Desmond and Sheingorn (2006), Hindman (1986).

36 Cf. Bull (2005) 20–3.

37 Mulryan and Brown (2006) xi.

38 Examples in Ceccarelli (2010).

39 Cleary (2007). *Bulfinch's Mythology* appeared in 1881, as a posthumous compilation of earlier collections, including *The Age of Fable, or Stories of Gods and Heroes* (1855).

40 Martin (2003) 2.

41 Plato, *Apology*, 21–2.

theory, likewise, offers no answer. From Vico to J. G. Frazer to Lévi-Strauss, theorists focus on 'real' myth, Greek or other (often Greek *and* other), on the affinities between different mythic systems, on the nature or deep structures of 'mythical thought' (Lévi-Strauss), on the status of myth as precursor to 'rational thought':[42] the strange half-life of classical myth beyond antiquity is, once again, hardly on the agenda.

What, then, might be the answer to our question? If (unlike the philosopher Hume) so many writers and artists have found myth 'good to think with', why should this be? – *why* and why *still*?

One relevant consideration is obvious enough. The enduring appeal of ancient myths is partly the appeal of specific ancient texts (and artworks) and their capacity to address changing concerns in different ages. Take Greek tragedy, grounded in the world of myth. This is a genre that has enjoyed a significant stage-presence from the first re-performance of an ancient script on a modern stage (Sophocles' *Oedipus Rex* at Palladio's Teatro Olimpico in Vicenza, in 1585) to the 'dawn of the third millennium';[43] and the concerns associated with, or read into, the *Oedipus*, from the heroic to the psychoanalytic, have certainly changed over time. Or take Ovid's *Metamorphoses*: if this text was a 'bible' for early-modern poets (and artists), it offers, equally, a repertoire of themes and behaviours that *we* find 'peculiarly modern' – including 'holocaust, plague, sexual harassment, rape, incest, seduction, pollution, sex-change, suicide, hetero- and homosexual love, torture, war, child-battering, depression and intoxication.'[44]

Yet this does more to explain the acceptability of ancient myth *in situ* than its re-employment, yesterday and today. More directly relevant is the contrary fact that in many cases, most obviously in recent generations, creative engagement with mythic material does not necessarily involve any specific ancient version. The dynamics are different.

Consider de Chirico's Ariadne paintings, a long, obsessive series of depictions of the abandoned heroine[45] – or, as it actually is, depictions of a *statue* of the abandoned heroine – displayed, and displaced, in a modern piazza. The paintings evoke a well-known Greco-Roman statue, the Sleeping Ariadne,[46] but none of them makes any pretence of narrative specificity that might point to a particular version of the tale; some carry Ariadne's name in the title, others (like *The Lassitude of the Infinite*, 1912) leave the familiar figure to interact both with the modern setting and with an abstract, but usually melancholy title, without mythic reference itself. And the

[42] Vico: *Scienza nuova* (1744); Frazer, esp. *The Golden Bough* (1911–15); Lévi-Strauss, esp. *Mythologiques* (1964–71). See generally Csapo (2005).

[43] Macintosh (2009) 70–3; Hall, Macintosh, and Wrigley (2004).

[44] Hofmann and Lasdun (1994) xi; cf. Barolsky (1998).

[45] Taylor (2002); the series begins in 1912 and continues into the 1970s. De Chirico: §33.

[46] Haskell and Penney (1981): no. 24. When first recorded (in XVI Rome), the statue, now in the Vatican Museum, was identified as Cleopatra (§5); she was relabelled as Ariadne in XIX.

physical displacement seems to enact the abandonment of which Ariadne is a plausible symbol.

By comparison with the art of de Chirico, literature inclines towards extended narrative. Yet even in narrative-mythic literature of de Chirico's age, and beyond, displacement – of various kinds – is characteristic again. In his Euhemeristic novel *Der Blaue Kammerherr* ('The Blue Chamberlain', 1949), Wolf von Niebelschütz creates a fantasy world by transposing Greek mythological characters into the Baroque age – with implicit reference to Richard Strauss's enigmatically 'comic' opera *Die Liebe der Danae* ('Danae's Love', 1938–40) – in a bid to come to terms with the condition of post-war Germany.[47] A displaced version of classical myth is evoked, and adjusted, as cover for engagement with contemporary issues.

Many works of recent decades conform to this pattern. Few are 'receptions' of anything specifiable – and even when they are, the degree to which the modern work resembles a particular ancient source can become almost incidental. Sartre's harsh drama *Les mouches* ('The Flies', 1943) presents a terrorist-killer Orestes and a cursed Argos, infested with blood-sucking insects. Besides Sartre's own existentialist preoccupations, the configuration inevitably calls to mind both Aeschylus' *Choephori* (without the flies) and the 'cursed' situation of German-occupied France; but it would be a quaintly academic audience that focused on Aeschylus, rather than the present 'curse', and felt the myth itself as something other than – to use the word again – *cover* (which is not quite the same as allegory) for the occupation.

Sarah Kane's play *Phaedra's Love* (1996) looks back to the distinguished line of 'Hippolytus' plays, from Racine to Seneca to Euripides.[48] In Euripides' version, Theseus' son Hippolytus, devoted to Artemis and repelled by sex, provokes Aphrodite to consume his stepmother Phaedra with obsessive desire for him, the outcome of which is Phaedra's suicide and Hippolytus' violent death. Kane's treatment is closer to Seneca's, though her emphasis on Phaedra also recalls Racine. Once again, though, the particularities of the alignment are hardly of the essence. The mythic-dramatic 'point' – and the overwhelming effect – is a jarring contrast between the sordid realities of modern life and the glamour associated with 'classical' myth as such; the opening spectacle of Hippolytus masturbating into a sock sets the tone.[49]

The Kane, the Niebelschütz, the Sartre, the de Chirico, are all very different – or not. In these, and many other modern cases, myth seems to operate like the human brain, engendering a kind of epiphenomenal consciousness, a secondary reality that operates independently of it. Myth mediates; it may itself impinge as *im*mediate; yet it is somehow detached from the outcome. But, then again, within the tradition, especially the earlier tradition, myth can work quite differently. With de Chirico's multiple Ariadnes, contrast their opposite: Titian's *Bacchus and Ariadne* (1523–4).

[47] Cf. Schori Bondeli (2005).

[48] Kane: Saunders (2002).

[49] Contrast the transposed glamour in Jules Dassin's film *Phaedra* (1962), where the Theseus character is a Greek shipping tycoon.

Titian's dynamic representation of the god's arrival to save the woman that Theseus abandoned succeeds in conveying a narrative in its entirety (from Theseus' ship, there in the distance, to the constellation – visible in daylight above Ariadne's head – with which the saviour god will assure her immortality).[50] The myth is retold – exuberantly reshown – in all its fullness, and the outcome *is* this exuberant reshowing.

And then with Kane's *Phaedra's Love*, compare *its* opposite (*si parva licet componere magnis* . . .),[51] Racine's *Phèdre* (1677). In Racine's play, Euripides (the chief point of reference) is in part accommodated to Jansenist Catholicism, whereby, despite her best efforts, the heroine is doomed to die, short of divine grace.[52] There is, in the event, an achieved parity between the 'Greek' action and characters and the preoccupations – ethical and psychological – explored in the drama: the exploration, above all, of the way that (as Racine declares in his preface) Phèdre herself, conflicted by her forbidden love for Hippolyte, is 'neither altogether guilty nor altogether innocent'. Her crime is 'punishment from the gods rather than an impulse of her own will', and, significantly, the reality of 'the gods' (active, and actively described, though not, as in Euripides, shown on stage) is not questioned.

At the end of Racine's play, his Thesée is concerned to forget his late wife ('if only the memory of her black deeds could die with her') and to appease 'the Manes' of his son by accepting Hippolyte's love Aricie as his daughter. The Manes – spirits of the dead – are Roman, not Greek; the significant detail of Aricie is (as the preface indicates) derived from Virgil;[53] and the aberrant asexuality of Euripides' Hippolytus has thus been drastically adjusted. Yet in his preface Racine insists that (with help from Plutarch, as well as Virgil) his aim has been 'to keep to the myth ["suivre la fable"] scrupulously'. And in essence the aim is achieved. For all his many adjustments, Racine has composed a drama in which 'the' myth is assimilated and sustained – and here *Phèdre*, like Titian's painting, is representative of innumerable compositions from the classicizing age.

In this light, Yeats's poem, 'Leda and the Swan' (1924), is an instructive modern example. Yeats begins with the assault ('A sudden blow'), dwells on the violent impregnation ('A shudder in the loins engenders there | . . . the burning roof and tower | And Agamemnon dead'), and adds an unexpected question at the end ('Did she put on his knowledge with his power?'). The poem assumes, rather than retells, the tale: the mortal Leda is raped by the swan that is the immortal Jupiter/Zeus ('*his* power'), and gives birth to Helen, cause of the Trojan war, whence both the 'burning' of Troy and 'Agamemnon dead'. Formally, the poem is a composite sonnet, half Shakespearean, half Petrarchan,[54] and the myth is composite too. Yeats's personal

50 The stars in daylight assume Ovid, *Metamorphoses*, 8. 176–82. Titian's depiction also borrows a Bacchic *thiasos* from Catullus, 64, 251–64.

51 Virgil, *Georgics*, 4. 176: 'if one may compare small with great'.

52 Goldmann (1955). Cf. p. 334 below.

53 'Aricia': *Aeneid*, 7. 761–2.

54 Shakespearean octave (*abab cdcd*), Petrarchan sestet (*efg efg*).

point of reference, it seems, was 'Michelangelo's image of Leda and the swan, a copy of which [he] kept by his desk as he wrote the poem'[55] – but Michelangelo's image has no burning, no Agamemnon, and no unexpected question. To any reader familiar with 'the' myth, Yeats's sonnet must seem to have made an idiosyncratic connection between a supernatural orgasm and historical contingency, between individual innocence ('Did she . . . ?') and momentous actions on the world stage: almost a lyric version of chaos theory. The poem's trajectory, certainly, invites reference to issues far beyond antiquity (and Yeats testified that his original intention was political commentary on modern history),[56] though in the event that reference remains as unspecific as the mythic source itself. Here, certainly, myth is conveyed with a powerful immediacy ('great wings', 'staggering girl'), yet not in full; and, as in the other modern examples, it is – still – detached from the outcome.

A provisional formula, then, is that premodern art and literature tend to assimilate myth, whereas compositions from – at least – the last hundred years or so tend to displace and detach. With the contrast in mind, we turn back to our question: *why* myth, and why *still*? The question has received remarkably little sustained attention, and we offer only a sketch of an answer.

The starting-point must be the distinctive nature of Greek myth, in the developed form it acquires in Greek poetry and art. Herodotus famously claimed that 'Homer and Hesiod' created the Greek gods' genealogies, epithets, spheres, and capacities.[57] One does not have to take the claim literally to acknowledge its force. Greek myth belongs to a 'real' religion, and yet the myth – and thus the religion too[58] – is so indebted to Greek writers and artists it becomes literary and artistic itself. In this developed form, Greek myth unites the inscrutable and the realistic,[59] the metaphysical and the experiential – as (say) Euripides' *Hippolytus* unites the arbitrary power of cosmic forces with the specifics of a young man's psycho-social condition and his stepmother's all-too-personal dilemma.

At the same time, a long series of poetic interventions, from Homer (and Hesiod) onwards, invests both individual myths and the mythic apparatus as a whole with a vast narrative interconnectedness, which the Roman appropriators (Ovid and others) further enhance. The complex product of this long process is both rich in interrelationships and yet insistent on the individual myths within it (the integrity of 'the' myth is secure). Conversely, with no theologians to control it, the apparatus is also (despite this integrity) strikingly adjustable in detail – and the more so, the more the entire system shifts away from any religious belief or practice and towards a free-standing repertoire of narratives and names.

[55] Albright (1994) 664. Michelangelo's actual 'image' is lost: the work is known from copies, including a (XVI) painting in the National Gallery, London.

[56] Ibid. 663–4.

[57] *Histories*, 2. 53.

[58] Cf. Hegel, *Ästhetik*, 2. 2, Introduction, 2.

[59] Contrast modern popular culture, where (in the latest of many dissociations) the two are compartmentalized into science fiction and fantasy, on the one hand, and TV soaps and 'reality' shows, on the other.

And yet crucially, despite this shift, the connotations of the metaphysical never disappear entirely. Classical myth retains its metaphysical reach, its engagement with perceived ultimate realities. In this sense, the instincts of the medieval Church were right: this is, and remains, a rival theology. In the same spirit, George Steiner (who *does* consider our question) points to 'myth and its commitment to transcendence'.[60] 'Transcendence' is not the *mot juste* (ancient myth and religion are – almost – all *immanence*, instead), but again his instinct is right. And it is (we suggest) the combination of this metaphysical presence with the experiential-realistic – along, indeed, with the narrative richness, the integrity of the individual myth, and yet the adjustability of the whole – that has ensured the continuance of the pagan mythic tradition, across (and beyond) the arts, in successive post-pagan ages. The responsiveness of different ages is then assisted by secondary factors: premodern Europe's, by the authority of the classical texts in which the myths are transmitted; the modern West's, by the Western tradition as a whole. Paradoxically, that is, even today when classical authors have long since lost *their* authority, classical myth retains something akin to authority, guaranteed by Euripides and Ovid, but also by de Chirico and Racine. And the sense of displacement that is so characteristic of modern reuses is distinctive testimony to the continuing force of *that* authority in its many alien settings.

On the modern side, though, it might be objected that in much mythical literature and art of the last hundred years, metaphysical reach is not conspicuous; and the same could be argued for the eighteenth century (Enlightenment thinkers might have reacted differently, though no more positively, if it had been). Without the metaphysical presence, conversely, the 'tyranny of Greece' that characterizes German Hellenism is inconceivable: think of, not just Nietzsche and Dionysus, but Schiller and 'The Gods of Greece', Hölderlin's *Hyperion*, Heine's 'Elemental Spirits'.[61] But the point is that, while the prominence of the metaphysical varies from case to case, the interconnectedness of the mythic apparatus – Greek, Greco-Roman, post-classical – ensures that its metaphysical premises are, ultimately, inescapable.[62]

One last example. In T. S. Eliot's *The Waste Land* (1922), the Philomela myth puts in another appearance. The setting is modern, a woman's dressing room, but with Shakespearean and other premodern overtones ('The Chair she sat in . . .').[63] And then:

> Above the antique mantel was displayed
> As though a window gave upon the sylvan scene
> The change of Philomel, by the barbarous king
> So rudely forced; yet there the nightingale
> Filled all the desert with inviolable voice

[60] Steiner (1984) 303: see ibid. 300–4.

[61] 'Die Götter Griechenlands' (1787); *Hyperion* (1797–9); 'Elementargeister' (1837).

[62] Cf. our discussion of 'the sublime' (§30).

[63] 'The barge she sat in . . .': *Antony and Cleopatra*, 2. 2.

And still she cried, and still the world pursues,
'Jug Jug' to dirty ears.
And other withered stumps of time
Were told upon the walls; staring forms
Leaned out . . .[64]

The 'barbarous king' is the rapist Tereus; and it is 'Philomel' (Shakespearean form) who 'changes' into the nightingale ('jug jug' is the nightingale's cry in Elizabethan English), now left to inhabit 'the desert' of a 'waste land' (wasted not least by warped sexuality).[65]

In this uncomfortable context, the myth takes its place among 'other withered stumps of time'. Besides hinting, painfully, at Philomela's mutilated tongue, the phrase picks up the 'heap of broken images' that is a premise of the poem and, on one level, its only hope ('These fragments I have shored against my ruins').[66] Like the 'antique mantel' and the – Miltonic – 'sylvan scene',[67] the myth belongs to the past ('withered stumps of time'), yet also the present ('and *still* the world pursues'). In Eliot's elliptical retelling,[68] only a single word ('change') refers, obliquely, to any remotely metaphysical presence (the change was the work of the gods), and yet that presence is conveyed, no less obliquely, by the placing of this mythic 'display' between two other hints. Immediately afterwards, we get the eerily unspecific 'staring forms', and shortly before, a typically ironic gesture: 'a golden Cupidon peeped out | (Another hid his eyes behind his wing)'. The powers, it seems, are still there: staring, hiding their eyes, peeping out. Between the eerie and the ironic, even in this most unpromising of settings, they – 'still' – make their presence felt.

64 *The Waste Land*, 97–106.

65 Contrast (e.g.) the connotations of the allusions to Cleopatra (n. 63 above) with Milton's innocent Eden (n. 67 below).

66 *The Waste Land*, 22, 430.

67 *Paradise Lost*, 4. 140 (the Garden of Eden).

68 The myth recurs, yet more elliptically, at 204–6.

§25

The City

Rome

Among the world's urban settlements, past or present, Rome is special.[1] 'First among cities', said Horace, in antiquity;[2] but what is so special is not the phenomenon of ancient Rome in itself, grand and powerful as ancient Rome was. The ancient city grows into an empire; but the same is true, on a smaller scale, of Babylon, of Carthage, of (briefly) Athens. Rather, what makes Rome so special is the extraordinary longer sequence – of which that ancient growth is indeed the first phase – from city to empire, but then from empire to heart, and head, of Western Christendom, and, finally, to capital of an Italy united, for the first time, as a nation-state.

At a time when over half the world's population lives in cities, 'the city' is the subject of extensive debate, not least in the expanding field of urban studies, whose preoccupations answer to ours in respect of urban pathology and renewal, not least.[3] In 1961, Lewis Mumford's pioneering study, *The City in History*, already offered a pointed comparison between the urban sprawls of our world and the 'overgrowth' of the ancient Roman 'megalopolis', which he read as a historic warning to today's politicians and planners.[4]

[1] Relevant overviews: Barkan (2010a), Bauer (2009), Blunt (1982), Bourgain (2003), Boutry (2003), Caldwell and Caldwell (2011), de Caprio (1987), Edwards (1996), Hibbert (1985), Kinney (2010), Krautheimer (1980), Maddalo (1990), Patterson (1984), Thompson (1971).

[2] 'Princeps urbium': *Odes*, 4. 3. 13.

[3] See e.g. Couch *et al.* (2003).

[4] Mumford (1961) 239: '[Ancient] Rome's chief contribution to city development is the negative lesson of her own pathological overgrowth.'

The Classical Tradition: Art, Literature, Thought, First Edition. Michael Silk, Ingo Gildenhard, and Rosemary Barrow.

Published 2017 by John Wiley & Sons Ltd.

Ancient Rome's 'overgrowth' notwithstanding, modern Rome sprawled to an unprecedented degree in the years of reconstruction after World War II, when new developments to house the urban poor were situated on the fringes of what more privileged spectators, and imaginers, think of as 'the' city. These unglamorous spaces were vividly depicted in the Italian neorealist cinema of the time. A representative case is De Sica's *Bicycle Thieves* (*Ladri di biciclette*, 1948), in which a working man searches the streets of Rome for his stolen cycle. The Rome that neorealism makes visible here includes 'no Colosseum, Vatican, Trevi Fountain, Roman Forum, or monuments, roads and buildings from Mussolini's EUR district'.[5] As we explore, precisely, the Rome of the Colosseum and the rest, we acknowledge this disquieting separation at the outset.

Given its history, there is, in any case, a series of different Romes: different, but interrelated. The ancient city was centred on the Forum and the Capitol; the medieval city, on the Vatican, the Lateran (Rome's cathedral), and the adjacent Lateran Palace (home of the popes until the fourteenth century); the modern city, encompassing all these and much more, looks down the axial Corso towards the Monumento a Vittorio Emanuele II, in front of the Capitoline Hill. And symptomatic of the interrelation of these different Romes are successive uses of that hill, once the symbolic site of ancient Roman power. In 1347, Cola di Rienzo assumed the title of tribune in a ceremony there. In 1538, with papal support, work began on Michelangelo's design for the Piazza del Campidoglio, on the summit, and in the same year the equestrian statue of Marcus Aurelius was removed from the Lateran to be sited there. In 1871, after Italian unification, a statue to Cola di Rienzo was erected. On the slope, and dominating the hill, stands the Victor Emmanuel Monument itself – designed in 1885, inaugurated in 1911, finished in 1935 – to commemorate united Italy's first king, who has his own equestrian statue there too. And during the inter-war years, the 'liberation' of the Capitoline from unwanted 'clutter' was one of many projects undertaken by Mussolini's Fascist regime.

For most of the nearly twenty-eight centuries since the reputed foundation of Rome, the city has been a special site for Christendom; and for centuries the city was under papal control. After the fall of the Western Roman empire, Rome was in the hands of – largely – Gothic or Byzantine rulers, but from the mid-eighth century, effective papal rule begins. Thereafter, popes run the city, more or less, until 1870, apart from a long period in the fourteenth (when the popes are in exile in Avignon) and some shorter periods, including a French occupation at the end of the eighteenth and the beginning of the nineteenth. And though the bishopric of Rome only attains full hegemony over Western Catholicism in the second millennium AD,[6] an ancient understanding of Rome as 'the eternal city' ('urbs aeterna')[7] takes on a new, and universal, Christian significance centuries before. At the same time, that

5 Piepergerdes (2007) 243.
6 Smith (2005).
7 E.g. Tibullus, 2. 5. 23; Ovid, *Fasti*, 3. 72; Ammianus, 14. 6. 1.

understanding is complicated by Christian preoccupations with the realm of the spirit, conclusively articulated by Augustine, in the early fifth century, in terms of the 'civitas dei', the 'city of God'. In the imaginary, henceforth, 'Rome' subsumes three separate, but (again) ultimately inseparable, relationships: the relationship of *this* eternal city with Augustine's visionary alternative, the other-worldly, everlasting 'city' of God; its relationship with the specifically worldly present, both within and beyond the city on the ground; and its relationship with its own pagan past. Even when Augustine himself is intent on a rigid distinction between the 'urbs' of Rome in this world and the 'civitas dei' in the next (his choice of a new word, 'civitas', for *that* city is symptomatic), a relationship is still apparent.

'The' city of Rome is thus a remarkable composite that encompasses the spiritual, the political, and a nexus of aesthetics, ideology, and practicalities on various levels. The practicalities include, not least, successive responses to the ancient city's physical remains. Except for buildings like the Pantheon that were rebranded with a Christian identity (§§11, 20), the Roman city's built relics were largely despoiled or neglected from the fifth century to the end of the fifteenth:[8] Raphael's appointment as superintendent of antiquities in 1514, though not spectacularly effective, signifies a new interest. Thereafter, the ancient remains, long-standing or newly excavated, become reference points in a complicated sequence of urban redesign.

A cluster of different Romes, then – but with continuities between them. If ancient Rome was already the 'eternal' city, it was also a site sacred to the gods ('deum . . . locus', in Ovid's words),[9] while many medievals – like Dante's contemporary, the chronicler Giovanni Villani – refer to 'the holy city of Rome'.[10] Beyond such slogans, however, there is a more unexpected continuity. In a quaint 'conversation' in *Blackwood's Edinburgh Magazine* for May 1889, one speaker points to 'a curious fact' – that 'Rome itself has given us no great names in literature or art.' And more specifically: 'None of the great Latin writers of ancient times in prose or poetry were Romans; and none of the great painters, poets, or writers of the Renaissance.'[11] The 'fact' is overstated, but not hugely. In antiquity, Julius Caesar is an exception, and in the Renaissance the painter Giulio Romano (as his name attests). Other native Romans, before and since, include the painter Artemisia Gentileschi (born in 1593), the poet-librettist Metastasio (1698), the dialect poet Belli (1791), the 'French' poet Apollinaire (1880), and the novelist Alberto Moravia (1907). Whether or not one detects 'greatness' here, it is indeed a remarkably short list, compared with – say – the 'great names' of Florence, even allowing for the difference, at crucial times, in population (in 1338, Villani estimated the population of Florence

[8] The modern sense of ancient Rome as dominated by the Colosseum is a representative outcome of this history; in antiquity *the* iconic building was the temple of Jupiter, in its successive versions, on the Capitol.

[9] *Tristia*, 1. 5. 70; likewise Livy, 5. 22. 2: cf. Brown (1967) 289.

[10] *Cronica* (1320s?), 8. 36. Rome is '(urbem) sacram' and 'sanctissimam' for Petrarch, *Invectiva contra eum qui maledixit Italiae* (1373), 3, following Seneca, *Epistulae*, 87. 41.

[11] Anon., 'Recent Conversations in a Studio'.

at 90,000, several times the size of Rome's – but then, by the end of the sixteenth century, Rome's numbers had grown to around 100,000).

It is, at all events, a 'curious fact' about Rome, and a significant one. This city has never been a place that creative figures come from, so much as one they go to: a city they visit, perhaps work and settle in, then respond to, and help to create images of. A strange phenomenon of a city, then: one where even ancient Romans could feel 'like strangers' ('tamquam hospites', as Cicero put it);[12] but also one from which forced removal was a dreadful fate (witness Cicero, again, and also Ovid, who lamented his exile loud and long).[13] And, as Mumford pointed out, even 'the Christian inheritors of Rome' still felt sufficiently at home to make it the 'cornerstone' of a new civilization, despite their 'searing memories of the arena and their grievous retreat in the catacombs'.[14] For the Christian Cassiodorus, amid the uncertainties of the sixth century, Rome was a city that 'cannot be called alien',[15] while in later ages, especially in and beyond the Romantic age, many visitors declare their allegiance. 'You become wonderfully attached to it', said Chateaubriand in 1804;[16] 'more intimately our home than even the spot where we were born', declared the novelist Hawthorne in 1860;[17] 'city of the soul' was Byron's phrase, in 1818;[18] while the Danish sculptor Thorvaldsen, who settled in Rome in 1797, celebrated the day of his arrival (8 March) as his 'Roman birthday'.

For visitors, Rome is a special place. What other city can claim such a long tradition of guide-books for visitors? – from modern tourists to pilgrims as early as the seventh century ('follow the Via Numentana to the lovely Church of St Agnes . . . restored by Pope Honorius').[19] What other city can claim a comparable tradition of visits from the great and the good, well before the modern age (when everyone goes everywhere)? In the first century AD, the apostles Peter and Paul were martyred there; in 303 the Emperor Diocletian came to inspect the city for the first time, twenty years into his rule; in 689 the West Saxon king Caedwalla came to be baptized (he was later buried in St Peter's); in 800 Charlemagne came to be crowned as 'Holy Roman Emperor', and in 1341 Petrarch to be crowned as laureate; in 1027 Cnut, king of Denmark and England, came to pray ('I judged it most profitable to seek the advocacy [of "the holy Apostle Peter"] with God');[20] in 1369 Byzantine Emperor

12 *Academica*, 1. 9.
13 Cicero, *Ad Atticum*, 3; Ovid, *Tristia* and *Ex Ponto*.
14 Mumford (1961) 238.
15 *Variae*, 4. 6.
16 *Lettre à M. de Fontanes sur la campagne romaine*.
17 *The Marble Faun*, ch. 36.
18 *Childe Harold's Pilgrimage*, 4. 78.
19 *Notitia ecclesiarum urbis Romae*. Some 'guides', however, cater less for visitors than for vicarious 'travellers' – thus (in XII) the *Mirabilia urbis Romae*: Miedema (1996), Summit (2000) 215. And at any given time very different descriptions might be available – e.g. Capgrave's *Solace of Pilgrims* (1449) and the 'Descriptio urbis Romae et de ruina eiusdem' in Book I of Poggio Bracciolini's *De varietate fortunae* (1448). See variously §§11, 14, 17, and Schudt (1930).
20 Cnut's letter to the English: Smith (2005) 272.

Ioannes V came to be converted to Catholicism; in 1510/11 Martin Luther came on a mission for his Augustinian monastery (on arriving, his talk was of 'hail, holy Rome', but a few weeks later, 'the holiest city' was now 'the worst');[21] in 1654 Queen Christina of Sweden abdicated and came to Rome as another Catholic convert (as a patron of opera, she was commemorated, after her death, by the foundation of the Arcadian Academy on the Janiculum).

Then again, Rome has attracted visitors of a less respectful kind. What other city has been so often looted, raided, sacked? – by the Gauls in 390 BC, then, in the Christian era, by Goths (410), by Vandals (455), by the Byzantine Emperor Constans II (663), by Saracens (846), by Normans (1084), by the German mercenaries of Emperor Charles V (1527). So familiar were external assaults during the Middle Ages that one chronicler imagined Rome as victim of such an unlikely foe as King Arthur.[22] But the assaults were real enough, and together with outbreaks of plague in the sixth and seventh centuries and a major earthquake in 847, they help to account for startling dips in the size of the population, estimated at a million, at its maximum, in antiquity (a figure only reached again in the twentieth century) – whereas, when Totila, king of the Goths, entered in 546, he is said to have found only a few hundred people inside the walls.[23] And along with Christian indifference, before and after, these violent events largely account for the disintegrated state of the pagan cityscape as we know it.

Yet, after the medieval age, Rome becomes a very different kind of destination – for artists. The great names of Renaissance and Baroque art and architecture are summoned to enhance the city and its Christian identity: Giotto and Piero della Francesca; Donatello and Mantegna; Raphael, Bramante, and Michelangelo; Titian and Caravaggio; Bernini and Borromini. And after the establishment of the Accademia di S. Luca in 1593, artists come from all over Europe to study, to work, to gain a reputation. By 1620 the critic Giulio Mancini (subsequently author of the first modern art-guide to the city)[24] could declare that there were too many French and Flemish artists coming and going in Rome to make a proper list.[25] Artists came from Spain (Velasquez, El Greco, Goya); from Britain (Joshua Reynolds, Robert Adam); from Germany (it was in Rome's Villa Albani in 1761 that Mengs painted the *Parnassus* that made his name; his friend Winckelmann came in 1755, the German Nazarenes in 1810). The French masters Claude Lorrain and Poussin both lived in Rome for years, and in 1666 the French established an Academy in the city, with a scholarship (the Prix de Rome) to enable students from the Parisian Académie Royale de Peinture et de Sculpture to study there; the institution survived until 1968. Prizewinners included Boucher (1723), Fragonard (1752), David (1774, after four

21 Weijenborg (1957).

22 Jean d'Outremeuse, in his *Ly Myreur des Histors* (late XIV), 1 (II. 218 Borgnet, 1869).

23 Procopius, *History of the Wars*, 7. 20. 9.

24 *Viaggio per Roma per vedere le pitture che si ritrovano in essa* (1623–4).

25 *Considerazioni sulla pittura*, 1. 5.

failed attempts),[26] and Ingres (1801), who later became Director (1835–40). In the course of the nineteenth century, Paris supersedes Rome as *the* place for the artist to be – but only after a stay in Rome has come to seem a *rite de passage* for the aspirational ('what upsets me is to see hordes of young French artists who think it's enough to be in Rome to become a great painter').[27]

With such a history and so many reflective visitors, Rome comes to seem, uniquely, a city of memories – with antiquity a prominent source. Rome is the place where 'all antiquity converges into one' (Humboldt).[28] It is 'the city of visible history' (George Eliot);[29] and 'he who stands on Mont Albano, and looks down on ancient Rome, has his mind peopled with the gigantic associations of the storied past' (the American painter, Thomas Cole).[30] The memories may be generalized and negative: 'everything is decadence, everything is memory, everything is dead' (Stendhal).[31] Alternatively, the memories are poignant and specific: 'as I first approached and entered the eternal city . . . I trod . . . each memorable spot where Romulus stood or Tully spoke or Caesar fell' (Gibbon).[32] In ancient Rome itself, Cicero spoke in such terms: 'when I saw our Senate House ['curiam nostram'] . . . I would think of Scipio, Cato, Laelius'[33] – while Virgil's Aeneas, on the future site of Rome, already contemplates the visible traces of 'men of the past'.[34] Retracing Aeneas' steps, in 1337, Petrarch converted the commemorative formula into a more inclusive set of remembrances: 'Remus died here . . . This is Trajan's Column . . . This is where Peter was crucified' (§29).

A city of memories, then, but – the *Bicycle Thieves* point, again – however unpalatable some of the memories in question ('Peter . . . crucified'), they privilege great individuals and momentous events, and elide the countless anonymous lives lived out in the squalid tenements of the ancient Subura, or the unrecorded horrors experienced during the successive catastrophes that helped to make Rome the strange composite it eventually became: 'bare of laurel, they live, dream, and die'.[35] In the terms favoured by the urban studies of our day, the 'memories' of a Petrarch or a Gibbon belong to the 'represented' rather than the 'everyday' city;[36] they help to construct an 'external' reality related to, but distinct from, the 'internal city', as most of its inhabitants would know it, at any stage of its development.[37]

26 Watteau also failed, in 1709, but was made a full academician in 1712.

27 François-Guillaume Ménageot, Director of the Academy: letter to the Comte d'Angiviller, 1 January 1788.

28 Letter to Goethe, 23 August 1804.

29 *Middlemarch* (1871–2), ch. 20.

30 'Essay on American Scenery' (1835).

31 *Rome, Naples et Florence en 1817* (1817): entry for 29 August 1817.

32 See §17 n. 1.

33 *De Finibus*, 5. 2.

34 *Aeneid*, 8. 312, 'virum monimenta priorum' (on the Palatine Hill).

35 Keats: p. 219 above.

36 Two of the chapter headings in Hubbard (2006).

37 Graham (2002) 1009–12.

With the physical city in mind, rather than its inhabitants (anonymous or great), Freud conjured up a vision of Rome as palimpsest, with a spatial simultaneity of different temporal moments, which he suggested as model for the human mind ('a psychic entity . . . in which all the earlier phases of development continue to exist alongside the most recent') – before himself dismissing such a notion of the city as 'unimaginable and even absurd'.[38] Unimaginable or not,[39] Freud's conception of the layered city has the effect of making the fragmentary past not only present but whole.[40] It thus eliminates much of the emotional force of the 'memories',[41] along with, perhaps, many of the city's particular characterizations and single images.

The city of memories has certainly generated a great variety of these. The holy city, the eternal city, the city of visible history, the city beset by King Arthur, is much else besides. The ancient image of a civilized Rome ruled by virtue, and virtuously ruling others, receives its classic statement in Livy's History and, more succinctly, in the words of Virgil's Anchises.[42] At the end of antiquity, it is reasserted, against the odds, by Cassiodorus ('vast temple of all the virtues').[43] Thereafter, if ancient Rome is under scrutiny, this positive image tends to be overlaid by a projection of imperial decadence – as already in the Book of Revelation (where Rome is 'the whore of Babylon'),[44] or as in Gibbon's majestic account of a declining empire – but without a specific focus on the city itself.

Meanwhile, ruined antiquity and moral turmoil provoke negative readings. 'Morals and walls, you are in ruins, aged Rome' is a representative tenth-century characterization.[45] The same source malevolently reinterprets an ancient palindrome that connected 'Roma' and 'amor', Rome and love: in the context of the desertion of the city by – even – its emperors, the proposition that 'love will come to you, Rome, with sudden passion' apparently becomes 'love will suddenly rush away'.[46] But at the close of the first millennium and in the opening centuries of the second, the preferred target is papal misbehaviour: taxation, simony, venality. In the twelfth century, one satirical tract deplores the power of two new saints, 'St Silver' and 'St Gold' ('Albinus' and 'Rufinus'),[47] while a Welsh cleric converts the accusation

[38] *Civilization and its Discontents* (*Das Unbehagen in der Kultur*, 1929/30), 1.

[39] Cf. Jacks (1993) 2.

[40] Cf. Barkan (1991) 13 and (2010b).

[41] Cf. Burckhardt: 'Part of the pleasure [*sic*] of Rome is that it keeps you forever guessing and arranging the ruins of the ages that lie so mysteriously, layer on layer' (letter to Karl Fresenius, 21 April 1846).

[42] *Aeneid*, 6. 851–3.

[43] *Variae*, 4. 6.

[44] 17. 3–4; the notion acquired renewed currency among Lutherans during the Reformation (as in Luther's own 'Babylonian Captivity of the Church', 1520).

[45] *Versus Romae*, 10: 'moribus et muris, Roma vetusta, cadis'. Likewise, Bernard of Morlaix, *De contemptu mundi* (mid-XII), 3. 737–8.

[46] *Versus Romae*, 12: 'Roma tibi subito motibus ibit amor'; the verse is first cited by Sidonius Apollinaris, *Epistles*, 9. 14 (late V).

[47] *Tractatus Garsiae*.

into an acronym of R-O-M-A itself ('radix omnium malorum avaritia': 'the root of all evil – greed').[48]

At the same time, Rome continues to attract favourable images. Its proud medieval emblem is the lion;[49] in Dante, the awesome impression Rome might make on a 'barbarian from the north' is a model, even, for his own amazement at the sight of Paradise;[50] and in Goethe, the old association with love becomes affirmative again – Rome would not be complete without it.[51] In this more positive vein, the long travails of the city engender sympathetic emotion, rather than moral critique. In a troubled Italy, with the 'Roman' Emperor remote and uninvolved, Dante's Rome (however awesome) is 'weeping, widowed, and lonely',[52] while Petrarch's is the Emperor's 'most desolate spouse'.[53] In comparable terms, but now with faded pagan glories nostalgically in mind, Byron's Rome is 'Niobe of nations' and 'Lone mother of dead empires'.[54]

Varied as these responses are, they have one thing in common: an elision of the topographical realities on which so much of the distinctive character of the composite city depends. One finds an engagement with topography, indeed, when Petrarch is walking through the city, or Thomas Cole looking down on it, or again, of course, in visual depictions like Turner's *Modern Rome* (§17). As we have seen, though, what takes precedence in Turner's painting is a nexus of symbolic values,[55] and the example has a representative significance. It is not so much that 'imagined' displaces 'real', but rather that particular connotations tend to overlay the primary, topographical denotation.[56] One possible reason for this is suggested by Walter Benjamin's reflections on the flâneur, the strolling spectator – a figure created by Paris, and a figure (Benjamin argues) that could not have been created by Rome, because in Rome pre-existing memories are simply so dominant:

> isn't the city too full of temples, enclosed squares, national shrines, to enter . . . the dreams of a passer-by . . . ? The great reminiscences, the historical frissons: these are all so much junk to the flâneur, who is happy to leave them to the tourist.[57]

[48] Walter Map, *De nugis curialium* (*c.* 1190); cf. I Timothy, 6. 10: Benzinger (1968) 111.

[49] Rather than the she-wolf, despite the antiquity of that symbol: Mazzoni (2010) 49–56.

[50] *Paradiso*, 31. 31–40. Dante's Rome: Davis (1957).

[51] *Römische Elegien* (1795), 1: 'Eine Welt zwar bist du, o Rom; doch ohne die Liebe | Wäre die Welt nicht die Welt, wäre denn Rom auch nicht Rom.' Cf. Rehm (1960) 167–80.

[52] *Purgatorio*, 6. 112–13: 'la tua Roma che piagne | vedova e sola'; 114, 'Cesare mio'.

[53] Letter to Charles IV (1350s): *Rerum familiarium*, 12. 1 ('desolatissimae sponsae tuae').

[54] *Childe Harold's Pilgrimage*, 4. 78–9.

[55] Cf. Baudelaire's Paris, where 'New palaces and scaffolding and blocks | And old suburbs are all symbols to me' ('Le Cygne', 1861).

[56] Even when an impression of 'life in the city' is given, as in Shakespeare's presentations of ancient Rome. For Miola (1983) 204, Shakespeare's Roman plays 'bring the ancient city to life'. 'To life', yes; 'the city', hardly. Cleopatra's vision of 'saucy lictors' and 'mechanic slaves with greasy aprons' is representative (*Antony and Cleopatra*, 5. 2).

[57] 'Die Wiederkehr des Flâneurs' (1929).

In Rome, likewise, the landmarks that acquire their own individual images, like the Colosseum, tend to be detached from topography too. That great monument has a long-standing association with Rome's 'eternal' status;[58] in the Hollywood epics of ancient Rome, very differently, it is the 'arena of arenas' and a context for Romans to persecute Christians;[59] for the art historian Federico Zeri, in 1981, it was simply 'one big urinal'; [60] for Byron, a 'noble wreck in ruinous perfection' (§17). In all these diverse characterizations, topography is secondary.

Conversely, though, the more explicitly that responses to Rome acknowledge its composite character, the more clearly the physical fabric of the city comes into view. This is apparent when Petrarch's dual concern for pagan antiquity and Christian order (§29) is brought to bear on Rome. In a *Canzone* seemingly addressed to Cola di Rienzo, Petrarch voices the hope that the megalomaniac tribune will be a 'father' to the city (the 'greater Father' apparently has other things on his mind); he must return the Rome of the Scipios, Brutus, and Fabricius to her former glory, so that 'my Rome shall be beautiful again' ('Roma mia sarà ancor bella!'); not least, he must repair 'the antique walls' and reverse the destruction of holy sites (mockingly accompanied by the sound of church bells).[61] Many verbal snapshots of the composite city work the same way. Robert Gernhardt's satirical poem 'Roma Aeterna' (1991) invokes 'The Rome of the fora, the temples, | The churches, the villas', before noting, bathetically, that the city has 'plenty of old building stock' ('viel alte Bausubstanz'). Rather like Turner, George Eliot's Dorothea sees Rome as 'ruins and basilicas, palaces and colossi, set in the midst of a sordid present'.[62] In such inclusive characterizations, allusion to ruins is common. In a pair of responding poems (the 'Rome elegies'), Hildebert, Archbishop of Tours in the early twelfth century, offers an admiring tourist's account of the ruined grandeur of the ancient city and its attendant divinities – then assumes the persona of the city herself to declare, in Augustinian mode, that 'through the laws and the efforts of these [pagans], I gained the world; a single Cross has given me Heaven'. And we recall Gibbon's vignette of how he first conceived his *magnum opus*, 'as I sat musing amidst the ruins of the Capitol, while the bare-footed friars were singing vespers in the Temple of Jupiter' (§17).[63]

Alternatively, the iconic monuments of pagan and Christian Rome are paired or, often, opposed. In Dumas's *Count of Monte Cristo*, Franz and Albert ask to be shown 'first St Peter's, then the Colosseum'.[64] On his second day in Rome, Charles Dickens asks his driver to take him to the Colosseum – but only after he has experienced St

58 Below, p. 320. Colosseum: cf. Hopkins and Beard (2005).

59 Mumford (1961) 232; cf. Fitzgerald (2001).

60 Lowenthal (1985) 403.

61 *Canzoniere*, 53. 29–56 and 82–4.

62 *Middlemarch*, ch. 20.

63 For Gibbon, 'Rome fell to ruin when the city became Christian and its new leaders destroyed or neglected the former monuments of its classical past': Summit (2000) 211.

64 *Le Comte de Monte-Cristo* (1844–5), ch. 33.

Peter's (which somehow provokes both 'a sensation never to be forgotten' and 'no very strong emotion').[65] For Stendhal, in 1817, St Peter's prompts 'admiration' – but he can only feel 'indignant' at the thought of monuments like the Colosseum and the Pantheon being pillaged for building-materials for churches.[66] Then again, the opposition can be compressed into a single instance. For the Marquis de Sade, in 1775, it was a shock to see the Pantheon itself, 'masterpiece of the *beau siècle* of Augustus', turned into 'a wretched, naked, stripped-down church' by 'that Ostrogoth, Urban VIII'.[67] Byron's vision of the Pantheon, by contrast, was magisterially inclusive: 'Shrine of all saints and temple of all gods, | From Jove to Jesus'.[68]

The construction of new architectural features and the treatment of old ones elicit strong responses. In the Middle Ages, when the remains of ancient Rome were rarely privileged, there were many who would have agreed that the old ruins should be left as witnesses to divine punishment.[69] Humanists began to see things differently. In his *Restoration of Rome* (*Roma instaurata*, 1444–6), the scholar Flavio Biondo suggests that posterity can judge which will last longer: 'restoration in marble . . . and bronze or restoration in letters'[70] – but as yet the implications of 'restoring', rather than imitating, pagan monuments are hardly faced.

After much hesitation and intermittent destruction, Renaissance popes eventually find ways of bridging the gulf between pagan and ecclesiastical Rome. One spectacular outcome is the church of Santa Maria degli Angeli, which Michelangelo designed inside the *frigidarium* of the delapidated Baths of Diocletian for Pope Pius IV in 1563–6. More brutal, half a century later, was the decision of Maffeo Barberini (as Pope Urban VIII) to remove ancient bronze beams from the portico of the Pantheon for reuse in the *baldacchino* of St Peter's. This was the act of vandalism that so affronted Sade, while, in its own day, it inspired a Latin *bon mot*: 'quod non fecerunt barbari, fecerunt Barberini' ('What the barbarians didn't do, the Barberini did').[71] At the opposite extreme, some new buildings extended hospitality to the old gods themselves, notably the *domus suburbana* built by Peruzzi for Raphael's patron, the Sienese banker Agostino Chigi, in 1508–11.[72] Richly decorated by (among others) Raphael, Sebastiano del Piombo, and Peruzzi himself, the villa was adorned with scenes from pagan mythology. Unlike the 'Ostrogoth', then, this *Agostino* had helped revive the *Augustan* age and (one humanist suggested) the 'gods and goddesses' of 'illustrious Rome' had 'come back from heaven, competing to bless the house'.[73]

65 *Pictures from Italy* (1846), 'Rome'.

66 *Rome, Naples et Florence en 1817*, entry for 21 September 1817.

67 *Voyage d'Italie* (1776), ch. 2.

68 *Childe Harold's Pilgrimage*, 4. 146.

69 Cf. the *Versus Romae* and Hildebert's elegies.

70 In the Dedication to Pope Eugenius IV.

71 Anon. (ascribed to 'Pasquino'). Barberini: Rietbergen (2006).

72 In Vasari's time, the building was 'the Chigi' ('Life of Raphael'); in 1580 it was acquired by Cardinal Alessandro Farnese, and is now the Villa Farnesina.

73 The Neapolitan Girolamo Borgia: Rowland (1984).

For many of today's visitors, Rome impinges, in large part, as a Baroque city, the creation of architects like Bernini and Borromini and the expansively-minded popes who commissioned them. This impression reflects notable individual monuments (like Bernini's colonnade in Piazza San Pietro, 1656–67), but also a preference for long straight thoroughfares (like the Via Sistina of Sixtus V, at the end of the previous century) and the 'asterisk type of avenue plan', both conceived in an 'undeviating military manner'.[74] The 'asterisk', indeed, was prefigured in the 1530s by Manetti's Piazza del Popolo and the roads radiating from it, and the 'undeviating' effect, more generally, by the axial symmetries of designs like Michelangelo's Piazza del Campidoglio in the same decade. Nevertheless, the Baroque grand design is something new. It is strikingly unlike the configurations of ancient Rome (the ancient city, even under Augustus, never acquired a coherent shape) and also strikingly influential. The grandly undeviating designs in later centuries by Haussmann for Paris, or Burnham and Bennett for Chicago, or the unrealized plans for London by Wren, Washington by L'Enfant, even Berlin by Speer, are all, arguably and ultimately, responses to Baroque Rome.

In Rome itself, the impetus towards the grandly undeviating reaches a peak with Mussolini's urban planning and the goal of 'Fascism in stone'.[75] Yet Mussolini's ambitious projects for the redesign of Rome were not entirely in line with those of his predecessors. Two premises of the new programme are noteworthy: the assertion of a direct relationship between ancient imperial Rome and its supposed contemporary equivalent; and the projection of the glories of the medieval and Renaissance city – in Fascist credos, widely, if confusingly, lumped together as 'medieval' – at the expense of the products of political 'decadence'. A good many styles and periods might be subsumed under this last heading, including the Baroque,[76] even though the ultimate inspiration for the grand, or grandiose, design was surely Baroque Rome itself.[77]

Mussolini's speeches of the mid-1920s give a vivid flavour of the new programme:

> We must liberate the whole of ancient Rome from the mediocre construction that disfigures it, but, alongside the Rome of antiquity and the Middle Ages, we must create the monumental Rome of the twentieth century.[78]

> In five years Rome will look . . . vast, ordered, powerful, as it was under Augustus . . . You will open up the areas round the theatre of Marcellus, the Pantheon, and the

[74] Mumford (1961) 289.

[75] Variously: Baxa (2010), Gentile (2007), Kallis (2012), Kirk (2006), Lasansky (2004), Painter (2005).

[76] Cf. Lasansky (2004) 3–6, 190–1.

[77] A more immediate point of reference for Fascism was the Victor Emmanuel Monument, with its scale, location on a symbolic axis, nationalist-ideological commitment to continuity with ancient Rome – but also a more overt relationship with Baroque Rome: cf. Atkinson and Cosgrove (1998), Bauer (2009).

[78] Speech at the Campidoglio, 21 April 1924.

> Campidoglio; everything created during the centuries of decadence must disappear. In five years we must be able to see the Pantheon from the Piazza Colonna. You will also free the majestic temples of Christian Rome from their parasitic accretions. The millennial monuments of our history must stand isolated and majestic.[79]

Though the Fascist project was never completed, the outcomes were significant. Notable classicizing monuments were built (like the Foro Italico, a sports complex constructed in 1928–31). Selected sites were excavated and selected monuments restored (with 'disfiguring' details removed). Slum clutter and unwanted buildings – even sixteenth-century houses and Baroque churches – were cleared to isolate and interrelate symbols of 'monumental' Rome. Whole districts were created (the EUR[80] and the Città Universitaria). And major roads, of the grandly undeviating kind, were constructed to connect existing monuments with new. In 1933 the Via dell'Impero (now the Via dei Fori Imperiali) was opened to connect the Piazza Venezia, where the Fascist government had its headquarters, to the Colosseum, while the Via della Conciliazione (work on which began in 1936) connected Castel Sant'Angelo to St Peter's: 'conciliation' making concrete 'the union of church and state imperative to Mussolini's political agenda'.[81]

The ironies associated with the Fascist project are many. One is the unmistakable continuity with that first phase of Baroque planning under Sixtus V (Mussolini himself could hardly have bettered Sixtus's decision, implemented in 1588, to put a statue of St Peter at the top of Trajan's Column, to replace the original, of Trajan himself).[82] Another is the very un-imperial effect of clutter produced by the toleration of newly revealed antiquities (like the remains of temples uncovered in the Largo Argentina, home of cats). And not the least piquant irony is that Mussolini's desire to erase the memory of the 'centuries of decadence' is echoed, in the post-war consciousness, by the response to his own constructions: in Rome, as elsewhere in Italy, Fascist sites themselves are now subject to the same 'politicized form of forgetting'.[83] But inevitably (as Freud might have pointed out) the city of memories subsumes these memories too. In 1935 Mussolini's chief consultant, the architect Antonio Muñoz, could declare, without fear of contradiction, that the urban profile of Rome now owed as much to Il Duce as to Augustus or the popes of the great age.[84]

79 Speech to the Rome City Council, 31 December 1925.

80 Designed for the Esposizione Urbanistica Roma, a major exhibition planned for 1942.

81 Kirk (2006) 756; cf. Kallis (2011).

82 Cf. Lasansky (2004) 4. A Piranesi etching ('Veduta delle due Chiese . . .', 1762) neatly conjoins imperial Rome and Christian triumph by foregrounding the – now Petrified – column along with the Church of the Most Holy Name of Mary (Nome di Maria), whose local cult Pope Innocent XI elevated into a universal celebration in the Catholic calendar after the defeat of the Ottomans at the Battle of Vienna (1683).

83 Lasansky (2004) 260–1.

84 *La Roma di Mussolini.*

Contemporary Rome has its own monuments: Renzo Piano's Parco della Musica (2002); Odile Decq's wing of the MACRO Museum of Contemporary Art (2010); Zaha Hadid's Maxxi Museum of twenty-first-century arts (2010); Paolo Desideri's Tiburtina railway station (2011). And yet again, the relation of this newest Rome to its predecessors becomes an issue, albeit aesthetic rather than political. For one commentator, Hadid's Maxxi is 'a masterpiece fit to sit alongside Rome's ancient wonders', with a 'huge overhang' at the entrance a 'much-warped version of a classical portico' that contrives to echo ancient form.[85]

One very different response to the composite city is appropriations of Rome beyond Rome itself. These include architectural citations, such as imitations of Trajan's Column in capital cities from Constantinople to Paris,[86] and visionary transpositions, like the Pantheon in Claude Lorrain's *Aeneas on Delos* (1672) [*Plate 7*], unmistakable among the buildings on the Greek island. Claude's painting draws on a variety of sources (notably Virgil and Ovid),[87] which yield a vision as authoritative as it is provoking. Aeneas has travelled to Delos to pray for guidance at the shrine of Apollo. Accompanied by his father, Anchises, and his son, Ascanius, he meets the priest-king Anius, shown here robed in white, pointing out the city to his visitors. In his many depictions of sunrise and sunset, remote distance and intricate foreground, water in motion, ruined and reconstructed buildings in juxtaposition, Claude repeatedly explores motions and juxtapositions across space and time.[88] Here, the siting of a Roman landmark in a Greek setting both speaks of such distinctive explorations and more specifically declares that Aeneas' destiny will lie in Rome, and that Rome itself is a city of motion and juxtaposition too.

A millennium before Claude, a more straightforward requisition of the city sees Christian Canterbury planned as 'a replica of Christian Rome',[89] while, across a yet wider time-span, new centres of power have imagined themselves as new Romes. Constantine's rival capital, Constantinople, was officially a 'new Rome' from 381; and in the early ninth century, Charlemagne's Aachen was hailed as a 'second Rome' and another 'new Rome'.[90] Charlemagne gave his seal the motto 'renewal of the Roman empire' ('renovatio Romani imperii'), which, two centuries later, his successor Otto III adjusted to 'renewal of the empire of the Romans' ('renovatio imperii Romanorum') – taking the words so literally that he tried running his empire from Rome itself, until driven out by the city's leading families in 1001 ('Rome was more useful as an idea than as a centre of government').[91] The title of 'Holy Roman

85 Rowan Moore in *The Observer* (London), 'New Review' section, 6 June 2010.

86 Respectively, the Column of Arcadius (erected in 402) and the Colonne de la Grande Armée on the Place Vendôme (designed for Napoleon in 1806–10).

87 *Aeneid*, 3. 73–98; *Metamorphoses*, 13. 623–79.

88 Cf. Roethlisberger (1989) 80.

89 Smith (2005) 286.

90 By Modoin, *Egloga*, 24, and the poet of *De Karolo rege et Leone papa*, 194.

91 Smith (2005) 276: Otto was the first 'emperor' to govern from Rome since early IV.

Emperor', conferred on Charlemagne during his visit to Rome in 800, was retained by successive emperors, nevertheless, until Napoleon eliminated the last traces of this 'empire' in 1806.

For the new powers in Constantinople and Aachen, the name of 'Rome' connotes authority and imperial succession. So it does again, after the fall of Constantinople in 1453, when the Russian tsars identify Moscow as a 'third Rome',[92] and then when Mussolini conjures up a new imperial Rome too – though one of the great founders of modern Italy, Giuseppe Mazzini, had already envisaged a democratic nation in that role, a century earlier: 'After the Rome of the emperors, after the Rome of the popes, there will be the Rome of the people'.[93] Midway between those two Italian 'third Romes', but decidedly closer to Mussolini's, is the Rome-in-progess depicted by Émile Zola in 1896: in the new Italy 'the blood of Augustus' still flows, and a 'third Rome' aspires to become 'new queen of the earth'.[94] Conversely, during the centuries when Rome's imperial sway was a distant memory, and the city itself a distant site for many, we find more innocent appropriations. A twelfth-century Welsh writer explains that Bardsey Island (Ynys Enlli), off the Welsh coast, was known as 'the Rome of Britain' – because 'it is situated on the very edge of the country, and also on account of the holiness and attractiveness of the place'.[95]

Needless to say, though, Zola's image, 'queen of the earth', is more typical of the way the city has been memorialized, from antiquity to the present day – almost irrespective of the power wielded, or not wielded, by the Rome of the time. In the fifth century AD, in the wake of the Gothic sack of Rome, the city is still 'queen of the world' ('regina . . . mundi') for Rutilius Namatianus;[96] 'mistress of the world' ('orbis . . . domina') in the tenth-century poem 'O Roma nobilis'; 'head' or 'capital' of the world ('orbis caput') in Ovid,[97] in Livy,[98] endorsed by Petrarch,[99] and in a wide range of medieval sources besides.[100] In antiquity, more expansively still, wordplay juxtaposing or simply equating 'urbs' (the city of Rome) and 'orbis' (the world) was commonplace ('the city and the world share the same space' was one Ovidian

[92] Lettenbauer (1961).

[93] Speech to the Rome Assembly, 9 March 1849. Mussolini: p. 316 above and Kallis (2012).

[94] *Rome*, ch. 8.

[95] The Book of *Llan Dáv*: Smith (2005) 286. 'By the early years of the second Christian millennium, Rome was Europe's "imagined community" *par excellence*, geographically marginal but symbolically central': ibid. 256.

[96] *De Reditu Suo*, 1. 47.

[97] *Fasti*, 5. 93.

[98] 5. 54. 7.

[99] *Rerum senilium*, 9. 1.

[100] From 1030, 'Roma caput mundi' ('Rome, head/capital of the world') was engraved on the imperial crown. In Notker Balbulus's *De gestis Caroli Magni* (late IX), 1. 26, Charlemagne's appearance in Rome becomes a visit from 'the head of the world to what had once been head of the world' ('caput orbis ad caput quondam orbis'). For Boccaccio (*Decameron*: Fifth Day, Third Story), yesterday's 'head' had become today's 'tail' ('Roma, la quale come è oggi coda così già fu capo del mondo'); cf. Bernard of Morlaix, *De contemptu mundi*, 3. 743.

version),[101] and this conceit, too, commended itself to later ages. For Erasmus, lamenting the sack of Rome in 1527, Rome's fall was 'the fall, not of a city, but of the world';[102] Jerome had said the same of the sack of Rome in 410.[103] 'Rome, you are a world indeed', Goethe acknowledged in 1795.[104] The equation retains its performative value, to this day, in the papal blessing to 'the city and the world', 'urbi et orbi' (notwithstanding the irony that the papal Vatican 'City' is now the world's smallest independent state).

Variations on the theme are many. It was Jean de La Fontaine, in 1693, who suggested that 'all roads lead to Rome'.[105] A thousand years earlier, as if by way of asserting the continuing relevance of Rome's pagan identity both to its world-status and its status as 'eternal' city, a saying, conventionally attributed to Bede, linked the equation to the city's most striking pagan monument: 'While stands the Coliseum, Rome shall stand; | When falls the Coliseum, Rome shall fall; | And when Rome falls – the World.'[106]

In the Western imaginary, Rome is both fixed to its site, layer on successive layer, and displaced, like the new Romes, like the Pantheon in Claude's Delos – or, again, like the ruined Rome of the poet Du Bellay's lament. Du Bellay's poignant 'Antiquities of Rome' were inspired by a four-year visit to the city (1553–7), and exquisitely rendered by Edmund Spenser, as 'Ruins of Rome', a generation later:

> Nouveau venu qui cherches Rome en Rome,
> Et rien de Rome en Rome n'apperçois . . .
>
> Thou stranger, which for Rome in Rome here seekest,
> And nought of Rome in Rome perceiv'st at all . . .[107]

For Du Bellay, here, 'Rome' is ancient Rome,[108] and, as such, a mere 'corpse' – even if 'her brave writings' have made her image 'through the world appear'[109] – but especially now that the spirit of those same 'brave writings' has been claimed, on behalf of French poetry and the French language, by this same Du Bellay not long

[101] 'Romanae spatium est urbis et orbis idem': *Fasti*, 2. 684.

[102] Letter to Jacopo Sadoleto, 1 October 1528.

[103] *Commentary on Ezekiel*, 1, Preface: 'in una urbe totus orbis interiit'.

[104] n. 51 above.

[105] 'Tous chemins vont à Rome': *Fables*, 12. 29. 4. Cf. Alan of Lille (XII), *Liber Parabolarum* (ch. 5), 483 (referring to Christian worshippers).

[106] Byron's translation, *Childe Harold's Pilgrimage*, 4. 145: 'Quandiu stat Colisaeus, stat et Roma. | Quando cadet Colisaeus, cadet et Roma. | Quando cadet Roma, cadet et mundus' (*Patrologia Latina*, ed. Migne, vol. 94, col. 543).

[107] *Les Antiquitez de Rome* (1558), 3; *Ruins of Rome* (*c.* 1590), 3: cf. Zarucchi (1997).

[108] Later in the sequence, though, Rome also 'Renews herself with buildings rich and gay' (*Antiquitez*, 27: Spenser's version). Du Bellay's Rome: McGowan (2000) 187–227.

[109] *Antiquitez*, 5 (Spenser's version). Cf. Du Bellay's *Romae descriptio* (composed in 1553), 130: 'And now dead Rome is her own tomb' ('ipsaque nunc tumulus mortua Roma sui est').

before.[110] The wider 'Rome' of classical literature, that is, has now moved to France – yet another 'translation' that competes with the ideal of Rome's renewal *in situ.*[111] But thanks to Du Bellay, and so many others, the ancient city has achieved 'immortality of reference in its very decomposition'[112] – while composite Rome, in which the ancient city is a continuing presence, reclaims the title of 'eternal' city with every recreation of its diverse images.

110 In the *Deffence* (1549) (§7).

111 'Translatio' versus 'resurrectio': cf. Stierle (2001).

112 Goldstein (1977) 35.

§26
Forms of Government

In these Western parts of the world, we are made to receive our opinions concerning the institutions and rights of commonwealths from Aristotle, Cicero, and other men, Greeks and Romans.

Thus the philosopher Thomas Hobbes in 1651.[1] What held true in the seventeenth century no longer holds true today. As in so many other spheres, those who pronounce on forms of government or their legitimacy rarely invoke classical authorities. They are more likely, instead, to defer to Enlightenment notions of universal rights (presumed to be self-evident and inalienable)[2] or the popular will ('in all forms of government, the people is the true legislator').[3] And yet there is no part of the cultural imaginary in which ancient experience (in long periods, conjoined with the authority of holy writ) has played a more direct role in shaping history, or remains, beneath the surface, a more formative influence still.

Most of the categories of Western thinking about the principles of communal life, and virtually all the customary labels, derive directly or ultimately from Greece or Rome: monarchy and oligarchy, aristocracy and democracy, nation and state,

1 *Leviathan*, 2. 21.

2 E.g. the right to 'life, liberty, and the pursuit of happiness' (the American *Declaration of Independence*, 1776) or to 'liberty, property, safety, and resistance to oppression' ('la liberté, la propriété, la sûreté et la résistance à l'oppression': the French *Déclaration des droits de l'homme et du citoyen*, 1789).

3 Edmund Burke, *A Tract on the Popery Laws* (1812), 3. 1.

The Classical Tradition: Art, Literature, Thought, First Edition. Michael Silk, Ingo Gildenhard, and Rosemary Barrow.

Published 2017 by John Wiley & Sons Ltd.

society and constitution, subject and citizen, politics and government itself. Even a Hannah Arendt, who argues that modern totalitarianism is historically unprecedented (§34), acknowledges the implications of this fact for an informed understanding of the political world. More fundamentally, though, the political theories and practices of antiquity, as read and reread in later ages, have yielded a repertoire of ideals to pursue and nightmares to avoid, that are built into the way Western political realities are constructed. Ancient categories condition the way we think about politics to this day.

Whether a given form of government, or its given name, belongs with ideals or nightmares is often a matter of debate. 'They that are discontented with monarchy call it tyranny': Hobbes again.[4] But it is not only the discontented who revalue terms of reference. In our world, two types of political organization enjoy widespread esteem: 'democracy' and 'republic'. Their cachet is such that even states that are, in any meaningful sense, neither (like the now defunct German Democratic Republic, 1949–90) have appropriated them for the purposes of self-advertisement, or to conceal abuses of power under a veneer of popular self-determination. But the modern inclination to bring these two ideals together tends to obscure the fact that 'democracy' (Greek) and 'republic' (Roman) derive from, and continue to reflect, two distinct political cultures.

Greek political thought focuses on the use and abuse of power; and Greek constitutional vocabulary tends to respond to the specific question, 'who rules and how?' According to Aristotle's classic schema, there are six basic forms of government, depending on the number of regents (one, few, or many) and on whether those in power exercise it in the community's interest or their own. The outcome, in Aristotle's thinking, is a threefold set of *good* forms – monarchy ('basileia'), aristocracy, and 'constitutional government' ('politeia') – and a matching set of *perverted* counterparts: tyranny, oligarchy, and (yes) democracy.[5] The Roman term 'republic', by contrast, designates a matter ('res') of common ('publica') property or interest, reflecting a preoccupation with communal values and contractual law. Unlike the Greek '-archy' and '-cracy' terms, 'republic' does not specify who rules, but elides the question of rule altogether, foregrounding contract and co-operation instead. From Polybius onwards, however, Greek observers look at the Roman 'res publica' with precisely the question of 'who rules?' in mind, and interpret it, in Greek terms, as a 'mixed constitution', with monarchical, aristocratic, and democratic elements held together by a principle of checks and balances; and in due course the principles detected here find their way, *mutatis mutandis*, into the codes and constitutions of the modern nation-state.[6]

Disconcerting as it may seem, most ancient theorists are, like Aristotle, hostile towards 'democracy'. Plato considers it the second worst form of government (little

[4] *Leviathan*, 2. 19.

[5] *Politics*, 3. 7–8. Aristotle considers monarchy the best of the good forms and tyranny the worst of the bad.

[6] Cf. Nippel (1980).

better than, and likely to degenerate into, tyranny), while for Aristotle himself it is simply rule by, and for, the mob. Even in the community-minded age of Enlightenment, such distaste is echoed in France, by Rousseau, and in America, by Madison (both suspect it leads to anarchy).[7] In fact, the consensus that upholds the positive connotations of the word is very recent,[8] while even today there remains sufficient scepticism about the 'democratic process' and its outcomes for Winston Churchill's quip to resonate: 'democracy is the worst form of government, except all those other forms that have been tried from time to time'.[9] A more general, and more radical, scepticism is already a feature of Enlightenment thinking ('Government, even in its best state, is but a necessary evil; in its worst state, an intolerable one');[10] in the nineteenth and earlier twentieth centuries, it is duly reflected in successive – now half-forgotten – anarchist experiments.

Between the end of antiquity and the present day, however, most of the ruling systems to be found in the Western world have involved either some form of monarchy (with kings, dictators, emperors, or princes) or some form of parliamentary democracy. And up to, and including, the early modern age, the prevailing form of government is hereditary monarchy. Throughout this period, kingship is sanctioned by scriptural chapter and verse, by appeals to divine law and a hierarchical cosmic order, and by 'classical' theory. By the Middle Ages the very term 'democracy' has all but disappeared from the political lexicon. An act of translation enables its re-entry into political discourse: William of Moerbeke's pioneering Latin version of Aristotle's *Politics* (*c.* 1260: §15). Its impact is immediate, first of all on Aquinas. In several of his writings, Aquinas defers to Aristotle's sixfold schema, but also gives it an original twist. In his *Summa*, he follows Aristotle in endorsing monarchy as the best of the good forms of government, but then goes on to argue that the very best type of monarchy will include an aristocratic and a democratic element;[11] and after going through his Aristotelian motions in a treatise on *Kingship*, he adds prescient thoughts on the possible legitimacy of tyrannicide.[12]

In the *Politics*, the Italian city-states find 'a new armoury of concepts' to challenge the notion that all governments are God-given,[13] but yet another 'Aristotelian' position is propounded by Dante. In *Monarchy* (*De monarchia*, *c.* 1312), Dante sets out to demonstrate three propositions: that monarchy is 'essential for the world's well-being'; that this essential monarchy is rightly identified with the Holy Roman

[7] See Rousseau's *Contrat social* (1762), 3. 4, and Madison's *Federalist* essay, no. 10 (1787): cf. Münkler (2003) 82–5.

[8] And – as the East German example suggests – is only in part explained by the relationship, or otherwise, between Athenian direct democracy and the representative democracies of the modern West.

[9] Speech in the House of Commons, 11 November 1947.

[10] Tom Paine, *Common Sense* (1776), ch. 1.

[11] 1. 2. 105. 1; cf. n. 5 above.

[12] *De regimine principum*, I (1360s?), 3 and 6. Aquinas's meditation on tyrannicide was anticipated by John of Salisbury's *Policraticus* (1159?), which collates precedents from history, Biblical and classical: Nederman (1988).

[13] Skinner (1988) 396.

Empire; and that 'the authority of the monarch' – specifically of the Emperor – 'derives directly from God'.[14] These propositions are argued with copious reference to Biblical texts, but also to 'the philosopher' (Aristotle) and other ancient sources – notably Virgil's *Aeneid*, which, for Dante, demonstrates that 'the Roman people were ordained by nature to rule'.[15] Ancient evidence is also invoked to support the surprising thesis that monarchy aims at individual liberty (the great model is 'the perfect monarchy of immortal Augustus').[16]

Across Renaissance Europe, ancient history, theory, and the revived tradition of Roman law are brought to bear, more comprehensively, on issues of political legitimacy. In an age of religious conflict, classical ideas are used to validate resistance to the perceived tyrannical conduct of royal regimes – and to formulate viable alternatives, grounded in parliamentary rights and civic ethics.[17] In sixteenth-century England, John Ponet, a Protestant writing in exile during Mary's reign, uses the notion of the body politic and the concept of natural law to turn episodes from ancient history into authoritative examples of opposition.[18] Ponet's definition of the tyrant as 'a monstre and cruell beast covered with the shape of a man' – hence a legitimate target for assassination – has a decidedly Ciceronian ring,[19] and Cicero figures prominently in arguments elsewhere. The *De Officiis* is an important point of reference in George Buchanan's 'Dialogue on the Law of Kingship among the Scots' (*De iure regni apud Scotos dialogus*, 1579), which redefines the relation of law and ruler by giving priority to the former. A few years later, in the wake of the Dutch rebellion against Philip II of Spain, an anonymous treatise, *Political Education*,[20] quotes from the *De Officiis* on its title page,[21] before adumbrating a programme of national education, civic cohesion, and an oath of allegiance to the Netherlands – an argument in large part derived from Cicero's treatise, not least the discussion of oaths in *De Officiis* 3.[22]

In sixteenth-century thought, direct challenges to monarchy alternate with a sometimes dispassionate realism, informed by classical moralizing. Early in the century, Machiavelli feels no compunction about advising 'princes' how to stay in power – though himself (with ancient experience much in mind) seemingly preferring 'republican' rule (§31). At the end of the century, Shakespeare has his Claudius

14 And not (contrary to papal opinion) from the papacy itself: *De monarchia*, 1. 2; 3. 16.

15 Ibid. 2. 6.

16 Ibid. 1. 12; 1. 16.

17 In the German territories, however, Protestant thinkers remain largely within the world of Biblical exegesis in arguing for the right of resistance against tyrannical – Catholic – regimes (as in the so-called Magdeburg Confession, 1550).

18 *A Shorte Treatise of Politicke Power* (1556).

19 Cf. *De Officiis*, 3. 32.

20 *Politicq onderwijs* (1582).

21 Along with a Biblical quotation (from Hebrews, 6. 16).

22 The oath was designed to exclude 'them' (Spanish sympathizers) from 'us' (Dutch nationalists). Cicero himself conducts comparable manoeuvres in his *Catilinarians* – followed by Saint-Just in revolutionary France (p. 328 below).

say, 'There's such divinity doth hedge a king'[23] – but this Claudius is also a regicide himself. Meanwhile, the 'divinity' of a monarch's position is often less remarked on than its cautionary aspects. As Montaigne observes, 'It's no use being called "Sire" or "Majesty" when the gout starts giving you trouble.'[24] Montaigne, too, reports with seeming impartiality on the contrasting positions taken up in 'a couple of Scottish books' – Buchanan's *De iure regni* and Blackwood's *Apologia* for Mary Stuart that responded to it:[25] 'for the man of the people [Buchanan], a king's position is worse than a cart-driver's, whereas the monarchist [Blackwood] places him a few steps above God.'[26] Montaigne's friend, Étienne de La Boétie, ponders, not the rights and wrongs of monarchy, but the phenomenon that its subjects acquiesce in it.[27] And even Jean Bodin's novel analysis of sovereignty (*De la république*, 1576), widely taken to be a vindication of French absolute monarchy, beyond popular challenge and justified by appeal to Roman law, is, arguably, 'evasive' on the propriety of absolutism itself.[28]

In seventeeth-century England, direct criticism of monarchy comes to the fore. A flamboyant example is Henry Parker's *Observations upon some of his Majesty's Late Answers and Expresses* (1642), written in response to Charles I's *Answer to the Nineteen Propositions*. Charles insisted that royalty derived from God and the law and was therefore supreme, above and beyond parliamentary interference. Arguing for the sovereignty of parliament as representative of the people, Parker deploys an array of classical techniques, from mythological invective ('the king . . . embrac[es] a cloud instead of Juno') to legal proof. [29] Under this last heading, he appeals to the legal principle, 'what affects everyone should be approved by everyone'[30] – a principle 'derived from the Roman law governing the management of waterways by private corporations', which then had a long career in canon law, and a presence in the 'guild-republicanism' of the later Middle Ages, before eventually becoming a surprise weapon in the struggle between parliament and king.[31]

In England, civil war, regicide, and Commonwealth government generate a range of polemical treatises. Among them is Milton's *Ready and Easy Way to Establish a Free Commonwealth, and the Excellence thereof, Compared with the Inconveniencies and Dangers of Readmitting Kingship in this Nation* (1660). Like so many others, Milton invokes Aristotle ('our chief instructor'), but as authority for the proposition that 'certain men at first, for the matchless excellence of their virtue above others,

23 *Hamlet*, 4. 5. 123.

24 *Essais*, 1. 42.

25 *Apologia pro regibus* (1581).

26 *Essais*, 3. 7. This impartiality, however, is itself 'placed' by a frank statement of personal preference ('I dislike all domination, by me or over me'), as well as by reflections on 'the disadvantages of high position' drawn from Plutarch and others.

27 *Discours de la servitude volontaire*, first published in full in 1577.

28 Franklin (1992) xiii.

29 Mendle (1995).

30 'quod omnes tangit ab omnibus approbari debet.'

31 Rahe (2000) 292.

or some great public benefit, were created kings by the people' – a suggestion that serves as a point of departure for the novel claim that monarchy is the most primitive form of government. Appealing to the notion of historical progress, Milton suggests that abuse of royal power and the response of 'prudent men' resulted in the deposition of tyrants and the establishment of free commonwealths in the more advanced civilizations. Any restoration of the monarchy now would be a national embarrassment: 'Why should we thus disparage and prejudicate our own nation?', he asks, dismissing any thought of 'a scarcity of able and worthy men united in council to govern us', and insisting that a single ruler is 'the natural adversary and oppressor of liberty'. Writing and thinking within the tradition of Roman historiography, with Sallust and Tacitus his particular inspirations, Milton condemns kingship as tantamount to slavery.

Today's republican commentators rightly emphasize Milton's classical models and foreground, more generally, the neo-Roman tradition of political thought in seventeenth-century England, but, more questionably, play down the importance of the Bible as a point of reference in the political debates of the time.[32] Karl Marx begged to differ. In *The Eighteenth Brumaire of Louis Bonaparte* (1852), he identified the passions (and illusions) of the Old Testament as the main source of inspiration behind England's 'bourgeois' revolution, whereas the heady mixture of ideas that helped to induce revolution in France, a century later, derived unmistakably from classical sources. For Marx, the French revolution resembled a Roman toga party: 'in Roman costume and with Roman phrases . . . Desmoulins, Danton, Robespierre, Saint-Just, Napoleon . . . carried out the tasks of their time: loosening the chains and setting up modern bourgeois society.'[33] Utterly unheroic and unimaginative itself, bourgeois society (Marx argued) required the delusional heroism of the revolutionaries and their imaginative use of Roman history to inspire it to action. Yet once the revolution was achieved, everything – 'antediluvian colossi and resurrected Romanicity' ('die vorsündflutlichen Kolosse und . . . das wieder auferstandene Römertum'), 'Brutuses, Gracchuses, Publicolas, tribunes, senators, and Caesar himself' – *everything* vanished, giving way to the administrative competence and commercial imperatives of sober thinkers like Benjamin Constant. This post-revolutionary generation was no longer concerned with the way that the ghosts of Roman history had played midwife to their new society – or the thought that France had 'repeated five hundred years of Roman history in a decade'.[34]

What such vivid characterizations miss, arguably, is the gradual development of the revolutionary cast of mind, and the contribution of earlier Enlightenment classicizing to it. In Act I of Voltaire's drama *Brutus*, Tarquin's messenger, Arons, and

[32] Cf. Skinner (2008). Bible: Pečar (2011).

[33] *Der achtzehnte Brumaire des Louis Bonaparte*, ch. 1; cf. generally Parker, H. T. (1937). Greek precedents played a secondary, and sometimes eccentric, role. During the constitutional debate of 1793, Hérault de Séchelles requested a copy of the laws of the Cretan king Minos from the curator of printed books at the Bibliothèque Nationale: Vidal-Naquet (1990) 221; cf. Hampson (1991) 47.

[34] Marx, *Der achtzehnte Brumaire*, 1; Sellers (2004) 356.

the eponymous Brutus himself dispute the pros and cons of monarchical and republican rule. Intriguingly, the censors at the time (the first performance was in December 1730) objected – but less to the articulation of republican sentiments than to Voltaire's arguments for an enlightened monarchy.[35] One way and another, a Romanizing-revolutionary constatation of ideas was already taking shape.

The invocation of exemplary figures and their *vertu* – given magnificent pictorial form by David (§21) – is only one of the ways classical reference helps to define the political imaginary of the age. In Cicero's oratory and the historians of the Roman republic (Sallust, in particular), revolutionaries trained in the classics find the eloquence and the ideology to acclaim civic patriotism and to castigate a corrupt regime – though also to engage in suicidal infighting.[36] On 29 October 1792, the Girondin Louvet de Couvrai denounced Robespierre for personal ambition in a speech modelled on Cicero's against Catiline.[37] On 5 November, Robespierre responded by claiming Cicero himself as authority. Notwithstanding a certain disregard for historical detail,[38] his invocation of the public good as a 'higher law' that overruled any concern for legality ('Citoyens, vouliez-vous une révolution sans révolution?')[39] was a deft use of Cicero, who insisted on the same principle to justify the illegal execution of the Catilinarians.[40] And a few days later, on 13 November, Louis Antoine de Saint-Just, 'Apostle of the Terror', went so far as to brand Louis XVI 'a second Catiline' and 'an enemy within', who fought his own people and should be treated as a foreign enemy: a re-enactment of the disenfranchisement that Cicero inflicted on Catiline and his followers, once fellow-citizens, now traitors and foes.[41]

Much of this 'Romanicity', no doubt, is 'posturing that came naturally to a classically-educated society'.[42] More substantial is the French Enlightenment theorizing from earlier in the century,[43] and here the most distinctive contribution comes from Montesquieu, novelist, historian,[44] and political thinker. In *The Spirit*

35 Schuckert (1989) 10.

36 Cf. Schama (1989) 169–70.

37 Jordan (1979) 52; cf. §3 n. 62.

38 As with his story of 'Clodius' accusing Cicero of 'violating the law' before Cicero 'gave an account of his administration' – when in fact the accusation came from Metellus, not Clodius, while Metellus' intervention actually prevented Cicero from giving his 'account'.

39 'Citizens, would you like a revolution *without* a revolution?'

40 *De Legibus*, 3. 8: 'salus populi suprema lex' ('the highest law is the safety/welfare of the people'). The central organ of Jacobin terror, the *Comité de salut public*, likewise sought to advance revolutionary policy through trials and executions that suspended legal procedure: Nippel (2003) 56. Subsequently, Tacitus' depictions of imperial tyranny served as reference points for opponents of the regime: Hammersley (2005) 151–6.

41 Elsewhere in his speech, Saint-Just identified a historical decline since the days of the late Roman republic, when tyrants like Caesar could be disposed of 'without any legal formalities': cf. Linton (2010).

42 Hampson (1991) 50.

43 Sometimes mediated by translations of classical-related English or Scottish texts: Baker (2001) 35.

44 His *Considérations sur la cause de la grandeur des Romains et de leur décadence* (1734) ascribes Roman 'greatness' to early republican virtue and liberties, and Roman 'decadence' to their loss.

of the Law (*L'Esprit des lois*, 1748), Montesquieu develops his own typology of political forms by both rejecting classical theory and reaffirming it. Like the Greek theorists of old, but with very different outcomes, he correlates given forms of government with dominant principles, associating democracy with civic virtue, aristocracy with moderation, monarchy with honour. His typology discards the distinction between good and bad forms of rule by the few and the many, but retains the differentiation between monarchy and despotism, while shifting the emphasis from rulers' motivations to a commitment to law (and educational advancement) and the need for autonomous subordinate institutions to check the exercise of power.[45] This affirmation of institutional checks and balances had momentous consequences, in theory and in practice. As Arendt pointed out, Kant's distinction between 'forms of domination' and 'forms of government' translates Montesquieu's new principle into 'two basic structures': republican government ('based on the division of powers, even if a prince is at the head of the state') and despotic government ('where the powers of legislation, execution, and judgment are not separated').[46] And in the Constitution of the United States, this principle found 'unequivocal expression.'[47]

In constitutional terms, the 'Union' presupposed by the 'United' States is largely the work of the *Federalist* papers (1787–8) by Alexander Hamilton, James Madison, and John Jay. In these essays the figure of the tyrant looms large – but (in the spirit of Aristotle and Plato) the Founding Fathers feared the tyranny of the people as much as royal tyranny.[48] As Madison put it: 'The accumulation of all powers, legislative, executive, and judiciary, in the same hands, whether of one, a few, or many, may justly be pronounced the very definition of tyranny.'[49] Arguing for a model of checks and balances on the perceived precedent of the mixed constitution of the Roman republic,[50] Madison opposed 'pure democracy', which (on the evidence of 'ancient Greece and modern Italy') he thought a recipe for 'turbulence and contention.' It was imperative to ensure personal security and the rights of property, but also to protect the 'obnoxious individual' and minority groups ('weaker parties') from the mob rule of the majority. Accordingly, he advocated 'representative democracy' (noting that it was 'modern Europe to which we owe the great principle of representation'). This solution – the election of delegates to represent the popular will – he called 'republican.'[51]

Whereas 'classical' principles had helped to validate the traditional monarchies of earlier centuries, the modes of political thought, legal principle, and civic value fostered by the classical experience now provided a decisive catalyst for 'the end

45 Further: Rahe (2001).

46 Arendt, 'On the Nature of Totalitarianism' (1950s?) (cf. §34).

47 Ibid.

48 Generally: Richard (1994).

49 *Federalist* papers, 47. Cf. Arendt, 'On the Nature of Totalitarianism': 'a democracy ruled by majority decisions but unchecked by law is just as despotic as an autocracy.'

50 Notional though the equilibrium of competing groups may have been: cf. Nippel (1980) 142–58.

51 *Federalist* papers, 10 and 14. The earliest definitive statement of 'representative' democracy is Hume's 'Idea of a Perfect Commonwealth' (1754).

of kings'[52] and the rise of the modern world-order. With some justification, then, Thomas Hobbes – a defender of royal authority – identified the classics as subversive texts that had promulgated discord and bloodshed:

> by reading of these Greek and Latin authors, men from their childhood have gotten a habit, under a false show of liberty, of favouring tumults and of licentious controlling the actions of their sovereigns and again of controlling those controllers, with the effusion of so much blood, as I think I may truly say: there was never anything so dearly bought as these Western parts have bought the learning of the Greek and Latin tongues.[53]

Since the British, American, and French 'tumults', the political potential of classical perspectives has often been dismissed. Many nineteenth-century thinkers followed Madison in arguing that the now favoured 'representative democracy', in any of its various modern forms, was different in kind from the 'direct' or 'pure' democracy practised in ancient Athens. It followed that the Greek experiment of popular rule was effectively irrelevant – either as a positive model or a cautionary tale. In France such a conclusion was reached by Benjamin Constant, in his 'Liberty of the Ancients in Comparison with the Liberty of the Moderns' (1819). Constant distinguished the ancient conception of 'liberty', which he interpreted as the freedom to participate in politics and shape a small-scale civic community directly, from a modern conception that found expression in the rule of law, absence of state interference, and the enjoyment of civil liberties; and ancient 'liberty', he argued, was hardly suited to a modern individualistic society in which the pursuit of commerce was paramount.

Thinkers of various kinds have taken a different view. Alexis de Tocqueville's *Democracy in America* sought to promote the study of the Greek and Latin classics as a counterweight to the egalitarian tendencies of the American experiment.[54] The cultural historian Jacob Burckhardt saw the democratic 'mob rule' of ancient Athens as a necessary warning, still, for modern times.[55] Anarchist readings have looked more sympathetically at that 'Athenian experience', and the extent to which it 'fully realised the universal nature of the democratic principle of equality'.[56] And some contemporary theorists have challenged Constant's dichotomy between 'ancient' and 'modern', advocating, for instance, the continuing value of 'neo-Roman' thought, including the republican notion of freedom as 'non-domination'.[57] Without ancient experience to draw on, the modern political imaginary would be – unimaginably – different.

52 Everdell (2000).
53 *Leviathan*, 2. 21.
54 *De la démocratie en Amérique* (1840): 'Pourquoi l'étude de la littérature grecque et latine est particulièrement utile dans les sociétés démocratiques'.
55 Cf. Flaig (2003).
56 Small (1964) 344. Cf. Richard Wagner: §31.
57 Pettit (1997); cf. Manville and Ober (2003).

§27

The Order of Things

In his lectures on *Logic*, published in 1800, Kant suggests that philosophy is concerned with four questions. These are: the metaphysical question, 'what can I know?'; the ethical question, 'what ought I to do?'; the religious question, 'what am I allowed to hope?'; and what (in eighteenth-century idiom) Kant calls the 'anthropological' question, 'what is a human being?' ('was ist der Mensch?') – with the first three subsumed under the fourth.[1]

What *is* a human being? Answers to this overriding question have varied throughout history. According to Foucault, 'the human being', special object of investigation for the 'human sciences', is a recent invention associated with epistemic shifts during the seventeenth and eighteenth centuries, and one that may be on the point of vanishing again, 'like a face drawn in sand on the sea shore'.[2] But epistemic paradigms notwithstanding, a concern with humanity and its place in the world is an enduring, even universal, feature of cultural imaginaries – and no less in an age when the overriding question is often answered, more or less reductively, with reference to DNA-sequences, the co-evolution of brain size and linguistic facility, or the ability to cook.[3]

Some model of what it is to be human, however implicit and intuitive, is a prerequisite of all communal living, as of all symbolic practice, from everyday discourse

[1] Kant, *Logik* (the so-called *Jäsche-Logik*), Introduction, 3.

[2] The concluding thought of Foucault's *Les Mots et les choses: Une Archéologie des sciences humaines* (1966): cf. Han-Pile (2010).

[3] Cf. Pasternak (2007).

The Classical Tradition: Art, Literature, Thought, First Edition. Michael Silk, Ingo Gildenhard, and Rosemary Barrow.

Published 2017 by John Wiley & Sons Ltd.

to literature and art.[4] The model may be universalizing, insofar as it focuses on the condition to which every member of our species is subject – the variable fortune and inevitable decline that end in mortality ('All human things are subject to decay', as Dryden put it): 'the human condition', in fact (Cicero's phrase, though in English usage only common from the 1930s).[5] Alternatively, the model is normative and selective, setting up benchmarks of excellence to be missed or exceeded. In such cases, the outcome may be that certain individuals or groups are deemed to be not 'human' at all, but superhuman (approximating to the divine) or subhuman (closer to animals). And these two models may co-exist. Cicero's notion of *humanitas*, for instance, subsumes both compassion for the weak, in acknowledgement of a shared 'humanity', and belief in the superiority of Roman civilization over the barbaric Other (as well as the superiority, within Roman civilization itself, of educated speakers).[6]

Then again, the model varies across cultures – as is already apparent in the art, the literature, and the thought of Rome, Greece, and the ancient Near East, to which the Hebrew Bible belongs. The symbolic constructions of the Near Eastern and Greek worlds evince a distinctive interest in cosmo- and anthropogenesis, and in the place of men and women (and men as against women) within (and as against) nature and the divine; the cultural imaginary of the Roman republic had other preoccupations, though these are increasingly adjusted to Greek thought from the third century BC onwards. But separately or in combination, the views that originate in the diverse cultural spheres of the ancient Mediterranean (Judaic and Christian, Greek and Roman) have had a profound impact on what 'being human' has meant ever since.

For our purposes, a special significance attaches to the various kinds of 'humanism' that have emerged since the demise of the ancient world.[7] As a period label, the word of course signifies the early Renaissance, its revival of classical Latinity, and the symbolic moment when Petrarch (fresh from uncovering Cicero's speech in praise of the poet Archias, the *Pro Archia Poeta*) draws inspiration from the phrase 'studia humanitatis' – 'human(e) classical studies' – in *that* speech for his own Coronation Oration of 1341.[8] But 'humanism' also subsumes various world-views in which humanity occupies a privileged position; hence, in academic usage,

[4] Cf. Barsch and Hejl (2000) 7 and, more generally, Trigg (1988).

[5] Dryden, *MacFlecknoe* (1682), line 1; Cicero, *Tusculan Disputations*, 1. 8. 15 ('humana condicio'), cf. de' Conti and Bracciolini, pp. 333–4 below. 'The human condition' entered educated idiom in the wake of the use of 'la condition humaine' as the title of an André Malraux novel (1933) and two René Magritte paintings (1933, 1935), but in French the phrase is established long before (e.g. Rousseau, *Émile*, 1: 1762). Earlier English usage lacks the universalizing implication: e.g. a review of de Staël's *De L'Allemagne*, in the *Edinburgh Review* 22 (October 1813), speaks of 'bettering the human condition'. Arendt's *The Human Condition* (1958) gives the phrase a rather different force (cf. §34).

[6] Gildenhard (2011) 201–16.

[7] Origin of the term: §4 n. 54.

[8] Variously: §3 n. 32; §29; Reeve (1996) 20–3.

a proliferations of humanisms, 'scholastic' and 'civic', 'Ovidian' and 'Christian', 'second' and 'third'.[9] And the semantics of 'humanism', already expansive, expand further by association with other 'big ideas' – individualism, secularism, rationalism, materialism, democracy.[10] In the perspective of the classical tradition, two aspects of humanist thought call for special attention: investment in classical views of humanity as secular alternatives to those enshrined in the Bible and elaborated in Christian theology; and the belief in the possibility of forming and improving human beings through education. We have touched on both elsewhere;[11] here, with a different emphasis, we bring the strands together.

From Petrarch onwards, the humanist validation of classical literature and its pagan contents frequently takes place within a Christian horizon; and 'Christian humanism' is an eminently appropriate label for, say, Ficino's reconciliation of classical and Judaeo-Christian ideas on the human soul.[12] Conversely, much humanist thought and practice tends to validate the classical as against the Biblical or, more broadly, the secular as against the religious.[13] For centuries, in the wake of Augustine, Christian theology defines humanity primarily by its subjection to an all-powerful divinity, by the stigma of original sin, and by what amounts to a devaluation of human existence in the here-and-now in favour of a life in Christ and a focus on the hereafter. In direct contrast, Renaissance humanists repeatedly endorse a conception of humanity that foregrounds our capacity for reason, the worldly imperatives of love and fame, and forms of self-realization independent of religious parameters and predicated on the inherent dignity of humankind.[14] The direct contrast often involves a specific engagement. Thus, Giannozzo Manetti's *De dignitate et excellentia hominis* ('On Human Dignity and Excellence', presented to the king of Naples in 1452: §8) is a response to a widely-read twelfth-century treatise 'On the Misery of the Human Condition' (*De miseria humanae conditionis*) by Lotario de' Conti (later Pope Innocent III).[15]

Yet direct contrasts and specific engagements are not the whole story. De' Conti himself planned a complementary treatise on the 'excellence' of human nature, while humanists are quite capable of revaluing human excellence downwards in classicizing terms. Poggio Bracciolini, for instance, produces his own *Misery of the*

9 Scholastic: Southern (1995). Civic: Hankins (2000). Ovidian: Zak (2010). Christian: Bequette (2007). Positing a sequence of humanisms is a German habit. Looking back to Renaissance humanism and XVIII/XIX neo-humanism (on which cf. Schauer 2005), Eduard Spranger identified a contemporary 'third humanism' in his 1922 speech, 'Der gegenwärtige Stand der Geisteswissenschaften und die Schule', followed by Stefan George's disciple Lothar Helbing (*Der dritte Humanismus*, 1932) and Werner Jaeger: cf. §16 and Stiewe (2011). Some philhellenic Germans of that time see the Romans (the first to imitate Greek culture) as the 'first humanists': Buck (1987) 13, 479 n. 1.

10 See Vaughn and Dacey (2003).

11 Esp. §§3–4.

12 In his *Theologia Platonica* (1469–74).

13 Petrarch himself is a complicated case: §29.

14 'Dignitas hominis', Cicero's phrase (*De Officiis*, 1. 30. 106): further, Pöschl (1989).

15 Murchland (1966).

Human Condition (1455), in which, with the help of the classics, he reactivates the pessimistic anthropology of the Church Fathers, ultimately advocating a Christian stoicism that identifies control over the passions as the only safeguard against the vagaries of fortune.[16] The idea of existence as a world of contingency ruled by the goddess of caprice is itself a classical conception that challenges Christian belief in divine providence – even if Boethius, in late antiquity, had already formulated an accommodation between the two (§3).[17]

Not everything, indeed, can be accommodated with everything else. In pagan Greece, tragedy is the 'anthropological' (or anthropological-existential) genre *par excellence*; but, as George Steiner has argued, the principle of divine benevolence in Judaeo-Christian thought makes the very notion of 'Christian tragedy' inherently problematic.[18] The implicit opposition here is eventually converted into the starkest of antitheses by Nietzsche ('Dionysus against the Crucified'),[19] though regarded more equivocally by his erstwhile friend Richard Wagner (for whom the 'pure human' is both a Greek achievement and yet also associable with Jesus and the ideal of human brotherhood: §31).

Appreciation of humanity's innate dignity goes hand in hand with the conviction that, to be fully realized, potential requires cultivation. Humanists insist that (as Erasmus put it) human beings, unlike flora and fauna, are 'not born, but formed' ('homines . . . non nascuntur, sed finguntur').[20] Erasmus and others are convinced that the best 'cultivation' is produced by a classical education, in part precisely because it involves the study of literary texts with a 'humanistic' world-view. This tradition of thought is summed up (in the 'second humanism') by Goethe: 'When we confront antiquity and . . . endeavour to use it to educate ourselves, we have a sense that only now do we become authentic human beings.'[21] And this same tradition is reduced to absurdity (at the fag-end of the *third* humanism) by the retiring head of a German academy (the aptly named 'humanistische Gymnasium') who could assure an approving audience, as late as 1966, that the humanity ('Menschentum') of anyone unable to read Plato in the original Greek must be compromised.[22] In the English-speaking world, meanwhile, the tradition, and the terminology, of humanist education is maintained more broadly, at university level, through the 'humanities' – a cluster of academic disciplines dedicated to the study and evaluation of human history and culture, with or without an explicit 'ancient' component, and with or without any such transformational pretension.[23]

16 Davies (1997) 17–18.

17 See esp. his discussion of 'the wheel of fortune': §3 n. 38.

18 'A notion in itself paradoxical': Steiner (1961) 31.

19 The last words of *Ecce Homo* (1888): §18.

20 *De pueris statim ac liberaliter instituendis* (1529).

21 *Maximen and Reflektionen* ('Aus Makariens Archiv', 1829), 660: 'Denn wenn wir . . . als ob wir erst eigentlich zu Menschen würden.' Contrast reservations in *Maxims* 658–9.

22 Erich Haag ('Wer Platon nicht im Urtext lesen kann, dem fehlt etwas zum vollen Menschentum'): Hartmann (1989) 17.

23 Cf. Nussbaum (1997), (2010), and Leavis (1948) on the 'English School'.

But quite apart from notions of humanism and 'humanity', antiquity has engendered a range of more specific figures of thought that have helped to shape the 'anthropologies' of the Western world. During the later middle and early modern ages, the correlation of microcosm and macrocosm associated with Plato's *Timaeus* exercises considerable influence, from Benvenuto da Imola's commentary on Dante (1375–80) to the ideology behind Palladian architecture (§30). Made available, in late antiquity, by Chalcidius' Latin version of Plato's text, Neoplatonic views of the human being as image of the universe (or, indeed, of God himself) belatedly commend themselves to a mind-set attuned to the Book of Genesis.[24] Centuries later, and without theological distractions, Plato's conception of the tripartite soul (articulated in the *Phaedrus* and the *Republic*) reappears, with suitable adjustment, in Freud's superego, ego, and id.[25]

Aristotle's legacy, as theorist of 'the human', is larger but more diffuse, and complicated by the contingent Greek experience on which his theories are commonly based. His celebrated definition of the human being as 'by nature' (*phusei*) a 'political animal' (*politikon zôion*)[26] is a prime instance. The formula has remained a point of reference for many political theorists, despite the fact that Aristotle's 'political' privileges the distinctive specifics of the classical Greek polis (supposedly the only institution within which human life can be properly fulfilled). The formula, again, assumes the hierarchy (uncontroversial in most ages) of gods, humans, animals – but also definitive contrasts between men and women, masters and slaves, parents and children, all presented as equally differences 'in nature'. Not only is politics, for Aristotle, the exclusive preserve of free male citizens. The notion of the 'natural slave' is his invention,[27] and his reflections on the 'natural' deficiencies of the female helped to underwrite misogyny for centuries: 'from "The Teacher" have come many of the standard Western arguments for the inferiority of womankind and for the political subordination of women to men in home and in society.'[28]

In the twentieth century in particular, minds no longer deferential to Aristotelian authority have repeatedly drawn attention to such unfashionable contributions to 'the reality in which we live'.[29] By contrast, assertions of womanly capability from earlier centuries, when the authority of Aristotle was much greater and more specific, rarely make the connection explicit. Yet, in challenging the institutionalized hierarchies of the time, the feminist protestations of a Christine de Pizan constitute an implicit challenge to Aristotle, too – and the same might be said of the embryonic egalitarianism of that late-medieval age: 'When Adam delved and Eve span, | Who was then the gentleman?' (John Ball's slogan, at the outbreak of the Peasants' Revolt in England, in 1381). Yet the peasants, at least, might have found a partial ally in

24 Kurdzialek (1971); generally, Barkan (1975).

25 See e.g. Price (1990), and more generally Armstrong (2005), Bowlby (2007).

26 *Politics*, 1. 2.

27 Ibid. 1. 5: cf. e.g. Heath (2008).

28 Horowitz (1976) 183.

29 Arendt: preface to the first edition of *The Origins of Totalitarianism* (1951).

the ancient Stoa. Against normative differentiation of human individuals into distinct 'natural' types, Stoic philosophy envisaged a common humanity beyond the contingent accidents of class or status. Centuries after the peasants' uprising, Enlightenment thinkers reaffirm the principle, and duly write it into the American *Declaration of Independence* (1776), with its claim that all human beings are created equal (the document, of course, says 'all men') and have certain fundamental rights in common.

No less dismissive of human stratification, but otherwise very different, is the great gospel of flux, Ovid's *Metamorphoses*. Ovid's poem is among the many points of reference for Pico della Mirandola's definition of humanity in his *De dignitate hominis* ('On Human Dignity', 1486: §8). Here, the human being becomes a metamorphic being, with the God-given freedom to move up or down the ontological ladder, and no fixed place in the order of things.

In Pico's early modern world and the medieval world before it, understandings of the human being and 'his' place in the cosmos are often mediated through numerical and other schematic systems. 'The ladder' – the *scala naturae* – is one such. Others include the circles of Dante's Hell, the 'Tree of Nature and Logic' of Dante's contemporary Ramon Llull, in which the universe of knowledge is schematized arboreally, and the 'great chain of being', which (like the ladder) subsumes and organizes the entire cosmos. No doubt because anything resembling such schemata survives today chiefly in Christian contexts (like the doctrine of the Trinity), this extensive apparatus tends to strike a modern mind as essentially Christian too – yet all of these systems are influenced by classical paradigms: the Aristotelian presence in Dante is representative.[30]

Many schemata share the same dual ancestry, including some that foreground numbers.[31] The schematic sevens are a case in point. In Biblical tradition, seven is special, from Genesis (as the number of days of Creation) to the Book of Revelation (as the ubiquitous symbolic number). Yet the 'seven ages of man', immortalized by Shakespeare's Jaques, are already established in ancient Greek medical theory.[32] So too – down the numerical scale – is the doctrine of the four temperaments or 'humours', based on the supposed balance, or imbalance, of the bodily fluids: blood, phlegm, bile, and black bile. Already explicit in a Hippocratic treatise, the aptly named *Nature of Man*, the doctrine is adumbrated within the Galenic corpus, and eventually correlated with the four elements (earth, air, fire, water), the four seasons, and even the four Evangelists. In the early modern era, the doctrine shapes literary understandings of human behaviour (Ben Jonson's *Every Man in His Humour*, 1598, is one among many), and with the perceived special status of 'melancholy'

[30] Dante: Boyde (1981). Llull, *Logica nova* (1303) ('Arbor naturalis et logicalis'): Johnston (1987) 157–75. *The Great Chain of Being* is the title of Lovejoy (1936); cf. Curtius (1953) 108–13 on Bernard Silvestris's *De universitate mundi* (*c.* 1150).

[31] Schimmel (1993) cites numerous examples.

[32] *As You Like It*, 2. 7; ps.-Hippocrates, *De Septimanis*.

(*melan-cholia*: preponderance of 'black bile') this antique schema extends its influence into the modern age.[33]

Greek constructions of the human are central to the visual imaginary too. As Guillaume Apollinaire, impresario of Cubism, observed, 'Greek art had a purely human conception of beauty: it took mankind as the measure of perfection'[34] – and the emphasis the Greeks gave the human form (and their reverence for the divine in human form) has ensured that Western visual culture, from the Renaissance onwards, is dominated by 'anthropological' conceptions. The contrast with Islamic tradition is noteworthy; so too, within Western traditions themselves, latter-day endeavours, in the wake of Cubism and other modernist movements, to create the non-representational, suprahuman, 'sublime' (§30).

Arguably the most remarkable single reception of classical 'anthropology' in the visual arts involves the Neoplatonic/Neopythagorean analogies between temple architecture, the geometry of the universe, and the proportions and symmetries of the human body (microcosm and macrocosm again), as posited by the Roman architectural theorist Vitruvius and visualized in Leonardo da Vinci's 'Vitruvian Man' (§30). More pervasive, though, is the reading of the human being in terms of the ideal body, male or female. The proposition is as fundamental to Renaissance and subsequent art as to the modern fashion industry, and it is a product, ultimately, of the classical tradition. Since the Renaissance, of course, classicizing art is peculiarly associated with the naked or near-naked body (§33), and a comparable association is apparent, again, in today's world, across a range of modern-cultural or popular-cultural forms, from photography to body-building.[35] If ancient texts educate the mind, ancient art can still inspire the properly-formed body. As Hollywood strong-man turned politician, Arnold Schwarzenegger, noted: 'at the end of the nineteenth century a new interest in muscle building arose, not muscle as a means of survival or of defending oneself, but a return to the Greek ideal – muscular development as a celebration of the human body.'[36]

But if today's world still finds ways to defer to the classical tradition, it also, and more representatively, challenges the tradition, and, with it, traditional understandings of humanity itself. For eighteen months, between 2005 and 2007, Marc Quinn's nude sculpture of the disabled artist Alison Lapper in an advanced state of pregnancy was displayed on the Fourth Plinth in London's Trafalgar Square, within sight of the National Gallery, where a wealth of 'traditional' nude paintings, from Titian to Cézanne, are on show. Through its nudity, its allusion to the Venus de Milo, its material (white Carrera marble), and its setting, *Alison Lapper Pregnant* duly evoked classical-body ideals, only to rewrite them in favour of human realities which the

[33] Ps.-Galen, *De Humoribus*; see variously Arikha (2007), Bell (forthcoming), Nutton (2010b), Schmidt (2007), esp. 1–17.

[34] 'La Peinture nouvelle: Notes d'art' (1912).

[35] Photography: Turner (2011).

[36] In his *Encyclopedia of Modern Bodybuilding* (1985): Wyke (1997b) 51. Cf. §12.

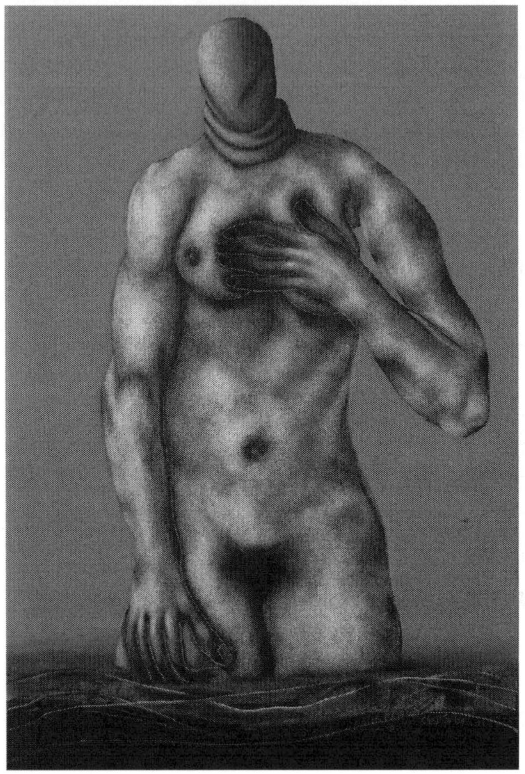

Figure 8 Chris Gollon, *Venus (I)*. Source: used by permission of the artist.

tradition has tended to repress and exclude. Quinn himself saw it in such terms – as a 'celebration of a wider notion of beauty and humanity'.[37]

Other contemporary artists have joined the fray. In a series of paintings on 'Being Human', another British artist, Chris Gollon, portrays Olympian deities in anything but classic fashion.[38] In Gollon's art, the traditional measures of the human body and its divine counterparts are subjected to a drastic refiguration. A prime example, from 2009, is *Venus (I)* [*Figure 8*], his brute reworking of Botticelli's *Birth of Venus* (*c.* 1485), an image that, for many, evokes the Renaissance 'rebirth' of classical ideals. Gollon's goddess, too, is rising from the sea, but unlike Botticelli's, her head is hooded, her physique is coarse, and she has dropped part of her pudica pose, revealing a black bush of pubic hair.

The uncomfortable questions posed by these works of Quinn and Gollon challenge humanism, its values, and its implications. Throughout its history, humanism has been a contested ideal, and is certainly so in recent times. Critiques have come

[37] Quinn (2006) 1.
[38] Gildenhard (2009).

from relativists, suspicious of any universalizing, from idiosyncratic voices like Heidegger's (for whom, not the human being, but Being itself has primacy), and from many who have felt that such value is undermined by modern barbarities (*If This Is a Man . . .*).[39] For some, the very 'meaning of the West' comes under scrutiny when humanism is at issue.[40] While several recent defenders have sought to reclaim humanism in terms of a 'transcultural' or strictly 'ontological' universality,[41] and in either case may well be speaking for a silent majority, there is no doubt that traditional understandings of distinctive human value are less easily articulated in the face of genetic manipulation, searches for extra-terrestrial life, and the prospect of ecological catastrophe. Some, indeed, believe that Western civilization has already entered a post-humanist phase, whose outcomes can hardly be predicted.[42]

> Concerned, but not disconsolate, we stand aside for the moment, contemplative beings who are permitted to be witnesses of these tremendous struggles and transitions. Alas – such is the magic of those struggles that anyone who looks must also join in![43]

[39] The English title of Primo Levi's first testimony to Nazi atrocity: *Se questo è un uomo* (1947). In that book, value survives: Epilogue, below.

[40] Cohen (2003) vii.

[41] Honig (2010), Levinas (2003), Rüsen and Laass (2009), Vaughn and Dacey (2003).

[42] Variously: Chambers (2001), Fuller (2011).

[43] Nietzsche, *The Birth of Tragedy*, 15.

Part IV

Making a Difference

§28
Preface

In Part IV of the book we consider some of the very different ways in which Western culture and its preoccupations have been shaped by particular ancient texts or by particular respondents to the ancient world from later ages. We discuss three such ways of 'making a difference', with each of the three discussions focused on a contrasting pair of case histories, on the premise that such contrasts are themselves a distinctive method of approaching, and illuminating, their subjects.

We begin, in §29, with a pair of 'originators': great creative-critical figures, whose importance within Western cultural history is inseparable from important rereadings of ancient culture. Various figures fit this description, from Augustine at the end of antiquity to Nietzsche in the nineteenth century. We look at a pair whose rereadings contributed significantly to the development of (respectively) Western poetry and art history, the Renaissance and German Hellenism: Petrarch, from the fourteenth century, and Winckelmann, from the eighteenth. Such figures are 'founders of a discourse', in Foucault's sense.[1] Their achievements recall what Auden said of Freud, 'To us he is no more a person | Now but a whole climate of opinion'[2] – except that the logic of 'being human' demands that we acknowledge all such originators as 'persons', still, as well.

In §30 our attention turns to texts. Certain writings from the ancient world have made a difference, by becoming 'points of departure' for new traditions. In some cases, this involves texts that were already notable points of reference in antiquity,

[1] 'Qu'est-ce qu'un auteur?' (1969).
[2] 'In Memory of Sigmund Freud' (1939).

The Classical Tradition: Art, Literature, Thought, First Edition. Michael Silk, Ingo Gildenhard, and Rosemary Barrow.

Published 2017 by John Wiley & Sons Ltd.

perhaps as leading representatives of a genre, like Plato's dialogues or Juvenal's *Satires*. More surprisingly, perhaps, some have had significantly more prestige and influence after antiquity than in antiquity itself. A distinctive Roman example here is Vitruvius' *De Architectura*. The treatise is hugely influential as a guide and sourcebook for architects and architectural theorists, from Renaissance Italy to eighteenth-century England (an unusual trajectory, in that the influence of practical texts is sharply restricted after the Renaissance: §5). In particular, the treatise provides the inspiration for 'the classical orders' and for an understanding of architecture in a human-existential perspective, both of which can claim a special significance in the Renaissance and beyond.

We pair the *De Architectura* with one of the most admired works of ancient literary theory, *On the Sublime*. The central surviving texts in this field present a curious set of contrasting case histories in their own right. Horace's *Ars Poetica* is an impressive poem by a great poet, and a central text for later antiquity, the Middle Ages, and the Renaissance. Aristotle's *Poetics* is a notable work by a great philosopher, but one with little direct influence in antiquity, and (unlike most of Aristotle) none on the Latin West in the Middle Ages. From the later Renaissance to the seventeenth century, the *Poetics* does become hugely influential on dramatic practice, helping to generate, above all, the powerful tradition of tragic drama in seventeenth-century France, but also to determine both the understandings and the practices of poetic language up to the Romantic age and beyond (§§22, 35). The case history of *On the Sublime* is different again. This is a Greek treatise with, seemingly, no status at all in antiquity, but a huge and continuing influence of the most eccentric kind, from the later seventeenth century to the present day. Given that the relation between the *De Architectura* and its legacy proves to be eccentric too, 'points of departure' is certainly an appropriate heading for both these texts.

Finally, in §31, 'Ideas and Action', we look at a relationship that has raised awkward questions for centuries. A life of thought and a life of action – the *vita contemplativa* and the *vita activa* – were variously evaluated in the Middle Ages and the Renaissance. When the alternatives become a one-way sequence – ideas *into* action – assessment can be peculiarly difficult. Our concern is with the phenomenon of innovators within the classical tradition who have 'made their difference' by developing programmes of action from classical sources. Such a pattern is not the norm. In the nineteenth century, Karl Marx is both a notable contributor to the classical tradition and the progenitor of a programme of action on an unprecedented scale, but the two are essentially separate. 'Philosophers have only interpreted the world in their various ways: the point is to change it': Marx's celebrated proclamation[3] is paradigmatic and self-evidently independent of ancient paradigms – even if precedents might be found in Plato, above all. Conversely, the cultural-political critiques sketched by (say) Michel Foucault, in more recent times, have been deeply implicated in classical-derived perspectives, but hardly in serious political *praxis* (perhaps their most characteristic failing, in the eyes of their Marxist critics).

[3] *Theses on Feuerbach* (composed in 1845), 11.

Intellectuals fascinated by politics have sometimes tried to act as educators, advisors, or ideologues to those in power – from Plato and Dionysius, tyrant of Syracuse, to Petrarch and Cola di Rienzo, to the notorious case of Heidegger and Hitler (§34). Rather differently, artists in various media – from Virgil to Sergei Eisenstein – have celebrated extraordinary deeds on the grand scale, often in return for patronage of one sort or another. And a related but distinctive case here is the composer Richard Wagner, celebrator of Germanic myth and (eventually) German nationhood, who (for years under the patronage of Ludwig II of Bavaria) directed his energies towards the creation of a new culture, centred on a new music-theatre on the Greek model.

Different again is the figure who first establishes a reputation in public life, and then, marginalized by age or circumstances, takes up his pen. In such cases, an autobiographical and apologetic subtext is a likely outcome, serving as a displacement activity or else as a means of retaining a voice in (or facilitating a return to) public affairs. A straightforward example from modern times is Winston Churchill, and, from antiquity, Cicero, who composed most of his philosophical corpus while politically marginalized, after Caesar's rise to the dictatorship. In destiny, if not in spirit, his kin from early modern times is the sometime public figure Niccolò Machiavelli, connoisseur of political theory and practice, ancient and modern; and our third contrasting pair consists of Machiavelli, from the sixteenth century, and Wagner, from the nineteeth.

§29
Originators

In a letter to his friend, the Dominican Giovanni Colonna, Petrarch, writing in Latin (as in most of his writings), recalls his first experience of Rome, in Colonna's company, in 1337:

> We would wander side by side . . . not only in the city but round the city ['nec in urbe tantum sed circa urbem'], and with each step find something to make us think and talk . . . Remus died here . . . Here poor Lucretia fell on her sword . . . Here Caesar triumphed . . . This is Trajan's Column . . . On this site, the story goes, the Sybil showed the infant Christ to the elderly Augustus . . . This is Augustus' house, on the Via Flaminia . . . This is where Peter was crucified . . . But . . . who today is more ignorant of the history of Rome than the citizens of Rome? . . . Nowhere is Rome less known than in Rome. Yet in truth, it is not just ignorance that I deplore – though what is worse than ignorance? – but the flight and exile of so many virtues. For who can doubt that if Rome did begin to know herself, she would rise again, on the spot ['ilico surrectura est']? . . . [W]ith the broken ruins before our eyes ['ruinarum fragmenta sub oculis'] . . . we talked about history . . . philosophy . . . art . . . you asked me to spell out my views on the origin of the liberal and mechanical arts . . . though I insisted I had nothing new to say, either of my own or from any other source.[1]

The studied precision so apparent here is characteristic of Petrarch's writing, Latin or Italian. One notes the fastidious balanced qualifications ('not only in the city but round the city'; 'either of my own or from any other source'). A pervasive

[1] *Rerum familiarium*, 6. 2.

The Classical Tradition: Art, Literature, Thought, First Edition. Michael Silk, Ingo Gildenhard, and Rosemary Barrow.

Published 2017 by John Wiley & Sons Ltd.

self-consciousness is evident, even in the protestations of conventional opinion ('nothing new to say'), alongside matter-of-fact acknowledgement of *idées reçues* ('the story goes'). The intense pressure of Petrarch's voluminous reading both shapes his proto-humanist Latin and underlies a striking oscillation between actual sights ('This is Trajan's Column') and superimposed 'memories' derived from ancient texts ('Remus died here').[2] 'One insatiable desire consumes me,' says Petrarch elsewhere: 'books.'[3]

All this is secondary, though, to the uncompromising antithesis between a glorious past, when Rome *was* Rome, and today's 'broken ruins' and absent virtues ('so many virtues'). The possibility of renewal, of some future hope, is allowed, but attenuated: Rome *would* 'rise again', *if* Rome could only 'begin to know herself'. Knowledge, it seems, is key ('what is worse than ignorance?'), but scarce ('Nowhere is Rome less known than in Rome'). On reflection, the assertive qualification added to the hope makes it more remote, not less: Rome would rise again – 'on the spot'?

Four centuries on, a relatable configuration of attitudes is visible in the writings of Winckelmann. The most celebrated of Winckelmann's works are the short *Reflections on the Imitation of Greek Painting and Sculpture* (*Gedanken über die Nachahmung der griechischen Werke in der Malerei und Bildhauerkunst*, 1755) and the much grander *History of the Art of Antiquity* (*Geschichte der Kunst des Altertums*, 1764). Between these two, and during the composition of the latter, he spent time in Naples, inspecting, in particular, the new finds at Herculaneum, which he reported in a *Letter on the Discoveries at Herculaneum* (*Sendschreiben von den herculanischen Entdeckungen*, 1762). This is a passage from the *Letter*, reviewing the quality of the utensils ('especially the vessels') lately brought to light by the excavators of the lost town:

> particular attention should be paid to their gracefulness ['Zierlichkeit'], in which none of our modern artists are able to match the ancients. Basically, their forms are founded on the principles of good taste ['guter Geschmack']; they resemble a beautiful young man who without conscious effort develops grace ['die Gratie'] in his bearing . . . Imitation of such grace could usher in an utterly different taste and lead us away from artifice ['das Gekünstelte'] towards nature, where art ['die Kunst'] can show itself. The beauty of these vessels comes through in the softly curving lines of their forms, which, as in beautiful young bodies, are emergent rather than fully grown . . . The sweet sensation on the eye from such forms is like the feel of delicate soft skin . . . [S]ensation ['Empfindung'] and reflection ['Überlegung'] should guide us towards the beautiful simplicity ['schöne Einfalt'] of the ancients . . . Once they recognised something as beautiful, they . . . stuck with it . . . [whereas] we lose our way in stupid imitation ['wir irren in törichter Nachahmung herum'].[4]

The differences between the Winckelmann and the Petrarch of these samples are plain enough. Winckelmann's sensibility (and not just his professional concern with

[2] Cf. §17 n. 54.

[3] *Rerum familiarium*, 3.18: 'una inexplebilis cupiditas me tenet . . . libris satiari nequeo.'

[4] *Sendschreiben* (1762), p. 62.

artefacts) is visual, not verbal. He insists on both 'sensation' and 'reflection', but it is the senses, and especially the 'sensation on the eye', that is determinative. Autopsy is central: 'the story goes' would have no place here.[5] Petrarch's 'insatiable desire' may be for books; Winkelmann's is for forms, for body and beauty, for 'beautiful young bodies'; it is not the moral-intellectual but the aesthetic, informed very obviously by the homoerotic ('a beautiful young *man*'), that confronts us. And if Petrarch is a proto-humanist, preoccupied with ancient Rome, Winckelmann is (almost) a proto-Romantic, inspired by the revelation of Hellenic art and beauty. And though most of the 'classical Greek' art he encounters throughout his career in fact consists of Greco-Roman copies, and though, in the passage quoted (as more generally) the awkwardness of finding Hellas in 'Roman' Herculaneum is implicit,[6] the terms in which he proclaims the merits of his Herculanean artefacts are the terms in which he sums up the merits of Greek art elsewhere. In particular, the 'beautiful simplicity of the ancients' here echoes the 'noble simplicity' famously conjoined with 'calm grandeur' that he ascribes to 'the Greek masterpieces' a few years earlier.[7] An incipient Romantic mind-set, meanwhile, is presaged by the antithesis between negative 'artifice' and positive 'art' and 'nature'.

Yet amidst these differences, Winckelmann shares with Petrarch a passion for the classical past, along with a profound dissatisfaction with the present[8] and a glimpse of a new age (sharper certainly in Winckelmann's case: '*could* usher in', '*should* guide'). Then again, in both cases, there is a perceptible contrast between the intensity of that passion and an undemonstrative acquiescence in the conventional. With Winckelmann, one sees this in the deference to 'good taste' (a guiding principle of the neoclassical age),[9] as also in his acceptance of the time-honoured principle of 'imitation'. On the one hand, today's world practises '*stupid* imitation'. On the other, the principle itself is sacrosanct: 'imitation' of Herculanean-Hellenic 'grace' is precisely what is required to 'usher in an utterly different taste'.[10] With Petrarch, one sees such acquiescence above all in his Christian allegiance – or, more precisely, in the matter-of-fact alternations of pagan and Christian in the catalogue of memories

[5] 'With the exception of the *Reflections*, Winckelmann's writings on classical art were expressions of his opinions about what he had seen and studied himself': Mattusch (2011) 52. Which does not, indeed, make him a pure empiricist: Decultot (2010).

[6] 'The eighteenth-century finds from Herculaneum and Pompeii . . . were discovered just in time for Winckelmann to include them in his chapter [4] on "Art of the Greeks" [in the *History*] . . . It is clear, however, that [he] was not entirely comfortable with the notion that Greek works had been found in Italy, for in the *History* . . . he rarely specified what date he wanted to assign to [them]': Mattusch (2011) 49.

[7] 'Edle Einfalt und stille Grösse': *Reflections*, 4.

[8] Though in the *Reflections*, in particular, Winckelmann praises Michelangelo, Raphael, Poussin, and other moderns.

[9] From Baltasar Gracián – for whom 'the hero' (§21) should have 'an exquisite taste' (*El Héroe*, 1637, ch. 5) – to Kant's *Kritik der Urteilskraft* (1790–3), where 'the judgement of taste' is presented as a 'subjective universal'. On the combination of 'taste' and Hellenism in Winckelmann, cf. Szondi (1974) 22–9.

[10] 'Grace': cf. p. 106 above.

and sights. In the larger and longer perspective of Petrarch's entire career, such 'alternations' can be seen to entail significant conflicts – yet the sense of acquiescence remains.

But one thing, above all, the two men share. Implicit in the passages quoted, and spelled out more fully elsewhere, is a personal engagement which both animates and informs new appraisals of the ancient world. Consider this self-revelation, from another of Petrarch's letters, which also shows just how distant, in his view, the prospects of renewal actually are:

> I am always talking and writing, not so much to assist our age ['saeculo meo'], whose wretchedness is now beyond hope ['iam desperata'], as to unburden myself and console my spirit . . . I write for myself, and when I am writing, I am in eager conversation with our ancestors ['cupide cum maioribus nostris versor'] in the only way I know; and I am happy to forget those that an unkind fate forces me to live among. All my mental powers I exert to escape from them and to seek out these others. Whereas the sight of the men of today seriously offends me, [just] remembering those and their magnificent deeds and glorious names fills me with unbelievable, incalculable joy . . . I am happier with the dead than the living.[11]

Petrarch's 'conversation' with his 'ancestors' has an intimacy about it (and elsewhere he does, literally, address letters to Cicero and others); so too his pessimism about 'our age'.

Compare the speech Petrarch delivers in Rome on the occasion of his laurel coronation in 1341: a Latin oration (the *Collatio laureationis*) inspired by Cicero's *Pro Archia*, which Petrarch had himself rediscovered, eight years earlier, and in which the orator Cicero praises the poet's calling, as the poet Petrarch does, rather differently, now. With reference to poetry in particular, and philosophy and 'the other arts' more broadly, Petrarch laments that, in his day, men are too preoccupied to attend to 'such studies' – unlike the age when poets were properly honoured: ancient Greece and, especially, Augustan Rome. He himself, meanwhile, is animated by three desires: to bring honour 'to this city, to my own city and to all Italy'; to win 'personal glory' ('propria gloria'); and to inspire others to follow in his path (he will be their guide, their 'dux'). There is no sense here that Petrarch actually foresees the Renaissance of which he is rightly regarded as a forerunner. Rather, he asserts his commitment to poetry and to antiquity, which for him is all one commitment; he proclaims his desire for glory and for the reflected glory that his own can bring to 'all Italy'; and he acknowledges the wish (*wish*, rather than conviction, or even hope) that others might be as he is: a poet and, by implication, a man of letters. The emphasis is hugely on the personal throughout.

Winckelmann's self-revelations are less tidy – but consider these observations, scattered across his correspondence and his formal publications:

[11] *Rerum familiarium*, 6. 4: to Giovanni Colonna, 25 September ?1342.

(*a*) 'From my youth, a love of art has been my strongest predisposition.'[12]
(*b*) 'In the masterpieces of Greek art, connoisseurs and imitators find not only nature at its most beautiful, but something beyond nature.'[13]
(*c*) 'The taste the Greeks bestowed on their works of art was unique.'[14]
(*d*) 'One must become as familiar [with Greek art] as with a friend.'[15]
(*e*) 'From my youth, my soul . . . has been possessed by friendship alone.'[16]
(*f*) 'I am one of the few who look on friendship as the highest earthly possession.'[17]

The seemingly contradictory claims that he, Winckelmann, is, and always has been, uniquely consumed by (*a*) 'a love of art' and by (*e*) (*f*) 'friendship' are conveniently, if superficially, reconciled by (*d*), where art – specifically Greek statuary – becomes 'a friend' itself. More fundamentally, the two allegiances have a common point of reference in his response to beauty, especially (and indissolubly) the beauty of young manhood and the beauty of Greek art. And the Greeks, he is convinced, both embodied and valued beauty like no others: 'among no other people has beauty been prized so highly.'[18] Winckelmann, said Goethe, 'we often find in the company of beautiful young men', who satisfied 'his two needs, for friendship and for beauty';[19] and (Winckelmann's own claim) 'the great artists among the Greeks' were inspired by the sight and thought of 'a beautiful youthful form' to create their art.[20] The distinction between the beauty of individual young men and the 'universal beauty and its ideal images' which he identifies as 'the way of the Greeks' he does, also, acknowledge,[21] but on the level of high theory, rather than in personal terms.

For some of Winckelmann's admirers, in the years after his death in 1768, his response to antiquity prompts thoughts of an affinity with the ancient world itself. For Herder, in 1777, Winckelmann's passion 'transported him to ancient Greece.'[22] In 1805, Goethe went further, reading Winckelmann's interrelated desires as the mark of 'a whole being', one within whom 'all qualities unite as one'. This, Goethe declared, was 'the happy lot of the ancients, especially the Greeks in their greatest age'; and Winckelmann both 'felt so close an affinity' to the ancient Greeks and had,

[12] *History*, Preface.
[13] *Reflections*, 1.
[14] Ibid.
[15] Ibid.
[16] Letter to Stosch, February 1765.
[17] Letter to Stosch, 16 September 1766.
[18] *History*, 1. 4. 1.
[19] *Winckelmann und sein Jahrhundert* (1805), 'Schönheit'.
[20] *History*, 1. 4. 2.
[21] Ibid.
[22] '. . . da zaubertest du dich liebevoll ins alte Griechenland': from the closing sentences of an unpublished essay, 'Denkmal Johann Winckelmann's'.

if anyone of his time had, 'just such an antique disposition'.[23] And in England, two generations down the line, Walter Pater picked up the theme:

> To most of us . . . the antique world . . . still remains faint and remote. To him . . . it early came to seem more real than the present.
>
> [F]rom a few stray antiquarianisms . . . Winckelmann . . . divines the temperament of the antique world, and that in which it had delight.
>
> This key to the understanding of the Greek spirit, Winckelmann possessed in his own nature, itself like a relic of classical antiquity.[24]

If Winckelmann, unlike Petrarch, failed to spell out in so many words his kinship with the ancient world, his admirers did it for him.

But now the nub of the matter: from their distinctive situations, both Winckelmann and Petrarch construct new valuations and appraisals of classical creativity and – on very different levels – reconfigure creativity itself; and though there is of course something 'objective' about their valuations, they retain the intensity of the personal engagements that give rise to them.

Winckelmann's *History* is his most decisive work. Here, in place of the Renaissance model of biographical and anecdotal art-criticism, epitomized by Vasari and Bellori, and with only a few prompts from ancient sources (§3),[25] Winckelmann invents art history in its now established sense.[26] His *History* frames individual works of art within a cultural context and a chronology determined by stylistic analysis, with a whole part of the book devoted to the changing 'External Circumstances in the Greek World', cultural and political.[27] In the process he helps to reorient the newly formulated category of 'the aesthetic' from a concern with pure sensation.[28] In his wake, criticism that combines formalist analysis and historicist contextualizing, in whatever proportions, becomes a norm.

In the *History*, Winckelmann adjusts the venerable tripartite schema of infancy, maturity, decay (§3), to the Enlightenment belief in progress, mapping Greek sculpture, in particular, onto the model, with the fifth and fourth centuries BC acclaimed as the high point of artistic achievement. But within that high-classical period, the

[23] 'Eine solche antike Natur': *Winckelmann und sein Jahrhundert*, 'Antikes'.

[24] Pater, 'Et Ego in Arcadia Fui', in his *The Renaissance: Studies in Art and Poetry* (1873). A version of the essay first appeared as 'Winckelmann' in the *Westminster Review*, January 1867.

[25] Goethe's essay already draws attention to the 'prompts' (*Winckelmann*, 'Mengs').

[26] Variously: Aebli (1991), Kaufmann (2001), Pommier (2003), Potts (1994), Testa (1999).

[27] Part 2, 'Nach den äusseren Umständen der Zeit unter den Griechen betrachtet'. Climatic conditions also inform his understanding of context: ibid. 1. 1.

[28] Cf. Ferris (2000) 8–9. The founding definition of aesthetics belongs to Alexander Baumgarten in 1750: this 'theory of the liberal arts' is also 'the science of sensory cognition' (beginning of the Prolegomena to his *Aesthetica*, 1).

designation of representative instances is, notoriously, less than impartial. In his ardent prose, it is not the female but the male body that is singled out, as representing the ultimate ideal. Informed, then, by his own sexual impulses – of which, indeed, his response to Greek art is more than 'simply a sublimation'[29] – his new ideal fuses the aesthetic with the homoerotic (a union acknowledged, more or less, by both Goethe and Pater).[30] For Winckelmann, the epitome of artistic achievement is the Apollo Belvedere, a statue he interprets (in the words of Alex Potts) as 'a complex intermingling of erotically charged beauty and sublime power and elevation.'[31] Imagined as poised in triumph after successfully dispatching the Pythian serpent, his Apollo combines (in his own terms) masculine vigour (mature 'virility') with delicate beauty ('eternal springtime'): the limbs are 'lofty structures' imbued with a 'soft tenderness.'[32] A personal imperative underlies his whole art-historical schema, as well as his understanding of Greece.

The distinctiveness of Winckelmann's response to the Apollo becomes apparent by comparison with its converse. This is Byron, creating a very different vision of heroic action and passive submission by making *his* Apollo the recipient of an eroticized female gaze:

> The shaft hath just been shot – the arrow bright
> With an immortal's vengeance; in his eye
> And nostril beautiful disdain, and might
> And majesty, flash their full lightnings by,
> Developing in that one glance the deity.
>
> But in his delicate form – a dream of love,
> Shaped by some solitary nymph, whose breast
> Longed for a deathless lover from above.[33]

If Winckelmann's case is complex, Petrarch's is more so, as his ventures are more diverse and, on several levels, more paradoxical. The poet who uses his *Canzoniere* to celebrate, and lament, his love for Laura, and to bring the Italian lyric and the sonnet form to a new 'classical' perfection, is also the pioneering humanist who emends the text of Livy, uncovers manuscripts of Cicero,[34] and lends his prestige to the cause of a Latin, rather than a vernacular Italian, culture (§13); his own Latin compositions range from the unfinished epic, *Africa*, to prose as various as the

[29] Gossman (1992) 238. The relationship is most direct in Winckelmann's comment on the head of a faun in his own collection: 'my Ganymede, which I can kiss without offence' ('mein Ganymedes, den ich ohne Ärgernis . . . küssen kann': letter to Schlabbrendorf, 19 October 1765). Cf. Davis (1996).

[30] See Potts (1994) and cf. Evangelista (2009) 33–4, Gustafson (2002) 37–67, Orrells (2011) 19–22, Wilson (2012) 135–203.

[31] Potts (1994) 118. Cf. §§5, 11 n. 8.

[32] *History*, 2. 4.

[33] *Childe Harold's Pilgrimage*, 4. 161–2 (1818).

[34] Petrarch as scholar: Reynolds and Wilson (1974) 113–17, 235–6.

treatise 'on famous men',[35] a 'Private Conversation' (the *Secretum*), and the collections of letters we have now dipped into. The pessimist, 'happier among the dead', nevertheless takes time off, in eloquent Latin, to urge Venice and Genoa to make peace, to beg the Pope (exiled in Avignon) to come back to Rome and the Emperor Charles IV to restore Italian unity, and, for a time, sees in the revolutionary Cola di Rienzo the auguries of a restored empire centred on Rome – though, then again, these and other transient enthusiasms remain essentially on the level of 'ideas', with little connection to 'the realities of practical politics'.[36] But at the same time (we have anticipated the point) this innovator is a conventional medieval thinker in his juxtaposition of the Christian and the classical, and also (this friend of monks, bishops, cardinals, and himself a sometime cleric) an essentially conventional, if also sophisticated, Christian.[37] Very unconventionally, though, he is his own editor – organizing the collections of 'Letters to Friends' (*Rerum familiarium*) and 'Letters of Old Age' (*Rerum senilium*) and, in addition, the collection of 366 Italian poems that make up the *Canzoniere*.

That 'Songbook', widely referred to under this Italian name,[38] Petrarch himself eventually labelled, in Latin, *Rerum vulgarium fragmenta*: 'Fragments in the Vernacular'.[39] The curiously self-deprecating title, the fact of its being in Latin, the fact that it is Petrarch's own title for his own collection (the first such collection since antiquity): all this has a representative significance. Petrarch's is a career of self-projection, self-fashioning, self-searching.[40]

The *Secretum* has a special significance. The work is a dialogue, seemingly composed in 1342/3 (though perhaps, like much of Petrarch's work, revised in later years)[41] between the two interlocutors, Francesco ('Franciscus') and Augustine ('Augustinus'), who readily invite interpretation in quasi-Freudian terms as Petrarch's classicizing ego and medieval superego. Widely taken to embody an ongoing psychological crisis, the dialogue between poet-scholar and saint lays bare a series of conflicting imperatives. In reading Augustine's *Confessions*, says Francesco, he feels he is reading 'the record of his own pilgrimage' towards Christian deliverance from worldly desires. That 'inner discord' ('intestina discordia') Augustine traces to

35 *De viris illustribus*: cf. §21.

36 Mann (1984) 39.

37 Conventional, likewise, in related domains: 'Petrarch was not, in our terms, an exciting or innovative literary critic' (Mann 1984: 31), though he was (e.g.) equivocal (*pace* Mann, ibid.) about the standard medieval practice of allegorizing Virgilian and other pagan poetry: *Rerum familiarum*, 4. 1; *Secretum*, 2. 16. His own neo-Virgilian eclogues, however, are allegorical themselves. Petrarch's medievalism, and the paradoxes of his humanism, are placed in the wider context of 'the foundation of Renaissance humanism in medieval Italy' by Witt (2012), (2000).

38 Also often referred to as the *Rime sparse* ('Scattered rhymes'); the collection is so described in line 1 of poem 1.

39 On the title(s), cf. Picone (2007) 9–13, Stierle (1998) 45–6.

40 Variously: Barolini (2009), Kablitz (2009), Mazzotta (1978), Tripet (1967).

41 Dotti (1993) vii–x.

a fundamental 'inconstancy' ('mobilitas') in Francesco's psychological make-up.[42] More particularly, says the saint, Francesco is shackled by two 'chains', love for Laura and the spurious immortality of glory, and the two have become one. Francesco's poetry is all word-play: he fell in love with the poetic 'laurel' and 'cultivated' it because it 'echoed her name' ('quicquid illi consonum fuit . . . coluisti') – and he 'longed for the laurel crown of poetry as immoderately as [he] had loved the lady herself.'[43] As with Winckelmann, one notes how classicism and personal desire interact.

But even without reference to these inner conflicts, Petrarch has problems of identity: with the language in which he writes and the age in which he lives. If Christian thinkers (not least, Augustine) saw history as a progression from pagan darkness to Christian light, Petrarch (for all his Christian commitments) turns this around: the glories of ancient Rome were followed by linguistic decay and intellectual darkness, which can only be redressed by a revival of the classical learning (and thus the Latinity) that he espouses. And though he never offers anything resembling a programme of action,[44] he does indeed identify the long Christian age as a 'middle age', with obvious implications for what comes after[45] – just as he does attach a huge symbolic importance to the laurel crowning in 1341.

That crown was awarded to Petrarch the poet, but in response to his Latin epic, the *Africa*, a narrative of Scipio Africanus and the Second Punic War. In the poem, Petrarch acclaims, as his literary ancestor, not the obvious candidate, Virgil, but the earlier Roman poet Ennius (contemporary with Scipio), who, as the founding father of Roman epic, had declared himself a reincarnated Homer.[46] Despite the fact that then, as now, Ennius' poetry only survived as scattered quotations, it is this symbolic figure against whom Petrarch places himself. Hopes for the future? – once again, the prospect comes elusively into view.

The language question underlies all Petrarch's work. In a letter of 1353, he refers to the writers of ancient Rome, collectively, as 'the absent masters of eloquence and rare jewels of the Italian tongue' ('absentes eloquii duces et rara quaedam linguae Italae ornamenta').[47] Consciously or not, this glorification of Latin as 'Italian' reverses Dante's treatment of Italian as a kind of vulgar-vernacular Latin with 'illustrious'

[42] *Secretum*, 1. 6, 15.

[43] Ibid. 3. 1–2.

[44] Not even in the late invective, *De sui ipsius et multorum ignorantia* ('On His Own Ignorance and the Ignorance of Many Others', 1370), sometimes identified as a humanist manifesto. This text concentrates its praises on *then* (there is much measured enthusiasm for Cicero, Plato, and others), with only a few positive noises for the man of learning ('doctus', 'literatus') *now*.

[45] Cf. §3. His *Epistula metrica*, 3. 33. 4–5, declares that 'there was and perhaps will be a happier age ('fuit et fortassis erit felicius aevum'), whereas 'our' age, the 'middle' one ('medium'), is all 'squalor' ('sordes'). Similarly (but without the 'medium'), *Africa*, 9. 446–7, 453–5.

[46] *Africa*, 2. 572–5 and 9. 179–391: Ennius, proem to *Annales* 1.

[47] *Rerum familiarium*, 24. 9. On Petrarch's own Latin, cf. Garin, Goldin Folena, and Rizzo in *Quaderni Petrarcheschi* 9–10 (1992/3).

prospects.[48] And Dante himself (the Dante who *did* choose Virgil) is certainly another 'absent master' against whom Petrarch places, and defines, himself.[49] His vernacular *Trionfi* ('Triumphs'), which he worked on for over twenty years, is an intensely personal poem in Petrarchan terms (with Laura once again a central point of reference), but also a moral exploration in Dantean metrical form (the *terza rima*) and Dantean narrative structure: the Petrarch figure, like his predecessor in the *Commedia*, interrogates figures from the past, who include Dante himself. Elsewhere, it is symptomatic that Petrarch's acknowledgement of Dante as 'our leader' in 'vernacular eloquence' should seem a doubled-edged compliment ('vernacular' is of course 'vulgaris');[50] symptomatic, too, that Dante's Christian-eschatological postulates can be challenged by a throw-away suggestion that the pagan Cicero might now be a denizen of Heaven – this, in a letter to the 'absent master' Cicero himself.[51]

And Augustine, whose *Confessions* represents a paradigm of introspective writing and a model of redemption by divine grace, is not the least of the 'masters' against whom, or at least through whom, Petrarch defines himself. Besides his place in the *Secretum*, Augustine figures significantly in the *Canzoniere*, where the whole collection is framed as an Augustinian exercise in retrospective confession. The sequence begins with the poet's infatuation with his mortal Laura, and 'my first youthful error', and ends with a prayer to the Virgin Mary, and hopes of inner 'peace',[52] thus announcing the sublimation of worldly desire ('for mortal beauty, deeds and words')[53] into spiritual love. As a personal-theological undertaking, but also as a literary conceit, this is a bold move. By her very name, Laura evokes the worldly glories of the laureate poet (as Petrarch's Augustine insists) – but equally she evokes the Ovidian nymph who becomes a laurel tree, along with the whole apparatus of Ovidian metamorphosis to which the tale belongs.[54] And these associations are pursued, overtly and repeatedly, in the earlier poems in the sequence above all. Indeed in one (the so-called 'canzone of transformations'), the poet describes his very existence in love as a series of metamorphoses, broadly prefigured in Ovid.[55]

Compare and contrast, inevitably, the Christian essence of Dante's Beatrice – the name, the figure as presented, the feelings she inspires, the place of honour she occupies within a cosmic system. Compare and contrast, too, the place of transformational paganism in the imaginary of the two poets. In Dante, Ovid helps to enable the articulation of an encounter, even, with the ultimate: to describe his sight of

48 *De vulgari eloquentia*: §13. On Petrarch's possible knowledge of Dante's text, cf. Gilson (2005) 21–53.

49 Baranski and Cachey (2009).

50 Cf. §13 (with n. 95).

51 *Rerum familiarium*, 24. 4. In the *Commedia*, Cicero is in Limbo: *Inferno*, 4. 141.

52 *Canzoniere*, 1. 3 and 366. 137.

53 Ibid. 366. 85.

54 Though cf. §10 n. 17.

55 *Canzoniere*, 23. In the last line of poem 70, Petrarch recalls 23 as a programmatic piece.

God, Dante resorts to an Ovid-inspired simile of the Argo, and Neptune's 'amazement' at that first ship.[56] In Petrarch, by contrast, the classical in its Ovidian incarnation threatens to disable the poet's Christian calling: pagan images merely seduce.

Petrarch, perhaps to the last, is conflicted. The last line of the self-reflective poem that introduces the second, would-be-spiritual, section of the *Canzoniere* declares: 'I see the better and cling to the worse.'[57] In spirit, the line recalls the Augustine of the *Confessions*.[58] In sense and antithetical shape, it is an almost verbatim translation of words uttered by Medea in Ovid's *Metamorphoses* ('video meliora proboque | deteriora sequor').[59] In sound, however, it presents an exquisite but painful assonantal sequence, in which the two elements of the first half are echoed and almost mocked by the elements of the second: 'et veggio 'l meglio et al peggior m'appiglio' – assonating words in a grammatical mismatch. The seemingly equal pulls of Petrarch's twin selves – classical and Christian, 'modern' and medieval – are enacted with agonizing delicacy and force. Goethe may have convinced himself that the Winckelmann he so admired was a whole and complete being; no-one could think this of Petrarch, least of all Petrarch himself.

Driven by their passion for antiquity, Winckelmann and Petrarch play central roles in momentous new developments in the worlds of letters and ideas. They engender new disciplines, on very different levels: art history and classicizing lyric verse. And both help to originate fundamental revaluations of Western cultural experience, the eventual outcomes of which are no less than Italian humanism and German Hellenism.

Inevitably, their achievements have come under critical scrutiny in later times. Winckelmann's identifications of 'Greek' art were soon challenged, not least in the light of new finds in Greece and the Near East.[60] A century after his death, his whole view of Greece was undermined by Nietzsche's argument that the qualities of beauty and calm order he associated with Greek sculpture, though indeed applicable to visual art, are superficial qualities; that behind this bright 'Apolline' surface (and Nietzsche's terminology itself acknowledges Winckelmann's choices) lies a deeper, disorderly, 'Dionysiac' reality, destructive yet essential for new creativity; and that in ancient Greece pre-eminently, but in culture generally, it is only through acknowledgement of the Dionysiac that Apolline beauty and order can itself arise.[61] And while, ultimately, Nietzsche's famous schema remains imponderable,[62] and though

56 *Paradiso*, 33. 94–6. Argonautica figure at length in *Metamorphoses* 7, with the Argo already introduced as the 'first ship' at 6. 721. Cf. Ginsberg (2011) 155–6.

57 264. 136.

58 Esp. *Confessions*, 8. 9–10.

59 7. 20–1.

60 Potts (1994) 30–1. The suspicion that Winckelmann was dealing with Greco-Roman copies was first voiced by his sometime friend, the painter Mengs: Potts (1980).

61 *The Birth of Tragedy* (1872). Winckelmann's German reception: Sünderhauf (2004), Uhlig (1988).

62 Silk and Stern (1981) 166–85, 225–96, 377–80.

Nietzsche was happy to acclaim Winckelmann's 'noble efforts' himself,[63] he no doubt made it impossible for a sculpture-centred aesthetic, ever again, to be given the kind of endorsement that once seemed axiomatic. More recently, the robust evaluations that characterize Winckelmann's understanding of art, and life, have become (to say the least) unfashionable, while the great tradition of art history he inaugurated has been subjected to criticism on not wholly unrelated grounds. In an age when a practising artist can say, 'I am not interested in art history, in the academics of styles, a succession of fads'[64] – and no-one is expected to blink at such equations – it can safely be said that the art world is not one that Winckelmann could approve. And yet it is his model of art and its development that remains, still, the inevitable point of departure.

Petrarch's brand of contemplative humanism was soon rejected even by some prominent representatives of the movement he helped to create;[65] recent scholars have insisted on the medieval quality of his Christian thought (in contrast, even, to the civic humanism that emerged in the Italian city-states of the twelfth century);[66] and many have questioned his paradigm of the (post)medieval.[67] A more fundamental problem is his espousal of Latinity as a normative standard for elite discourse. However comprehensible in its own terms, Petrarch's example did little, in the end, but complicate Italy's 'language question', while in the short term his prioritizing of scholarly Latin over – even – his own creative poetry in Italian helped, in the eyes of many, to engender a 'period without poetry' (a 'secolo senza poesia').

The *Canzoniere* itself has had a rather different legacy. For some, the word 'Petrarchism' came to connote (in Winckelmann's phrase) 'stupid imitation': mannerism, empty conceits, formal sophistication for its own sake, 'petrification' in fact. But without this example of classic, and classic*al*, formality, it is hard to imagine the existence of anything like Pléiade poetry or Shakespeare's sonnets ('anti-Petrarchan' though both, sometimes, are).[68] And with good reason, 'the sonnet' remains one of the most familiar of all poetic forms, to this day.

Ultimately, all these legacies are dependent on the extraordinary engagements with the classical past that these two great originators lived for and by. 'You don't *learn* anything when you read him,' said Goethe of Winckelmann, 'you *become* something.'[69] Winckelmann's personal intimacy with his Greeks, and Petrarch's with his Romans, are themselves examples of 'becoming', which can be related, in turn, to the strange tally of identifications perceived by the two men and by others – from Petrarch's 'love' and 'glory' (united in Laura and the laurel) to Winckelmann's 'friendship' and 'art' (which meet in his response to male beauty). Becomings breed becomings, making a difference.

63 *The Birth of Tragedy*, 20.
64 Louise Bourgeois in a 1988 interview: Bourgeois (2005) 166.
65 Notably Bruni.
66 Cf. Witt (2000) 497.
67 See e.g. Ascoli (1991) 6.
68 Variously: Forster (1969), Greene (1991), Kennedy (1994), Meozzi (1934).
69 'Man . . . *wird* etwas.': in Eckermann, *Gespräche mit Goethe* (1836/48), 16 February 1827.

§30

Points of Departure

The ten books of Vitruvius' *On Architecture* (*De Architectura*) cover a range of topics, from architecture and town planning (I) to temples (III–IV) and other public buildings (V), from private houses (VI) to civil and military engineering (X). In our overview of the visual arts (§11), we noted the influence of Vitruvius on the architectural practice of Alberti, Palladio, and Jones. For that same era, the *De Architectura* (especially its first six books) serves as an aid – sometimes far from straightforward – to reading Roman ruins; to urban design (an example is Bernini's final design for the Piazza San Pietro, 1656); to scenography, theatre building, and the acoustic properties of such buildings; to the development of a technical terminology for buildings and their component parts; to the evolution of 'the classical orders'; and, most broadly, to the status and new theoretical scope of architecture in the classicizing age.[1]

'It is well known,' says architectural historian Alberto Pérez-Gómez, 'that the discipline [of architecture] had been "promoted" to the sphere of the liberal – that is, "mathematical" – arts during the Renaissance.'[2] The proposition serves to demarcate a cluster of related developments whereby, within the cultural world of fifteenth- and sixteenth-century Italy, architects aspire to be 'artists' and thinkers (§11), and ancient precept plays a key role in translating the understanding of a

[1] Variously: Friedman (2010); Hart (2010), Howard and Moretti (2009) 6–8; Clarke (2003), Moressi (1988), Pagliara (1986). 'Orders': n. 28 below.

[2] Pérez-Gómez (1993) 1.

The Classical Tradition: Art, Literature, Thought, First Edition. Michael Silk, Ingo Gildenhard, and Rosemary Barrow.

Published 2017 by John Wiley & Sons Ltd.

hierarchical cosmos into the 'orders and meanings' to be 'embodied in the built world'.[3] In these developments, Vitruvian authority is paramount.

In the opening pages of his treatise, Vitruvius argues that 'architectural learning' ('architecti scientia') is a matter of technical know-how and craftsmanship, but also of 'letters' ('litterae'): of mathematics, history, philosophy, music, medicine, law, and astronomy.[4] The proposition is duly endorsed in the first treatise 'on architecture' since the ancient world: Alberti's *De re aedificatoria*, composed in 1452 and printed in 1485, a year before the first printed edition of the *De Architectura* itself. Critical though he is of aspects of Vitruvius' treatise (from its language[5] to the mismatch between its descriptions and the – often later – Roman ruins still visible), and boldly declaring that modern architects should be inspired by the ancients 'and their doctrines' to produce 'something of their own invention',[6] Alberti too insists that the architect must have 'a thorough insight into the noblest and most curious sciences'.[7]

If an overt appeal to humane letters aligns Alberti's treatise with Vitruvius', so too do the cultural pretensions of his Latin – and his patronage (§11). The *De re aedificatoria* was instigated by Leonello d'Este and presented to Pope Nicholas V after d'Este's death; the *De Architectura* was dedicated to Augustus. Carefully positioned both in and out of alignment with Vitruvius, Alberti's work represents a new beginning, both for architectural theory and also for the *De Architectura* itself. Up to this point, the text had little direct influence, on architectural design, at least.[8] In late antiquity an epitome was produced by Faventinus, material from which finds its way into Isidore's *Etymologiae*, in the seventh century. In Charlemagne's court there are limited signs of renewed interest: a Carolingian manuscript of the text from which all other known copies derive; the director of building in Aachen (Einhard) who asks for help with Vitruvius' 'obscure vocabulary';[9] Vitruvian influence on a few ecclesiastical buildings in the centuries following.[10] By the fourteenth century, the treatise is well known in Florence (Petrarch and Boccaccio are among its readers), and then around 1414 Poggio Bracciolini publicizes his 'discovery' of a new manuscript in St Gallen.[11] The more significant responses to Vitruvius soon follow.

3 Ibid.

4 *De Architectura*, 1. 1–10.

5 *De re aedificatoria*, preface to book 6. The linguistic criterion neatly avoided 'the contradiction of taking authority from a Roman source while disagreeing with it at the same time': Betts (2000) 245.

6 *De re aedificatoria*, 1. 9, tr. James (Giacomo) Leoni (1726); cf. Alberti's praise of Brunelleschi in the preface to his *Della pittura* (1435–6): Smith (1992) 19–39.

7 *De re aedificatoria*, preface (tr. Leoni).

8 Medieval reception of Vitruvius: Conant (1968), Schuler (1999).

9 'Verba et nomina obscura ex libris Vitruvii': undated letter to Vussin.

10 Kruft (1994) 31.

11 Ciapponi (1960); the significance (though hardly the symbolism) of the '(re)discovery' has been exaggerated (Clarke 2002). The transmission as a whole: Weiskittel and Reynolds (1983).

Like Alberti, successive architectural theorists steered their own paths between reverence for the *De Architectura* and assertions, or reluctant admissions, of independence. Even for the most determined Vitruvian, a degree of independence was inevitable, given the discrepancies between surviving ruins and the master's descriptions, but especially because the text had originally been accompanied by illustrations, whose loss, centuries earlier, meant that descriptions might often be realized in alternative ways. The loss proved an obstacle to understanding, but also a creative opportunity.[12] The first illustrated edition was Fra Giocondo da Verona's (1511), but the most celebrated set of illustrations accompanied Daniele Barbaro's Italian translation of 1556,[13] in the form of woodcuts by Palladio. Compromises with Vitruvian doctrine were in any case embodied in such notable treatises as Serlio's *Architecture and Perspective* (*Tutte l'opere d'architettura e prospetiva*, 1537–51), Vignola's *Five Orders of Architecture* (*Regola delle cinque ordini d'architettura*, 1562), and Palladio's own *Four Books on Architecture* (*I quattro libri dell'architettura*, 1570). The title of Serlio's first volume, 'General Rules of Architecture . . . for the most part ['per la magior parte'] in accordance with Vitruvius', is symptomatic – not least because Serlio's starting point is that 'the great architect' is 'infallible'.[14]

As late as the opening decades of the eighteenth century, 'Vitruvius' is still a hallowed name. In 1729, Matthäus Daniel Pöppelmann, designer of the Zwinger in Dresden, proudly associates his Baroque masterpiece with Vitruvian principle;[15] between 1715 and 1725, the Scottish architect Colen Campbell acclaims the *De Architectura* in the very title of his *Vitruvius Britannicus*; and in 1731, Alexander Pope's 'Epistle' to the patron of architects, Lord Burlington, invokes (along with Burlington) the triad of Inigo Jones, Palladio, and Vitruvius himself: 'Jones and Palladio to themselves restore, | And be whate'er Vitruvius was before'[16] – this, in implicit celebration of the status of Vitruvius, as well as the Vitruvian affinity of Palladio's and Jones's designs. Yet, all this time, there were discrepancies between Vitruvian precept and classicizing practice, not just for a Pöppelmann, but for a Palladio too. As early as his illustrations for Barbaro's translation, for instance, Palladio was committed to the questionable belief that the ancients customarily used temple pediments, along with columned porches, in private houses, as his reconstruction of the 'House of the Ancients' makes clear;[17] and his own designs, like the Villa Barbaro at Maser (1550s), translate the belief into memorable new constructions. For Palladio, Vitruvius was 'master and guide';[18] but misinterpretations of the

[12] Cf. Carpo (2001) 16–22, Gros (2006). As late as 1662, Fréart de Chambray was still lamenting the loss of Vitruvius' 'profiles and lineal models': *Idée de la perfection de la peinture demonstrée par les principes de l'art*, ch. 1.

[13] Giocondo's edition was notable also for its correction of manuscript errors and its restitution of Greek technical terms. Translations of Vitruvius: §15.

[14] *Tutte l'opere*, 3. 131; 3. 46.

[15] *Vorstellung und Beschreibung des Zwingergartens zu Dresden.*

[16] Epistle 4. 193–4.

[17] Likewise, *I quattro libri*, 2. 16.

[18] Ibid. preface.

De Architectura, misidentifications of archaeological remains, and selective appeals to other ancient evidence[19] combined to generate a remarkable hybrid of – what had been, in ancient Rome – the distinct spheres of the monumental and the domestic.

Meanwhile, a more subtle series of adjustments was under way. Esteem for Vitruvius in the age of Palladio is inseparable from a larger world view, according to which the universe (the macrocosm) is governed by mathematical relationships embodied (on the microcosmic level) in architecture, as again in music (the climactic version of that argument is the astronomer Kepler's *Harmonice mundi*, or 'World Harmony', 1619).[20] Vitruvius himself relates building to the circle of the heavens and the zodiac, as well as to musical harmony,[21] and in the same spirit the Renaissance now accords the human body 'a central role in architectural thinking', with architecture 'not seen as an autonomous realm of artistic expression, but as a mediation between the universe and man.'[22]

Of special importance here is Vitruvius' use of the human body as paradigm for the ideal proportions of temple structures and his description of the perfectly shaped man ('homo bene figuratus'), who, with arms and legs extended, conforms to the geometry of a circle and a square.[23] In Fra Giocondo's Vitruvius, the description is illustrated in two separate woodcuts, but some years earlier (1480s?) Leonardo had given 'Vitruvian Man' his most enduring image: a pen-and-ink drawing in which a nude male figure stands in two superimposed positions, with arms and legs apart, simultaneously inscribed within square and circle. In point of fact, this positioning adjusts rather than illustrates the text, as does Leonardo's extension of the arms to a position where the fingertips are level with the top of the head (in Vitruvius the angle is lower, and the arms form lines passing through the navel). As a demonstration of staticity and movement in the human body, however, Leonardo's drawing not only makes a contribution to the quest for ideal proportion in architecture, but becomes a paradigm for figure painting, as well as an endlessly familiar cultural reference.[24]

In the Vitruvian context to which the 'perfectly shaped man' belongs, the idealized human form is related to the Platonic-Pythagorean valuation of perfect numbers, as well as 'perfect' geometrical forms.[25] Vitruvius' key terms are 'symmetry'

19 See Clarke (2003) 103–4, 143, 161; cf. Pellecchia (1992).

20 Classic modern discussion: Wittkower (1949).

21 *De Architectura*, 9. 1–6; 5. 3. 8–5. 4.

22 Pallasmaa (2011) 579–81.

23 *De Architectura*, 3. 1. 3.

24 Recent examples: Andrew Leicester's *Tin Man* (2001) converts the 'man' into a gigantic robotic statue of stainless steel; Michael Chang's installation *Vitruvian Woman* (2009) uses multiple video monitors to project the female, rather than male, body – anticipated by Australian artist Dorothea White's *Sex Change for Vitruvian Man* (2005). In the popular arena, Leonardo's image features in Hollywood films from *Hackers* (1995) to *Harry Potter and the Prisoner of Azkaban* (2004); as iconic symbol (from 2002), on Italy's 1-euro coin.

25 *De Architectura*, 3. 1. 1–9.

('symmetria') and 'proportion' ('proportio'): symmetry is said to depend on proportion, and proportion itself on modularity (the interrelation of parts and whole). In full: 'Without symmetry and proportion, no temple can have a logic to its design ['rationem . . . compositionis']: that is, unless its elements [literally, 'limbs': 'membra'] have a precise logic to them like those [limbs] of a perfectly shaped man.' And: 'proportion is the modular correspondence ['commodulatio'] of a given component of the elements to the whole work, and the logic of symmetries ['rationem symmetriarum'] is based on this correspondence.'[26]

Vitruvius' exposition here is focused explicitly on temple construction, not on the design of columns. Despite that, it becomes determinative for the Renaissance conception of 'the classical orders': a system of approved column-types and entablatures. The terminology of 'orders' (plural) is itself foreign to Vitruvius, who specifies only the 'kinds' ('genera') of temple building (three kinds: Doric, Ionic, Corinthian), and refers to 'order' ('ordinatio', singular) quite separately, as one of the principles of architecture as a whole (in effect, the principle of numerical ratios), on a level with 'proportion' and 'symmetry' themselves: 'order is the measured commensurability ['modica . . . commoditas'] of the elements of a work individually, and the adjustment of proportion to symmetry collectively.'[27] Not exactly pellucid, but clearly distinct from the new Renaissance conception of 'orders' as column types (eventually five in number), now understood as detachable, autonomous entities.

Competing to find a new, yet still authoritative, synthesis, successive theorists adjust their conceptions and their Vitruvius, as appropriate.[28] To the three Vitruvian types, Alberti adds, first the Tuscan, then, with specific reference to columns and their capitals, the Italic or Composite;[29] Serlio subsequently produces a codified system of what now become the canonical five orders. The mathematical specifics of the Vitruvian proportions are adjusted too. Vignola prefers his own measurements from Roman ruins, as later does Palladio, albeit *his* measurements differ less markedly from Vitruvius' prescriptions (just as his new designs – in their symmetry and proportion, at least – correspond most closely to the Vitruvian text). In its theory, as in its practice, Renaissance architecture retains its kinship with Vitruvius – more or less.

As late as 1672, Charles Le Brun, Director of the French Royal Academy, can still appeal directly to Vitruvius as specific authority for the proposition that 'the architect must have a thorough understanding of proportion' based on 'the proportions of the body';[30] but this is now the age of 'ancients' and 'moderns', and it is in this context that the architect Claude Perrault (brother of the 'modernist', Charles

[26] Ibid. 3. 1. 1.

[27] Ibid. 4. 1. 3; 1. 2. 2.

[28] Cf. Payne (1999). Development of the orders: Mitrovic (1999), Onians (1988), Pauwels (1989), Thoenes and Günther (1985). Raphael, among others, contributed, as did medieval schemata: Onians (1988) 147–9, Rowland (2006).

[29] *De re aedificatoria*, 1. 9; 7. 8.

[30] 'Sentiments sur le discours du mérite de la couleur par M. Blanchard'.

Perrault) initiates the first decisive rejection of the Vitruvian-Renaissance synthesis, understanding the orders as a culturally determined outcome of human design: notions of architectural propriety are relativized. Along with editions of Vitruvius (1673/84), Perrault published a complementary work, in 1683, *Order of the Five Kinds of Column According to the Method of the Ancients* (*Ordonnance des cinq espèces de colonnes selon la méthode des anciens*). This title, and much of the content of the work itself, seem to guarantee deference to Vitruvian orthodoxy. On the contrary: 'those who have written on architecture all contradict each other'; 'proportions that follow the rules of architecture' are pleasing like 'the proportions of a fashionable mode of dress'; 'exaggerated respect for antiquity' is misplaced; 'reason' may be on one side and 'authority' on the other; and 'since most proportions in architecture are arbitrary . . . there is nothing to prevent us from adjusting established proportions or . . . inventing others'.[31] On any links between the human body, architecture, and the cosmos at large, Perrault is silent, but will no doubt have agreed with his brother Charles, who detected, in mankind, 'no proportion ['nulle proportion'] and no connection with those great [heavenly] bodies ['ces grands corps'] that are infinitely distant from us'.[32]

What Perrault initiates, in fact, is a first, momentous subversion of 'meaning in the embodied order'.[33] A significant official abandonment of such meaning comes, again in France, a century later. In the Napoleonic era, the newly founded École Polytechnique reassigns architecture to technology and science; and in his 'Lectures on Architecture' (1802–5), Jean Nicolas Louis Durand, professor at the École, singles out for criticism the principle that was central to Vitruvian, and then Renaissance, understandings: 'the human body bears no formal equivalence ['analogie'] to any architectural body and cannot be imitated in its proportions'.[34] Vitruvius has lost his authority; and in the course of the nineteenth century, appeal to the *De Architectura* wanes, even as a template for classicizing architecture – with the increasingly obvious gulf between Vitruvian-Renaissance tradition and the domestic architecture uncovered at Pompeii and Herculaneum a contributory factor. The text is accused of misrepresentation;[35] in northern Europe and the USA, the Greek Revival looks to new archaeological finds, not real or imagined Vitruvian norms; and Vitruvius' historical accounts are treated without respect.[36] Conservative architectural practice that might pass for deference to the *De Architectura* survives here and there

[31] *Ordonnance*, preface and 2. 7.

[32] *Parallèle des anciens et des modernes*, vol. 4 (1692: p. 52), dialogue 5.

[33] Pérez-Gómez (1993) 1.

[34] *Précis des leçons d'architecture données à l' École Polytechnique*, vol. 2 (1805), 'Discours préliminaire'.

[35] Ganzert (1990).

[36] E.g. Gottfried Semper (*Der Stil in den technischen und tektonischen Künsten*, 1860–3) on the evolution of the Doric temple (Hvattum 2003: 29–35) and Alois Riegl, in the introduction to his 'history of ornament' (*Stilfragen. Grundlegungen zu einer Geschichte der Ornamentik*, 1893), on the acanthus motif. Cf. Wittman (2007) on XVIII France.

(on the eve of World War I, Antonio Sant'Elia's 'Manifesto of Futurist Architecture' pooh-poohs the 'young Italian architects' who still 'obstinately persevere with the rules of Vitruvius, Vignola and Sansovino'),[37] but, over the first half of the twentieth century, even a sense of the historical importance of the text diminishes: influential works from Bernard Bosanquet (*History of Aesthetic*, 1892/1904) to Arnold Hauser (*Social History of Art*, 1951) ignore Vitruvius altogether; in Croce's *Aesthetic* (*L'Estetica*, 1902/11), he gets a single mention, in passing.

But then things change again. In what may, at the time, have seemed a capricious act of modernist revaluation, Le Corbusier's Modulor system aspires to revive both 'the tradition of systemic proportional harmony' and 'architecture's connection with the human body'.[38] And though 'Vitruvian' designs of more recent decades often incline, simply, to superficial eclecticism (Johnson and Burgee's 'One International Place' in Boston, 1987: a forty-six-floor skyscraper lit by repetitive 'Palladian' windows),[39] some of today's notable theorists, conversely, have insisted that the Vitruvian-Renaissance understanding be upheld, itself, as a living ideal. In this spirit, 'Vitruvian House' (1990), by architect-historian Thomas Gordon Smith, in South Bend, Indiana [*Figure 9*], asserts the endeavour to revive a truly Vitruvian mode of design;[40] the search is on for 'a new Vitruvius for the twenty-first century';[41] the 'relation of body and architecture' is, once again, urgently debated;[42] and architecture is seen, anew, as 'the art of reconciliation between ourselves and the world'.[43]

In a long perspective, in fact, responses to Vitruvius, and to the Vitruvian legacy more generally, from Alberti to Durand and beyond, take on a larger meaning: as stages in an ongoing struggle between two views of architecture, as humane art and technological practice, and, more fundamentally still, as a more-than-human and less-than-human understanding of existential realities (§27). In this embodiment of the classical tradition, the stakes, it turns out, could hardly be higher.

If the autonomous development of the classical orders is among the noteworthy facets of the Vitruvian legacy, a yet larger instance of autonomy confronts us in the case of Longinus and the sublime.[44] 'Longinus' is a name joined to a text: in itself, merely the less implausible of two unconvincing guesses by some unknown

[37] 'L'Architettura Futurista. Manifesto': published in *Lacerba* (Florence), 1 August 1914.

[38] Pallasmaa (2011) 585: Le Corbusier, *Le Modulor* (1948), *Modulor* 2 (1955).

[39] Cf. Venturi's design for a remodelled version of Mount Vernon: Hersey (1988) 152–4.

[40] Complete with (controversial) Ionic temple front (p. 360 above): further, John (2001).

[41] Salama (2007). Likewise for 'new Palladians': Sagharchi and Steil (2010).

[42] Bacci and Melcher (2011); Bloomer and Moore (1977); Dodds and Tavernor (2002); cf. Rykwert (1996).

[43] Pallasmaa (2005) 72. Cf. Pallasmaa (2011), Pérez-Gómez (2011) 577, Salama (2007).

[44] Historical overviews of 'the sublime': Aguado (1994), Axelsson (2007), Costelloe (2012), Saint-Girons (2005), Shaw (2006), Till (2006). Much discussion is confused by conflation of the term and its possible referents (the sublime in Lyotard is different in kind from 'the sublime in Aeschylus'): typical examples in Etlin (2012), Marot (2007).

Figure 9 Thomas Gordon Smith, 'Vitruvian House'. Source: used by permission of the artist-architect.

Byzantine scholar, who attached the two names ('Dionysius or Longinus', in a table of contents) to a surviving tenth-century manuscript of the treatise, *On the Sublime*; [45] and, since the Renaissance, this name stands in lieu of author. Today's classical scholars commonly flag this untidy set of circumstances by keeping the name in scare-quotes: 'Longinus'. In our book he is plain Longinus, because this is what he has been called throughout the centuries of his eccentric influence.

On the Sublime – the Greek title is *Peri Hupsous*, 'On Height' – is a fragmentary rhetorical treatise (around a third is lost), seemingly composed in the first century AD as a reply to an earlier treatise of the same name by a fellow-rhetorician, Caecilius. Unlike most rhetorical works, from antiquity or thereafter, it is strikingly innovative.

Beyond the fact that it was copied in the tenth century, there is little sign of any knowledge of the treatise between antiquity and the fifteenth century, when new copies were made.[46] Serious interest, among the learned, begins in the mid-sixteenth. The first printed editions are Robortelli's in 1554 and Manutius's in 1555. A series of editions and Latin translations follow. The first published vernacular translation (into Italian, by Niccolò Pinelli: *Dell'altezza del dire*) comes as late as 1639 – a

[45] Russell (1964) xxii–xxiii.

[46] Ibid. xxvi–xxviii, xlix–l.

sufficient indication of the marginal status of the work, up to this point. The learned few appreciated its distinctiveness (in 1644, Milton brackets its author with Plato and Aristotle, among others);[47] most readers remained unaware of its existence.

It was the French translation by Nicolas Boileau-Despréaux in 1674[48] that announced Longinus to a wider public and – with his title, *Traité du sublime* ('Treatise on the Sublime') – gave 'the sublime' to the French, English, and Italian languages ('das Erhabene' became the accepted German equivalent) and a new concept to the world. *Peri Hupsous* had already been Latinized as 'de sublimi orationis genere' ('on the sublime sort of discourse') by Robortelli;[49] 'the sublime', as an open-ended noun-phrase, is effectively Boileau's contribution.

Longinus' treatise is a mixture of technical analysis, compositional advice, and reflections on the decline of literature – but also a unique meditation on high thinking, high feeling, high writing, the effects of such 'heights' on the reader, and the writerly gifts needed to attain the heights. The influence exerted by the treatise on later ages depends on these last preoccupations; and, with hindsight, the crucial moments are those when Longinus locates the sublime, beyond Greek literature, in the Hebrew Bible:

> the lawgiver of the Jews . . . who grasped the power of divinity . . . writes at the start of his Laws: 'God said' – what? – 'let there be light, and there was light' –

and in, and beyond, the grand workings of the physical world:

> The universe cannot satisfy the range of human speculation and thought, and our conceptions often exceed the limits of our surroundings. Look . . . at the excess, the grandeur, the beauty . . . [W]e admire, not tiny streams, but the Nile, the Danube, the Rhine, and the Ocean . . . the fires of heaven . . . the craters of Etna . . . the eruptions . . . It is always the exceptional that excites our wonder –

and in words, but not in visual art:

> In art we admire accuracy . . . we expect a statue to resemble a man, but in literature we look for something higher than the human.[50]

Two less substantive aspects of the treatise also proved significant. The passion and force of Longinus' criticism soon prompted sympathetic readers to see a

[47] *Of Education, to Master Samuel Hartlib*. Cf. Gilby (2006) 1–5 and Martin (2012) on receptions in France.

[48] Assisted by some complementary 'reflections' in 1692–4: *Réflexions critiques sur quelques passages du rhéteur Longin*.

[49] Similarly, Manutius: 'De sublimi genere dicendi'. The now standard 'De sublimitate' is not established before the 1694 edition by the Dutch scholar, J. Toll. The Latin neuter 'sublime' is used as a noun in Tanneguy Lefèvre's 1663 edition: cf. Martin (2012) 84–5. Details of early editions/translations: Marin (1967) 7–11, Weinberg (1950).

[50] *De Sublimitate*, 9. 9; 35. 3–5; 36. 3.

paradigm of the sublime in his own writing. As Pope put it, in 1709: 'Whose own example strengthens all his laws, | And is himself the great sublime he draws.'[51] Significant in a different way was Longinus' unparalleled emphasis on effect rather than style. Boileau saw this clearly: 'By "sublime" Longinus did not mean what the rhetoricians ['les orateurs'] call the sublime style, but rather the extraordinary and the marvellous.'[52] Some resisted the point, even decades later (in 1755, Johnson's *Dictionary of the English Language* defines 'the sublime' as 'the grand or lofty style', adding, testily: 'a Gallicism, but now naturalized'); but interest in the new concept only grew.

'The sublime', that is, becomes both fashionable critical currency ('A forward critic often dupes us | With sham quotations *peri hupsous*')[53] and the object of intensive critical scrutiny, especially in Britain[54] (fast becoming the centre of critical-aesthetic debate), then later in Germany. First comes a period of sporadic usage, highly deferential to Longinus ('undoubtedly, after Aristotle, the greatest critic among the Greeks': Dryden in 1677),[55] in which the sublime is related, for instance, to the poetry of Milton (whose 'distinguishing excellence' is 'the sublimity of his thoughts': Addison, in 1712).[56] There follows, though, an era of focused discussions that seek to elucidate the sublime independently of its Longinian source. John Baillie's *An Essay on the Sublime* (1747) foregrounds the incommensurable, especially in nature ('where an object is vast and . . . uniform, there is to the imagination no limits of its vastness, and the mind runs out into infinity');[57] and in 1757 Edmund Burke's *A Philosophical Enquiry into the Origin of Our Ideas of the Sublime and Beautiful* pursues this theme more decisively by detaching, for the first time, sublimity from beauty, and leaving Longinus (to whom the distinction would have been incomprehensible) to one side. For Burke, the sublime arises from 'whatever is in any sort terrible'; and its occasions vary from 'obscurity' to 'power' to 'greatness that approaches, or seems to approach, infinity', which is 'sublime to a high degree'.[58] Then again, Burke anticipates the more rarified association between the sublime and the limits of representation that will concern a much later age. In Milton's vision of Hell as a 'universe of death', he identifies 'a very great degree of the sublime' – and 'two ideas not presentable but by language'.[59]

[51] *Essay on Criticism*, 679–80. So already Boileau ('en parlant du sublime, il est lui-même très sublime': preface) and, before Boileau, Stefan von Castrobello ('quid enim praeter ipsam sublimitatem ipso Longino sublimius?'), in a letter of March 1612 to Gabriele dalla Pietra ('De Petra'), included in the latter's 1612 edition. The French prose stylist Guez de Balzac was criticised as 'too sublime' ('trop sublime') in the wake of such writings as his *Entretiens* (1657): Martin (2012) 79.

[52] *Traité du sublime*, preface.

[53] Swift, 'On Poetry: A Rhapsody' (1733), 271–2.

[54] Axelsson (2007), Monk (1935), Wood (1972).

[55] 'The Author's Apology for Heroic Poetry and Poetic Licence', prefixed to *The State of Innocence*.

[56] *The Spectator* 279 (19 January 1712).

[57] *Essay*, 2.

[58] *Enquiry*, 1. 7; 2. 8.

[59] Ibid. 5. 7; *Paradise Lost*, 2. 622: cf. Shaw (2006) 52–3.

Henceforth, the sublime is a category with an independent life and an object of systematic enquiry. The classic text here is Kant's *Critique of Judgement* (*Kritik der Urteilskraft*, 1790/3). Drawing on Burke in particular, and without much reference to Longinus, to literature, to art of any kind, Kant distinguishes the sublime ('das Erhabene') and the beautiful ('das Schöne') on a strictly affective basis, with a new precision. For Kant the faculty of judgement generates 'the feeling of beauty' out of the harmony felt in relating the imagination to the understanding; it generates 'the feeling of sublimity' out of the conflict between imagination and reason.[60] The feeling of the sublime is provoked by wildness, chaos, disorder, desolation,[61] but more precisely, 'nature is sublime in those of its phenomena whose intuition brings the idea of infinity with it'.[62] However, 'the sublime is not to be sought in the things of nature, but only in our own ideas', 'in the mind . . . not in the natural object', in 'the unattainability of nature . . . *as a presentation of ideas*'.[63] The contrast between beauty and sublimity is not itself (Kant insists) an opposition, but the 'ideas' are indeed opposed: 'the beautiful is connected with the form of [an] object . . . with boundaries. The sublime . . . is to be found in a formless object, in which or through which *boundlessness* is presented [within our ideas]'.[64]

The infinite and the boundless: these lie at the heart of the Kantian sublime. Distinguishing 'the mathematical sublime' (occasioned by the infinitely huge) from 'the dynamic sublime' (occasioned by the infinitely powerful), Kant subsumes both under the heading of the absolute: 'that which is *absolutely great* we call *sublime*.'[65]

The sublime is not in itself a Romantic category, but, with its infinities, its unattainabilities, its links with wildness and desolation, it inevitably feeds into romanticism. Unlike Kant, though, the Romantics are not systematic thinkers. In the Romantic age, accordingly, the 'sublime' label is attached to almost anything felt to be special and profound. For Victor Hugo, in 1827, it is attached to 'the soul . . . purified by Christian morality', and contrasted with the grotesque;[66] for Jean Paul, in 1804, humour (in contrast to other categories of the comic) is 'the sublime in reverse' ('das umgekehrte Erhabene');[67] for Leopardi, in 1829, 'Beauty and its moral feeling is always sublime', as is 'every poetic feeling or thought';[68] for Blake, around 1808, 'singular and particular detail' in art is 'the foundation of the sublime';[69] for Coleridge, in 1794, ''Tis the sublime of man | . . . to know ourselves | Parts and

60 *Critique*, 2. 27.

61 Ibid. 2. 23.

62 Ibid. 2. 26.

63 Ibid. 2. 25; 2. 26; 2. 29 (our emphasis). Within Kantian philosophy, there are moral implications here (cf. Merritt 2012), though hardly for Kant's successors.

64 Ibid. 2. 23 (Kant's emphasis).

65 Ibid. 2. 25–7; 2. 28–9; 2. 25 (Kant's emphases).

66 Preface to *Cromwell*.

67 *Vorschule der Ästhetik*, 1. 7. 29.

68 'Il bello, e il sentim. morale di esso, è sempre sublime'; 'Ogni sentim. o pens. poet. . . . è . . . sublime': notebook entry (*Zibaldone*) for 22 April 1829.

69 Note on Reynold's *Discourses* (I, p. 58): Bentley (1978), 2. 1471.

proportions of one wondrous whole.'[70] In 1798, Wordsworth claims to have felt, in nature, 'a sense sublime | Of something far more deeply interfused',[71] and his fellow Romantics duly associate the sublime, even satirically, with Wordsworth himself. Keats speaks of 'the Wordsworthian egotistical sublime', while for Byron 'simple Wordsworth' conveys his message in 'Christmas stories tortured into rhyme', which (maybe) 'contain the essence of the true sublime'.[72]

More significantly, a new set of connections and oppositions emerges. 'Gothic art is sublime,' declares Coleridge in 1818: 'On entering a cathedral . . . my whole being expands into the infinite.'[73] The equation of 'Gothic' with sublimity might look like yet another random association; but given the more established opposition between Gothic and Greek (§3), the equation can be seen to belong to a larger opposition between (on the one hand) beauty and the Hellenic and (on the other) sublimity and the Hebraic. A reading of the distinctive 'sublimity' of the Old Testament – the Prophets and the Psalms, rather than the bit of Genesis that so impressed Longinus – had been current for decades: we find it in Robert Lowth's *Lectures on the Sacred Poetry of the Hebrews*, in the 1750s,[74] and then again in Herder's *On the Spirit of Hebrew Poetry* (*Vom Geist der ebräischen Poesie*, 1782). Now, with Kant's decisive advocacy of the distinction between sublime and beautiful, and in an age that defers to Winckelmann's identification of the beautiful and the Greek, the whole oppositional schema falls neatly into place.

The new opposition is variously acknowledged. In 1815 Wordsworth contrasts 'the prophetic and lyrical parts of the Holy Scriptures' with the writings of 'ancient Greece and Rome' on the grounds that:

> the anthropomorphitism [*sic*] of the pagan religion subjected the minds of the greatest poets in these countries too much to the bondage of definite form, from which the Hebrews were preserved by their abhorrence of idolatry. This abhorrence was almost as strong in our great epic poet [Milton] . . . However imbued the surface might be with classical literature, he was a Hebrew in soul; and all things tended in him towards the sublime.[75]

In 1802, Chateaubriand's *Genius of Christianity* opposes both Gothic cathedrals to Greek temples and the Bible to Homer, with 'le sublime' firmly attached to the former against the latter.[76] In the 1820s, Hegel's *Lectures on Aesthetics* insist that in ideal(izing) art 'everything is clear and transparent' ('alles klar und durchsichtig'),

[70] 'Religious Musings', 126–8.

[71] 'Tintern Abbey', 96–7.

[72] Keats, letter to Woodhouse, 27 October 1818; Byron, *English Bards and Scotch Reviewers* (1809), 237, 245–6.

[73] 'European Literature', lecture 2.

[74] The title of George Gregory's 1787 English version of Lowth's *Praelectiones academicae de sacra poesi Hebraeorum* (1753).

[75] Preface to *Poems* (1815).

[76] *Le génie du Christianisme*, 2. 6.

that classical Greek myth and religion belong to that sphere of artistic representation, and that the Old Testament God is beyond that sphere and *therefore* 'sublime'.[77] Then, some decades later, in a rare appeal to the sublime, Matthew Arnold restates the whole schema with reference to the German Jewish poet, Heinrich Heine:

> He himself had in him both the spirit of Greece and the spirit of Judea; both these spirits reach the infinite, which is the true goal of all poetry and all art – the Greek spirit by beauty, the Hebrew spirit by sublimity. By his perfection of literary form, by his love of clearness, by his love of beauty, Heine is Greek; by his intensity, by his untamableness, by his 'longing which cannot be uttered', he is Hebrew.[78]

Arnold's association of 'the infinite' with 'all art', and with Greece as well as 'Judea', blurs the contrast, no doubt. What the divorce of 'sublimity' from 'the Greek spirit' makes crystal clear, is how far Longinus has been left behind.

Yet while some are preoccupied with Hebraic sublimity, others, especially in Germany, are constructing a new link between Greece and the sublime – though again without reference to Longinus – in respect of one of the great Greek achievements: tragedy. Unlike other influential modal terms (from realism to the absurd), the sublime in its literary applications has never been associated with a specific movement or with set examples. Many, indeed, like Addison, Burke, and Wordsworth, have found it in Milton, but others (like Vico and Coleridge) in Dante;[79] alongside the Greek tragedians and Homer, Longinus detected it in the historian Xenophon and the love-poet Sappho;[80] Lyotard (we shall see) identifies it in Proust and Joyce. Now, though, for the first and only time, a specifiable literary-generic affiliation comes into view.

A loose connection with tragedy is on record as early as 1660 – even before Boileau's Longinus – when the tragedian Corneille acclaims a supremely 'sublime' *kind* of tragedy: a 'kind', supposedly 'cathartic', associated with externally imposed changes of fortune.[81] More broadly, in his first reflections 'On the Feeling of the Beautiful and the Sublime', in 1764, Kant suggests that 'tragedy is distinct from comedy . . . chiefly in that [tragedy] arouses the feeling for the sublime, [comedy] for the beautiful' (comedy of manners, no doubt, with its elegant resolutions).[82] Picking up the correlation, in two essays 'On the Pathetic' ('Über das Pathetische', 1793) and 'On the Sublime' ('Über das Erhabene', 1801), Schiller associates sublimity distinctively with the newly identified aesthetic-existential category of 'the

[77] *Vorlesungen über die Ästhetik* (first published in 1835/42), 1. 1. 3. b. 2. 3. c; 2. 2. Introduction, 2; 1. 2. 2. b. 2.

[78] 'Heinrich Heine', in *Essays in Criticism*, First Series (1865). Cf. Arnold's reflections on 'Hebraism and Hellenism' in *Culture and Anarchy* (1869), 4 (p. 244 above).

[79] Vico, 'Discoverta del vero Dante' (*c.* 1730); Coleridge, *Biographia Literaria* (1817), 16.

[80] *De Sublimitate*, 8. 1; 10. 1–3.

[81] 'Discours de la tragédie' ('du genre le plus sublime'): cf. Gilby (2006) 35–45.

[82] 'Beobachtungen über das Gefühl des Schönen und Erhabenen', 2.

tragic',[83] and, in particular, with the tragic sufferer and his assertion of moral freedom in the face of an uncomprehending and incomprehensible universe. A generation later, Schopenhauer, too, insists that 'our pleasure in tragedy belongs, not to the feeling of the beautiful, but to the feeling of the sublime', with tragedy itself 'the summit of poetic art' (this, because uniquely, among the 'poetic arts', it demonstrates the worthlessness of existence).[84] And in *The Birth of Tragedy* (1872), Schopenhauer's erstwhile disciple, Nietzsche, invokes the association, unexpectedly but vividly, once more. In a moment of existential crisis, early-Greek Dionysiac man 'looks into' the true 'horror and absurdity' of existence, feels revulsion, but is saved by art:

> Art alone can turn these thoughts of revulsion . . . into ideas compatible with life: these ideas are the *sublime* ['das Erhabene'], as the artistic taming of horror, and the *comic* ['das Komische'], as artistic release from the nausea of the absurd.[85]

Nietzsche's 'sublime' is the prototype of tragedy, which (like Kant and so many others: §22) he presents as the opposite of comedy. And his argument assumes, not only the tragedy/comedy opposition, but a contrastive pairing of 'the sublime' and 'the *ridiculous*', which surely represents the most significant entry of the sublime into general usage. The essence of the new pairing is that, though opposites, the two categories are somehow adjacent; and its ultimate source, seemingly, is Boileau. Longinus' treatise looks critically at modes of writing, like bombast, that aspire, but fail, to be sublime, and an example (from Aeschylus) is dismissed as 'derisory', rather than 'terrifying'; in Boileau's translation this comes out as 'ridiculous' ('ridicule', rather than 'terrible').[86] Nine years later, one of the 'New Dialogues of the Dead' (1683), by Fontenelle, has a speaker (Scarron) boast of a burlesque version of the *Aeneid*, which proves 'that the grand and the ridiculous are so close, they touch' ('le magnifique et le ridicule sont si voisins qu'ils se touchent'). In England, another ten years on, John Dennis adjusts Fontenelle's *bon mot* more strictly to the terminology of Boileau/Longinus, having a speaker in *his* 'first dialogue' in *The Impartial Critic* (1693) come up with this:

> Has not Scarron impudently diverted all Europe at the expense of Virgil . . . ? Upon which an ingenious Frenchman [Fontenelle] has made this observation, that as all human grandeur is but folly, so sublimeness and the ridiculum [*sic*] are very nearly related.

[83] The notion of 'the tragic' ('das Tragische', 'le tragique') is formulated, essentially as an extrapolation from Greek tragedy, as early as the 1750s (Billings, forthcoming, ch. 2), but is first decisively articulated by Schelling, *Philosophische Briefe über Dogmatismus und Kritizismus* (1795), letter 10.

[84] *Die Welt als Wille und Vorstellung*, 2. 3. 37 (1844) and 1. 51 (1819).

[85] *Birth*, 7: Nietzsche's emphases.

[86] *De Sublimitate*, 3. 1 (Boileau's ch. 2): *ek tou phoberou . . . pros to eukataphronêton*. Boileau uses 'ridicule', again, for a case of frigidity in *De Sublimitate*, 4. 7 (his ch. 3).

In the age of Kant, the opposition crystallizes into a formula. 'From the sublime to the ridiculous is only one step': so said Napoleon of the retreat from Moscow in 1812 (§3), and Tom Paine had already said something similar in 1795.[87]

Formulaic usage aside, the sublime is largely absent from critical-aesthetic debate as the nineteenth century wears on[88] (both the usages by Arnold and Nietzsche are isolated), and in the opening decades of the twentieth century too. When it does resurface, it is in the unexpected context of visual art: more specifically, the presumed incapacity of figurative depiction to represent the sublime.

The unexpected voice here belongs to the American abstract expressionist painter, Barnett Newman. In a 1948 essay, 'The Sublime Is Now', Newman acclaims the sublime as a 'feeling of exaltation' not founded on any 'objective rhetoric'. Appealing to surrealism, also to 'the Gothic or Baroque', where 'the sublime consists of a desire to destroy form', Newman announces a new 'sublime art', which must be wholly divorced from any feeling for formal beauty. Detecting equivocations in Kant and Hegel (and Longinus as well), Newman commends Burke for a total separation of the sublime from form ('to me Burke reads like a surrealist manual'). In this revisionist argument, the extremes with which the sublime has long been associated are located exclusively in the subjective mind: in 'man's natural desire for the exalted, for a concern with our relationship to the absolute emotions'. And in 1951 Newman proceeds to paint a massive canvas, *Vir Heroicus Sublimis* ('Heroic Sublime Man'), as enactment of this new sublime.

A generation on, the cause of revisionist theorizing, along with Newman's argument too, is taken up by the French postmodernist, François Lyotard. Lyotard invokes the sublime in a variety of contexts – from a 1982 essay, 'Presenting the Unpresentable: The Sublime', to a provocative 1984 discussion of the 'Sublime Aesthetic of the Hired Killer',[89] to his 1991 book (focused on and named after Kant's *Critique*), *Lessons on the Analytic of the Sublime* (*Leçons sur l'analytique du sublime*). Looking back variously, then, to Kant, to Newman, and also to others,[90] Lyotard retains, but reinterprets, the distinction between beauty and sublimity. In broad terms, he reads the beautiful as convention and conformity (which assume a unity of human experience), the sublime as the radical, subversive opposite. This new schema has a political dimension, among others,[91] but its most productive application is to art, visual and other.

[87] 'The sublime and the ridiculous are often so nearly related that it is difficult to class them separately': *The Age of Reason*, 2. Contrast Jean-Paul on 'das Lächerliche' and 'das Erhabene', *Vorschule der Ästhetik*, 1. 7. 24–5.

[88] Unless derivatively – for Wagner, Beethoven has transported music from the merely beautiful to 'the absolute sublime' ('das durchaus Erhabene': *Beethoven*, 1870) – or regressively: 'the sublime is not distinct from what is beautiful' (Ruskin, *Modern Painters*, 1843, 1. 2. 3).

[89] 'Esthetique sublime du tueur à gages': ch. 3 of *L'Assassination de l'expérience par la peinture, Monory*.

[90] E.g. to Derrida's 1978 *La vérité en peinture*, 1. 4. The sublime has exercised other recent theorists, e.g. Slavoj Žižek, who relates it in neo-Lacanian terms to the impossible 'Real' (*The Sublime Object of Ideology*, 1989): cf. Hoffmann (2006).

[91] See esp. *Le Différend* (1983).

Central to postmodernism is a suspicion of any claim to find fixed points, values, or principles outside the 'indeterminacy' of experience – or as Lyotard himself famously labels it, 'incredulity towards metanarratives'.[92] In his case, such 'incredulity' subsumes, not least, resistance to the premise of an objective reality behind realist representation, and accordingly provokes a disdainful reading of realism itself ('somewhere between academicism and kitsch').[93] Commending Newman's assertion of the sublime against the figurative, Lyotard construes the sublime as central to the postmodern concern with the incommensurable;[94] and taking his bearings, now, from Kant, he applauds, as the heart of the Kantian sublime, 'the incommensurability of reality to concept': the 'feeling of the sublime' is 'the transport that leads all thought to its limits'.[95]

Lyotard's perspectives are historical, but his preoccupations are essentially with the contemporary, and, by way of elucidating the condition of modern and contemporary art, he offers a new distinction, between the 'melancholic' sublime and what he calls the 'novatio' sublime.[96] The basis of the melancholic is a Romantic striving for communion with the absolute: doomed to fail, but driven to press on. The novatio mode is quite distinct. It is characteristic of avant-garde art, perhaps in any age,[97] but specifically in the modern age: art that uses technical innovation to assert the limits of representation. Against conventional narratives and 'documentary' art, then, he acclaims painters like Newman and writers like Proust and Joyce. In *Ulysses*, for instance, Joyce 'puts forward the unpresentable in presentation itself',[98] while in general the creative art of today is directed towards 'exploring the unsayable and the invisible'.[99]

In one particular, though, Lyotard reverts to Kant. In the *Critique*, Kant glances at the Old Testament commandment, 'Thou shalt not make unto thee any graven image, or any likeness of any thing', and comments: 'Perhaps there is no passage more sublime in the Jewish law.'[100] For Lyotard this is a crucial insight into the importance of 'a representation that represents nothing', which prefigures 'minimalist and abstractionist endeavours to escape the figurative prison': 'art that enables us to see only by making it impossible to see'.[101]

At which point – though Lyotard himself is silent here – one is irresistibly reminded of both the Romantic association of the sublime with the Hebraic and,

92 *La Condition postmoderne* (1979). Cf. 'The Sublime and the Avant-Garde' (1984).

93 'Réponse à la question: qu'est-ce que le postmoderne?' (1982).

94 'Presenting the Unpresentable'; 'The Sublime and the Avant-Garde'; 'L'Instant, Newman' (1984).

95 'The Sign of History' (1982). Cf. Nietzsche, *Birth of Tragedy*, 15, where, at the 'limits' of knowledge, man 'stares into the ineffable' and 'logic coils up and bites its own tail'.

96 'Qu'est-ce que le postmoderne?'

97 'Whatever age it makes an appearance in, modernity cannot exist without a shattering of belief and without uncovering reality's "lack of reality" ': ibid.

98 Ibid.

99 'La Philosophie et la peinture à l'ère de leur expérimentation' (1981).

100 2. 29.

101 'L'Instant, Newman'; 'Qu'est-ce que le postmoderne?'

indeed, of Longinus' own pioneering appeal to Genesis. And *pace* Lyotard, one is tempted to go further. The implication of these connections is that the subversive enactment of the limits of thought, of the unpresentable *beyond* presentation, ultimately points to *the metaphysical beyond*. For Lyotard, all *meta*physics must belong to the *meta*narratives towards which postmodernism feels such incredulity. And yet the sublime surely has what one might call a momentum towards the metaphysical,[102] which – to his credit, and in defiance of all his own incredulities – Lyotard's own analyses help to uncover.

For us, the long history of the sublime – the concept, in all its elusive versions – is peculiarly illuminating. It vividly illustrates the extraordinary shapes that the classical tradition can take: the tangents, disconnections, reconnections. Juxtaposing this Longinian legacy with the Vitruvian is illuminating too (and not only because both prove to have existential-metaphysical affinities). The two case histories involve multiple interactions between the visual, the verbal, and the conceptual, but interactions made manifest in unpredictably different ways, and indeed at different times. The 'classical' sublime comes into full view in the late seventeenth century, at precisely the time when Vitruvian classicism is first seriously challenged; and the single most consequential development of the concept of the sublime (by Kant, in Germany) is almost simultaneous with the decisive rejection of Vitruvianism (by Durand, in France). Conversely, the same year (1948) sees late-modernist reassertions of the sublime (by Newman) and of neo-Vitruvianism (by Le Corbusier). More fundamentally, though: our two texts have not served as 'authorities' for centuries, and yet the categories and perspectives they have engendered – as 'points of departure' – retain a comparable power to this day.

[102] Relatedly, 'religious ideas' have long been seen as 'the most proper to give . . . sublimity to a discourse': Dennis, 'The Grounds of Criticism in Poetry' (1704), 4. Cf. Weiskel (1976) 3: 'without some notion of the beyond, some credible discourse of the superhuman, the sublime founders'; likewise, Brady (2012) 175: 'what seems to distinguish the sublime from awe, wonder, and other neighboring concepts is . . . its very metaphysical quality.'

§31

Ideas and Action

'If he wants to hold on to power, a prince must learn how not to be good.' 'If you have to choose, it is much safer to be feared than loved.' 'Reprehensible actions may be justified by their outcomes; and a good outcome will always justify them.' 'Our religion has shown us the truth and the true path, but . . . rather than men of action, it glorifies humble and contemplative men . . . a mode of life that seems to have left our world weak.'[1]

These are among the many specimens of Machiavelli's realism that caused his writings to be put on the Index (in 1559) and his name to become a byword for ruthless cynicism: 'we doubt whether any name in literary history be so generally odious' (Macaulay).[2] Odious or not ('perfection in politics' was Nietzsche's estimate),[3] Machiavellian realism presupposes a distinctive mode of engagement with the ancient world, and a distinctive understanding of the relation between that engagement and the world of action.

Niccolò Machiavelli was born in Florence in 1469. After a humanist education,[4] he entered public life and in 1498, following the downfall of Savonarola, was appointed to the position of second chancellor of the Florentine republic. Unlike the bookish humanists who conceived of writing as living (or *vice versa*), he was, from the first, a man of action, whose service to the republic of Florence was the

[1] Machiavelli, *The Prince*, 15 and 17; *Discourses*, 1. 9 and 2. 2.

[2] 'Machiavelli' (*Edinburgh Review*, 1827).

[3] In a note of 1887/8: Colli and Montinari (1967–), 8. 2. 267. Cf. §8 n. 13.

[4] Seemingly without Greek: cf. e.g. Mansfield (1979) 206. General biography: Viroli (1998).

The Classical Tradition: Art, Literature, Thought, First Edition. Michael Silk, Ingo Gildenhard, and Rosemary Barrow.

Published 2017 by John Wiley & Sons Ltd.

centre of his life. Between 1498 and 1512, he worked in the second chancery of the Palazzo Vecchio, a branch of civic government primarily responsible for internal affairs; but he was also called on to give administrative support to the committee overseeing foreign affairs, the so-called 'Ten of War'. In this capacity, he was sent on various diplomatic missions, to the France of Louis XII, the court of Cesare Borgia, the Rome of Pope Julius II – all privileged sites for observing at first hand some of the early modern world's most unscrupulous brokers of power – until 1512, when his career in government came to an abrupt end. The Florentine republic succumbed to the superior military might of Spain, and the Medici family, in exile since 1494, returned to power. Machiavelli was dismissed from his post and, the following year, accused (wrongly) of collusion with an anti-Medicean conspiracy. The outcome was prison, then forced retirement on his farm, outside Florence, where he died in 1527.

In a celebrated letter to the Florentine ambassador in Rome, Francesco Vettori, Machiavelli describes his shrunken existence during the earlier years of what, for him, amounted to miserable exile. His daylight hours are spent on petty squabbles over firewood, on snaring thrushes, on backgammon or cards, on reading love poetry (he mentions Dante and Petrarch, Tibullus and Ovid). The contrast with his active role in politics could hardly have been greater. Yet each evening, a 'quasi-Eucharistic' experience beckons as he turns his mind to more congenial pursuits:

> Come evening, I go back home, into my study. At the door, I take off my everyday clothes, covered with mud and dirt, and put on royal or courtly robes. Now suitably dressed, I step into the ancient courts of ancient men, where I am welcomed most warmly and feast on food reserved for me, the food I was born for. Without compunction, I talk to these men and ask them about the motives behind their actions ['della ragione delle loro actioni']; and they, in their humanity ['humanità'], answer me; and for four hours I feel no boredom, forget my problems, have no fear of poverty, no apprehension of death. I lose myself in them completely.[5]

The idea of imaginary dialogue with figures from classical antiquity and the topos of 'food for thought' prompt thoughts of Petrarch's *Familiares*;[6] and, at first sight, Machiavelli indeed seems to approach the classics in the spirit of a Petrarch, eagerly striking up a conversation with the ancients and sifting their works for useful lessons. But Machiavelli's engagement is very different. Crossing the threshold into his study is not so much a prelude to an audience with the great writers of the past as a return to the grandeur of public affairs. Through his books, he enters a world out of time, in which he can hold conversations with the powerful individuals of classical antiquity on the same terms as he did, so recently, with the great men of his own day. And in his interviews, he does not seek out classical authors as such; rather, he interrogates the men of action who populate their narratives. This exercise

[5] Letter to Vettori, 10 December 1513. 'Eucharistic': Bárberi Squarotti (1987) 65–9.

[6] Cf. Bec (1976).

will inevitably have involved texts – though here Machiavelli passes over his actual reading in silence – but it does not grant those texts any normative force. Conversely, he has no interest in the hermeneutics of historical difference of either the nostalgic or the antiquarian sort that preoccupied many of his contemporaries. His interviews with the great men of the past have one overriding purpose: to understand the timeless logic of power politics, past, present, and future. But what looks like a means of temporary escape from his current misfortune is also a way to regain political relevance – and Machiavelli duly goes on to inform Vettori that he has already set down some of his findings in a little book ('opuscolo'), to be dedicated to Giuliano de' Medici in the hope of patronage.

The 'little book' – subsequently known as *Il principe* (*The Prince*), and eventually dedicated to Giuliano's nephew, Lorenzo – was first printed in 1532, after Machiavelli's death. During the years of effective exile, marked otherwise only by a few, more or less abortive, attempts to re-enter public life, this was one of several notable compositions in a range of genres: *Belfagor*, a novella; *Mandragola*, a comic drama of adultery (composed, probably, in 1518 and performed privately in Florence, that same year); a dialogue, *Arte della guerra* (*The Art of War*, printed in 1521); *Istorie fiorentine* ('Histories of Florence', completed in 1525); and his most substantial contribution to political thought, the *Discorsi sopra la prima deca di Tito Livio* (*Discourses on the First Ten Books of Livy*), written between 1513 and 1518, and eventually printed, again after his death, in 1531. All these diverse works were written in prose, and in Tuscan Italian, not Latin:[7] here, as elsewhere, Machiavelli displays his independence of humanist norms.

In one respect, the title of the *Discourses* is misleading. Livy is the main source and provides a rough chronological framework for Machiavelli's reflections, but these are less reflections *on* Livy than thoughts arising, primarily, *from* Livian material, which at the same time appeal freely to a wide variety of additional written sources, both 'modern' and, especially, ancient, from Plutarch to Sallust, and Tacitus to Xenophon.[8] Conversely, the title of *The Prince* is apt enough,[9] insofar as here (and this is the ultimate reason for Machiavelli's ill repute) he is content to assume the entitlement of autocratic rulers to exercise and retain power – whereas the *Discourses* deal with republics, as well or instead, and, in broad terms, indicate a calculated preference for republican government.[10]

In the letter to Vettori, Machiavelli effectively adumbrates the programme that defines both the *Discourses* and *The Prince*, while in the dedicatory letter that

[7] He also addresses the language question directly in an 'Essay on Our Language' (*Discorso intorno alla nostra lingua*, 1523–4). Machiavelli and literature: Ascoli and Kahn (1993), Bárberi Squarotti (1987), Sullivan (2000).

[8] Lists in Walker (1950), 2. 271–305. Recent scholarship stresses the role of Lucretius: Rahe (2007), cf. Brown (2010).

[9] The original title – cited in Machiavelli's letter to Vettori – was in Latin, 'De principatibus' (in effect, 'On States with a Prince/Princeps'); it became (in Italian) *Il principe*, in the first printed edition.

[10] *Discourses*, 1. 1–10.

accompanied *The Prince*, he spells out his qualifications for the task. Pointing to a 'knowledge of the actions of great men' ('la cognizione delle azioni degli uomini grandi') as his most valuable asset, he identifies its two sources. It derives from a long experience of contemporary affairs ('una lunga esperienzia delle cose moderne') and from ongoing readings in their ancient equivalent ('una continua lezione delle antique'), both of which he has examined and reflected on with great care ('con gran diligenzia lungamente escogitate ed esaminate'). By comparison with the humanists of his day, Machiavelli thus articulates a novel position. He foregrounds personal experience, and gives it the same status as knowledge acquired by reading the ancient authorities (a status enacted by the parallel construction of 'lunga . . . cose moderne' and 'continua . . . antique'); implicitly he transforms those authorities from normative guides into banks of data; and in formulating his arguments he puts an unqualified emphasis on independent judgement.

In the dedication attached to the *Discourses*, Machiavelli reiterates the fundamentals – the autopsy and the knowledge of history – that provide the data on which rational analysis must rely: 'I have set down everything I know and everything I have learnt from long experience and constant study of worldly affairs' ('una lunga pratica e continua lezione delle cose del mondo'). Once again: knowledge is not grounded in the assimilation of pre-formulated wisdom; rather, it demands an independent assessment of events, whether ancient or contemporary or (in the event) both. With good reason, Machiavelli sees his approach to politics as a radical break with orthodoxy, and flaunts his originality by comparing it to Columbus's voyage across the Atlantic.[11] Unsurprisingly, he dismisses humanist eloquence as irrelevant to his project: 'I have not embellished my work by filling it with rounded periods, high-sounding words or fine phrases . . . [T]he scope of the material and the importance of the subject should [by themselves] ensure its appeal.'[12]

At the centre of Machiavelli's outlook are heterodox universalizing axioms about human nature, the socio-political sphere, and the supranatural environment. The validity across times and cultures that he ascribes to his insights makes it possible to learn something of contemporary relevance from ancient history: 'in all peoples there are the same desires and the same inclinations'.[13] Thereby he maintains a powerful practical imperative: the identification of recurrent patterns and regularities in politics renders the future to some extent predictable and thus serves as a guide to successful action – which may well mean action by 'the prince', or the ruling elite, in the world as it is, and not the world as moralizing thinkers (past or present) might wish it to be.

Notoriously, one of Machiavelli's premises is that 'all men are wicked', or, more specifically, that 'men are ungrateful, fickle, false, afraid of danger, greedy for gain' and that 'men only do good out of necessity':[14] a set of bleak convictions that contrasts

11 Cf. Walker (1950), 1. 80–93.

12 Dedication to *The Prince*.

13 *Discourses*, 1. 39.

14 *Discourses*, 1. 3; *The Prince*, 17; *Discourses*, 1. 3.

starkly with the optimistic anthropology one tends to find in humanism and its classical sources (Cicero, Aristotle, Plato), and which one finds again in Rousseau and the Romantics. Equally unsettling to his contemporaries is his amoral reinterpretation of *virtù*, which, according to Machiavelli, manifests itself in the acquisition and maintenance of power.[15] In general humanist usage, this much-used term looks back to the Roman understanding of *virtus* as the cluster of qualities that define a man ('vir'), from purposeful ('manly') capability to moral worth, but with the emphasis on the latter. Machiavelli puts the emphasis firmly on the former: the ruthless Cesare Borgia, for instance, rose to power through his great 'virtue'.[16] Turning the civic ethics of Cicero's *De Officiis* on its head (Cicero had argued that whatever is morally right is also expedient), Machiavelli, too, eliminates the possibility of conflict between expediency and moral rectitude, but does so largely by eliding morality altogether: he assesses figures or communities by the amoral criterion of success – by whatever means necessary, from deceit to, even, fratricide.[17]

Machiavelli's unconventional thinking manifests itself again in the way he conceives of the forces and dynamics that determine the historical evolution of civic communities, not least in his exploration of the factors involved in the rise of Rome from city-state to world empire. Against the conviction, broadly common to humanist circles and their ancient sources, that unity and harmony are essential for a civic community or state to survive, Machiavelli ponders the case of the ancient Roman republic, characterized as it was by constant friction between the ruling elite and the people. And his bold conclusion is that strife and discord can be positive, insofar as they further liberty and generate imperialist energies.[18] Ironically enough, the expansionist energies unleashed in Rome resulted in the transformation of a republican form of government into an imperial regime that eventually caused the destruction of 'all republics and civic institutions' elsewhere, before succumbing to destruction itself.[19] This is one of many junctures in Machiavelli's thinking where a genealogical connection between ancient history and presentist concerns is apparent. The repercussions of this historical development, he argues, can still be felt today. As a consequence of the Roman experience, cities everywhere have struggled to revive republican forms of government 'except in a very few parts of that empire'[20] – one of which happens to be northern Italy.

Machiavelli's distinctively principled thoughts on the world of politics subsume reflections on the larger environment – supranatural, even *super*natural – as he tries to master, on the theoretical level, the challenge of how to impose one's will on

15 Humanist/Machiavellian readings of *virtus*: Skinner (1978) 88–94, (2000) 35–53; cf. Mansfield (1996) 6–56.

16 *The Prince*, 7.

17 *Discourses*, 3. 10, on Romulus.

18 One contemporary reaction was Francesco Guicciardini's 'Considerazioni intorno ai "Discorsi" del Machiavelli' (?1530); cf. Gilbert (1965).

19 *Discourses*, 2. 8.

20 Ibid. 2. 2.

circumstances: a challenge that he himself (self-proclaimed victim of the 'malignity of fortune')[21] had conspicuously failed to meet in practice. From Herodotus and the tragic playwrights of fifth-century Athens onwards, a long tradition of thought insists on the futility of any such endeavour, in the face of the arbitrary or inscrutable nature of divine will and the consequent unpredictability of the universe within which humans, individually or collectively, are required to operate. This outlook finds personified expression in the Greek goddess *Tuche* and her Roman equivalent *Fortuna*: 'chance'. In due course, Christian authors accommodate the randomness of fortune to the notion of divine providence,[22] and the seemingly irrational forces that buffet humans in the here-and-now acquire new meaning within the larger frame of reference of the Christian afterlife. Fickle fortune now becomes an *ancilla dei*, a 'handmaid of God' that reconciles the experience of injustice with the requirements of theodicy and, for good measure, allows soldiers of Christ to prove their mettle.

Meanwhile, though, some Roman sources uphold a different view: Fortuna does not scatter her goods at random, but shows meritocratic preferences – hence, for instance, the adage, 'fortes fortuna adiuvat', 'fortune favours the brave' (or 'helpeth hardy man to his empryse', as Chaucer put it).[23] In conformity with this principle, the warlords of the Roman republic, Sulla and Caesar above all, claimed a special relationship with fortune; and it is this tradition of thought that Machiavelli (along – for once – with other humanist authors) reactivates.[24] In his terms, a manly strength of purpose (*virtù*) enables the individual to impose his will on circumstances. But rather than looking to etymological word-play ('fortes fortuna') to make his point, Machiavelli chooses a racier idiom that plays on Fortune's gender: 'Fortune is a woman ['la fortuna è donna'] and if you want to stay on top of her, you have to use force and treat her roughly. You will find that this is the type she gives in to, more than to men that come at her timidly.'[25]

What Machiavelli seeks to address is a perceived discrepancy between political theory and his own experience of political practice, and equally a contradiction between the conventional moralizing use of the classical authorities and his own sense of their capacity to support a quite different outlook. His first-hand knowledge of politics undermines the moral imperatives which the educated world of his day had learned to associate with the ancient texts. The classics and those who upheld them as normative points of reference had failed, therefore, both in utilitarian and analytical terms – and yet, far from rejecting the classical sources, Machiavelli reclaims them.

Like Cicero, in an earlier age, Machiavelli turns his own past career in politics into the central aspect of his authorial self-fashioning. But Cicero turned to normative

21 The December 1513 letter to Vettori speaks of 'questa malignità di questa mia sorta'.

22 Notably Boethius: §3.

23 *Troilus and Criseyde*, 4. 601.

24 Cf. Poppi (1988) and more generally Parel (1992).

25 *The Prince*, 25. Cf. Falco (2004), Pitkin (1983) 138–69.

principles to cope with personal and political disaster, and formulated an alternative vision to catastrophic *Realpolitik*, aiming to align, protreptically, reality with theory. In a revolutionary move, Machiavelli inverts the alignment.[26] Declaring allegiance to the true and permanent lessons of ancient history, he seeks to align theory with the principles of action. The outcome is a radical inflection of tradition: a 'classical' solution that involves a break with the classical and classicizing commonplaces that define his age.

If Machiavelli's project is illuminated by comparison with Cicero, in antiquity, it is illuminated in a different way by comparison with Richard Wagner, four centuries on. The juxtaposition – unexpected, no doubt – has a typological value: it shows up two contrasting ways in which the classical past can help to shape aspirations and imperatives to action, in an imperfect world.

Like Machiavelli's, Wagner's life (1813–83) is full of notable names. His correspondents range from the French poet Baudelaire to the Russian anarchist Bakunin and the German Chancellor Bismarck. His fellow-composer Liszt became his father-in-law when he married Liszt's daughter, Cosima; King Ludwig II of Bavaria became his devoted patron; for a few years, the young Nietzsche was his enthusiastic friend.

All this reflects a life of achievement. Wagner composed some of the most admired musical dramas in the operatic repertoire – writing words, as well as music, sometimes conducting, eventually directing: *Der fliegende Holländer* (*The Flying Dutchman*, premiered in 1843), *Tannhäuser* (1845), *Lohengrin* (1850), *Tristan und Isolde* (*Tristan and Isolde*, 1859), *Die Meistersinger von Nürnberg* (*The Mastersingers of Nuremberg*, 1868), *Parsifal* (1880) and the four-part *Ring* cycle: *Der Ring des Nibelungen* (*The Ring of the Nibelung*, premiered in 1876). The *Ring* – *Das Rheingold* (*The Rhine-Gold*), *Die Walküre* (*The Valkyrie*), *Siegfried*, and *Götterdämmerung* (*Twilight of the Gods*) – took nearly thirty years to plan, compose, revise, and perform. Intended to reinvent the culture that produced it, the *Ring*, in its Bayreuth setting, is perhaps the most ambitious work of art in Western history; the specially designed Bayreuth festival theatre, and the festival itself, with the first complete performance of the *Ring* its inaugural event, were ambitious ventures in their own right.

Wagner is one of the great musical innovators. He aimed to supersede traditional 'number-opera' and its sequences of recitative, aria, chorus, and ensemble. In its place, from *Lohengrin* onwards, he pioneered the integrated 'music-drama' (*not* his favoured term).[27] Integration was achieved by various means, but in the *Ring*, above all, partly by a principle of musical-thematic continuity in the shape of the

[26] Cicero and Machiavelli: Colish (1978) 85–6.

[27] See his essay 'Über die Benennung "Musikdrama"' ('On the Name "Music-Drama"', 1872). The term originates in the 1830s: Dahlhaus (1971) 9. Up to and including *Lohengrin*, Wagner's 'operas' are so called; then (e.g.) *Tristan* is an 'Action' ('Handlung') and the *Ring* a 'Festival Play for the Stage' ('Bühnenfestspiel').

celebrated 'leitmotifs' (again, *not* . . .)[28] – this, as one contributory element to the fusion of drama, music, and poetry in the 'total work of art': the *Gesamtkunstwerk* (yet again, *not* . . .):[29] No less innovative is his bold harmonic usage, especially in *Tristan* (its 'wandering tonality' a precursor, even, of Schoenberg's 'atonal chromatic mode of composition').[30]

Wagner's influence has been huge, within the realm of music ('I am not a Wagnerian,' said Puccini, but 'like every other modern musician, I have been influenced by Wagner'),[31] and also beyond. The *Gesamtkunstwerk* ideal evoked responses across the modernist movements – from Mallarmé to Kandinsky to the Bauhaus (where architect-designer Gropius and theatre director Piscator envisaged a 'total theatre') – while the ideal still resonates in the world of digital technology ('The Total Work of Art: From Bayreuth to Cyberspace').[32] Bayreuth itself inspired the modern 'music festival', from Salzburg to Woodstock. The 'Tristan chord' is 'by far the most analysed collection of four notes in Western music'.[33] An array of eminent figures from beyond the musical arena have investigated Wagner: Baudelaire and Nietzsche, George Bernard Shaw and Thomas Mann, Adorno, Badiou, and Žižek[34] – this, in response both to his art and to the Wagner 'phenomenon', including his appropriation by the Nazi regime and Wagner's own nationalism and anti-Semitism that provoked it.[35]

And Wagner is implicated in the classical tradition. Like the German Hellenists of an earlier generation, Wagner looks to Greece, but with a difference.[36] Apart from a few trifles (including jottings, in 1849, for an 'Achilleus' drama),[37] the classical world plays no overt part in his creative work. His mature musical dramas are set in the world of medieval legend, or late-medieval historical fiction (*Meistersinger*), or pre-medieval Nordic myth (the *Ring*). Where the classical world figures explicitly is in his prose and his expository thoughts: in Cosima Wagner's diaries (which seek

[28] E.g. in *Opera and Drama* (1852), 3. 5–6, Wagner speaks of 'musical motifs' and 'principal themes'. 'Leitmotif' was popularized by Hans von Wolzogen: Grey (2008b) 87.

[29] The term was invented by Karl Trahndorff, *Ästhetik* (1827): Dieckmann (1988). Wagner uses it in *Art and Revolution* (1849) and 'The Art-Work of the Future' (1849–50), but avoids it thereafter.

[30] Schoenberg, *Harmonielehre* (1911): Grey (2006) 65.

[31] Interview in *Neue Zeitschrift für Musik*, 1912.

[32] The title of Smith, M. W. (2007). Influence of the *Gesamtkunst* ideal: Bablet (1995), Finger and Follett (2011), Fornoff (2004), Wöll (1984).

[33] Deathridge (2008) 114.

[34] Baudelaire, 'Richard Wagner et Tannhäuser à Paris' (1861); Nietzsche, *Die Geburt der Tragödie* (1872), 'Richard Wagner in Bayreuth' (1876), *Nietzsche Contra Wagner* and *Der Fall Wagner* (both 1888); Shaw, *The Perfect Wagnerite* (1898); Mann, *Wagner und unsere Zeit* (essays collected in 1963); Adorno, esp. *Versuch über Wagner* (written in 1937/8, published in 1952); Badiou and Žižek in Badiou (2010).

[35] Provoked also (debatably) by 'totalitarian' implications of the 'total' work of art: Michaud (2003). Wagner's anti-Semitism (endlessly discussed): Grey (2008c).

[36] Wagner and the Greeks: overviews in Lloyd-Jones (1982) 126–42, Schadewaldt (1970). See also: Ewans (1982); Foster (2010) (but see n. 65 below); Lee (2003); Silk and Stern (1981); Wilberg (1996). Cf. variously: Deathridge (2008) 102–9, Goldhill (2008), Roller (1992), Ruehl (2003).

[37] He also arranged and translated Gluck's *Iphigénie en Aulide* (1771–3) for performance in 1847.

to transcribe his daily thoughts and words, from 1869 onwards); in his autobiography, *Mein Leben* (*My Life*, 1880); in his voluminous essays on music, theatre, aesthetics, cultural history, and politics, which strive to articulate the convictions behind his developing practice.

Like his art, the convictions change over time, sometimes drastically. Rarely are the changes confronted in his prose, however – ideas are simply adjusted or replaced, without comment – and this endless slippage makes the essays anything but a straightforward commentary on his mind-set or his creative work. Worse, their idiom is often bizarre and their mode of argument elliptical. Their importance, nonetheless, is inescapable.

For our purposes, the single most important essay is *Die Kunst und die Revolution* (*Art and Revolution*), written in the summer of 1849: this is the essay that spells out, most fully, the significance of Greece for Wagner's project.

The context of the essay is noteworthy. Wagner decided on a musical career after an unremarkable early life in Dresden and Leipzig. In 1843 the proverbial struggling composer became second conductor at the Dresden court opera. There he stayed until the wave of political uprisings that began in Paris, in 1848, spread to Dresden itself. His active involvement as a republican and, broadly, a socialist (with Bakunin, 'on the barricades') led to a warrant for his arrest in May 1849. He fled to Switzerland, where he stayed, on and off, first in Zurich, then near Lucerne, until 1872. Now married to Cosima (since 1870) and supported by Ludwig (since 1864), he moved to Bayreuth, in Bavaria, to put his festival project into action.

Art and Revolution, then, was composed and published in 1849, in the wake of Wagner's revolutionary activities. This and two other 'Zurich essays' that follow, 'Das Kunstwerk der Zukunft' ('The Artwork of the Future', published in 1850) and *Oper und Drama* (*Opera and Drama*, 1852), all declare a commitment to ancient Greece. Wagner's 'Hellenism' first began with a schoolboy enthusiasm for Greek mythology;[38] then and later he made abortive attempts to learn the language;[39] in Dresden, in the 1840s, he read Greek literature extensively.[40] The work that impressed him, above all, was Aeschylus' *Oresteia*, in the translation by Johann Gustav Droysen, which he studied in 1847: 'My ideas about the meaning of drama, and particularly theatre, were crucially shaped ['entscheidend . . . gestaltet'] by the experience.'[41] The passion for Aeschylus, and the *Oresteia* in particular, never left him. In June 1880, he read the *Agamemnon* to Cosima, 'transfigured, inspired, all one with his reading'; in his own reported words, the play achieved 'perfection' on every level, 'religious, philosophical, poetic, artistic'.[42] And among his last words of all: 'My admiration ['Bewunderung'] for [Aeschylus] never stops growing.'[43]

[38] See Wagner's open letter to Nietzsche, 12 June 1872, and *Mein Leben*: Altmann (1923), 1. 17.

[39] Ewans (1982) 15–16.

[40] Also some classical scholarship: Foster (2010) 1–6, 269–94.

[41] Droysen, *Des Aischylos Werke* (1832/41). *Mein Leben*: Altmann (1923), 1. 469.

[42] Cosima Wagner, *Tagebücher*, 23–24 June 1880.

[43] A final entry added to Cosima's *Tagebücher* by his stepdaughter Daniela, after his death on 12 February 1883.

In *Art and Revolution*, 'admiration' for Aeschylean Greece is unqualified. The opening paragraph insists that 'modern art is merely one link in the chain of Europe's overall artistic development; and this development begins with the Greeks.' In line with the title, meanwhile, the preface proposes to uncover 'the meaning of art as outcome ['Ergebnis'] of the life of the state'. The essay acclaims Aeschylean drama in its festival setting: 'the highest conceivable form of art'; the triumphant creation of the Greek 'people'; a 'religious festival', where the people 'streamed in their thousands' to hear their poet proclaim 'the great tale of necessity told through the mouths of [the people's] gods and heroes'. And yet the Athenian community went astray, and tragedy with it. What follows is centuries of decline: Roman 'imitation' and 'brutality' (here, as often, Wagner connects morality, political structure, artistic innovation, by phraseological gesture, rather than argument) – then 'the fresh Germanic nations', but soon 'Christian self-loathing', the 'so-called Renaissance', the 'hypocrisy' of French neoclassicism, and today's worship of commerce (the god of 'five per cent') and trivial 'entertainment': prosaic plays, inconsequential operas, 'civilized corruption and Christian dull-wittedness ['Stumpfsinn']'.

At its Aeschylean peak, the public art ('öffentliche Kunst') of Greece expressed the 'deepest and noblest' consciousness of the people; as such, it was 'conservative'. Greek theatre belonged to the people, ours to the moneyed classes. Today, what is 'deepest and noblest' is 'denunciation of our public art'. True art now lives in the private consciousness; as such, it must be revolutionary. And in frank contradiction of so many Romantic hopes (§3), Wagner declares: 'No, we do not want to be Greeks again; for *we* know what the Greeks did not know and, not knowing, were doomed.' In Greece, unified tragic art suffers a 'revolutionary' shift as early as the Periclean age, with Sophocles, before fragmenting into 'rhetoric, sculpture, painting, music, etc.', duly revived, as separate arts, in the Renaissance. In each separate art, 'great minds have created marvels' – Shakespeare and Beethoven are singled out – but 'the one true art has not been reborn . . . It cannot be reborn; it must be born anew.' Paradoxically, only 'the great revolution of mankind, whose beginnings once destroyed Greek tragedy, can regain this art.' Modern civilization values mankind instrumentally – it marginalizes 'man alive' ('der wirkliche lebendige Mensch')[44] – but revolution can create 'a nobler universalism'. Art will direct the revolution towards a new 'brotherhood of man', in which humanity is 'free and united', the separate arts meet once more in tragic drama – and 'this art will be conservative again'. A 'free and independent' public will sustain the theatre ('most powerful of all artistic institutions'), to which, as in antiquity, they will have free admission. And Wagner concludes by invoking the brotherhood of man, the dignity ('Würde') of man, and Jesus and Apollo: 'the two most sublime ['erhabensten'] teachers of mankind'.

The switch from a rare moment of practical policy ('free admission') to this astonishing peroration ('Jesus and Apollo') is characteristic. The precise relationship

[44] Cf. D. H. Lawrence: 'the only thing that is anything . . . man alive, and live woman' ('Why the Novel Matters', published posthumously in *Phoenix*, 1936).

between Wagner's diverse hopes remains forever elusive. In lieu of practicalities, his stock-in-trade is sweeping denunciations of the negative and assertions of the positive, its consummate value, its own ultimate unity. The unified community and the unified work of art are themselves, ultimately, united – in Wagner's mind. In his writing, such unities are established by a rhetoric of alignments and oppositions: the alignment of Apollo and Jesus (but *not* world-hating Christianity) is representative.

In this essay one can find most of the *idées fixes* that characterize Wagner's subsequent outlook (though nationalism tends to displace 'universalism' and enthusiasm for political revolution soon fades).[45] But at this mid-point in his creative career, with *Tannhäuser* and *Lohengrin* behind him (the latter composed, though not yet performed), and Bayreuth and the masterpieces of *Tristan* and the *Ring* still to come, one has a sense of new directions. Praise of Attic tragedy and Beethoven, but scorn for opera, implies an aspiration, spelled out more fully in *Opera and Drama*, to translate the power and authority of the modern symphonic tradition into myth in dramatic form. In the years leading up to the Zurich essays, this new 'mythic' orientation is apparent, both from Wagner's reading – not only Aeschylus, but also the Eddas and other Nordic saga-material – and from his drafts, which include (in 1848) a sketch of a drama on 'The Nibelung Myth' and a libretto for 'Siegfrieds Tod' ('The Death of Siegfried', a first version of *Götterdämmerung*). Work on the music of the *Ring* would not begin until 1853 (and on the music of *Tristan*, not until 1856).

Not quite all of Wagner's positives were yet in place. In its diagnosis of human alienation and endorsement of secular (but spiritual) value, *Art and Revolution* is indebted to the post-Hegelian philosopher Ludwig Feuerbach (whose *Principles of the Philosophy of the Future – Grundsätze der Philosophie der Zukunft*, 1843 – also helped to shape Wagner's slogans). A more momentous influence to come was the philosophy of Schopenhauer, which Wagner encountered 'as a gift from heaven' in 1854.[46] Yet Schopenhauer served to reinforce rather than redirect: 'His central idea, the final negation of the will to live, . . . is the only means of redemption ['einzig erlösend'] . . . [though] not new to me.'[47] Not new, indeed: throughout Wagner's career, renunciation and redemption, often in a distinctively Wagnerian context of sacrificial love, are among his favourite themes, from *The Flying Dutchman* to *Tristan* to *Parsifal* (whose closing words, 'redemption for the redeemer' – 'Erlösung dem Erlöser' – sum up the continuity of his idiosyncratic neo-Christianity as well).[48]

In one respect, allegiance to Schopenhauer complicated the project. What was the status of music in relation to the other arts? For Wagner, 'absolute music' – 'music divorced from the art of poetry'[49] – had reached its highest form, but

[45] Wagner's anti-Semitism (implicit in the tirades against commerce) becomes fully overt in 'Das Judentum in der Musik' ('Jewishness in Music'), published under a pseudonym in 1850.

[46] Letter to Liszt, ?16 December 1854.

[47] Ibid.

[48] Cf. his letter to Hans von Wolzogen, 17 January 1880.

[49] Letter to Ferdinand von Biedenfeld, 17 January 1849.

effectively a dead end, in the symphonies of Beethoven (in Wagner's mind, his great predecessor).[50] Elsewhere in the Zurich essays, especially *Opera and Drama*, he rewrites the hierarchy of the operatic arts: theatrical representation ('drama') comes first, music (expression of emotion) second, words ('poetry') third. Drama is 'the end', and music 'a means', whereas in opera 'a means of expression (music) has been made the end, and the end of expression (drama) a means.'[51]

A remarkable position, this, for the future composer of the *Ring* and, especially, *Tristan*, where magnificent music dominates from start to finish – and indeed for a devotee of Greek tragedy, where drama and the poetic word are dominant, and music a virtual appendage (not only is music confined to the lyric portions: in its monophonic simplicity, it will have borne no relation to the orchestral sophistications of the nineteenth century, or their 'expressive' power). But Schopenhauer's position was different again. In his philosophy, the everyday world is one of secondary illusion, from which drama, at its tragic best, offers an escape in the sense of a 'demonstration of the vanity of all human undertakings', whereas music has a superior significance altogether, penetrating metaphysical reality and revealing 'the innermost nature of the world': for Schopenhauer, 'at the highest creative level, words were redundant'.[52] Faced with these multiple contradictions, Wagner's successive prose writings make valiant attempts to square circles and reconcile irreconcilables.[53] His artistic development, mercifully, proceeded regardless.

In *Art and Revolution*, at all events, the essence of Wagner's project is on display: the unified community, coming together at a religious festival to experience unified musical tragedy and its mythic material (product of the community's 'insight into the nature of things and men')[54] – and then the Feuerbachian vision of the 'free' human individual, crystallized here in the phrase 'man alive' and elsewhere in appeals to the 'pure, essential human' ('das Reinmenschliche'), which, like the dramatic festival, is first cultivated by the Greeks.[55]

On one level, the entire project is one of innumerable instantiations of the Lacanian 'yearning for the whole'. In historical terms, it recalls the particular yearnings of the German Romantic generation, where the aspiration to recombine the arts is commonplace,[56] and where Schiller, for one, contrasts the fragmentation of modern culture with the cultural unity of ancient Greece.[57] The difference is the emphasis

[50] Wagner and Beethoven: Kropfinger (1974).

[51] *Opera and Drama*, 3, and introduction to 1.

[52] Silk and Stern (1981) 327, 55; Schopenhauer, *Die Welt als Wille und Vorstellung* (1819/44), 2. 3. 37 and 1. 3. 52.

[53] Cf. Silk and Stern (1981) 53–7, 137–40, 239–42.

[54] 'Die Wibelungen' ('The Wibelungs', 1849).

[55] *Opera and Drama*, 2. 6 ('das, was das Wesen der menschlichen Gattung, als solcher, ausmacht'); 'Artwork of the Future', 3. 1.

[56] Cf. Schefer (2011). This aspiration in fact precedes the Romantics: see e.g. John Brown's *Dissertation on the . . . Separations . . . of Poetry and Music* (1763).

[57] See esp. *Über die ästhetische Erziehung des Menschen* (1795).

Wagner gives to music – and the commitment he shows in attempting to translate these ideals into action.

It is easy to criticise Wagner's view of Greece. History has to be squashed, and actualities adjusted, to make the Athenian 'community' the effective creator of Greek myth. The Greek dramatic festivals have as much to do with the 'entertainment' that Wagner scorns as with the religion he commends. And (quite apart from the remarkable notion of a 'revolutionary' Sophocles) the idea that tragedy at its Aeschylean peak was 'conservative' (*because* communal) ignores its exploratory treatment of 'epic' heroism (obvious in the *Oresteia*), of dominant womanhood (in the Oresteian Clytemnestra), even of religion.

Easy, too, to identify discrepancies between the Greek paradigm and Wagner's project, as eventually realized in the *Ring*. Like the *Oresteia*, the *Ring* is a connected cycle, but a very different sort of cycle. Its characters and plot – adapted freely from the abstruse material of the sagas – define a conflict, on a cosmic scale, between power and love. The conflict is initiated by the theft of the Rhine-gold, and its fashioning into a ring in which earthly power resides, and resolved by the love-struck Brünnhilde's sacrifice of the ring, and herself, which precipitates the destruction of the gods: love overpowers power itself. Such an allegory, foreign to Greek tragedy, is only one of many un-Greek features of Wagner's *Ring*.[58] Not only is its music unrelatable to any Aeschylean 'equivalent' (albeit, in an audacious pun, Wagner identified the musical commentary provided by his *orchestra* with the role of the tragic chorus in the Greek *orkhestra*).[59] The *Ring*'s 'concocted mythology' (unrelated to a living religion) is far removed from the traditional mytho-religious materials that formed the 'inner landscape' of Athenian audiences,[60] while the whole momentum of the cycle is devoted to 'exploring the world of inner feeling in a way which is quite alien to the spirit of Aeschylus'.[61]

For good measure, Wagner's best efforts to make Bayreuth 'a festival of German art' and a 'real religious necessity',[62] and his festival theatre an indoor equivalent of a Greek theatrical space, largely went astray. The theatre, based on designs by Gottfried Semper, had novel features: an ingenious amphitheatrical auditorium, without social stratification, and a darkened auditorium and concealed orchestra pit. The overall effect (in Thomas Mann's words), was 'a kind of theatrical Lourdes, a grotto of miracles for a weary twilight age that yearns for some kind of faith', while the whole Bayreuth phenomenon embodied 'not the spirit of the nation, but simply one artist's supreme ambition'.[63] (Mann might have added that, where Athenian festivals had competing playwrights, Bayreuth was all Wagner.) Privately, Wagner

[58] Like many modern artists, Wagner uses myth as 'cover': §24.

[59] See Silk (1999c) 213–17. Of *Götterdämmerung*, Act III, Wagner said, 'I have composed a Greek chorus . . . to be sung by the orchestra': Cosima, *Tagebücher*, 29 September 1871.

[60] Steiner (1961) 322–3; cf. Ewans (1982) 56–62.

[61] Ibid. 45.

[62] Letters to Ludwig, 1 October 1874, and Hans von Bülow, 15 February 1852.

[63] 'Leiden und Grösse Richard Wagners' (1933); 'Versuch über das Theater' (1908).

was dissatisfied, too, especially with his audiences: moneyed, paying customers, 'all in fancy dress and make-up', a world away from his original vision of a 'free' community: 'Now I've created the invisible orchestra, I'd like to invent the invisible theatre'.[64]

There is, certainly, direct influence on Wagner's creative work (especially the *Ring*) from Greek tragedy (especially the *Oresteia*).[65] The *Ring* and the *Oresteia* have in common the cyclical form; a huge tale of striving and vengeance; a god-driven cosmology; and a trajectory from the divine to the human (*Eumenides* closes with a human processional acclaiming reconciliation among the gods, the *Ring* with human survivors contemplating the gods' collective 'twilight'). Then there are 'Aeschylean' moments, like Sieglinde's nightmare (both vision and reality) in *Walküre*, Act II, recalling the lyric dialogue between Cassandra and chorus in the *Agamemnon*.[66]

But the Aeschylean traces in Wagner's work pale into insignificance beside the triumphant modernity of the music, the 'inner feeling', and the inner values that are everywhere evident. Wagner is 'the modern artist *par excellence*,' said Nietzsche in 1888: 'the Cagliostro of modernity.' And 'confronted with the labyrinth of the modern soul, where could [one] find a more qualified guide?'[67] Wagner's intimates might see him as a new Aeschylus,[68] but he knows he is not – and *no*, he does not even *want* to be . . . He wants to create, not Aeschylean tragedy, but 'near-tragedy' – 'the compromise of an age which did not believe in the finality of evil'.[69] He wants to explore, not the societal loyalties of Greek heroes, but the emotional compulsions of the modern 'subjective' individual,[70] whose passions define the nineteenth-century novel, as they define *Tristan* and the *Ring*.[71] And that 'Aeschylean' end of *Götterdämmerung* – Brünnhilde's 'redeeming' self-sacrifice and the love that drives her to join her Siegfried in death ('die Liebe nur sein!' – among her last words – 'only love!')[72] – all this is modern in a very special way. This love that destroys gods, and lets human beings inherit the earth, is Christianity translated into Wagnerian-redemptive worldly love: God was among us, so loved the world, *died* for us, that we might live. Insofar as Wagner's resolution satisfies on the mythic-dramatic level,

[64] Cosima, *Tagebücher*, 23 September 1878.

[65] Scrutinized/overstated by Ewans (1982). Misrepresented by Foster (2010); cf. Ewans (2010). The 'Aeschylean' *Prometheus* also influenced the *Ring* – Ewans (1982) 256–60 – and is itself invoked in *Art and Revolution*.

[66] Ewans (1982) 141–5. Wagner thought the Cassandra scene 'the most perfect thing human art has ever achieved': Cosima, *Tagebücher*, 18 November 1874.

[67] *Der Fall Wagner*, 5, and preface.

[68] Cosima, letter to Nietzsche, 26 August 1869; Nietzsche, letter to Erwin Rohde, 3 September 1869; Cosima, *Tagebücher*, 4 October 1869; Nietzsche, 'Richard Wagner in Bayreuth', 4.

[69] Steiner (1961) 133.

[70] A Hegelian contrast: see Hegel's *Ästhetik*, 3. 3. 3. c. c. 3. B–c (*sic*); cf. Silk and Stern (1981) 322–5.

[71] Cf. Nietzsche, *Der Fall Wagner*, 9.

[72] Cf. Wagner, letter to August Röckel, 25/26 January 1854.

it does so by tacit appeal to this nexus – reshaped, in irresistibly modern form, for an age of the death of God, or gods. But meanwhile (in case the dramatic resolution is insufficient), the *Ring* is resolved, musically, by – no less irresistibly modern – an overwhelming recapitulation of musical themes from the whole cycle.

Where, then, does all this leave Wagner and the Greeks? What, ultimately, is their contribution to his project? Details apart, the Greeks form no part of Wagner's edifice. They are, rather, part – but a crucial part – of the scaffolding. Some interpreters have invested the Greeks with a more direct significance, whereby, for instance, 'Wagner's Hellenism and his anti-Semitism are integrally connected',[73] with the Greeks paradigmatic for a nationalist project, the Jews as the cosmopolitan Other. Such a schema is not persuasive: not because there is any doubt about the anti-Semitism, but because Wagner himself never articulates this opposition,[74] and complicates any thought of it by an alignment between the Jews and the nationalist-minded French,[75] which assumes the special significance of French opera. In France, opera had acquired the status of a national art-form as early as the founding of the Académie Royale de Musique in 1669.[76] In dismissing traditional opera and nominating Beethoven as his predecessor, Wagner is affirming the superiority of the symphonic Germans over the operatic French (and, not least, over the dominant figure in mid-nineteeth-century French opera, the German-Jewish composer, Meyerbeer).

'No, we do not want to be Greeks again'. It is no coincidence that Wagner's Greek allegiances hardly surface within his vast influence,[77] or indeed within the perspective of his chief critics. Here, Nietzsche is a revealing case. In 1872, at the height of his Wagnerian commitment, Nietzsche acclaims Wagner as the modern successor to Aeschylus (and Sophocles), heralding the birth of a new 'tragic age'.[78] In 1876, by way of a last hurrah and though now deeply ambivalent, Nietzsche affirms the 'affinity' between Wagner and Aeschylus himself.[79] Yet once he has finally renounced Wagner, later that decade, his copious critiques of his former idol freely condemn Wagner's nationalism and anti-Semitism, mischievously identify Wagner as spiritually French ('Very modern . . . Very Parisian. Very *decadent*'),[80] but say hardly a word about (or even against) the Greek connection. And it is no coincidence, either, that *Tristan*, Wagner's most achieved and most quintessentially Wagnerian work ('he

73 Goldhill (2008) 461–2.

74 Despite eventually seeing the Jews as 'the enemy of the pure human' ('reine Menschheit': letter to Ludwig, 22 November 1881), alongside his view of the Greeks (p. 386, above).

75 The French and the Jews are common targets in (esp.) Wagner's essay, 'Was ist deutsch?' ('What is German?', 1865/78).

76 Fulcher (1987).

77 Bayreuth provoked a few classicizing imitations, notably the 'Fêtes d'Orange' (1894), held in the Roman amphitheatre at Orange and featuring Saint-Saëns's 'Hymne à Pallas-Athènè'.

78 *The Birth of Tragedy*, 19: Silk and Stern (1981).

79 See n. 68 above.

80 *Der Fall Wagner*, 9. 'Decadence': Silk (2004c).

says he has produced nothing new since'),[81] with all its consummate inner feeling and 'uninterrupted music' ('ununterbrochene Musik'),[82] has nothing Greek about it at all.

Wagner is a composer who puts great emphasis on performance, and a music-dramatist for whom only his own theatre will do. He is a man of action, certainly, and he thinks of action when he thinks of art. Art should 'give light at a time rich in deeds' ('sie . . . leuchten soll während einer tatenreichen Zeit').[83] His musical-theatrical goal, he wrote in 1872, was 'deeds of music made manifest' ('ersichtlich gewordene Taten der Musik').[84] Deeds *of* music, or deeds lit up *by* music: like so much else, this relationship is never determined. What *is* determined is that the deeds belong to the here-and-now, not to the past, Greek or other.

Between the cases of Wagner and Machiavelli – theoretically-minded music-dramatist and diplomat turned political theorist – there are obvious differences. But the two have one crucial thing in common: both use antiquity to assist a project or programme of action, without feeling any obligation to *imitate* antiquity. Demonstrations of the way Wagner models this or that aspect of the *Ring* on the *Oresteia* are, in the final analysis, off the point. In fundamentals, Wagner is as remote from the spirit of Winckelmann or Weimar classicism as Machiavelli is from *his* fellow humanists.

However, like most of antiquity's imitators, great or small, both believe that we can (even must) learn from antiquity. Like, but significantly unlike. Machiavelli converts the ancient authorities into a databank, for present and future reference; Wagner, into a stage in a process of construction that (like scaffolding . . .) is to be out of sight, even out of mind, in the event. In different degrees, both (like the imitators) accept the validity of the classical example, across cultures. Machiavelli's commitment to learn from antiquity depends on his faith in the universality of behaviour. That kind of transculturalism is shared by Wagner in one sense (the 'pure human' that informed the Greek world must inform ours now), but not in another: *no*, we cannot and do not even want to *try* and be Greeks again. Among the significant makers of the classical tradition – and the wider, modern world – the two present a provoking comparison and contrast.

[81] Cosima, *Tagebücher*, 26 March 1879 – twenty years after *Tristan* was composed. In 1860, Wagner had already decided that, after *Tristan*, there were 'no new essential truths' for him to 'uncover': letter to Mathilde Wesendonck, 2 May 1860.

[82] Wagner's own description: Cosima, *Tagebücher*, 4 October 1881.

[83] Ibid. 21 December 1870.

[84] 'Über die Benennung "Musikdrama"'.

Part V

Contrasts and Comparisons

§32
Preface

Intermittently, in the course of this book, we have distanced ourselves from the fashionable preoccupation with 'reception of antiquity' at the expense of other modes of the classical tradition.[1] In Part V, rather, we focus on what might well be considered as cases of reception in their own right – though in §35 'engagements with earlier engagements' (§1) figure prominently as well, and in §33, arguably, we have something approaching the evolution of an archetype.

As in Part IV, the cases chosen involve juxtaposition, but here the outcomes are comparisons of a more direct kind. We consider three sets of three creative figures in the contrasting fields of painting (§33), political thought (§34), and poetry (§35). Each of these sections seeks to illuminate, not just the individual figures, but the respective fields themselves, by critical comparisons between the individuals and their place within the tradition – while our juxtaposition of the three sections points an implicit contrast between the three fields, the responses to antiquity (direct or indirect) characteristic of each, and the different kinds of issues that arise in each.

Three painters, then; three political thinkers; and three poets – with, in each case, a particular point of reference. The painters are Titian, David, and de Chirico, with a focus on the female nude. Like the painters, the poets belong to different periods: Milton, Tennyson, and Eliot – and our emphasis, here, is on poetic language. The thinkers, by contrast, all belong to the twentieth century: Arendt, Popper, Leo Strauss – and here the common point of reference is the sombre phenomenon of Nazi atrocity and the modern totalitarian state.

[1] Or (as it sometimes is) a fashionable habit of subsuming, under the rubric of 'reception', any instance or aspect of the tradition that comes to scholarly notice.

The Classical Tradition: Art, Literature, Thought, First Edition. Michael Silk, Ingo Gildenhard, and Rosemary Barrow.

Published 2017 by John Wiley & Sons Ltd.

§33
Painting

If you find it helpful to copy the work of others . . . take as your model a mediocre sculpture rather than an exceptional painting. From painted objects we only train the hand in making a likeness; from sculptures we learn both to represent a likeness and to assess the correct light.[1]

From the Renaissance, and for centuries (§4), formal art training, in line with Alberti's advice, laid stress on drawing from antique sculptures and casts. This practice had a profound impact on representations of the nude, and not only because (as Rembrandt's pupil, van Hoogstraten, put it), a hard surface does not behave like 'soft skin'.[2] Poses, proportions, and types that had once evolved, and were eventually prescribed, for white marble were now translated onto a painted canvas; representations of living humanity were required to conform, more or less, to a standardized set of mathematical calculations; and the painted nude was thus accommodated to the 'ideal nature' or 'general nature' that critics from Winckelmann to Sartre would come to identify as the hallmark of the classical sculptural form.[3] Meanwhile, the exclusion of women from fifteenth-century workshops

1 Alberti, *De pictura*, Part 3.

2 *Introduction to the Advanced School of Painting* (*Inleyding tot de hooge schoole der schilderkunst*, 1678), 6. 6.

3 Winckelmann, *Reflections on the Imitation of Greek Works in Painting and Sculpture* (1755), 1, on the nude sculptures of the Greeks: 'their model was an ideal nature'. Sartre, 'The Search for the Absolute' (in the Alberto Giacometti exhibition catalogue, Pierre Matisse Gallery, New York, 1948): the classical sculptor believes 'he can eliminate his own [individual] glance, and sculpt human nature in general.'

The Classical Tradition: Art, Literature, Thought, First Edition. Michael Silk, Ingo Gildenhard, and Rosemary Barrow.

Published 2017 by John Wiley & Sons Ltd.

helped to institutionalize the principle that the female form, in particular, could only be studied by copying sculpture.[4] For the foreseeable future, therefore, images of the female nude would be associated with antique models.

In sixteenth-century Venice, Giorgione's *Sleeping Venus* (1509) established the distinctive topos of the reclining nude. The artist derived his female types from sculptural sources; and both the sleeping motif and the pudica pose of his Venus are familiar in ancient sculpture from the fourth century BC onwards.[5] In the wake of Giorgione's painting, Venice now became a new centre of production for classicizing representations of the female nude, with Titian (who completed some of the incidental detail of the *Sleeping Venus*) inheriting Giorgione's mantle as the leading innovator in the field. Titian's *poesie*, a set of mythological paintings commissioned by Philip II of Spain, are significant on several levels. Derived from Ovid's *Metamorphoses*, these pictorial 'poems' offer both a commentary on the Latin text and a demonstration of the power of pictorial art to challenge the descriptions of poetry; they also contrive to display the female form from a beguiling variety of different angles.[6] Of Philip's Titians, only one – the *Venus and Adonis* (1555) – is connected with a specific sculptural prototype (this one, with the Hellenistic Grimani altar),[7] but elsewhere Titian's many Venuses look more closely to their Greco-Roman sources. *Venus Anadyomene* (*c.* 1525) recreates Apelles' masterpiece from textual description and surviving sculptural types,[8] while *Woman in a Fur Coat* (1536–8) and *Venus with a Mirror* (*c.* 1555) recall the distinctive double pudica pose of the Medici Venus. That celebrated statue, though today firmly ensconced in the canon of ancient art, actually has no recorded find spot or date of rediscovery and indeed is not recorded at all until the seventeenth century, by which time it is a prized possession in the Villa Medici in Rome.[9] Yet whether or not the Medici Venus herself serves as a model for Titian, there is no doubt that he looks to the many Venus variants which (like the Medici) derive from Praxiteles' fourth-century masterpiece, the Aphrodite of Cnidos.[10]

4 Cf. Bernstein (1992).

5 Though the complex poses found in frescoes of the Fondaco dei Tedeschi might suggest life study: Battisti and Krumrine (1982).

6 In a letter to Philip (1554) discussing the shipment of *Venus and Adonis*, Titian writes: 'And since the *Danae*, which I have already sent to Your Majesty, is seen from the front, I wanted to vary this in the other *poesia*, showing the figure from the opposite side, so that the room they are to hang in will be more pleasing ['grazioso'] to the eye. Soon I shall send you the *poesia* of Perseus and Andromeda, which will offer yet another view, different from these; and the same with Medea and Jason'. Cf. Rosand (1978) 41. Titian and Ovid: cf. Martindale (1993) 60–4.

7 Goffen (1997) 242 n. 98.

8 The Anadyomene type is already familiar in the medieval period: Heckscher (1956). Venice could not offer Renaissance artists the wealth of monumental sculptures unearthed in Rome, but smaller decorative items were well represented in Venetian collections: Brown (1997), Favaretto (1990).

9 Haskell and Penny (1981) cat. 88.

10 Bober and Rubinstein (1986) 59 ascribe to the Venus pudica type 'an almost continuous history in Medieval and Renaissance art'. Pudica statues possibly known to Titian: Goffen (1997) 133 n. 86. Cnidian Aphrodite's reception in post-classical art: Barrow (2005) (from which some of the material in this section derives).

Praxiteles' statue (which only survives in Hellenistic and Roman copies) evokes the mythical voyage of Aphrodite across the Mediterranean. Stopping to wash the sea's foam from her body, the goddess is shown undressing for a bath or else dressing after the bath is over. In a single pudica motion, her right hand moves to conceal her body and her left hand holds a garment. Is she dropping her garment, or reaching for it in order to cover herself? The pose is appropriated by the sixteenth-century Venetian school: in Giorgione's painting, Venus' hand rests lightly on her genitals; in Titian's *Venus of Urbino* (1538), her fingers curl enticingly around the area she purports to cover. This ambiguous pose raises another set of questions. It has been read as an uncontroversial emblem of chastity,[11] and as an unmistakable erotic signal.[12] More widely, at least, there is a recent consensus that mythological subject matter in general sanctions erotic representation,[13] and that classical sculpture in particular offers an aesthetic prototype for representation of the sensual nude. The classical-sculptural form may be, in the poet Swinburne's words, 'noble and nude and antique';[14] but (like Swinburne's poetry) it also carries a latent erotic charge, which, no doubt, is felt more strongly, and also felt to be more problematic, in some eras than in others. 'Every young sculptor,' says Nathaniel Hawthorne, in Swinburne's own day, 'seems to think that he must give the world some specimen of indecorous womanhood, and call it Eve, Venus, or a Nymph, or any name that may apologise for a lack of decent clothing.'[15]

In art-historical terms, the female nude has come to transcend conventional categorization: it has become both a symbol of the classical tradition in art and emblematic of art itself. So emblematic, indeed, that in the neoclassical age commentators assume it. 'Artists!,' declared Alexander Pope in 1734, 'To draw the naked is your true delight.'[16] Conversely, in the age of modernist rebellion, manifesto-writers single it out for rejection. For Boccioni and his fellow-Futurists in 1912, the nude typifies the traditions that they must 'fight against', at least for the time being (though even they feel obliged to acknowledge its underlying truth-to-art): 'We demand, *for ten years*, the total suppression of the nude in painting.'[17] For centuries, artists operate within a broadly comparable structure of visual certainties, and one

11 Himmelmann (1985) 52–3.

12 Gaston (1995/6), esp. 250–1.

13 Hope (1976) speaks of the 'alibi of a classical subject' with reference to the eroticism of Titian's mythological paintings; Talvacchia (1999) 46 n. 28, of the 'cloak of mythology' that allowed Titian to use a portrait of Cardinal Alessandro Farnese's mistress for the face of *Danae*, commissioned by the Cardinal and hung publicly in his residence; Gaston (1995/6) 254, of Bronzino's classical-subject paintings as 'mythologically sanctioned' images of desire.

14 'Dolores' (1866), stanza 7.

15 *The Marble Faun* (1860), ch. 14 (Miriam speaking).

16 'Epistle to a Lady', 187–8.

17 'Futurist Painting: Technical Manifesto' (Italian original, 1910), from the 1912 English version in the Sackville Gallery catalogue – where the whole sentence is in italics. Female nudes in the academic tradition had been an *avant-garde* target for decades: see (e.g.) Huysmans on 'Cabanel's peaches-and-cream Venus' ('L'Exposition des Indépendents en 1881': *L'Art moderne*, 1883).

of these – from Botticelli (in Alberti's century) to Matisse (in the Futurists' own) – is the female nude, and the viewer's familiarity with the female nude, in the tradition of the Cnidian Aphrodite. Indeed, both before and after the Futurist protests, creative challenges to the nude's traditional form (painted or sculpted), and to all its attendant associations, only confirm the power of its continuing presence within the widening horizons of Western art. In 1865 Manet's notorious *Olympia* subverted audience expectations by showing a real woman in place of a goddess, while a century later Larry Rivers presented a racially-aware reworking of what was now a cultural stereotype with *I Like Olympia in Black Face* (1970).

The long reception of the classicizing pictorial nude has been much discussed, but less attention has been paid to the meaning of the reproduction of ancient nude statuary in painting. Does a sculptural nude on a painted canvas – like the painted female form itself – also inscribe the body with its latent erotic associations? For Titian, certainly, the painted sculptural figure seems to have an erotic significance, even without the actualized fleshiness of the 'real' body. In the *Worship of Venus* (1518–20), a recognisable variant of the Cnidia type appears, as a statue, in the right-hand corner of the canvas, with the pudica pose in the form of a hand clutching at drapery which slides down the hips to reveal the body [*Plate 8*]. This modified pose recalls the Celestial Venus type, a Cnidia variant also known from Roman copies.[18] But Titian does not imitate a specific type; he draws on and develops a now long-standing tradition with his own high-Renaissance variations. Unmistakably, the face of *his* Venus is not in the idealized style of pre-Hellenistic sculpture, but sharply individualized. Here Titian makes a statue look like a woman rather than *vice versa*.

The distinction between marble and flesh can be profitably reconsidered in the light of modern art-historical debates about the female nude. In 1956 Kenneth Clark distinguished nudity and nakedness in terms of an opposition between aesthetic identification and material reality, only for John Berger (sixteen years later) to reject such tidy categories, in favour of the dynamic of viewer and viewed and the objectification of the female body that Berger associated it with.[19] More recently, feminist art historians have challenged and problematized Berger's own argument, which tends to ignore socio-historical context, medium, and mode of production, and to assume an exclusively male viewership.[20] More particularly, Lynda Nead reads the aesthetic category of the nude itself as a way of controlling the unruly female body: woman, made up of an undisciplined mass of flesh, fat, and orifices, can be disciplined by idealized and inviolable artistic transformation.[21] We can add, then, that a marble statue, necessarily smooth, cool and (literally) impenetrable, is an ideal

[18] See Falomir (2003) cat.11, who notes that one such copy was in the Grimani collection and probably on display in Venice in early XVI.

[19] Clark (1956); Berger (1972).

[20] McDonald (2001), Nead (1992), Pointon (1992).

[21] Nead (1992) 2.

vehicle within which to contain (though also still to imply) female fleshiness and sexuality. To this extent, a pictorial nude *based on* a classical sculpture and a painting *of* a statue can be seen to share a common meaning.

Titian's *Worship of Venus* was one of two works he painted for Duke Alfonso d'Este that derived from an ecphrasis in Philostratus' *Imagines*, a work of the Greek Second Sophistic. The text was chosen by the duke (or his advisors), and the completed work was placed in a camerino in his castle, which was eventually adorned with paintings by Bellini, Dosso Dossi, and Titian himself.[22] Philostratus' description begins, 'Look, cupids [*erôtes*] are gathering apples',[23] and Titian, accordingly, presents his viewers with a chaotic assemblage of cupids gathering their fruit, all dancing, hunting, playing, and fighting. The scene is presided over by the statue of Venus mounted on a pedestal. In Philostratus, it is the (Greek) goddess herself who oversees the celebrations in her honour: 'Please, look at Aphrodite.'[24] By choosing to portray the goddess in plastic form, Titian conveys a powerful sense of her presence. The painter, his patron, and his audiences could all assume such an assured knowledge of ancient anthropomorphic imagery that a standing female nude of the Cnidia type was immediately recognisable as a Venus, in a way that any representation of a 'real' woman was not.[25] Here, then, it is the statue that manifests a presence, both erotic and divine.

By the eighteenth century, the continuum of ancient statuary and its understandings provides a set of artistic paradigms, beyond controversy or challenge, for painters in Continental Europe, Britain, and America. Sculptural forms serve as a compelling prototype for the representation of the Greco-Roman mythological nude, while actual statues, along with architecture and other artefacts, enliven history paintings. The neoclassical nude exudes a cool elegance rather than the ripe fleshiness of her Renaissance predecessor, but representations of statuary in painting show more continuity than change. Painted in pre-revolutionary France, David's *Paris and Helen* (1788) is based on the episode in *Iliad* 3 where Paris is whisked away from battle into Helen's boudoir,[26] and features a statue of Venus/Aphrodite standing on a pedestal in its left-hand corner [*Plate 9*]. An imitation of the Victorious Venus, the figure holds her slipping drapery with one hand, while the other

[22] Ancient ecphrasis and Renaissance painting: Rosand (1990). D'Este's camerino: Cavalli-Björkman (1987), Shearman (1987).

[23] Philostratus, *Imagines*, 1. 6. 1.

[24] Ibid. 1. 6. 7.

[25] The original commission for the camerino paintings was secured by Fra Bartolommeo, who died before its completion, but in a 1517 drawing of the *Worship of Venus*, he, too, depicts the goddess as a statue on a pedestal.

[26] Whereas David's Revolutionary paintings, often drawn from early Roman history (§21), politicize masculine courage and self-sacrifice, Korshak (1987) 102 finds in *Paris and Helen* 'a metaphor for the French monarchy's narcissism and evasion of duty on the eve of the French Revolution'. Contrast Dowley and Korshak (1988).

hand, arm outstretched, holds a golden apple. Except for an added diadem in her hair, as befits a goddess, David's Venus is an exact copy of a statue in the Barberini collection.[27]

In Renaissance Venice, artists had licence to adapt classical models freely; now, in an age of archaeological discovery, adjustments have a restorative function. Among a clutter of objects portrayed – from Jean Goujon's sixteenth-century Louvre Caryatids to a Pompeian-type tripod brazier – David's statue is part of a *mise-en-scène* calculated to evoke the authoritative past. David and other artists choose settings, costumes, and accessories suggestive of historical validity; but, as the wide-ranging provenance of the artefacts demonstrates here, in what purports to be Homeric Troy, it is a broadly conceived authenticity rather than any periodizing accuracy that is felt to be appropriate. At the same time, this Venus/Aphrodite claims a narrative significance beyond the archaeological. It is Paris' bestowal of the prized apple on the goddess that started the Trojan war, and it is also this goddess that snatched the Trojan prince away from duty and danger. In the painting, Aphrodite's eschewal of warfare is illustrated by Paris' discarded weaponry: a bow rests on the pedestal, while the statue's outstretched arm supports his quiver strap.

In David's preparatory drawings, an actual Cupid rather than a statue of Aphrodite was used to convey the active presence of love,[28] but the artist eventually rejected such a configuration in favour of a sculpture that signifies the presence of the goddess herself. Although Paris is the only fully nude figure, Helen's transparent chiton surmounted by falling red himation echoes Aphrodite's own semi-draped form; and if the Spartan queen is depicted at a moment of blushing modesty, her sexual presence is embodied in the Aphrodite statue instead. In David's Aphrodite, as in Titian's Venus, female sexuality is once again contained within the boundaries of the aesthetic form of a statue.

Modernist art practices reject archaeological detail and text-based narrative, along with the idealized classicizing nude. Even so, the Cnidia (her variants and copies) maintains her place in twentieth-century painting, in the work of Giorgio de Chirico, at one time, himself, an associate of the Futurist Carlo Carrà. De Chirico's *The Uncertainty of the Poet* (1913) [*Plate 10*] is typical of the artist's Metaphysical period, in which architectonic spaces are populated by solitary figures, inanimate objects, mysterious shadows. In de Chirico's painting, the torso of a nude Aphrodite sits uneasily in a modern setting. The torso faces a bunch of plantains,[29] while a steam train hurtles past in the distance. Placed in a disconcertingly illogical alignment, the statue's significance as an aesthetic ideal is undermined, and its acknowledged high-art status and meaning within the art-historical canon

[27] Coche de la Ferté and Guey (1952) 146.

[28] See e.g. a pen and black-ink and grey-wash sketch dated 1786 in the Getty Museum.

[29] Critics have (mis)identified the fruit as bananas rather than plantains: Barrow (2005) 346, Cowling and Mundy (1990) 73, Gale (1988) 275.

challenged.[30] Both literally and figuratively Aphrodite has been knocked off her pedestal.

De Chirico's statue is not modified (as in Titian) or restored (as in David); instead, it is presented in terms ordinarily recognisable to the modern viewer: a damaged plaster cast of a once complete marble original. Such a fragmented antiquity is not a new visual trope. Even in the Renaissance, certain statues were left unrestored (§§11, 17). In the nineteenth century, Rodin reinstated the incomplete body in the shape of finished sculptures derived from antique fragments[31] (and one recalls the way that Rilke, Rodin's sometime secretary,[32] found his Apollo torso compelling despite, or because of, its missing head: §14). But in de Chirico's painting, the torso's fragmentary state, like one of Pound's 'broken statues' (§4), seems to offer a commentary on the place of the classical in the modern world. The remnants of antiquity are worn, damaged, hopelessly incongruous. And the very title, 'the uncertainty of the poet', proclaims the distance of this modern world from the confident creativity of earlier ages. 'The best lack all conviction', as the poet Yeats put it, a few years later.[33] In de Chirico's disquieting vision, the formal and spiritual relationships of a whole tradition, like the statue itself, appear broken.

But the lesson of de Chirico's painting, and of its sculptural nude, is not exhausted by this sobering exegesis. Textual references in antiquity confirm that the original Cnidia was widely read as an erotic representation of the goddess of sexual love.[34] Titian's Venus and David's Aphrodite retain an erotic significance, but de Chirico's cast, without legs, arms, or head, surely has none, except insofar as absence suggests presence, by force of habit – or here by the juxtaposition of phallic plantains, which seem to draw attention to the torso's lack of sexual allure. For this Italian painter, it may be, the exotic, African connotations of the plantain evoke something quite different: Italy's imperial expansionist policies, especially across northern Africa, in this modern age. Yet the fruit's own exotic modernity (seemingly so different from Titian's apples) is not clear-cut either. Banana and plantain domestication has been traced back to south-east Asia between 5000 and 8000 BC, and their first introduction to Europe is actually associated with the Indian campaign of Alexander the Great in 327 BC.[35] Perhaps 'the uncertainty of the poet' is prompted by the challenge

[30] Cf. Baldacci (1983) 27–8. In this period de Chirico's work presents comparable assortments of objects: in *The Song of Love* (1914), the head of the Apollo Belvedere rests next to a rubber glove; in *The Philosopher's Promenade* (1913), a Hellenistic-type head of Zeus shares its space with two artichokes. The seeming inspiration for such juxtapositions is Cézanne's *Still Life with Plaster Cupid* (*c.* 1895): Taylor (2002) 35.

[31] Rodin was inspired by sculpture collections in Paris and London, and even bought pieces himself. His letter to Helene von Nostiz (10 October 1910) declares: 'Now I have made a collection of mutilated fragments, some of them real masterpieces. I spend time with them and they teach me'. Cf. Lampert (2006) 250 and p. 237 above.

[32] Rilke and Rodin had a noteworthy relationship: Potts (2000) 61–101.

[33] 'The Second Coming', composed in January 1919.

[34] Notably: Pliny, *Natural History*, 36. 21; Lucian, *Erotes*, 13–17.

[35] Gowen (1995) 4.

of alien, cosmopolitan disruption – or perhaps it is a more open-ended, more positive, uncertainty. Are we to find disharmony and discontinuity here? Or instead an unexpected reassurance, whereby a long-forgotten contact is recuperated and restored, and the classical emblem of artistic tradition evokes a lost relationship, even, in the most unlikely setting? De Chirico's torso may relieve the Aphrodite statue of her erotic function, but the truncated sculptural body, it may be, wins a paradoxical victory. Now the female form is no longer a mere vessel for containment, and, beyond sexuality (and even gender) itself, her broken image intimates a new dialogue.

§34
Political Thought

'After Auschwitz, writing poems is barbaric': Theodor Adorno's dictum is less a call for silence than an admission of the complicity of high culture – *even* poetry – in the barbarity of state-sponsored genocide.[1] It acknowledges, but also queries, the 'abyss' between Nazi Germany's 'fabrication of corpses'[2] and the values and traditions of Western civilization. Along with such other murderous systems as Stalin's in the USSR, the Nazi regime epitomizes what Eric Hobsbawm called 'the age of extremes':[3] 'extremes' sometimes ascribed to factors specific to Germany, sometimes explained in terms of totalitarianism in general.[4] And for Karl Popper, Leo Strauss, and Hannah Arendt, such a focus on the totalitarian is fundamental to their contrasting attempts to offer a systematic reappraisal of Western political thought, its classical roots, and their contemporary relevance.

These three influential figures shared a common background. All were Jewish émigrés from the Third Reich who fled to the safety of the English-speaking world, where they were to enjoy distinguished academic careers. Popper left Vienna in

[1] 'nach Auschwitz ein Gedicht zu schreiben, ist barbarisch': Adorno, 'Kulturkritik und Gesellschaft' (1951). Cf. Diner (1988), Gubar (2003).

[2] Arendt, '"What Remains? The Language Remains"', in *Essays in Understanding, 1930–1954* (1994).

[3] Hobsbawm (1994).

[4] See Jesse (1999). German-specific explanations include: the 'special road' ('Sonderweg') by which Germany, as a 'belated nation', reached modernity (Wehler 1973); a nexus between German high culture and the Holocaust (Steiner 1969, Stern 1978); and the peculiar virulence of German anti-Semitism (Goldhagen 1996).

The Classical Tradition: Art, Literature, Thought, First Edition. Michael Silk, Ingo Gildenhard, and Rosemary Barrow.

Published 2017 by John Wiley & Sons Ltd.

1936, then went to New Zealand, and finally to the London School of Economics (1949–69); Strauss, who had left Germany to study in Paris in 1932, spent time in England and New York, before becoming a professor of political science at the University of Chicago (1949–67); and Arendt, who escaped from the Gestapo in 1933 and an internment camp in newly defeated France in 1940, eventually held positions at various institutions in the United States, including the New School for Social Research in New York (1967–75).[5]

But in each case the biography and the contribution to political thought transcend the confines of professional scholarship. Of Arendt, Ernest Gellner wrote: 'Her life is a parable, not just of our age, but of several centuries of European thought and experience'[6] – and the same might be said of Popper and Strauss as well. Notwithstanding their institutional affiliations, moreover, the trio stand apart from the academic mainstream. In one way or another, the thinking of all three has significant links with active politics. And each responds to the plenum of Western thought from Greek antiquity to the present, addressing contemporary issues from within these broad historical parameters, albeit from radically different premises and with radically different outcomes. And if the phenomenon of totalitarianism is central to their shared concerns, so too is the role of cultural tradition, the power of ideas, and the reassessment of (among other ancient figures) Plato. In a very real sense, then, the three case studies add another chapter to our story of classical paradigms and their contribution to Western political thought (§26).

Before the Nazi occupation of Austria in 1938, Karl Popper's claim to fame was his contributions to the history and philosophy of science.[7] The *Anschluss* now prompted him to apply a strikingly rational intelligence to politics. The result was his *magnum opus*, *The Open Society and Its Enemies*, largely written during World War II and first published in 1945. Popper called it 'a fighting book', 'an attempt, with the very moderate means at my disposal, to help to fight the war' – but also to shape the subsequent peace.[8] His immediate targets are Hitler and Stalin, but his arguments address their presumed antecedents: Plato, Hegel, and Marx. While connections between Stalin and the philosophies of Hegel and (especially) Marx are obvious enough, correlating Plato and Hitler may seem far-fetched or, as Popper himself suggested, 'absurd'.[9] Yet he developed a remarkable theory of political history to give plausibility to the thesis that one could wage war on Hitler by a critique of Plato.

5 Popper: Edmonds and Eidinow (2001), Hacohen (2000), Popper (1976). Strauss: Sheppard (2006), Smith (2009b). Arendt: Kristeva (2001), Young-Bruehl (1982).

6 Gellner (1987) 75.

7 In his *Logik der Forschung* (1934) and elsewhere, Popper famously theorized the relation between science and 'falsifiability'.

8 'The Theory of Totalitarianism. A Talk on The Open Society' (1946).

9 Ibid. Elsewhere Popper uses a pun to link the two: Hitler claimed to be *Gröfaz* ('Grösster Feldherr aller Zeiten': 'greatest commander of all time'), Plato was *Gröphaz* ('Grösster Philosoph aller Zeiten': 'greatest philosopher . . .'): Frede (1996) 75.

For Marx, as for Hegel before him, history centres on human conflict. For Popper, Western history is a Manichean struggle between two opposite types of societal organization: 'closed' ('tribal', 'primitive', 'totalitarian') and 'open' ('liberal'). Closed societies are beholden to authority; they police critical thought and dissent; and they give precedence to the collective over the individual. Then again (Popper suggests), their conception of historical reality is defective: it is informed by beliefs that are surely false, notably the supposition that history operates according to laws that enable the future to be predicted (a position he calls 'historicism').[10] And these erroneous belief-systems are used by ideologues as the basis for comprehensive social engineering, with disastrous consequences. Open societies, conversely, value individuals and their moral agency and accountability; they are committed to freedom, critical thinking, and rational analysis. Progress from a closed form of societal organization to an open form is both possible and desirable, but not inevitable. In fifth-century Athens, the Greeks took the first steps towards an open society – most significantly in the person of Socrates: critical thinking and rational analysis were his lifeblood. But at times of social upheaval, the seeming virtues of a closed society have a dangerous appeal. After any 'opening', a reactionary totalitarianism is liable to arise in response (*almost* a law of history, this). In classical Athens, reaction came with Plato. The political programme adumbrated in the *Republic* is a call for autocracy, eugenics, racialism, and socio-political engineering, with Plato 'the first to respond to . . . a real social need very similar to the one to which Hitler later responded, by cunningly exploiting it'.[11]

Popper's reading of Plato, as not merely authoritative advocate of a closed society but also direct precursor of fascism, was and continues to be controversial.[12] As Melissa Lane points out, the context of his critique helps to explain its impetus. In 1930s Germany, Plato was much in vogue as a political authority, among members of the circle of Stefan George,[13] for instance. In his Rector's Speech at the University of Freiburg, in 1933,[14] Martin Heidegger, too, invoked Plato to help define the task facing the contemporary German student: 'Arbeitsdienst' ('service in work'), 'Wehrdienst' ('military service'), and 'Wissensdienst' ('service to learning'). Thereby, Heidegger reaffirmed a version of the social groupings in Plato's ideal state, with its farmers and artisans, its guardians, and its philosopher-king(s).[15]

With his bold argument from the margins, Popper succeeded in establishing 'openness' as an important complement to 'democracy'. At the same time, he offered

10 Popper first thought of calling his book 'False Prophets: Plato – Hegel – Marx': Popper (1976) 113.

11 'The Theory of Totalitarianism'.

12 Bambrough (1967), Frede (1996), Taylor (1997).

13 Lane (2001) 121–8, 152, with reference to such works as J. Bannes, *Hitlers Kampf und Platons Staat* (1933); cf. Lane (1999).

14 'Die Selbstbehauptung der deutschen Universität'.

15 The speech concludes with a quotation from *Republic* 497d: 'All great things are precarious' ('Alles Grosse steht im Sturm'). In her 'appreciation' of Heidegger on the occasion of his eightieth birthday, Arendt likens Heidegger's endorsement of Hitler to Plato's involvement with the tyrants of Syracuse: both ended up courting 'tyrants and leaders' ('Martin Heidegger at Eighty', 1971).

a message of hope: the gullible might fall under the 'spell' of false prophets, but once confronted with rational argument, followers of ideologues would no doubt recognise the error of their ways. This disconcerting optimism is only one of the problematic features of his position. Arguably, he not only overestimated the power of ideas but also underestimated the significance of tradition (as, indeed, he himself suspected).[16] More fundamentally, the very notion of 'open' and 'closed' societies was soon criticised as an 'oversimplification', while many protested that there was 'more to learn from Plato' than 'empiricists' like Popper supposed.[17] Yet, whatever else, Popper had helped to re-establish Plato's contemporary relevance for the English-speaking world.[18] When, in the early post-war years, Bertrand Russell declared that his book had 'brilliantly' exposed Plato as a champion of 'injustice, cruelty, and opposition to progress',[19] he spoke as a representative of intellectual activism, as much as of academic philosophy. Popper's work impinged on both.

In his commitment to scientific enlightenment and its values, and his distrust of authority and tradition, Popper is the mirror image of Leo Strauss. Following Heidegger, Strauss saw the modern West as a world in crisis, precisely because of 'the pervasive belief in Western progress and enlightenment': the urgent need was to recognise 'the self-destructive nature of modern rationality and the philosophical limits of modern natural science'.[20] Like Heidegger, too, Strauss looked for a remedy in the ancient sources of Western civilization, which, however, he located not just in Greek philosophy,[21] but also in the revealed law and morality of the Biblical tradition.

On one level, Strauss's thought, before and after his exile, shows a striking continuity. In the early 1930s, he had already identified Western history as a succession of wrong turns, each pushing Western man further and further away from traditional wisdom. The Enlightenment freed itself by fighting tradition with tradition: a conception of science that originated in Greece finally undid the Aristotelian-scholastic view of the world, while principles of altruism derived from the Bible challenged intolerance within established religion. Then, in the nineteenth century, a further radicalization put into question such principles themselves (and here, like many others, Strauss saw Nietzsche as the decisive figure). Absolute freedom, 'anarchy', 'polytheism of values', was the unhappy outcome.[22]

We find the same figures of thought in Strauss's writings a quarter of a century later. Modernity (he now argued) came in waves, each initiated by a great thinker, each changing the 'moral climate' of the West. The first such thinker was Machiavelli,

16 'Towards a Rational Theory of Tradition' (1949), in *Conjectures and Refutations* (1963).

17 Rosen (1967) 178.

18 Anticipated by Richard Crossman's *Plato Today* (1937): Crossman was an Oxford philosopher and subsequently a leading Labour Party politician in post-war Britain.

19 Russell (1967) 114–5: a lecture originally delivered in 1946.

20 Mewes (1995) 105.

21 Heidegger: cf. §6.

22 'Die geistige Lage der Gegenwart' (1932).

whose radical break with earlier traditions of political philosophy was continued by Hobbes; the second was Rousseau; and the third, Nietzsche. And Strauss proceeded to correlate innovations in thought with developments in politics: 'The theory of liberal democracy, as well as of communism, originated in the first and second waves of modernity; the political implication of the third wave proved to be fascism.'[23] This enabled him to claim that 'the crisis of modernity is . . . primarily the crisis of modern political philosophy'. Perhaps unexpectedly, though, he conceded that, under liberal democracy, 'the theoretical crisis does not necessarily lead to a practical crisis'. For democracy was the only modern form of government that derived 'powerful support from a way of thinking which cannot be called modern at all: the premodern thought of our Western tradition.'[24]

Strauss thus advocated, not further 'progress', but a revalidation of the two sources of Western civilization and their dominant presence in premodern culture. Irreconcilable as Jerusalem and Athens, the Bible and Greek philosophy, might be,[25] their wisdom offered a way out of the modern malaise of moral relativisms and denials of ultimate value,[26] with the systematic rereading of selected classic texts the remedy prescribed.[27] Strauss's patient exegesis of ancient, medieval, and early modern thinkers, however, was conducted in a very particular, 'non-historicist' spirit. Thucydides and Aristophanes, Plato and Aristotle, Maimonides and his Arabic predecessors (Alfarabi, Avicenna, Averroes), Machiavelli, Spinoza, and Hobbes: these and others were submitted to scrupulous readings that resisted the supposed relativity of thought to its 'historical situation'. The outcome of such 'historicist' relativizing must be 'a questionable mixture of interpretation and critique'. His own recommendation was rather to 'understand' the thought of the past 'as exactly as possible as it was actually understood by its authors',[28] but without limitation to its (or their) original context. Great thinkers, who pursue the important questions of existence, of value, of ultimate meaning, are universal thinkers.

Strauss's *On Tyranny* (1948), a close reading of Xenophon's dialogue *Hiero*, involves a significant critical engagement with totalitarian politics, and is in many ways his representative work. In the introduction, he identifies a failure of modern political science to understand totalitarianism. For him, the modern totalitarian phenomenon is effectively ancient tyranny empowered by the technological capabilities that modern science has made possible. Even though his own generation

[23] 'The Three Waves of Modernity' (1959).

[24] Ibid.

[25] 'The Western tradition does not allow of a synthesis of [these] two elements, but only of their tension: this is the secret of the vitality of the West': 'Thucydides: The Meaning of Political History' (1960s), in Pangle (1989).

[26] See esp. 'Relativism' (1961).

[27] With premodern philosophy broadly 'superior' insofar as it insists on the question, 'Why does human life need philosophy?': see *What is Political Philosophy?* (1959), ch. 3, and 'How to Begin to Study Medieval Philosophy' (1944), in Pangle (1989).

[28] Introduction to *On Tyranny: An Interpretation of Xenophon's Hiero* (1948).

had come 'face to face with . . . a kind of tyranny that surpassed the boldest imagination of the most powerful thinkers of the past', contemporary political science had 'failed to recognize it'. This failure was paradoxical, but symptomatic. Whereas earlier ages, even without 'direct experience of actual tyranny', nevertheless understood it very well, 'our' political science had lost sight of *their* understanding. It was true that many contemporaries, 'disappointed or repelled by present-day analyses of present-day tyranny', had found, in Plato and other classical thinkers, pointers to 'the horrors of the twentieth century'. But one crucial text had been overlooked, 'the only writing of the classical period . . . explicitly devoted to the discussion of tyranny and its implications, and to nothing else': Xenophon's *Hiero*. As such, this text was 'indispensable'.[29]

Strauss is an eloquent champion of political-philosophical thinking at its most strenuous and far-reaching. But though he abhorred 'creeping conformism',[30] as a thinker in his own right he belongs with those that Nietzsche characterized as the founders of philosophical schools,[31] thinkers with doctrines and followers, like Plato or Hegel, not with experimental thinkers (however powerful their legacy) like Socrates or Nietzsche himself (Strauss's penchant for the esoteric only makes this more apparent).[32] As such, Strauss has exercised a remarkable influence on successive generations of – North American – scholars and writers (and, less directly, on American political life). Much has been written about this (for and against),[33] but less on his status as spokesman for the classic texts, Greek or other. Given Strauss's restrictive insistence on authorial understandings, but given also the intimate relation (which he hardly acknowledges) between reading, interpretation, and evaluation, his position is – to say the least – awkward. The classic texts, it seems, are to be the focus of a reader's attention, and they are to be read scrupulously in that authorial spirit, therefore without the free critical impartiality which, indeed, must involve challenging, or at least standing outside, their premises (historical or other). But if they are not read with a free critical impartiality, how can a reader know that they *are* – that they deserve to be treated as – classic texts? Strauss reads Xenophon (and others) authorially, as 'the natural way of reading the work of a wise man'.[34] But without the critical impartiality – without the 'mixture of interpretation and critique' that he ascribes to 'historicism', but which is surely a prerequisite of any and all productive reading – how can even he identify 'wisdom' and know that Xenophon *is* a 'wise man'? Then again, given that 'Strauss's overriding allegiance was to Socratic philosophy, not to the classical city [the polis and its ideals] or even to

[29] Ibid.

[30] *What is Political Philosophy?*, ch. 3.

[31] First in a set of notes on 'Wissenschaft und Weisheit im Kampfe' (1875): Colli and Montinari (1967–) 4. 1. 172–96; cf. Silk (2007c) 45–6.

[32] Cf. Lampert (2009).

[33] Variously: Burnyeat (1985), Norton (2004), Pangle (1989), Zuckert and Zuckert (2006).

[34] *On Tyranny*, Introduction.

classical art',[35] and also that he seems tolerant (and not merely 'understanding') of Plato's notorious dismissal of the masterpieces of Homer and Greek tragedy,[36] one is left to ponder how far classic texts, ultimately, profit from such a champion.

Like Strauss, Hannah Arendt had a youthful passion for philosophy and the life of thought.[37] But things changed with the burning of the Reichstag in 1933 and the Nazi oppression that followed. Only active resistance would do: 'from that moment on I felt responsible.'[38] But it was the behaviour of fellow-intellectuals that shaped her response – the spectacle of friends, acquaintances, and even the great Heidegger (her erstwhile lover), submitting to the policies of National Socialism ('Gleichschaltung'). As Plato had once abandoned politics, in disgust, when the Athenian state put Socrates to death,[39] she turned her back on dispassionate thought: 'I never forgot that. I left Germany dominated by the idea – of course somewhat exaggerated: Never again! I shall never again get involved in any kind of intellectual business.'[40] And in a reversal of Plato's switch, she turned to politics – politics in practice, but in theory too – and in the years that followed she proceeded to rethink the entire Western tradition of political thinking.[41]

Like Strauss, Arendt diagnoses a cataclysmic undoing of 'our tradition of political thought'. That tradition had 'its definite beginning in the teachings of Plato and Aristotle', but 'a no less definite end in the theories of Karl Marx'. For Arendt, it is Marx who transvalues Plato's regression from political life by locating philosophy and its truths not 'outside the affairs of men and their common world but precisely in them'.[42] Kierkegaard (who challenged 'the basic assumptions of traditional religion') and Nietzsche (who did the same for 'traditional metaphysics') join Marx in announcing the age of 'confusion and helplessness . . . in which we live today'.[43] Yet unlike Strauss or Popper, Arendt does not ascribe a decisive influence to individual thinkers in the historical process. Rather, 'the break in our history' is the outcome of 'a chaos of mass-perplexities on the political scene and of mass-opinions in the spiritual sphere which the totalitarian movements, through terror and ideology, crystallized into a new form of government and domination'.[44]

35 Pangle (1989) xxiv.

36 See the closing pages of 'The Problem of Socrates' (1958), in Pangle (1989).

37 '"What Remains?"'.

38 Ibid.

39 Plato, *Epistle* 7.

40 '"What Remains?"'. While Arendt does not name names, the case of Heidegger is paradigmatic here: see her fable 'Heidegger the Fox' (1953) in *Essays in Understanding*. Arendt and Heidegger: Ludz (2011), Steiner (1995), (1999).

41 See her 'Philosophy and Politics' (1954) (published in 1990, in *Social Research* 57) and cf. Villa (1996).

42 'Tradition and the Modern Age', in *Between Past and Future: Eight Exercises in Political Thought* (1968).

43 Ibid.

44 Ibid.

Where Popper assimilates the totalitarian to the tribal and the primitive, and Strauss to ancient tyranny, Arendt insists that the pernicious ideologies and catastrophic politics of the twentieth century cannot be comprehended in terms of established categories. In *The Origins of Totalitarianism* (1948), she denies the direct applicability of the long Aristotelian tradition of political thought, and situates fascism and also communism (both concerned to eliminate freely chosen political action) in the distinctively modern context of racist and imperialist ideology. But then, in her later writings, she sets out to reconstruct a meaning and purpose for humanity that might answer the totalitarian challenge.[45]

If the past has lost its authority, it has not lost its value. Arendt neither rejects the possibility of recovering insights from tradition, like Popper, nor seeks to resuscitate the superior wisdom of the past, like Strauss. Rather, she revisits and rethinks the past in a critical spirit (one is reminded, up to a point, of Machiavelli), in search of precedents for those phenomena she has learnt to value for the present and the future: the free play of opinion, citizens in dialogue, personal responsibility, sound judgement, authentic political action. This search entails a harsh reappraisal of philosophical arguments against an open, democratic society; and here, particular targets are Plato and Heidegger, even though her mode of thought sometimes reflects Heidegger's own.[46]

In her recuperative enterprise, Arendt draws on the two – or, as she presents it, *four* – cultural formations that have shaped the Western tradition of political thought: Christianity and Judaism (with its 'hidden tradition'), ancient Greece and ancient Rome.[47] Then again, she points approvingly to later departures, in particular Enlightenment thinking (Kant's, above all)[48] and the American revolution. The latter, she interprets as a new foundation, even if the founders were inspired by Roman models;[49] her interest in Rome distinguishes her from Popper or Strauss, and reflects, precisely, the importance of Roman thought, and figures of thought, within such later developments. Again, she addresses the lives, as well as the ideas, of significant individuals: of Socrates, who practised philosophy in a public space, a citizen among citizens;[50] of Cicero; of Aristotle.[51] She revisits distinctive moments, in fifth-century Athens or revolutionary America, but also distinctive concepts, such

[45] See esp. *The Human Condition* (1958) and the posthumously published *Life of the Mind* (1978). Variously: Heuer *et al.* (2011), Villa (2000).

[46] See e.g. 'What Is Existential Philosophy?' (German original, 1948), in *Essays in Understanding*.

[47] See e.g. *The Jew as Pariah: A Hidden Tradition* (1944) and (Greece and Rome) Euben (2000), Hammer (2002), Taminiaux (2000). Her interest in Christian thought began early, with a 1929 dissertation (supervised by Karl Jaspers), *Der Liebesbegriff bei Augustin*.

[48] 'Kant's so-called moral philosophy is in essence political': 'Concern with Politics in Recent European Philosophical Thought' (1954), in *Essays in Understanding*.

[49] 'The Revolutionary Tradition and Its Lost Treasure', in *On Revolution* (1963).

[50] Cf. Canovan (1990).

[51] Arendt's theory of action is 'the systematic renewal of the Aristotelian concept of *praxis*': Habermas (1983) 174. Cf. (in a wider context) Gutschker (2002).

as the Roman idea of authority and the Christian conception of 'freedom from politics' ('politically perhaps the most relevant part of our Christian heritage' and 'one of the most important negative liberties we have enjoyed since the end of the ancient world').[52] And she perceives, with great clarity, the crucial link between the classical tradition and 'being human': 'Husserl and Hofmannsthal are both classicists, if classicism is the attempt – by means of an utterly rigorous imitation of the classic vision, which is to say of man's sense of being at home in the world – to conjure up a new home from a world perceived as alien.'[53]

All in all, Arendt's example is as telling as any of her particular arguments. She uses an impressive familiarity with Western history and its traditions, hidden or broken, Jewish or Christian, Greek or Roman, to recover insights that might assist the project of rethinking the human condition in the aftermath of the abyss.

Putting these three case studies side by side prompts several related lines of thought: about the capacity of specialist scholarship to initiate a wider debate (Popper's book is a well-documented example); about the role of the public intellectual in the – almost – contemporary world[54] (Strauss, in particular, may have deplored the condition of the Western world as he found it, but the world he deplored gave him the scope to work out and propagate his ideas); about the relation between the personal traumas of émigré figures and the gain their migration brings to the host culture (the trauma and the gain are most intimately connected in Arendt's case); and – for us, the most immediate concern – about the continuing power of classical antiquity to suggest new modalities, within the continuum, or even *dis*continuum, of political culture. As Arendt observed, with reference to a Kafka 'parable' and a Tocqueville insight into modern America, 'it is the future that sends man's mind back into the past "up to the remotest antiquity".'[55]

52 'The Revolutionary Tradition' and 'What Is Authority?' (in *Between Past and Future*).

53 'What is Existential Philosophy?' Cf. §27.

54 Strauss died in 1973, Arendt in 1975, Popper in 1994.

55 Preface to *Between Past and Future*.

§35

Poetry

Now sleeps the crimson petal, now the white;
Nor waves the cypress in the palace walk;
Nor winks the gold fin in the porphyry font.
The fire-fly wakens; waken thou with me.
Now droops the milk-white peacock like a ghost,
And like a ghost she glimmers on to me.
Now lies the earth all Danaë to the stars,
And all thy heart lies open unto me.

Such exquisite formality, and such a conclusive classical allusion, surely belong to a classicizing age. Not strictly true: the passage comes from Tennyson's *The Princess*, published in 1847, a year before Dickens brought out *Dombey and Son* and Marx and Engels their *Communist Manifesto*, when Wagner was busy creating 'modern' music in *Lohengrin* and Courbet visual realism in the *Burial at Ornans*. Indeed, the wider themes of *The Princess* (women's education, above all) have a 'modern'-realist flavour themselves, while the Danae allusion – startling in its erotic charge – is less directly classical in spirit than might be supposed.[1] In its technical features, however,

[1] In antiquity the princess impregnated by Jupiter/Zeus is a suffering rather than a titillating figure (see e.g. Sophocles, *Antigone*, 944–50), except for unwittingly inspiring the rape in Terence, *Eunuch*, 584–606. Tennyson looks rather to artistic images like Titian's *Danae* (§33 n. 13).

The Classical Tradition: Art, Literature, Thought, First Edition. Michael Silk, Ingo Gildenhard, and Rosemary Barrow.

Published 2017 by John Wiley & Sons Ltd.

this passage, like Tennyson's poetry in general, is decidedly classicizing: archaizing idioms ('waken thou') and inversions ('Now sleeps'); singulars for plurals ('the crimson petal');[2] ubiquitous parallel structures, from matching noun-epithet phrases ('the gold fin in the porphyry font') to simple repetitions ('with me'/'to me'/'unto me').

Such technical usage satisfies an expectation of poetic elevation, derived (via Keats, Milton, Spenser, and the Petrarchan tradition) from the ancient doctrine formulated by Aristotle ('poetic *lexis* should be clear but not low')[3] and restated, to subsume the principle of decorum, by rhetoricians like Quintilian ('correct, clear, ornate, and appropriate').[4] The principle depends as much on what isn't allowed (above all, the colloquial) as on what is: an 'isn't' would seem out of place.[5] Everything is subordinated to an ideal of stylized formality, in this instance distantly Virgilian perhaps.[6]

The effect of this classicizing, however, is not to suggest any specific antiquity (Virgilian or other), while, correlatively, the substantive elements of Tennyson's description (although exotic) evoke no specific exotic locale either (contrast, say, Yeats's Byzantium).[7] Then again, nothing here evokes timelessness, the way Turner's *Modern Rome* does (§17). Tennyson's *where* and *when* are unplaceable, because scrupulously unparticularized.[8] Compare Eliot's reading of Milton:[9]

> His language is . . . artificial and conventional . . . The imagery in *L'Allegro* and *Il Penseroso* is all general:
>
> While the ploughman near at hand
> Whistles o'er the furrowed land,
> And the milkmaid singeth blithe,
> And the mower whets his scythe,
> And every shepherd tells his tale
> Under the hawthorn in the dale.
>
> It is not a particular ploughman, milkmaid, and shepherd that Milton sees (as Wordsworth might see them).[10]

[2] Synecdoche: see e.g. Quintilian, *Institutio Oratoria*, 8. 6. 20; 9. 3. 20.

[3] *Poetics*, 22: cf. p. 160 above.

[4] *Institutio Oratoria*, 11. 3. 30 (of oratorical language, in the first instance).

[5] Contrast conversational touches in Tennyson's Prologue ('And what's my thought').

[6] Cf. the incantatory plangencies of Virgilian love-talk: *Eclogues*, 1. 38–9; *Georgics*, 4. 465–6; *Aeneid*, 4. 307–8.

[7] Tennyson's princess is 'the Eastern Queen of romance': Jordan (1988) 87. Her country, likewise, is loosely 'Eastern' (Persian? Arabian?).

[8] The 'aesthetic of particularity' that Christ (1975) associates with Victorian poetry is most certainly inapplicable to Tennyson in this characteristic mode.

[9] The essay (from 1936) is (re)titled 'Milton I' in Eliot's collection *On Poetry and Poets* (1957), 138–45: cf. n. 37 below.

[10] 'Singulars for plurals' (common to the Milton and the Tennyson) themselves paradoxically make general. Any thought of specific singularity ('there was only *one* crimson petal?') is unwanted and subversive.

The citation of Wordsworth is to the point. All such usage is challenged by Wordsworth's arguments, in the Preface to *Lyrical Ballads* (half a century before *The Princess*), in favour of 'a selection of the language really spoken by men'.[11] That formula (which may or may not seem adequate for Wordsworth's own poetry)[12] Wordsworth himself represents as a rejection of neoclassical usage; but it is, more fundamentally, a rejection, for 'modern' poetry, of classicizing technique as such.

If Tennyson and Milton agree in the use (though hardly the degree) of classicizing technique, they differ sharply in other ways. One thing that Tennyson does not offer is the close engagement with antiquity that characterizes the generic classicism of Milton's age.[13] Take *Paradise Lost* and the issue of free will. Following a 'Stygian council', some of Milton's rebel angels amuse themselves by singing 'their own heroic deeds', but complain 'that fate | Free virtue should enthrall to force or chance'; others (converting that complaint to 'discourse more sweet') –

> Others apart sat on a hill retired,
> In thoughts more elevate, and reasoned high
> Of providence, foreknowledge, will and fate,
> Fixed fate, free will, foreknowledge absolute,
> And found no end, in wandering mazes lost.[14]

The topic permeates the poem. In particular, 'the Almighty Father' proclaims what Milton articulates as definitive truth – Satan and the other rebels were created free:

> So were created, nor can justly accuse
> Their Maker, or their making, or their fate,
> As if predestination overruled
> Their will, disposed by absolute decree
> Or high foreknowledge. They themselves decreed
> Their own revolt, not I. If I foreknew,
> Foreknowledge had no influence on their fault.[15]

A world of theological debate underlies these magnificent formulations. Milton scholars relate God's position to arguments between rival schools of Protestant thought: against Calvinist determinism, Milton is asserting a version of the Arminian doctrine of human (or angelic) freedom.[16] No less relevant, though, are his intellectual underpinnings in pagan antiquity. Like the fallen angels who evoke Homer's Achilles (singing 'their own heroic deeds'),[17] those who get lost in the

11 In the 1802 Preface: Brett and Jones (1965) 254 (with this ideal explicitly opposed to 'devices to elevate the style': ibid. 250). Cf. §13.

12 Attridge (1988) 46–89, Uhlig and Regier (2010), Ward (1984).

13 Milton and antiquity: Hopkins (2010b), Martindale (1986), Parker (1937). 'Generic': §22.

14 *Paradise Lost*, 2. 506–61.

15 Ibid. 3. 112–18.

16 See e.g. Fallon (2007) 182–202.

17 Cf. *Iliad*, 9. 189.

paradoxes of 'providence, foreknowledge, will and fate' call to mind (say) the paradox ascribed to Agamemnon's decision to sacrifice Iphigeneia, in Aeschylus' play ('Under compulsion's yoke he strapped himself'),[18] while God's pronouncement recalls Homer's exasperated Zeus:

> Look at the way that mortals blame us gods.
> From us, they claim, comes evil – when themselves,
> By their own crimes, suffer beyond due ordinance.[19]

From which, however, complications arise. Can Milton's God really take a tip from Homer's Zeus? Milton himself seems to have entertained such thoughts,[20] but it is one thing for deviant angels (Satan, above all) to behave like pagan beings (§21); it is quite another for God to emulate his pagan (non-)equivalents.[21] Commitment to the norms of generic classicism has consequences – even, or especially, for so grand a project as Milton's.

Complications associated with Milton's classicism arise most notoriously from his language. Here, the early *Lycidas* (1638) is paradigmatic. This lament for a dead friend is an allegorical pastoral, such as the Virgil of the *Eclogues* might have recognised, with its generic markers ('Sicilian' Muses and 'singing' shepherds) and its abundance of elevated features ('Yet once more, O ye laurels, and once more, | Ye myrtles brown, with ivy never sere')[22] – but also its phraseology, transplanted from Virgil's Latin. Milton has 'Alas! what boots it . . . | To . . . strictly *meditate* the thankless *Muse*?[23] – where Virgil had written: 'silvestrem tenui *Musam meditaris* avena'.[24]

Throughout his poetry, and not least in *Paradise Lost*, Milton's classicizing technique encompasses extremes, including radical Latinizing, in pursuit of the high style.[25] As such, it duly engenders a series of critiques, from the early eighteenth century[26] to the mid-twentieth. Thus, Addison:

18 *Agamemnon*, 218: *anankas edu lepadnon.*

19 *Odyssey*, 1. 32–4 (. . . *huper moron*): cf. Blessington (1979) 47–8. In later antiquity, the terms of debate are impressively intellectualized by Aristotle, *Ethics*, 3. 1, and Augustine, *City of God*, 5. 9–10.

20 See *The Doctrine and Discipline of Divorce* (1644), 2. 3, and the closing arguments of the unfinished *Christian Doctrine*, 1. 4 (cf. Hopkins 2010b: 30).

21 Cf. Empson on Yvor Winters's view that 'Milton's form is such that he must . . . reduce [his God and additional supernatural agents] to something much nearer the form of the Homeric gods than their proper form': Empson (1965) 91–2 (cf., generally, 91–146). Milton himself stresses the differentiation between God and pagan gods ('devils to adore for deities', 1. 373), by equating the pagans with the fallen angels themselves (1. 730–48 etc.).

22 *Lycidas*, 133, 10–11, 1–2 (with archaic 'ye'; formal repetition of 'once more'; inversion and generic epithet in 'myrtles brown').

23 Ibid. 64–6.

24 *Eclogue*, 1. 2: 'You *meditate* [practise] the woodland *Muse* [i.e. music] on a slender straw [pipe].' There are also less challenging echoes, like *Lycidas*, 77, 'Phoebus . . . touched my . . . ears', alongside *Eclogues*, 6. 3–4, 'Cynthius aurem | vellit'.

25 In principle, then, an extreme case of generic propriety. Milton's idiom is far more demotic in his prose: Davies (1970).

26 Earlier still, if one counts Dryden's remarks on Milton's 'Grecisms' and 'Latin elegancies' in his 'Discourse Concerning . . . Satire' (1693).

> Milton . . . has infused a great many Latinisms, as well as Grecisms, and sometimes Hebraisms, into . . . his poem . . . [H]is style, though admirable in general, is in some places too much stiffened and obscured by the frequent use of those methods which Aristotle has prescribed for the raising of it.[27]

> [T]he language of this great poet . . . is often too much laboured, and sometimes obscured, by old words, transpositions and foreign idioms.[28]

In 1734 Jonathan Richardson was more sweeping, but also more tolerant:

> Milton's language is English, but 'tis Milton's English; 'tis Latin,'tis Greek English; not only the words, the phraseology, the transpositions, but the ancient idiom is seen in all he writes.[29]

Johnson, in 1779, was famously critical:

> through all his greater works there prevails an uniform peculiarity of diction, a mode and cast of expression, which bears little resemblance to that of any former writer, and which is so far removed from common use, that an unlearned reader . . . finds himself surprised by a new language . . . [T]he truth is that . . . he had formed his style by a perverse and pedantic principle. He was desirous to use English words with a foreign idiom.[30]

Similarly, Keats, on Milton's greatest work:

> *Paradise Lost* though so fine in itself is a corruption of our language . . . A northern dialect accommodating itself to Greek and Latin inversions and intonations.[31]

With a new twist, Coleridge was less judgemental:

> The connexion of the sentences and the position of the words are exquisitely artificial, but the position is rather according to the logic of passion or universal logic, than to the logic of [English?] grammar. Milton attempted to make the English language obey the logic of passion as perfectly as the Greek and Latin. Hence the occasional harshness in the construction.[32]

In Victorian England, Matthew Arnold echoed Richardson in accentuating the positive: 'this master in the great style of the ancients is English.'[33] Meanwhile, strikingly,

[27] *The Spectator* 285 (26 January 1712).

[28] Ibid. 297 (9 February 1712).

[29] *Explanatory Notes and Remarks on Milton's Paradise Lost.*

[30] *Life of Milton*: Hill (1905), 1. 190–1. Johnson adds: 'One source of this peculiarity was his familiarity with the Tuscan poets: the disposition of his words is . . . frequently Italian'. Cf. Thomas Warton's 'Preface to Milton's Poems' (1785) and (more recently) Hale (1997) 125–7, Prince (1954).

[31] Letter to George and Georgiana Keats: 21 September 1819.

[32] Lectures of 1818, 'Lecture X', in *Literary Remains* (1836).

[33] 'Milton' (1888): §4 n. 24.

Wordsworth's rejection of neoclassicism targets, not Milton, but the eighteenth century.[34] It was left to literary modernism, espousing a sharper version of Wordsworth's argument, to produce the most trenchant critiques from the post-Wordsworthian age. First, Ezra Pound, in 1917:

> He tried to turn English into Latin; to use an uninflected language as if it were an inflected one . . . : 'Him who disobeys me disobeys.'[35]

Then Leavis, who granted that 'the Grand Style, at its best, compels us to recognize it as an impressive stylization', but insisted on the 'extreme and consistent remoteness of Milton's medium from any English that was ever spoken':

> [Such stylization] . . . became . . . habitual to him; but habituation could not . . . sensitize a medium so cut off from speech . . . 'Milton wrote Latin as readily as he did English.' . . . But however admirable his Latin . . . to latinize in English is quite another matter.[36]

And then Eliot, whose identification of Miltonic idiom as 'artificial and conventional' was preliminary to the charge: 'Milton writes English like a dead language.'[37]

'Dead language': it was argued, more specifically, by Eliot and by Leavis, that Milton's idiom tends to obviate, not just 'particularity', but the creative use of language epitomized by Shakespearean writing, where 'the combinations of words . . . enlarge the meanings of the individual words joined', and where 'the words seem to do as they say.'[38] These charges were countered, in part, by Christopher Ricks's appeal to the 'enhancing suggestions' and enactmental effects observable in individual Miltonic contexts[39] and often identified by eighteenth-century commentators, trained (we might add) in the categories of ancient rhetorical theory, where such effects are identified and approved. Thus, on the fallen angels who struggled to make philosophical sense

> Of providence, foreknowledge, will and fate,
> Fixed fate, free will, foreknowledge absolute,
> And found no end, in wandering mazes lost –

[34] See esp. (in the 1800 Preface) Brett and Jones (1965) 249 (Shakespeare and Milton) versus 252–3 (Gray).

[35] 'Notes on Elizabethan Classicists': Pound (1954) 238. The reference is to *Paradise Lost*, 5. 611–12.

[36] Leavis (1936) 50–2, from a chapter first published in *Scrutiny* 2 (1933).

[37] From 'Milton I' (n. 9 above), originally an article in *Essays and Studies*, 1936: Eliot (1957) 138, 141. In 1947 Eliot qualified his criticism, in a less compelling essay, 'Milton II': ibid. 146–61.

[38] Eliot, 'Milton I' (1957: 140); Leavis (1936) 55.

[39] Ricks (1963), where 'enhancing suggestions' (Bagehot's phrase) is the title of ch. 3 (78–117). Contrast the argument that Milton's language 'is in fact as remote and artificial as is thought' (Lewis 1942: 60) – but rightly so, because remote subjects demand it (ibid. 40–61).

Addison comments that Milton, 'to humour the perplexity, makes a kind of labyrinth in the very words that describe it.'[40]

Recent disputants, going further, have argued either (unconvincingly) that the scope or nature of Milton's Latinizing has been overstated[41] or (more persuasively) that some, at least, of the Latinisms add specific force to their contexts. As Kenneth Haynes remarks, the very title *Paradise Lost* embodies the constructive use of a Latinate construction: this is 'the Latin way of saying "the loss of paradise"'; Milton's phrase 'insists on the loss of paradise, to prevent paradise even from being imagined, except on condition of its imminent loss.'[42] Haynes, again, comments on Milton's use of a Greek construction already appropriated, in Miltonic fashion, by Virgil. Eve takes the apple and 'Greedily she ingorged without restraint, | And knew not eating Death.'[43] 'The unusual syntax' (Haynes suggests) succeeds in concentrating several distinct meanings: 'Eve did not know (. . . she was ignorant . . .) *while* she was eating death; she did not know *what* she did (she ate death); she did not know the *eating*, devouring power of death.'[44]

Classicizing technique (like ancient poetry itself) can indeed satisfy both classical and supra-classical demands. Yet in Milton's case the problem remains. Alongside the felicities is an extensive residue of elevation for elevation's sake, which encompasses a kind of Latinate translationese – as in *Lycidas*, or Pound's 'me disobeys', or strikingly un-English negatives: 'Nor did they not perceive the evil plight | In which they were'; 'And thus with words not sad she him received.'[45] Ultimately, the problem remains because, in idiom, the English language, however Romancified lexically, is too alien to Roman(ce) practice for Latinate high-style writing to be sustained without significant complications. The extreme character of Milton's idiom, identified by critics from very different eras, remains an issue for debate, as much as an achieved ideal.

Eliot's response to Milton's language deserves attention for its relevance to his own poetry, as well as to Milton himself. His critique belongs to a lifelong commitment 'to purify the dialect of the tribe' and a lifelong concern with the problematic of poetic language as such in an uncongenial world: 'That was a way of putting it – not very satisfactory: | A periphrastic study in a worn-out poetical fashion.'[46] Like

40 Addison, *The Tatler* 114 (1709): Ricks (1963) 78. On comparable stylistic enactments, cf. e.g. Quintilian, *Institutio Oratoria*, 8. 3. 17 and 9. 4. 126.

41 Cf. Fowler (1980) 11–21 and Corns (1990) 199. Such revisionism defies the clear consensus of Milton's earlier readers (*pro* or *con*) (whose Latin, it has to be said, is generally superior to that of the revisionists themselves). The fundamental problematic (cf. p. 426 below) is in any case unaffected. Hale (1997) adds interesting perspectives, while accepting Milton as a Latinizer (ibid. 105–30).

42 Haynes (2003) 79.

43 *Paradise Lost*, 9. 791–2: cf. Virgil, *Aeneid*, 2. 377.

44 Haynes (2003) 79 (his italics).

45 *Paradise Lost*, 1. 335–6, 12. 609. Compare/contrast Martindale (1986) 41–7 on Milton's 'metaphrastic' tendencies; and Ricks's suggestion (1963: 17–20, 147–50) that Milton writes worst when most direct.

46 *Four Quartets* (1943), 'Little Gidding' II and 'East Coker' II.

Wordsworth, Eliot never properly signals the relation of his project to the classical tradition – the relation, to put it bluntly, of the 'worn-out poetical fashion' to the techniques of elevation that Aristotle and Quintilian prescribed and Milton took to extremes. And this is remarkable: because as early as 1928 Eliot pronounced himself 'classicist in literature' (along with 'royalist in politics' and 'anglo-catholic in religion');[47] because his verse plays (especially *Murder in the Cathedral*, 1935, and *The Family Reunion*, 1939) have unmistakable Greek-tragic points of reference (from the chorus in the former to the Furies in the latter); because a significant relationship with antiquity is repeatedly flagged by Greek or Latin epigraphs to his poems (from 'Mr Apollinax', 1917, to *The Waste Land*, 1922, to *Four Quartets*, 'Burnt Norton', 1943); because in his essay, 'Tradition and the Individual Talent' (1920), Eliot insists that 'the whole of the literature of Europe from Homer . . . has a simultaneous existence and composes a simultaneous order'; and because in two critical essays and one unfinished poem, 'Coriolan' (1931), he assigns a special place of honour to Virgil.[48]

Elusively connected with Shakespeare's classical-subject *Coriolanus*, 'Coriolan' resembles the earlier and more achieved *Waste Land* in its enactment of cultural fragmentation, its plurality of idioms and modes (from the satirical to the lyrical), its juxtapositions of disparate items. The poem presents a modern world of processions and committees ('And now come the Mayor and the Liverymen') and a cast of characters, mostly British and prosaic ('Arthur Edward Cyril Parker is appointed telephone operator'), but partly old Roman ('Now come the virgins bearing urns'). The juxtapositions are largely ironic, and to the ironic mix is added one unmistakable reference to the Coriolanus saga – and one to Roman Virgil:

> A commission is appointed
> To confer with a Volscian commission

('Coriolanus' was so named after capturing the Volscian city of Corioli)

> About perpetual peace: the fletchers and javelin-makers and smiths

(the poem's opening procession featured 'machine guns', and the like, in modern mode; now the weaponry is antique)

> Have appointed a joint committee to protest against the reduction of orders.
> Meanwhile the guards shake dice on the marches
> And the frogs (O Mantuan) croak in the marshes.
> Fireflies flare against the faint sheet lightning –

This 'flare' and the drawn-out rhythms and alliteration of the last line, along with the harsh pararhyme of the lines preceding ('marches'/'marshes'), combine to recall

47 In his preface to 'For Lancelot Andrewes'.
48 Eliot and 'tradition': Klein (2003), Lucy (1960).

the World War I of Wilfred Owen ('Wearied we keep awake because the night is silent | Low, drooping flares confuse our memory of the salient');[49] and 'Mantuan' is Virgil;[50] but whereas machine guns preannounce the world of World War, Virgil is unexpected, if only because his Rome is five hundred years later than the Volsciana –

> What shall I say?
> Mother mother
> Here is the row of family portraits, dingy busts, all looking remarkably Roman,
> Remarkably like each other, lit up successively by the flare
> Of a sweaty torchbearer, yawning.
> O hidden under the . . .

The marks of omission (Eliot's) conceal 'dove's wing', to judge from an earlier sequence, and this and other traces of unattached (but 'lyrical') Christian imagery promise relief from the otherwise relentless oscillation between worldly pretension and prosaic deflation (even the 'flare' of the fireflies turns into the flare of a 'sweaty' torchbearer).

The fragmented idiom in such sequences – though less programmatic than in *The Waste Land* ('These fragments I have shored against my ruins': §24) – is equally telling. As a technique of poetic *lexis*, nothing could be more abrasively anti-classical, flouting the whole tradition of consistent decorum and appropriate elevation. Such abrasiveness is central to Eliot's writing. The very title of his earliest consequential poem (1915) embodies it: *The Love Song* (reassuringly traditional-sounding) *of J. Alfred Prufrock* (prosaic, modern, deflating). That title announces the problem and the quest: how to reconcile tradition (classical, at bottom) with the contemporary fragmented-eclectic world.

In 'Coriolan', the ancient Roman presence is itself, in large part, prosaic and deflating: 'shake dice', 'dingy busts', 'sweaty torchbearer'. Even 'the virgins bearing urns' get their prosaic come-uppance in a sequence of Latinate ingenuity that contrasts with, but once again gives way to, Christian hope:

> If the mactations, immolations, oblations, impetrations,
> Are now observed
> May we not be
> O hidden

Conversely, the appeal to Virgil ('O Mantuan'), in parallel form to the repeated 'O hidden', seems to associate itself with that Christian hope, prefiguring the tenor of Eliot's two essays.

In 'What Is a Classic?' (1944), Eliot pronounces Virgil the paradigm of a 'classic' writer, where 'classic' implies 'maturity' – of mind, manners, language – and 'perfection of the common style', such as no English poet has ever achieved. Virgil is 'the

[49] Owen, 'Exposure' (1917).
[50] Mantua was Virgil's birthplace.

consciousness of Rome and the supreme voice of her language' and can claim 'the centrality of the unique classic; he is at the centre of European civilization'.[51] Regarding English poetry, Eliot notes the paradox that 'the style of Milton is not a classic style', precisely because his masters were 'not English, but Latin and to a less degree Greek'; that the nearest to classic writing in English is the poetry of Pope (whose 'classical qualities', however, were 'obtained at a high price – to the exclusion of some greater potentialities of English verse'); and that in Dante's *Comedy*, if anywhere, 'we find the classic in a modern European language'.[52]

In 'Virgil and the Christian World' (1951), the comparison with Dante is pursued, to Dante's advantage: his Christian 'vision' is superior, in fact supreme. 'We are all, so far as we inherit the civilization of Europe, still citizens of the Roman Empire', whereas Virgil, supreme consciousness of that empire, 'made of Roman civilization in his poetry something better than it really was', and is rightly Dante's 'guide and teacher' only up to a certain point.[53]

Virgil's momentary presence in 'Coriolan' makes – coded – sense. Brief as it is, this engagement is more consequential than (say) the obvious uses of Greek tragedy in his plays.[54] The 'Mantuan' represents order:[55] the opposite, positive ideal to the fragmented eclecticism of the contemporary 'waste land'.[56] As embodiment of writerly 'maturity', moreover, he constitutes, not indeed an attainable ideal, but a supreme point of reference – on linguistic grounds, as much as any other. The Latinate sequence in 'Coriolan' ('Mactations . . . impetrations') now takes on a sharper irony in the light of Eliot's critical placings of Virgil ('the unique classic') and the Latinizing Milton ('greatest of all eccentrics')[57] and his own endeavour 'to purify the dialect of the tribe'. Classicizing technique is insupportable in our modern age, except on ironic terms.[58]

If Eliot projects a distinctive Virgil, so too does Tennyson – but Tennyson has, ultimately, no investment in his projection. This may well seem a surprising judgement, not least with Tennyson's late poem, 'To Virgil' (1882), in mind:

> I salute thee, Mantovano,

(the poem was commissioned by the Virgilian Academy of Mantua, and 'Mantovano' – 'O Mantuan', in English – was what Dante had once called Virgil)[59]

[51] Eliot (1957) 53–71, esp. 56–60, 68.

[52] Ibid. 58–60.

[53] Ibid. 121–31, esp. 125, 130–1. Dante and Virgil: §§7, 13.

[54] Despite the paucity of allusion to Virgil in his poetry elsewhere (e.g. *The Waste Land*, 92). Greek tragedy and the plays: Tanner (1970).

[55] The 'busts' in 'Coriolan' (presumably of ancestors displayed in the ancient atrium) are 'dingy', but at least 'all correctly inscribed', and their Roman precision, albeit ironized, compares favourably with droopy modernity ('I a tired head among these heads').

[56] With this 'special relationship' itself a symptom of eclecticism (§10). A differently focused discussion of the relationship: Martindale (1996).

[57] 'Milton II': Eliot (1957) 155.

[58] Cf. the use of 'Augustan' couplets for the seduction scene in *The Waste Land* (III).

[59] *Purgatorio*, 6. 74.

I that loved thee since my day began,
Wielder of the stateliest measure
ever moulded by the lips of man.

And this graceful tribute is combined with a series of complimentary characterizations which read plausibly enough: 'Roman Virgil' as 'lord of language', above all. But Virgil is also invoked as

Thou majestic in thy sadness
at the doubtful doom of human kind,

and this thought serves to provoke the Victorian poet's own 'sadness'. *His* sadness, though, is attached, not to any 'doubtful doom', but to the poignant distance between Virgil's world and ours:

Now thy Forum roars no longer,
fallen every purple Caesar's dome . . .[60]

All things indeed perish with time:

Now the Rome of slaves hath perished –

but are we to feel the loss of ancient slavery, even, as poignant? The parallelism, and the majestic-melancholy flow, suggest it, until Tennyson draws back –

and the Rome of freemen holds her place.

Yet that momentary suggestion is no accident. Tennyson both acclaims and resists the contemporary world,[61] while distance and loss constitute a uniquely affecting preoccupation which underlies much of his most haunting poetry, and not least his classical-subject poems. The understanding of Tennyson as 'the poet of loss' is a critical commonplace, but what needs to be insisted on, in the context of the classical tradition in particular, is that, for this poet, the past *as such* is identified with loss: 'O Death in Life, the days that are no more.'[62]

'Frater, Ave atque Vale' (1883) is ostensibly the outcome of a trip to Catullan territory in northern Italy. This short piece looks back to two poems by Catullus, a celebration of Sirmio, on Lake Garda, and a lament at his brother's grave.[63] Symptomatically, it is a sombre phrase from the lament ('Brother, Hail and Farewell') that provides Tennyson's title, and this poem too that redirects Tennyson's mood from cheerful travelogue –

[60] Cf. Horace's 'purple tyrants' ('purpurei tyranni'): *Odes*, 1. 35. 12.

[61] See e.g. Stott (1996).

[62] The last line of 'Tears, Idle Tears', from *The Princess*. Among recent critics, Joseph (1992) reads Tennyson as 'the Victorian poet of loss' (ibid. 10), without quite making the point about 'the past as such'.

[63] Catullus 31 and 101, respectively.

> There to me through all the groves of olive in the summer glow –

to shared sorrow –

> There beneath the Roman ruin where the purple flowers grow
> Came that 'Ave atque Vale' of the poet's hopeless woe –

except that, as 'Roman *ruin*' indicates, Tennyson's sorrow is generated less by the circumstances of Catullus' own 'woe' and more by the simple fact that Catullus belongs to the lost past (behind or beneath the oddly symbolic 'purple flowers': compare 'every purple Caesar's dome', in 'To Virgil'). This becomes unmistakable in the next line:

> Tenderest of Roman poets *nineteen-hundred years ago.*

What really affects Tennyson is our distance from this past poet – not this past poet's loss of his brother at all.[64]

This perspective is fundamental to Tennyson's response to the classical, whether Roman or Greek.[65] Even in poems focused on very specific dilemmas, like 'Tithonus' (1860) or 'Lucretius' (1868), the sense of loss is never far away. In 'Tithonus', the hero whose goddess-lover made him immortal, but forgot to stop his ageing, looks back in dismay to 'days far-off', when he was, still, young. In 'Lucretius', more subtly, the great Epicurean, poisoned and frenzied, confronts the creatures of ancient myth, whose existence (or at least presence) his philosophy had rejected, including the goddess Venus, famously invoked in the 'rich prooemion' to his great poem,[66] 'In lays that will outlast thy Deity.' The strange paradox of *that* formulation feels personal. It is as if Tennyson is using Lucretius' distance from the mythic world as, once again, a figure for his own, quite different, distance from that past: a distinctive version of 'myth as cover' (§24), indeed.

Tennyson's lost pasts can be directly personal, as most notably in his *In Memoriam A. H. H.* (1850):

> He is not here; but far away
>   The noise of life begins again,
>   And ghastly through the drizzling rain
> On the bald street breaks the blank day.[67]

[64] Our italics. The plangency of the poem is intensified by the way its remarkable rhyme-scheme ('glow'/'grow'/'woe' etc.), together with the closing reference to 'Catullus' all-but-island', evokes 'The Lady of Shalott' (1832), Tennyson's classic depiction of frustrated Arthurian romance: 'And up and down the people *go*, | Gazing where the lilies *blow* | Round an *island* there *below*.' There may also be a more surprising point of 'reference' here, Edward Lear's 'Yonghy-Bonghy-Bo' (1877): Silk (2000) 398–401.

[65] Overview of relevant material: Markeley (2004).

[66] Lucretius, *De Rerum Natura*, 1. 1–49.

[67] *In Memoriam*, 7 (with 'On . . . day' another classical-patterned line like 'Nor . . . font' in *The Princess*). Even in this poem, the 'local occasion' for melancholy can be a 'pretext': Joseph (1992) 19.

Alternatively, loss can involve frustrated hope, as in the early 'Mariana' (1830), an Elizabethan-age fantasia on the theme of Shakespeare's love-lorn 'Mariana in the moated grange'.[68] In a context remote from classical antiquity, it is instructive to find the emotional configuration that is associated with the classical elsewhere:

All day within the dreamy house
The doors upon their hinges creaked;
The blue fly sung in the pane . . .
Old faces glimmered through the doors,
Old footsteps trod the upper floors,
Old voices called her from without.
  She only said, 'My life is dreary,
  He cometh not,' she said.

As so often, the writing is generalized ('the moated grange was no particular grange', Tennyson noted),[69] but also arrestingly sensuous. 'The blue fly sung in the pane': appalling dull stillness, conveyed by long monosyllables. 'Sung in the pane': or *pain*, as it also surely is. (Tennyson 'seems to see with his ear', said Poe;[70] 'seems to *feel*' would be better.) In the gothic-atmospheric enactment of dreariness and dreaminess, 'old faces', 'footsteps', and 'voices' sensualize lost past, alongside 'her' refrain: 'He cometh not'. But do the old faces (etc.) have any close relation to this 'she' or indeed to the unforthcoming 'he'? And does it even matter whether they do or not?[71] The evocation of loss has a kind of self-sufficiency; significantly, the question whether it might be transmuted or transcended seems not to arise.

In 'Ulysses' (1833), a transmuting or transcending is, for once, attempted. In this imagined continuation of Homer's *Odyssey*, a few years on, our hero is in Ithaca, dissatisfied, with recollections of 'windy Troy' spurring him on to new adventure ('I cannot rest from travel'). The poem develops a theme, not directly from the *Odyssey* (though a final journey is briefly foretold there), but from Dante's *Inferno*, where the hero describes his last, fatal voyage, motivated by 'burning desire' ('l'ardore') for 'knowledge of the world'.[72] By Tennyson's own admission, the poem was 'written under the sense of loss and [the sense] that all had gone by, but that, still, life must be fought out to the end.'[73] That resolve animates the famous closing lines:

68 Tennyson's epigraph, alluding to *Measure for Measure*, 3. 1.

69 Quoted by Ricks (1987), 1. 205.

70 *Democratic Review*, December 1844.

71 'The images [in 'Mariana'] are presences that are a substitute for "his" absence, and . . . are held together by the emotions evoked by that absence': Hair (1991) 53.

72 *Odyssey*, 11. 121–37; *Inferno*, 26. 97–8. Dante's account (on which: Epilogue, below) has no ancient source: Stanford (1954) 180–1. Tennyson aligns his version with Dante's by using the Roman-derived 'Ulysses', like Dante's 'Ulisse' (*Inferno*, 26. 75); contrast Tennyson's Grecizing 'Lotos-Eaters' (Latin 'lotus', Greek 'lotos').

73 Quoted by Ricks (1987), 1. 613.

though
We are not now that strength which in old days
Moved earth and heaven, that which we are, we are . . .

Even here, though, we get the emotionally charged 'old days', and another such moment is identifiable earlier on. Despite approving words for 'mine own Telemachus', Ulysses' Ithaca is reduced to a few negatives – 'barren crags', a 'still hearth' (stillness can be as disturbing as the 'noise of life' in Tennyson), and an 'aged wife' – and the contrasting positive lies ahead:

It may be that the gulfs will wash us down:

(as happens in Dante)

It may be we shall touch the Happy Isles,
And see the great Achilles, whom we knew.

It is not, in the end, *new* knowledge that Tennyson's Ulysses yearns for, but the recapturing of his known past – and that 'touch' conveys the 'ardour' behind the yearning, as well as a poignant and paradoxical immediacy.[74]

A companion piece, 'The Lotos-Eaters' (1832), expands an episode from the *Odyssey*, where Odysseus/Ulysses and his men are *en route* to Ithaca from Troy.[75] The poem begins almost as 'Ulysses' ends: '"Courage!", he said, and pointed toward the land'. Here, though, on landing, the men eat the 'enchanted' lotos and succumb to a determined indolence: 'Oh rest ye, brother mariners, we will not wander more.' Their 'choric song' (of which that line marks the close) begins with exquisite languor, articulated in exquisite sound:

There is sweet music here that softer falls
Than petals from blown roses on the grass.

The landscape, generalized as usual, is party to the languor:

And in the stream the long-leaved flowers weep,
And from the craggy ledge the poppy hangs in sleep.

But then there is also a charming evocation of real Ithaca, yet one that turns into a rationalizing desire to let that real world go and, in the very act of letting go, into the habitual sense of lost past. Without a doubt, 'all hath suffered change'. 'Our sons inherit us', perhaps –

74 Felicitously, Tennyson makes 'The Islands of the Blessed Ones' (Hesiod, *Works and Days*, 171 etc.) 'the *Happy* Isles' – as they would be for Ulysses if he 'touched' them.

75 9. 82–104 (but there, unlike here, Odysseus' men are saved from the lotos).

Or else the island princes over-bold
Have eat our substance, and the minstrel sings
Before them of the ten years' war in Troy
And our great deeds, as half-forgotten things.

That 'half-forgotten' bites, like the 'whom we knew' in 'Ulysses'.

'Oenone' (1832) presents another world of exquisite sound –

There lies a vale in Ida, lovelier
Than all the valleys of Ionian hills[76] –

and a victim of lost love:

Mournful Oenone, wandering forlorn
Of Paris, once her playmate on the hills.

And 'now the noonday quiet holds the hill . . . | The purple flower droops.' To another irrecoverable past ('once') is attached a familiar set of disparate, but more or less classicizing, attributes: exquisite sound; purple and stillness;[77] and generalized singulars ('*the* purple flower'). Substantively, though, any objective connection with classical antiquity here is purely notional.

Tennyson uses the past – *any* past – to activate a preoccupation with loss, which is essentially preoccupation with the pain of distance,[78] not with any specifics of the loss itself.[79] The pain is vested in classical subjects and non-classical subjects, in Ulysses' 'old days' and Mariana's 'old faces'. His response to the past has, itself, a generalized quality; and the elusively generalized items that populate his 'historic' landscapes – 'the fire-fly', 'the purple flower' – seem to sum it up. In terms of specifiable commentary on the classical, Tennyson hardly registers[80] – unlike Eliot, and quite unlike Milton.

The very different poetic achievements of Tennyson and Eliot raise hard questions about the possibilities of classicizing in an increasingly recalcitrant age. Tennyson's exquisite technical usage is, on reflection, hard to reconcile with his deeper preoccupations, even in poems on classical themes: the past is painfully lost – but

76 Astonishingly, these two lines are almost entirely open syllables (without consonant clusters) and voiced sounds (there is no /p/, /t/, /k/, /č/, /f/, /θ/, /s/, /š/, and just one voiceless glottal fricative /h/). Tennyson's sensitivity to sound: cf. Hair (1991) 61–73.

77 This particular 'stillness' has unrelated classical connections: Silk (2004d) 365–7.

78 That distance expands and contracts. Ulysses is ostensibly three years away from heroic existence ('Ulysses', 29), but when he looks back to the 'old days' in Troy, it feels more like three thousand (*Tennyson's* distance). Conversely, the thought of seeing 'the great Achilles, whom we knew' makes *this* loss suddenly immediate.

79 Cf. Joseph (1992) 209: 'between the object-focused mourning and objectless melancholy . . . the latter is primary.' Joseph goes on (ibid. 210) to relate Tennyson's condition to the Lacanian 'primal lack'.

80 'Tennyson's classical vision is harder to frame,' says Joseph (1992) 136. Indeed.

a harmonious version of its idiom prevails? Eliot's radically innovative technique is more immediately disjunct from the classicism that constitutes, for him, an unattainable ideal. Both writers occupy distinctive, but ultimately provocative, places in the classical tradition. By comparison with both, Milton's place in the tradition is straightforward and coherent, however extreme his classicizing (and however far from 'the classic', in Eliot's sense, he must therefore be). Milton's use of classical form to tell Christian-Biblical story (the Paradise epics, the Samson drama) has in itself a clear logic, in terms of the norms of his age: the grand genres to express the highest truths and the hardest mysteries. The special problems that his technique raises – problems at their most apparent with a language like English? – transcend his age, and admit of a critical solution only at the deepest level of poetic theory: what is special about poetry, that it should demand a special kind of language?[81] It is no accident that it should be the work of a great poet, in the focus of a great tradition, that brings such a question to the fore.

[81] The subject of Silk (forthcoming).

Epilogue

'Classical' connotes value, and 'tradition' continuity. Within the classical tradition, value is at its most problematic when trivialized by false notions of reflected glory: the notion that people are made superior 'on account of their classical education' (§4), or 'great painters' by being in Rome (§25), or creative figures by adhering to a prestigious conventional genre (§22). And value, within the tradition, is at its most unassailable in the truly creative achievements of the towering figures who have shaped Western culture under the direct influence of the ancient world – and who continue to shape it, even when the continuity of Western culture itself is seen to be breached (§34).

Continuity is a term of value in its own right, though not always of positive value. It is less than a positive in any age when 'convention' threatens to stifle growth – hardly a danger in our age, which has the opposite problem: a suspicion of conventions altogether. 'This is our true bondage,' wrote D. H. Lawrence: 'this is the agony of our human existence, that we can only feel things in conventional feeling-patterns. Because when these feeling-patterns become inadequate . . . then we are in torture.'[1] Contrast Gombrich: 'Even the greatest artist – and he more than others – needs an idiom to work in. Only tradition, such as he finds it, can provide him with the raw material.'[2] For centuries, the continuities of the classical tradition met Gombrich's 'need' – in art, in literature, and in thought, as well. The tradition continues in our age; but outside popular culture, which lives by conventionalized

[1] 'The Good Man' (first published in *Phoenix*, 1936).

[2] Gombrich (1963) 126. Cf. Steiner (1998) 485.

The Classical Tradition: Art, Literature, Thought, First Edition. Michael Silk, Ingo Gildenhard, and Rosemary Barrow.

Published 2017 by John Wiley & Sons Ltd.

idioms, Gombrich's truth is one that our age has yet to relearn: the conventionalized heroics of Hollywood's *Gladiator* (§12), or indeed of Las Vegas's Caesars Palace (§§11, 20), have, in this sense, a lesson for 'even the greatest artist'. Meanwhile, Lawrence's contrary proposition is indisputable – except that it is the creative figures (like Lawrence himself), and especially the towering figures, who transcend 'bondage' and, in their different spheres, show how new 'patterns' are created, perhaps by radical innovation, but still by affirming continuity in the end. Michelangelo and Nietzsche, Picasso and Montaigne, Shakespeare and Dante: continuity with ancient experience helps to make their new 'patterns' possible.

But the continuity of the classical is reflected in archetypes, too, and in reflexes (as we have called them), and in responses to responses (our paradigm was Eliot on Milton: §§1, 35). And reflected, again, institutionally: in education most directly, but also in libraries, galleries, and museums; in urban planning and Grand Tours; in programmatic translation and authorized language. Our endeavour to make sense of the classical tradition, and thus offer a significant perspective on Western culture itself, is only possible because of these continuities.

Traditions can be contested; and most of the towering figures at some point contest the classical tradition; but the tradition is renewed even then. Amidst the horrors and degradations of Auschwitz, Primo Levi drew strength from Dante's line: 'you were not made to live like animals' – a bitter, but also uplifting, instance of response to a response. The words are those of Ulysses exhorting his men to new quests, words recounted now by Ulysses himself to Virgil, Dante's guide in Hell:

> you were not made to live like animals,
> but to pursue excellence and knowledge.
>
> fatti non foste a viver come bruti,
> ma per seguir virtute e canoscenza.[3]

In Auschwitz, Levi quotes the passage, from memory, to a fellow-prisoner, but also hears it himself, and it was –

> as if I was hearing it for the first time too: like a trumpet-blast, like the voice of God. For a moment I forget where I am or who I am.[4]

In Dante, though, the words are not God's, but those of a self-assertive pagan explorer; and in Dante's Christian world-view, self-assertive exploration, without sanctity or due ethical restraint (and 'virtute' is more mastery than morality), can only be suspect, captivating though it may be.[5] The classical is contested. And yet,

[3] *Inferno*, 26. 119–20.

[4] *Se questo è un uomo*, ch. 11.

[5] 'Dante the poet has [Ulysses] drowned by God; Dante the judge condemns him to hell; and even Dante the character and author will later repeat that Ulysses' "varco" ['path'] was indeed "folle" ['mad']': Boitani (1994) 40. Ulysses is in any case portrayed as devious and dishonest (*Inferno*, 26. 55–63), one of his many guises down the centuries: Hall (2008d), Stanford (1954).

Figure 10 British Library piazza, London. Source: © The British Library Board. Asset 066442.

for Levi, the words affirm human value and its survival;[6] his response cancels Dante's own – but it is Dante's own that makes it possible: the continuity remains.

Our closing thought is prompted by personal circumstance. It concerns Colin St John Wilson's new British Library building (1997), where some of this book was researched and written. The concourse in front of the library offers a view of the building [*Figure 10*] whose overall rhythm and particular detail – the oblong tower and the clock, above all – evokes (of all unlikely precedents) a range of de Chirico's paintings from his Metaphysical period (§§24, 33), with their towers and clocks, their steam trains, and their classicizing statues: *The Soothsayer's Recompense* (1913) [*Figure 11*], *La gare Montparnasse* (1914), *Ariadne's Afternoon* (1913). A postmodern in-joke on the architect's part, perhaps, but in any case an implicit enactment of classical continuities in the shape of a response to a response, yet again. In the evocative view of the library, there is no train visible – but then, behind the library

6 Cf. §§16, 27.

Figure 11 Giorgio de Chirico, *The Soothsayer's Recompense*. Source: Philadelphia, Philadelphia Museum of Art. Oil on canvas, 53 3/8 × 70 7/8 inches (135.6 × 180 cm). The Louise and Walter Arensberg Collection, 1950.© DACS 2013. Photo ©2013, The Philadelphia Museum of Art/Art Resource/Scala, Florence.

is the grand Victorian railway station at St Pancras, where steam trains once came and went. There is no classicizing statue here, either[7] – but then, the library itself is replete with items (including books of, and on, classicizing statuary) that embody the tradition in all its different ages and its diverse forms. Visible or invisible, the continuity remains.

[7] Paolozzi's statue of Newton ('After Blake'), on the concourse, is hardly classicizing in any relevant sense.

Bibliography

Ackroyd, P. R. *et al.* (1963–70), *The Cambridge History of the Bible*, 3 vols, Cambridge.

Adams, J. N. (2003), *Bilingualism and the Latin Language*, Cambridge.

— (2007), *The Regional Diversification of Latin, 200 BC–600 AD*, Cambridge.

Adams, N. (1983), review of Saalman (1980), *Art Bulletin* 65: 513–15.

Adorno, T. W. and Horkheimer, M. (1972), *Dialectic of Enlightenment*, tr. J. Cumming, New York.

Aebli, D. (1991), *Winckelmanns Entwicklungslogik der Kunst*, Frankfurt a. M.

Aguado, M. I. P. (1994), *Ästhetik des Erhabenen: Burke, Kant, Adorno, Lyotard*, Vienna.

Albright, D. (1994), W. B. Yeats, *The Poems*, rev. edn, London.

Allan, D. (2003), 'André Malraux and the Challenge to Aesthetics', *Journal of European Studies* 33: 23–40.

Allen, D. C. (1970), *Mysteriously Meant: The Rediscovery of Pagan Symbolism and Allegorical Interpretation in the Renaissance*, Baltimore, Md.

Allen, P. (1982), 'The Role of Myth in Racine', in Aspley *et al.* (1982): 93–116.

Allen, T. W. (1908), 'The Epic Cycle', *Classical Quarterly* 2: 64–74.

— (1924), *Homer: The Origins and the Transmission*, Oxford.

Altmann, W. (1923), Richard Wagner, *Mein Leben*, 2 vols, Leipzig.

Amarasinghe, U. (1962), *Dryden and Pope in the Early Nineteenth Century*, Cambridge.

Andersen, Ø. and Haarberg, J. (2001) (eds), *Making Sense of Aristotle: Essays in Poetics*, London.

Anderson, L. (2005), *A Place in the Story: Servants and Service in Shakespeare's Plays*, Newark.

Andrews, R. (1999), 'The Cinquecento: Theatre', in P. Brand and L. Pertile (eds), *The Cambridge History of Italian Literature*, rev. edn, Cambridge: 277–98.

Annas, J. (2006), 'Seneca: Stoic Philosophy as a Guide to Living', in J. Welchman (ed.), *The Practice of Virtue*, Indianapolis: 156–69.

The Classical Tradition: Art, Literature, Thought, First Edition. Michael Silk, Ingo Gildenhard, and Rosemary Barrow.

Published 2017 by John Wiley & Sons Ltd.

Arasse, D. (1985), 'Giulio Romano e il labirinto di Psiche', *Quaderni di Palazzo Te* 3: 7–18.

Arikha, N. (2007), *Passions and Tempers: A History of the Humours*, New York.

Armstrong, R. H. (2005), *A Compulsion for Antiquity: Freud and the Ancient World*, Ithaca, NY.

Ascoli, A. R. (1991), 'Petrarch's Middle Age: Memory, Imagination, History, and the "Ascent of Mt. Ventoux"', *Stanford Italian Review* 10: 5–43.

Ascoli, A. R. and Kahn, V. (1993) (eds), *Machiavelli and the Discourse of Literature*, Ithaca, NY.

Aske, M. (1985), *Keats and Hellenism*, Cambridge.

Aspley, K. *et al.* (1982) (eds), *Myth and Legend in French Literature*, London.

Assmann, A. and Assmann, J. (1987), 'Introduction', in id. (eds) *Kanon und Zensur: Archäologie der literarischen Kommunikation II*, Munich: 7–27.

Astington, J. H. (2001), 'Playhouses, Players and Playgoers in Shakespeare's Time', in M. de Grazia and S. Wells (eds), *The Cambridge Companion to Shakespeare*, Cambridge: 99–113.

Atkinson, D. and Cosgrove, D. (1998), 'Urban Rhetoric and Embodied Identities: City, Nation, and Empire at the Vittorio Emanuele II Monument in Rome, 1870–1945', *Annals of the Association of American Geographers* 88. 1: 28–49.

Attridge, D. (1988), *Peculiar Language*, London.

Auden, W. H. (1963), *The Dyer's Hand*, London.

Axelsson, K. (2007), *The Sublime: Precursors and British Eighteenth-Century Conceptions*, Berne.

Ayres-Bennett, W. and Jones, M. C. (2007) (eds), *The French Language and Questions of Identity*, London.

Babbitt, S. M. (1985), *Oresme's Livre de Politiques and the France of Charles V*, Philadelphia.

Bablet, D. (1995) (ed.), *L'oeuvre d'art totale*, Paris.

Bacci, F. and Melcher, D. (2011) (eds), *Art and the Senses*, Oxford.

Bach, A. (1970), *Geschichte der deutschen Sprache*, 9th edn, Heidelberg.

Badiou, A. (2010), *Five Lessons on Wagner* (with Afterword by S. Žižek), London.

Baehr, P. and O'Brien, M. (1994), *Founders, Classics and the Concept of a Canon*, London.

Baeumer, M. (1976), 'Nietzsche and the Tradition of the Dionysian', in J. C. O'Flaherty *et al.* (eds), *Studies in Nietzsche and the Classical Tradition*, Chapel Hill: 165–89.

Baines, P. and Rogers, P. (2007), *Edmund Curll, Bookseller*, Oxford.

Baker, K. M. (2001), 'Transformations of Classical Republicanism in Eighteenth-Century France', *Journal of Modern History* 73: 32–53.

Bakhtin, M. (1968), *Rabelais and His World*, tr. H. Iswolsky, Bloomington, Ind.

Baldacci, P. (1983), 'Le classicisme chez Giorgio de Chirico', *Cahiers du Musée National d'Art Moderne* (Paris) 11: 18–31.

Baldi, P. (2002), *The Foundations of Latin*, Berlin and New York.

Bambrough, R. (1967) (ed.), *Plato, Popper and Politics*, Cambridge.

Bann, S. (1984), *The Clothing of Clio: A Study of the Representation of History in Nineteenth-Century Britain*, Cambridge.

Baranski, Z. G. and Cachey, T. J., Jr. (2009) (eds), *Petrarch and Dante*, Notre Dame, Ind.

Barber, C. L. (1959), *Shakespeare's Festive Comedy*, Princeton.

Bárberi Squarotti, G. (1987), *Machiavelli o la scelta della letteratura*, Rome.

Barberini, M. G. and Gaspari, C. (1994), *Bartolomeo Cavaceppi: Scultore romano 1777–1799*, Rome.

Barkan, L. (1975), *Nature's Work of Art: The Human Body as Image of the World*, New Haven.

— (1986), *The Gods Made Flesh: Metamorphosis and the Pursuit of Paganism*, New Haven.
— (1991), *Transuming Passion: Ganymede and the Erotics of Humanism*, Stanford.
— (1999), *Unearthing the Past: Archaeology and Aesthetics in the Making of Renaissance Culture*, New Haven.
— (2010a), 'Rome: II. Renaissance and After', in Grafton, Most, and Settis (2010): 848–50.
— (2010b), 'Rome, History, and the Spolia-of-the-Mind', in Kocziszky (2010): 89–102.
Barnes, T. (1981), *Constantine and Eusebius*, Cambridge, Mass.
Barolini, T. (1984), *Dante's Poets*, Princeton.
— (2009), 'The Self in the Labyrinth of Time (*Rerum vulgarium fragmenta*)', in V. Kirkham and A. Maggi (eds), *Petrarch: A Critical Guide to the Complete Works*, Chicago: 33–62.
Barolsky, P. (1998), 'As in Ovid, So in Renaissance Art', *Renaissance Quarterly* 51: 451–74.
— (2011), 'Giotto's Fleeing Apostle', *Arion* 18: 116–22.
Barrow, R. J. (2001), *Lawrence Alma-Tadema*, London.
— (2005), 'Praxiteles to de Chirico: Art and Reception', *International Journal of the Classical Tradition* 11: 344–68.
— (2007), *Creating Continuity with the Traditions of High Art: The Use of Classical Art and Literature by Victorian Painters, 1860–1912*, Lewiston, NY.
— (2010), 'Toga Plays and Tableaux Vivants: Theatre and Painting on London's Late-Victorian and Edwardian Popular Stage', *Theatre Journal* 64: 209–24.
Barsch, A. and Hejl, P. M. (2000), 'Zur Verweltlichung und Pluralisierung des Menschenbildes im 19. Jahrhundert: Einleitung', in id. (eds), *Menschenbilder. Zur Pluralisierung der Vorstellung von der menschlichen Natur (1850–1914)*, Frankfurt a. M.: 7–90.
Bartel, H. and Simon, A. (2010) (eds), *Unbinding Medea: Interdisciplinary Approaches to a Classical Myth from Antiquity to the 21st Century*, Oxford.
Barthes, R. (1953), *Le degré zéro de l'écriture*, Paris.
— (1957), *Mythologies*, Paris.
— (1968), 'L'Effet de Réel', *Communications* 11: 84–9.
— (1984), *Le bruissement de la langue*, Paris.
Bate, J. (1993), *Shakespeare and Ovid*, Oxford.
— (1995), *The Arden Shakespeare: Titus Andronicus*, London.
Bately, J. M. (2000), 'The Literary Prose of King Alfred's Reign: Translation or Transformation?', in P. E. Szarmach (ed.), *Old English Prose*, New York: 3–27.
Battisti, E. and Krumrine, M. L. (1982), '"Desiderare una ignuda": Giorgione e Michelangelo attraverso l'indagine cinesica', *Artibus et Historiae* 6: 37–73.
Baudrillard, J. (1981), *Simulacres et simulation*, Paris.
Bauer, F. J. (2009), *Rom im 19. und 20. Jahrhundert: Konstruktion eines Mythos*, Regensburg.
Baumstark, M. (2010), 'Hume's Reading of the Classics at Ninewells, 1749–51', *Journal of Scottish Philosophy* 8: 63–77.
Baxa, P. (2010), *Roads and Ruins: The Symbolic Landscape of Fascist Rome*, Toronto.
Beadle, R. (2004), 'Masks, Mimes and Miracles', in P. Holland and S. Orgel (eds), *From Script to Stage in Early Modern England*, London: 32–42.
Beard, M. (2000), *The Invention of Jane Harrison*, Cambridge, Mass.
Beard, M. and Henderson, J. (1994), 'PLEASE DON'T TOUCH THE CEILING: The Culture of Appropriation', in S. Pearce (ed.), *Museums and the Appropriation of Culture*, London: 5–42.
Beaton, R. (2007), 'The Greek Novel and the Rise of the European Genre', in J. Mander (ed.), *Remapping the Rise of the European Novel*, Oxford: 225–33.
— (2009), 'Korais and the Second Sophistic', in Georgakopoulou and Silk (2009): 341–54.

Bec, C. (1976), 'De Pétrarque à Machiavel: à propos d'un topos humaniste (le dialogue lecteur/livre)', *Rinascimento* 16: 3–17.

Becker, E.-M. (2005) (ed.), *Die antike Historiographie und die Anfänge der christlichen Geschichtsschreibung*, Berlin.

Bein, T. (1990), 'Orpheus als Sodomit. Beobachtungen zu einer mhd. Sangspruchstrophe mit (literar)historischen Exkursen zur Homosexualität im hohen Mittelalter', *Zeitschrift für deutsche Philologie* 109: 33–55.

Bell, M. G. (forthcoming), *Melancholia: The European Malady.*

Bell, M. J. (1989), 'The Study of Popular Culture', in M. T. Inge (ed.), *Handbook of American Popular Culture*, Westport, Conn.: 1459–84.

Belluzzi, A. (1989) (ed.), *Giulio Romano*, Milan.

Beltramini, G. and Burns, H. (2009), *Palladio*, London.

Benitez, E. (2004), 'On Literal Translation: Robert Browning and the *Agamemnon*', *Philosophy and Literature* 28: 259–68.

Benn, M. B. (1962), *Hölderlin and Pindar*, The Hague.

Benner, D. (2003), *Wilhelm von Humboldts Bildungstheorie*, 3rd edn, Weinheim.

Bennett, T. (1979), *Formalism and Marxism*, London.

Bentivoglio, E., *et al.* (2001), *Donato Bramante*, Bologna.

Bentley, G. E. (1978), *William Blake's Writings*, 2 vols, Oxford.

Benzinger, J. (1968), *Invectiva in Romam: Romkritik im Mittelalter vom 9. bis zum 12. Jahrhundert*, Lübeck.

Bequette, J. P. (2007), *Christian Humanism*, Lanham, Md.

Berger, J. (1972), *Ways of Seeing*, London.

Berger, J. and Luckmann, T. (1967), *The Social Construction of Reality*, London.

Berić-Djukić, V. (1988), 'Ist die deutsche Verbstellung dem lateinischen Einfluss zuzuschreiben?', in P. Wiesinger (ed.), *Studien zum Frühneuhochdeutsch*, Göppingen: 219–26.

Berman, A. (1984), *L'Épreuve de l'étranger: culture et traduction dans l'Allemagne romantique*, Paris.

Bernstein, J. G. (1992), 'The Female Model and the Renaissance Nude: Dürer, Giorgione, and Raphael', *Artibus et Historiae* 26: 49–63.

Berschin, W. (1988), *Greek Letters and the Latin Middle Ages*, tr. J. C. Frakes, Washington, DC.

Berthold, G. (1958), *Cézanne und die alten Meister*, Stuttgart.

Bettini, M. (2001), *Classical Indiscretions: A Millennial Enquiry into the State of the Classics*, tr. J. McManamon, London.

Betts, R. J. (1993), 'Structural Innovation and Structural Design in Renaissance Architecture', *Journal of the Society of Architectural Historians* 52: 5–25.

— (2000), 'Si come dice Vetruvio: Images of Antiquity in Early Renaissance Theory of Architecture', in A. Payne *et al.* (eds), *Antiquity and Its Interpreters*, Cambridge: 244–57.

Biermann, V. (1997), *Ornamentum. Studien zum Traktat De re aedificatoria des Leon Battista Alberti*, Hildesheim.

Billings, J. (forthcoming), *The Genealogy of the Tragic: Greek Tragedy and German Philosophy*, Princeton.

Binns, J. W. (1978), 'Latin Translations from Greek in the English Renaissance', *Humanistica Lovaniensia* 27: 128–59.

— (1990), *Intellectual Culture in Elizabethan and Jacobean England*, Leeds.

Blanc, P. (1986), 'La construction d'une utopie néo-urbaine. Rome dans la pensée, l'action et l'oeuvre de Petrarque de 1333 à 1342', in D. Poirion (ed.), *Jérusalem, Rome, Constantinople. L'image et le mythe de la ville au Moyen Age*, Paris: 149–68.

Blanchot, M. (1971), 'Traduire', in id., *L'Amitié*, Paris: 69–73.

Blanning, T. C. W. (2010), *The Romantic Revolution*, London.

Blanshard, A. (2007), 'From *Amor Socraticus* to *Socrates Amoris*: Socrates and the Formation of Sexual Identity in Late Victorian Britain', in Trapp (2007a): 97–116.

Blanshard, A. and Shahabudin, K. (2011), *Classics on Screen: Ancient Greece and Rome on Film*, London.

Blessington, F. C. (1979), *Paradise Lost and the Classical Epic*, London.

Bloomer, K. C. and Moore, C. W. (1977) (eds), *Body, Memory, and Architecture*, New Haven.

Blumenberg, H. (1983), *The Legitimacy of the Modern Age*, tr. R. M. Wallace, 2nd edn, Cambridge, Mass.

Blunt, A. (1967), *Nicolas Poussin, I. Text*, London.

— (1982), *Guide to Baroque Rome*, London.

Bober, P. and Rubinstein, R. (1986), *Renaissance Artists and Antique Sculpture*, London.

Bockris, V. (1998), *Muhammad Ali in Fighter's Heaven*, London.

Bodmer, F. (1944), *The Loom of Language*, London.

Boitani, P. (1994), *The Shadow of Ulysses*, tr. A. Weston, Oxford.

Bolgar, R. R. (1954), *The Classical Heritage and Its Beneficiaries*, Cambridge.

— (1971) (ed.), *Classical Influences on European Culture, AD 500–1500*, Cambridge.

Boon, K. (2005), 'Heroes, Metanarratives, and the Paradox of Masculinity in Contemporary Western Culture', *Journal of Men's Studies* 13: 301–12.

Boone, R. (2000), 'Claude de Seyssel's Translations of Ancient Historians', *Journal of the History of Ideas* 61: 561–75.

Booth, M. R. (1981), *Victorian Spectacular Theatre, 1850–1910*, London.

Boroughs, R. (1995), 'Oscar Wilde's Translation of Petronius: The Story of a Literary Hoax', *English Literature in Transition* 38: 9–49.

Botley, P. (2002), 'Learning Greek in Western Europe, 1476–1515', in Holmes and Waring (2002): 199–241.

— (2004), *Latin Translation in the Renaissance*, Cambridge.

Boucher, B. (1998), *Andrea Palladio: The Architect in His Time*, London.

Bourdieu, P. (1979), *La distinction: critique sociale de jugement*, Paris.

Bourdieu, P. and Darbel, A. (1991), *The Love of Art: European Museums and Their Public*, tr. C. Beattie and N. Merrimon, Cambridge.

Bourgain, P. (2003), 'Image de Rome dans la littérature (Moyen Âge)', in Levillain (2003): 833–7.

Bourgeois, L. (2005), *Destruction of the Father, Reconstruction of the Father: Writings and Interviews, 1923–1997*, ed. M. L. Bernadac *et al.*, London.

Bourqui, C. (1999), *La Commedia dell' Arte. Introduction au théâtre professionel italien entre le XVIe et le XVIIIe siècles*, Paris.

Boutry, M.-P. (2003), 'Image de Rome dans la littérature (époque moderne et contemporaine)', in Levillain (2003): 838–52.

Bovée, C. L. (2003), *Contemporary Public Speaking*, 2nd edn, San Diego.

Bowersock, G. W. (2007), Lorenzo Valla, *On the Donation of Constantine*, Cambridge, Mass.

Bowlby, R. (2007), *Freudian Mythologies: Greek Tragedy and Modern Identities*, Oxford.

Bowra, C. M. (1945), *A Classical Education*, Oxford.

Boyde, P. (1981), *Dante, Philomythes and Philosopher: Man in the Cosmos*, Cambridge.

Braden, G. (2004), 'Plutarch, Shakespeare, and the Alpha Males', in Martindale and Taylor (2004): 188–208.

— (2010), 'Astérix', in Grafton, Most, and Settis (2010): 83–4.

Brady, E. (2012), 'The Environmental Sublime', in Costelloe (2012): 171–82.
Brams, J. (1997), 'L'édition critique de l'Aristote Latin: le problème des révisions', in S. G. Lofts and P. W. Rosemann (eds), *Editer, traduire, interpréter*, Louvain-la-Neuve: 39–53.
Bremer, J. M. (1969), *Hamartia*, Amsterdam.
Brett, R. L. and Jones, A. R. (1965), Wordsworth and Coleridge, *Lyrical Ballads*, rev. edn, London.
Brilliant, R. (2000), *My Laocoön*, Berkeley.
Brink, C. O. (1971), *Horace on Poetry: The 'Ars Poetica'*, Cambridge.
— (1986), *English Classical Scholarship: Historical Reflections on Bentley, Porson and Housman*, Cambridge.
Bristol, M. D. (1989), *Carnival and Theater: Plebeian Culture and the Structure of Authority in Renaissance England*, New York.
Brodey, I. S. (2008), *Ruined by Design: Shaping Novels and Gardens in the Culture of Sensibility*, London.
Brombert, V. (1969) (ed.), *The Hero in Literature*, New York.
Brophy, J. and Partridge, E. (1965), *The Long Trail: Soldiers' Songs and Slang, 1914–18*, rev. edn, London.
Brower, R. A. (1971), *Hero and Saint: Shakespeare and the Graeco-Roman Heroic Tradition*, Oxford.
Brown, A. (2010), *The Return of Lucretius to Renaissance Florence*, Cambridge, Mass.
Brown, P. (1967), *Augustine of Hippo*, London.
Brown, P. F. (1997), *Venice and Antiquity: the Venetian Sense of the Past*, New Haven.
Brown, S. A. (2004), 'Philomela', *Translation and Literature* 13: 194–206.
Brownlee, K. (1993), 'Dante and the Classical Poets', in R. Jacoff (ed.), *The Cambridge Companion to Dante*, Cambridge: 141–60.
Buck, A. (1987), *Humanismus. Seine europäische Entwicklung in Dokumenten und Darstellungen*, Freiburg.
Buddensieg, T. (1971), 'Criticism and Praise of the Pantheon in the Middle Ages and the Renaissance', in Bolgar (1971): 259–67.
Budelmann, F. (2007), '*Trojan Women* in Yorubaland; Femi Osofisan's *Women of Owu*', in Hardwick and Gillespie (2007): 15–39.
— (2009) (ed.), *The Cambridge Companion to Greek Lyric*, Cambridge.
Budelmann, F. and Haubold, J. (2008), 'Reception and Tradition', in Hardwick and Stray (2008): 13–25.
Bull, M. (2005), *The Mirror of the Gods: Classical Mythology in Renaissance Art*, London.
Bullough, D. A. (2004), *Alcuin: Achievement and Reputation*, Leiden.
Burdick, W. L. (1938), *The Principles of Roman Law and Their Relation to Modern Law*, Rochester, NY.
Burke, P. (1969), *The Renaissance Sense of the Past*, London.
— (1992), *The Fabrication of Louis XIV*, New Haven.
— (2007), 'Translations into Latin in Early Modern Europe', in P. Burke and R. Po-chia Hsia (eds), *Cultural Translation in Early Modern Europe*, Cambridge: 65–80.
— (2009), *Popular Culture in Early Modern Europe*, 3rd edn, Farnham.
— (2010a), 'Popular Culture', in Grafton, Most, and Settis (2010): 765–7.
— (2010b), 'Progress and Decline', in Grafton, Most, and Settis (2010): 782–5.
Burnett, C. (2005), 'Arabic into Latin', in P. Adamson and R. C. Taylor (eds), *The Cambridge Companion to Arabic Philosophy*, Cambridge: 370–404.

Burns, H. (2003), *La città bianca: continuità e innovazione nell'architettura di San Pietroburgo, 1762–1825*, in N. Navone and L. Tedeschi (eds), *Dal Mito al Progetto. La cultura architettonica dei maestri italiani e ticinesi nella Russia neoclassica*, vol. 2, Lugano: 455–501.

Burns, N. T. and Reagan, C. J. (1975) (eds), *Concepts of the Hero in the Middle Ages and the Renaissance*, Albany, NJ.

Burnyeat, M. (1985), 'Sphinx Without a Secret', *New York Review of Books* 32. 9: 30–6.

Burroughs, C. (1988), 'Palladio and Fortune: Notes on Sources and Meaning of the Villa Rotonda', *Journal of the History of Architecture* 18: 59–61.

Burrow, C. (2004), 'Shakespeare and Humanistic Culture', in Martindale and Taylor (2004): 9–27.

Burton, P. (2005), 'George Orwell and the Classics', *Classical and Modern Literature* 25: 53–75.

Bush, D. (1932/3), 'Wordsworth and the Classics', *University of Toronto Quarterly* 2: 359–79.

Butterfield, D. and Stray, C. (2009) (eds), *A. E. Housman, Classical Scholar*, London.

Buxton, R. G. A. (1999) (ed.), *From Myth to Reason? Studies in the Development of Greek Thought*, Oxford.

— (2009), *Forms of Astonishment: Greek Myths of Metamorphosis*, Oxford.

Calder, W. M. (1966), 'Die Geschichte der klassischen Philologie in den Vereinigten Staaten', *Jahrbuch für Amerikastudien* 11: 213–40.

— (1983), U. von Wilamowitz-Moellendorff, *Selected Correspondence 1869–1931*, Naples.

— (1985), 'Ecce Homo: The Autobiographical in Wilamowitz's Scholarly Writings', in Calder *et al.* (1985): 80–110.

Calder, W. M. *et al.* (1985) (eds), *Wilamowitz nach 50 Jahren*, Darmstadt.

Caldwell, D. and Caldwell, L. (2011) (eds), *Rome: Continuing Encounters between Past and Present*, Farnham.

Cameron, A. M. (1997), 'Hellenism and the Emergence of Islam', *Dialogos* 4: 4–18.

Campbell, J. W. P. (2008), *Building St Paul's*, London.

Canitz, A. E. C. (1996), '"In our Awyn Langage": The Nationalist Agenda of Gavin Douglas's *Eneados*', *Vergilius* 42: 25–37.

Cannon-Brookes, P. (1992), 'The Nature of Museum Collections', in J. M. A. Thompson *et al.*, *Manual of Curatorship*, Oxford: 500–12.

Canovan, M. (1990), 'Socrates or Heidegger? Hannah Arendt's Reflections on Philosophy and Politics', *Social Research* 57. 1: 135–65.

Carne-Ross, D. S. (1962), 'Structural Translation: Notes on Logue's *Patrokleia*', *Arion* 1. 2: 27–38.

— (1989), 'Jocasta's Divine Head: English with a Foreign Accent', *Arion* n. s. 1: 106–41.

Carpenter, T. H. and Faraone, C. A. (1993) (eds), *Masks of Dionysus*, Ithaca, NY.

Carpo, M. (2001), *Architecture in the Age of Printing*, tr. S. Benson, Cambridge, Mass.

Carrier, D. (1993), *Poussin's Paintings*, Philadelphia.

Caruso, C. and Laird, A. (2009) (eds), *Italy and the Classical Tradition: Language, Thought and Poetry 1300–1600*, London.

Cary, G. (1956), *The Medieval Alexander*, Cambridge.

Casapullo, R. (1999), *Storia della lingua italiana. Il Medioevo*, Bologna.

Castiglione Morelli, V. (1999) (ed.), *A Giuseppe Fiorelli nel primo centenario della morte*, Naples.

Castor, G. (1964), *Pléiade Poetics*, Cambridge.

Catterson, L. (2005), 'Michelangelo's Laocoon?', *Artibus et Historiae* 26. 52: 29–56.

Cavalli-Björkman, G. (1987) (ed.), *Bacchanals by Titian and Rubens*, Stockholm.

Cavallo, G. *et al.* (1989) (eds), *Le biblioteche nel mondo antico e medievale*, Bari.

Cave, T. (1979), *The Cornucopian Text*, Cambridge.

— (2006), 'Locating the Early Modern', *Paragraph* 29: 12–26.

Cave, T. and Castor, G. (1984) (eds), *Neo-Latin and the Vernacular in Renaissance France*, Oxford.

Ceccarelli, P. (2006), *Friedrich Gottlieb Welcker e l'antiquaria napoletana: carteggi Gervasio - Welcker e Minervini - Welcker*, San Severo.

— (2010), 'Sostratos (23)', *Brill's New Jacoby*, http://referenceworks.brillonline.com/entries/brill-s-new-jacoby/sostratos-23-a23, accessed 22 July 2013.

Celant, G. *et al.* (2004) (eds), *Robert Mapplethorpe and the Classical Tradition: Photographs and Mannerist Prints*, New York.

Centanni, M. (2010), 'Alexander the Great', in Grafton, Most, and Settis (2010): 25–31.

Ceram, C. W. (1967), *Gods, Graves and Scholars: The Story of Archaeology*, tr. E. B. Garside and S. Wilkins, New York.

Chadwick, W. (1980), *Myth in Surrealist Painting 1929–1939*, Michigan.

Chambers, I. (2001), *Culture After Humanism*, London.

Chance, J. (1994), *Medieval Mythography, 1: From Roman North Africa to the School of Chartres, A.D. 433–1177*, Gainesville, Fla.

— (2000), *Medieval Mythography, 2: From the School of Chartres to the Court at Avignon, 1177–1350*, Gainesville, Fla.

Chandler, J. (1984), 'The Pope Controversy: Romantic Poetics and the English Canon', *Critical Inquiry* 10: 481–509.

Charles, D. (2005), 'Aristotelianism', in T. Honderich (ed.), *The Oxford Companion to Philosophy*, 2nd edn, Oxford: 51–4.

Chartier, R. (1994), *The Order of Books: Readers, Authors, and Libraries in Europe between the Fourteenth and Eighteenth Centuries*, Stanford.

Chastel, A. and Cevese, R. (1990) (eds), *Andrea Palladio: nuovi contributi*, Vicenza.

Chaurand, J. (1999), *Nouvelle histoire de la langue française*, Paris.

Chavy, P. (1981), 'Les traductions humanistes du début de la Renaissance française', *Canadian Review of Comparative Literature* 7: 284–306.

Choay, F. (2001), *The Invention of the Historic Monument*, tr. L. O'Connell, Cambridge.

Christ, C. T. (1975), *The Finer Optic: The Aesthetic of Particularity in Victorian Poetry*, New Haven.

Christian, K. W. (2010), *Empire Without End: Antiquities Collections in Renaissance Rome, c. 1350–1527*, New Haven.

Christidis, A.-F. (2007) (ed.), *A History of Ancient Greek*, Cambridge.

Ciapponi, L. A. (1960), 'Il De architectura di Vitruvio nel primo umanesimo', *Italia Medievale e Umanistica* 3: 59–99.

Ciccolella, F. (2007), *Donati Graeci: Learning Greek in the Renaissance*, Leiden.

Clackson, J. and Horrocks, G. (2007), *The Blackwell History of the Latin Language*, Chichester.

Clark, K. (1956), *The Nude: A Study in Ideal Form*, New York.

— (1969), *Civilisation*, London.

Clark, W. (2006), *Academic Charisma and the Origins of the Research University*, Chicago.

Clarke, C. C. and Clarke, M. C. (1878), *Recollections of Writers*, London.

Clarke, G. (2002), 'Vitruvian Paradigms', *Papers of the British School at Rome* 70: 319–46.

— (2003), *Roman House - Renaissance Palace: Inventing Antiquity in Fifteenth-Century Italy*, Cambridge.

Clarke, M. and Penny, N. (1982) (eds), *The Arrogant Connoisseur: Richard Payne Knight*, Manchester.

Clarke, M. L. (1959), *Classical Education in Britain, 1500–1900*, Cambridge.

Classen, C. J. (2003), *Antike Rhetorik im Zeitalter des Humanismus*, Munich.

Cleary, M. S. (2007), *Myths for the Millions: Thomas Bulfinch, His America, and His Mythology Books*, Frankfurt a. M.

Clingham, G. and Smallwood, P. (2009) (eds), *Samuel Johnson After 300 Years*, Cambridge.

Coche de la Ferté, E. and Guey, J. (1952), 'Analyse archéologique et psychologique d'un tableau de David: Les amours de Paris et d'Hélène', *Revue archéologique* 10: 129–61.

Coffin, D. R. (1994), *The English Garden: Meditation and Memorial*, Princeton.

Cohan, S. (1997), *Masked Men: Masculinity and the Movies in the Fifties*, Bloomington, Ind.

Cohen, R. A. (2003), 'Introduction: Humanism and Anti-Humanism - Levinas, Cassirer, and Heidegger', in Levinas (2003): vii–xliv.

Cohen, S. (2000), 'The Early Renaissance Personification of Time and Changing Concepts of Temporality', *Renaissance Studies* 14: 301–28.

Cohen, T. (1999), 'High and Low Art, and High and Low Audiences', *Journal of Aesthetics and Art Criticism* 57: 151–6.

Colish, M. A. (1978), 'Cicero's *De Officiis* and Machiavelli's *Prince*', *Sixteenth-Century Journal* 9. 4: 80–93.

Colli, G. and Montinari, M. (1967–), Nietzsche, *Werke, Kritische Gesamtausgabe*, Berlin.

Coltman, V. (2006), *Fabricating the Antique: Neoclassicism in Britain, 1760–1800*, Chicago.

— (2009), *Classical Sculpture and the Culture of Collecting*, Oxford.

Colvin, S. (1998), '"Die Zung ist dieses Schwert": Classical Tongues and Gendered Curricula in German Schooling to 1908', in Y. L. Too and N. Livingstone (eds), *Pedagogy and Power: Rhetorics of Classical Learning*, Cambridge: 47–66.

Comparetti, D. (1997), *Virgil in the Middle Ages*, tr. E. F. M. Benecke, intr. J. M. Ziolkowski, Princeton.

Conant, K. J. (1968), 'The After-Life of Vitruvius in the Middle Ages', *Journal of the Society of Architectural Historians* 27: 33–8.

Connor, M. A. (2010), 'Real American Heroes', in D. Rubin and J. Verheul (eds), *American Multiculturalism After 9/11: Transatlantic Perspectives*, Amsterdam: 93–104.

Considine, J. (2008), *Dictionaries in Early Modern Europe*, Cambridge.

Conti, C. (2007), *A History of the Restoration and Conservation of Works of Art*, tr. H. Glanville, Oxford.

Cook, B. F. (1985), *The Townley Marbles*, London.

Cooley, A. E. (2003), *Pompeii*, London.

Cooper, T. (1991), 'The History and Decoration of the Church of San Giorgio Maggiore in Venice', Diss. Michigan.

Copeland, R. (1991), *Rhetoric, Hermeneutics and Translation in the Middle Ages*, Cambridge.

Copeland, R. and Sluiter, I. (2009), *Medieval Grammar and Rhetoric: Language Arts and Literary Theory, AD 300–1475*, Oxford.

Corfield, P. (2007), *Time and the Shape of History*, New Haven.

Corns, T. N. (1990), *Milton's Language*, Oxford.

Corrie, M. (2006), 'Middle English: Dialects and Diversity', in Mugglestone (2006): 86–119.

Corsi, M. (1939), *Il teatro all' aperto in Italia*, Rizzoli.

Costazza, A. (2007), 'Herders Übersetzungstheorie zwischen Linguistik, Ästhetik und Geschichtsauffassung', *Germanisch-Romanische Monatsschrift* 57: 135–49.

Costelloe, T. M. (2012) (ed.), *The Sublime: From Antiquity to the Present*, Cambridge.

Costil, P. (1943), 'La question homérique et l'evolution du goût littéraire en France', *Annales de l'Université de Grenoble* 19: 95–168.

Cotton, H. *et al.* (2009) (eds), *From Hellenism to Islam: Cultural and Linguistic Change in the Roman Near East*, Cambridge.

Couch, C. *et al.* (2003) (eds), *Urban Regeneration in Europe*, Oxford.

Couch, H. N. (1946), 'Translation in the Classics', *Journal of Higher Education* 17: 351–8.

Cowling, E. and Mundy, J. (1990), *On Classic Ground: Picasso, Léger, de Chirico, and the New Classicism, 1910–1930*, London.

Cox, V. (2009), 'Leonardo Bruni on Women and Rhetoric: *De Studiis et Litteris* Revisited', *Rhetorica* 27: 47–75.

Cox-Rearick, J. (2000) (ed.), *Giulio Romano: Master Designer*, New York.

Craddock, P. B. (1984), 'Edward Gibbon and the Ruins of the Capitol', in Patterson (1984): 63–82.

Craig, A. (1962), *The Banned Books of England and Other Countries*, London.

Craig, H. (1950), *The Enchanted Glass: The Elizabethan Mind in Literature*, Oxford.

Crawford, K. (2010), *The Sexual Culture of the French Renaissance*, Cambridge.

Cremona, J. (1965), 'Dante's Views on Language', in U. Limentani (ed.), *The Mind of Dante*, Cambridge: 138–62.

Croce, B. (1922), *Aesthetic*, tr. D. Ainslie, rev. edn, London.

Crome, K. (2004), *Lyotard and Greek Thought: Sophistry*, Basingstoke.

Crook, J. M. (1972), *The Greek Revival: Neo-Classical Attitudes in British Architecture, 1760–1870*, London.

Crow, T. (1985), *Painters and Public Life in Eighteenth-Century Paris*, New Haven.

Csapo, E. (2005), *Theories of Mythology*, Oxford.

Cubberley, E. P. (1920), *The History of Education*, London.

Cucchi, A. (1983), 'Concezioni grammaticali dell' Alto Medioevo', *Lingua e Stile* 18: 47–73.

Cuno, J. (2008), *Who Owns Antiquity? Museums and the Battle Over Our Ancient Heritage*, Princeton.

Curren, B. A. (2012), 'The High Renaissance, Classicism, and Antiquity: Thoughts on a Tradition and Its Discontents', in J. Burke (ed.), *Rethinking the High Renaissance*, Farnham: 27–55.

Curtis, P. *et al.* (2007), *Towards a New Laocoon*, Leeds.

Curtius, E. R. (1953), *European Literature and the Latin Middle Ages*, tr. W. R. Trask, London.

Cyrino, M. (2005), *Big Screen Rome*, Oxford.

Dahlhaus, C. (1971), *Wagners Konzeption des Musikdramas*, Regensburg.

Damerini, G. (1956), *L'isola e il cenobio di San Giorgio Maggiore*, Venice.

Dannhauser, W. J. (1974), *Nietzsche's View of Socrates*, Ithaca, NY.

Davies, H. S. (1970), 'Milton and the Vocabulary of Verse and Prose', in Watson (1970): 175–93.

Davies, M. (1997), 'Poggio Bracciolini', in J. Kraye (ed.), *Cambridge Translations of Renaissance Philosophical Texts, vol.1: Moral Philosophy*, Cambridge: 17–28.

Davis, C. T. (1957), *Dante and the Idea of Rome*, Oxford.

Davis, T. (1991), *Actresses as Working Women*, London.

Davis, W. (1996), 'Winckelmann's "Homosexual" Teleologies', in N. B. Kampen (ed.), *Sexuality in Ancient Art*, Cambridge: 262–76.

Dawson, G. (1994), *Soldier Heroes: British Adventure, Empire and the Imagining of Masculinities*, London.

Day, K. (2008), '"What Makes a Man to Wander?": *The Searchers* as a Western Odyssey', *Arethusa* 41: 11–49.

Deathridge, J. (2008), *Wagner: Beyond Good and Evil*, Berkeley.

de Caprio, V. (1987) (ed.), *Poesia e poetica delle rovine di Roma*, Rome.

Decultot, E. (2010), 'Erlebte oder erträumte Antike? Zu Winckelmanns geplanten Griechenlandreisen', in Kocziszky (2010): 125–40.

Dejean, J. (1989), *Fictions of Sappho 1546–1937*, Chicago.

Delisle, J. and Woodsworth, J. (1995) (eds), *Translators Through History*, Amsterdam.

de Lubac, H. (1959/1990), *Medieval Exegesis, 1: The Four Senses of Scripture*, tr. M. Sebanc, Edinburgh.

de Man, P. (1971), *Blindness and Insight*, Oxford.

Derrida, J. (1980), 'The Law of Genre', tr. A. Ronell, *Glyph* 7: 202–13.

Desmond, M. (2006), *Ovid's Art and the Wife of Bath: The Ethics of Erotic Violence*, Ithaca, NY.

Desmond, M. and Sheingorn, P. (2003), *Myth, Montage, and Visuality in Late Medieval Manuscript Culture: Christine de Pizan's Epistre Othea*, Ann Arbor.

Devereux, J. A. (1975), 'The Textual History of Ficino's *De Amore*', *Renaissance Quarterly* 28: 173–82.

de Vocht, H. (1951), *History of the Foundation and Rise of the Collegium Trilingue Lovaniense, 1517–1550*, Louvain.

Dickerman, E. H. and Walker, A. M. (1996), 'The Choice of Hercules: Henry IV as Hero', *Historical Journal* 39: 315–37.

Dieckmann, F. (1988), 'Vom Gesamtkunstwerk', *Bildende Kunst* 36: 298–9.

Di Marzio, C. (1941), 'Verdi come esempio', in *Verdi. Studi e memoria* [no editor cited], Rome: 3–8.

Diner, D. (1988) (ed.), *Zivilisationsbruch. Denken nach Auschwitz*, Frankfurt a. M.

Dionisotti, A. C. (1995), 'Claude de Seyssel', in M. H. Crawford and C. R. Ligota (eds), *Ancient History and the Antiquarian*, London: 73–89.

Di Pasquale, S. (2002), *Brunelleschi. La costruzione della cupola di Santa Maria del Fiore*, Venice.

Dirnoff, P. (1936), *La Vie et l'oeuvre d' André Chenier jusqu' à la révolution française, 1762–1790*, Paris.

Dodds, G. and Tavernor, R. (2002) (eds), *Body and Building: Essays on the Changing Relation of Body and Architecture*, Cambridge, Mass.

Donald, R. D. (2001), 'Masculinity and Machismo in Hollywood's War Films', in S. M. Whitehead and F. J. Barrett (eds), *The Masculinities Reader*, Cambridge: 170–83.

Donohue, A. A. (1995), 'Winckelmann's History of Art and Polyclitos', in W. G. Moon (ed.), *Polykleitos, the Doryphoros and Tradition*, Madison, Wis.: 327–53.

Doody, M. A. (1996), *The True Story of the Novel*, New Brunswick, NJ.

Dotti, U. (1993) (ed.), Francesco Petrarca: *Secretum*, Rome.

Dowley, F. H. and Korshak, Y. (1988), 'An Exchange on Jacques Louis David's Paris and Helen', *Art Bulletin* 70: 504–20.

Dowling, L. (1994), *Hellenism and Homosexuality in Victorian England*, Ithaca, NY.

Downes, K. (1994), 'Sir Christopher Wren, Edward Woodroffe, J. H. Mansart, and Architectural History', *Architectural History* 37: 37–67.

Downey, G. (1955), 'Education in the Christian Roman Empire', *Speculum* 32: 48–61.

Drerup, E. (1930–32), *Die Schulaussprache des Griechischen von der Renaissance bis zur Gegenwart*, 2 vols, Paderborn.

Droge, A. J. (1989), *Homer or Moses? Early Christian Interpretations of the History of Culture*, Tübingen.

Dronke, P. (1968), *Medieval Latin and the Rise of European Love-Lyric, vol. 1: Problems and Interpretations*, 2nd edn, Oxford.

Dunbar, R. (2007), 'Why Are Humans Not Just Great Apes?', in Pasternak (2007): 37–48.

Duncan, C. (1995), *Civilizing Rituals: Inside Public Art Museums*, London.

Dunn, R. D. (1984), William Camden, *Remains Concerning Britain*, Toronto.

Durkin, P. (2009), *The Oxford Guide to Etymology*, Oxford.

Dyer, R. (1997), *White*, London.

Dyson, S. L. (1998), *Ancient Marbles to American Shores: Classical Archaeology in the United States*, Philadelphia.

— (2006), *In Pursuit of Ancient Pasts: A History of Classical Archaeology in the Nineteenth and Twentieth Centuries*, New Haven.

Eagleton, T. (1976), *Criticism and Ideology*, London.

Earl, G. P. (2005), 'Video Killed Engaging VR? Computer Visualizations on the TV Screen', in S. Smiles and S. Moser (eds), *Envisioning the Past: Archaeology and Time*, Oxford: 204–22.

Easterling, P. E. (2004), 'General Introduction', in R. C. Jebb, *Sophocles: Plays. Oedipus Tyrannus*, Bristol: 7–30.

Ebeling, F. (2007), *The Secret History of Hermes Trismegistus: Hermeticism from Ancient to Modern Times*, tr. D. Lorton, Ithaca, NY.

Eco, U. (1984), *Semiotics and the Philosophy of Language*, Bloomington.

— (1986), *Faith in Fakes: Travels in Hyperreality*, tr. W. Weaver, London.

— (1995), *The Search for the Perfect Language*, tr. J. Fentress, Oxford.

Edelstein, W. (1965), *Eruditio et sapientia. Weltbild und Erziehung in der Karolingerzeit*, Freiburg.

Eden, K. (2012), *The Renaissance Rediscovery of Intimacy*, Chicago.

Edmonds, D. and Eidinow, J. (2001), *Wittgenstein's Poker: The Story of a Ten-Minute Argument between Two Great Philosophers*, London.

Edwards, C. (1996), *Writing Rome*, Cambridge.

Edwards, J. (2009), *Language and Identity*, Cambridge.

Edwards, T. (2006), *Cultures of Masculinity*, London.

Eicher, H. (1972) (ed.), *'Romantic' and Its Cognates: The European History of a Word*, Toronto.

Eisner, R. (1993), *Travelers to an Antique Land: The History and Literature of Travel to Greece*, Ann Arbor.

El-Abbadi, M. (2004), 'The Alexandria Library in History', in Hirst and Silk (2004): 167–83.

Eliot, T. S. (1957), *On Poetry and Poets*, London.

Elliott, C. D. (1994), *Technics and Architecture: The Development of Materials and Systems for Building*, Cambridge, Mass.

Ellis, R. (1989) (ed.), *The Medieval Translator*, Cambridge.

Ellmann, R. (1988), *Oscar Wilde*, London.

Elsner, J. (2010), 'Tourism and Travel', in Grafton, Most, and Settis (2010): 939–42.
Elsner J. and Cardinal, R. (1994) (eds), *The Cultures of Collecting*, London.
Empson, W. (1965), *Milton's God*, rev. edn, London.
Erlich, V. (1973), 'Russian Formalism', *Journal of the History of Ideas* 34: 627–38.
Esterhammer, A. (2008), *Romanticism and Improvisation, 1750–1850*, Cambridge.
Etlin, R. A. (2012), 'Architecture and the Sublime', in Costelloe (2012): 230–73.
Ettmayer, K. von (1916), 'Vulgärlatein', in W. Streitberg (ed.), *Geschichte der indogermanischen Sprachwissenschaft seit ihrer Begründung durch Fr. Bopp*, II. 1. 231–80, Strasbourg.
Euben, J. P. (2000), 'Arendt's Hellenism', in Villa (2000): 151–64.
Evangelista, S. (2009), *British Aestheticism and Ancient Greece*, London.
Evans, J. (2010), 'Astronomy', in Grafton, Most, and Settis (2010): 89–96.
Everdell, W. R. (2000), *The End of Kings*, Chicago.
Ewans, M. (1982), *Wagner and Aeschylus: The Ring and the Oresteia*, London.
— (2010), 'Wagner's *Ring* Cycle and the Greeks', *Philological Quarterly* 89: 337–40.
Fabb, N. (1997), *Linguistics and Literature*, Oxford.
Falco, M. J. (2004) (ed.), *Feminist Interpretations of Niccolò Machiavelli*, University Park, Pa.
Fallon, S. M. (2007), *Milton's Peculiar Grace*, Ithaca, NY.
Falomir, M. (2003) (ed.), *Tiziano*, Madrid.
Fanelli, G. and Fanelli, M. (2004), *Brunelleschi's Cupola*, Florence.
Fantina, R. (2005), *Ernest Hemingway: Machismo and Masochism*, New York.
Farrington, B. (1967), *The Faith of Epicurus*, London.
Favaretto, I. (1990), *Arte Antica e Cultura Antiquaria nelle Collezioni Venete al Tempo della Serenissima*, Rome.
Fay, H. C. (1952), 'George Chapman's Translation of Homer's *Iliad*', *Greece and Rome* 21: 104–11.
Feeney, D. C. (1998), *Literature and Religion at Rome*, Cambridge.
Feilden, B. M. (1982), *Conservation of Historic Buildings*, London.
Felch, J. and Frammolino, R. (2011), *Chasing Aphrodite: The Hunt for Looted Antiquities at the World's Richest Museum*, Boston, Mass.
Fer, B. (2000), 'Some Translucent Substance, or the Trouble with Time', in C. B. Gill (ed.), *Time and the Image*, Manchester: 69–78.
Ferguson, W. K. (1948), *The Renaissance in Historical Thought*, Boston, Mass.
Ferris, D. S. (2000), *Silent Urns: Romanticism, Hellenism, Modernity*, Stanford.
Ferruolo, S. (1998), *The Origins of the University: The Schools of Paris and Their Critics, 1100–1215*, Stanford.
Fiedrowicz, M. (2000), *Apologie im frühen Christentum. Die Kontroverse um den christlichen Wahrheitsanspruch in den ersten Jahrhunderten*, Paderborn.
Field, S. (1994), *Screenplay*, 3rd edn, New York.
Figal, G. (2008), 'Nietzsches Dionysos', *Nietzsche Studien* 37: 51–61.
Figueira, D. M. (2002), *Aryans, Jews, Brahmins: Theorizing Authority Through Myths of Identity*, Albany, NY.
Finger, A. and Follett, D. (2011) (eds), *The Aesthetics of the Total Artwork*, Baltimore.
Finley, M. I. (1956), *The World of Odysseus*, rev. edn, London.
Finn, C. (2004), *Past Poetic: Archaeology in the Poetry of W.B. Yeats and Seamus Heaney*, London.
Fish, S. (1980), *Is There a Text in This Class? The Authority of Interpretive Communities*, Cambridge, Mass.
Fisher, P. (1975), 'The Future's Past', *New Literary History* 6: 587–606.

Fitzgerald, W. (2001), 'Oppositions, Anxieties, and Ambiguities in the Toga Movie', in Joshel *et al.* (2001): 23–49.

Flaig, E. (2003), 'Jacob Burckhardt, Greek Culture, and Modernity', in Gildenhard and Ruehl (2003): 7–45.

Flannery, K. (2001), *Acts Amid Precepts: The Aristotelian Logical Structure of Thomas Aquinas' Moral Theory*, Washington, DC.

Flashar, H. (1995) (ed.), *Altertumswissenschaft in den 20er Jahren*, Stuttgart.

— (1997) (ed.), *Tragödie. Idee und Transformation*, Stuttgart.

Förster-Nietzsche, E. (1912), *Der junge Nietzsche*, Leipzig.

Ford, P. (2007), *De Troie à Ithaque: reception des epopees homériques à la Renaissance*, Geneva.

Fornoff, R. (2004), *Die Sehnsucht nach dem Gesamtkunstwerk: Studien zu einer ästhetischen Konzeption der Moderne*, Hildesheim.

Forster, L. (1969) (ed.), *The Icy Fire: Five Studies in European Petrarchism*, Cambridge.

Foster, D. H. (2010), *Wagner's* Ring *Cycle and the Greeks*, Cambridge.

Foster, K. (1977), *The Two Dantes and Other Studies*, London.

— (1982), *Petrarch: Poet and Humanist*, Edinburgh.

Fowler, A. (1980), Milton, *Paradise Lost*, corr. edn, London.

— (1982), *Kinds of Literature*, Oxford.

Fowler, R. (2004) (ed.), *The Cambridge Companion to Homer*, Cambridge.

Frakes, J. C. (1988), *The Fate of Fortune in the Early Middle Ages: The Boethian Tradition*, Leiden.

France, P. (1982), 'Myth and Modernity: Racine's *Phèdre*', in Aspley (1982): 227–42.

— (1985), 'Eloquence révolutionnaire et rhétorique traditionelle', *Saggi e ricerche di letteratura francese* 24: 143–76.

— (2000) (ed.), *The Oxford Guide to Literature in English Translation*, Oxford.

France, P. and Gillespie, S. (2008), 'General Editors' Foreword', in R. Ellis (ed.), *The Oxford History of Literary Translation in English, vol. 1: To 1550*, Oxford.

Francis, A. J. (1977), *The Cement Industry, 1796–1914: A History*, London.

Frank-Job, B. (2003), 'Romana lingua - vulgare illustre - italiano. Kategorisierungen der Muttersprache in Italien', in Grimm *et al.* (2003): 15–37.

Franklin, J. H. (1992), Jean Bodin, *On Sovereignty*, Cambridge.

Frede, D. (1996), 'Platon, Popper und der Historizismus', in E. Rudolph (ed.), *Polis und Kosmos: Naturphilosophie und politische Philosophie bei Platon*, Darmstadt: 74–107.

Freedman, L. (2004), 'Titian and the Classical Heritage', in P. Meliman (ed.), *The Cambridge Companion to Titian*, Cambridge: 183–204.

Freund, W. (1957), *Modernus und andere Zeitbegriffe des Mittelalters*, Cologne.

Friedman, D. (2010), 'City Planning', in Grafton, Most, and Settis (2010): 202–5.

Frow, J. (2006), *Genre*, London.

Frye, N. (1957), *Anatomy of Criticism*, Princeton.

Fubini, R. (2003), *Humanism and Secularization from Petrarch to Valla*, tr. M. King, Durham, NC.

Fuhrmann, H. (2003), *Cicero und das Seelenheil, oder: wie kam die heidnische Antike durch das christliche Mittelalter?*, Munich.

Fuhrmann, M. (1959), 'Friedrich August Wolf', *Deutsche Vierteljahrsschrift für Literaturwissenschaft und Geistesgeschichte* 33: 187–236.

Fukuyama, F. (1992), *The End of History and the Last Man*, London.

Fulcher, J. F. (1987), *The Nation's Image: French Grand Opera as Politics and Politicized Art*, Cambridge.

Fuller, S. (2011), *Humanity 2.0: What It Means to be Human, Past, Present and Future*, London.

Fumaroli, M. (1980), *L'âge de l'éloquence: Rhétorique et 'res literaria' de la Renaissance au seuil de l'époque classique*, Geneva.

Funnell, P. (1982), 'The Symbolical Language of Antiquity', in Clarke and Penny (1982): 50–64.

Fusco, L. (1982), 'The Use of Sculptural Models by Painters in Fifteenth-Century Italy', *Art Bulletin* 64: 175–94.

Fusco, L. and Corti, G. (2006), *Lorenzo de' Medici: Collector and Antiquarian*, Cambridge.

Fyler, J. M. (2007), *Language and the Declining World in Chaucer, Dante and Jean de Meun*, Cambridge.

Gadol, J. (1969), *Leon Battista Alberti: Universal Man of the Early Renaissance*, Chicago.

Gaimster, G. B. (2000), 'Sex and Sensibility at the British Museum', *History Today* 50. 9: 10–15.

Gáldy, A. M. (2009), *Cosimo I de' Medici as Collector*, Newcastle.

Gale, M. (1988), 'The Uncertainty of the Painter: De Chirico in 1913', *Burlington Magazine* 130: 268–76.

Galinsky, K. (1972), *The Herakles Theme: The Adaptations of the Hero in Literature from Homer to the Twentieth Century*, Oxford.

— (1992), *Classical and Modern Interactions: Postmodern Architecture, Multiculturalism, Decline and Other Issues*, Austin, Tex.

— (2010), 'Hercules', in Grafton, Most, and Settis (2010): 426–9.

Gamble, D. R. (2008), '"Maitres antiques": The *Bucoliques* of André Chenier and the Neoclassical Mode', *Dalhousie French Studies* 83: 17–22.

Gamel, M.-K. (2007), 'Sondheim Floats Frogs', in Hall and Wrigley (2007): 209–30.

Ganzert J. (1990), 'Zweimal zur Vitruv-Interpretation', *Opuscula Romana* 18: 107–14.

García y García, L. and Jacobelli, L. (2001), *Louis Barré, Museo Segreto*, Pompeii.

Gargiani, R. (1994), *Auguste Perret*, Milan.

Garin, E. (1992/3), 'Petrarca latino', *Quaderni Petrarcheschi* 9–10: 1–9.

Garland, R. (2004), *Surviving Greek Tragedy*, London.

Gaston, R. W. (1995/6), 'Sacred Erotica: The Classical *Figura* in Religious Paintings of the Early Cinquecento', *International Journal of the Classical Tradition* 2: 238–64.

Gaunt, S. (1989), *Gender and Genre in Medieval French Literature*, Cambridge.

Gellner, E. (1987), 'From Königsberg to Manhattan', in id., *Culture, Identity, and Politics*, Cambridge: 75–90.

Genette, G. (1966, 1969, 1972), *Figures I, II, III*, Paris.

Gentile, E. (2007), *Fascismo di pietra*, Rome.

Georgakopoulou, A. (2009), 'Greek-Language Standardizing, Past, Present and Future', in Georgakopoulou and Silk (2009): xi–xxviii.

Georgakopoulou, A. and Silk, M. S. (2009) (eds), *Standard Languages and Language Standards: Greek, Past and Present*, Farnham.

Giacardi, L. (2006), 'From Euclid as Textbook to the Giovanni Gentile Reform (1867–1923)', *Paedagogica Historica* 42: 587–613.

Gilbert, F. (1965), *Machiavelli and Guicciardini: Politics and History in Sixteenth-Century Florence*, Princeton, NJ.

Gilby, E. (2006), *Sublime Worlds: Early Modern French Literature*, London.

Gildenhard, I. (2003), 'Philologia Perennis? Classical Scholarship and Functional Differentiation', in Gildenhard and Ruehl (2003): 161–203.

— (2009), 'A Postmodern Prometheus', in D. Tregunna and T. Pickeral (eds), *Being Human: Paintings by Chris Gollon*, London: 36–9.
— (2011), *Creative Eloquence: The Construction of Reality in Cicero's Speeches*, Oxford.
Gildenhard, I. and Ruehl, M. (2003) (eds), *Out of Arcadia: Classics and Politics in Germany in the Age of Burckhardt, Nietzsche and Wilamowitz*, London.
Gildenhard, I. and Zissos, A. (2007), 'Barbarian Variations: Tereus, Procne, and Philomela in Ovid (*Met.* 6.412–674) and Beyond', *Dictynna* 4: 2–18.
Gillespie, S. and Rhodes, N. (2006) (eds), *Shakespeare and Elizabethan Popular Culture*, London.
Gilson, S. (2005), *Dante and Renaissance Florence*, Cambridge.
Ginsberg, W. (2011), 'Dante's Ovid', in J. G. Clark *et al.* (eds), *Ovid in the Middle Ages*, Cambridge: 143–59.
Ginzburg, C. (1976), *Il formaggio e i vermi. Il cosmo di un mugnaio del '500*, Turin.
Gnilka, C. (1984), *Chresis. Die Methode der Kirchenväter im Umgang mit der antiken Kultur I. Der Begriff des 'rechten Gebrauchs'*, Basel.
— (1993), *Chresis. Die Methode der Kirchenväter im Umgang mit der antiken Kultur II. Kultur und Conversion*, Basel.
Goff, B. E. (2005) (ed.), *Classics and Colonialism*, London.
Goff, B. E. and Simpson, M. (eds) (2008), *Crossroads in the Black Aegean: Oedipus, Antigone, and Dramas of the African Diaspora*, Oxford.
Goffen, R. (1997), *Titian's Women*, New Haven.
Goldhagen, D. J. (1996), *Hitler's Willing Executioners: Ordinary Germans and the Holocaust*, New York.
Goldhill, S. (1984), *Language, Sexuality, Narrative: The Oresteia*, Cambridge.
— (2002), *Who Needs Greek? Contests in the Cultural History of Hellenism*, Cambridge.
— (2007a), 'Naked and O Brother, Where Art Thou? The Politics and Poetics of Epic', in B. Graziosi and E. Greenwood (eds), *Homer in the Twentieth Century*, Oxford: 245–68.
— (2007b), *How to Stage Greek Tragedy Today*, Chicago.
— (2008), 'Wagner's Greeks: The Politics of Hellenism', in Revermann and Wilson (2008): 453–80.
Goldin Folena, D. (1991), *Volgarizzare e tradurre*, Turin.
— (1992/3), 'Petrarca e il medioevo latino', *Quaderni Petrarcheschi* 9–10: 459–87.
Goldmann, L. (1955), *Le dieu caché: étude sur la vision tragique dans les Pensées de Pascal et dans le théâtre de Racine*, Paris.
Goldstein, L. (1977), *Ruins and Empire: The Evolution of a Theme in Augustan and Romantic Literature*, Pittsburgh.
Gombrich, E. H. (1963), *Meditations on a Hobby-Horse*, London.
— (1966), *Norm and Form: Studies in the Art of the Renaissance*, London and New York.
— (1995), *The Story of Art*, 16th edn, London.
Goodkin, R. E. (1991), *The Tragic Middle: Racine, Aristotle, Euripides*, Madison, Wis.
Gossman, L. (1992), 'Death in Trieste', *Journal of European Studies* 22: 207–40.
Goulemot, J. (1994), *Forbidden Texts: Erotic Literature and Its Readers in Eighteenth-Century France*, Cambridge.
Gowen, S. (1995) (ed.), *Bananas and Plantains*, London.
Goyens, M. *et al.* (2008), *Science Translated: Latin and Vernacular Translations of Scientific Treatises in Medieval Europe*, Leuven.
Grabar, O. (1990), 'From Dome of Heaven to Pleasure Dome', *Journal of the Society of Architectural Historians* 49: 15–21.

Grafton, A. (1983a), 'Protestant versus Prophet: Isaac Casaubon on Hermes Trismegistus', *Journal of the Warburg and Courtauld Institutes* 46: 78–93.

— (1983b), 'Polyhistor into *Philolog*: Notes on the Transformation of German Classical Scholarship, 1780–1850', *History of Universities* 3: 159–92.

— (1993a), *Joseph Scaliger: A Study in the History of Classical Scholarship*, 2 vols, Oxford.

— (1993b), 'The Vatican and Its Library', in id. (ed.), *Rome Reborn: The Vatican Library and Renaissance Culture*, Washington, DC: 3–45.

— (1997), *Commerce with the Classics: Ancient Books and Renaissance Readers*, Ann Arbor.

— (2000), *Leon Battista Alberti: Master Builder of the Italian Renaissance*, Harmondsworth.

Grafton, A., Most, G. W., and Settis, S. (2010) (eds), *The Classical Tradition*, Cambridge, Mass.

Grafton, A., Most, G. W., and Zetzel, J. E. G. (1985), F. A. Wolf, *Prolegomena to Homer, 1795*, Princeton.

Graham, B. (2002), 'Heritage as Knowledge: Capital or Culture', *Urban Studies* 39: 1003–17.

Gramsci, A (1975), *Letteratura e vita nazionale*, rev. edn, Turin.

Gray, B. (1969), *Style: The Problem and Its Solution*, The Hague.

Grayson, C. (1960), *A Renaissance Controversy: Latin or Italian?*, Oxford.

— (1965), '*Nobilior est vulgaris*: Latin and Vernacular in Dante's Thought', in *Centenary Essays on Dante* (Oxford Dante Society), Oxford: 54–76.

— (1998), *Studi su Leon Battista Alberti*, ed. P. Claut, Florence.

Greenblatt, S. (1980), *Renaissance Self-Fashioning: From More to Shakespeare*, Chicago.

— (1988), *Shakespearean Negotiations: The Circulation of Social Energy in Renaissance England*, Berkeley.

— (1990), *Learning to Curse*, London.

Greene, E. (1996) (ed.), *Re-Reading Sappho: Reception and Transmission*, Berkeley.

Greene, R. G. (1991), *Post-Petrarchism: Origins and Innovations of the Western Lyric Sequence*, Princeton.

Greenfield, J. (2007), *The Return of Cultural Treasures*, Cambridge.

Greenhalgh, M. (1989), *The Survival of Roman Antiquities in the Middle Ages*, London.

— (2009), *Marble Past, Monumental Present: Building with Antiquities in the Medieval Mediterranean*, Leiden.

Greer, M. R. (2000), 'Decolonizing the Middle Ages: Introduction', *Journal of Medieval and Early Modern Studies* 30: 431–48.

Grendler, P. F. (1988), 'Printing and Censorship After 1550', in Schmitt *et al.* (1988): 21–53.

— (1989), *Schooling in Renaissance Italy: Literacy and Learning, 1300–1600*, Baltimore.

— (1995), *Books and Schools in the Italian Renaissance*, Aldershot.

— (2002), *The Universities of the Italian Renaissance*, Baltimore.

Grey, T. S. (2006), 'Magnificent Obsession: *Tristan* as the Object of Musical Analysis', in N. Bacht (ed.), *Music, Theatre and Politics in Germany, 1850–1950*, London: 51–78.

— (2008a) (ed.), *The Cambridge Companion to Wagner*, Cambridge.

— (2008b), 'Leitmotif, Temporality, and Musical Design in the *Ring*', in Grey (2008a): 85–114.

— (2008c), 'The Jewish Question', in Grey (2008a): 203–18.

Grimm, R. R. *et al.* (2003) (eds), *Italianità. Ein literarisches, sprachliches und kulturelles Identitätsmuster*, Tübingen.

Gros, P. (2006), 'Les illustrations du "De architectura" de Vitruve. Histoire d'un malentenda', *Collection de l'École française de Rome* 366: 363–88.

Gross, K. (1992), *The Dream of the Moving Statue*, Ithaca, NY.

Gubar, S. (1996), 'Sapphistries', in Greene (1996): 199–218.

— (2003), *Poetry After Auschwitz: Remembering What One Never Knew*, Bloomington, Ind.

Gumpert, M. (2001), *Grafting Helen: The Abduction of the Classical Past*, Madison, Wis.

Gunn, S. (2006), *History and Cultural Theory*, Harlow.

Gurd, S. A. (2005), *Iphigenias at Aulis: Textual Multiplicity, Radical Philology*, Ithaca, NY.

Gurstein, R. (2002), 'The Elgin Marbles: Romanticism and the Waning of Ideal Beauty', *Daedalus* 131: 88–100.

Gürtler, J. D. (1831–5), *Fr. Aug. Wolfs Vorlesungen über die Alterthumswissenschaft I–V*, Leipzig.

Gustafson, S. E. (2002), *Men Desiring Men: The Poetry of Same-Sex Identity and Desire in German Classicism*, Detroit.

Gutas, D. (1998), *Greek Thought, Arabic Culture: The Graeco-Arabic Translation Movement in Baghdad and Early 'Abbâsid Society*, London.

Guthmüller, B. (1997), *Mito, Poesia, Arte. Saggi sulla Tradizione Ovidiana nel Rinascimento*, Rome.

Gutschker, T. (2002), *Aristotelische Diskurse. Aristoteles in der politischen Philosophie des 20. Jahrhunderts*, Stuttgart.

Habermas, J. (1981), 'Modernity versus Postmodernity', *New German Critique* 22: 3–14.

— (1983), *Philosophical-Political Profiles*, Cambridge, Mass.

Hachmeister, G. L. (2002), *Italy in the German Literary Imagination*, Rochester, NY.

Hacohen, M. H. (2000), *Karl Popper – The Formative Years, 1902–1945: Politics and Philosophy in Interwar Vienna*, Cambridge.

Hair, D. S. (1991), *Tennyson's Language*, Toronto.

Hale, J. K. (1997), *Milton's Languages*, Cambridge.

Hall, E. (1999), 'Classical Mythology in the Victorian Popular Theatre', *International Journal of the Classical Tradition* 5: 336–66.

— (2008a), 'Putting the Class into Classical Reception', in Hardwick and Stray (2008): 386–400.

— (2008b), 'Ancient Pantomime and the Rise of Ballet', in E. Hall and R. Wyles (eds), *New Directions in Ancient Pantomime*, Oxford: 363–77.

— (2008c), 'Navigating the Realms of Gold: Translation as Access Route to the Classics', in Lianeri and Zajko (2008): 315–40.

— (2008d), *The Return of Ulysses: A Cultural History of Homer's Odyssey*, London.

Hall, E., Macintosh, F., and Taplin, O. (2001) (eds), *Medea in Performance, 1500–2000*, rev. edn, Oxford.

Hall, E., Macintosh, F., and Wrigley, A. (2004) (eds), *Dionysus since 69: Greek Tragedy at the Dawn of the Third Millennium*, Oxford.

Hall, E. and Wrigley, A. (2007) (eds), *Aristophanes in Performance, 421 BC–AD 2007*, London.

Hall, H. G. (1984), *Comedy in Context: Essays on Molière*, Jackson, Miss.

Hall, R. A. (1974), *External History of the Romance Languages*, New York.

Hall, S. (1980), 'Cultural Studies: Two Paradigms', *Media, Culture and Society* 2: 57–72.

— (1981), 'Notes on Deconstructing the Popular', in R. Samuel (ed.), *People's History and Socialist Theory*, London: 227–49.

Halliwell, S. (1986), *Aristotle's Poetics*, London.

— (2000), 'Classical Philosophy', in France (2000): 375–80.

Hamesse, J. and Fattori, M. (1990) (eds), *Rencontres de cultures dans la philosophie médiévale: traductions et traducteurs de l'antiquité tardive au xiv siècle*, Louvain-la-Neuve.

Hammer, D. (2002), 'Hannah Arendt and Roman Political Thought', *Political Theory* 30: 124–49.

Hammersley, R. (2005), *French Revolutionaries and English Republicans: The Cordeliers Club, 1790–1794*, London.

Hampson, N. (1991), 'The Heavenly City of the French Revolutionaries', in C. Lucas (ed.), *Rewriting the French Revolution*, Oxford: 46–68.

Hankins, J. (1990), *Plato in the Italian Renaissance*, 2 vols, Leiden.

— (1991), 'The Myth of the Platonic Academy of Florence', *Renaissance Quarterly* 44: 429–75.

— (2000) (ed.), *Renaissance Civic Humanism*, Cambridge.

Hanoosh, M. (1986), 'Painting as Translation in Baudelaire's Art Criticism', *Forum for Modern Language Studies* 22: 22–33.

Han-Pile, B. (2010), 'The "Death of Man": Foucault and Anti-Humanism', in T. O'Leary and C. Falzon (eds), *Foucault and Philosophy*, Chichester: 118–42.

Hansen, W. (1998), *Anthology of Ancient Greek Popular Literature*, Bloomington, Ind.

Harbus, A. (2007), 'Metaphors of Authority in Alfred's Prefaces', *Neophilologus* 91: 717–27.

Hardison, O. B. (1986), 'Tudor Humanism and Surrey's Translation of the *Aeneid*', *Studies in Philology* 83: 237–60.

Hardwick, L. and Gillespie, C. (2007) (eds), *Classics in Post-Colonial Worlds*, Malden, Mass.

Hardwick, L. and Stray, C. (2008) (eds), *A Companion to Classical Receptions*, Malden, Mass.

Harke, H. (2002), *Archaeology, Ideology, and Society: The German Experience*, Frankfurt.

Harper, G. M. (1974), *Yeats's Golden Dawn*, London.

Harpham, G. G. (2009), 'Roots, Races and the Return to Philology', *Representations* 106: 34–62.

Harris, J. (1994), *The Palladian Revival: Lord Burlington, His Villa and Garden at Chiswick*, New Haven.

Harris, J. (2007), *Pompeii Awakened: A Story of Rediscovery*, London.

Hart, V. (2007), *Nicholas Hawksmoor: Rebuilding Ancient Wonders*, New Haven.

— (2010), 'Theater Architecture', in Grafton, Most, and Settis (2010): 933–4.

Hart, V. and Hicks, P. (1998) (eds), *Paper Palaces: The Rise of the Renaissance Architectural Treatise*, New Haven.

Hartmann, R. (1989), 'Als sie rot sahen: Die APO-Jahre am Uhland-Gymnasium', in *Schola Anatolica: Freundesgabe für Hermann Steinthal*, Tübingen: 17–25.

Haskell, F. (2000), *The Ephemeral Museum: Old Master Paintings and the Rise of the Art Exhibition*, New Haven.

Haskell F. and Penny, N. (1981), *Taste and the Antique: The Lure of Classical Sculpture 1500–1900*, New Haven.

Haskins, C. H. (1972), *The Rise of Universities*, Ithaca, NY.

Hatty, S. E. (2000), *Masculinities, Violence and Culture*, London.

Hay, D. (1957), *Europe: The Emergence of an Idea*, Edinburgh.

Hayes, J. C. (2009), *Translation, Subjectivity, and Culture in France and England, 1600–1800*, Stanford.

Haynes, K. (2003), *English Literature and Ancient Languages*, Oxford.

Heath, M. (2008), 'Aristotle on Natural Slavery', *Phronesis* 53: 243–70.

Heckscher (1956), 'The Anadyomene in the Medieval Tradition', *Nederlands Kunsthistorisch Jaarboek* 7: 1–38.

Heidegger, M. and Fink, E. (1970), *Heraklit*, Frankfurt a. M.

Hein, H. S. (1966), 'Schopenhauer and Platonic Ideas', *Journal of the History of Philosophy* 4: 133–44.
Heller, W. (2010), 'Mime and Pantomime', in Grafton, Most, and Settis (2010): 591–2.
Hemmerle, O. B. (2006), 'Crossing the Rubicon into Paris: Caesarian Comparisons from Napoleon to de Gaulle', in M. Wyke (ed.), *Julius Caesar in Western Culture*, Oxford: 285–301.
Henderson, D. E. (2007), 'From Popular Entertainment to Literature', in R. Shaughnessy (ed.), *The Cambridge Companion to Shakespeare and Popular Culture*, Cambridge: 6–25.
Hepp, N. (1968), *Homère en France au xviième siècle*, Paris.
Herman, J. (1990), *Du latin aux langues romanes*, Tübingen.
— (2000), *Vulgar Latin*, tr. R. Wright, University Park, Pa.
Herrick, M. (1946), *The Fusion of Horatian and Aristotelian Literary Criticism, 1531–1555*, Urbana.
Hersey, G. (1988), *The Lost Meaning of Classical Architecture*, Cambridge, Mass.
Herzog, R. and Koselleck, R. (1987) (eds), *Epochenschwelle und Epochenbewusstsein*, Munich.
Hetzler, F. M. (1988), 'Causality: Ruin Time and Ruins', *Leonardo* 21: 51–5.
Heuer, W. (1992), *Citizen. Persönliche Integrität und politisches Handeln: Eine Rekonstruktion des politischen Humanismus Hannah Arendts*, Berlin.
Heuer, W. *et al.* (2011) (eds), *Arendt-Handbuch: Leben – Werk – Wirkung*, Stuttgart.
Hexter, R. J. (1986), *Ovid and Medieval Schooling*, Munich.
Hibbert, C. (1985), *Rome: The Biography of a City*, New York.
Highet, G. (1967), *The Classical Tradition*, corr. edn, Oxford.
Hill, G. B. (1905), Samuel Johnson, *Lives of the English Poets*, 3 vols, Oxford.
Himmelmann, N. (1985), *Ideale Nacktheit*, Opladen.
Hindman, S. (1986), *Christine de Pizan's 'Epistre Othéa': Painting and Politics at the Court of Charles VI*, Toronto.
Hinz, V. (2001), *Nunc Phalaris doctum protulit ecce caput: antike Phalarislegende und Nachleben der Phalarisbriefe*, Munich.
Hirsch, E. D. (1967), *Validity in Interpretation*, New Haven.
Hirst, A. and Silk, M. S. (2004) (eds), *Alexandria, Real and Imagined*, Aldershot.
Hobsbawm, E. (1994), *The Age of Extremes: The Short Twentieth Century, 1914–1991*, London.
Hobsbawm, E. and Ranger, T. (1983) (eds), *The Invention of Tradition*, Cambridge.
Hoffmann, T. (2006), *Konfigurationen des Erhabenen. Zur Produktivität einer ästhetischen Kategorie in der Literatur des ausgehenden 20. Jahrhunderts*, Berlin.
Hofmann, M. and Lasdun, J. (1994) (eds), *After Ovid: New Metamorphoses*, London.
Hogben, L. (1943), *Interglossa*, Harmondsworth.
Hogg, R. M. *et al.* (1992–2001), *The Cambridge History of the English Language*, 6 vols, Cambridge.
Hoggart, R. (1957), *The Uses of Literacy: Aspects of Working Class Life*, London.
— (2004), *Mass Media in a Mass Society*, London.
Holmes, C. and Waring, J. (2002) (eds), *Literacy, Education and Manuscript Transmission in Byzantium and Beyond*, Leiden.
Holmes, R. (1980), *Shelley on Love*, Berkeley.
Holtorf, C. (2008), *Archaeology Is a Brand! The Meaning of Archaeology in Contemporary Popular Culture*, Oxford.
Honig, B. (2010), 'Antigone's Two Laws: Greek Tragedy and the Politics of Humanism', *New Literary History* 41: 1–33.

Hooper-Greenhill, E. (1999) (ed.), *Museum, Media, Message*, London.

Hope, C. (1976), 'Problems of Interpretation in Titian's Erotic Paintings', in *Tiziano e Venezia: Convegno Internazionale di Studi*, Venice: 111–24.

Hopkins, D. (2010a), *Conversing with Antiquity: English Poets and the Classics, from Shakespeare to Pope*, Oxford.

— (2010b), 'Milton and the Classics', in P. Hammond and B. Worden (eds), *John Milton: Life, Writing, Reputation*, Oxford: 23–41.

Hopkins, K. and Beard, M. (2005), *The Colosseum*, London.

Hornsby, C. (2000a) (ed.), *The Impact of Italy: The Grand Tour and Beyond*, London.

— (2000b), 'Introduction, Or Why Travel?', in ead. (2000a): 1–25.

Horowitz, M. C. (1976), 'Aristotle and Woman', *Journal of the History of Biology* 9: 183–213.

Horrocks, G. (1997), *Greek: A History of the Language and Its Speakers*, London.

Horstmann, A. (1979), 'Der Mythosbegriff vom frühen Christentum bis zur Gegenwart', *Archiv für Begriffsgeschichte* 23: 7–54, 197–245.

Howard, D. and Moretti, L. (2009), *Sound and Space in Renaissance Venice: Architecture, Music, Aesthetics*, New Haven.

Howard, S. (1982), 'William Blake: The Antique, Nudity, and Nakedness', *Artibus et Historiae* 3: 117–49.

— (1992), 'Albani, Winckelmann and Cavaceppi: The Transition from Amateur to Professional Antiquarianism', *Journal of the History of Collections* 4: 27–38.

— (2003), 'Michelangelo and Greek Sculpture', in J. Feifer *et al.* (eds), *The Rediscovery of Antiquity: The Role of the Artist*, Copenhagen: 37–62.

Howell, A. C. (1946), '*Res et Verba*: Words and Things', *English Literary History* 13: 131–42.

Howells, R. (2003), *Visual Culture*, Cambridge.

Hubbard, P. (2006), *The City*, London.

Hull, E. M. (2010), 'Comic Books', in Grafton, Most, and Settis (2010): 225.

Hunt, L. (1983), 'Hercules and the Radical Image in the French Revolution', *Representations* 2: 95–117.

Huntington, D. C. (1968), 'Robert Adam's *mise-en-scène* of the Human Figure', *Journal of the Society of Architectural Historians* 27: 249–63.

Huntington, S. P. (1997), *The Clash of Civilizations and the Remaking of World Order*, New York.

Hvattum, M. (2003), *Gottfried Semper and the Problem of Historicism*, Cambridge.

Idorn, G. (1997), *Concrete Progress: From Antiquity to The Third Millennium*, New York.

Ijsewijn, J. (1990), *Companion to Neo-Latin Studies*, Louvain.

Inglebert, H. (1996), *Les romains Chrétiens face à l'histoire de Rome: histoire, Christianisme et Romanités en Occident dans l'antiquité tardive (IIIe–Ve siècles)*, Paris.

Iori, T. (2001), *Il cemento armato in Italia dalle origini alla seconda guerra mondiale*, Rome.

— (2009), *Pier Luigi Nervi*, Milan.

Iser, W. (1991), *Das Fiktive and das Imaginaire. Grundzüge einer Literaturanthropologie*, Frankfurt a. M.

Isermeyer, C. A. (1967), 'Die Villa Rotonda von Palladio', *Zeitschrift für Kunstgeschichte* 30: 207–21.

Ishii, K. (1999), *Membrane Designs and Structures in the World*, Tokyo.

Jacks, P. (1993), *The Antiquarian and the Myth of Antiquity: The Origins of Rome in Renaissance Thought*, Cambridge.

Jaggard, D. (2004), 'Dionysus versus Dionysus', in P. Bishop (ed.), *Nietzsche and Antiquity*, Rochester, NY: 277–94.

Jakobson, R. (1959), 'On Linguistic Aspects of Translation', in R. A. Brower (ed.), *On Translation*, Cambridge, Mass.: 232–9.

— (1960), 'Closing Statement: Linguistics and Poetics', in Sebeok T. (ed.), *Style in Language*, New York: 350–77.

James, H. (1991), 'Cultural Disintegration in *Titus Andronicus*: Mutilating Titus, Vergil and Rome', in *Themes in Drama* 13: 123–40.

James, S. (1997), 'Drawing Inferences: Visual Reconstructions in Theory and Practice', in B. L. Molyneaux (ed.), *The Cultural Life of Images: Visual Representation in Archaeology*, London: 22–48.

Jameson, F. (1991), *Postmodernism, Or the Cultural Logic of Late Capitalism*, London.

Janson, H. (1967), 'The Equestrian Monument from Cangrande della Scala to Peter the Great', in A. R. Lewis (ed.), *Aspects of the Renaissance*, London: 73–85.

Jarvis, S. (1995), *Scholars and Gentlemen: Shakespearean Textual Criticism and Representations of Scholarly Labour, 1725–1765*, Oxford.

Jauss, H. R. (1983), 'The Paradox of the Misanthrope', *Comparative Literature* 35: 305–22.

— (2005), 'Modernity and Literary Tradition', tr. C. Thorne, *Critical Inquiry* 31: 329–64.

Jeanneret, M. (2003), *Éros rebelle. Littérature et dissidence à l'âge classique*, Paris.

Jebb, R. C. (1883), Sophocles, *The Oedipus Tyrannus*, Cambridge.

— (1899), *Humanism in Education*, London.

Jencks, C. (2002), *The New Paradigm in Architecture: The Language of Post-Modernism*, New Haven.

Jenkins, I. (1992), *Archaeologists and Aesthetes in the Sculpture Galleries of the British Museum, 1800–1939*, London.

Jenkyns, R. (1980), *The Victorians and Ancient Greece*, Cambridge, Mass.

Jens, W. and Seidensticker, B. (2003) (eds), *Ferne und Nähe der Antike: Beiträge zu den Künsten und Wissenschaften der Moderne*, Berlin.

Jesse, E. (1999) (ed.), *Totalitarismus im 20. Jahrhundert. Eine Bilanz der internationalen Forschung*, Baden-Baden.

John, R. (2001), *Thomas Gordon Smith and the Rebirth of Classical Architecture*, London.

Johns, C. M. S. (1994), 'Portrait Mythology: Antonio Canova's Portraits of the Bonapartes', *Eighteenth-Century Studies* 28: 115–29.

Johnson, D. E. (2007), '*As If* The Time Were Now: Deconstructing Agamben', *South Atlantic Quarterly* 106: 265–90.

Johnston, M. D. (1987), *The Spiritual Logic of Ramon Llull*, Oxford.

Jokilehto, J. (1999), *A History of Architectural Conservation*, Oxford.

Jolibert, B. (1999), *La commedia dell' arte et son influence en France du XVIe au XVIIIe siècle*, Paris.

Jones, A. F. (1970), 'Science and English Prose Style, 1650–75', in Watson (1970): 194–230.

Jordan, D. P. (1979), *The King's Trial: The French Revolution vs. Louis XVI*, Berkeley.

Jordan, E. (1998), *Alfred Tennyson*, Cambridge.

Joseph, G. (1992), *Tennyson and the Text*, Cambridge.

Joshel, S. R. *et al.* (2001), *Imperial Projections: Ancient Rome in Modern Popular Culture*, Baltimore.

Kablitz, A. (2009), 'Aufbruch zur Neuzeit? Petrarca und das Ende des Mittelalters', in P. Geyer and K. Thorwarth (eds), *Petrarca und die Herausbildung des modernen Subjekts*, Bonn: 45–55.

Kahr, M. M. (1978), 'Danaë: Virtuous, Voluptuous, Venal Woman', *Art Bulletin* 60: 43–55.

Kajanto, L. (1989), 'A Humanist Credo: Poggio Bracciolini on the Meaning of *studia humanitatis* and *virtus*', *Arctos* 23: 98–119.

— (1994), 'Poggio Bracciolini's *De Infelicitate Principum* and Its Classical Sources', *International Journal of the Classical Tradition* 1: 23–35.

Kaldellis, A. (2008), *Hellenism in Byzantium*, Cambridge.

Kallendorf, C. W. (1999), *Virgil and the Myth of Venice: Books and Readers in the Italian Renaissance*, Oxford.

— (2002), *Humanist Educational Treatises*, Cambridge, Mass.

— (2007), *A Companion to the Classical Tradition*, Malden, Mass.

— (2010), 'Education', in Grafton, Most, and Settis (2010): 292–9.

Kallis, A. (2011), '"Reconciliation" or "Conquest"? The Opening of the Via della Conciliazione and the Fascist Vision for the "Third Rome"', in Caldwell and Caldwell (2011): 129–52.

— (2012), 'The "Third Rome" of Fascism: Demolitions and the Search for a New Urban Syntax', *Journal of Modern History* 84: 40–79.

Kandl, J. (2001), 'The Politics of Keats's Early Poetry', in S. J. Wolfson (ed.), *The Cambridge Companion to Keats*, Cambridge: 1–19.

Karmon, D. (2011), *The Ruin of the Eternal City: Antiquity and Preservation in Renaissance Rome*, Oxford.

Kasparek, J. L. (1977), *Molière's Tartuffe and the Traditions of Roman Satire*, Chapel Hill.

Kaster, R. A. (1988), *Guardians of Language: The Grammarian and Society in Late Antiquity*, Berkeley.

Kaufmann, T. D. (2001), 'Antiquarianism, the History of Objects, and the History of Art before Winckelmann', *Journal of the History of Ideas* 62: 523–41.

Kaufmann, W. (1974), *Nietzsche: Philosopher, Psychologist, Antichrist*, 4th edn, Princeton.

Kavanagh, J. H. and Lewis, T. E. (1982), 'Interview: Etienne Balibar and Pierre Macherey', *Diacritics* 12: 46–51.

Kay, S., Cave, T. and Bowie, M. (2003), *A Short History of French Literature*, Oxford.

Kelly, C. (2000), 'Tolstoy', in France (2000): 592–4.

Kelly, L. G. (1979), *The True Interpreter: A History of Translation Theory and Practice in the West*, Oxford.

Kelsey, F. W. (1908), 'Is There a Science of Classical Philology?', *Classical Philology* 3: 369–85.

Kennedy, D. (2004), 'British Theatre 1895–1946: Art, Entertainment, Audiences', in B. Kershaw (ed.), *The Cambridge History of British Theatre*, Cambridge: 3–33.

Kennedy, W. J. (1994), *Authorizing Petrarch*, Ithaca and London.

Kermode, F. (1975), *The Classic: Literary Images of Permanence and Change*, Cambridge, Mass.

Kessler, E. and Maclean, I. (2002) (eds), *Res et Verba in der Renaissance*, Wiesbaden.

Keys, M. M. (2006), *Aquinas, Aristotle and the Promise of the Common Good*, Cambridge.

Kidson, F. (1901), *The Minstrelsy of England*, London.

Kiefer, F. (1979), 'The Conflation of Fortuna and Occasio in Renaissance Thought and Iconography', *Journal of Medieval and Renaissance Studies* 9: 1–27.

Kimbell, D. R. B. (1991), *Italian Opera*, Cambridge.

King, D. N. (1991), *The Complete Works of Robert and James Adam*, London.

King, M. and Rabil, A. (1983), *Her Immaculate Hand: Selected Works By and About the Women Humanists of Quattrocento Italy*, Binghamton, NY.

King, R. (2000), *Brunelleschi's Dome: The Story of the Great Cathedral in Florence*, London.
Kinney, D. (2010), 'Rome: I. Antiquity to Renaissance', in Grafton, Most, and Settis (2010): 839–48.
Kirk, T. (2006), 'Framing St. Peter's: Urban Planning in Fascist Rome', *Art Bulletin* 88: 756–76.
Kitzbichler, J. *et al.* (2009), *Theorie der Übersetzung antiker Literatur in Deutschland seit 1800*, Berlin.
Klein, J. (2003) (ed.), *T. S. Eliot, Poeta Doctus. Tradition und die Konstitution der klassischen Moderne*, Frankfurt.
Klibansky, R. (1981), *The Continuity of the Platonic Tradition During the Middle Ages*, 2nd edn, Munich.
Kocziszky, E. (2010) (ed.), *Ruinen der Moderne: Archäologie und die Künste*, Bonn.
Korshak, Y. (1987), 'Paris and Helen by Jacques Louis David: Choice and Judgement on the Eve of the French Revolution', *Art Bulletin* 69: 102–16.
Kortum, H. (1966), *Charles Perrault und Nicolas Boileau. Der Antike-Streit im Zeitalter der klassischen französischen Literatur*, Berlin.
Krause-Tastet, P. (1999), *Analyse der Stilentwicklung in politischen Diskursen während der Französischen Revolution (1789–1794)*, Frankfurt.
Krautheimer, R. (1980), *Rome: Profile of a City, 312–1308*, Princeton.
Kraye, J. (1996) (ed.), *The Cambridge Companion to Renaissance Humanism*, Cambridge.
Kristeller, P. O. (1956), *Studies in Renaissance Thought and Letters*, Rome.
— (1986), 'Marsilio Ficino and His Work After Five Hundred Years', in G. C. Garfagnini (ed.), *Marsilio Ficino e il ritorno di Platone*, Florence: 15–196.
Kristeller, P. O. *et al.* (1960–2003) (eds), *Catalogus Translationum et Commentariorum: Mediaeval and Renaissance Latin Translations and Commentaries*, Washington, DC.
Kristeva, J. (1969), *Semiotikè*, Paris.
— (2001), *Hannah Arendt*, New York.
Kropfinger, K. (1974), *Wagner und Beethoven*, Regensburg.
Kruft, H.-W. (1994), *A History of Architectural Theory: From Vitruvius to the Present*, tr. R. Taylor *et al.*, New York.
Kubler, G. (1962), *The Shape of Time: Remarks on the History of Things*, New Haven.
Kunze, M. (1991), *The Pergamon Altar: Its Rediscovery, History and Reconstruction*, Mainz.
Kunzle, D. (1997), *Che Guevara: Icon, Myth, and Message*, Los Angeles.
Kurdzialek, M. (1971), 'Der Mensch als Abbild des Kosmos', in A. Zimmermann (ed.), *Der Begriff der Repraesentatio im Mittelalter*, Berlin: 35–75.
Lambert, J. (2008), 'Medieval Translations and Translation Studies: Some Preliminary Considerations', in Goyens *et al.* (2008): 1–10.
Lampert, C. (2006) (ed.), *Rodin*, London.
Lampert, L. (2009), 'Strauss's Recovery of Esotericism', in Smith (2009a): 63–92.
Lane, M. (1999), 'Plato, Popper, Strauss, and Utopianism: Open Secrets?', *History of Philosophy Quarterly* 16: 119–42.
— (2001), *Plato's Progeny: How Plato and Socrates Still Captivate the Modern Mind*, London.
Lapidge, M. (1979), 'Aldhelm's Latin Poetry and Old English Verse', *Comparative Literature* 31: 209–31.
Larrabee, J. A. (1943), *English Bards and Grecian Marbles*, New York.
Lasansky, D. M. (2004), *The Renaissance Perfected: Architecture, Spectacle, and Tourism in Fascist Italy*, University Park, Pa.
Lavin, I. (1980), *Bernini and the Unity of the Visual Arts*, New York.

Leach, A. F. (1911), *Education Charters and Documents*, Cambridge.
Leach, R. (1985), *The Punch and Judy Show*, Athens, Ga.
Leavis, F. R. (1932), *New Bearings in English Poetry*, London.
— (1936), *Revaluation*, London.
— (1948), *Education and the University*, London.
Lebègue, M. R. (1966), 'De la Brigade à la Pléiade', in R. Antonioli *et al.* (eds), *Lumières de la Pléiade*, Paris: 13–20.
Lee, M. O. (2003), *Athena Sings: Wagner and the Greeks*, Buffalo, NY.
Lee, R. W. (1967), *Ut Pictura Poesis: The Humanistic Theory of Painting*, New York.
Leedham-Green, E. S. (1996), *A Concise History of the University of Cambridge*, Cambridge.
Lefevere, A. (1992), *Translation/History/Culture*, London.
Lehmann, K. (1945), 'The Dome of Heaven', *Art Bulletin* 27: 1–27.
Leitgeb, M.-C. (2003), '"Da ward die Liebe . . ." Der platonische Erosmythos in einem Fragment zu Hölderlins Hyperion', *Wiener Studien* 116: 259–76.
— (2004), *Liebe und Magie: die Geburt des Eros und Ficinos De Amore*, Enzersdorf.
Leonard, M. (2010) (ed.), *Derrida and Antiquity*, Oxford.
Leonhardt, J. (2005), 'Petrarcas Liebe zu Cicero oder: Latein und die Sünde der Lust', in U. Auhagen *et al.* (eds), *Petrarca und die römische Literatur*, Tübingen: 35–55.
Lepschy, G. (2009), 'In Nomine Patria et Filia', *Plurilinguismo* 16: 177–82.
Lettenbauer, W. (1961), *Moskau, das Dritte Rom*, Munich.
Levillain, P. (2003) (ed.), *Dictionnaire historique de la papauté*, rev. edn, Paris.
Levin, G. (2007), 'Modern and Postmodern Art and Architecture', in Kallendorf (2007): 371–92.
Levinas, E. (2003), *Humanism of the Other*, tr. N. Poller, Urbana.
Levine, J. (1984), 'The Battle of the Books and the Shield of Achilles', *Eighteenth Century Life* 9: 33–61.
— (1991), *The Battle of the Books*, Ithaca, NY.
Levine, L. W. (1998), *Highbrow/Lowbrow: The Emergence of Cultural Hierarchy in America*, Cambridge, Mass.
Levinson, M. (1988), *Keats's Life of Allegory*, Oxford.
Lewis, C. S. (1942), *A Preface to Paradise Lost*, London.
Lianeri, A. and Zajko, V. (2008) (eds), *Translation and the Classic*, Oxford.
Liberman, R. E. (1997), 'The Architectural Background', in M. Hall (ed.), *Raphael's School of Athens*, Cambridge: 64–84.
Licht, M. (1985), '"I Ragionamenti": Visualizing St. Peter's', *Journal of the Society of Architectural Historians* 44: 111–28.
Linton, M. (2010), 'The Man of Virtue: The Role of Antiquity in the Political Trajectory of L. A. Saint-Just', *French History* 24: 393–419.
Lloyd-Jones, H. (1982), *Blood for the Ghosts: Classical Influences in the Nineteenth and Twentieth Centuries*, London.
Lockspeiser, E. (1962), *Debussy: His Life and Mind, vol. 1: 1862–1902*, London.
Lockwood, D. P. (1918), 'Two Thousand Years of Latin Translation from the Greek', *Transactions of the American Philological Association* 49: 115–29.
Lockwood, L. (1984), *Music in Renaissance Ferrara, 1400–1505*, Oxford.
Lodge, R. A. (1993), *French: From Dialect to Standard*, London.
Losemann, V. (1977), *Nationalsozialismus und Antike*, Hamburg.
Louis, M. K. (1999), 'Family Secrets, Family Silences: The Language of the Heart in Swinburne's "Itylus"', *Victorian Poetry* 37: 453–64.

Loukaki, A. (2008), *Living Ruins, Value Conflicts*, Aldershot.
Louth, C. (1998), *Hölderlin and the Dynamics of Translation*, Oxford.
Lovejoy, A. O. (1936), *The Great Chain of Being*, Cambridge, Mass.
Lowe, D. (2009), 'Playing with Antiquity: Videogame Receptions of the Classical World', in D. Lowe and K. Shahabudin (eds), *Classics for All: Rewriting Antiquity in Mass Cultural Media*, Cambridge: 62–88.
Lowe, N. J. (2000), *The Classical Plot and the Invention of Western Narrative*, Cambridge.
Lowenthal, D. (1985), *The Past Is a Foreign Country*, Cambridge.
Lowry, M. (1979), *The World of Aldus Manutius: Business and Scholarship in Renaissance Venice*, Oxford.
Lucey-Roper, M. (2006), 'Discover Babylon', *Museums and the Web 2006*, http://www.museumsandtheweb.com/mw2006/papers/lucey-roper/lucey-roper.html, accessed 22 July 2013.
Lucy, S. (1960), *T. S. Eliot and the Idea of Tradition*, London.
Ludz, U. (2011), 'Briefwechsel: 10.4. Martin Heidegger', in Heuer *et al.* (2011): 154–8.
Lynch, S. J. (1998), *Shakespearean Intertextuality*, Westport, Conn.
McClellan, A. (1994), *Inventing the Louvre: Art, Politics, and the Origins of the Modern Museum in Eighteenth-Century Paris*, Cambridge.
McDonald, H. (2001), *Erotic Ambiguities: The Female Nude in Art*, London.
MacDonald, W. L. (1976), *The Pantheon: Design, Meaning and Progeny*, Cambridge, Mass.
McFarlane, I. D. (1986), 'The Renaissance Epitaph', *Modern Language Review* 81: xxv–xxxv.
McGowan, M. M. (2000), *The Vision of Rome in Late Renaissance France*, New Haven.
Macintosh, F. (1995), 'Under the Blue Pencil: Greek Tragedy and the British Censor', *Dialogos* 2: 54–70.
— (1997), 'Tragedy in Performance', in P. Easterling (ed.), *The Cambridge Companion to Greek Tragedy*, Cambridge: 284–323.
— (2008a), 'Performance Histories', in Hardwick and Stray (2008): 247–58.
— (2008b), 'An Oedipus for Our Times? Yeats's Version of Sophocles' *Oedipus Tyrannos*', in Revermann and Wilson (2008): 524–47.
— (2009), *Oedipus Tyrannus*, Cambridge.
Macintosh, F. *et al.* (2005) (eds), *Agamemnon in Performance: 458 BC to AD 2004*, Oxford.
Mack, P. (2002), *Elizabethan Rhetoric: Theory and Practice*, Cambridge.
Mackie, G. (2004), 'Publishing Notoriety: Piracy, Pornography, and Oscar Wilde', *University of Toronto Quarterly* 73: 980–90.
McLaughlin, M. L. (1995), *Literary Imitation in the Italian Renaissance: The Theory and Practice of Literary Imitation in Italy from Dante to Bembo*, Oxford.
— (1996), 'Humanism and Italian Literature', in J. Kraye (ed.), *The Cambridge Companion to Renaissance Humanism*, Cambridge: 224–45.
McNeil, D. O. (1975), *Guillaume Budé and Humanism in the Reign of Francis I*, Geneva.
Maddalo, S. (1990), *In figura Romae: immagini di Roma nel libro medievale*, Rome.
Maguire, L. E (2009), *Helen of Troy: From Homer to Hollywood*, Oxford.
Mainstone, R. J. (1977), 'Brunelleschi's Dome', *Architectural Review* 162: 156–66.
Mainz, V. (2007), 'Bringing the Hemlock up: Jacques-Louis David's Socrates and the Inventions of History', in Trapp (2007a): 249–67.
Makdisi, G. (1989), 'Scholasticism and Humanism in Classical Islam and the Christian West', *Journal of the American Oriental Society* 109: 175–82.
Malamud, M. (2001), 'The Greatest Show on Earth: Roman Entertainments in Turn-Of-The-Century New York City', *Journal of Popular Culture* 35: 43–58.

— (2009), *Ancient Rome and Modern America*, Oxford.
Malcolm, N. (1998), 'Charles Cotton, Translator of Hobbes's *De cive*', *Huntington Library Quarterly* 61: 259–87.
Maleuvre, D. (2000), 'David Painting Death', *Diacritics* 30: 25–38.
Mann, N. (1984), *Petrarch*, Oxford.
Manni, P. (2003), *Trecento toscano: la lingua di Dante, Petrarca e Boccaccio*, Bologna.
Mansfield, H. (1979), *Machiavelli's New Modes and Orders: A Study of the Discourses on Livy*, Ithaca, NY.
— (1996), *Machiavelli's Virtue*, Chicago.
Mantello, F. A. C. and Rigg, A. G. (1996) (eds), *Medieval Latin: An Introduction and Bibliographical Guide*, Washington, DC.
Manville, B. and Ober, J. (2003), *A Company of Citizens: What the World's First Democracy Teaches Leaders about Creating Great Organizations*, Boston, Mass.
Marchand, S. L. (1996), *Down from Olympus: Archaeology and Philhellenism in Germany, 1750–1970*, Princeton.
Margolin, J.-C. (1971), 'Érasme et le verbe', in id., *Érasme, l'Alsace, et son temps*, Strasbourg: 87–110.
Marin, D. (1967), *Bibliography of the 'Essay on the Sublime' (Peri Hupsous)*, Bari.
Marin, L. (1995), 'Panofsky et Poussin en Arcadie', in id., *Sublime Poussin*, Paris: 126–50.
Markeley, A. A. (2004), *Stateliest Measures: Tennyson and the Literature of Greece and Rome*, Toronto.
Markiewicz, H. (1987), '*Ut Pictura Poesis*: A History of the Topos and the Problem', *New Literary History* 18: 535–58.
Marot, P. (2007) (ed.), *La littérature et le sublime*, Toulouse.
Martin, É. M. (2012), 'The "Prehistory" of the Sublime in Early Modern France', in Costelloe (2012): 77–101.
Martin, R. P. (2003), *Myths of the Ancient Greeks*, New York.
Martindale, C. (1986), *John Milton and the Transformation of Ancient Epic*, London.
— (1993), *Redeeming the Text: Latin Poetry and the Hermeneutics of Reception*, Cambridge.
— (1996), 'Ruins of Rome: T. S. Eliot and the Presence of the Past', *Arion* 3: 102–40.
— (2006), 'Thinking Through Reception', in C. Martindale and R. F. Thomas (eds), *Classics and the Uses of Reception*, Oxford: 1–13.
— (2008), 'Dryden's Ovid: Aesthetic Translation and the Idea of the Classic', in Lianeri and Zajko (2008): 83–109.
Martindale, C. and Taylor, A. B. (2004) (eds), *Shakespeare and the Classics*, Cambridge.
Maslen, R. W. (2000), 'Myths Exploited: The *Metamorphoses* of Ovid in Early Elizabethan England', in Taylor (2000): 15–30.
Mason, H. A. (1972), *To Homer Through Pope*, London.
Matthews, J. F. (1975), *Western Aristocracies and Imperial Court, A.D. 364–425*, Oxford.
Mattusch, C. C. (2011), Johann Joachim Winckelmann, *Letter and Report on the Discoveries at Herculaneum*, Los Angeles.
Matzner, S. (2010), 'From Uranians to Homosexuals: Philhellenism, Greek Homoeroticism, and Gay Emancipation in Germany, 1835–1913', *Classical Receptions Journal* 2: 60–91.
Mayr, E. (1982), *The Growth of Biological Thought*, Cambridge, Mass.
Mazrui, A. (1997), 'Note' [no title], *Language in Society* 26: 469.
Mazzocco, A. (1993), *Linguistic Theories in Dante and the Humanists*, Leiden.
Mazzoni, C. (2010), *She-Wolf: The Story of a Roman Icon*, Cambridge.

Mazzotta, G. (1978), 'The *Canzoniere* and the Language of the Self', *Studies in Philology* 75: 271–96.

Mendle, M. (1995), *Henry Parker and the English Civil War: The Political Thought of the Public's 'Privado'*, Cambridge.

Menze, C. (1975), *Die Bildungsreform Wilhelm von Humboldts*, Hanover.

Meozzi, A. (1934), *Il petrarchismo europeo*, Pisa.

Merritt, M. M. (2012), 'The Moral Source of the Kantian Sublime', in Costelloe (2012): 37–49.

Mewes, H. (1995), 'Leo Strauss and Martin Heidegger: Greek Antiquity and the Meaning of Modernity', in P. Graf Kielmansegg *et al.* (eds), *Hannah Arendt and Leo Strauss: German Émigrés and American Political Thought After World War II*, Cambridge: 105–20.

Meyer, E. (1969), *Heinrich Schliemann, Kaufmann und Forscher*, Göttingen.

Mezzatesta, M. P. (1984), 'Fray Antonio de Guevara, and the Ideal of the Perfect Prince in the Sixteenth Century', *Art Bulletin* 66: 620–33.

Michaud, E. (2003), 'Oeuvre d'art totale et totalitarisme', in J. Galard and J. Zugazagoitia (eds), *L'oeuvre d'art totale*, Paris: 35–65.

Michelakis, P. (2009), 'Greek Lyric from the Renaissance to the Eighteenth Century', in Budelmann (2009): 336–51.

Miedema, N. R. (1996), *Die Mirabilia Romae: Untersuchungen zu ihrer Überlieferung*, Tübingen.

Migliorini, B. and Griffith, T. G. (1984), *The Italian Language*, rev. edn, London.

Miller, D. A. (2000), *The Epic Hero*, Baltimore.

Millward, M. (1996), *A Biography of the English Language*, 2nd edn, Fort Worth.

Milroy, J. (1977), *The Language of Gerard Manley Hopkins*, London.

— (1992), 'Social Networks and Prestige Arguments in Sociolinguistics', in K. Bolton and H. Kwok (eds), *Sociolinguistics Today*, London: 146–62.

Minnis, A. J. (2001), *Magister Amoris: The Roman de la Rose and Vernacular Hermeneutics*, Oxford.

Minnis, A. J. and Scott, A. B. (1988), *Medieval Literary Theory and Criticism, c. 1100–c. 1375: The Commentary Tradition*, Oxford.

Minsaas, K. (2001), 'Poetic Marvels: Aristotelian Wonder in Renaissance Poetics and Poetry', in Andersen and Haarberg (2001): 145–71.

Miola, R. S. (1983), *Shakespeare's Rome*, Cambridge.

— (1994), *Shakespeare and Classical Comedy*, Oxford.

Mitrovic, B. (1999), 'Palladio's Theory of the Classical Orders in the First Book of *I quattro libri dell'architettura*', *Architectural History* 42: 110–40.

— (2004), *Learning from Palladio*, New York.

Mittelstrass, J. (1979), '*Phaenomena bene fundata*: From "Saving the Appearances" to the Mechanisation of the World-Picture', in R. R. Bolgar (ed.), *Classical Influences in Western Thought, A.D. 1650–1870*, New York: 39–59.

Mohr, W. (1974), 'Bemerkungen zur Verfasserschaft von *De regimine principum*', in J. Möller and H. Kohlenberger (eds), *Virtus Politica*, Stuttgart: 127–45.

Momigliano, A. (1963), 'Pagan and Christian Historiography in the Fourth Century AD', in id. (ed.), *The Conflict between Paganism and Christianity in the Fourth Century*, Oxford: 79–99.

— (1980), *Saggezza straniera: l'ellenismo e le altre culture*, Turin.

Mommsen, T. E. (1942), 'Petrarch's Conception of the "Dark Ages"', *Speculum* 17: 226–42.

Monk, S. H. (1935), *The Sublime: A Study of Critical Theories in Eighteenth-Century England*, New York.

Morales, H. (2007), *Classical Mythology: A Very Short Introduction*, Oxford.

Moressi, M. (1988), 'Humanistic Interpretations of Vitruvius in the Fifteenth Century', in T. H. Mäkelä (ed.), *Canon*, Princeton: 81–100.

Morini, M. (2006), *Tudor Translation in Theory and Practice*, Aldershot.

Mortier, R. (1974), *Le poétique des ruines en France*, Geneva.

Moss, A. (2003), *Renaissance Truth and the Latin Language Turn*, Oxford.

Most, G. W. (1999), 'From Logos to Muthos', in Buxton (1999): 25–47.

— (2002a), 'Heidegger's Greeks', *Arion* 10: 83–98.

— (2002b) (ed.), *Disciplining Classics: Altertumswissenschaft als Beruf*, Göttingen.

Moul, V. (2006), 'Ben Jonson's *Poetaster*: Classical Translation and the Location of Cultural Authority', *Translation and Literature* 15: 21–50.

— (2010), *Jonson, Horace and the Classical Tradition*, Cambridge.

Mousourakis, G. (2003), *The Historical and Institutional Context of Roman Law*, Aldershot.

Mugglestone, L. (2006) (ed.), *The Oxford History of English*, Oxford.

Mukerji, C. (2006), 'Tacit Knowledge and Classical Technique in Seventeenth-Century France: Hydraulic Cement as Living Practice among Masons and Military Engineers', *Technology and Culture* 47: 713–33.

Mullett, M. and Scott, R. (1981) (eds), *Byzantium and the Classical Tradition*, Birmingham.

Mulryan, J. and Brown, S. (2006), *Natale Conti's Mythologiae Translated and Annotated*, Tempe, Ariz.

Mumford, L. (1961), *The City in History*, New York.

Münkler, H. (2003), 'Republik, Demokratie und Diktatur. Die Rezeption von drei antiken Begriffen im politischen Denken der Neuzeit', in Jens and Seidensticker (2003): 69–97.

Munro, H. A. J. (1886), *Titi Lucreti Cari De Rerum Natura*, Cambridge.

Murchland, B. (1966), *Two Views of Man: Pope Innocent III – On the Misery of Man; Giannozzo Manetti – On the Dignity of Man*, New York.

Murdoch, B. (1996), *The Germanic Hero: Politics and Pragmatism in Early Medieval Poetry*, London.

Murphy, J. J. (1974), *Rhetoric in the Middle Ages*, Berkeley.

Murray, G. (1908), *Greek Historical Writing and Apollo*, Oxford.

Murray, J. (1897), *The Autobiographies of Edward Gibbon*, 2nd edn, London.

Murray, P. A. (1999), 'What is a *Muthos* for Plato?', in Buxton (1999): 251–62.

Myrsiades, K. (2007), 'Reading the Gunfighter as Homeric Epic', *College Literature* 34: 279–300.

Nabokov, V. (1955), 'Problems of Translation: *Onegin* in English', *Partisan Review* 22: 496–512.

Nead, L. (1992), *The Female Nude*, London.

Nederman, C. J. (1988), 'A Duty to Kill: John of Salisbury's Theory of Tyrannicide', *Review of Politics* 50: 365–89.

Neeley, G. S. (2000), 'Schopenhauer and the Platonic Ideas', *Idealistic Studies* 30: 121–48.

Négrel, E. and Sermain, J.-P. (2002) (eds), *Une expérience rhétorique: l'éloquence de la révolution*, Oxford.

Newey, V. (1994), 'Keats, History, and the Poets', in N. Roe (ed.), *Keats and History*, Cambridge: 165–93.

Nicholson, K. (1990), *Turner's Classical Landscapes*, Princeton.

Nicoll, A. (1931), *Masks, Mimes and Miracles: Studies in the Popular Theatre*, London.

Niebuhr, R. (1943), *The Nature and Destiny of Man*, vol. 2, London.

Nield, S. (2004), 'Popular Theatre, 1895–1940', in B. Kershaw (ed.), *The Cambridge History of British Theatre*, vol. 3, Cambridge: 86–109.

Nippel, W. (1980), *Mischverfassungstheorie und Verfassungsrealität in Antike und früher Neuzeit*, Stuttgart.

— (2003), 'Antike und moderne Freiheit', in Jens and Seidensticker (2003): 49–68.

Nisbet, G. (2008), *Ancient Greece in Film and Popular Culture*, 2nd edn, Bristol.

Noble, A. (1991), *From Art to Archaeology*, London.

Norman, L. F. (2011), *The Shock of the Ancient: Literature and History in Early Modern France*, Chicago.

Norman, R. (1979), 'Aristotle's Philosopher-God', in J. Barnes *et al.* (eds), *Articles on Aristotle, 4, Psychology and Aesthetics*, London: 93–102.

Norton, A. (2004), *Leo Strauss and the Politics of American Empire*, New Haven.

Norton, G. P. (1984), *The Ideology and Language of Translation in Renaissance France and Their Humanist Antecedents*, Geneva.

Novati, F. (1905), *Attraverso il medioevo*, Bari.

Nussbaum, M. C. (1997), *Cultivating Humanity: A Classical Defense of Reform in Liberal Education*, Cambridge, Mass.

— (2010), *Not For Profit: Why Democracy Needs the Humanities*, Princeton.

Nuttall, A. D. (1996), *Why Does Tragedy Give Pleasure?*, Oxford.

— (2003), *Dead From the Waist Down: Scholars and Scholarship in Literature and the Popular Imagination*, New Haven.

Nutton, V. (2010a), 'Humors', in Grafton, Most, and Settis (2010): 467.

— (2010b), 'Medicine', in Grafton, Most, and Settis (2010): 573–9.

Nyrop, K. (1899–1930), *Grammaire historique de la langue française*, 6 vols, Copenhagen.

Onians, J. (1988), *Bearers of Meaning: The Classical Orders in Antiquity, the Middle Ages and the Renaissance*, Princeton.

Orrells, D. (2011), *Classical Culture and Modern Masculinity*, Oxford.

O'Sullivan, M. J. (1980), 'Running Division on the Groundwork: Dryden's Theory of Translation', *Neophilologus* 64: 144–59.

Pade, M. (2011) (ed.), *On Renaissance Academies*, Rome.

Page, D. L. (1955), *Sappho and Alcaeus*, Oxford.

Pagliara, P. N. (1986), 'Vitruvio da testo a canone', in S. Settis (ed.), *Memoria dell'antico nell'arte italiana, vol. 3: Dalla tradizione all'archeologia*, Turin: 3–85.

Paine, A. B. (1912), *Mark Twain, A Biography*, New York.

Painter, B. W. (2005), *Mussolini's Rome: Rebuilding the Eternal City*, New York.

Pallasmaa, J. (2005), *The Eyes of the Skin: Architecture and the Senses*, Chichester.

— (2011), 'Architecture and the Existential Sense', in Bacci and Melcher (2011): 579–98.

Pangle, T. L. (1989), *The Rebirth of Classical Political Rationalism: An Introduction to the Thought of Leo Strauss*, Chicago.

Panofsky, E. (1930), *Hercules am Scheidewege: und andere antike Bildstoffe in der neueren Kunst*, Leipzig.

— (1936), '"Et in Arcadia Ego": On the Conception of Transience in Poussin and Watteau', in R. Klibansky and H. J. Paton (eds), *Philosophy and History: Essays Presented to Ernst Cassirer*, Oxford: 223–54.

— (1955), '"Et in Arcadia Ego": Poussin and the Elegiac Tradition', in id., *Meaning and The Visual Arts*, New York: 295–320.

— (1960), *Renaissance and Renascences in Western Art*, Stockholm.

Parel, A. (1992), *The Machiavellian Cosmos*, New Haven.

Parker, H. T. (1937), *The Cult of Antiquity and the French Revolutionaries*, Chicago.

Parker, J. (2001), *Dialogic Education and the Problematics of Translation in Homer and Greek Tragedy*, Lewiston, NY.

Parker, W. H. (1988), *Priapea: Poems for a Phallic God*, London.

Parker, W. R. (1937), *Milton's Debt to Greek Tragedy in 'Samson Agonistes'*, Baltimore.

Parry, R. (2008) (ed.), *Museums in a Digital Age*, London.

Parslow, C. C. (1995), *Rediscovering Antiquity: Karl Weber and the Excavations of Herculaneum, Pompeii and Stabiae*, Cambridge.

Pasternak, C. (2007) (ed.), *What Makes Us Human?*, Oxford.

Patterson, A. (1984) (ed.), *Roman Images*, Baltimore.

Pattison, R. (1979), *Tennyson and Tradition*, Cambridge, Mass.

Paul, J. (2013), *Film and the Classical Epic Tradition*, Oxford.

Paulsen, F. (1919–21), *Geschichte des gelehrten Unterrichts auf den deutschen Schulen und Universitäten vom Ausgang des Mittelalters bis zur Gegenwart*, 2 vols, 3rd edn, Leipzig.

Pauwels, Y. (1989), 'Les origines de l'ordre composite', *Annali d'architettura* 1: 29–46.

Payne, A. (1999), *The Architectural Treatise in the Italian Renaissance*, Cambridge.

Pearsall, D. (1987), 'Gower's Latin in the *Confessio Amantis*', in A. J. Minnis (ed.), *Latin and Vernacular: Studies in Late-Medieval Texts and Manuscripts*, Cambridge: 13–25.

Pečar, A. (2011), *Macht der Schrift. Politischer Biblizismus in Schottland und England zwischen Reformation und Bürgerkrieg*, Munich.

Pellecchia, L. (1992), 'Architects Read Vitruvius: Renaissance Interpretations of the Atrium of the Ancient House', *Journal of the Society of Architectural Historians* 51: 377–416.

Pepin, R. E. (2008), *The Vatican Mythographers*, New York.

Perelman, C. and Olbrechts-Tyteca, L. (1958), *Traité de l'argumentation: La nouvelle rhétorique*, Paris.

Pérez-Gömez, A. (1993), 'Introduction', in Claude Perrault, *Ordonnance for the Five Kinds of Columns After the Method of the Ancients*, tr. I. K. McEwen, Chicago: 1–44.

— (2011), 'Architecture and the Body', in Bacci and Melcher (2011): 579–98.

Perl, J. (2010), 'Modernism in Art', in Grafton, Most, and Settis (2010): 595–8.

Perry, J. (2001–2), 'Ancient *Collegia*, Modern Blackshirts: The Study of Roman Corporations in Fascist Italy', *International Journal of the Classical Tradition* 8: 205–16.

Perry, M. (1993), 'The Grimani Cameos in Renaissance Venice', *Journal of the Warburg and Courtauld Institutes* 56: 268–74.

Pettit, P. (1997), *Republicanism: A Theory of Freedom and Government*, Oxford.

Pfeiffer, R. (1961), *Philologia Perennis*, Munich.

— (1976), *History of Classical Scholarship from 1300 to 1850*, Oxford.

Piana, M. (2009), 'San Giorgio Maggiore e le cupole lignee lagunari', *Annali di Architettura* 21, http://www.cisapalladio.org/cisa/annali.php, accessed 22 July 2013.

Picone, M. (2007), 'Petrarca e il libro non finito', in id. (ed.), *Il Canzoniere. Lettura micro et macrotestuale*, Ravenna: 9–23.

Piepergerdes, B. J. (2007), 'Re-envisioning the Nation: Film Neorealism and the Postwar Italian Condition', *ACME* 6. 2: 231–57.

Pirrotta, N. (1969), *Li due Orfei: da Poliziano a Monteverdi*, Turin.

Pitkin, H. F. (1983), *Fortune Is a Woman: Gender and Politics in the Thought of Niccolò Machiavelli*, Berkeley.
Plattard, J. (1910), *L'Oeuvre de Rabelais*, Paris.
Plommer, H. (1973), *Vitruvius and Later Roman Building Manuals*, Cambridge.
Pointon, M. (1992), *Naked Authority: The Body in Western Painting, 1830–1908*, Cambridge.
Polak, B. H. (1948–9), 'De Invloed van enige Monumenten der Oudheid op het Classicisme van David, Ingres en Delacroix' *Nederlands Kunsthistorisch Jaarboek* 11: 287–315.
Polcari, S. (1988), 'Mark Rothko: Heritage, Environment and Tradition', *Smithsonian Studies in American Art* 2. 2: 32–63.
Polenz, P. von (2000), *Deutsche Sprachgeschichte vom Spätmittelalter bis zur Gegenwart*, vol. 1, 2nd edn, Berlin.
Pomian, K. (1990), *Collectors and Curiosities: Paris and Venice 1500–1800*, tr. E. Wiles-Portier, London.
Pommier, E. (2003), *Winckelmann, inventeur de l'histoire de l'art*, Paris.
Popper, K. (1976), *Unended Quest: An Intellectual Autobiography*, London.
Poppi, A. (1988), 'Fate, Fortune, Providence and Human Freedom', in Schmitt *et al.* (1988): 641–67.
Porter, J. I. (2000), *Nietzsche and the Philology of the Future*, Stanford.
Pöschl, V. (1989), *Der Begriff der Würde im antiken Rom und später*, Heidelberg.
Posner, R. (1996), *The Romance Languages*, Cambridge.
Potts, A. D. (1980), 'Greek Sculpture and Roman Copies, I: Anton Raphael Mengs and the Eighteenth Century', *Journal of the Warburg and Courtauld Institutes* 65: 150–73.
— (1994), *Flesh and the Ideal: Winckelmann and the Origins of Art History*, New Haven.
— (2000), *The Sculptural Imagination: Figurative, Modernist, Minimalist*, New Haven.
Pound, E. (1952), *The Spirit of Romance*, Norfolk, Conn.
— (1954), *Literary Essays*, ed. T. S. Eliot, London.
Powell, C. (1987), *Turner in the South: Rome, Naples, Florence*, New Haven.
— (2003), 'On the Wing Through Space and Time: The Dynamics of Turner's Italy', *Forum for Modern Language Studies* 39: 190–201.
Pozzo, R. (2004) (ed.), *The Impact of Aristotelianism on Modern Philosophy*, Washington, DC.
Price, A. W. (1990), 'Plato and Freud', in C. Gill (ed.), *The Person and the Human Mind*, Oxford: 247–70.
Price, B. B. (1996), 'The Effect of Patronage on the Intellectualization of Medieval Endeavors', in Wilkins and Wilkins (1996): 5–18.
Prince, F. T. (1954), *The Italian Element in Milton's Verse*, Oxford.
Prins, Y. (1999), *Victorian Sappho*, Princeton.
Pritchard, C. (2003) (ed.), *The Changing Shape of Geometry*, Cambridge.
Proctor, R. (1900), *The Printing of Greek in the Fifteenth Century*, Oxford.
Provine, R. R. (2000), *Laughter: A Scientific Investigation*, London.
Quain, E. A. (1945), 'The Medieval *Accessus ad Auctores*', *Traditio* 3: 215–64.
Quinn, M. (2006), *Fourth Plinth*, Göttingen.
Radke, G. M. (2007) (ed.), *The Gates of Paradise: Lorenzo Ghiberti's Renaissance Masterpiece*, New Haven.
Rahe, P. A. (2000), 'Situating Machiavelli', in Hankins (2000): 270–308.
— (2001), 'Forms of Government', in D. H. Carrithers *et al.* (eds), *Montesquieu's Science of Politics: Essays on The Spirit of Laws*, Lanham, Md: 69–108.
— (2007), 'In the Shadow of Lucretius: The Epicurean Foundations of Machiavelli's Political Thought', *History of Political Thought* 28: 30–55.

Rashdall, H. (1936), *The Universities of Europe in the Middle Ages*, rev. F. M. Powicke and A. B. Emden, 3 vols, Oxford.
Rawnsley, A. (2001), *Servants of the People: The Inside Story of New Labour*, rev. edn, London.
Redpath, T. (1973), *The Young Romantics and Critical Opinion, 1807–1824*, London.
Rees, R. (2009) (ed.), *Ted Hughes and the Classics*, Oxford.
Reeve, M. D. (1996), 'Classical Scholarship', in Kraye (1996): 20–46.
Rehm, W. (1960), *Europäische Romdichtung*, 2nd edn, Munich.
Reid, J. D. (1993), *The Oxford Guide to Classical Mythology in the Arts, 1300–1990s*, Oxford.
Reinhardt, K. (1960), *Tradition und Geist*, ed. C. Becker, Göttingen.
Renfrew, C. (2003), *Figuring It Out: What Are We? Where Do We Come From? The Parallel Visions of Artists and Archaeologists*, London.
Renger, A.-B. and Issler, R. A. (2009) (eds), *Europa – Stier und Sternenkranz. Von der Union mit Zeus zum Staatenverbund*, Göttingen.
Renger, A.-B. and Solomon, J. (2012) (eds), *Ancient Worlds in Film and Television: Gender and Politics*, Leiden.
Revermann, M. and Wilson, P. (2008) (eds), *Performance, Iconography, Reception: Studies in Honour of Oliver Taplin*, Oxford.
Reynolds, L. D. (1983) (ed.), *Texts and Transmission: A Survey of the Latin Classics*, Oxford.
Reynolds, L. D. and Wilson, N. G. (1991), *Scribes and Scholars: A Guide to the Transmission of Greek and Latin Literature*, 3rd edn, Oxford.
Ricard, P. (1989), *A History of the French Language*, 2nd edn, London.
Richard, C. J. (1994), *The Founders and the Classics: Greece, Rome, and the American Enlightenment*, Cambridge, Mass.
Richards, K. and Richards, L. (1990), *The Commedia dell'Arte: A Documentary History*, Oxford.
Ricks, C. (1963), *Milton's Grand Style*, Oxford.
— (1987), *The Poems of Tennyson*, 3 vols, 2nd edn, London.
— (1988), *A. E. Housman, Collected Poems and Selected Prose*, Harmondsworth.
— (2002), *Allusion to the Poets*, Oxford.
Ricks, D. (1989), *The Shade of Homer: A Study in Modern Greek Poetry*, Cambridge.
Ricoeur, P. (1978), *The Rule of Metaphor*, tr. R. Czerny, London.
Ridley, G. (2006), 'The Rhetoric of Liberty: Playing to the Crowd in the American and French Revolutions', in S. Manning and P. France (eds), *Enlightenment and Emancipation*, Cranbury, NJ: 63–80.
Ridley, R. T. (1992), *The Eagle and the Spade: Archaeology in Rome during the Napoleonic Era*, Cambridge.
Riedel, V. (1976), *Lessing und die römische Literatur*, Weimar.
Riehle, W. (2004), 'Shakespeare's Reception of Plautus Reconsidered', in Martindale and Taylor (2004): 109–21.
Rietbergen, P. (2006), *Power and Religion in Baroque Rome: Barberini Cultural Policies*, Leiden.
Rizzo, S. (1992/3), 'Il latino del Petrarca e il latino dell'umanesimo', *Quaderni Petrarcheschi* 9–10: 349–65.
Robbin, T. (1996), *Engineering a New Architecture*, New Haven.
Roberts, D. H. (2008), 'Translation and the "Surreptitious Classic": Obscenity and Translatability', in Lianeri and Zajko (2008): 278–311.
Robin, D. (2000), *Cassandra Fedele: Letters and Orations*, Chicago.
Robins, R. H. (1989), *General Linguistics*, 4th edn, London.

Robinson, A. (2002), *The Life and Work of Jane Ellen Harrison*, Oxford.

Roe, N. (1997), *John Keats and the Culture of Dissent*, Oxford.

Roethlisberger, M. G. (1989), 'The Dimension of Time in the Art of Claude Lorrain', *Artibus et Historiae* 20. 10: 73–92.

Röhl, J. C. G. (2001), *Wilhelm II: Der Aufbau der persönlichen Monarchie*, Munich.

Rohrbach, E. (1996), 'H. D. and Sappho: "A Precious Inch of Palimpsest"', in Greene (1996): 184–98.

Röhrs, H. (1995), *Der Einfluss der klassischen deutschen Universitätsidee auf die Higher Education in Amerika*, Weinheim.

Roller, D. W. (1992), 'Richard Wagner and Classical Antiquity', *Ars Musica Denver* 4. 2: 3–24.

Root, R. K. (1903), *Classical Mythology in Shakespeare*, New York.

Rosand, D. (1978), *Titian*, New York.

— (1990), 'Ekphrasis and the Generation of Images', *Arion* 1: 61–105.

— (2004), 'Inventing Mythologies: The Painter's Poetry', in P. Meilman (ed.), *The Cambridge Companion to Titian*, Cambridge: 35–57.

Rosand, E. (1991), *Opera in Seventeenth-Century Venice*, Berkeley.

Rosen, S. H. (1967), 'Political Philosophy and Epistemology', in Bambrough (1967): 171–86.

Rosenmeyer, T. G. (1969), *The Green Cabinet: Theocritus and the European Pastoral Lyric*, Berkeley.

Rothwell, W. (1968), 'The Teaching of French in Medieval England', *Modern Language Review* 63: 37–46.

— (2001), 'English and French in England After 1362', *English Studies* 82: 539–59.

Rowland, I. D. (1984), 'Some Panegyrics to Agostino Chigi', *Journal of the Warburg and Courtauld Institutes* 47: 194–9.

— (2006), 'Raphael, Angelo Colocci, and the Genesis of the Architectural Orders', in M. W. Cole (ed.), *Sixteenth-Century Italian Art*, Oxford: 511–36.

— (2007), 'Baroque', in Kallendorf (2007): 44–56.

— (2011), 'The Fra Giocondo Vitruvius at 500', *Journal of the Society of Architectural Historians* 70: 285–9.

Rüegg, W. (1946), *Cicero und der Humanismus: formale Untersuchungen über Petrarca und Erasmus*, Zurich.

Ruehl, M. (2003), '*Politeia* 1871: Nietzsche *Contra* Wagner on the Greek State', in Gildenhard and Ruehl (2003): 61–86.

Runnels, C. N. (2007), *The Archaeology of Heinrich Schliemann: An Annotated Bibliographic Handlist*, Boston.

Rüsen, J. and Laass, H. (2009) (eds), *Humanism in Intercultural Perspective*, Bielefeld.

Russell, B. (1967), 'Philosophy and Politics', in Bambrough (1967): 109–34.

Russell, D. A. (1964), *'Longinus', On the Sublime*, Oxford.

— (2001), Quintilian, *The Orator's Education, I: Books 1–2*, Cambridge, Mass.

Rykwert, J. (1955), Leone Battista Alberti, *Ten Books on Architecture*, London.

— (1996), *The Dancing Column: On Order in Architecture*, Cambridge, Mass.

— (1999), *The Palladian Ideal*, New York.

Rykwert, J. and Rykwert, A. (1985), *The Brothers Adam*, London.

Saalman, H. (1980), *Filippo Brunelleschi: The Cupola of Santa Maria del Fiore*, London.

Sagharchi, A. and Steil, L. (2010), *New Palladians: Modernity and Sustainability for 21st-Century Architecture*, London.

Said, E. W. (1979), 'The Text, the World, the Critic', in J. V. Harari (ed.), *Textual Strategies: Perspectives in Post-Structuralist Criticism*, Ithaca, NY: 161–88.

Saint-Girons, B. (2005), *Le Sublime, de l'antiquité à nos jours*, Paris.

Salama, A. M. (2007), 'Nikos A. Salingaros: A New Vitruvius for 21st-Century Architecture and Urbanism?', *ArchNet-IJAR: International Journal of Architectural Research* 1: 114–31.

Salmon, F. (2000), *Building on Ruins: The Rediscovery of Rome and English Architecture*, Aldershot.

Sandys, J. E. (1908), *A History of Classical Scholarship, II–III*, 2nd edn, Cambridge.

— (1921), *A History of Classical Scholarship, I*, 3rd edn, Cambridge.

Saunders, G. (2002), *'Love Me or Kill Me': Sarah Kane and the Theatre of Extremes*, Manchester.

Schadewaldt, W. (1970), 'Richard Wagner und die Griechen', in id., *Hellas und Hesperien*, vol. 2, Zurich: 341–405.

Schaefer, U. (2006) (ed.), *The Beginnings of Standardization: Language and Culture in Fourteenth-Century England*, Frankfurt a. M.

Schama, S. (1989), *Citizens: A Chronicle of the French Revolution*, London.

Schapiro, M., Janson, H. W., and Gombrich, E. H. (1970), 'Criteria of Periodization in the History of European Art', *New Literary History* 1. 2: 113–25.

Schauer, M. (2005), 'Friedrich Immanuel Niethammer und der bildungspolitische Streit des Philanthropinismus und Humanismus um 1800', *Pegasus-Onlinezeitschrift* 5. 1: 28–45.

Schefer, O. (2011), 'Variations on Totality: Romanticism and the Total Work of Art', in Finger and Follett (2011): 29–51.

Scherer, M. R. (1964), *The Legends of Troy in Art and Literature*, New York.

Schimmel, A. (1993), *The Mystery of Numbers*, Oxford.

Schlatter, R. (1945), 'Thomas Hobbes and Thucydides', *Journal of the History of Ideas* 6: 350–62.

Schmidt, H. J. (1969), *Nietzsche und Sokrates*, Meisenheim am Glan.

Schmidt, J. (2007), *Melancholy and the Care of the Soul: Religion, Moral Philosophy and Madness in Early Modern England*, Aldershot.

Schmitt, C. B. *et al.* (1988) (eds), *The Cambridge History of Renaissance Philosophy*, Cambridge.

Schnapp, A. (1996), *The Discovery of the Past: The Origins of Archaeology*, London.

Schori Bondeli, R. (2005), *Der postmoderne Kammerherr. Niebelschütz und sein 'unzeitgemässer' Nachkriegs-Roman*, Berne.

Schreiner, K. (1987), '"Diversitas temporum" – Zeiterfahrung und Epochengliederung im späten Mittelalter', in R. Herzog and R. Koselleck (eds), *Epochenschwelle und Epochenbewusstsein*, Munich: 381–428.

Schrift, A. D. (1990), *Nietzsche and the Question of Interpretation*, New York.

Schröbler, I. (1953), *Notker III von St. Gallen als Übersetzer und Kommentator von Boethius' De Consolatione Philosophiae*, Tübingen.

Schröder, E. (1913), 'Studiosus Philologiae', *Neue Jahrbücher für das klassische Altertum* 32: 168–71.

Schuckert, L. (1989), 'Citoyen Brutus. Aktualisierungen der Antike in der Französischen Revolution', *Der Altsprachliche Unterricht* 32. 4: 5–21.

Schudt, L. (1930), *Le guide di Roma*, Vienna.

Schuler, S. (1999), *Vitruv im Mittelalter. Die Rezeption von 'De architectura' von der Antike bis in die frühe Neuzeit*, Cologne.

Schwartz, P. H. (1988), 'Equestrian Imagery in European and American Political Thought', *Western Political Quarterly* 41: 653–73.
Scott, C. (2000), 'Branding: Positioning Museums in the 21st Century', *International Journal of Arts Management* 2. 3: 35–9.
Scott, J. A. (1921), *The Unity of Homer*, Berkeley.
Screech, M. A. (1979), *Rabelais*, London.
— (2003), Michel de Montaigne, *The Complete Essays*, rev. edn, London.
Searle, J. (1996), *The Construction of Social Reality*, London.
Seidensticker, B. (2003), 'Der glückliche Sisyphos. Zur Präsenz des antiken Mythos', in Jens and Seidensticker (2003): 151–75.
Seifert, A. (1986), 'Von der heiligen zur philosophischen Geschichte', *Archiv für Kulturgeschichte* 68: 81–117.
Sellers, M. N. S. (2004), 'The Roman Republic and the French and American Revolutions', in H. I. Flower (ed.), *The Cambridge Companion to the Roman Republic*, Cambridge: 347–64.
Sergl, A. (1998), 'Das Problem des Chors im deutschen Klassizismus: Schillers Verständnis der *Iphigenia auf Tauris* und seine *Braut von Messina*', *Jahrbuch der deutschen Schillergesellschaft* 42: 165–94.
Serianni, L. and Trifone, P. (1993–4) (eds), *Storia della lingua italiana*, 3 vols, Turin.
Settis, S. (2006), *The Future of the Classical*, Cambridge.
— (2010), 'Classical', in Grafton, Most, and Settis (2010): 205–6.
Seznec, R (1953), *The Survival of the Pagan Gods: The Mythological Tradition and Its Place in Renaissance Humanism and Art*, tr. B. F. Sessions, New York.
Shaw, P. (2006), *The Sublime*, Abingdon.
Shearman, J. (1967), *Mannerism*, Harmondsworth.
— (1987), 'Alfonso d'Este's Camerino', in '*Il se rendit en Italie*': *Études offertes à André Chastel*, Rome and Paris: 209–29.
Shepard, A. and Powell, S. D. (2004) (eds), *Fantasies of Troy: Classical Tales and the Social Imaginary in Medieval and Early Modern Europe*, Toronto.
Sheppard, E. R. (2006), *Leo Strauss and the Politics of Exile*, Waltham, Mass.
Short, I. (1992), 'Patrons and Polyglots: French Literature in Twelfth-Century England', *Anglo-Norman Studies* 14: 229–49.
Shvidkovsky, D. (1996), *The Empress and the Architect: British Architecture and Gardens at the Court of Catherine the Great*, New Haven.
Sichel, W. (1911), 'The English Aristophanes', *Fortnightly Review* 90: 681–704.
Silk, M. S. (1997), 'Sing For Our Time Too', *Times Literary Supplement* 4942 (19 December): 3–4.
— (1999a), 'Words That Say What They Mean', *Times Literary Supplement* 5046 (17 December): 16–17.
— (1999b), 'Review of Guy Lee, *Horace: Odes*', in *The Eagle* (St John's College, Cambridge): 78–81.
— (1999c), '"Das Urproblem der Tragödie": Notions of the Chorus in the Nineteenth Century', in *Drama* 7 (Stuttgart): 195–226.
— (2000), *Aristophanes and the Definition of Comedy*, Oxford.
— (2001), 'Aristotle, Rapin, Brecht', in Andersen and Haarberg (2001): 173–95.
— (2004a), 'Shakespeare and Greek Tragedy: Strange Relationship', in Martindale and Taylor (2004): 241–57.
— (2004b), *Homer, The Iliad*, 2nd edn, Cambridge.

— (2004c), 'Nietzsche, Decadence, and the Greeks', *New Literary History* 35: 587–606.
— (2004d), 'Alexandrian Poetry from Callimachus to Eliot', in Hirst and Silk (2004): 353–72.
— (2007a), 'Poetic Presences', *International Journal of the Classical Tradition* 14: 220–7.
— (2007b), 'Translating/Transposing Aristophanes', in Hall and Wrigley (2007): 287–308.
— (2007c), 'Nietzsche's Socrateases', in Trapp (2007b): 37–57.
— (2009a), 'The Invention of Greek', in Georgakopoulou and Silk (2009): 3–31.
— (2009b), 'Lyric and Lyrics: Perspectives, Ancient and Modern', in Budelmann (2009): 373–85.
— (2010), 'Daughter of Ancient Darkness', *Times Literary Supplement* 5579 (5 March): 10–11.
— (2012), 'Literary Theory and the Classics', in S. Hornblower *et al.* (eds), *The Oxford Classical Dictionary*, 4th edn, Oxford: 845–50.
— (2013), 'The Greek Dramatic Genres: Theoretical Perspectives', in E. Bakola *et al.* (eds), *Greek Comedy and the Discourse of Genres*, Cambridge: 15–39.
— (forthcoming) *Poetic Language in Theory and Practice*, Oxford.
Silk, M. S. and Stern, J. P. (1981), *Nietzsche on Tragedy*, Cambridge.
Simons, P. (1994), 'Lesbian (In)Visibility in Italian Renaissance Culture: Diana and Other Cases of *donna con donna*', *Journal of Homosexuality* 27: 81–122.
Simonsuuri, K. (1979), *Homer's Original Genius: Eighteenth-Century Notions of the Early Greek Epic (1688–1798)*, Cambridge.
Singerman, J. E. (1986), *Under Clouds of Poesy: Poetry and Truth in French and English Reworkings of the Aeneid, 1160–1513*, New York.
Sinisgalli, R. (2011), Leon Battista Alberti, *On Painting*, Cambridge.
Siry, J. M. (2008), 'Perspectives on American Tall Buildings', *Journal of Urban History* 35: 186–95.
Skinner, Q. (1978), *The Foundations of Modern Political Thought, vol. 1: The Renaissance*, Cambridge.
— (1988), 'Political Philosophy', in Schmitt *et al.* (1988): 389–452.
— (2000), *Machiavelli: A Very Short Introduction*, Cambridge.
— (2008), 'What Does It Mean to Be a Free Person?', *London Review of Books* 30. 10: 16–18.
Small, M. (1964), 'Athenian Democracy', *Anarchy* 45: 329–45.
Smith, C. (1992), *Architecture in the Culture of Early Humanism: Ethics, Aesthetics and Eloquence 1400–1470*, Oxford.
Smith, J. J. (2006), 'From Middle to Early Modern English', in Mugglestone (2006): 120–46.
Smith, J. M. H. (2005), *Europe After Rome: A New Cultural History, 500–1000*, Oxford.
Smith, M. M. (2007), *Sensing the Past: Seeing, Hearing, Smelling, Tasting, and Touching in History*, Berkeley.
Smith, M. W. (2007), *The Total Work of Art: From Bayreuth to Cyberspace*, New York.
Smith, S. B. (2009a) (ed.), *The Cambridge Companion to Leo Strauss*, Cambridge.
— (2009b), 'Leo Strauss. The Outlines of a Life', in Smith (2009a): 13–40.
Solodow, J. B. (2010), *Latin Alive: The Survival of Latin in English and Romance Languages*, Cambridge.
Solomon, J. (2001), *The Ancient World in Cinema*, 2nd edn, Cambridge, Mass.
Solterer, H. (1995), *The Master and Minerva: Disputing Women in French Medieval Culture*, Berkeley.

Soros, S. W. (2006) (ed.), *James 'Athenian' Stuart 1713–1788: The Rediscovery of Antiquity*, New Haven.
Southern, R. W. (1995), *Scholastic Humanism and the Unification of Europe*, Oxford.
Sowerby, R. (2000), 'Aristophanes', in France (2000): 367–70.
Spencer, J. R. (1966), Alberti, *On Painting*, rev. edn, New Haven.
Spierenburg, P. (1998), *Men and Violence: Gender, Honor, and Rituals in Modern Europe and America*, Columbus, Ohio.
Stack, J. (2000), 'Artists into Heroes: The Commemoration of Artists in the Art of Giorgio Vasari', in M. Rogers (ed.), *Fashioning Identities in Renaissance Art*, Aldershot: 163–76.
Stanford, W. B. (1941), 'Gerard Manley Hopkins and Aeschylus', *Studies: An Irish Quarterly Review* 30: 359–68.
— (1954), *The Ulysses Theme*, Oxford.
St. Clair, W. (1967), *Lord Elgin and the Marbles*, Oxford.
Steen, J. (2008), *Verse and Virtuosity: The Adaptation of Latin Rhetoric in Old English Poetry*, Toronto.
Stein, P. (1963), 'The Influence of Roman Law on the Law of Scotland', *Juridical Review* 8: 205–45.
— (1999), *Roman Law in European History*, Cambridge.
Steiner, G. (1961), *The Death of Tragedy*, London.
— (1967), *Language and Silence*, London.
— (1969), 'An den deutschen Leser', in id., *Sprache und Schweigen*, Frankfurt a. M.: 7–10.
— (1984), *Antigones*, Oxford.
— (1995), 'The New Nouvelle Héloïse? Hannah Arendt's Self-Abasing Love for Heidegger', *Times Literary Supplement* 4828 (13 October): 3–4.
— (1998), *After Babel*, 3rd edn, Oxford.
— (1999), 'The Magician in Love: Heidegger's Correspondence with Hannah Arendt and the Light Shed on His Philosophy - and His Politics', *Times Literary Supplement* 5000 (29 January): 3–4.
Stern, J. P. (1975), *Hitler: The Führer and the People*, Glasgow.
Stevens, L. C. (1950), 'How the French Humanists of the Renaissance Learned Greek', *Proceedings of the Modern Language Association* 65: 240–8.
Stevenson, J. (2005), *Women Latin Poets: Language, Gender, and Authority, from Antiquity to the Eighteenth Century*, Oxford.
Stierle, K. (1998), *Petrarca. Fragmente eine Selbstentwurfs*, Darmstadt.
— (2001), '"Translatio" e "Resurrectio". Due miti di identità Europea', in C. Ossola (ed.), *Europa: miti di identità*, Venice: 77–96.
— (2003), *Francesco Petrarca: Ein Intellektueller im Europa des 14. Jahrhunderts*, Darmstadt.
Stiewe, B. (2011), *Der 'Dritte Humanismus'. Aspekte Deutscher Griechenrezeption vom George-Kreis bis zum Nationalsozialismus*, Berlin.
Storey, R. F. (1978), *Pierrot: A Critical History of a Mask*, Princeton.
Stott, R. (1996) (ed.), *Tennyson*, Harlow.
Stray, C. (1998), *Classics Transformed: Schools, Universities, and Society in England, 1830–1960*, Oxford.
— (2005) (ed.), *The Owl of Minerva: The Cambridge Praelections of 1906*, Cambridge.
Striner, R. (1990), 'Art Deco: Polemics and Synthesis', *Winterthur Portfolio* 25. 1: 21–34.
Stroh, W. (2007), *Latein ist tot, es lebe Latein! Kleine Geschichte einer grossen Sprache*, Berlin.

Struve, T. (2004), 'Cola di Rienzo: ein Traum von der Erneuerung Roms und die antike *lex regia*', in id., *Staat und Gesellschaft im Mittelalter*, Berlin: 204–29.
Sullivan, M. A. (1992), 'Bruegel's "Misanthrope": Renaissance Art for a Humanist Audience', *Artibus et Historiae* 26: 143–62.
Sullivan, V. B. (2000) (ed.), *The Comedy and Tragedy of Machiavelli*, New Haven, Conn.
Summerson, J. (1964), *The Classical Language of Architecture*, London.
— (1990), *The Unromantic Castle and Other Essays*, London.
Summit, J. (2000), 'Topography as Historiography: Petrarch, Chaucer, and the Making of Medieval Rome', *Journal of Medieval and Early Modern Studies* 30: 211–46.
Sünderhauf, E. S. (2004), *Griechensehnsucht und Kulturkritik: Die deutsche Rezeption von Winckelmanns Antikenideal 1840–1945*, Berlin.
Szondi, P. (1974), *Poetik und Geschichtsphilosophie*, ed. S. Metz *et al.*, vol. 1, Frankfurt a. M.
Talvacchia, B. (1999), *Taking Positions: On the Erotic in Renaissance Culture*, Princeton.
— (2010), 'Pornography', in Grafton, Most, and Settis (2010): 767–71.
Tamani, G. (1992), 'Traduzioni ebraico-latine di opere filosofiche e scientifiche', in I. Zinguer (ed.), *L'hébreu au temps de la Renaissance*, Leiden: 105–14.
Taminiaux, J. (2000), 'Athens and Rome', in Villa (2000): 165–77.
Tanner, R. G. (1970), 'The Dramas of T. S. Eliot and Their Greek Models', *Greece and Rome* 17: 123–34.
Tavoni, M. (1984), *Latino, grammatica, volgare. Storia di una questione umanistica*, Padua.
Tavoni, M. *et al.* (1998), 'Renaissance Linguistics', in G. Lepschy (ed.), *History of Linguistics: III, Renaissance and Early Modern Linguistics*, New York: 1–148.
Taylor, A. B. (2000) (ed.), *Shakespeare's Ovid: The* Metamorphoses *in the Plays and Poems*, Cambridge.
Taylor, C. (2004), *Modern Social Imaginaries*, Durham.
Taylor, C. C. W. (1997), 'Plato's Totalitarianism', in R. Kraut (ed.), *Plato's Republic: Critical Essays*, Lanham, Md.: 31–48.
Taylor, M. R. (2002) (ed.), *Giorgio de Chirico and the Myth of Ariadne*, Philadelphia.
Taylor, T. J. and Toolan, M. (1996), 'Recent Trends in Stylistics', in Weber (1996): 87–91.
Testa, F. (1999), *Winckelmann e l'invenzione della storia dell' arte*, Bologna.
Theodorakopoulos, E. (2010), *Ancient Rome at the Cinema*, Exeter.
Thoenes, C. and Günther, H. (1985), 'Gli ordini architettonici: Rinascita o invenzione?', in M. Fagiolo (ed.), *Roma e l'antico nell'arte e nella cultura del cinquecento*, Rome: 261–310.
Thomas, S. (2008), *Romanticism and Visuality*, London.
Thompson, D. (1971), *The Idea of Rome from Antiquity to the Renaissance*, Mexico City.
Thomson, P. (2004), 'Clowns, Fools and Knaves: Stages in the Evolution of Acting', in J. Milling and P. Thomson (eds), *The Cambridge History of British Theatre*, vol. 1, Cambridge: 207–21.
Thorslev, P. L. (1962), *The Byronic Hero*, Minneapolis.
Thuillier, J. (1960), 'Pour un *corpus poussinianum*', *Actes du Colloque Poussin* 2: 49–238.
Tierno, M. (2002), *Aristotle's Poetics for Screenwriters: Storytelling Secrets from the Greatest Mind in Western Civilization*, New York.
Till, D. (2006), *Das doppelte Erhabene. Geschichte einer Argumentationsfigur von der Antike bis zum Beginn des 19. Jahrhunderts*, Tübingen.
Timpanaro, S. (2005), *The Genesis of Lachmann's Method*, tr. G. W. Most, Chicago.
Toolan, M. J. (1990), *The Stylistics of Fiction*, London.

Torrell, J.-P. (2005), *Saint Thomas Aquinas: The Person and His Work*, Washington, DC.
Tosh, J. (2005), *Manliness and Masculinities in Nineteenth-Century Britain*, London.
Toynbee, P. (1968), *A Dictionary of Proper Names and Notable Matters in the Works of Dante*, rev. C. S. Singleton, Oxford.
Trapp, M. B. (2007a) (ed.), *Socrates from Antiquity to the Enlightenment*, Aldershot.
— (2007b) (ed.), *Socrates in the Nineteenth and Twentieth Centuries*, Aldershot.
Trask, R.L. (2000), *The Dictionary of Historical and Comparative Linguistics*, Edinburgh.
Trigg, R. (1988), *Ideas of Human Nature*, Oxford.
Tripet, A. (1967), *Pétrarque, ou la connaissance de soi*, Geneva.
Tritter, J.-L. (1999), *Histoire de la langue française*, Paris.
Tucker, H. F. (1983), 'Tennyson and the Measure of Doom', *Proceedings of the Modern Language Association* 98, 8–20.
Tuckwell, W. (1907), *Reminiscences of Oxford*, 2nd edn, London.
Turner, M. (2011), *Exposed: Photography and the Classical Nude*, Sydney.
Tuve, R. (1947), *Elizabethan and Metaphysical Imagery*, Chicago.
Twycross, M. and Carpenter, S. (2002), *Masks and Masking in Medieval and Early Tudor England*, Aldershot.
Uhlig, L. (1988), *Griechenland als Ideal. Winckelmann und seine Rezeption in Deutschland*, Tübingen.
Uhlig, S. H. and Regier, A. (2010) (eds), *Wordsworth's Poetic Theory: Knowledge, Language, Experience*, Basingstoke.
Untermeyer, L. (1964), *Robert Frost*, Washington, DC.
Usener, H. (1907), *Vorträge und Aufsätze*, Leipzig.
Vance, N. (1997), *The Victorians and Ancient Rome*, London.
van den Abbeele, G. (1992), *Travel as Metaphor: From Montaigne to Rousseau*, Minneapolis.
van der Zande, J. (1998), 'The Microscope of Experience: Christian Garve's Translation of Cicero's *De Officiis* (1783)', *Journal of the History of Ideas* 59: 75–94.
Vandiver, E. (2008), 'Homer in British World War One Poetry', in Hardwick and Stray (2008): 452–65.
— (2010), *Stand in the Trench, Achilles: Classical Receptions in British Poetry of the Great War*, Oxford.
van Eck, C. (1998), 'The Structure of *De Re Aedificatoria* Reconsidered', *Journal of the Society of Architectural Historians* 57: 280–97.
Vassallo, S. (2007), 'Antiquities Without Provenance: The Original Sin of the Field', in R. F. Rhodes (ed.), *The Acquisition and Exhibition of Classical Antiquities: Professional, Legal and Ethical Perspectives*, Notre Dame, Ind.: 81–91.
Vasunia, P. (2011), *Greece, Rome, and the British Empire*, Oxford.
Vaughan, W. and Weston, H. (2000) (eds), *David's The Death of Marat*, Cambridge.
Vaughn, L. and Dacey, A. (2003), *The Case for Humanism: An Introduction*, Lanham, Md.
Venuti, L. (2008), *The Translator's Invisibility: A History of Translation*, 2nd edn, London.
Vickers, B. (1985), 'The Royal Society and English Prose Style: A Reassessment', in B. Vickers and N. S. Struever (eds), *Rhetoric and the Pursuit of Truth: Language Change in the Seventeenth and Eighteenth Centuries*, Berkeley: 3–76.
— (2002), *Shakespeare, Co-Author*, Oxford.
Vidal-Naquet, V. (1990), 'La place de la Grèce dans l'imaginaire des hommes de la révolution', in id., *La démocratie grecque vue d'ailleurs*, Paris: 211–35.
Villa, D. R. (1996), *Arendt and Heidegger*, Princeton.

— (2000) (ed.), *The Cambridge Companion to Hannah Arendt*, Cambridge.
Vincenti, R. (2010), 'Law, Roman', in Grafton, Most, and Settis (2010): 512–19.
Vineis, E. and Maierù, A. (1994), 'Medieval Linguistics', in G. Lepschy (ed.), *History of Linguistics, II. Classical and Medieval Linguistics*, London: 134–315.
Vinti, F. (1995), *Giulio Romano pittore e l'antico*, Florence.
Viroli, M. (1998), *Il sorriso di Niccolò: storia di Machiavelli*, Rome.
Visser, A. S. Q. (2005), *Johannes Sambucus and the Learned Image: The Use of the Emblem in Late-Renaissance Humanism*, Leiden.
Vitale, M. (1978), *La questione della lingua*, 2nd edn, Palermo.
Vogt-Spira, G. (2003), 'Warum Vergil statt Homer? Der frühneuzeitliche Vorzugsstreit zwischen Homer und Vergil', *Poetica* 35: 323–44.
Wade, N. J. and Swanston, M. T. (2001), *Visual Perception*, 2nd edn, Hove.
Wadsworth, P. A. (1987), *Molière and the Italian Theatrical Tradition*, Birmingham, Ala.
Waite, G. (2000), *Old English Prose Translations of King Alfred's Reign*, Cambridge.
Waith, E. M. (1962), *The Herculean Hero*, London.
— (1975), 'Heywood's Women Worthies', in Burns and Reagan (1975): 222–38.
Walker, D. P. (2000), *Spiritual and Demonic Magic: From Ficino to Campanella*, University Park, Pa.
Walker, L. J. (1950), *The Discourses of Niccolò Machiavelli*, 2 vols, London.
Wallraff, M. (2006) (ed.), *Julius Africanus und die christliche Weltchronistik*, Berlin.
Walzer, P. (1958), 'On the Arabic Versions of Books A, a and L of Aristotle's *Metaphysics*', *Harvard Studies in Classical Philology* 63: 217–31.
Waquet, F. (2001), *Latin: Or the Empire of the Sign – An Account of the Social Connotations of Latin, 1500–1800*, London.
Ward, J. P. (1984), *Wordsworth's Language of Men*, Brighton.
Warren, G. L. (1990), *Translation as Re-Creation in the Roman de Troie*, Ann Arbor.
Warshaw, J. (1920), 'The Epic-Drama Conception of the Novel', *Modern Language Notes* 35: 269–79.
Waswo, R. (1987), *Language and Meaning in the Renaissance*, Princeton.
Watkin, D. (2000), 'The Architectural Context of the Grand Tour: The British as Honorary Italians', in Hornsby (2000a): 49–62.
Watkins, D. (1989), *Keats's Poetry and the Politics of the Imagination*, London.
Watson, G. (1962), John Dryden, *Of Dramatic Poesy and Other Critical Essays*, 2 vols, London.
— (1970) (ed.), *Literary English Since Shakespeare*, Oxford.
Waxman, S. (2008), *Loot: The Battle over the Stolen Treasures of the Ancient World*, New York.
Waywell, G. (1992), 'Art', in R. Jenkyns (ed.), *The Legacy of Rome: A New Appraisal*, Oxford: 295–327.
Webb, T. (1976), *The Violet in the Crucible: Shelley and Translation*, Oxford.
Weber, J. J. (1996) (ed.), *The Stylistics Reader: From Roman Jakobson to the Present*, London.
Wehler, H.-U. (1973), *Das deutsche Kaiserreich, 1871–1918*, Göttingen.
Weijenborg, R. (1957), 'Dokumente zu Luthers Romreise', *Antonianum* 33: 147–202.
Weimann, R. (1978), *Shakespeare and the Popular Tradition in the Theater*, Baltimore, Md.
Weinberg, B. (1950), 'Translations and Commentaries of Longinus, *On the Sublime*, to 1600: A Bibliography', *Modern Philology* 47: 145–51.
Weiskel, T. (1976), *The Romantic Sublime: Studies in the Structure and Psychology of Transcendence*, Baltimore, Md.
Weiskittel, S. F. and Reynolds, L. D. (1983), 'Vitruvius', in Reynolds (1983): 440–5.
Wellek, R. (1955), *A History of Modern Criticism, 1750–1950*, vol. 1, London.

— (1970), 'The Name and Nature of Comparative Literature', in id., *Discriminations: Further Concepts of Criticism*, New Haven: 183–8.

Wellek, R. and Warren, A. (1963), *Theory of Literature*, 3rd edn, Harmondsworth.

Wells, R. H. (2000), *Shakespeare on Masculinity*, Cambridge.

Westfall, R. S. (1972), 'Newton and the Hermetic Tradition', in A. G. Debus (ed.), *Science, Medicine and Society in the Renaissance*, vol. 2, New York: 183–98.

Whitehead, A. N. (1929), *Process and Reality: An Essay in Cosmology*, Cambridge.

Whitehead, S. M. (2002), *Men and Masculinities*, Cambridge.

Wickert, L. (1964), *Theodor Mommsen. Eine Biographie, II: Wanderjahre. Frankreich und Italien*, Frankfurt a. M.

Wiebenson, D. (1973), 'The Two Domes of the Halle au Blé in Paris', *Art Bulletin* 55: 262–79.

Wilamowitz(-Moellendorff), U. von (1895), Euripides, *Herakles*, 3 vols, 2nd edn, Berlin.

— (1913), *Sappho und Simonides*, Berlin.

— (1926), *Reden und Vorträge*, 2 vols, 4th edn, Berlin.

— (1928), *Erinnerungen, 1848–1914*, Leipzig.

Wilberg, P.-H. (1996), *Richard Wagners mythische Welt*, Rombach.

Wiles, D. (1987), *Shakespeare's Clown: Actor and Text in the Elizabethan Playhouse*, Cambridge.

Wilkins, D. G. and Wilkins, R. L. (1996) (eds), *The Search for a Patron in the Middle Ages and the Renaissance*, Lewiston, NY.

Williams, B. (1993), *Shame and Necessity*, Berkeley.

Williams, R. (1976), *Keywords*, London.

Wilson, N. G. (1983), *Scholars of Byzantium*, London.

— (1992), *From Byzantium to Italy: Greek Studies in the Italian Renaissance*, London.

Wilson, W. D. (2012), *Goethe, Männer, Knaben*, Berlin.

Wilton, A. (1976), 'Blake and the Antique', *British Museum Yearbook* 1: 187–218.

Winckelmann, J. (1988), Max Weber, *Gesammelte Aufsätze zur Wissenschaftslehre*, 7th edn, Tübingen.

Winkler, M. M. (2001) (ed.), *Classical Myth and Culture in the Cinema*, rev. edn, Oxford.

Winterer, C. (2002), *The Culture of Classicism: Ancient Greece and Rome in American Intellectual Life, 1780–1910*, Baltimore, Md.

— (2007), *The Mirror of Antiquity: American Women and the Classical Tradition, 1750–1900*, Ithaca, NY.

Wippel, J. F. (2004), 'Thomas Aquinas' Commentary on Aristotle's *Metaphysics*', in J. J. E. Gracia and J. Yu (eds), *Uses and Abuses of the Classics: Western Interpretations of Greek Philosophy*, Aldershot: 137–64.

Witt, R. G. (2000), *In the Footsteps of the Ancients: The Origins of Humanism from Lovato to Bruni*, Leiden.

— (2012), *The Two Latin Cultures and the Foundation of Renaissance Humanism in Medieval Italy*, Cambridge.

Wittenburg, A. (2010), 'Olympia und Delphi – Deutsche und französische Archäologen in Neuen Griechenland', in Kocziszky (2010): 221–44.

Wittkower, R. (1949), *Architectural Principles in the Age of Humanism*, London.

Wittman, R. (2007), 'The Hut and the Altar: Architectural Origins and the Public Sphere in Eighteenth-Century France', *Studies in Eighteenth Century Culture* 36: 235–59.

Wlosok, A. (1990), 'Zur Geltung und Beurteilung Vergils and Homers in Spätantike und früher Neuzeit', in id., *Res Humanae – Res Divinae*, Heidelberg: 476–98.

Wöll, S. (1984), *Das Totaltheater. Ein Project von Walter Gropius und Erwin Piscator*, Berlin.

Wolosky, S. (1995), *Language Mysticism: The Negative Way of Language in Eliot, Beckett, and Célan*, Stanford.

Wood, T. E. B. (1972), *The Word 'Sublime' and Its Context, 1650–1760*, The Hague.

Woodward, C. (2001), *In Ruins*, London.

Woodward, W. H. (1897), *Vittorino da Feltre and Other Humanist Educators*, Cambridge.

Woolf, D. R. (2010), 'Biography', in Grafton, Most, and Settis (2010): 127–30.

Worsley, G. (1995), *Classical Architecture in Britain: The Heroic Age*, New Haven.

Worstbrock, F. J. (1965), '*Translatio artium*: über die Herkunft und Entwicklung einer kulturhistorischen Theorie', *Archiv für Kulturgeschichte* 47: 1–22.

Wright, R. (1982), *Late Latin and Early Romance in Spain and Carolingian France*, Liverpool.

— (1991) (ed.), *Latin and the Romance Languages in the Early Middle Ages*, London.

— (2002), *A Sociophilological Study of Late Latin*, Brepols.

— (2008) (ed.), *Latin vulgaire, latin tardif, VIII*, Hildesheim.

Wyke, M. (1997a), *Projecting the Past: Ancient Rome, Cinema and History*, London.

— (1997b), 'Herculean Muscle: The Classicizing Rhetoric of Bodybuilding', *Arion* 4: 51–79.

Yablon, N. (2007), '"A Picture Painted in Fire": Pain's Reenactments of *The Last Days of Pompeii*, 1879–1914', in V. C. Gardner Coates and J. L. Seydl (eds), *Antiquity Recovered: The Legacy of Pompeii and Herculaneum*, Los Angeles: 189–205.

Yates, F. A. (1964), *Giordano Bruno and the Hermetic Tradition*, London.

Young, D. C. (1984), *The Olympic Myth of Greek Amateur Athletics*, Chicago.

Young, P. H. (2003), *The Printed Homer*, Jefferson, NC.

Young-Bruehl, E. (1982), *Hannah Arendt: For Love of the World*, New Haven.

Zak, G. (2010), *Petrarch's Humanism and the Care of the Self*, Cambridge.

Zarucchi, J. M. (1997), 'Du Bellay, Spenser and Quevodo Search for Rome', *French Review* 71: 192–203.

Zedelmaier, H. (2003), *Der Anfang der Geschichte*, Hamburg.

Zimmermann, R. (1989), *Künstliche Ruinen*, Wiesbaden.

Ziolkowski, J. (1990) (ed.), *On Philology*, University Park, Pa.

Ziolkowski, T. (2008), *Minos and the Moderns: Cretan Myth in Twentieth-Century Literature and Art*, Oxford.

Zucker, P. (1961), 'Ruins: An Aesthetic Hybrid', *Journal of Aesthetics and Art Criticism* 20: 119–30.

Zuckert, C. and Zuckert, M. (2006), *The Truth About Leo Strauss*, Chicago.

Index

In this index, names of historical individuals are normally cited with birth and death dates or centuries. As elsewhere, dates are AD unless specified as BC; but a few AD dates are shown as such to avoid possible ambiguity. All BC dates, and some AD, are cited by century. A mark of ? or *c.* before one of two dates refers only to that date, not to both. Names with de/da/von etc. are indexed under their customary headword, as, Balzac, de Man, Du Bellay, Este, Goethe, Goya, Leonardo etc. Page numbers in italics denote text figures; '*Plate 1*' (etc.) refers to a colour plate (between pp. 370 and 371).

The Classical Tradition: Art, Literature, Thought, First Edition. Michael Silk, Ingo Gildenhard, and Rosemary Barrow.

Published 2017 by John Wiley & Sons Ltd.

Plate 1 William Blake, *Albion Rose* (Glad Day): see §3, p. 27. Source: © The Trustees of the British Museum.

The Classical Tradition: Art, Literature, Thought, First Edition. Michael Silk, Ingo Gildenhard, and Rosemary Barrow.

Published 2017 by John Wiley & Sons Ltd.

Plate 2 Francesco Xanto Avelli da Rovigo, maiolica dish (1532) representing the Laocoon: see §11, p. 106. Source: New York, Metropolitan Museum of Art. Approximately Rackham's shape 14. Diameter: 10 1/4 inches (26 cm). Robert Lehman Collection, 1975. Inv. 1975.1.1129© 2013. Image copyright The Metropolitan Museum of Art/Art Resource/Scala, Florence.

Plate 3 Calum Colvin, *Brief Encounter*: see §11, p. 117. Source: used by permission of the artist.

Plate 4 Nicolas Poussin, *The Arcadian Shepherds*: see §14, p. 171. Source: Paris, Louvre.

Plate 5 J. M. W. Turner, *Modern Rome: Campo Vaccino*: see §17, p. 224. Oil on canvas. Size: Unframed: 91.8 × 122.6 cm (36 1/8 × 48 1/4 inches) Framed [outer dim]: 122.6 × 153.4 × 11.1 cm (48 1/4 × 60 3/8 × 4 3/8 inches). Source: The J. Paul Getty Museum, Los Angeles.

Plate 6 Umberto Boccioni, *Unique Forms of Continuity in Space*: see §17, p. 239. Source: New York, Metropolitan Museum of Art. Bronze; h. 48, w. 15-1/2, d. 36 inches (121.9 × 39.4 × 91.4 cm). Bequest of Lydia Winston Malbin, 1989. Acc.n.1990.38.3© 2013. Image copyright The Metropolitan Museum of Art/Art Resource/Scala, Florence.

Plate 7 Claude Lorrain, *Aeneas on Delos*: see §25, p. 318. Source © The National Gallery, London (NG1018).

Plate 8 Titian, *Worship of Venus*: see §33, p. 397. Source: Madrid, Prado. © 2013. Photo: Scala, Florence.

Plate 9 Jacques-Louis David, *Paris and Helen*: see §33, p. 398. Source: Paris, Louvre. Oil on canvas, 146 × 181 cm. © 2013. DeAgostini Picture Library/Scala, Florence.

Plate 10 Giorgio de Chirico, *The Uncertainty of the Poet*: see §33, p. 399. Source: Private Coll. peinture, 106 × 94 cm.